Challenging Chicago

Challenging
Chicago

UNIVERSITY OF ILLINOIS PRESS

Coping with Everyday Life, 1837–1920

Perry R. Duis

URBANA AND CHICAGO

This book is printed on acid-free paper.

Library of Congress Cataloging-in-Publication Data

Duis, Perry, 1943—
Challenging Chicago : coping with everyday life, 1837–1920 / Perry R. Duis.
p. cm.
Includes bibliographical references (p.) and index.
ISBN 0-252-02394-3 (acid-free paper)
1. Sociology, Urban—Illinois—Chicago.
2. City and town life—Illinois—Chicago.
3. Social mobility—Illinois—Chicago.
4. Chicago (Ill.)—Social life and customs.
5. Chicago (Ill.)—Social conditions.
6. Chicago (Ill.)—Economic conditions.
I. Title.
HN80.C5D85   1998
307.76'09773'11—dc21
97-45252
CIP

For Barb, and Moe, and Betty,
and The Loving Memory of Jack
My Heroes, Always

Contents

Acknowledgments   ix
Introduction   xi

PART ONE   ON THE MOVE
1   Coping with a New Sense of Place   3
2   Counting Minutes and Miles   42

PART TWO   A ROOF OVERHEAD
3   Housing Strategies   67
4   Living in the Inherited City   89

PART THREE   FOOD
5   The Risky Business of Food   113
6   Eating Out   145

PART FOUR   SPARE MOMENTS
7   Reducing Risk and Taking Control   169
8   Amusements, Crowds, and Morals   204

PART FIVE   HARD WORK
9   Chicago Is Work   243
10   Getting Ahead on Your Own   274

PART SIX   AVOIDING DISASTER

     11   Time, Risk, and Family Finances   297

     12   The Institutional Trap   316

CONCLUSION   COPING WITH URBAN LIFE   347

     Notes   359
     Selected Bibliography   409
     Index   413

Acknowledgments

WORK on this book began early in 1978 with a telephone call from Don Klimovich, an old friend who was then an editor at *Chicago* magazine. His question: Would Glen Holt, another old friend, and I be interested in writing a monthly column on Chicago history? Glen and I had been coauthors on other works, and we agreed. Each of us sent in samples of his work. (Although we coauthored the column, we never collaborated on any one piece.) Grant T. Dean, the reference librarian of the Chicago Historical Society, suggested a title for the column, and "Chicago As It Was" made its debut in April of that year. Over the next seven years there were seventy-eight offerings of the column, which attracted a large and steady readership. Glen left the masthead in January 1983 to pursue his career in St. Louis, where he is today executive director of that city's public library system; his seventeen excellent columns do not appear in this book. I continued "Chicago As It Was" until August 1985, when the magazine's new management and I agreed that the idea had run its course and did not fit the new format.

Since that time, Richard L. Wentworth, director of the University of Illinois Press, has asked me several times to consider bringing out a collection of my pieces. In 1994, I finally agreed, adding some of the fourteen pieces that first appeared in *Chicago History,* the journal of the Chicago Historical Society. In all of these articles, the goal was originality. At the time they were written, virtually every one was the only thing published on its subject. Over the years, various other authors have used information from them, often without attribution. My pieces were based almost entirely on primary sources, although they were footnoted in neither of their original places of publication. None of the works appears here in its original form; all of them have undergone varying amounts of rethinking, re-researching, and rewriting. The most painful part of the operation was having to omit a large number of them.

As a consequence of its heritage, *Challenging Chicago* attempts to appeal to both the scholar and the general reader. This book contains a scholarly theme and enough smaller arguments to keep urban historians busy with analysis and reinterpretation. At the same time, most general readers are at ease with works based on primary sources, and footnotes do not cause their eyes to glaze over. I have always felt that the division that has developed between academic and popular history is both artificial and unnecessary. In this effort, I have tried to take my cue from one who had bridged both worlds of readership with great skill and success, Daniel J. Boorstin, who is in many ways still my mentor.

The writing of a book is a lonely journey that is made more pleasant by help and encouragement along the way. The largest intellectual debt of gratitude, of course, goes to Glen E. Holt. Our friendship has never been more than a phone call away. In addition, all of my colleagues at the University of Illinois at Chicago, whose history department is a remarkable intellectual community, have always had words of encouragement. Gerald Danzer was kind enough to read and critique my proposal for the book, while my colleagues at UIC have always been willing to listen to my ideas. I thank each of them.

Others who helped along the way include Mary Ann Bamberger, Special Collections librarian at the University of Illinois at Chicago; the three most recent directors of the Chicago Historical Society, Harold Skramstad, Ellsworth Brown, and Douglas Greenberg; as well as other members of the CHS staff: Archie Motley, Linda Evans, Ralph Pugh, Jan McNeil, Emily Clark, Russell Lewis, Rosemary Adams, and the late Scott LaFrance. In her role as editor and friend, the late Fannia Weingartner had an enormous influence over my writing.

The staffs of the Illinois State Historical Library and of the libraries at the University of Chicago, University of Illinois at Chicago, Northwestern University, and the College of DuPage, as well as those at the public libraries of Chicago and Naperville, have also been helpful. Through the years, I have traded references and ideas with many friends, including Frank Jewell, Dominic Pacyga, Arnold Hirsch, Rita Rhodes, David R. Johnson, Howard Rabinowitz, Paul M. Green, Zane Miller, Michael Ebner, Kenneth T. Jackson, Carl Smith, Lew Erenberg, Susan Hirsch, Ellen Skerrett, David Cherry, John Daly, the late Frank Lederer, and David Goldfield. My editor at the University of Illinois Press, Carol Bolton Betts, kept the footnotes accurate and the text from wandering away from the point; it was a joy working with her. The completion of this book was greatly aided by a research leave at the Humanities Institute of the University of Illinois at Chicago.

The greatest aid and comfort came from my wife, Cathy, and our son, Tim, who graciously endured research trips, piles of books, boxes of notes, and my frequent disappearances into "the pit" to work.

Introduction

Go to your library and look up the word "coping" in the catalog. You will find references to books and videos that tell how to manage the problems of stress, aging parents, alcoholism, delinquent children, and a spectrum of other social problems. A magazine bearing the word as its title deals with oncology. The literature is both voluminous and most frequently sad. What separates these works from studies of the general ills that afflict our society is their private and personal dimension. The literature of coping is an iconography of the crises that tens of thousands of families discuss in hushed tones behind closed doors in the quiet hours of the night after the children are asleep. With varying degrees of success, those who face the challenges of life's problems attempt to devise strategies that involve several steps of action that individuals and families can take. Usually, they begin with the discovery of the symptoms of a problem, then move on to verifying its existence, informing (and sometimes confronting) other people involved, then mapping out a plan of action. The latter often depends on what are sometimes called "coping devices," which are mental mindsets or planned responses. At some stage, contact with others similarly afflicted may be part of dealing with the difficulty. Follow-up advice often includes assessment of success or failure, prevention of backsliding, and recognition of signs of other potential problems before they develop.

The millions of all social classes who flocked to American cities also needed to resort to survival strategies. Urban life was a new experience for most of them. Raised on farms and in small towns, both here and abroad, they were often unprepared for what lay ahead. Many found that cities were far more congested, crowded, dangerous, unpleasant, immoral, and unhealthy than they had anticipated. Some of them did not stay. But the vast majority did remain in Chicago and other cities, and in order to survive they had to find strategies, ways to cope with urban life and challenges. Sometimes the action was an unthinking reflex action; other times it was carefully planned. Often the response was solitary, one of thousands or millions of individual stitches in the social fabric; other times it involved a group or was even an institutional reaction that grew out of a society that demanded complex answers to equally complex social needs. The purpose of this study is to examine a sample of the kinds of challenges people faced; it also attempts to blend examples of successful adaptation with those of failure.

This book is organized around the myriad daily decisions made by individuals and families as they came to grips with obtaining the essentials of city life. It begins with what was perhaps most basic, the struggle to get from one part of town to another. The first chapter deals with short-range mobility; the second, with a wider metropolitan movement. In one way or another, much of what happens in the rest of the book depends on the mobility described in the first two chapters. Chapters 3 and 4 examine how the ability to move about affected where people lived, why they moved, where they were headed, and what they encountered when they got there. Mobility also plays an important role in chapters 5 and 6, which treat the sometimes difficult task of obtaining foods that were consumed both at home and around the city. Chapters 7 and 8 consider how people used their mobility, both geographical and social, to improve their lives by seeking out healthy endeavors, as well as the new forms of entertainment that helped them escape daily cares. Ultimately, those who sought these amusements had to face issues of morality. Chapter 9 is an examination of the ways people avoided pitfalls in finding employment and includes as an example the story of the difficulties encountered by African-American restaurant and hotel waiters in their efforts to shape their future by joining together to form unions. Chapter 10 explains how some groups of Chicagoans met the challenges of the city by creating their own futures through independent employment and self-motivated study. The last two chapters focus on serious problems that could ruin family plans. Chapter 11 deals with the sometimes perilous decisions involved in making ends meet and putting money aside, and the sad consequences of families' spending more than they earned. The last chapter focuses on those who had the most difficulty coping with city life, often becoming entrapped in an institutional "safety net" of the day, which was supposed to protect them. The book's conclusion examines some of the larger reasons why coping was necessary, as well as the general themes that run through the survival experience. These include such abstract notions as the role of time in shaping everyday life, the role of privacy, and, most important of all, the manner in which city living brought with it an unprecedented number and variety of risks. There is a logical progression through these topics, but this format also affords the casual reader ready answers to such basic questions as How did Chicagoans find housing? and How did traffic problems differ from today?

The history that unfolds here is not the same one that many general books on Chicago tell. It is not about architectural innovation, the arts, rapid industrial growth, or a myriad of other triumphs that marked the rise of a great metropolis. Others have done a superb job of that.[1] Nor is this a comprehensive social history of Chicago. In a sense, to be complete, such a book would have to tell the story of each of millions of people, for all humans deal with their social and cultural environments in different ways. Nor is this a definitive summary of any of Chicago's major subject areas, some of which are worthy of independent volumes. Instead, this book attempts to enlighten by means of a series of examples drawn from several areas of social history. The main action of most of the chapters falls roughly between the Civil War and 1920, but "postscripts" at the end of each chapter will give the reader some idea of what happened in the intervening years down to the time of this writing.

In some ways, this is a catalog of what *could* go wrong with city living, not what *did* go wrong for everyone. While some of the stories told here ended in failure and even suicide, the overwhelmingly vast majority did not. Nor should readers come to the mistaken conclusion that all of the misfortunes and challenges described here befell any one individual or family. The majority of city dwellers may have grumbled about the inconvenience of transit but faced no particular crisis in finding food, shelter, employment, or any other necessity. Generally, the lower you were on the social ladder, the more of these ills you might have encountered.

Overall, this book demonstrates that most Chicagoans, even the very poor, did find ways to come to grips with the new experience of urban living. A great city is the testament of their success.

PART ONE

On the Move

1   Coping with a New Sense of Place

AN 1897 *Chicago Tribune* feature wondered "Why Chicago Millions Go to Other Cities." The article pointed out that each year the city's wealthy, worth some $130 million, spent most of their time abroad, on the East Coast, or in other parts of the nation—everywhere except in the city where they had made their fortunes. Such prominent family names as Field, Leiter, Nickerson, and Armour were among those of the "absentee landlords." The explanations were varied. Local booster and real estate broker Dunlap Smith exclaimed that only the idlers left town, but most of the people interviewed by the paper believed that well-to-do Chicagoans fled because of the city's unpleasantness. The extremes of the seasons were unavoidable, but the reasons most often mentioned were noise, smoke, congestion, and physical danger. "People . . . refuse to stay where they are suffocated in smoke and soiled in dust; and where their eyes are offended in filthy streets, their ears deafened with clanging bells on the level or roaring trains overhead; and where they can go out with safety only in the most circumscribed limits."[1] The *Tribune* feature was but one in a string of complaints about a conspicuous failure of American cities: the sense of danger and unpleasantness that pervaded urban public places. Although Chicago's boosters puffed with grandiloquent pride, the real transformation from a rural trading post to an industrial metropolis took place largely in the streets, in the evolution of difficulties people encountered while trying to get from here to there.

This story had several broad themes. One involved an unending sorting-out process during which the city rearranged itself from a chaotic patchwork of undifferentiated activities, classes, and land uses to a more rational pattern of specialized functions. This mechanism was the inevitable byproduct of economic growth, but it also sprang from a conscious desire to segregate or isolate something deemed undesirable by the public.[2]

A second theme reflected how the use of new technologies to get more quickly from one place to another tended to force citizens to rethink how they used the roadways. As the years passed, Chicagoans became increasingly irritated with those who used the streets for selfish purposes. This impatience, in turn, led directly to a third theme. This was the growing belief among many Chicagoans that their city was a corporate social entity in which everyone had a stake in the common environment of the public place. Even the wealthy, who could buy a measure of isolation from the unpleasantness of life, were aware that an inefficient street cost them money in the form of slow delivery time and wasted employee wages.

In the final theme, the evolution of the public street was also directly related to the tightening definition of what space was public and what was private. All urbanites, including Chicagoans, differentiated the physical space of the city according to the degree of public access. As spatial entities, urban areas have always been differentiated according to three types of use, the interrelationships of which reveal much about the evolution of society. First, there has been the *public space,* owned—in theory at least—by all citizens in common and open to everyone for reasonable use. This space included the streets, sidewalks, park lands, waterways, public buildings, and the sky. At the opposite end of the spectrum was the *private space,* such as the home and other types of property closed to public access. An outsider who entered did so as a guest or by the power of a court order.

The third category of urban space was a hybrid of the other two and can be labeled *semipublic space.*[3] Its definition, control, and use generated many controversies because it was privately owned yet usually open to public access. Such space proliferated in number and type during the last part of the nineteenth century. Churches and charitable institutions such as Jane Addams's Hull-House formed one type of semipublic space, but such space could more often take the form of stores, depots, restaurants, hotels, and other commercial institutions. As the numbers of citizens using these semipublic areas grew, questions arose about safety, police control, etiquette, and morality. What rights of safety did the visitor or customer enjoy? Who could be excluded? How much access did the police have? How did the semipublic place differ from the private club? As life in the city grew more complex and crowded, Chicagoans had to face these difficult new questions.

First Steps toward Modernization, 1833–50

On paper at least, Chicago was a beautiful and orderly place. In 1830 the Illinois and Michigan Canal Company hired a surveyor named James Thompson to create a plat map of the future city. Although the riverbank that dominated the site was irregular and contained a number of inlets and swamps, his design imposed a uniform grid of blocks on land tucked between the junction of the branches of the Illinois River and Lake Michigan. He gave the streets imposing names, mostly those of presidents, and added alleys so that the new city would avoid some of the crowding found in older cities of the East. There were woods along the northern shore and a gently diverted river mouth. A village of a few hundred people could dream of looking like a city.[4]

None of this resembled the real Chicago. The first crisis of the paper vision came in determining who owned what. Initially, the trustees who ran the Town of Chicago between 1833 and 1837 were more interested in determining who had access to the choice lots next to the river than they were in dealing with the problems of mobility on land.[5] When they finally got around to laying out the streets, they had to force property owners to pull their informally located buildings back within their property lines; structures that could not be moved were destroyed.[6] The authorities also had to defend public property from the dumping of private refuse. The 1833 town charter had empowered its government to "prevent and remove nuisances," and the first public-health ordinance prohibited the disposal of dead animals in the Chicago River. Four years later, the act that incorporated the city allowed the Common Council to specify that "No dung, dead animal or putrid meats and fish or decayed vegetables [were] to be deposited in any street, avenue, lane or public square."[7]

The streets were more efficient on paper. The unpleasantness of the real thoroughfares contributed to the difficulty of getting from here to there. The lack of sidewalks forced pedestrians to walk on the sides of the road, where debris, garbage, stray animals, mud, standing water, and dust impeded daily travel. Even the most affluent found themselves confronting pigs in the street or cleaning mud spatters from their clothing. Through the 1840s, petitioners implored the Common Council to force landowners to install sidewalks, which was done on a block-by-block basis. The most successful plea was for access to a church. But even when wooden walkways were constructed, they failed to extend far from Lake Street, then the most important road. People living in the cluster of houses and inns near the junction of the river branches were among the first to realize the inconvenience of life on the early urban fringe.[8]

No one could escape some kind of unpleasantness in public places. In part, this was because the ability of Chicagoans to cope with the situation was compromised by primitive technologies and limited funds. The cost of pipes and catch basins precluded installation of any type of storm sewer, so that when the streets sank out of sight into the mud, the city fathers could do little more than order another load of stones dumped at the appropriate places. Even simple wooden planking, the first hard street surface, did not appear in Chicago until 1844.[9] When a portion of a bridge rotted away, often in the spring, carpenters would replace it with timbers that had been prudently stockpiled for use during winter shipping shutdowns. A broken chain or pulley created a crisis that could be solved only by a blacksmith.[10] The only readily available resource was human muscle. The 1837 charter, which legally transformed the town into a city government, contained a provision that the government could demand three days' labor from adult male citizens to keep the roads in repair. Most Chicagoans found it easier to pay a fine than comply, giving rise to the principle of property taxes. Larger public works projects routinely encountered opposition from those who complained that they were located too far away to justify their sharing the burden of cost.[11]

There were few places of refuge from the hopeless mess of the street. Chicago's semipublic spaces were themselves unpleasant. Dismal and poorly lighted stores sold merchandise that was neither attractively displayed and organized nor reliably supplied. What the owners had on their shelves was usually what they could grab from the cargoes of ships that were being unloaded at the river. Prudent retail customers hoarded what they could while it was available.[12] Years later, pioneers fondly remembered inns, which were the other principal type of social gathering place, and nights spent singing to the tunes of Mark Beaubien's fiddle. But the same inns were also described as small, filthy, noisy, and rude, often occupying the attic of a private cabin. Guests freely interacted with the proprietor's household, leaving an unclear distinction between what space was private and what was not. The requirement that two or three strangers sleep in a bed added to the confusion. Only gradually did the young city's growth and the impersonality of competition force the standards to improve. The Lake House, built at Kinzie and Rush Streets in 1835, offered one welcome alternative. It was one of the earliest brick buildings, its furnishings were grand, and it reputedly introduced napkins and a printed bill of fare to Chicago.[13]

Chicagoans tried to muster some pride in their streets and public places, which were supposed to provide integrative and noncommercial functions as they did in eastern cities. For many years Chicagoans listened for one of their most prominent African-American citizens, the town crier John Ellis Clark, who strolled the night calling out the time, reuniting lost children with their parents, and checking the condition of the streets. Chicago's mayors traditionally delivered their inaugural speeches from the steps of City Hall to the throngs gathered in the square. Funeral corteges and public processions on the thoroughfares marked the passing of important men.[14] On happier occasions, bands and vividly colored banners added visual stimulation to the excitement of a parade. July Fourth commemorations included cannon shots, which were reminders of the military victories necessary to guarantee liberty. By 1849, fireworks, as well as long-winded patriotic orations, marked the occasion.[15]

But even the uses of public places that were supposed to instill municipal patriotism became disorderly. Clashes between supporters of national political parties marred election time, which was meant to be an occasion for civic unity. Rival volunteer fire companies, who loved to strut in parades, were frequently more interested in claiming first arrival at the scene of a fire than they were in extinguishing the flames. In both cases, the losers frequently picked fights with the winners. And complaints about drunken mayhem invariably followed the celebration of July Fourth. One bizarre incident took place in 1837. A crew dredging the Chicago River had earlier discovered a cannon believed to be a relic of the 1812 Fort Dearborn massacre, and city crews had rehabilitated it for use during Independence Day observance. A family at home several blocks from the celebration heard the roar of the cannon, followed a few seconds later by a loud thump on their roof. They were horrified to discover that it was the severed arm of Joseph Schoneker, a German immigrant who was in charge of the big gun. The sadness did not end there. In the years that followed, Schoneker lost his job because he could no longer work, and he tried unsuccessfully several times to collect compensation from city government.[16]

City Space in Transition, 1850–71

The middle decades of the nineteenth century saw Chicago's population expand dramatically. In 1848, the beginning of railroad construction and the completion of the Illinois and Michigan Canal stimulated an unprecedented growth spurt in the city.[17] A populace of 4,170 in 1837 became 29,963 in 1850 and 109,260 in 1860, and it was on its way to three times that figure by the time of the Great Fire in 1871. As the numbers rose, transportation difficulties grew worse and increasingly interfered with the need to travel to a job, transact business, purchase the necessities of life, or even find a pleasureful moment in one of the city's new commercial leisure spots.

The two decades between 1850 and the Great Fire brought steam power and iron building fronts to the city, signaling the beginning of a limited technological revolution in its public places. Progress was uneven. The city continued to install crude wooden sidewalks only when the complaints and petitions of pedestrians seemed more indignant than the replies of property owners who did not want to bear the burden of paying for the convenience of strangers. Mud, dust, and deep holes were everywhere. In the absence of adequate city street-cleaning services, store owners crossed the line between public and private responsibility and paid youthful "crossing sweepers" to brush aside the muck from narrow paved paths so that pedestrians could cross from one block to another at the corners.[18]

Modernization was slow. The first change was in the street itself. The demands placed on it by heavy traffic frequently exceeded the level of building technologies that a government operating under stringent budgets could afford. This forced a hierarchy of surfaces based primarily on how heavily a street was used. Outlying minor residential streets were still graded stone or dirt, while "Nicholson paving" was most commonly used elsewhere after 1854. This surface had been introduced as an experiment on Western Avenue seven years earlier. It was composed of uniformly cut 4" × 6" blocks, set grain-end up, with strips of board placed between the rows for stability. A coating of hot tar acted as a preservative and gave vehicles a smooth surface on which to travel. The city began installing limestone blocks on many downtown streets in 1855. All of this drove up costs. The 1860s marked a turnaround in the city's infrastructure investment. During the wartime year of 1862, only $42,635 was spent on roads and sewers; in 1870, thanks to a new tax levy law, that item in the city budget had risen to $2.8 million.[19]

The street was also becoming a technological corridor. In 1855 the fear of disease as the result of poor drainage forced the Common Council to approve the installation of an expensive new sewer system designed by Ellis Chesbrough, an engineer. He convinced the aldermen that the only way to create an effective system in a city that was so close to lake level was to start over on top of the existing streets. His plan necessitated raising the street grade as much as sixteen feet above the old surface. The soil under the uplifted street provided not only room for the proper run-off pitch for sewer lines but also space for new water pipes and gas mains. The city held the dirt-filled core in place by erecting long walls at the curb lines. This new barrier, in turn, forced adjacent property owners either to lift their structures onto new, taller foundations or to be content to have their front windows look forlornly across a pit and into a blank wall. For years, however, the sidewalks in front of downtown structures were left uneven; elevated sections might drop suddenly to segments at the old level.[20]

Technological change became visible above the new street surface as well. In 1849 the Chicago Gas Light and Coke Company received its state charter, and on September 4, 1850, the first gas street lights flickered on. The new system, which retained the lamplighter as part of the army of those employed in the streets, was more reliable than the older one using oil lamps.[21] By 1848 telegraph wires had begun to festoon some major streets, and within a decade the demand for instant communication to the other side of the city or across the nation saw these fragile strands drape parts of the urban landscape. In 1864 the growing need for rapid responses from police and fire departments prompted the installation of alarm boxes, which became familiar sidewalk fixtures.[22]

Chicago's bridge development underwent a similar midcentury transformation from simple to complicated technology. In 1856, various designs of wooden spans along the river—all of which had operated with indifferent results—ultimately gave way to an iron swing bridge at Rush Street, the first of its type built in the West. The whole structure pivoted on a pier positioned in the middle of the river, and it had far greater reliability and speed than any of its predecessors. The success of the swing span made it the prototype for several decades to come, but its huge cost forced an end to the legal tradition that required nearby property owners to share construction costs. The following year, the new iron bridge at Madison Street became the first constructed entirely at city expense. By 1870 a total of twenty-seven bridges of all types spanned the river.[23]

While these structures were marvels in their time, they still did not solve the problem of connecting Chicago's three land divisions so that people could cross the river in and out of the downtown without long delays. This problem grew in proportion to the city's increasing contact with its rural hinterland. The town that had once been a backward landing point at the southwestern end of the Great Lakes system became one of the nation's busiest ports. Docks lined the Chicago River. Then, as the city quickly embraced the new technology of the railroad to became its national hub, Chicago became the interface between the two transportation forms. The substantial lake commerce that passed through the main branch of the river tied up bridges and frustrated thousands of daily commuters and rail passengers on their way to and from depots that were on the "wrong side." By the 1850s being "bridged" was costing frustrated teamsters thousands of dollars in time wasted while they waited for boats to pass. The lengthy commuting delays were serious enough to affect property values and divert development to South Side neighborhoods.[24]

In 1853 engineers began studying the possibility of going under the river, but nothing was done until two years later when William Butler Ogden, former Chicago mayor and head of the Galena and Chicago Railway, suggested that the city could follow the lead of European cities and build a system of river tunnels at major streets to accommodate passengers. The other railroads balked at his demand that they contribute to the cost because the arrangement would aid access to their depots, and they quarreled over proposed divisions of assessments. The depression that followed the Panic of 1857 added another delay, as did the apparent lack of local technological knowledge. In 1858, the Common Council voted to advertise in New York newspapers, asking anyone who knew how to dig tunnels to contact Chicago officials. The outbreak of the Civil War further stalled the project, but on July 27, 1866, the city was finally ready to embark on a modest undertaking, a single tunnel to the West Side at Washington Street. But the impressive groundbreaking ceremony was followed by months of frustration. After cave-ins drove the first contractor into bankruptcy, Ellis Chesbrough took over supervision of the task, and on New Year's Day 1869 the city celebrated the opening of a new portal to the West Side.[25] Its enormous popularity led to the construction of another tube at LaSalle Street in 1871. On a typical day that year, the North Side tube carried 2,015 foot passengers and 528 vehicles, while 2,395 pedestrians and 1,396 wagons and carriages passed through its West Side counterpart.[26]

Although Chicago's streetscape was inching its way into the technological age, getting around still depended entirely on human legs or horseflesh. By the 1850s, Chicago's function as a railroad hub allowed it to become the great interchange through which the midwestern agricultural bounty was collected for movement to the east; but the iron horse also enabled it to act as a funnel for gathering and marketing the region's production of live horses. By 1851, one Randolph Street firm alone was handling 3,000 head annually, and a few years later the local press proclaimed the city to be the nation's leading horse market.[27] That role reached critical importance during the Civil War, when the Union Army advertised throughout the Midwest offering the top price in gold for the finest animals. During the last half of 1861, the federal government bought 8,332 of the 11,165 horses sold in the city, and two years later the army erected a corral bounded by State, Clark, Twenty-second, and Twenty-third Streets that could hold 2,000 head for testing. Chicagoans flocked to the area to see army cowboys in action.[28] The horse trade continued to grow after Appomattox. Sales barns clustered on the Near South Side, especially along Dearborn and Wabash, and newspaper feature writers spoke in awe of the hundreds of horses that passed through the markets each day. Meanwhile, near the Union Stock Yard, which opened in 1865, investors built the huge Dexter Park Pavilion, with an 800-seat theater and a 1,150-horse capacity, itself a tourist attraction.[29]

Possession of a horse was a visible sign of social status. Those who could afford to buy one of their own could travel around the city above the mud and muck of the streets. The youthful founders of the village treated their mounts as pets and raced them along the banks of the river. By the early 1850s, equestrianism had become a fad among fashionable men and women. "Every evening," noted the *Daily Democratic Press* in 1855, "as soon as the sun is low in the west, couples are encountered cantering through the more quiet streets, and frequently a whole cavalcade comes sweeping down the avenues." The children even clamored for rocking horses. During the decades that followed, riding schools, high-fashion riding dress, and equestrian shows continued to amuse the wealthy, and park officials added bridle paths in the 1890s to accommodate them.[30]

With horses readily available at low prices, Chicago never lacked horsepower for wagons, cabs, and other vehicles of work, or as a four-legged energy source for lifting construction materials and running other light machinery. The horse also made possible the most important transportation innovation of midcentury. Chicago's site, flat and lacking natural barriers except for the river, encouraged the population to disperse toward cheaper land on the periphery. The resulting increase in traveling times, in turn, made horseless Chicagoans especially interested in new forms of transportation that would get them from here to there as quickly and as mudfree as possible. The first step came during the early 1850s, when Frank Parmelee and Warren Parker began operating omnibuses—urban versions of stage coaches—between the railway stations and hotels. Parmelee established regularly scheduled fixed routes that reached as far as two miles from the center of downtown. But his omnibuses encountered great difficulty negotiating the muddy and rutted streets, jostling and sometimes stranding his passengers. These problems inspired attempts to operate his vehicles on planks embedded in the roadway, but the boards failed to stay in place. The obvious solution was to install permanent rails in the streets. The plan had been introduced two decades earlier in New York, but the potential passenger traffic in Chicago remained too small and scattered to warrant the investment. In 1854 a pair of Illinois Central Railroad employees made the first attempt to construct a horse-drawn railway, but they ran out of money. The Panic of 1857 further delayed the opening of the first successful line until April 25, 1859, when Frank Parmelee and Henry Fuller's Chicago City Railway Company introduced the technology of mass transit to the city.[31]

The equipment proved to be a nightmare to operate. The weight of the car and the frequent stops and starts exhausted the animals after traveling only a few miles of a route. The company had no choice but to own and maintain a large herd—usually seven horses for each car—which also required a large force of blacksmiths, grooms, hostlers, and barn hands as well. Many of the animals perished each year because of falls, rough handling, or other urban hazards.[32] Some tinkerers attempted to attach spring mechanisms to push each car to a more rapid start, but there was little that technology could do to alleviate the strain on the animals. Street-railway interests on the periphery were experimenting with an alternative, miniature steam locomotives, or "dummies," but city officials predicted havoc from frightened horses and exploding boilers and banned their use within municipal borders.[33]

Although passengers were sheltered from the rain and the street muck by horsecars, service frequently aroused their anger. The top speed was six miles an hour, but most of the time the pace was not much faster than walking. With stops, passengers were lucky to make four miles, or about thirty-two blocks, in an hour's journey. This left the expanding fringe of the city still beyond the range of a reasonable commuting time.[34] Soaring operating costs encouraged the company to reduce the number of cars, which increased headways between runs and forced customers to cope with overcrowding. Horsecars had been in business only a month when the *Journal* complained, "We vote the State Street Horse Railway a nuisance. The cars are so jammed and crammed that it is almost impossible to get aboard."[35]

Who Owns the Streets? 1850–70

The ubiquitous presence of the horse created a deceptively unprogressive image of midcentury Chicago as simply a dense version of a frontier town. Animal power was still critical, but by 1870 the streets were well on their way to becoming a collection of other systems designed to move people, energy, information, and goods around the city with greater efficiency. At the same time, these new technologies were beginning to alter public attitudes toward the streets, sidewalks, parks, and public buildings. These transitions were subtle, often merely hints of ideas that would mature later, but they were important steps toward changing the manner of getting from place to place in the modern city.

The first change, which grew out of a sense of crowding, came from the need to substitute written traffic rules for what had formerly been left up to courtesy. Between 1850 and 1870 the Common Council not only specified speed limits but also enacted other restraints on drivers that were meant to prevent or at least untangle traffic jams. In June 1855, for instance, a new law determined which vehicles had the right-of-way in crossing bridges. Those running straight ahead could cross first, those on side streets to the right went next, and those on the left were last. Seen in a larger context, the statute required the individual driver to sacrifice a bit of immediate freedom in order to enjoy the larger benefit of the more efficient use of city streets.[36]

The growing number of nuisance complaints through the midcentury years indicated that Chicagoans were becoming less tolerant of the unpleasantness they had to encounter. What might have been appropriate in rural areas was now thought to interfere with the rights of others in a city that reached 300,000 by 1870. New laws prohibited loud noises, offensive smells, and unsightly structures, even when they were on private property. The city also expanded and refined its antidumping powers. But conditions saw little improvement. Visitors described the streets as nearly impassible with mud, manure, and garbage, the sources of which had remained anonymous. The river, another form of public space, had also become an open sewer. In 1860, Franc Wilkie, a local newspaper humorist, complained that the river "can not be crossed in small boats on account of its exhalations . . . a combination of sulphurated hydrogen, the odor of decaying rodents, and the stench of rotting brassica [cabbage]."[37] The unseemly nature of urban public places was an accepted hazard of travel in early Chicago. On occasion, an angry letter or editorial would appear in the press, but concern never reached the level needed to sustain a reform movement.

Another, and less anonymous, barnyard survival within the borders of industrializing Chicago was the presence of livestock and its odors. Although housed on private property, hens and milk cows directly influenced the character of nearby public areas. Carter Harrison II described the neighborhood around Ashland Boulevard and Jackson Street in the 1860s as "semi-pastoral," with vegetable gardening and small farm animals, and "a smokehouse in the back yard."[38] Franc Wilkie's tongue-in-cheek commentary described North Siders as consisting of "men, women, children, dogs, billy-goats, pigs, cats, and fleas."[39] Mrs. O'Leary's cow was more famous for its alleged role in starting the Great Fire of 1871, but the bovine was significant in this context because it was a farm animal housed just a mile from the center of the business district.[40] Although decidedly rural and unpleasant to many people, keeping pigs, cattle, and chickens in Chicago was legal as late as 1890, so long as the animals did not share living space with the family and the owner received the approval of the city health department. This policy allowed separate regulations for the rural fringe neighborhoods and the densely settled core of the city.[41]

Most pre-Fire Chicagoans accepted the legitimacy of the commercial uses of public spaces. The strong tradition of free trade included virtually limitless access to the streets as places to make sales, post advertising, and cart goods. Marketplaces and peddling (both described in detail in later chapters) were the most visible profitmaking uses. The only real controversy arose when businesses crossed the property lines between their stores and the public spaces outside and began to interfere with traffic. A forest of advertising signs not only lined rooftops but also hung over the sidewalks. When weather permitted, merchants piled their goods on the walkways to attract the attention of passersby. By 1857 these practices had become such a nuisance that Mayor "Long John" Wentworth issued a special decree demanding that merchants withdraw to within their property lines. When the offenders failed to comply, Wentworth organized a raid. Under cover of darkness, he personally tore down dozens of sidewalk obstructions, described by the press as "show-cases, milliners' bonnet-blocks, merchants' boxes, grocers' barrels, barbers' poles, saloon signs, literary depot advertisers, and other articles too numerous to mention." Wentworth's personal crusade proved futile in the long run, for by the late 1860s whole sides of buildings had become signboards, and huge banners hung across streets. Commerce had triumphed over the aesthetics of the public place.[42]

Although streets and sidewalks were busy commercial centers in pre–Civil War Chicago, many citizens still regarded most public places with some measure of fear and disdain. The sidewalks became home to the poorest urbanites who had nowhere else to live; if citizenship provided little else, common ownership of the city's public places at least carried with it the right, within the limits of vagrancy and loitering laws, to live on the street or illegally squat there.[43] There was increasing concern about the open brazenness of footpads (today's muggers), rowdies, and prostitutes who helped to create and perpetuate the negative image of the city as a predominantly violent and lawless place. Initially, the problem grew from the makeup of the "frontier town" population, unattached young men, many of them Irish immigrants who had arrived to work on the Illinois and Michigan Canal.

With fair frequency the press reported victims' being accosted and beaten on the streets or dragged from carriages and robbed in broad daylight. "Complaints are made of outrages committed nightly upon persons walking the streets," declared the *Daily Democrat* in 1849. "Ladies out alone after night fall are in danger of being insulted by ruffians; and indeed many males are afraid to walk the streets without going around and avoiding the alleys and being careful of the corners."[44] As early as the 1850s, Chicago newspapers also began complaining about the presence of packs of youths wandering the streets. When they were not brawling or vandalizing public property or stealing from gardens, they were pawning stolen goods or selling them to junk dealers.[45]

The perception of street danger also grew from Chicago's role as a crossroads. Farmers coming to town to sell livestock were easy prey to thugs and con artists who lay in wait along roads leading into town.[46] The rapid multiplication of Chicago's rail passenger traffic also introduced tens of thousands of strangers to the city's streets, and those who became victims helped spread the city's bad reputation across America. The budding convention business, which got under way in 1847 and reached a peak with the Republican national meeting of 1860, also brought in easy marks. As early as 1859 the city's reputation inspired a New York publisher to issue *Tricks and Traps of Chicago,* a guide that warned of "sandbaggers," real estate speculators, and the attractive "grisettes," or waitresses, at saloon halls. Hackmen were often co-conspirators. "Scalpers" met trains and talked travelers into rides to overpriced hotels. One man, "Allspice," was reportedly lured into a cab and taken to a rough district where he was forced to buy an expensive bottle of wine and was then drugged and robbed. The locally published *Chicago after Dark* (1868) perpetuated the city's reputation as a crime-ridden center. Improved travel helped make Chicago a major crossroads for professional criminals; a quick rail exit from other cities brought them likely as not to the new metropolis.[47]

Individuals coped with the situation in a variety of ways, including staying off the street at night. But there was also a collective public response to this disorder that took several forms. At one extreme, Chicago's first execution, that of John Stone in 1840, was a civic affair attended by over 2,500 people of all classes, men, women, and children "of every condition of life."[48] Other crimes obviously required more subtle reactions. In 1858 the growing sense that Chicago was sinking into disorder resulted in the reorganization of an ineffective constabulary into a professionalized police department. Believing that quick response to emergencies enhanced the sense of street safety, city officials divided the force into precincts, with police officers originally housed in market buildings and later in their own halls throughout town. In 1858, Mayor John C. Haines equipped the force with standard blue uniform coats and stars; his successors retained the tradition. Despite a jurisdictional dispute between the mayor and the governor, who controlled the Chicago police from 1861 through 1876 by his appointments to a commission, city officials agreed that the police on the street should become more visible symbols of authority to engender a feeling of security and order.[49]

A third response to street danger was less organized and more subtle. As bad as conditions often were, there was a growing belief that Chicago's public spaces could serve unifying and practical purposes. For example, two of the functions of the post office, which had long been a social gathering place, were dispersed into the streets during the 1860s in the form of collection boxes and letter carriers. At the same time, the strategic location of police and fire alarm boxes made citizens feel a bit safer.[50] The streets adjacent to newspaper and telegraph offices served an informational function when people gathered to see the posting of election returns. During the tense war years, crowds assembled to read the latest war news dispatches posted in front of newspaper offices. And the middle decades of the century saw the first public clocks installed on the government-owned market halls, as well as on downtown commercial buildings and a few factories.[51] Finally, public mourning moved from indoor meetings to elaborate outdoor services, especially when the deceased was a president or ex-president. Schools and businesses closed, somber bunting draped buildings, and church bells tolled. The most notable instance was the city's elaborate memorial to Abraham Lincoln, which employed a chorus of thousands and a procession that wound its way through heavily decorated streets. The local reburial of groups of Civil War soldiers occasioned similar outpourings. And when former President Ulysses S. Grant died in 1885, his Chicago cortege included an elaborate, but empty, coffin.[52]

While these positive uses did help to improve the public's perception of the street, three developments during the late 1860s foreshadowed the ways in which Chicagoans would cope with the problems of their public places in the future. The first prescient change, which took place in 1869, involved what was perhaps the first organized nongovernmental intrusion of one group of interests into the manner in which someone else used the public street. The issue was the treatment of horses. Most animals undoubtedly received adequate care as pets or valuable economic assets, but many others were beaten, forced to pull overweight loads, left outdoors all winter, and abandoned when they were old or dying. Horses that were driven too fast for conditions skidded and fell on slippery streets. When teaming companies lost money, they cut the animals' oat rations to near-starvation levels.[53] In 1869 the General Assembly passed a tough anticruelty law, and that same year the Illinois Society for the Prevention of Cruelty to Animals (ISPCA) was founded. The ISPCA built drinking fountains, many of which accommodated dogs, cats, and people at different spouts, and operated a horse ambulance. Renamed the Illinois Humane Society in 1871, it warned, prosecuted, and educated offenders, while carrying on a parallel crusade to aid another helpless group, destitute and abused children.[54] In 1899 the Anti-Cruelty Society joined the field and sponsored such events as workhorse parades, which encouraged owners to clean up their everyday beasts of burden and march them with pride.[55]

The ISPCA was significant as a model of one way in which Chicagoans were learning to cope collectively with the problems of urban life. The first stage involved individuals coming in contact with those who were similarly distressed by what they saw. These people, not yet formally organized, noticed the problem of animal cruelty, then defined the issue so clearly that they, in effect, invented it. Then they lobbied the state legislature for a bill that they drafted, and after it became law, they set themselves up as the organization that became the principal enforcer. In later years, those interested in issues as diverse as smoke pollution and juvenile delinquency would employ the same approach.[56]

The protest formula worked especially well because it united those whose individual outcries would have had no impact. In 1869, for instance, the Chicago City Railway converted its entire system to rear-entry "bobtail cars," on which riders were forced to push their way through the crowd to the front to deposit their money in the farebox, which was located next to the driver, who was the lone onboard worker. The bobtail intensified another problem that was beginning to make public transit even more unpleasant. Driver-collectors were so occupied with the horses that they could not watch what was going on behind them. There were frequent complaints about drunken, odoriferous passengers who smoked, spat, told off-color jokes, and otherwise menaced more-sensitive fellow riders with little interference from the driver. In 1875, angry riders banded together to form the Citizens' Protective Association. As a mass protest, its members got on the bobtail but refused to make any effort to pay the fare. When the company roughed up women boycotters, the press castigated the company for excessive force. The size of the protest grew to the point that revenues virtually disappeared, forcing the company to restore fare collectors and larger cars.[57] The model was clearly set for the future: coping with a shared problem by discovering others with the same concerns, publicizing the problem, organizing a protest, and applying public pressure where it could produce reform.

The second development of the late 1860s involved park lands. Chicago's nickname, "The Garden City," had been derived from the landscaping and vegetable plots on private land, not public spaces. The public city of the pre–Civil War era had been homely and utilitarian, with little effort expended in the beautification of public places. "The behemoth Trade swallows up everything," bristled the *Tribune* in 1853. "Still we say parks—give us public parks. They are the 'lungs of the metropolis.' Let us breathe or we and our children die."[58] There was a small fountain in Court House Square, and on Sundays young men and women strolled down an informal "promenade" along a pleasant stretch of Michigan Avenue. But the parks that existed before the late 1860s were not necessarily regarded as benefiting the whole city. Dearborn Park, located downtown, was frequently occupied by tent meetings and balloon launches. Union and Washington Squares, though designed to improve generally the quality of life in the immediate community, were inadequate and too small. The creation of Lincoln Park in 1863 gave some promise of what lay ahead, but even that space remained unattractive because it had been an active cemetery until 1859, and the removal of remains continued into the 1870s.[59]

Then, in 1869, the legislature created a ring of major parks and boulevards several miles beyond the perimeter of the city. The parks' significance lay in the fact that they were artificial landscapes of plantings, carefully designed and aesthetically utopian. They were to be everything the streets were not: quiet, orderly, free from commercial intrusion, and safe. Although only twigs in a mud hole in 1869, the parks promised to mature into middle- and upper-class sylvan retreats. Planners and the commissioners who ran the parks afterward dealt with the demand for active sports by carefully segregating playing fields from the quiet, more contemplative areas.[60]

The third change that appeared in its incipient form in the 1860s involved a parallel effort to escape the horrors of the street. As most of Chicago's public places became increasingly unattractive, the semipublic places that benefited from private ownership became correspondingly more desirable as retreats and alternative spaces. The railroads were in several ways responsible for this development. Profits, competition, direct all-rail routes to eastern cities, and huge increases in the number of passengers transformed the depots. The era of the small, wooden shanties was beginning to give way to the grand age of the "terminal," a symbolic as well as practical beginning and end to the rail journey. In such structures as the Illinois Central–Michigan Central Depot on the lakefront and the Galena and Chicago Union Station built at Kinzie and Wells, the train shed shielded passengers from the rain and snow, while the waiting room of each new depot became less narrowly utilitarian and more commodious and decorative. In 1866, for instance, the newly opened Lake Shore and Michigan Southern–Rock Island Railroad station boasted a 542-foot train shed, access to the platforms without crossing tracks, and a grand waiting room.[61]

Chicago's emergence as a rail hub meant that no trains merely stopped in the city; they began or ended their runs there. Travelers on their way through had to get from one line's terminal to another, supplying a depot-to-depot "transfer trade" for hacks or Frank Parmelee's coaches. Recognizing the potential in this arrangement, the *Chicago Daily Democrat* in 1850 editorialized against the idea of a union station; it argued that if the railroads built several depots in scattered parts of the town, the streets and sidewalks "would be lively all the time [because] produce, merchandise and passengers would change here," while only a few would benefit from a unified depot.[62]

The paper's wish came true. The travelers also provided a clientele for the city's large hotels, which by the late 1860s were emerging from an atmosphere of utility to one of elegance. For example, the Grand Pacific, which opened in 1870, was co-owned by the Lake Shore and Michigan Southern and the Rock Island railroads, whose depot was nearby. The elegant hotel, which covered most of a square block, boasted a conservatory, several posh dining rooms, and elevators to all floors. Each of its 550 rooms was equipped with a "new electric annunciator" to summon service. Potter Palmer opened a similarly sumptuous hotel only months before the Great Fire destroyed both structures.[63]

The most significant feature of the Grand Pacific was its glass-domed court, under which carriages unloaded. This enabled travelers to avoid the unpleasantness of the street and the numerous "baggage smashers" who gathered outside of hotels and offered to cart travelers' luggage. Thus, an affluent traveler could retreat to what amounted to a city within a city. The arriving passenger could take a Parmelee bus to a hotel, then alight in a privately owned place that could shield visitors and provide elegant accommodation for selected strangers. As semipublic places, hotels and depots—along with restaurants and entertainment spots (which are discussed later)—were attractively decorated, clean, well lighted, and secure from unpleasant and dangerous people. Like the parks, the semipublic places promised to be everything that the streets were not.[64]

Self-Dissolving Solutions, 1880–1910

The technological advances of city life before 1870 helped transform Chicago's street life, but the horsecars, gaslights, hotels, and bridges proved to be only the beginning. In the four decades following the Great Fire, revolutions in communications, transportation, and building technology remade the downtown areas and changed the manner in which Chicagoans would reach the center of the city from their homes. At the same time, Chicagoans expressed a deepening concern about the state of their public places, which underwent the most rapid transformation after 1880. The flood of transportation technology shifted the nature of the street from a place of commerce to a conduit of transit, a means of moving through the city as quickly as possible. The relaxed stroll and casual dickering with a vendor began to give way to the rush hour. And with this change came a new attitude concerning who might use the streets and for what purpose. The appropriation of public property for private business that had been tolerated in earlier years now provoked an urgent outcry. The question Who owns the city? elicited a strong answer that the streets, at least, belonged to the people.

Some elements remained the same. The horse continued to dominate the social life of the street. Newspaper features introduced readers to the milk horse that stopped by a saloon every day for a beer, and recounted the way in which draft animals pulled police wagons, fire engines, cabs, omnibuses, and thousands of wagons.[65] Horses were also an important economic feature of the city because they figured in several dependent industries. For instance, Chicago became a leading center for the manufacture of saddles and other riding equipment because the slaughter of cattle and pigs produced large amounts of leather as a byproduct. At the turn of the century, there were 280 firms enrolled in the Carriage and Wagon Manufacturers Association of Chicago. And the decoration of those vehicles became a separate specialty pursued by 44 other local members. There were several manufacturers of horseshoes, nails, trim, varnish, tires, decals, and the lamps and oils used on wagons. And by 1895 there were 245 blacksmiths, 398 horseshoers, and 325 livery stables that rented equipages. In addition, a number of grain suppliers, who were centered in the Haymarket area of Randolph Street, provided the necessary food link between the farm and the city.[66]

But the horse was basically a rural animal and was prone to cause monumental urban problems. Large and powerful, it could do great harm on a crowded street. The sudden noises of the city resulted in runaway teams and wrecked carriages that dotted the accident lists. Many young men on horseback could not resist the temptation to dash down a crowded urban street at a country road gallop. Moreover, the horse was an investment with an independent personality.

Its impatience and need for food and water placed a limit on how long it could be left unattended outside of a stable, thus affecting the amount of time its rider had to visit or to conduct his or her business. The want-ads were often filled with queries about animals that had ambled away because their owners had failed to hitch them properly. When tied at the curb, unattended mounts often managed to move into a perpendicular position and blockade the streets.[67] There was also no way to "lock up" a horse, making thievery an easy and common crime. Like auto theft years later, the object stolen became the means of escape. But branding one's animal to deter theft only decreased its resale value.[68] Ultimately, horses were rural survivors in an urban setting. Because stables generated noise, smell, flies, and traffic, they became an urban necessity that everyone wanted only in someone else's neighborhood.[69] The tons of manure, or "road apples," lent an obvious unpleasantness to the streetscape, and the cost of sweeping it all strained the city budget.[70]

Another negative aspect of Chicago's dependence on the horse became apparent in the fall of 1872. On October 11, some animals that had been imported from Canada fell ill in a stable on West Jackson. The "Horse Epizootic" that had raged in other parts of the country had arrived in Chicago. The effects on the city for the next three months were devastating. The equine death toll for one six-week period reached 1,150, halting virtually all urban commerce. Horse-drawn streetcars ceased operation, while oxen were pressed into service to haul the few wagons still moving. As people carted their merchandise through the streets, the sound of their footsteps dominated the rush hour. The *Chicago Times* observed that the epizootic did more for temperance than closing barrooms on Sunday because brewers were unable to deliver beer to saloons. The disease finally abated during the Christmas season, only to return in a milder form three years later.[71]

The shortcomings of the horse as a means of transportation hastened the introduction of the cable car, which was probably the most significant turning point in Chicago's transportation history. This form of propulsion had been developed in 1873 in San Francisco, where horsedrawn vehicles had great difficulty operating on the steep hills, especially during rainy weather. The new system replaced the horse with a moving underground cable that was contained in a deep slot located beneath and between the tracks. The "steel rope" moved at a steady speed on a complicated network of pulleys powered by large steam engines. The operator used two levers to control the car. One was a "grip," a device that reached through the bottom of the car into the slot and either held onto the moving cable or released it. The other lever applied the brakes to the wheels to stop the car.[72]

The cable car arrived in Chicago in January 1882. Its advocates saw it as an important advancement over the horsecars: it was faster, cheaper to operate, and could free the transit companies from the problem of maintaining hundreds of horses. But the cable system had serious flaws. Much of the slot chamber and all of the pulleys and cables were iron or steel, and the installation process was slow because it had to be precise or it would not work. At a cost to the private investors of more than $100,000 a mile, the system was too expensive

Clark Street, 1857. Uneven sidewalks created by raising the street grade made walking an adventure. (Unless noted otherwise, illustrations are from the collection of the author.)

Lake Street, 1857. An omnibus, which seems bound for a collision with a private carriage, lumbers by a sidewalk used for a mixture of commercial and pedestrian activities.

Dearborn and Madison Streets, 1890. As a fixed-route vehicle, the streetcar (cable car) could not move around obstacles, thus becoming another impediment to the flow of traffic.

North Clark Street, 1890. Crossing a street became a perilous venture in muck and traffic. Note the police call box at the corner, to the left.

Outside the Chicago Horse Show, Coliseum, 1906. For many families, such as that of
lunchroom chain owner John R. Thompson, whose son is shown at the left, a horse was
a part of everyday life. The annual horse show brought together dealers, equipment
manufacturers, and families of dreamers, much as the annual Chicago Auto Show would
do later. (Chicago Historical Society, DN004153)

Adams Street looking east from State Street, postcard view, around 1900. Growth in the volume of street and sidewalk traffic often outpaced the development of discipline and order.

Rush Street Bridge, around 1900. A postcard view captures a common experience: being "bridged" by a passing ship. Note the industrial nature of the downtown river edge and the dock for ships to Milwaukee and Racine.

SECTIONAL VIEW OF LA SALLE STREET TUNNEL.

LaSalle Street Tunnel system, early 1870s. The first effort to use technology to overcome the problem of urban congestion utilized tunnels under the crowded river, which served as the port of Chicago.

CHICAGO, ROCK ISLAND AND PACIFIC R. R. DEPOT.

Chicago, Rock Island, and Pacific Rail Road depot, sometime between 1897 and 1903. This advertising drawing illustrates how pedestrians coming from the station gained access to the "iron highway" of the elevated system over the streets.

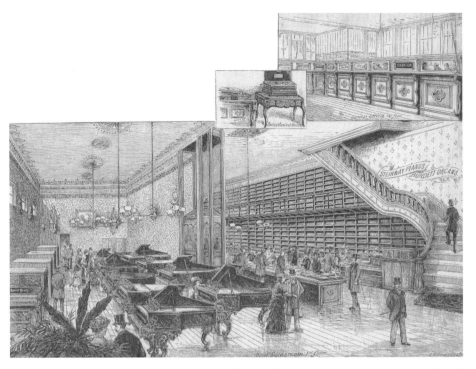

Lyon and Healy Music Store interior, around 1880. Pleasant commercial interiors offered an escape from the congestion and unpleasantness of the street outside.

Office of the American Express Company, 1880s. Business offices in the expanding downtown were models of efficiency and order compared with the street.

to install outside of densely settled districts. But investors ultimately built eighty-two miles of lines in Chicago, making it the largest cable car system in the world.[73]

The new form of street transportation showed its vulnerability during the ebb and flow of urban traffic. Because the cable could bear only so much weight pulling on it at any given point, the system worked best when the cars were distributed fairly evenly throughout the system. The element of time was critical because the cable car functioned least efficiently when it was most needed. Rush hour became a particular problem because tens of thousands of riders wanted to go in the same direction at the same time and the weight of the cars could snap the steel ropes on which everything depended. As a result, the metal strands that made up the cables could easily stretch or fray and become tangled in their pulleys or in the grip mechanism, causing the driver to lose control of the car. Operating the system required practiced skills, and inexperienced gripmen were known to throw passengers to the floor by "grabbing" the cable too quickly. The inflexibility of the cable speed caused the cars to start too rapidly in the congested districts while seeming to move at a snail's pace in the outlying neighborhoods. Cold Chicago winters meant that the cable slot had to be set much deeper in the ground than in San Francisco to be safely below the frostline. This meant that the grip from the car had to be longer to reach the sunken cable, making the mechanism subject to more frequent breakdowns and the slot more likely to fill with frozen manure and other street debris during the winter. Finally, the moving cable created an audible rumble under the street, unnoticed during the daytime but an annoyance to nearby residents during the quiet hours of the night.[74]

The cable system represented a tendency toward technological centralization. Just as the gas company filled its lines from a few large "gas houses," where coal was baked into lighting gas and coke, transit became dependent on a few power plants that moved the cables along a grid. There was no way to isolate the impact of breakdowns. A cable break could shut down an entire line, create a corridor of indignation, and elevate blood pressure among thousands of passengers forced to become pedestrians without warning. Angry complaints forced the cable companies to keep hundreds of horses available for emergency use.[75] Thus, the replacement of the horse was an urban technological trade-off. On the one hand there was the advantage of convenience, greater speed, and the thrill of being modern. On the other hand, a price had to be paid in the form of a dependence on a fragile, centrally powered technology that disadvantaged greater numbers of people when it failed to work properly.

The cable lines represented an investment of millions in the public streets, but the system was barely finished before its replacement was imminent. The electric streetcar, or trolley, invented in Richmond, Virginia, by Frank Sprague in 1887, had its first public demonstration that year at a Chicago railway exposition. Transit engineers and investors quickly appreciated its advantages. The lower installation costs of suspending a wire over the street made it feasible to extend service into outlying districts that generated too few riders for cable cars to operate profitably. Despite problems of ice accumulation on the wires, they were easier to maintain than the cable slots. The trolley cars could be crowded together and even linked in trains during rush hours. The first Chicago electric streetcar line opened in 1890 on a stretch of Ninety-third Street on the Southeast Side, and sixteen years later the entire length of what had been the cable car system was electrified. Both the horsecars, which had been relegated to lightly patronized feeder lines, and the cable cars stopped running in 1906.[76]

Electric cars forced riders to confront a new set of problems. The motors could accelerate so quickly that standing passengers were forced to grab for the straps or anything else fixed to the cars to avoid being pitched to the floor. Higher speeds and larger cars meant more serious accidents; dozens of careless pedestrians were run down each year. The casualty toll leveled off only after an 1890 city ordinance required the addition of a "safety fender" to scoop up people who wandered into the path of the car.[77] And finally, there was a constant fear that the overhead wires might fall. A newspaper had greeted the prospect of electric cars with a headline warning of "DEATH IN THE AIR," and the city council had initially relegated the new form of propulsion to outlying districts. The press no doubt fueled rumors that the streetcar companies were involved in some kind of conspiracy to keep the public from knowing about safer power systems, such as underground conduits or batteries. These fears, along with the belief that the wires would ruin the appearance of the streets, stymied efforts to introduce the electric trolley downtown until 1901. As was the case with the steam dummy, outlying neighborhoods enjoyed more advanced technologies sooner than did the center of the city. But there was a price for progress. Those who lived nearest the lines suffered the most inconvenience because of noise and crowds. The electric trolley might provide faster service, but its wires and posts defaced property and brought urban hazards into residential neighborhoods. And in all cases, the rush-hour crowds made property along the heavily traveled principal streets less desirable for those who lived nearby.[78]

While the most visible of the new street-corner technologies involved public transit, private vehicles were evolving as well. The basic horsedrawn commercial wagon proved easily adaptable to many designs and uses. There were such exotic styles as a baker's wagon, equipped with double-pane glass to keep the contents warm; oil tankers; insulated ice wagons; pie carriers with compartments opening from the sides of the body; and furniture wagons with large doors. Taxis evolved into such forms as herdics and hansoms, while private carriages came in several sizes and styles. Citizens on the way to the mental hospital rode in the asylum van, while those bound for jail bounced along in the "Black Maria." In the mid-1880s the Chicago Police Department claimed credit for inventing patrol wagons, drawn by fast horses and specially equipped with warning bells, irons to detain prisoners, and stretchers, as well as hooks and other emergency rescue equipment.[79]

The mechanization of the street and its crowding with commercial vehicles and transit cars gradually forced a significant change in attitude toward the use of public places in Chicago. Congestion aroused concern over street safety. Speeding and reckless drivers had always been a problem: as early as 1851 the Common Council had tried to enact a workable speed limit law. During the

1880s the Citizens Association, a private reform group, began a campaign to slow down wagons, hacks, and even fire engines. But the measurement of speed was still a crude science, and specific limits, such as "six miles per hour," were finally defined, not very helpfully, by the courts as "about as fast as a horse can trot and keep moving."[80]

The people of Chicago were angered by the way in which individuals seemed to be taking over the streets for private economic gain and paying nothing for the privilege.[81] The expanding city was constantly short of government revenues, and in the 1880s officials began to discuss license fees for all types of stores and trades, including peddlers. Chicago teamsters were particular targets, in part because of the "call boxes" they placed on street corners to receive express packages and messages.[82] Many citizens were upset when teaming companies made sales duties part of the drivers' job, effectively adding hundreds more aggressive street salesmen to the crowded thoroughfares.[83] The carriers used heavy wagons with narrow tires to reduce the amount of drag on the horses. The practice created considerable damage to the street surfaces, but the companies resisted control. Just after the turn of the century, some angry citizens formed a Chicago Wide Tire Association to call attention to the problem and force team owners to pay for damage to the streets. Association members darted through traffic measuring rim widths and the group lobbied in the press and Chicago City Council chambers for a new law. In 1903 the city's aldermen enacted corrective legislation, but political pressure slowed its enforcement for another two years. Only the direct orders of Mayor Edward F. Dunne, in office from 1905 to 1907, and the determination of his public works commissioner, the newspaper heir Joseph Medill Patterson, finally forced compliance.[84]

The general issue of conducting private business on the public streets was at the center of the great debates over franchises for the new utilities and transit companies. Technological development was expensive; each innovation required a higher capital investment, while the expansion of gas, telephone, and electrical service created massive grids of trunk lines over and under the major streets. The new utilities also benefited from economies of scale. A large gas plant could produce more volume than several smaller ones and at a lower cost per unit. The same was true for electric companies, while transit lines could easily share generating stations and realize a new efficiency from longer routes. This aroused a strong desire by the utilities to expand beyond the narrow confines of a small section of the city. More important, investors demanded long-term operating rights to guarantee a return on their money. Technically, a cable car company was required to tear up its tracks and cable slots at the end of its franchise, at a cost of $100,000 a mile, making a short-term contract ruinous. Thus, utilities demanded exclusive rights over larger territories and for extended periods of time.[85]

The public reaction created an uproar that lasted for decades. Suspicious citizens saw every franchise grant as an unfair right to use common public space in perpetuity for a pittance. Gas and horsecar lines had provoked a few complaints at midcentury, but the later developments of cable cars, electric trolleys, and electric service focused unprecedented public attention on the franchise grants by the city council and the Illinois General Assembly. Beginning in 1868, charges of payoffs to legislators surrounded nearly every franchise grant; bribes were part of the cost of doing business, which, it was rumored, could be passed on to consumers. Political reform groups argued that the companies returned little or nothing to the people whose commonly owned space was being used; high rates, poor service, and the inconvenience of torn-up streets were the citizens' rewards.[86]

While most Chicagoans could only cuss and cope with the problems of getting from here to there, one individual came to personify the cause of their problems. For sixteen years, the bulk of the criticism over shoddy service and corrupt franchise deals was aimed at Charles Tyson Yerkes. He had made his first fortune selling municipal bonds for his native Philadelphia, and questionable practices had landed him in prison for seven months in 1873. After paying off his Pennsylvania creditors, Yerkes sought new opportunities further west and settled in Chicago in 1881, where a lucrative stock and bond business soon gave him the funds to invest in street railways. In 1886 he gained control over the Chicago West Division Railway Company, and over the next few years he bought out forty-six smaller, outlying companies, most of which were marginal operations that had been built to lure home buyers to subdivisions.[87]

Yerkes and his operations angered the public, while his poor relations with the press only made him look more villainous. Service was substandard. Cars ran infrequently and they were always packed with people. His famous remark—"It is the people who hang to the straps who pay you your big dividends"—became the battle cry of an anti-Yerkes crusade. Chicagoans gradually learned that he had issued stock to himself in amounts far beyond the value of his lines and then squeezed huge dividends per share, which he deposited in his own bank accounts. When reformers complained, he issued a stream of public relations pamphlets and even bought the *Chicago Inter-Ocean* in 1897 to use in defense of his reputation. Opposition to Yerkes mounted steadily. Because he kept his companies in the form of separate legal entities, riders were denied the right of free transfer, even though all profits went into the same hands. Various "Strap-hangers Leagues" and other citizens' protest groups tried unsuccessfully to organize boycotts and withhold fares. Yerkes was even vilified in literature as the fictional Frank Cowperwood, an evil character created by the novelist Theodore Dreiser. Ironically, as city life was creating irascible crowds, the people found a sense of unity in their hatred of the "Traction baron."[88]

Technological Coping: Creating Layers of Loop

By the 1890s, traffic on the Chicago River, which had become one of the busiest ports in North America, effectively cut off the downtown from two-thirds of the city. Midcentury technology proved inadequate to the task of solving the problem. The initial enthusiasm prompted by the Washington and LaSalle Street tunnels soon waned. The tubes were too expensive, too narrow, and their entranceways too steep for heavily laden teams. By the mid-1880s, the tunnels had begun to leak, and the aldermen gladly turned them over to streetcar companies in exchange for the cost of upkeep. A private transit company built a third streetcar-only tunnel at Van Buren Street in 1893; it would be the last of its type. Between 1906 and 1916, all three had to be lowered to allow larger vessels to use a deepened river above them.[89] Instead of going under the river, most daily commuters chose to risk being "bridged" by ships that caused the movable spans to be opened. Since federally regulated maritime transport had right-of-way over locally regulated land transport, shipping could disrupt even a rush hour. And, while Chicagoans complained vociferously, many found the rush hour a universal excuse for being late for work.[90]

Despite these difficulties, the bridges and tunnels were, in a sense, operating too efficiently. By the 1890s, downtown congestion had moved from curiosity to crisis, with too many people trying to move about in too little space. The culprit was the technological improvement in public transit, which extended the distance commuters could travel in the same amount of time. This not only opened up whole new districts to subdivisions, but also increased the number of people drawn to the downtown to shop, work, and be entertained. At the same time, the downtown could not grow horizontally to accommodate the new users because of the lake to the east, the river to the north and west, and a wall of railway tracks leading into railway stations to the south. Transit riders also tended to avoid walking too far from a convenient ring, or loop, of tracks by which the streetcars turned themselves around for outbound trips. In place by the early 1880s, the "Loop" soon came to refer to the downtown blocks within the trackage as well. This tendency to remain compact both promoted and was intensified by new skyscrapers and department stores, whose workers and shoppers jammed the streets during rush hours and at noontime. Downtown Chicago sprawled vertically at an increasing rate. In 1913 one architect, August Gatzert, noted:

> Consider the bank building nearing completion upon one half block bounded by Adams, LaSalle, Quincy and Fifth Avenue [now Wells Street]. I am told that the occupancy of that twenty-two story structure will embrace 7,000 people. In former times, when our six- and eight-story buildings were erected with large office rooms and more hall space, it took nearly three blocks in our downtown district to house 7,000 people. What does that mean? It means the concentration of the business of other days into one-sixth of its former street area, with a slowing up of movement due to crowding.[91]

Moreover, soaring property values made it feasible for developers and architects of new structures to include multiple subbasements, and this "underground age," as one writer called it, further added to the street congestion above.[92] The result: more people and activities filled streets and sidewalks, which could not easily be widened because of the soaring property values that the crowds helped to create. Chicago was choking on its own prosperity.[93]

The traffic jam was becoming the symbol of this new kind of city. Wagons, horses, carriages, streetcars, pushcarts, and pedestrians scrambled together into immobile knots of inefficiency that were all the more difficult to untangle because of the variety of vehicles involved. Some observers directly blamed an excess of individualism. In 1899, for instance, the *Chicago Post* grumbled about hacks: "An utter disregard for the rights of others is becoming altogether too common in drivers. They delay streetcars, block crossings, and frequently involve other vehicles in the most complicated tangles by their innate selfishness. All rights are theirs, and all parts of the street they happen to want to occupy are theirs. . . . They have no regard for anything but the upraised club of the corner policeman, and they frequently do not hesitate to swear at him."[94]

The problem of vehicular and especially pedestrian crowding was aggravated by an ironic surplus of conveniences. The letter box, for instance, had dispersed through the streets one of the most important functions of the post office, the collection of mail. Similarly, electric alarm boxes brought instantaneous contact with police and fire departments, while clocks on posts kept those without timepieces on schedule. Corner newsstands made the information in newspapers and magazines easily accessible, but an "iron newsboy," the earliest newspaper vending machine, seemed more intrusive. The Woman's Christian Temperance Union and others provided drinking fountains for those who did not want to enter a saloon or restaurant to slake their thirst. The Humane Society provided watering troughs for horses and dogs. And at a few intersections there were public benches to make the wait for a streetcar more tolerable. Individually, each was a convenience, a remnant of the mid-nineteenth-century idea that public places should provide positive unifying functions for citizens. But placed too near each other on a crowded street in an era when most people walked from place to place, they easily became a collective annoyance.[95]

Ironically, the inefficiency of the crowded street created an entrepreneurial opportunity that contributed further to the hazard of the traffic jam. Messengers on bicycles could squirt through traffic, sometimes recklessly, and could complete vital links to other businesses and the telegraph office. This was especially important in communications—in the case of legal documents, for instance—that required the movement of a paper or a product. Not even the proliferation of the telephone and telegraph could help the situation. By the turn of the century, there were reputedly more than three thousand people involved in this trade in the Loop alone, and as late as 1914 there were still some 850 minors delivering telegrams downtown.[96]

Just as Chicagoans had conquered the problem of crossing the river by building efficient bridges and tunnels, they once again sought to address problems with solutions that were primarily technological. The telephone, which had helped create the skyscraper by allowing corporate offices to remove themselves from factories, gained rapid acceptance because of its ability to transcend the crowd. In effect, its wires, along with those of the telegraph, created a layer of communications space, much in the same manner that tall buildings multiplied the rentable space on a lot.[97]

The layer of wires over Loop streets, in turn, helped inspire the idea that multilevel public areas could carry several types of traffic with plenty of room for each. As early as 1883, visionaries began proposing systems of moving platforms above downtown Chicago's streets, but nothing came of any of the schemes.[98] The principle was finally given a practical demonstration at the World's Columbian Exposition ten years later. Initially, a system of moving sidewalks was to link several areas of the massive fairgrounds, but the owners of a chair-pushing concession used their influence to relegate this technological wonder to an amusement pier extending into the lake.[99]

Several promoters tried and failed to adapt moving sidewalks to downtown. Between 1892 and 1902 there were at least six proposals for elevated walkways that would have removed pedestrians from traffic hazards and the unpleasantness left by horses. The more spartan plans called for fixed platforms with translucent floors that would permit the light to reach the sidewalk below. Deluxe models, such as one proposed by the noted architect J. L. Silsbee, employed a continuously moving platform with seats.[100] None of the projects was built. They were too costly, and property owners objected to the light blockage and overhead noise. Meanwhile, the city council banned skybridges of any type as an illegal private usurpation of the public space.[101]

Some sidewalk proposals were linked to plans for another type of downtown layer. Chicagoans had begun talking about the idea of an "el" in 1869, the year that New York built its first steam-powered elevated. Over the next quarter-century more than seventy corporations were formed to build elevated tracks in Chicago, but nothing had been constructed. Some ventures were obviously fraudulent; others were proposed by those who lacked the technical expertise of bridge building needed to carry out construction. But one Chicago-based company, the Hannah Railway, had actually built one of the New York lines. Hannah's proposal to run a bridge railroad over Clark Street from Lincoln Park to Twenty-second Street was realistic. But costs, the lack of population density, political maneuvering, fears for public safety, and vociferous objections to building over the street stalled the project.[102]

It took the potential profit generated from carrying millions of visitors to the World's Columbian Exposition to inspire the capitalization of the first line, the Chicago and South Side Rapid Transit Railroad. Built in 1892 between Twelfth Street and Jackson Park, it was steam powered and nicknamed the "Alley El" because of its back-of-the-lot route. Despite the fact that the company slid into bankruptcy during the depression of the mid-1890s, work began on elevated routes to the north, northwest, and west during the next few years. Within a decade, the el system that served the city for the next century was in place.[103]

Initially, the elevated lines suffered in popularity among commuters because they stopped a few blocks from the periphery of downtown. In 1894, however, streetcar baron Charles T. Yerkes began construction of an extension of the Lake Street line east from Halsted toward the lake. Through political bribery and bullying property owners, Yerkes overcame objections to completion in 1897 of the four sides of a "Union Loop," which allowed el trains from four lines to circle the central business area and reverse direction without having to back up or encounter dead-end bumper posts, the same function that the original trolley loop performed for streetcars. The system also facilitated transfer from one line to another, although the lack of free transfers saved riders no money.[104]

While the new elevated structure put riders far above the chaos of the streets, many Chicagoans complained that it caused more problems than it solved. Many protested that the steam locomotives that were first used on the line were "an infringement on the public right," because they rained soot and sparks on the traffic and pedestrians below.[105] Yerkes replaced the engines with new electrified motors, but some pedestrians were even more frightened by falling electrical sparks.[106]

The construction of the el in 1897 proved poor timing for Yerkes, who launched a campaign to extend the franchises of his companies that same year. His so-called Humphreys Bills called for forty-year renewals, with only a minimal percentage of revenues going back to city coffers in return for the use of the street. After the Illinois Senate passed the bills, word leaked out that Yerkes had planned to spend fifty thousand dollars to influence votes in the state legislature. Mayor Carter Harrison II, who had been elected on the cry "The Streets Belong to the People," led civic leaders to pressure state representatives to reject the senate's action and kill the Humphreys Bills. Yerkes quickly countered with the Allen Bills, which granted the city council greater flexibility in establishing the terms of the franchise. Both houses of the assembly and the governor approved these measures, which shifted the conflict to the council. Six more months of debates, threats, bribes, protest meetings, and exposés brought the issue to a resolution in December 1898, when the Allen Bills were defeated. Yerkes realized that his influence in Chicago was waning, and during the following year he sold his holdings for ten million dollars and moved to New York. With his departure, Chicagoans lost a uniquely unifying target for their anger.[107]

Even with Yerkes out of the way, his Union Loop and its shadows and obtrusive posts remained. Critics pointed to the problems caused by Boston's 1894 subway and called for the replacement of the Chicago elevated structure even before it was completed. But in 1907 downtown business operators accepted the fact that the Chicago el was permanent and formed the Loop Protective Association to improve its worst features. Association members proposed alterations that called for the floors and roofs of platforms to be reconstructed in translucent glass and the stations to be rebuilt under the tracks so that they would cast smaller shadows on the streets. They also argued that a crushed stone roadway under the tracks would absorb much of the deafening roar transmitted by ties bolted directly to the support structure. Brighter paint on the girders would reduce what the association called the "gloom and oppression" created by dismal stations. Except for brighter coats of paint that were applied many years later, none of the association's proposals was adopted.[108]

The safety of the elevated lines occasionally became an issue. The lines' unimpeded route allowed them to travel at higher speeds, greatly increasing the danger of collisions. Derailments were obviously more of a hazard because the trains could fall from the structure. That fear was realized in 1896, 1908, and 1913, when elevated train cars tumbled to the ground; fortunately, the cars were empty and no one was injured. There were additional hazards in the crowding of passengers who boarded and left the cars on platforms of limited size rather than on the street surface. Accidents, sometimes fatal, occurred when the doors closed on people who were not fully in the car.[109]

Chicagoans generally enjoyed more success in coping with congestion by creating subterranean solutions. Firemen had long feared entanglement in utility wires that hung over sidewalks, and the press had long bemoaned the fate of hapless pedestrians who might be under lines that fell during ice storms. During the 1880s, the city became one of the first in the nation to require utility companies to bury their downtown lines to provide safety and avoid what city leaders called a "New York type of ugliness." By the end of the century most wires were off the main streets in the Loop.[110]

The pressure to remove telephone and telegraph lines, however, developed into one of the most controversial projects in the city's history. In 1898, the Illinois Telephone and Telegraph Company quietly received a state charter to install an underground conduit for its wires. Instead, secret work began the following year in the basement of Alderman Johnny Powers's Madison Street saloon. In April 1902 the public discovered that what was really being built was an elaborate system of freight tunnels 40 feet beneath the surface. When the network was finally completed in 1909, 62 miles of track connected dozens of stores and office buildings. A fleet of 117 miniature locomotives pulled more than 3,000 miniature gondolas that hauled coal and deliveries to the subbasements and carted away ashes and refuse. The tunnel system not only helped building managers avoid surface congestion, but also impeded the growth of the teamsters' union by providing an alternative means of delivery.[111]

Meanwhile, the underground empire continued to expand. A proposal in 1881 to build an underground railway from the South Side to Evanston never materialized, but others got to carry out plans to burrow beneath Chicago. Besides the new utility lines that were made necessary by the growing forest of skyscrapers, two new underground delivery systems responded to the need to move information more efficiently from a central point to locations scattered throughout the congested Loop. One system was built in 1892 by the City Press Association, a cooperative venture sponsored by the city's newspapers to gather and distribute information about petty crime and less significant news events. It installed several miles of a pressurized tube system that carried dispatches from its central news bureau to the city rooms of its member papers.[112] A decade later, postal authorities realized that heavy traffic was impeding the delivery of mail from the central post office to the four largest railroad terminals. The American Tube Service Company received the contract to build an elaborate tube system. In both cases, compressed air pushed capsules containing messages, letters, and packages through greased brass pipes buried deep in the ground at speeds of as much as thirty miles per hour, far faster than anything moved on the surface. As with the cable car lines, the tradeoff for efficiency was the monumental problem that resulted when the systems failed. The capsules occasionally became lodged in the tubes, especially where joints had shifted position, and the resulting snags could tie up the whole system in a manner much like traffic jams on the surface. Because everything was buried and the location of the trouble could seldom be determined exactly, workers had to dig up blocklong sections of pipe in search of an elusive capsule.[113]

In a sense, the underground tube systems were the ultimate symbol of downtown urban technology. They existed because of the crowding in the city center. They involved a complicated technology doing the job that had once been handled by simpler methods. They handled information, the flow of which was a major urban commodity consolidated in the heart of the city. They were a technological solution to what was basically an economic-social-political problem, that is, the concentration of too many activities in too limited a space.

Finally, the tubes shared the fate of other attempts to cope with the problems of the Loop: by becoming so popular that they became overloaded and broke down frequently, they became self-defeating solutions. The river tunnels demonstrated that the more permanently constructed the solution to the problem, the more easily it became obsolete because it could not be expanded. The el avoided the immobile traffic jam below, but it also complicated the problem it was supposed to solve; its convenience attracted even more riders downtown and deposited all of them on limited stretches of sidewalk beneath its stations. The el also failed to improve upon one of the most serious drawbacks to surface transportation: the sardinelike crowding within the cars. The buried electrical conduits proved so successful that they had to be dug up and replaced by higher capacity lines, while modern trucking and the elimination of the coal-fired boiler made the freight tunnel system a forgotten relic.

The Rise of the Anti-City: The Golden Age of the Semipublic Chicago

By the last decades of the nineteenth century, Chicago was beginning to pay the price for maturity. Factories filled the skies with smoke, and the noise of commerce roared in the streets. The public ways presented an image of bustling prosperity, as well as an air of maturity that the citizens of the young metropolis were so anxious to generate. But behind the facade was a concern about risk: the electric wires, the speeding streetcars, a fire in a tall building, pickpockets, beggars, germs—all increased the possibility of injury or at the very least an encounter with something repulsive or irritating. As if to insulate themselves from the unpleasantness and dangers outside, Chicagoans eagerly flocked to an expanding array of semipublic places. Visiting these downtown destinations became a way of rewarding oneself for overcoming the difficulties of getting from here to there. It is crucial to note that these semipublic amenities mirrored the complexity of the city by being multifunctional. Like the factory, they centralized as many related activities and served as many groups of customers and clients as possible under one roof. The logic of centralization had triumphed over dispersal and disorganization.

The world of commercial spaces, privately owned but open to the public, symbolized the rising city. That happened in part by default. Chicago was remarkably devoid of great public buildings. It had no great cathedrals. Its city hall and courthouse buildings were architecturally undistinguished and shoddily built, and its museums were still small, with modest collections.[114] Instead, Chicagoans poured their talents, energies, and money into the construction of magnificent private commercial buildings, soaring office towers, large department stores, impressive railroad stations, and grand hotels. There was money in attracting crowds, and the competitive atmosphere demanded that each new structure be more elaborate than the last. Yet, at the same time, these places provided a practical escape from the street, a virtual anti-city within the city.[115]

The hotel was the archetypal semipublic place. Rebuilding on the ruins of the Great Fire, contractors worked around the clock to construct replacements for wrecked hostelries. The Grand Pacific, the Palmer House, and the Tremont tried to turn disaster into advantage by introducing appointments even more lavish than those in their pre-Fire buildings. Potter Palmer, for instance, initiated a private coach line that greeted guests at the railway stations and delivered them to his hotel's elegant entrance, which was adorned with statues said to be "the most costly and elaborate works of art ever used to ornament any building in the country." There was a grand staircase—increasingly relegated to an ornamental role by elevators—and a grand entryway rotunda, whose overhead balconies became "popular places of resort for both ladies and gentlemen and from which the busy scene below can be enjoyed." Locals, some of them permanent residents, as well as travelers could enjoy the hotel. There was a huge domed restaurant, ballrooms of several sizes, and a richly furnished billiard parlor for men. In their search for comfort as well as grandeur, hotels added barber shops, hairdressers, newsstands, and other services that made it unnecessary to venture outside for basic needs.[116]

The rise of the department store was marked by a similar tendency to provide lavish indoor appointments and to bring together a great many goods and services under one roof. Architectural innovations helped make this possible. More spacious floor areas with improved lighting and ventilation resulted from the introduction of iron and steel frames to building construction. Electricity brought merchandise under uniform illumination in all parts of the store and at all hours, and escalators and elevators made it possible to stack floor after floor of departments, each of them specialized and logically arranged. New services—restaurants, waiting rooms, beauty parlors, dentists' offices, checkrooms, offices in which to purchase theater tickets or arrange travel plans, and even a day nursery where children could romp on real grass and sand—spurred the competition. These amenities allowed shoppers, especially women, to arrive downtown by commuter train, do their shopping, and never set foot on the public street. But most important of all, by essentially bringing together a city full of stores, each reduced in size and efficiently designed, and by offering the most popular merchandise, the department store made shopping a form of recreation. Show windows were still important for luring customers inside; once there, Chicagoans found that the interior aisle had become a risk-free replacement for the public street.[117]

During the post-Fire years the city's railway stations underwent a similar transition. The growth of passenger service gradually forced railroad lines to shift many of their freight operations to the city's periphery, where cheaper expansion space was available for yards. Competition for passengers, the growing size of the ridership on both intercity and suburban trains, and the entrance into Chicago of new trunk lines that shared the burden of new construction costs—all prompted the rebuilding of rail stations during the 1880s. The element of boosterism made Chicagoans realize that their depots gave visitors their first impressions of the city. The press complained loudly about the condition of the West Side station of the Chicago and Alton, and the Pittsburgh, Fort Wayne, and Chicago. The *Tribune* reprinted the unkind comments of the *Toledo Blade:*

> Chicago is a great city, and its buildings as a whole are massive and grand, but the worst hovel in all that great city, and the one that causes an exclamation of contempt to escape the beholder's lips each time he sees it, is the depot. . . . The paint has long since been worn off by the action of the weather, and the woodwork on the inside is thickly covered with a deposit of grease and dirt that makes it very variegated in appearance. The floor is covered by a thick three-ply carpet of tobacco quids. . . . It is almost a disgrace that those roads should consent to use such a depot.[118]

The foul little building was eventually replaced by a new Union Station in 1881. Not to be outdone, two groups of railroads constructed new depots of their own: Dearborn Station on Polk Street in 1883 and a Grand Central Station at Wells and Harrison in 1890. To the north, the Chicago and North Western built its new Wells Street Station in 1882. It is almost a cliché to call these elaborate structures "gateways," or grand symbolic entranceways to the city. They were virtually cities in themselves, and most of them benefited those leaving Chicago rather than the new arrivals. In these stations, as well as in the Illinois Central Depot (1892), the LaSalle Street Station (1905), and the new North Western (1911) and Union (1925) Stations, the services essential to travelers and commuters were consolidated on one site. Clothing stores, food services of varying prices, laundries, and apothecaries often were under the same roof with a jail and a small hospital. The new North Western Station was arranged to cater to the different needs of three major types of passengers. Long-distance travelers on their way to destinations in the northern states and regions served by the connecting Union Pacific Railroad benefited most from the large waiting room, small sleeping rooms, and major restaurants; those arriving in the morning could nap and dine before the departure of their afternoon West Coast trains. The second group, the commuters, could also take advantage of these facilities before embarking on an evening on the town. The last group, immigrants on their way to farms in the west, used separate waiting and dining facilities that were designed to protect them from temptations and the disreputable characters of the outside city.[119]

Of all these impressive structures, the greatest monument to the crowd was the Auditorium Building. Everything about it reflected the most favorable attitude toward semipublic places. It was huge, touted as the tallest and most massive structure in the world when it opened in 1889. It was also fireproof, an important consideration in a city once nearly consumed by flames and at a time when catastrophes in other cities made Chicagoans fear another conflagration. Despite its enormous seating capacity, the structure was extremely versatile. An advertising book described the future uses of its giant theater for political and trade conventions, mass meetings, lectures, operatic performances, balls, promenade concerts, charity fairs, and concerts by choral associations and orchestras. To maximize the building's moneymaking potential, its ground floor spaces were to be used for commercial purposes while a luxurious hotel and an office section provided other steady sources of revenue. "Externally, the building is almost Roman," boasted the promoters, "but internally it is American, and one may go further and say Chicagoan."[120]

The Auditorium Building became the prevailing symbol of civic progress, and promoters boasted about every feature. Its observation tower was the tallest point in the city, its restaurant and hotel were luxuriously appointed, and the acoustics in the theater, which was reputedly the largest room in the world, approached perfection. The building's promoters had also tried to relate its interior functions to the best characteristics of the city outside. Michigan Avenue was still the great social artery of Chicago, with traffic that consisted mainly of carriages rather than drays. The lakefront park, though hardly elegant since Illinois Central trains operated nearby, was at least open. Bicycle clubs congregated weekly at the Auditorium, and the nearby harbor sheltered the yachts of the wealthy. There was still hope that the city's smoke nuisance could be reformed, and there was a general belief that the new building would have a beneficial effect on its physical environment. Thus, the privately owned Auditorium was a multifunctional "department store" offering physical comforts to all who could afford its rates.[121]

Semipublic places easily became self-selective retreats from the streets, which were perceived as dangerous places where one might come face to face with the homeless poor and the unassimilated immigrant. The private aspect of the semipublic place then became important. The posh decor of the department store doubtless intimidated the poor into staying outside, just as the price of a ticket kept them outside a theater or a maitre d' barred their entry into a fine restaurant. Depots, where authorities could demand to see the rail tickets of those they suspected were not passengers, were usually populated by police detectives who were there to apprehend fugitives.[122]

Conclusion

It is obvious that there would not have been a Chicago without a way to get from here to there. But citizens had to pay a price of inconvenience, unpleasantness, and danger. They had to cope with a dense population, the pushing and the closeness of the crowd, and the frustration of being trapped in a slow mass. They were angered at the lack of choice in the matter. The persons who coughed at you, sat next to you in a restaurant, or handled the items you contemplated purchasing were not individuals of your selection.

But the most distinctive characteristic of getting anywhere in the city was that it was both a collective nightmare and an individual misery. Coping had to come on both levels. Public coping took the form of writing angry letters to the newspapers, organizing reform groups such as the ISPCA, enacting laws, and adopting new technologies. Chicagoans could thus respond as a group, often to a clearly identifiable enemy such as transit companies. Coping on the individual level involved choosing among alternatives. These included retreating into the semipublic world of hotels, department stores, restaurants, and other places that were clean, orderly, and safe. The parks people visited were sylvan and public, but these spaces were controlled to provide a similarly planned environment. Chicagoans also adapted in individual ways by making small decisions—finding an uncrowded alternative to rush hour routes, leaving early to avoid being bridged, or even moving away from the city altogether.

The semipublic space also became an important coping mechanism. As a destination, it made the journey worthwhile. Not all spaces of this type were grand and lavishly appointed. Neighborhood saloons, apothecary shops, and grocery stores afforded customers the opportunity to visit, hear local gossip, use the rest room, make phone calls, and otherwise find pleasureful moments in retreat from the outside world. In return, customers usually felt obliged to spend a little money.[123] Other types of semipublic spaces were treated differently, especially when they were associated with employment. Architects of office structures lavished great attention on the appearance of lobbies, which took on new importance when elevators transformed the small building into the skyscraper. But the owners of these structures were far less willing to take responsibility for the safety of their tenants on the same elevators.[124] Similarly, factory owners were unwilling to admit that their buildings were anything but private space; only when states enacted worker health and safety regulations was management forced to recognize their semipublic status.[125] Churches and social settlement houses were another exceptional category of semipublic place, the former even taking on the protective function of an asylum.

All of this was in sharp contrast to the external city, the outdoor space that remained largely utilitarian. The characteristics of its appearance came mainly from the privately owned buildings that lined the sidewalks. Even when clean, a street in the slums was still a slum street. Such commercial intrusions as signs and display windows and of course the architecture itself determined the character of business streets. Except for the creation of parks and a few boulevards, which were retreats from the average streets, there would be no sustained effort to beautify most other public places until the famous Burnham Plan of 1909. And in contrast to the attractiveness of the department store, the depot, and the hotel, public places were regulated by a series of prohibitive laws that attempted to modify behavior and create a new sense of urban discipline. Ironically, a city where the greatest difficulty had been simply getting from point to point now had to cope with the problem of too many people traveling too fast and complaining that the streets were too crowded with users.

There was a grand irony in the rise of the semipublic city. Its grandeur was an index of a city's size and maturity, the evidence boosters mustered to prove Chicago's emergence. Smaller cities could not have supported anything the size of the Auditorium. Yet, by being a safe, clean, and orderly place of escape, the semipublic world of hotels, train stations, restaurants, and theaters simultaneously became the anti-city, everything that Chicago was not.

Postscript

The horse, which had been the dominant motive power for most forms of urban transportation, was in eclipse by the end of the century. The drawbacks of animal power had prompted unending and expensive efforts to replace it. New technologies relegated Old Dobbin to branch line service until 1906, when horsecars were eliminated altogether. That same year the temperamental cable cars also stopped running; their replacements, the trolleys, continued to operate until 1957.[126]

By the middle of the twentieth century, nearly all of the layer-creating solutions to the question of Loop crowding had become outmoded. The postal tubes lasted only until June 30, 1918.[127] The LaSalle Street tunnel was last used in 1939; the Van Buren and Washington Street tubes closed in the early 1950s.[128] In the case of the freight tunnels, a new underground system crippled the old one. Construction of the new transit subways in State (completed in 1943) and Dearborn (1951) Streets disrupted the freight tunnel network, which ceased operating in 1950.[129] Teletype machines finally replaced the City News Bureau tube system in the early 1960s.[130] But remnants of the past survive. Motorists of North LaSalle Street still dodge the entrance to a tunnel as they approach the Traffic Court building south of Hubbard Street. The Washington Street viaduct under the North Western Station conceals another underground entrance beneath its unused center lane. Loop excavations still yield occasional fragments of a pneumatic tube system, and, although few people had heard of it before it flooded on April 13–14, 1992, a freight railway system has existed forty feet below downtown streets since the beginning of the century. Overhead, Chicago's most functional antique, its century-old el structure, still carries thousands of passengers each day. While interesting to urban archaeologists and tourists, these remains are also important as symbols of an earlier "crisis of the Loop," when business leaders actually worried about *too many* people flocking downtown to work and shop.

Each succeeding generation claimed to answer the question of who owned the streets by giving control to certain interests. The transit lines underwent another unification under Samuel Insull during the 1920s. The founder of Commonwealth Edison, widely revered for his business genius, Insull was so hated for his monopolistic tactics that he became the Yerkes of a new age. When he fell into bankruptcy during the Depression, the rail lines operated under federal receivership through World War II.[131] By then Chicagoans were convinced that public ownership was preferable to private profit. They finally achieved that goal in 1946 with the creation of the Chicago Transit Authority. There was some dismay when the new agency promptly raised fares and closed branch elevated lines. Meanwhile, the private Chicago Surface Lines bus routes became part of the CTA in 1952. Public transit has failed to win very many friends in the succeeding half-century. Riders have felt underserved and unhappy. Declining federal subsidies and dwindling ridership have meant that trains and buses run at less frequent intervals. Between rush hours they virtually disappear; much of the system no longer runs around the clock, leaving night workers stranded. The alternate-stop "A" and "B" trains gave way to slower all-stop service. Meanwhile the bus fleet is aging. Ironically, the public agency is trying to save itself by eroding the principle on which it was created. By selling its equipment to investors and leasing it back, the CTA is returning to private ownership, if not private operation. It is also considering the takeover of some its bus routes by outside companies.

Physical vestiges of the earlier years remain, including several car barns that made the transition to modern businesses; Chicago Bulls star Michael Jordan, for instance, opened a popular restaurant in an old horsecar building. Another remnant of an earlier age, streetcar tracks, had been left in place and frequently surface during street construction. The quiet efficiency of the streetcar has regained recognition in most recent years. During the early 1990s, Mayor Richard M. Daley promoted a plan for a Central Area Circulator that would have linked the West Side railroad stations, the Loop, and North Michigan Avenue districts with "light rail" service that looked suspiciously like the old streetcar service.

One generation's headache can become another's dream.

2 Counting Minutes and Miles

DURING the predawn hours of February 9, 1888, Amos J. Snell awakened to the sound of a burglar in the first-floor drawing room of his mansion at Washington and Ada Streets on the West Side. The sixty-four-year-old millionaire, clad in a nightshirt and stockings, rose from his bed, grabbed a revolver, and went to the door of his room. Instead of sneaking downstairs, he stood at the top of the landing and shouted a challenge that awakened his cook and a maid, who had been asleep in their third-floor quarters. Then, in rapid succession, shots were exchanged. Snell aimed downward and hit a door and a wall of the drawing room below, but two of the three bullets fired at him by the intruder found their mark, his bright white nightshirt no doubt making him an easy target even in poor light. One bullet lodged in his chest; the other exploded in his head. He probably died before he hit the floor.[1]

A few hours later Snell's coachman came in from his quarters above the stable to start the day's fires. He had failed to hear the gun battle because of the noise from carriages taking revelers away from a party that was breaking up nearby. When he entered the house, he found a bullet hole in a door, the hysterical servants hiding in their rooms, and his employer dead in a pool of blood in the main hallway. The shocking news reached the papers that afternoon. Chicago was stunned; how could one of its leading citizens meet such a fate? A few days later, after the sculptor Leonard Volk had made a death mask of the millionaire, a long funeral cortege accompanied the sable-lined casket to its final resting place at Rose Hill Cemetery.[2]

Although the murder of Amos Snell generated nationwide headlines and publicity, the subsequent investigation never produced a firm suspect, let alone an indictment. The route of entry had been through a kitchen door, and an abandoned case found in the drawing room contained the burglary tools that had also been used to pry open a small safe that contained non-negotiable securities. Most puzzling of all, however, the bullets that felled Snell had come from two revolvers of different calibres. Were there two perpetrators, or was there an effort to make the authorities think there were two? The best of the skimpy evidence pointed to one Willie Tascott, the ne'er-do-well son of a Chicago paint manufacturer. When investigators searched Tascott's rooming house, acting on a tip from a suspicious landlady, they found a check that had probably been stolen from Snell. Later in the morning of the murder, Tascott had apparently left Chicago for St. Paul, where a few days later he conversed briefly with an acquaintance who evidently knew nothing of the investigation back in Chicago. After that, Tascott was never to be seen again. The lack of a photograph of the man hampered police efforts to advertise his whereabouts. For years afterward the police tracked down literally thousands of leads. The trail gradually grew stale, with only occasional newspaper features to mark the anniversary of the crime. And for a generation afterward, "Where's Willie Tascott?" became the local name for the "hide-and-seek" game among the city's children.[3]

All of Chicago acted shocked at Snell's murder, but a large number of the region's residents may have had some motive to kill him. For decades he had been alternately one of the most admired and hated men in Chicago. When he had arrived from New York in 1845, he had twenty-two dollars in his pocket; at his death, he was regarded as probably the largest individual landlord in the city, owning, among other things, 360 marble-front houses. The years that lay between were blessed with lucky investments. Snell had spent his first six years in Illinois operating an inn in Schaumburg, then a dusty country village, before moving to Jefferson Township, several miles closer to the city. Here he obtained a lucrative contract to supply firewood to the Chicago and North Western. In 1865 he noticed that a broken-down road ran parallel to the railroad for part of its route. He discovered that it was the old North West Plank Road, a remnant of a midcentury road-building technique that employed wooden boards set on top of tracklike "stringers" to provide a relatively smooth surface. "Corduroy roads," as they became known, seldom worked properly; settling and flooding dislodged the boards.[4] But Snell had discovered three important facts: the route was a toll road beyond the city limits; growing numbers of prosperous farmers were swelling the ranks of travelers; and, he could buy the road for only $20,000 from county officials who had taken control of it in 1865 and were unaware of its true value.

In 1870 the "Snell Toll Road," a route followed by today's Milwaukee Avenue to suburban Wheeling, went into business. Snell improved the road with a new gravel surface but claimed that he had to erect toll gates at closer intervals to pay for it.[5] As the years passed, the roadway deteriorated, but farmers on their way to market or on holiday excursions to beer gardens and picnic groves found the direct route so convenient that they had no real alternative. One newspaper reported that Snell, who kept adding additional toll gates, took in as much as $790 on a single Sunday, with the daily average of around $400. When the West Division Railway Company built a huge new barn for its horse-drawn streetcars at Armitage Road and Milwaukee in 1878, the company reportedly had to pay Snell $100,000 to cross his road. "Banker Snell," however, had to hire a security force to counter the vandalism perpetrated by his captive and increasingly unhappy customers.

It took a while after Snell's death for customers to realize it, but his demise meant that the last of the old toll roads had lost a tenacious owner who had been willing to send his guards chasing after nonpaying interlopers. Snell had died without a will, and when his widow, Henrietta, who had been out of town at the time of the murder, and their children tried to assume control of the road, the courts refused to recognize it as an asset. She brought suit, but on the night of April 30, 1890, a mob attacked the toll house and gates near the intersection of present-day Fullerton and Milwaukee Avenues. They stoned the collector, roughed up the guards, and tore down and burned the gate. When Snell's survivors complained to city officials, Assistant Corporation Counsel Clarence Darrow informed them that the gates had never been legal. Soon, travelers began using the road without paying, and on May 14, 1890, the Illinois Supreme Court declared that the whole toll road had been operating illegally since its purchase. Altogether, it had been a bad month for the Snell family.[6]

The saga of this murder is significant not only because the case remains unsolved. To Chicagoans of the late nineteenth century, Amos J. Snell symbolized a defiant impediment to the free movement between city and suburb. The story really centered on the ability to get from here to there. The growth of the city involved much more than an increase of population; expanding size meant coping with geographical expansion and with counting travel times in hours and miles, rather than minutes and blocks. The rise of the new and congested Loop was made possible because of the growth of a transportation network across the region that made it accessible to the masses for work, business, and leisure. Even before he died, Snell had come to represent the dead hand of the past, an old technology and a limited, narrow-minded view of transportation. Ultimately, the story of regional transportation also became an object lesson in human adaptation to new technologies that would redefine local travel, extending it beyond city boundaries, as well as down city streets. It was also a study in the expansion of choice. Initially, the only alternatives were shoe leather, the steam engine, or horseflesh. But inventions and innovations provided new choices. The ways people used them would provide new meanings to the word "coping."

Getting Home behind Steam: The Rise of the Commuter

Joke: An Englishwoman asks a Chicago and North Western conductor, "Is this train going to Heavanston?" "No," he replies, "This train goes to Helgin."[7]

Effective transportation always involved a difficult tradeoff. In the congested city of the horsecar, cable car, and streetcar, movement was slow and measured in blocks, but passengers could board cars at every corner. Few people had to walk any great distance to get home because parallel lines were often located only a few blocks apart and it was easy to transfer at intersecting routes. The creation of the elevated lines in the 1890s, however, introduced an alternate type of mobility. The "iron highway" took riders across the city at faster speeds and did not stop at every corner, but accessibility declined because passengers were funneled through stations located a few blocks apart. The ultimate step in this evolution involved the commuter railroad, which would prove to be the fastest yet least accessible way to travel across the region. Steam locomotives accelerated slowly, forcing railroads to seek a balance between the mechanical efficiency of infrequent stops and the need to stop often enough to maximize the ridership. In the process, the depot assumed a special meaning for rail commuters.

Determining the date when suburban service began in Chicago depends on definition. Because the city's first rail operation, which started on October 25, 1848, went only as far as present-day Oak Park, it was technically a suburban run. But the development of regular passenger schedules did not take place until early in the next decade. By 1850, citizens of the Fox River Valley were requesting more frequent service. Shortly before the Galena and Chicago Union line reached Elgin in January of that year, a Chicago newspaper gave its tongue-in-cheek explanation for the demand for more trains: Fox Valley bachelors wanted to be able to steal into Chicago for a night of revelry and return home before their neighbors and mothers awakened. The G&CU soon added special suburban "accommodation cars" to its trains, but it was not until June 1854 that the line announced plans for commuter-only trains.[8] Two years later, a new south lakefront resort called Hyde Park was born when Paul Cornell, a young lawyer-developer, convinced the Illinois Central Railroad to stop at a depot he had erected; soon, the railway began operating a special train just for commuters.[9]

The next forty years saw a dramatic increase in suburban ridership. The Galena and Chicago Union (later the West Line of the Chicago and North Western, now the Union Pacific) carried a total of 37,000 passengers during the entire first year, but by the early 1880s such roads as the Illinois Central transported 250,000 suburban-only passengers per month on 56 daily trains. An 1884 survey of commuter service revealed that 15 railroads operated 301 daily trains over nearly 500 miles of track serving half a million residents outside of Chicago and untold thousands from stops within the city limits. A decade later, ridership was estimated at 100,000 a day, or 30 million annually. One 1913 study counted 123,188 daily suburban passengers arriving and departing on 746 trains pulling 3,229 cars. Fueled by the availability of cheap suburban land, fear of another major Chicago fire, and the hard sell of subdividers—who often counted railroad officials among their investors—the commuter boom became a significant aspect of getting from here to there.[10]

Despite their swelling ranks, the suburbanites were a group whose diversity often made them unhappy with the train service. Some wanted more early morning "working-man's trains" to serve the needs of janitors, construction workers, and others who needed to be on the job by dawn.[11] Many women complained about the lack of midday runs that would allow them a few hours to shop in the city between the times they needed to be home to care for their families.[12] Other suburb dwellers were angry when the elimination of some of the lightly patronized late-hour "theater trains" shortened their evening's entertainment in Chicago.[13]

Conditions aboard the trains were not always ideal. The private ownership of the line and the requirement of a ticket to ride technically made the railroad car a semipublic place, separate from the public street. But those limitations did not always keep out drunken rowdies, who occasionally terrorized night-owl passengers before being ejected. Quite predictably, riders froze in the winter and stewed in their soot-speckled summertime sweat.[14] Jefferson Park residents along the North Western grumbled that the trains were seldom on time and that conductors did not want to stop long enough to allow a safe entrance or exit.[15] Another common complaint: "petty" conductors who would not allow a commuter's mother-in-law to borrow his monthly pass for an occasional Saturday shopping excursion.[16]

Equipment was another issue. It was not until late in the century that the lines began experimenting with equipment especially designed for suburban operation. Until then, the cars were usually old and obsolete hand-me-downs from intercity service; aisles and doors were too small to accommodate the quick entrance and exit of crowds who were eager to get to work or to their homes as soon as possible. The locomotives were invariably the oldest and least reliable. When the North Western and other suburban lines discontinued suburban baggage service in the early 1880s, commuters were left to contend with hauling home their Loop purchases. "Packages," grumbled one observer, "will tumble out of scanty racks and crush the silk plug hats of the just and unjust." Cars were often crowded. "Twelve more months will go by," groused the *Tribune* in 1883, "and the Society for the Prevention of Cruelty to Animals will refuse to recognize that commuters are animals, and the General Superintendent of the railroad will refuse to recognize that they are anything but animals."[17]

The railroads quickly discovered that relieving the problems of one group of commuters simply created new difficulties with which another would have to cope. For instance, improvement in service invariably pitted those living in the most distant suburbs against those closer to downtown. Commuters constantly complained about the slow schedules, but as the carriers responded with faster and more frequent service, they encountered opposition from city dwellers along the line whose neighborhoods were disrupted by the additional noise and smoke. Speedier trains meant greater danger, and every time the 5:02 express roared into a hapless wagon at a grade crossing, aldermen heard from their constituents. As early as 1870, city officials began discussing the dream of elevating high-speed main lines, or at least requiring crossing guards.[18] When the railroads balked at the costs of the proposals, the Illinois General Assembly passed a law in 1877 that enabled local officials to impose speed limits ranging from eight to twelve miles an hour within incorporated areas. That led to years of litigation and additional speed restrictions imposed by the Chicago City Council.[19]

The most bitter fight focused on what was undoubtedly the region's least successful suburban operation. In 1871, a group of residents living in Lake View

Township east of the Chicago and North Western talked the rival Chicago and Milwaukee into constructing a parallel northward line that would run a few blocks west of Lake Michigan to Evanston. The following year, the Milwaukee Road got permission to use half of Southport Avenue for part of its new route. But when work began in 1874, not only did the railroad face a legal challenge that ended up in the U.S. Supreme Court, but angry residents stormed the construction site each night and tore up the tracks.[20] The northern part of the line was completed into Evanston in 1883, while mobs were still destroying track on Southport Avenue.[21] When service finally got under way Lake View residents fumed over the lack of stations, the high fares, and the speed of the "Limiteds" that seemed to cater to the "Holy Hole" of Evanston at the expense of close-in riders. They retaliated in 1890 by convincing Chicago aldermen to impose a twelve-mile-per-hour limit in Lake View Township, increased to twenty if the railroads fenced their tracks and provided crossing gates and watchmen. The law sparked the *Tribune*'s tongue-in-cheek suggestion of adding sleeping cars to commuter trains, as well as a protest meeting of 1,500 angry outlying suburbanites who demanded a fare reduction on the Evanston Division because of the slowed schedule.[22]

The "Battle of Lake View" taught the carriers that it was ultimately cheaper to raise their tracks and build viaducts than it was to irritate riders and tie up equipment in snail's-pace operations. The railroads saw the obvious advantages in having what amounted to their own layer of the city. They also could not ignore the loss of 326 people in grade crossing accidents in the city during 1892, or the fact that the problem only grew worse with the development of outlying rural lands that Chicago had annexed in 1889. But the proposed improvement was massive and expensive. In 1892 one newspaper estimated that Chicago's 179.22 square miles contained 1,403.66 miles of surface railway tracks that made over 3,000 street grade crossings. Finally, on February 23, 1893, the city council bent to the pressure and voted to require that the major lines be elevated or depressed sixteen feet below grade. By the end of the century, most of the main lines in the more densely populated parts of the city were safely operating on their own level. Some Chicagoans, however, grumbled that their neighborhoods had been surrounded by ugly walls just for the convenience of suburbanites.[23]

Commuters constantly felt exploited. They swore and shook their fists when they were sidetracked for the fast intercity "varnish," for "special" trains carrying railroad directors, or even for high-priority freight.[24] Angry suburbanites viewed the fares they paid as the predictable financial backbone of railroads that lavished attention on everything else while treating daily riders very shabbily. Illinois Central riders complained that the line charged them two to four times the cost of parallel transit lines. *Skandinaven,* a Swedish paper, angrily suggested that commuters refuse to pay more than three cents a mile and demanded that the federal government investigate fare gouging.[25]

Over the years, those making the daily suburban trek developed a folklore, perhaps as a way of coping with problems through humor, ritual, or just a sense of camaraderie. Newspaper columnists described suburban women who passed the travel time by knitting and commuters who left concerts and plays early lest they miss the last train home. Since many suburbs had poor street lighting or none at all, commuters had a difficult time finding their way to and from the station, especially during the dark winter months. Most carried lanterns, which the railroad allowed to be stored in the station house during the daytime. Over the years, the smell of kerosene became so associated with commuting that it became a means of identifying a fellow rider. The hasty morning departure from home became another part of the folklore. Cartoonists depicted the suburban-ite breakfasting with coat and hat perched on the back of his chair, ready for the dash to the train.[26]

Newspaper reading during the long rides was another common aspect of the commuting experience, and this disturbed observers who were upset over what they deemed an increasing amount of "trash" in the press. In 1873, the *Chicago Illustrated Journal* complained:

> The railway newspaper reader offends against eyes, nerves, brain, mind, and manners. His daily ride should be social; it should release his mind from serious occupation; it should give to his brain and nerves something as near relaxation as possible; it should spare the much abused and much endangered eye-sight. Every suburban town about our great cities should have an extensive blind asylum, and a university of insane hospitals adapt-ed to all classes of the lunatic. . . . By and by it will appear that city folk go to the bad generally by rail, because of their habit of dreadful misusing, over a newspaper, their hours of journeying to and fro.[27]

The railroads responded to the commuters' complaints by claiming that they, too, were unhappy about their suburban "burden." Plodding trains re-quired heavy expenditures for crew wages, in part because most older engines were seldom powerful enough to haul trains of more than five cars. Equipment had to be cleaned and moved around twice each day, although it was in service for only a few hours. The low fares—roughly two cents a mile through much of the late nineteenth century—barely met the expenses generated by the up-keep of dozens of suburban stations, each of which had to have an agent. Be-cause they were on the trains so many hours, commuters filed a disproportion-ate number of personal injury lawsuits; one line claimed that such litigation ate up more than 11 percent of its gross suburban revenue. The carriers complained loudly that the freight and long-distance passenger service had to subsidize money-losing commuter operations, especially after the lower fares of the ele-vated transit systems built in the 1890s cut revenues by luring away riders from closer-in stations.[28]

Commuters, on the other hand, saw competition as the only real source of relief. Parallel lines, especially to the South Side, forced carriers to institute improvements in the form of additional tracks to reduce delays and headways, or the intervals between trains. A few rail companies even added such luxuries as dining cars.[29] When plans for a competing elevated line or narrow-gauge steam systems were announced, the railroads responded with swift reductions in fares, hoping to discourage potential investors. But in one instance, the Rock

Island dropped eighteen trains when the Chicago and Northern Pacific introduced its suburban service.[30] After the turn of the century, the construction of three interurban lines—the South Shore, the North Shore, and the Chicago, Aurora, and Elgin—presented a new challenge. The new electric lines were cleaner and quieter, and the trains could accelerate faster, reach higher speeds, and stop more smoothly than the steam "teakettles." To counter its interurban threat, the Illinois Central boldly announced electrification plans of its own in 1895. The conversion finally came in 1926.[31]

Unloved by riders, by operators, and by Chicagoans through whose neighborhoods they operated, suburban trains were regarded as an indispensable evil, even in the days of rapid growth that preceded the automobile and the expressway. The lines helped to integrate the economy of the region, so much so that in 1900 merchants from as far away as fifty miles asked the railroads to raise fares because of trade lost to Chicago.[32] Ultimately, tens of thousands of commuters thought the delays and uncomfortable conditions to be worth the reward of homes of their own at the other end of the line.

The Automobile Comes to Chicago

At the dawn of the century most Chicagoans would probably have agreed that the automobile would never supplant the good old horse. But a decade later, the world had changed, and the horseless carriage was well on its way toward displacing animal power. As that transformation took place, it opened a new chapter in the debate about the nature of streets, who controlled them, and for what purpose. Most important of all, Chicagoans would have to cope with a clash of transportation technologies. A machine that worked with greatest efficiency when speedily covering great distances and at the fastest speeds in the distended city increasingly vied with horses and streetcars for domination of the congested city streets.

Out of the clashing claims on city space emerged the question of what constituted reasonable risk. Coping with city life had always involved the potential for injury or death on the dangerous streets. Runaway horses, barrels tumbling from wagons, slippery crossings, coal hatches left uncovered on sidewalks, falling signs or streetcar wires—all led to individual family tragedies that had for decades filled the short-notice columns in the daily press. Innovations in public transit only added to the difficulty. For instance, the electric trolley accelerated so quickly that pedestrians frequently failed to get out of its way. Finally, the speed and maneuverability that were the advantages of the automobile also made it the most dangerous form of transport ever introduced to the street. Unlike the transit company that operated by franchise and had its name painted on the side of the car, the automobile was privately owned, making culpability much more difficult to prove.

Like many great inventions and discoveries, the concept and creation of the automobile grew from multiple origins. The first appearance of the machine on Chicago's streets probably came in 1892, when William Morrison of Des Moines brought his mysterious electric carriage to show to a prospective manufacturer. John B. McDonald, the head of the American Storage Battery Company, not only bought the invention, but he also became Chicago's first auto commuter when he began using it to get from his home on the West Side to his LaSalle Street office. The following year, the company exhibited one of the Morrison electrics at the World's Columbian Exposition, where visitors also viewed Gottlieb Daimler's petrol-powered "motorcycle" from Germany. At that time, the automobile was still a curiosity with little practical value.[33]

The second stage in the evolution of a new technology involved the struggle to gain legitimacy. Chicagoans found it difficult to take the earliest autos seriously. Promoters spent the next decade using attention-getting public spectacles and shows to convince the general public that the flimsy contraptions would hold together. Demonstrations of the most impractical of uses were also essential to convince the public that the vehicles were durable, safe, and had practical applications. That principle—along with selling sensationalist newspapers—was the real motive behind the Chicago *Times-Herald*'s sponsorship of America's first automobile race. Held on Thanksgiving Day 1895, the run from Jackson Park to Waukegan covered a hundred miles, and the winner, J. Frank Duryea, averaged seven and a half miles per hour.[34]

Numerous endurance runs and races followed, including a continuous run on a wooden track at the first Chicago Automobile Show, March 23–31, 1901. Here, many of the twenty thousand visitors enjoyed a free ride that demonstrated that the device would neither fall apart nor kill them. Over the next decade, the annual winter auto shows would be an effective means of breaking down resistance to cars by making them more familiar to the masses.[35]

The next step in introducing and disseminating the automobile made fortunes for the enterprising Chicagoans who could teach the general public how to use it. One example was Charles Coey, who used his popularity as a racing driver to open one of the area's first driving schools in 1901. Students each spent eight weeks and one hundred dollars learning how to repair as well as drive the machines. Coey, who later expanded into the taxicab business and began manufacturing his own car, the Coey-Mitchell, promised that high wages would await graduate chauffeurs and "mechanicians."[36]

Although some among the upwardly mobile working class may have recognized a new technological future in the automobile, the cost of many innovations and the certain dangers involved in the auto's use limited the ranks of purchasers to wealthy people who were daring enough to take risks. By 1903, there were 1,461 registered drivers in Chicago. Most of them came from wealthy families who saw the auto as a fashionable replacement for the bicycle, whose status slipped when mid-1890s mass production considerably lowered its price.[37] The auto, moreover, was the ideal way to get to the country club, that new elite institution that was springing up on the suburban periphery. During the early years of the century there was more than a tinge of class sentiment in the manner in which newspapers reported the arrest of some millionaire's son or daughter for speeding, or "scorching," or for scaring some hapless pedestrian.[38]

Elite women found it fashionable to be seen in an auto, and designers offered stylish wardrobes for that purpose. Even women who could not afford a car could still be "up to the minute" by following the latest fad: a small dab of gasoline behind the ear to give the popular aroma of the hour. But many women did drive. Varying accounts give the honor of being the first to either Mrs. C. E. Woods or Miss Julia Bracken, both of whom were among the ten women on the road by 1900.[39]

During the next phase in the acceptance of the new automobile technology, the rapid expansion in the numbers of cars on the road caused some observers to note that they were beginning to have an impact on the city. But at this point the ownership ranks were still small enough that problems of congestion and pollution had not yet surfaced. In fact, it was easy for wealthy owners to promote the special benefits of the car as a solution to two of Chicago's most annoying environmental problems: horse manure and smoke. Horses required rough street surfaces of stone or brick, and when Old Dobbin left behind his ineluctable calling card, it lodged between the paving blocks and became almost impossible to sweep away. Spring rains turned manure into a smelly soup, while summer heat dried it to the point where winds kicked up eye-stinging clouds. A concern that the swirling dust might harbor germs prompted health officials to ban outdoor dining facilities in restaurants as well as food vending from open containers.[40] Moreover, the size of the animals meant that when they expired, there was little the owner could do except walk away. The city was left with the task of picking up thousands of dead horses from the streets each year. Car enthusiasts insisted that the replacement of horses with automobiles, which did not decay and were too valuable to abandon, would make Chicago a safer and healthier place.[41] At the same time, they argued that everyone would benefit from the smooth, easy-to-clean asphalt pavement that automobilists needed for the protection of their balloon tires.[42]

Another kind of cloud also disturbed environmentalists. Heavy smoke poured not only from factories and domestic heating boilers, but also from the locomotives that pulled hundreds of commuter trains in and out of the city each day. Efforts to force the railroads to electrify their metropolitan trackage failed—in the 1920s the Illinois Central became the exception—and the trend toward suburban housing made the problem seem worse each year. At the same time, many believed that auto drivers would themselves be healthier than pedestrians or rail commuters because they could avoid contact with germs. The crusade against tuberculosis that emerged during the first decade of the new century included war on open-faced sneezers, expectorators, and others who flooded the streetcar or el with microbes. Even when its sides were only waterproof cloth, the auto became a way to carry private space into the street; this provided safety not only from criminals but also from unseen threats.[43]

Then there was the matter of traffic. Car owners quickly appreciated the auto's speed and its independence from railroad scheduling and began driving to the Loop. So many of them complained about the surface on the Rush Street Bridge, the main portal to the North Side, that the city put down a smooth macadam pavement.[44] A few bold newspaper writers expanded on that idea and argued that the auto both would and *should* replace the streetcar. The automobile could dart in and out of tight traffic, and, if disabled, could be pushed to

The old Turnpike Gate at Milwaukee Avenue and Fullerton Avenue, from a photograph taken the morning after its destruction by fire in 1889.

Fire-damaged toll road gate, Milwaukee and Fullerton Avenues, 1889. Area residents celebrated the murder of Amos Snell and the defeat of his stranglehold over Milwaukee Avenue by burning down his main toll booth.

South Park Depot, Grand Boulevard, Illinois Central Railroad, 1880s. Local commuter stations gave riders an elegant sendoff each morning and served as busy hubs of outlying communities, such as South Park, near present-day Jackson Park.

Kenilworth Station, Chicago and North Western Railway, early 1920s. The rustic stone station bearing the town's logo symbolized the affluent ambience of the North Shore suburbia.

Automobile excursion, ca. 1915. For many families, the car was more significant for the leisure-time freedom it gave to explore the rural Midwest than it was as a way to get to work.

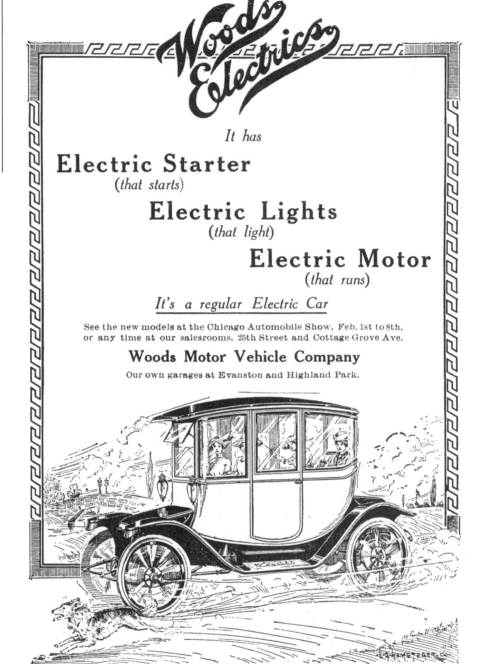

Woods Electrics

It has

Electric Starter
(that starts)

Electric Lights
(that light)

Electric Motor
(that runs)

It's a regular Electric Car

See the new models at the Chicago Automobile Show, Feb. 1st to 8th,
or any time at our salesrooms, 25th Street and Cottage Grove Ave.

Woods Motor Vehicle Company
Our own garages at Evanston and Highland Park.

Woods Motor Vehicle advertisement, Garrick Theatre program, February 2, 1913. The Woods was one of several electric autos that were being promoted as fashionable, easy to operate, and reliable—not as more friendly to the environment than the gasoline rivals.

Auditorium Hotel, Michigan Avenue and Congress Street, postcard view, around 1910. Those who dined at the summer restaurant saw automobiles replace horses in their view of Grant Park below.

Automobiles on North Michigan Avenue, late 1920s. Once touted as a solution to street congestion, the car soon became fully capable of plugging the streets.

the side of the street; by contrast, the lumbering streetcar, which could not stray from its tracks to go around obstructions, blocked everything behind it. Furthermore, the cavalier way in which traction companies treated their customers and monopolized the streets irritated many reform-oriented Chicagoans. It was easy to view automobile drivers as brave, independent taxpayers seeking to reclaim the right to use the public streets that their tax dollars built and maintained. Yet individual owners also realized that they could not depend solely on the influence of wealthy fellow drivers. In December 1899 they formed the Chicago Motor Club to focus lobbying efforts on behalf of its members, who saw the advantages of coping through purposeful organization.[45]

Environmentalists of that day were seemingly unaware that they were supporting the automobile for the wrong reasons, but municipal officials quickly realized that the machine caused as many problems as it solved. First, there was the problem of fuel. Gasoline, which had been denounced as a dangerous poison as early as the 1880s, was far more volatile than kerosene or any other petroleum product that average citizens were accustomed to handling.[46] Chicago's fire chief agonized over the possibility that another Great Fire could erupt if an exploding tank in one blazing garage touched off a chain reaction.

Chicagoans were also becoming increasingly aware that the automobile's ability to move quickly from here to there could become a problem. The advantage of the machine lay not primarily in its comfort or its power to plow through Chicago winters, but rather in its speed and its capability to avoid streets with transit lines. Both of these features made it especially attractive to those traveling the distended city. The negative tradeoff was the greatly increased potential for human injury, especially among those who were unaware of the new dangers. In 1899, a man named Frank Raymond had the dubious distinction of becoming the city's first auto fatality when he stepped in front of a taxi on Michigan Avenue. This led to demands that the machine be licensed.[47]

Because of the new risks, calls arose for some sort of test of driving competency, prompting the city council to pass the city's first driver's license ordinance on July 6, 1899. It established a Board of Examiners of Operators of Automobiles. This agency included the Chicago health commissioner, who passed judgment on an applicant's physical abilities—color blindness and epilepsy were disqualifiers—and the city engineer and city electrician, who assessed mechanical knowledge of the machine.[48] Arthur J. Eddy, an industrialist and novelist, reportedly got the first license, but the test was actually so simple that a thirteen-year-old girl reportedly received a permit as well. What would prove to be the most significant part of the law may have been the eight-miles-per-hour speed limit it imposed and its specification that each vehicle be equipped with a lamp, adequate brakes, and a gong or bell.[49]

In 1902, the continuing problem of speeding and accidents aroused the concern of city officials. Mayor Carter Harrison II reportedly became enraged when he heard that one man claimed that he could make the six-mile trip between the Union League Club and the Saddle and Cycle Club in twelve minutes. The rate of thirty miles an hour was more than three times the speed of the rest of the traffic. Harrison vowed to send all speeders directly to jail rather than fine them.[50] The uproar forced the aldermen to tighten the law on December 8, 1902. Not only did drivers have to sound their alarm bells at pedestrian crossings and install a second braking system, they were now forced to wear numbered badges.[51] Five months later, they were also forced to put numbered tags on their vehicles as well, and yet another revision of the law in 1903 made it mandatory that owners supply their own tags, which had to conform to specifications.[52]

No one anticipated the backlash that resulted among the monied, especially concerning the license plate requirement. Some owners complained that they were being inconvenienced and publicly identified as being reckless, all because of the actions of a few. Although Honore Palmer, hotel owner Potter's son and head of the Chicago Auto Club, personally favored the law, some members of the organization labeled it "class legislation" that had been created by a group they called "automobile anarchists," who had no cars and were jealous of those who did.[53] The same class attitude was evident when A. C. Banker of the Chicago Motor Club told a *Record-Herald* reporter that a driver who has a female passenger in his car should not stop when a policeman asks him to, because it "saves a man's appearance." Two weeks earlier, Banker had been arrested for speeding.[54] Judge Murray F. Tuley upheld the tag law in July 1903, declaring the auto to be the most dangerous thing ever unleashed on the streets of Chicago. But tag opponents led by Banker won a restraining order and, later, an appellate decision with the argument that because horses, which often exceeded eight miles per hour, did not have licenses, it was unfair to require tags of automobiles.[55] Meanwhile, the commissioners of Chicago's larger parks—the twenty-two park systems in the city would not be unified as the Chicago Park District until 1934—began issuing operating permits of their own because much early pleasure driving was done in the sylvan reserves.[56]

In 1904 the city council had to start over with a new licensing ordinance that set the minimum driving age at eighteen and required full use of arms and legs, good eyesight and hearing, and freedom from heart disease and a "drug habit." The speed limit rose to ten miles per hour.[57] The *Record-Herald* noted that the easiest way police could locate violators was to check the streets outside of elite clubs; the paper also condemned opponents as "certain persons of considerable property who denounce labor agitators and talk a lot about law and order," but who want to break laws that apply to them.[58] The Chicago Motor Club, which the *Record-Herald* claimed had "recovered from its fanciful flight into a utopia of selfishness," not only supported the law, but provided touring cars so that the police might pursue "scorchers" and other law violators.[59]

At no time in Chicago's history had so many of its most substantial citizens been cast in the role of lawbreakers, and the problem did not stop at the city border. To the dismay of the promoters of Sheridan Road, which ran north from the city to the Wisconsin border, the care in designing it as a corridor led to its unfortunate transformation into a racetrack. Its wide and well-marked route allowed scorchers to escape from one municipal jurisdiction to another before understaffed police forces could apprehend them. Midnight racing became especially popular because the streets were clear and law enforcement was at its lowest manpower level. One wealthy scofflaw and "injunction enthusiast," John Farson, led police on a six-mile chase over the Chicago portion of the route.[60] By 1906 the load of cases generated by drivers on Sheridan Road prompted Evanston to establish a special traffic court, but the social class of the offenders guaranteed that they would not find themselves hauled before a judge. Chauffeurs delivered the fines on behalf of their employers, while drivers were allowed to give testimony over the telephone rather than face the embarrassment of appearing in court. The trial of one prominent lady was held at her convenience in the back seat of her car.[61]

Meanwhile, the soaring accident rate became an especially serious problem near congested areas; in 1905, an average of nearly one driver in four was involved in some type of mishap.[62] That year, there was a rash of collisions near bridges, and several autos broke through the chains that blocked the roadway when the swing spans were turned. This brought calls for a law requiring autos to come to a full stop before crossing bridges, but the *Record-Herald* editorialized against it as a "useless restraint on liberty of movement."[63] One alderman wanted autos banned completely from downtown between the hours of five and seven in the evening.[64] Mayor Edward F. Dunne, who held office in 1905–7, responded to the problem by insisting that he interview and test license applicants personally. He summoned lawbreakers to his office for a tongue lashing. But he was later forced to admit that small fines paid over and over again amounted to no more than a fee to break the law; he proposed that violators should be jailed instead.[65] In reality, of course, he did not control the municipal court, which continued the previous practices.

The problem was compounded by the difficulty in establishing precedents in traffic law. In one notable case, Dunne felt that he could not revoke the city auto license of the first driver apprehended for drunken driving because the man was not in control of his actions and therefore could not be held responsible for what he did. That decision prompted temperance groups to demand that a pledge of total sobriety be required of each licensee.[66] By 1906, the *Record-Herald* expressed an opinion shared by increasing numbers of people: "The pedestrian's first feeling toward the auto was one of envy. Now it is the feeling that in the hands of inconsiderate people, it can be dangerous."[67]

The automobile's ability to race across the distended city also created confusion over which level of government should license the vehicle and which would license the driver. The state of Illinois took over vehicle licensing in 1907, in large part because of the great number of suburbanites who objected to being forced to obtain a Chicago license to drive on the city streets. But in February 1908 the Chicago City Council amended the licensing law once more, this time requiring plates for any vehicle transporting people; this included carriages, wagons, and hacks.[68] The new law withstood all challenges, at least until the closing days of 1911, when the Illinois General Assembly voted to enact its own license law. By this time, the increased geographical mobility of automobilists made it logical to override a patchwork of local licensing regulations with a uniform state license.[69] The Chicago aldermen decided to retain their license system and continued to collect fees from unhappy motorists until 1915, when the Illinois Supreme Court invalidated the collection of local license fees when the state issued plates.[70]

By 1910, most of the initial enthusiasm for the auto's urban benefits had cooled. Positive comments came largely from the swelling ranks of owners.[71] Most publicity was negative. Bankers fretted that deposits were declining because people were "squandering" their money on cars. The meek "putt-putt" of the early machines gave way to louder noises as defiant drivers found ways to bypass mandatory mufflers.[72]

Parking was emerging as yet another new headache. In years past, comparatively few horses had been used for commuting to the Loop. Equestrians who did spend the day downtown felt compelled to put their animals into a private stable. There were practical limits to the time that a horse could be expected to stand tethered to a curb; there was no practical way to lock up the horse, and if left too long, the animals wandered away or occasionally became impatient and bit pedestrians. But the auto could remain at the curb indefinitely. When the streets became clogged with parked cars in 1909, the city council passed a one-hour "standing limit," yet another source of conflict with owners. In 1912, defenders of the public parks were shocked to read of a proposal to park automobiles in Grant Park. The city also began to complain that it now had to haul away disabled and abandoned automobiles, as well as horses.[73] And the image of the autoist as young, daring, stylish, and athletic also gave way to another perception. The *Record-Herald* ran a story about how Chicago tailors could spot an automobile owner: he was reportedly "swelled up" in the wrong places from lack of exercise.

Perhaps the most dismaying aspect of the developing image of the automobile was the manner in which it began transforming wrongdoing. By 1910, auto theft had emerged as one of the fastest growing crimes. The speed and anonymity of the machine proved a perfect way to escape from a crime scene and evade the police. The full impact of the automobile on crime became clear on the night of December 2, 1912, when a pair of gangs, given the name Auto Bandits by the press, began an extended spree of robbery and murder on the North Side. The young men, two of whom were chauffeurs, stole cars, terrorized and robbed the owners of dozens of small businesses, escaped police dragnets, and taunted the precinct houses with phone calls until the capture of the last of them over ten weeks later.[74]

As frightening as these escapades were to Chicagoans, they would, of course, prove minor compared with the use of the automobile during the heyday of the gangs during the 1920s. The "one-way ride" did not take place in a buggy, and somehow it is difficult to imagine Al Capone escaping a crime scene in a streetcar.

It took a while, but Chicagoans finally discovered that solutions to problems could also become problems.

Conclusion

The foregoing discussion of the means of getting from here to there demonstrates that the way one group coped with a problem often created a difficulty for someone else: The old Snell toll road that was hailed as progressive in the nineteenth century became an unappreciated impediment for later travelers. Commuter trains polluted in-city neighborhoods and ran over pedestrians, while autos increased the street danger for everyone. During Chicago's early decades, transportation problems had been mired in slowness and in inflexible routes and schedules; now they were caused by speed and a driver's ability to change course and head almost anywhere and at any time. The result was an elevated level of risk.

Chicagoans who traveled across longer distances tended to view the world differently from those who walked or rode mass transit. Commuting of all types, even by foot, tended to promote a view of the city and its region as a series of corridors. The daily trek went past the same familiar landmarks, which ceased being part of the scenery and became measuring devices that allowed a quick calculation of progress toward the destination. The string of towns "along the line" shaped the commuter's perception of the world. This linear thinking bordered on being anti-city because most urban functions became impediments to travel. The street, which had been a multifunctional place, was seen in increasingly narrow terms as a path for traffic to move with as few interruptions as possible. The auto displaced the horse, an improvement in public health, but there was a tradeoff. The familiar peddlers, gawking pedestrians, rambunctious children, piles of horse manure, distracting street signs, and other hallmarks of the street became dangerous obstacles, especially when the question of speed entered the picture. For these reasons, and not merely because of jealousy or dislike of the wealthy, the working class easily viewed the automobile as a dangerous and selfish appropriation of common space. The Milwaukee Road's ill-fated Evanston Division represented a similar threat that was even more serious because it brought the commuter train away from its familiar stone right-of-way to invade what had been a residential street.

Social class played an obvious role in this story. Money meant that automobile drivers could insulate themselves from the city through which they traveled. Even the side curtains and sheet-metal work of the early automobile provided a buffer around the driver and passengers. And riding companions were there by invitation, not accident. Commuter-train riders may have been less well off financially than the autoists, but they often thought of themselves as luckier than those who had to ride slow, crowded streetcars. Streetcar riders usually encountered less jostling by the crowd than did pedestrians, who also had to contend more directly with the weather.

The higher income that often enabled commuting by car also allowed one to use this daily mobility to one's own advantage, to separate home and work, city frenzy and sylvan quiet, weekday "city house" from weekend "country home," and even the immorality of urban vice and the moral purity of a liquor-free town. The ability to view the city and its region in terms of miles rather than blocks meant being able to build contrasts into one's life; those geographical choices were not available to the poor. The irony came from the fact that the auto aroused intense social class resentments because it was such a publicly visible symbol of wealth. As a result, early drivers found their mobility limited when they began to realize that the possibility of attack made it too dangerous to drive through some poor neighborhoods.

Finally, the automobile driver may be regarded as taking part in a special type of coping. Like the peddler, he or she wanted to come to terms with the city on an individual basis, one on one. There was even less of an emphasis on joining associations than there had been among bicycle riders. The automobilist's self-view was that of a pioneer, perhaps a little purer and prouder than the herds of strap-hangers that were left in the exhaust during the commute to work. Streetcar riders were victims, dupes of corruption. From this viewpoint, it was natural to resist the imposition of traffic rules. It was also possible to deny—in the face of the facts—that the auto had created new risks.

Many of these attitudes would, of course, change in the decades after the Model T and the growing supply of used "machines" brought the cost of owning an automobile within the reach of working-class families. By the end of the 1920s, automobile traffic jams had begun to replace the tangles of wagons and horses. And once more, someone's solution became someone else's problem.

Postscript

Old Dobbin was doomed. During the last two decades of the nineteenth century, the ranks of Chicago horses reportedly dropped by 20 percent. The replacement of the horsecar by the cable car and especially the reliable trolley was one factor in the demise of the equine city.[75] But the rise of the automobile and its freight-hauling counterpart, the truck, proved to be the final challenge. One 1899 estimate pegged the cost of maintaining a horse at $3,000 a year, compared with $1,900 for a motorized delivery wagon. Mass production of vehicles widened that differential.[76] Horses routinely lost the battle over pavement surfaces to trucks, and drivers were even forced to equip their wagons with wider tires to limit the damage to the asphalt.[77] In 1907 there were still 77,000 horses left in the city, but the numbers were thinning.[78]

By 1910, the horse-related industries were striving to protect a declining market. A new National Carriage Dealers Protective Association tried to demonstrate the superior comfort and style of its product in an exhibition at the Coliseum, but to no avail.[79] In one of the saddest rear-guard actions of any dying industry, the Chicago-based Horse Association of America opened its doors in 1920 to keep alive the interest in animal power on the farm and in the city. A blitz of handbills and news releases argued that draft horses were cheaper to maintain, more powerful, more reliable, and more fun to own than a motor truck.[80] But it was a lost cause. Horse-drawn wagons survived in milk delivery longer than in most other cartage uses because the animals could be trained to make all of the stops in a route by themselves, freeing the driver to concentrate on carrying bottles to and from the door.

Years later, there was a flurry of prohorse sentiment when Chicagoans faced tire and gasoline rationing during World War II. Some delivery services did return to hoof power, but it proved to be just a brief flirtation. Except for horse racing and equestrian hobbies, the urban horse faded into oblivion, and until carriages made their 1980s return and the Chicago Police Department restored mounted patrols, the animal had all but disappeared from the city's public places.

On September 30, 1983, Chicago finally came to grips with a new horse-and-buggy age. The open carriages that plied Near North streets may have charmed tourists, but they did not mix well with taxis, buses, and rush-hour commuters. So the city was compelled to issue guidelines as to when and where the horse-drawn vehicles could operate. This contest between the hoof and mechanical locomotion was not new, but for the first seventy-five years of the city's history, even after the invention of the automobile, Old Dobbin had the right-of-way.[81]

Commuter rail service not only survived the rise of the automobile but continued to thrive despite highway improvements. In 1926 the Illinois Central completely electrified its suburban line, but steam engines survived on other roads into the mid-1950s. In 1950 the Burlington railroad became the first to introduce new air-conditioned double-deck "gallery" cars. The North Western (now Union Pacific) line did the same six years later, completely converting to diesel power and introducing "push-pull" trains on which the locomotive always remained at the north or west end of the train. During inbound runs the engineer utilized a cab built into the last car and the train appeared to be backing up toward Chicago. With the windows now sealed, it was no longer possible to spot commuters by looking for the locomotive soot speckles on their white shirts or blouses—or by sniffing for kerosene.

Despite the upgrades, the private carriers claimed huge operating losses and by the early 1970s were threatening to discontinue several lines. The South Shore line continues as America's last interurban railway, but only with a heavy subsidy. The creation of the Regional Transportation Authority (RTA) in 1974 provided a funnel for state and local tax funds to make up operating deficits for lines under private operation and to buy outright and run the commuter routes of defunct railroads, such as the Milwaukee Road. Metra, the suburban rail system operating under the RTA, continues to provide excellent diesel and electric service, but not everyone is happy. Some suburbs are served by only a handful of trains each day, and the lines remain entirely focused on downtown destinations. Fares have risen. Rail officials are left with a delicate balancing act of finding money to run their systems and upgrade aging equipment, while trying to avoid driving away customers by increasing fares. There are also complaints that express service to the outermost stations poses a danger to the inner suburbs through which the fast trains operate. A tragic accident in October 1995, in which a Union Pacific–Metra train hit a school bus at seventy miles an hour and killed seven students, brought calls for speed limits that were reminiscent of the demands in the "Battle of Lake View" a century earlier. Lengthy investigations attributed the 1995 accident to the design of the crossing and concluded that imposing speed limits on trains would not significantly reduce vehicular hazards.

The mansion that was the scene of the Snell crime continued to attract curiosity seekers until it was razed in 1923. When Snell's widow, Henrietta, died in 1900 the property was turned over to trustees who continued to manage it until the deaths of her three daughters. The youngest child, Grace Henrietta, eloped with a coachman at age fifteen, married five more times, and over the years made several appeals for larger allowances. When she died in 1941 at the age of seventy-five, the estate was still worth $1.5 million. Three years later most of the property was sold at auction and the proceeds divided among eleven heirs.[82]

Willie Tascott never was apprehended and the murder of Amos J. Snell remains unsolved.

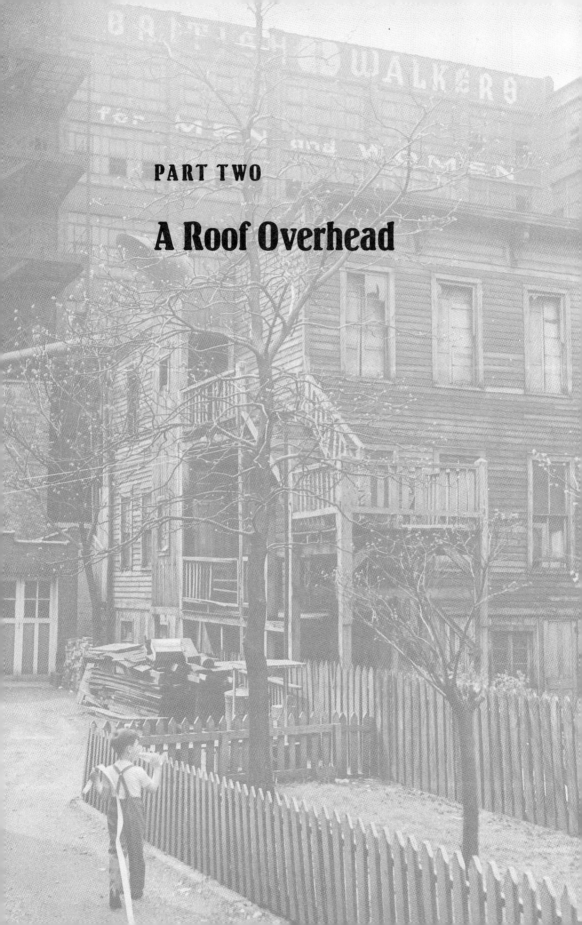

PART TWO

A Roof Overhead

3   Housing Strategies

HISTORY has lost track of the James Van Cleeve family. Their moment of fame came in September 1890, when the *Chicago Post* asked readers to fill out ballots extolling the virtues of their favorite suburb. Tens of thousands eagerly mailed in entries that bubbled with enthusiasm for the cleanliness, beauty, safety, house quality, transportation convenience, and general livability of their towns. Everyone wanted to be a suburbanite. The paper gave in to the demands of residents from the Town of Lake, Jefferson, Hyde Park and Lake View that they be included in the contest, even though these outlying townships had been annexed to the city in July of the previous year. Morton Park won the contest with over 13,000 votes and Dauphin Park was a close second. The third-place finisher was Grossdale, now part of Brookfield. The *Post* received over 12,000 entries from there, including one from the James Van Cleeve family. Their ballot explained that ten months earlier, when their daughter had become the first child born in the town, they expressed their admiration for the place by naming her "Grossie Dale."[1]

For most Chicagoans, the process of finding a new home did not lead to the satisfaction enjoyed by the Van Cleeve family.[2] The search for a place to live was a frequently frustrating experience of trial and error that was made more difficult by the rapid growth and evolution of the city. Such factors as industrialization, improvements in transportation, innovations in housing technology, and fads and fashions complicated the choice of alternatives that was already circumscribed by a family's income level. And looming over the whole process in a city of housing shortages was the risk that a family might end up having to tolerate someplace unsatisfactory or unhealthy, or even having no home at all.

"No Codfish Aristocracy": Suburbs, Subdivisions, and Security

Finding a place to live was a contest, a war of the marketplace involving thousands of small battles that took place every day across the city. On one side was the consumer and the dream of the perfect home. Whatever its outward manifestation, that dream was rooted in a vision of the future that included predictability and risk management. The buyer hoped for a stable neighborhood, increasing value, freedom from the dangers of the city. Pitted against that dream were the realities of urban life. The developer or seller was principally interested in generating the maximum profit. Nonetheless, the quest for the perfect home often failed because of uncontrollable events and the rapid changes of an urbanizing metropolis. In the middle of the contest was the subdivision, the multihouse development whose appeal, whether warranted or not, lay in the promise of its future, rather than the reality of its past.

The search for shelter had been a difficult task for most people caught up in the mud and the speculative madness of the pioneer city. The first generation of prospective homeowners had to cope with shortages of materials and limitations in technology. Crude solid-wall log dwellings not only used large amounts of relatively scarce wood, but they were also impossible to move. Gradually, people who wanted to own a home were able to gain the skills to build the place themselves if they used the balloon-frame design attributed to George Snow, a lumber dealer and carpenter who first utilized it in the construction of St. Mary's Roman Catholic Church in 1833. Although knowledge of the technique quickly diffused throughout the community, inefficiency and occasional difficulty in obtaining sawed lumber and nails tended to limit construction, drive up prices, and push the population of the growing town into rooming houses and tiny dwellings.[3] The first indication of change came in 1837 when a local physician named Dr. William B. Egan erected a row of four inexpensive frame houses and charged high rent; it was Chicago's first subdivision.[4] But, decades before the idea of mass production became popular, no one else saw the advantage of adapting the principle to housing. The general disinterest in owning a home grew out of the transient nature of Chicago's pioneer population. Young men who merely wanted to make a quick fortune before moving on wanted no commitment to anything as permanent as home ownership. Some land deals were tainted by fraud perpetrated on unsuspecting out-of-towners who bought useless swamp.[5]

By the 1850s, however, the ideas of mass-produced housing and subdivided land joined to create the first housing boom that was aimed at the growing numbers of families. Some of these early buyers faced a dilemma. They realized that government and charitable institutions had traditionally used the urban fringe as an exile for the unwanted. Institutions, many of them accommodating juvenile delinquents (Illinois Industrial Training School), alcoholics (Martha Washington Home), the insane (Cook County Insane Asylum), prisoners (House of Correction), and "fallen women" (Erring Woman's Refuge), as well as garbage dumps, dog pounds, and temporary pesthouses for those with contagious diseases, had historically dotted the countryside.[6]

But much of Chicago's surrounding land remained undeveloped and relatively inexpensive, because it was, as the title of a popular booklet of the time put it, *Out of Town*.[7] The answer for prospective homeowners was to go beyond the immediate fringe and away from some of the old roads, and the vehicle that made it possible was the commuter train. After the early 1850s, steam railroads and the later omnibuses and horsecars provided access to those outlying lands, opening up a wide range of choices for the potential home buyer. Many were reluctant to move too far out at first. For instance, in 1855, the J. A. Marshall Company was unable to sell most of the 250 lots put up for auction at its Chittenden plot, seven miles out on the Chicago and Milwaukee Railroad; the subdivision languished until Rose Hill Cemetery was established across the tracks in 1859.[8]

During the post–Civil War years other factors helped propel that outward movement, two of them in 1869. One was the creation of a broad ring of new parks and interconnecting boulevards that encircled Chicago several miles from the edge of settlement. Developers such as Paul Cornell, a young lawyer and associate of Stephen Douglas who owned adjacent lands, were among the most prominent park proponents. Those who sought to avoid the periodic epidemics that afflicted the city were doubtless impressed by the argument that the presence of tree-covered park land would reduce the incidence of disease for those living nearby.[9]

That same year the Illinois General Assembly also approved legislation that facilitated the creation of building and loan societies. These thrift institutions enabled working-class savers to borrow against an accumulated balance and purchase a home. Investors quickly formed the new Chicago Building and Loan Association and offered seven house plans approved by one of its trustees, the architect W. W. Boyington. These ranged from a tiny four-room, $600 wooden duplex to an expansive ten-room, $5,000 house on a corner lot. The steady accumulation of even a small amount of wealth provided not only a road map of sorts toward a goal, but also a cushion for the unforeseen.[10]

Another factor was the entry into the area housing market of large-scale corporations owned by anonymous investors, which often included railway companies. These firms developed logical marketing plans pitched at particular parts of the housing market. The Highland Park Land Company, for instance, offered relatively expensive lots and homes for the emerging elite of the metropolis. It excluded liquor and manufacturing. Similarly, in 1869 R. T. Race bought a farm along the North Western railroad, platted lots, and built fifteen substantial houses. Race tried to play upon the popularity of Washington Irving's novels by naming his development Irvington, later changing it to Irving Park.[11] By contrast, in 1869 the Maywood Land Company intentionally developed a multiclass town with a strong industrial base. Its offerings ranged from substantial frame houses for middle-class managers down to fairly modest housing that workers could afford. Maywood was also virtually alone in encouraging industry, which by the mid-1870s included a plow company and what would become one of the world's largest producers of tin cans.[12]

Some companies found that it was often easier to sell land closer to the fringes of town. During the 1860s, for example, two developers, Charles and Joel

Wicker, laid out Wicker Park.[13] On the West Side, a former Kentuckian named Samuel J. Walker built a district of fine homes along Ashland Avenue and sold many of them to well-to-do families who had recently arrived from the South. By 1873, Walker had fifteen hundred acres inside the city limit under development.[14] Meanwhile, to the south, Paul Cornell founded the towns of Hyde Park, Grand Crossing, and several other suburbs that are now city neighborhoods.[15] Gradually, the railroad dissolved not only the distance from town, but also the resistance to traveling it on a daily basis.

Buyers found that most of these new subdivisions and towns were planned on a traditional grid. While this practice did make it simpler to understand exactly the size of the lot and created a sense of order, the result was not very exciting. Most developments—especially those pitched at working-class buyers—also lacked distinguished architectural design, offering instead a formula of a limited number of standardized plans that expedited construction but produced what were later considered monotonous subdivisions. Designers of other developments were eager to exploit any irregularities in the dinner-plate flatness of most of the Chicago region. The undulating landscape of many parts of the North Shore made it much more difficult to lay out grids and rendered the area more attractive to elite buyers. But to the west, where the land was generally flat, landscape architects had to make the best of even the most modest knolls. For instance, when H. W. S. Cleveland, the designer of Lake Forest, laid out "West Hinsdale," present-day Clarendon Hills, his curvilinear streets enhanced the gentle hillsides. The most famous exception to the grid, however, was Riverside. In 1869 the new land company brought in Frederick Law Olmsted, the landscape architect famous for designing New York City's Central Park. Faced with flat acreage, he designed curved streets and greenery-shrouded lots. Olmsted's partner, Calvert Vaux, along with the Chicagoan William LeBaron Jenney, best-known for his later invention of the steel-framed office building, drew up the home plans, which were as pleasant and distinctive as their setting.[16]

While developers appealed to different segments of the market, most were really selling security and predictability. Several placed restrictions on the minimum value of houses erected there, as well as deed restrictions that guaranteed that incoming neighbors would not bring with them unwanted businesses or other nuisances. Developers who required that buyers erect the houses were, in effect, allowing them to visualize the future character of the place. Many of the towns also offered pre-installed public amenities, which freed new homeowners from the burden of having to cope with the inconveniences that were an inevitable part of municipal evolution. It was also common for developers to construct a depot as an inducement to the railroad to stop long-distance trains there or establish a commuter run. The rail carriers, which often owned land-company stock, were only too happy to offer service as a way to enlarge their passenger business.[17]

The developers also carefully prepared the town's public and semipublic spaces. They constructed commercial and civic buildings—usually a store, a school, and a municipal building, often adding a central downtown square and parks. They gave free lots to congregations willing to build new churches as an inducement to relocate. It was easy for a developer to draw contrasts between his planned community and the inner-city chaos of unfinished streets and haphazardly created utilities. For buyers, the more complete the package of established amenities, the less they need worry that the work would never be done.[18]

While Edison Park claimed that "future health and prosperity are assured by our attitude and healthful surroundings," the emphasis in many places was on the way that technological progress would assure vitality, safety, and growing property values. Maywood boasted that Gen. William Sooy Smith, a distinguished architectural engineer, was in charge of all improvements. Oak Park had the latest macadamized street. Several places touted their "advanced" water systems that distributed pure artesian well water, while J. L. Cochran, a developer, emphasized that every one of the houses in Edgewater was equipped with Edison's electric light system. Only Wilmette among the higher-priced towns seemed to take pride in resisting the amenities, although in 1890 the *Post* could note that newcomers were forcing a change.[19]

The subdividers hammered their message through creative, as well as aggressive, merchandising that no potential home buyer could miss. The only medium readily available was print, but Chicago's preeminence as America's center for the printing of timetables, mail-order catalogs, travel brochures, and elaborately illustrated throwaways made it possible for land companies to issue bales of eye-catching handbills, brochures, and newspaper layouts. Some developments, such as Edgewater and Kenilworth, always spelled out their names in distinctive typefaces that became easily recognizable trademarks. Advertisers used print size to emphasize the price, location, and size of the property, or whatever else they considered to be the most attractive feature. Extensive use of illustrations and easily understood symbols also made it possible to lure those with only a limited understanding of English. But in some ads, lines of small type delivered the sales pitch, which sometimes made light of competitors. "No codfish aristocracy, criminals, toughs, or saloons," announced the ads for E. H. Prince and Company's Downers Grove subdivision.[20]

The fancier suburbs and subdivisions also sold potential buyers on the secure future that grew out of social selectivity and solidarity. Residents were members of an identifiable group. One Oak Park resident boasted to a reporter, "Everything gives one the idea of a perfectly organized community—a community in the welfare of which one and all take active pride and interest." Hinsdale residents added that they "had no desire to 'boom'" their town because "its location is such that it will not attract residents whose employment gives neither the time nor the means to live at this distance out."[21]

Predictability and security also extended to social relationships. Ownership had its own filtering effect, but in addition residents of many subdivisions and suburbs could join the two types of institutions that provided selected companionship. One was a church, by which most established denominations were represented. By the early 1890s, however, many towns took even greater pride in that other type of institution, the club. Even Evanston promoters were quick to point out that the "old Puritan days" were over and that "the new liberal blood infused in the town of late years gives it enough liberality to escape bigotry and leaves just enough bigotry to act as a safeguard and check." To some extent, the club assumed the role of social center in many towns. Operating out of sometimes elaborate clubhouses, clubs sponsored athletic and literary groups, dances, holiday parties, outings, and "closed theatricals" whose audiences were composed only of other members.[22]

Suburbs were also careful to emphasize that the environment was safe for children. One newspaper feature on Hinsdale boasted: "They [parents] can feel that their precious charges are surrounded by the best and most refined social atmospheres. No iniquitous dens exist to tempt the innocent youth. . . . The schools are excellent, embracing all of the advantages of the public school system without that objectionable feature to be noticed in cities—a mixed attendance from every social grade. The children are of equal social rank."[23]

The advertising allowed prospective buyers to imagine that their future homes were everything their present ones were not, offering space instead of congestion, quiet instead of the urban din, greenery instead of monotonous brick, safety instead of the danger of street crime and another Great Fire, and health instead of disease. Although the breadwinner still had to cope with city problems during workdays, his family could live in splendid isolation. The ads depicted life on the fringes of Chicago as an endless vacation, and to emphasize that point, the larger companies constructed adjacent resort hotels, with reduced room rates for potential home buyers.[24] The Glen Ellyn Hotel and Springs Company, on the shores of Lake Ellyn, called itself "The Future Saratoga of the West." Its advertising featured illustrations that exaggerated the size of the lake and the height of the hills surrounding it. In every case, if the development had a riverfront, it was transformed into a rustic carriage drive with ornate well houses and bandstands that implied future summer evening concerts. Perhaps the most spectacular of these embellishments was the observation tower that Maywood built in the early 1870s. Bearing a remarkable resemblance to the external framing of today's John Hancock Center, it was 124 feet tall and offered a splendid view of the countryside—and of the thriving town below.[25]

Prospective buyers could select from a bewildering choice of developers and towns, but the most popular home builder was Samuel E. Gross, the most prolific developer in Chicago's history.[26] He arrived in the city in 1865, sold houses for a while, and then, when he lost his business in the 1870s depression, became an equally unsuccessful playwright. (Years later he won a lawsuit when a judge decided that he, not Edmond Rostand, was the creator of the character Cyrano de Bergerac.)[27] By 1881 S. E. Gross and Company was back in the housing business, and during the next ten years it sold more than thirty thousand lots and built thousands of houses in twenty-one subdivisions. These included Dauphin Park on Chicago's South Side, as well as the Van Cleeves' Grossdale.[28]

There were several reasons for Gross's success, especially among those whose more modest means might have kept them out of Hinsdale or the North Shore. They, too, were interested in security, but of a slightly different variety. The size and number of Gross's subdivisions functioned as self-advertising, and

Chicagoans who wanted to minimize the risk of losing their investment saw him as a safe bet. His liberal credit terms required as little as $100 down and $10 a month. Socially mobile "Gross families" could also move up through a sequence of increasingly opulent homes and subdivisions. His prices began at as little as $1,000 for four rooms at Forty-seventh and Laflin to $5,000 for a substantial dwelling in a North Side development. His vacant-lot prices ranged from $100 to $2,500. He seldom foreclosed on a mortgage, regardless of the prevailing economic conditions, and that fact eased the fears of those only marginally able to afford a house. This made him so popular among Chicago's working class that in 1889 union leaders tried, unsuccessfully, to persuade him to run for mayor.[29]

Gross also became famous for his unconventional and much-imitated marketing techniques. Believing that hotel discounts and brochures were not enough to lure city folk, he chartered streetcars and whole suburban commuter trains to funnel weekend throngs—often as many as five thousand people at a time—into his circus tents for free meals and entertainment, as well as into his sales tents for a carefully rehearsed pitch. The experience introduced prospects to the idea that commuting was not only a tolerable part of fringe living, but it could even be pleasureful.[30] Gross's competitors quickly caught on to his methods, much to the advantage of potential buyers. During the summer of 1890 alone, a family, whether looking for a home or simply in search of an afternoon of free entertainment and food, could literally travel to a different development every Sunday. One afternoon saw McElroy, Keeney, and Company, which was selling a thousand-lot plot between Fifty-fifth and Sixty-third Streets, near the lake, serve fifty-five whole roasted cows, sheep, and hogs to the more than ten thousand potential buyers the developer had attracted out to the property on free trains. Not to be outdone, the E. A. Hill firm put together special Sunday celebrations that included not only Rock Island train rides to its Englewood on the Hill development, but also a concert by the Chicago Zoave Prize Band. The highlight of the afternoon was the launch of fifty skyrockets, each bearing a certificate worth ten dollars toward the purchase of a lot. That season's buyers could also ride free to McLean, Bierbach's Edison Park or its Kervin addition to Oak Park, or to Gross's Dauphin Park and Grossdale, or to McElroy and Keeney's addition to Clarkdale, as well as to Downers Grove, Glen Ellyn, and other sites. Smaller companies, which collectively built as many houses as the giants in the field, could only optimize their lack of competitive advantage. One of them, S. M. Bloss and Company, no doubt played on the name recognition of S. E. Gross and Company and offered free excursions to its West Maywood development. Another developer, William Boldenweck, advertised, "No Brass Band, Balloon Ascension, nor Lots Given Away, but sold at prices to come within the reach of every man, woman, and child." The "no-such-thing-as-a-free-lunch" implication was clear.[31]

But despite all of these assurances about the future, there were failures. Developments were not immune to urban disasters of all types. Some of the first generation of railway suburbs, including Homewood and Canfield, fell victim to the Panic of 1857. An 1870 outbreak of ague (malaria) sharply reduced interest in Riverside, and in attempting to bring back potential buyers, the development company's use of Pullman cars and exclusive showings scared away many prospects who thought the place more expensive than it was. The Panic of 1873 and subsequent depression forced the perfect town into bankruptcy from which it did not recover until early in the next decade. Fires could also be a problem. On the windy afternoon of May 8, 1889, children playing in the sun with a magnifying glass started a blaze outside a recently finished church in west suburban Moreland. Before the volunteer fire department could bring it under control, a devastating fire destroyed seventy houses and a dozen commercial structures.[32]

As the years passed, the open and uncrowded fringe proved to be a dissolving fantasy. Dozens of new developments hugged the commuter lines that fanned out from the city, while extensions of surface and elevated transit lines penetrated areas closer to Chicago's border. A patchwork of tracts gradually filled in much of a wide band of truck farms that once encircled the city.[33]

The turning point for many of these areas came with annexation—against the will of nearly a majority—in the summer of 1889. Many fringe residents demanded that the press report neighborhood activities as if they resided outside the city's borders. Mostly, however, they had to turn that suburban desire for predictability into community activism, which was meant to head off later problems. By 1894 dozens of neighborhood improvement associations dotted the annexed districts, enough to form a citywide federation of groups. That same year, residents began pressuring their aldermen to introduce ordinances banning saloons in precincts, then whole wards. It was easy to claim that the "liquor element" and its potential for attracting vice and crime was a neighborhood destabilizer that demanded preventive action. In 1907, Chicago adopted local option, which allowed residents to place neighborhood prohibition on the ballot, and within two years two-thirds of the city was dry.[34]

However they were marketed and whoever ended up living in them, the thousands of houses built by late-nineteenth-century developers forever changed the Chicago landscape. In 1890, Chicago could boast that its citizens were more comfortably housed than were New Yorkers. Whereas Gotham's 312,766 families lived in only 81,828 buildings, Chicago's 220,320 families filled 127,871 structures. Only 12 percent of New York families owned their own homes, compared with 35 percent in Chicago. Among major cities, only Philadelphia, with its tradition of tiny row houses, had a broader base of home ownership than Chicago had.[35]

The heritage of mass-produced housing that Gross and his contemporaries developed formed a legacy for the later giants in land development—Van Vlissingen, McIntosh, and Brannigar in the 1920s, and the others who followed. These developers may have been less flamboyant, but they continued to responded to changes in their buyers' lifestyles. They paid attention to factors that began to shape fringe housing development, including the way their buyers got from here to there. During the 1920s Samuel Insull, the utilities mogul, used his access to electricity to improve service on elevated lines and on the new high-speed interurban lines around which the suburbs of Niles Center (present-day Skokie), Mundelein, and Westchester thrived. At the same time, the Chicago, Aurora, and Elgin line and the newly electrified Illinois Central commuter service stimulated suburban building booms to the west and south, respectively.[36] Other developers responded to the automobile, which allowed subdivisions to expand away from public transit and steam commuter lines, by helping to promote the idea of a system of hard-surface limited-access highways.[37]

Later developers were also just as adept at targeting customers and creating personalities for their developments. In the 1920s they simulated the relaxed atmosphere of the country club, with winding roads and asymmetrically massed foliage that were compatible with the popular English cottage-style architecture.[38] There was also historical continuity in that fact that during the same decade, more than a hundred thousand families bought new bungalows built within Cook County, the bulk of them constructed in small rows by medium or large developers with funds provided by building and loan associations.[39]

Most important of all, developers through the decades knew how to respond to such intangibles as the desire of fringe and suburban home buyers to create a feeling of order, safety, predictability, and escape from urban assaults on the senses. The story of how Chicago embraced the idea of subdivisions was part of a larger fact: ultimately, home was a destination that made the daily travail of commuting worth the experience.

The Curse of May First: Moving Day

The noises are as much a part of spring as the first robin or opening day at the ballpark. Trucks roar, dollies rattle, and grunts and groans (and a few choice words) pour out from beneath heavy sleeper-sofas. It's one of Chicago's oldest customs: May first, moving day.

It is difficult to tell when the custom arrived in the city; it was already well established in New York when Chicago was still in its infancy. Its origins were tied to habits of spring housecleaning, the end of the school year, and the beginning of the construction season, as well as the May Pole celebrations that symbolized the reawakening of outdoor vegetation. However the custom got started, by 1847 Chicago's *Western Citizen* could note: "As the First of May approaches, the majority of those who are not so fortunate as to have houses of their own are looking out for a shelter for themselves and families for the coming year. We are imminently [*sic*] a migratory people."[40]

By the 1870s the May moving day had become an annual ritual. During the next thirty years as many as one-third of all Chicago households changed residences annually in what amounted to musical chairs played with houses. Families put themselves through the ordeal for a multitude of reasons. Like immigrants from foreign shores, they uprooted themselves and fled discomfort and danger for someplace more pleasant and safe. Concern about periodic epidemics and fires, a change in economic status, crowded conditions, fear, noise, schools—the reasons for relocating were endless.[41] Every new housing unit constructed and each fad in style was a beacon attracting one future occupant, while the house or tenement left behind was paradise for someone else. And

CHICAGO
BUILDING AND LOAN ASSOCIATION,

FOR THE

Promotion of Industry and Economy among the People, and to Encourage
Young Men, and persons of Limited Income, to Save their
Earnings to procure themselves a Homestead.

INCORPORATED MAY 1869.   CAPITAL $500,000.00
IN SHARES OF $100 EACH,

Payable in Monthly Installments, at the Company's Office, No. 125 Dearborn
Street, near Madison, during the last week in each month.

COTTAGE No. 1,

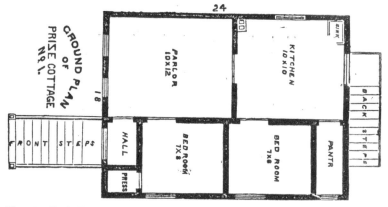

Plan of a Single Tenement Cottage, to cost not exceeding $600 when erected in Chicago.
Complete in itself, but suitable to form a part or wing of a larger building.

Chicago Building and Loan Association advertisement, from *Statistical and Historical Review of Chicago* (1869, p. 65). A "tenement" was a desirable thing when it was new, cost only six hundred dollars, and could be yours for easy monthly installments.

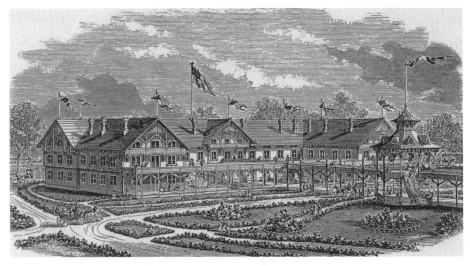

Riverside Hotel, from *Riverside in 1871* (Chicago: Riverside Improvement Co., 1871). The town, planned by Frederick Law Olmsted and Calvert Vaux, included a resort hotel that catered to prospective buyers, as well as those seeking a brief escape from the city.

Sales office, Britiganwood, Virginia and Peterson Avenue, 1920s. A roof sign and garish diagonal stripes made developer Joel Britigan's showroom and sales office distinctive. The auto was symbolic of the subdivision's independence from public transit.

Edgewater advertisement, *Chicago Tribune,* June 10, 1888. The casual elegance of the homes made Edgewater one of the most popular subdivisions on the North Side. The rendering of architect J. L. Silsbee's design is the work of young "Frank Lloyd Wright, Del[ineator]."

Moving Day cartoon, *Chicago Tribune,* April 25, 1897. The problems of household moving confronted as much as a third of all Chicagoans each spring.

South Shore Motor Express truck, ca. 1920. The speed of the gasoline-powered truck and its ability to travel long distances revolutionized household moving.

The Pattington advertisement, Colonial Theatre program, February 2, 1913. The large Irving Park Road apartment complex lured tenants with luxury features—and two ways to get to the Loop.

each improvement in transportation brought new commuters to the ranks, while simultaneously the outward movement of industries to cheap land brought with it employees who moved to avoid a long daily trek to work.

Market determinants—among them the amount of new housing available—directly controlled the number of families on the move and the intensity of the annual scramble. When mild winter conditions allowed an abundance of new construction, competition lowered prices and lured more people into changing addresses. At times when the city's population increase shot far ahead of the number of new units, those who already had places were inclined to stay put, even though high demand tended to "deter landlords from seeking to retain good tenants by attention to those details every householder prizes."[42]

Each type of housing unit catered to a particular market. Some of the city's wealthy resided in hotels, where full food and cleaning services complemented the luxurious appointments. Although suites were available, most of this class of Chicagoans were singles or childless couples and they were able to put concern about convenience above that of space.[43]

The most elastic of the various forms of nineteenth-century housing was at a somewhat lower economic level than the luxury residential hotel. This was the transplanted eastern institution of the boardinghouse, which usually supplied morning and evening meals as well as a room. When William Corkran, the new librarian of the Chicago Historical Society, and his wife arrived from New York City in March 1868, they encountered their first "westerners" in a boardinghouse:

> What a mixture of people. There was a Mrs. Wright, a great big fat vulgar woman, dressed in the most pretentious style, married to a pale, sickly little man, one of the many hundreds of real estate brokers, or agents, who made a living in a manner that would puzzle the most cunning to find out. Next to them was a thin, pale looking woman, also dressed in flounces and silks, having some dozen rings on her fingers; by her side was seated a heavy, rough-looking man, whose coarse clothes and beard made him appear like a master mason, but who in fact was a prominent commission broker. Besides these were two or three dry goods clerks, dressed in the most fancy manner, while a poor little dressmaker sat at the end of the table, near my landlady's three sons.
>
> The supper consisted of the most plain and unhealthy collection of edibles, namely: Hot bread, hot biscuit, hot cakes, cold meat and pickles, was devoured by men with a rapidity perfectly astonishing. No sooner was this eating match concluded, than the first over would hurry off, without saying a word, and so on to the last.
>
> Few words had been spoken, as western people are not a talkative lot. Yet each one in turn had addressed us some remarks, always beginning with, "Chicago is a great city."[44]

Most of the pre-Fire boardinghouses were single-family structures that sat in the way of retailing as it expanded southward across the present-day Loop. Another type of living arrangement appeared in commercial structures themselves. The lack of elevators made it more difficult to rent out anything above the third floor of a building as offices or stores. Building owners attracted residential tenants by partitioning the top floors into as many as fifty sleeping rooms and then leasing the whole floor to a landlord who would sublet the spaces to individuals and families. This form of rooming house arrangement, which was called "living in blocks," was ideal for bachelors who did not want structured eating arrangements, but it had drawbacks. Invariably, not only was such a building inadequately soundproofed and vulnerable to fire, but it was also ideally designed to house a brothel.[45]

The Great Fire of 1871 and the construction of elevators in the new buildings ended living in blocks and left the downtown with virtually no residential population. Instead, technological obsolescence and changing fashions expanded the ranks of the boardinghouses after that fire. Although Chicago's leading families tended to remain in their mansions on high-prestige streets for many years, they often found it easier to build anew than to retrofit an older house with the new advances in heating, plumbing, and lighting. This was particularly the case when architectural styles that had been popular gave way to new ones, and when once-fashionable neighborhoods declined. Prairie Avenue, for instance, had been home to the Pullmans, the Fields, and other elite families who built there in the 1870s and 1880s. By the mid-1890s the deaths of Chicago's first-generation mercantile and industrial leaders left the street with the nickname "Widow's Row." By 1910, virtually all of the old residents were gone, and roomers were beginning to move in. On the North Side, the lavish home of Perry Smith, chief legal counsel to the North Western Railway, became another boardinghouse. The same happened on the West Side's Ashland Avenue district and on some streets north of the river.[46] Heavier traffic, an influx of industry and commercial buildings, and the presence of lower-class people on the street could spell doom for any neighborhood adjacent to downtown. In one of his "Stories of the Streets and of the Town" columns, George Ade described the uncomfortable situation one remaining well-off family encountered when impoverished gawkers gathered outside their fence and ruined their lawn party. For them, it was a sign that it was time to move.[47]

The boardinghouses that grew up varied considerably in quality. Many of even the more respectable couples had begun their married lives in what were termed "private" boardinghouses, where the clientele was select, the furniture up-to-date, and the food often brought to the table by servants. It was understood that their situation was a temporary stop on the way to home ownership. Each step down the price scale brought with it the need to contend with a less convenient location, more threadbare and uncomfortable appointments, less careful screening of tenants, and poorer food quality.[48] The bottom of the line was the minimal accommodation known as the "furnished room." Declining price meant a clientele less likely to own and more certain to move. Occasionally, it also meant that residents of a building who fell behind in mortgage payments found themselves evicted and their possessions on the curb.[49]

Many of the residents of the poorer-quality boardinghouses were single women on their own—"adrift" was the widely used description—who faced particular difficulties finding accommodations that were safe and respectable, yet affordable. A number of the young women had voluntarily chosen to live by themselves; others were in boarding and rooming houses because of widowhood and divorce. But in most instances, they were guided in their choice of housing by their low wages.[50] Some turned to charities for help, but most could only minimize spending where possible by walking to work, finding free amusements, and moving to the cheapest-possible quarters. Instead of viewing their plight with sympathy, many Chicagoans opposed the lifestyle altogether. In 1873 the *Tribune* carried a bitter exchange of letters. On one side were low-paid, self-supporting women who described their struggles to live on their own. On the other were anonymous men who thought that the only proper place for women outside of the home was in domestic service.[51] By the end of the century, single women on their own raised fewer eyebrows, especially if they lived at the Eleanor Club, the Three Arts Club, or other facilities that offered a more protected and predictable social environment as well as rooms. Others who lived independently were viewed as particularly vulnerable to recruitment into the city's booming vice trade.[52] In the case of both men and women, the boardinghouse functioned as a symbol of the lonely urban dweller, pitiable because he or she lacked attachment to either people or place.[53]

For many Chicagoans, the boardinghouse was a brief stopover on the way to respectability. As upwardly mobile couples acquired furniture and started families, the rental of a house became the next logical step toward independence, but many complained about the inconvenience of the search. Often, this meant traipsing through neighborhoods to hunt for notices tacked to doors by landlords who failed to advertise in the newspapers. Some would-be tenants turned to rental agents, but they later complained that the listings supplied them misrepresented the houses and their neighborhoods. One 1873 *Tribune* feature described the wanderings of a hapless husband who found one house too far from the streetcar, another whose present occupant would not allow him in the door, and others unacceptable because of trash in the back yard, an oversized stove that filled a kitchen, unfinished interiors, and a previous tenant who demanded that he buy the stove and water heater. When he finally found the ideal place and went back to the agent, he discovered that the place had already been rented.[54]

The announcement that a boardinghouse couple was "going into housekeeping" was often followed by unforeseen problems. The cost of "fitting up" a place was often more than they estimated. They had to learn how to shop for food, and someone had to do the cooking and cleaning. That usually meant the expense of servants. It was easy for those who were used to a convenient boardinghouse to be charmed into renting an attractive house on a quiet outlying street only to discover afterward that it resulted in an impossibly inconvenient commute. Those who lacked the resolve could readily become nostalgic about the rooming house and its insolent servants, slightly threadbare furniture, and barely tolerable food.[55]

One answer to these problems was a type of housing that was designed to accommodate transiency and to minimize maintenance by tenants. As early as 1869 local writers had begun to advocate "the Parisian apartment plan" for Chicago. During the latter part of the 1870s some of the regular hotels had begun to evolve into what were called "family hotels," which catered to permanent guests. With the addition of independent food preparation equipment, they evolved into the apartment.[56] The construction of the Beaurivage, Chicago's first "French flat" building, in 1878 gave the trend respectability. Its spacious quarters attracted prominent families and signaled the beginning of the "flat craze," which would quickly sweep Chicago and give potential tenants a choice among several new buildings. Once apartments overcame the stigma of shared dwellings with a common entrance—a popular definition of a tenement—they quickly attracted large numbers of families and bachelors who were willing to sacrifice a bit of space and privacy for a convenient location. Meanwhile, the introduction of leases added an element of stability to the landlord-tenant relationship.[57]

Apartments were not universally popular. Residents complained about the noise from adjacent units, the cramped quarters, and the often domineering character of the janitor—"the presiding genius of the flats," George Ade called him—whose control over heat and repairs often led him to assume a haughty attitude that angered tenants.[58] There were concerns about safety, especially after a faulty heating system caused a fire that swept through the Beaurivage on the night of January 5, 1884. There was also the risk that, like the weakest link in a chain, the most careless tenant could accidentally kill the most careful.[59] But by the early 1880s, apartment life had already become fashionable, and landlords had discovered how fickle tenants could be. It was easier to reject an offer of a lease extension than it was to sell property, and flat-dwellers were eager to take advantage of their mobility and an occasional abundance of choices. Every year or two they could move to a place with the latest architectural style or such innovations as stained-glass windows, steam heat, elevators, electricity, pantries, and speaking tubes that linked apartments with their fancily decorated lobbies. Some faddists moved annually, proclaiming it easier than conducting a thorough spring cleaning; one newspaper quoted Ben Franklin to the effect that "three house-cleanings were equal to one removal, and three removals to one fire." By 1909, one newspaper believed that 95 percent of what it termed "habitual movers" were flat-dwellers.[60]

The annual mobility of so many Chicagoans was a continuing source of concern to some observers. "A love of change makes up for the love of home," the *Tribune* had grumbled in 1874. Two years later, the paper editorialized that those who moved often "usually do not own houses and have no taxes to pay." Others were convinced such rootlessness indicated the lack of a stake in society, which fostered political radicalism; the only cure was putting every family in its own home. Decades later, critics were still warning that nomadic apartment dwellers were a subversive force that destroyed the social stability necessary for family and neighborhood life. In 1910, the Edgewater Improvement Association grumbled that "apartment buildings have been the ruin of most neighborhoods in this city because their occupants have allowed themselves to be influenced by the narrow-minded and unamerican among them who are forever proclaiming that they 'don't do what they don't have to do.'"[61]

Others were willing to link annual mobility to strains in family structure. Some writers blamed the disruption of moving on social-climbing wives who were too anxious to move to the latest fashionable neighborhood or whose gossiping had made them unwelcome where they lived. Others were quick to point out that many husbands found revenge in managing to be elsewhere when the van arrived, leaving their harried wives to supervise the transplant.[62]

Class stereotypes also reinforced the negative image of moving. For those of comfortable means, moves were reputedly less frequent, completely voluntary, and often surrounded by charming customs. For instance, when the John J. Glessner family moved to their new house at Eighteenth Street and Prairie Avenue in 1887, they built a final fire on the hearth of their old home, then transported the glowing coals across town and used them to light the first fire in their new home. Many families also took the occasion to retell the stories of the *lares* and *penates,* the Roman household gods.[63]

But for others, the move from flat to flat constantly exposed families to the need to make new friends, as well as to strangers who were not always reputable. In one incident, a young man took over a furnished apartment, advertised its contents for sale, collected deposits from a dozen buyers, and fled with the proceeds.[64] Others moved to dodge bill collectors and landlords trying to collect back rent. The *Tribune* warned that unusual nighttime activity often meant that a family was about to "skip." By the 1880s, there were at least two lessor's organizations, one of them, the three-thousand-member Chicago Landlords' Protective Bureau, had a substantial deadbeat blacklist against which members could check applicants.[65]

For the very poor, eviction or the search for more sanitary and safe tenements often led to the transfer of their meager possessions every few months. Their stay in one place was often so brief that they used neighborhood saloons as permanent mailing addresses.[66] The final step down the scale of class and permanence was homelessness, where identity through address was on a day-by-day basis.

Whatever the causes of the move, the local press had a field day describing it. Columnists vividly described the chaotic scene ("the streets are alive with teams of furniture") and used imagery ranging from parades ("a larger and more picturesque procession than Independence Day") to nomads ("a huge caravan").[67] Observers familiar with Charles Darwin tried to tie moving day to the evolutionary characteristics of migrating animals.[68] Several writers noted that the event caused families to lose all sense of privacy. Some families tried to reduce the cost of moving by hauling small goods on the streetcar. "One lady on the Randolph line," noted the *Tribune* in 1880, "was encumbered with the marble top of a wash-stand, three chromos, a caged canary bird, and an oil lamp, while another moving farther south struggled manfully in the attempt to retain possession of a sprinkling can, three potted geraniums, a poodle dog, four umbrellas, and a dozen oranges." What had been hidden behind lace curtains was now open to inspection by neighborhood gossips and gapers. The old horsehair sofa, so carefully kept from the view of visitors, was now in transit from the front door to the curb. Status-conscious new arrivals in a neighborhood were also aware that unpacking the van at the new abode could create an initial image of themselves that would be difficult to change. The solution: conceal old furniture under covers and bury it at the center of the load. Also, make sure that the movers were sober and orderly, lest neighbors think that your family could not afford a reliable firm.[69]

Most Chicagoans, however, faced moving day with a highly developed set of fears. There was, first of all, a superstition that Friday moves brought bad luck, just as a ship launched on Friday would surely sink, or, according to the *Tribune,* a child born on Friday would be hanged or go to Congress. The weather presented an obvious peril. Most people expected it to rain, but there was also an occasional unforeseen May Day blizzard.[70] And those who were unfortunate enough to plan a move on May 1, 1905, found that teamsters had gone on strike. Out-of-town moves were even more disaster prone. Household items were packed into crates and barrels that were at the mercy of the railroads as well as the movers. Labels could become detached and lost, the containers dropped or robbed, and a lifetime accumulation of household goods misrouted to freight houses across the country.[71]

The unregulated nature of the moving business could also present an opportunity for extortion. It was not unusual for van owners to refuse to offer written contracts, then suddenly raise their rates after the goods had been loaded. The quality of the moving crew frequently left Chicagoans in an apoplectic rage. Before the early 1900s, the once-a-year nature of the business discouraged express companies from hiring special equipment or expert workers. So many cartage crews were filled with incompetent temporaries that each year's moving season was followed by inevitable lost-and-found ads seeking the whereabouts of dressers and chairs that had tumbled into the street somewhere along the way. Furniture repair places were especially busy mending detached chair arms and torn cushions, while home furnishings dealers took advantage of the situation by suggesting that it was easier for families to dispose of their old furniture before moving and buy new goods that would be delivered to their next address.[72]

By the early years of the new century, the May-first custom was under intense criticism. Chicago's health commissioner announced a new indictment: The annual transplant of people could spread diseases across the city in a matter of days. His efforts to get the city council to pass an ordinance requiring the fumigation of residences between tenancies failed, although the aldermen did approve a law establishing standard moving rates in 1910. But the dispersed nature of the moving business, with individual crews negotiating with clients in private, left the new law virtually unenforceable, and people who complained found their goods deposited on the curb.[73]

As the twentieth century progressed, conditions improved with the introduction of several innovations that encouraged more professional standards and efficiency in the industry. Chicago architects created specially designed warehouses, constructed in safe neighborhoods, which facilitated long-term storage and the coordination of out-of-town routing. Some of these were particularly attractive, the notable example being the W. C. Reebie and Company building. Its Clark Street facade reflected the Egyptian design fad of the 1920s.[74]

Meanwhile, the introduction of motor trucks improved speed and safety records and simplified intercity moves. Now, whole truckloads of household goods could remain together instead of being divided into many crates and shipped as railway freight. The intercity mobility factor, in turn, led to the creation of nationwide companies that linked local movers. Locally, the most important development of that type grew out of the old Werner moving company, which was taken over by the Kennelly family in 1919. Werner-Kennelly, as it became known, formed the centerpiece for the creation of Allied Van Lines in 1929. Its founder, Martin Kennelly, would serve as Chicago's mayor during 1947–55.[75]

Meanwhile, increasingly bitter battle lines were being drawn between landlords and tenants. Building owners found themselves at the mercy of carpenters and painters, whose work had to be done during the short interval between the departure and arrival of tenants. Lessors also complained that screening tenants took too much time.[76] Many landlords turned to longer leases as a way of countering the "moving habit," and on March 14, 1911, the Chicago Real Estate Board went on record favoring "flexible leases," thus breaking the May-first monopoly.[77] Tenants complained about anything that compromised their mobility, and when housing shortages and rents soared during World War I and the years that followed, they began to react. The more prosperous working families among them sought to buy homes, especially the small "Chicago bungalows" that were beginning to appear in a broad crescent of neighborhoods around the perimeter of the city.[78] Those who had no choice either doubled up in apartments or put their goods in storage and moved back to boardinghouses and cheap hotels. But others began to defy rent increases and refused to move. Thousands joined tenants protective leagues, which pooled resources and fought evictions in the courts. The skirmishes lasted throughout the decade, only to be increased by the onset of the Great Depression.[79]

Yet despite the changes, old customs and superstitions of moving day survived. In 1931 Martin Kennelly noted that many owners feared bad luck if they ever moved back to a place where they had once lived, or if they carried an old broom, a partial loaf of bread, or a used bag of salt into their new place. They refused to remove calendars from the walls of their old abode and nailed a horseshoe over the door of their new one.[80]

Many Chicagoans continue those traditions today—and tremble at the thought of May first.

Conclusion

The story of housing, especially among those of at least some means, reveals an essential contradiction that existed within the metropolis. On one hand, there was the city of perpetual motion and change. Many Chicagoans admired growth and boasted that "their" skyscrapers displaced smaller structures and that "their" suburbs were spreading across the countryside. Where people lived was part of that picture, as was the instability of household moves, boardinghouses, and the turnover of apartment residents. Even the neighborhood savings and loan was a destabilizing factor if the goal of its depositors was a new home elsewhere.

Yet there was another side to the Chicago psyche that admired and demanded fixedness and predictability. Most of the barons of industry and merchant princes remained in their homes until death, and their widows lived out their days amidst the memories of an old house. Temperance advocates talked of the saloon in terms of an enemy invading middle-class districts, while describing churches and other institutions as anchors. And neighborhood improvement associations railed at apartments and anything else that might threaten their members' hard-earned investment in their single-family homes. Citywide zoning, adopted in 1923 by the city council, was another effort to control change. For the most part, stability was sought as the necessary counterbalance to the unforeseen. But, as the 1919 race riots and other forms of bigotry demonstrated, the goal of neighborhood stability had its dark side; it could fuel ethnic and racial intolerance, even violence.

Postscript

The fringe of the city and its suburbs continued the process that began more than a century ago. After the Depression and World War II gave way to the 1950s and the massive postwar building boom, it became fashionable among city dwellers to denigrate suburbia as an assembly-line product. Everything that had been attractive about fringe development several decades earlier became reason to condemn it. Malvina Reynolds's popular song complained of "little houses all made out of ticky-tacky," those rows of dull, look-alike suburban homes that housed dull, act-alike people. William H. Whyte's *The Organization Man* examined conformist lives in the new community of Park Forest, while the architecture critic Jane Jacobs, in her book *The Death and Life of the Great American Cities,* decried large-scale "cataclysmic building" as a delayed-fuse time-bomb of decay. Jacobs blamed urban decay on the construction of row after row of houses that had been built all at once and that now seemed destined to fall into disrepair all at once. Although the indictments may have been largely true, what most critics of large-scale subdivisions failed to realize was that, in an earlier age, virtually all of Chicago and its older suburbs had been developed in precisely the way they condemned.[81]

What of moving day? Although the beginning of October has become a second choice for ending and beginning leases, May first remains a favorite moving day. Chicagoans have only to go to their windows and listen.

And we do not know what happened to Grossie Dale Van Cleeve.

4 Living in the Inherited City

THE Piszazeks were shocked when officers from the Rawson Street (now Concord Place) Police Station arrived at their front door one day in March 1894 and inquired about the purchase of their new house. Mr. Piszazek claimed that he had paid $165 for the structure and produced a bill of sale as proof. But the police informed him that it was, in fact, a stolen house, removed from its foundation on Elston Avenue a few days earlier and carted several blocks to the Piszazeks' lot on Dudley (now Honore) Street.[1]

The unusual theft that created their plight, however, was but one aspect of a complex industry that provided one solution to the problem of shelter for thousands of Chicagoans each year: a change in location without a change of houses. The incident also reflected a larger problem. Those with the most modest means usually ended up living in historical remnants of an earlier era. The lifestyle that grew from those homes and the neighborhoods that surrounded them was characterized by the kind of instability and risks that those of greater wealth tried to avoid.

Moving the Past: The House Has the Right-of-Way

House moving in Chicago began in the dark. In December 1833, members of the First Presbyterian Church became concerned about a squatter building that had been put up on a lot the congregation had purchased for a new building. The occupant refused to vacate. During the night a vigilante group from the church attached chains to the little wooden structure and dragged it with oxen to a "no-man's-land" near the river. The idea soon caught on in a more planned and pleasant way, and by the end of the 1830s house moving had become an established business.[2] The small size of most Chicago buildings and the rapid adoption of balloon-frame construction, which gave structures light weight, strength, and flexibility, made the job relatively easy. Even amateurs could learn how to place a heavy wheel assembly under a home, hitch up a team, and move the house as well as its furnishings to a new site. "The business of moving buildings has opened brisk this spring," noted the *Chicago Journal* in 1845, "and we observe a large number on the stocks, ready to wheel into the street at the word of command." In a rapidly growing city with a chronic housing shortage, such preservation of older buildings was also financially attractive.[3]

Chicago's efforts to raise its street grade during the 1850s brought a whole new technology to the industry. The elevation of the roadway created an obvious problem for an adjacent building owner, who faced the dilemma of allowing the first floor to be overshadowed by the street or coming up with the money to raise the structure as much as sixteen feet and have a new first floor and foundation built under it. Most chose the latter, and house raisers used new types of jacks and shoring timbers so effectively that multistory hotels could be lifted without cracking the plaster or disturbing the sleeping guests.[4]

The work not only made such engineer-entrepreneurs as George Pullman wealthy, but also brought a new sophistication to the methods of moving brick and stone buildings of enormous size. Weight and width were the major concerns for Chicago's pioneer house movers, Chester and Simmeon Tupper, and their competitors. The largest structures were cut from their utilities, then jacked up from their original foundations, placed on greased skids resembling railroad tracks, and then pushed down the street by horizontal jacks at a slow, steady pace.[5]

Meanwhile, the proficiency of Chicagoans at creating structures at the opposite end of the weight-and-size spectrum contributed to the development of other house-moving skills. In 1866 the factory of "Major" Lyman Bridges began constructing prefabricated housing that was "already made, and ready to put up on any lot in the city or to ship to the country." Buyers could choose among five models that featured from three to seven rooms. The completion of the transcontinental railroad in 1869 opened new markets for Chicago's ready-made housing in the West, where lumber was scarce. The premade, bolt-together sections also permitted both farmers and city people who lacked expertise in carpentry to erect a house in hours without having to pay a skilled carpenter. The same technology allowed easy demounting, dismantling, and removal to another location.[6]

The house-moving industry mushroomed after the Great Fire of 1871. During the rebuilding, the practice became entangled in the argument over whether Chicago should enact a total ban on any wooden house construction or relocation within designated "fire limits." The city council finally enacted a compromise ordinance that allowed the relocation of wooden structures in all but a few districts, a great victory for the working class and for house movers.[7]

The outward expansion of the business district was an even more important force in the razing or removal of hundreds of residences each year. In 1872, for instance, one depot project alone put fifty houses in transit. At the same time, the construction of new streets through fringe farmlands meant that old buildings were suddenly in the center of what would soon become major thoroughfares.[8] By the 1880s, house moving was so popular that it created a variety of problems. Serious traffic delays developed when "tramp houses," as one newspaper called them, blocked some neighborhood streets for weeks. Streetcar service was often interrupted by laggard homes caught on the tracks.[9] Fires also burst from improperly disconnected gas lines. But what was most distressing for many residents of new lot subdivisions was the unexpected appearance of older, woebegone structures that threatened property values when they were rolled into place among new buildings of much higher price. Just as human tramps occasionally upset the social sifting-out process of the city by showing up at the doors of mansions, tramp houses had the potential of disrupting the normally efficient process of sorting people by income and where they lived.[10]

The difficulties created by an unregulated business forced the city council to revise the building code in June 1883. House movers were required to take out a license, post a ten-thousand-dollar bond, and pay a five-dollar permit fee for each move. Park commissioners also had to approve any move across a boulevard, and any trek over streetcar lines had to be done at night. To prevent portable slums, no building worth less than half its original value could be moved, and property owners in the destination neighborhood had to sign a petition of approval.[11] Despite the new restrictions, the industry continued to thrive during the last decades of the nineteenth century. The number of permits issued climbed from 726 in 1884 to a record high 1,710 in 1890, when 33,992 linear feet, or 6.4 miles, of building frontage changed locations in a single year.[12]

Almost any house-moving job became a free public spectacle for the hundreds of people who gathered to marvel at the combination of engineering skills and brute strength. As the years passed, an increasing number of the buildings moved were made of brick, and some were as tall as three and four stories. Some also traveled long distances. One small house was reportedly moved all the way from Twenty-first Street on the South Side to Lill Street in Lake View, a distance of over fifty blocks. Such spectacular projects usually led the press and the public to treat house moving with a measure of awe. The public image of house movers changed to "brutish," however, during the rare instances where movers uprooted the wrong structure, destroyed it in transit, or were accused of stealing it. In one sad case, an immigrant named Stanislaus Janochowski bought a house and began moving it before he discovered that the destination lot was no longer available. A city ordinance, which stipulated that West Side moves that started north of Madison Street could be made only in a northward or westward direction, prevented him from returning it to its original site. The structure sat for several days in the middle of a busy street before the desperate owner found a suitable lot.[13]

During the late nineteenth century, movers were also increasingly willing to tackle large and complex nonresidential structures. In 1891 engineers lifted the old Madison Street swing-span bridge onto submerged scows and floated it a block down the river, where it became the new Washington Street Bridge.[14] A Chicago engineer named Harvey Sheeler, who invented and patented much of the industry's equipment, moved a 6,652-ton church at Michigan Avenue and Twenty-third Street about fifty feet. In another one of Sheeler's moves, the five-story, half-block-square Tyler and Hippach Mirror Company was shifted 220 feet in 1910 to make way for the new Chicago and North Western terminal. At the time, Sheeler claimed that the glass company was the largest building that had ever been moved.[15]

One of the most unusual jobs was the 1890 removal of the first Ashland Block (1872) to make way for the construction of a second building (1892) of the same name. The seven-story original structure was moved in many sections, from Clark and Randolph over a mile to the corner of Twelfth Street (now Roosevelt Road) and Michigan Avenue, where the segments were rejoined. Here it briefly became offices for John Alexander Dowie, an evangelist and faith-healer, before being remodeled into the Hotel Imperial in time for the World's Columbian Exposition. Later used by the Illinois Central Railroad as an office building, it made a third move of only eighty-five feet in 1923. These peregrinations gave the first Ashland Block another distinction. It stood until 1973, outlasting its replacement, the second Ashland Block, which had been razed in 1949 to make way for the Greyhound Bus Terminal.[16]

Despite these achievements, house movers gradually found themselves limited by Chicago's emerging transportation system. The replacement of cable cars by overhead electric trolley lines was the first major problem. Bold movers cut the wires and disrupted service. Charles T. Yerkes, the transportation baron, tried to charge house movers for crossing his tracks, but city officials sided with the movers and ordered streetcar companies to lift wires to accommodate tall structures.[17] Ultimately, the need to move people and things from here to there above grade resulted in wall-like barriers that sliced across neighborhoods. The construction of the elevated rail system after 1891 was the first of these permanent impediments, followed in the next decade by the elevation of steam railway track onto embankments. Not only did hundreds of neighborhood streets now terminate at dead ends, but engineers found it virtually impossible to move anything larger than a small bungalow through the viaducts. The industry was never able to recapture its earlier pace, but Chicago ingenuity ultimately triumphed in some cases. A few tall houses, for instance, were loaded onto barges and floated on the river or lake for part of their journey.[18]

The gradual adoption of Daniel Burnham's 1909 Plan of Chicago, which mandated the widening of several major streets, gave house movers some additional work. Among the dozens of structures that had to be relocated on their lots was St. Francis of Assisi Church, which was shifted thirty-two feet back to accommodate the widening of Roosevelt Road in May 1917; its parish house was picked up and moved down a side street. The most spectacular job was probably the transit of the imposing Our Lady of Lourdes Church. In March 1929 it was not only moved across Ashland Avenue but also turned forty-five degrees.[19]

At least there was no question about those two being stolen buildings.

Goose Island Memories: Contending with the Slums

There probably should never have been slums in Chicago. It was not crowded onto an island like Manhattan, forced onto a peninsula like Boston, or pinched between two rivers like Philadelphia. Instead Chicago had cheap, limitless land on which to erect balloon-frame houses that were built in a few days with abundant Wisconsin lumber. "The German, Swede or Hollander has built himself a cottage-dream of the Fatherlands," noted one writer, "sometimes erected a little barn for temporary habitation, then adding a second floor, later moving to the covered basement of his proposed residence, and building gradually above until he has a two or three-story house." Such descriptions had a ring of optimism, but not everyone shared it. Congested and bad housing proved to be as much a part of Chicago's story in its youth as it was in its old age, ultimately forcing two groups to find ways to cope with the slums: those who lived in them and the community at large that struggled with the problems they created.[20]

No place reflected the sad history of Chicago's slum housing better than one of the city's most storied districts, Goose Island. Located little more than a mile up the North Branch of the river from the Loop, it is today a largely desolate stretch of industrial land. Few who use busy Halsted and Division Streets even notice that they have crossed an island with a past. The side streets are still there—Weed, Hooker, Bliss, and others whose names once evoked immediate and intense images of crime, disease, and hopelessness.[21]

During the 1830s, Goose Island was still an uninhabited out-of-town area, but it had already been swept up in the feverish land speculation triggered by plans for the construction of the Illinois and Michigan Canal. Although greater fortunes were to be made along the South Branch of the Chicago River, which would later carry the canal traffic, direct water access inflated North Branch values as well. In 1832, Charles Taylor bought eighty acres of the future Goose Island site from the federal government for $100. He sold it twenty days later for $545. During the next three years the price per acre mushroomed from the original $1.25 to $550. The bubble burst during the panic and depression of 1837, and land values collapsed everywhere, including the broad crescent-shaped fringe that surrounded Chicago.[22]

The riverfront location of the island had already attracted a few early industries, including a sawmill and a shipyard that in 1836 turned out a steamboat named the *James Allen*. But most of Goose Island sat unoccupied and undeveloped as owners patiently waited for the value to climb back to its purchase price. Before another decade passed, however, Chicagoans were beginning to hear about the island for other reasons. In 1847 a blight began to affect the potato vines in southwest Ireland, and, rather than pay taxes to support the extenants' stay in the poorhouse, three large landholders in Kilgubbin, County Cork, and County Mayo evicted their peasants and paid for their passage to America. The immigrants landed in New York penniless, but a labor broker who was aware of the shortage of workers in Chicago paid for their boat transportation west. When they finally arrived, the Kilgubbin families found little work. Faced with impending cold weather, they followed the path to survival taken by many of the city's homeless poor: they found some unoccupied land on the periphery of town, erected shacks, and became squatters.[23]

By settling on the fringe, Goose Islanders became part of a housing pattern common to American cities of the period. In an era before commutation made escape to the suburbs possible and the smoke and noise of industry made it desirable, the wealthy remained largely in the center of cities, a convenient walk or carriage ride away from downtown businesses. Chicago's first elite housing consisted of centrally located marble-front row houses and freestanding mansions cooled by the breezes of the nearby lake. Each step down the economic ladder, however, brought housing that was progressively farther from downtown, as well as increasingly uncomfortable. The heavy port traffic on the Chicago River also effectively cut off the North and West Sides, retarding the escalation of land values compared with those of the booming South Side, which enjoyed bridge-free access to downtown. Therefore, the urban fringe lands like Goose Island, which were mainly held for speculative resale, were fair game for squatters.[24]

As a consequence, by the late 1840s, Chicago found itself ringed by districts bearing prosaic names. "Conley's Patch," to the south of downtown, was obviously Irish, while "Laramie" and "Cheyenne" indicated that they were to the west. "Kilgubbin" joined the list. Because the land along the North Branch sat unused while speculator-owners watched its value increase, the Kilgubbin Irish were able to erect shacks from cast-off materials. Chicago's position as a major lumber distribution center made it easy to crib a board here and a plank there. The initial Kilgubbin settlement occupied a strip between Kinzie and Franklin Streets and the river. Nearby was a clay island formed at the confluence of the North and South Branches. Seasonal flocks of birds had prompted the nickname Goose Island, which quickly became associated in the public mind with the new residents less than a mile to the north.[25]

The squatters took the Goose Island name with them when they moved upstream to a larger peninsula of neglected land near present-day Chicago Avenue and Halsted Streets. Their new shanties, which were sometimes as large as three rooms, were densely populated with children and animals. In 1855 one newspaper carried a description of what was likely a Goose Island household:

> One of our policemen enumerates the inmates of an Irish cabin in the West Division into which he casually stepped one day last week. It was ten feet by sixteen, and contained, exclusive of furniture, one woman and five children, a dog with a litter of puppies, a cat and kittens, three pigs, a hen with a dozen chickens, and a calf six weeks old. On asking for the cow, he was informed that "she was only gone away for a little bit, but would be back again soon most likely." There was no sign for "Boarders" nailed up beside the door.[26]

The livestock wandered at will, while the geese took over a small inlet that had been created at a bend of the river by a brickmaker who had begun to extract clay. Many of the Goose Island men found work in the McCormick Reaper Company (on the site of the present-day Tribune Tower) or on the docks and canal boats. Their wives took in laundry in quantities that made long lines of fluttering wash a part of the newspaper illustrations of the place.[27]

Ultimately, the growth of Chicago's population from fifty thousand in 1850 to twice that in 1860, along with the city's budding industrialization, forced changes in Goose Island. William Butler Ogden, who had served as Chicago's first mayor, saw the potential of the location. In 1853 he formed the Chicago Land Company, and among the many parcels it purchased was the flat marshy crescent along the North Branch that was now occupied by the Kilgubbin settlement. Ogden occasionally grumbled about having to chase "Paddies" off his land, but the major threat to the residents came when his company enlarged the digging operations at the clay inlet to make bricks to sell to builders. By 1857 excavation had created a canal along a north-south axis that rejoined the river half a mile to the north, and Goose Island really became an island. Although the city had annexed the area in 1855, the channel was not officially declared part of the river until a decade later, after the new waterway had been dredged to a depth of ten feet and a width of fifty feet. In 1866 the city built the first substantial wooden bridge between the main channel and the island at Halsted and a few years later constructed similar spans on Division and Weed Streets. Chicago's island now bore the unofficial name "Ogden's Island."[28]

By then, the squatters had to contend with industry, which had already begun to encroach on the periphery of the city. Chicagoans had long attempted to exile the smoke and noise of manufacturing, such as Charles Cleaver's South Side soap works, to the same broad swathe of open land that edged the town.[29] Goose Island was ideally surrounded by a river that provided a ready supply of water, a limitless industrial sewer, and excellent dock sites. In 1857 the North Chicago Rolling Mills opened on the North Branch near the present North Avenue bridge. On April 24, 1865, the company rolled the first steel rail produced in America.[30] The People's Gas Light and Coke Company began buying land on the mainland just to the east of the island at the close of the Civil War. A few years later, it opened a large "gas house" where furnaces extracted flammable gas from baked coal. This "gas light" was piped across Chicago to illuminate buildings and streets. The company's fires and sulphurous fumes filled the night sky, giving nearby neighborhoods the collective name of "Little Hell" long before the term became associated with the crowded district of teeming tenements nearby. The new industries provided work for the men of the island but gradually pushed their shanties northward.[31]

The emerging problem of slums in places like Goose Island produced little public concern during midcentury. Bad housing was largely located outside of the city limits and most people were optimistic that the shacks they tolerated during Chicago's infancy would disappear as a natural result of the city's spectacular growth.[32] Chicagoans were then willing to blame any housing problems on the temporary shortages caused by people arriving in the city at a faster rate than new housing could be constructed to accommodate them. "We hear of as many as three or four families residing under one roof on account of the scarcity of tenements," noted the *Daily Democrat* in 1852. "Where are our builders?"[33] The Chicago press responded in the same manner when the Civil War brought crowds of factory workers. Intense shortages, which led to habitation of places that would normally have been torn down, were also thought to be only temporary. The only times the presence of rundown houses aroused major concern was when midcentury epidemics such as cholera seemed to sweep poor areas first, then pose a threat to the rest of the city.[34]

During the postbellum years, the same lack of natural barriers to growth and the general abundance of land that promoted the development of new fringe subdivisions also had an unfortunate effect of instilling a false confidence that Chicago could not have a permanent slum problem. This optimism, in turn, created a laissez-faire attitude toward building and land use laws that virtually guaranteed that a crisis would develop. While other large cities eventually learned the lesson of overbuilding and regulated the amount of the lot that property owners could cover with structures, Chicagoans were left to develop an unfortunate local tradition: When owners erected new houses on their lots, they skidded the old ones backward, either attaching them as additions or leaving them freestanding. In some cases, a series of as many as three or four rear structures extended all the way to the alley. Chicagoans' inclination to save what they thought was a serviceable edifice was often strengthened by the prospect of additional rent money that the rear buildings could bring.[35] Thus, where downtown Chicago sprawled upward, its poor neighborhoods increased their population densities by filling in every privately owned square foot of space.[36]

Chicago's housing problem deteriorated even more in the wake of the Great Fire of 1871, as most of the hundred thousand left homeless tried to crowd into the surviving housing stock. Often, those most willing to take in roomers lived in housing to the west and south of downtown that was already on the verge of deterioration. The conflagration spared the squatters of Goose Island, although the thousands of refugees who temporarily joined them made the settlement even more congested.[37]

The Great Fire, which burned itself out in the tiny shacks of Scandinavians on the fringe of the North Side, also led to a controversial effort to prevent future problems in the rebuilt district. Many of those who had once owned small wooden houses on the North Side were now left to crowd refugee areas in Lincoln Park, some of them occupying the dirt holes left in the process of transforming the old cemetery into park lands.[38] The circumstances heightened social-class tensions when the Common Council began to debate an end to further wooden construction within the city limits. Reformers represented the interests of the city's elite, who were fearful of further fire devastation and the impact on insurance rates. They viewed all-brick construction as an investment in a safer future. By contrast, members of the North Side German working class who had been burnt out of their homes were convinced that they could not afford to rebuild in brick and that a fire-limits law was intended to push them out of the city. Thus, what seemed like a reform was actually a threat to the survival of the working class. Debate over the issue produced heated rhetoric, a minor riot, and a compromise measure that proved self-defeating because of loopholes. It permitted temporary wooden structures for emergency housing without placing a time limit on the emergency. It also did not apply retroactively to the two-thirds of the city left unburnt and did not limit the practice of moving existing frame structures into the supposedly all-brick district.[39]

Other changes followed. During the decade after the fire, areas bordering the river became increasingly industrial. Lumber, stone, and coal yards also took advantage of Goose Island's access to the river. In 1872 the Chicago and Pacific Railroad constructed its terminal just east of the river, opposite the south end of the island, and announced plans to build a line to the West Coast. Although the railroad failed in 1879 and was absorbed in the Chicago, Milwaukee, and St. Paul system a year later, the tracks that ran the length of the island attracted a number of new commercial ventures. Goose Island renters and squatters found themselves pushed further north and away from the river. The transformation of Goose Island was one example of the displacement of the old peripheral squatters' districts around the city. Eventually, such industries as printing, baking, confectionery, and garment manufacture would occupy the old squatters' fringe to the south and west, furniture factories would dominate the northwest, and farm implement manufacture, the north. Warehouses would take most of the rest. There was an irony in this: land that had once been occupied by squatters, who were among society's most mobile people, was being taken for industrial purposes, which was generally the most immobile and permanent type of land use because machinery was too hard to move.[40]

By the 1880s, ship building, charcoal baking, and so many other smaller industries had also been established on Goose Island and nearby riverfront that the Chicago Fire Department stationed one of its fireboats on the island's northern tip.[41] New symbols of Chicago's daring entrepreneurship began to appear when Philip D. Armour decided that he could expand his fortune beyond meat packing by buying and reselling western wheat destined for eastern tables. In 1887, he built a huge storage elevator to hold his purchases until the price was right. Soon afterward, eastern speculators began buying vast quantities of wheat, driving the price to record-high levels. The easterners hoped that when Chicago grain merchants discovered that the city's elevators could not supply the amounts of grain they had promised to deliver, they would be forced to buy the easterners' holdings at inflated prices. But Armour's new elevator saved the day, and the Chicagoans filled the orders. When the grain war was renewed in 1893, Armour again found himself promising more than he could store, but this time his trading rivals were fellow Chicagoans led by the interests of Cudahy, another meat packer and grain speculator. With millions of bushels of grain already enroute to Chicago from western farms, Armour was forced to build new storage space to rescue his reputation and financial empire. Three hundred carpenters worked around the clock for almost a month to build three more grain elevators, and he was victorious. For years these looming structures, among the largest in the country, dominated the island's landscape and cast shadows on the small houses below. Yet another grain war resulted in new elevators in 1897.[42]

The Great Fire catastrophe, the housing problems that followed, and the rapid industrialization of the old squatter fringe eventually dispelled the notion that Chicago was free of slums. Since 1833, health authorities had exercised the right to inspect private homes during epidemics and order the cleanup of unsanitary conditions. Though the germ theory of disease causation would not gain acceptance until a half-century later, both doctors and the general public suspected that what smelled foul might cause cholera, typhoid, and other scourges. Maps and reports clearly linked the presence of disease with poorly drained and poorly housed neighborhoods. In 1874, the fear of diphtheria brought the first effort to normalize what had been emergency powers. It took three ordinances, an act of the Illinois General Assembly, and seven more years of frustration before health officials were given the power to approve or veto plans for future buildings, as well as inspect existing ones.[43]

Optimists greeted the passage of the new 1881 housing ordinance with the confident prediction of a quick demise for the slum. Instead, it became clear that the teams of inspectors, often understaffed and vulnerable to bribes, barely made a dent in the problem. Tenements were now emerging as a matter of foremost civic concern. The ranks of reformers, then confined largely to a few church charities and the Citizens Association, which was led by business owners, hoped that the new tactic of publicizing the problem would shock the city into passing a strict housing code. Reporters accompanied health inspectors on their daily rounds and penned sensational newspaper exposés that were adorned with artists' sketches of the misery. While the columns implied that slum residents themselves were largely responsible for the squalid conditions, they bore two additional implications. First, all citizens ultimately suffered at least indirectly the effects of the slum; there was no real escape. Second, there was an interconnection between social ills and the way in which slum conditions contributed to "squalor, discomfort, intemperance, herding like cattle, filth, chronic disease, sweeping epidemics and decimation by death, the little children being the chief victims, family disruption, growth in immorality and vicious habits, and the creation of and fostering of crime." In other words, environment as well as innate character created society's problem citizens.[44]

The press was essentially correct in its assessment of the problems of survival, but there was also a relationship between the slum and the process of urbanization. First, by the 1880s, urban housing had seen enormous technological progress, but it was unevenly distributed across cities. The fruits of change benefited the wealthy first, who were able to upgrade heating, lighting, plumbing, and communications systems or move. But the poor in Chicago and other places had become inheritors of the city as a hand-me-down urban artifact. Slum dwellers, by contrast, faced whole neighborhoods that were frozen in outmoded technologies. Water came from a backyard well, often still in use despite health department condemnation, while attempts to pipe water into the building were often the handiwork of unlicensed and uninformed plumbers. Toilet facilities consisted of a pit in the basement floor or a rear building. Heat came from coal stoves and light from oil lanterns for want of connections for gas lighting.[45]

City government had been negligent in upgrading antiquated utilities in poor districts. Water mains consisted of wooden pipes, reminders of an era when iron was almost a precious metal. A *Chicago Post* investigation in 1896 revealed that much of the near west Nineteenth Ward had no sewers; what served as a sewer was little more than a pit in the ground. Meanwhile, private gas and electric companies were unwilling to invest in infrastructure where few could afford to become customers. People's Gas would not put lines onto Goose Island until 1928. Thus, the utilities grids that were the pride of developments on the far-flung reaches of the region were ironically absent less than a mile from Chicago's epicenter. This also meant that the portions of the old squatters' periphery of the 1850s that had remained residential had become a technological vacuum half a century later.[46]

At the same time, the wooden buildings that predominated in pre-Fire neighborhoods deteriorated more quickly than those made of stone or brick. And the low, horizontal configuration of Chicago's slums meant that they were frequently built on makeshift foundations. It was common practice to rest a frame house directly on cedar posts driven into the earth, but many small houses simply sat on the ground. Such structural flaws were less common in the multistory tenements, such as those found in New York.[47]

The poor were also trapped in an outdated social artifact. Over time, urban growth fostered the natural tendency of cities to sort themselves out according to social and economic factors. Commercial and industrial facilities generally followed the availability of transportation; factories hugged the river and the railroad, not vice versa. Transportation improvements and new housing developments on the fringe also made it easy for those who could afford it to live elsewhere. Residential buildings of various types, stores, warehouses, and small factories, which had been mixed or in close proximity during Chicago's infancy, gradually drifted into districts and residential neighborhoods that tended to define themselves by income and ethnicity. As we have seen, wealth meant the ability to remove one's family physically from the congestion, noise, and physical dangers of nonresidential districts. Every improvement in the ability to get from here to there confirmed that fact.[48]

By contrast, those with few resources inherited what was left behind. The outward movement should have ensured that vacant units would increase the housing opportunities for those who remained in the inner city, enabling them to move up to something better. But several factors intervened. Impoverished neighborhoods and those who lived there suffered because the urban sorting process was incomplete. The poor were the last central-city dwellers to give up the rural remnant of farm animals because chickens and milk cows were a source of income. One longtime resident remembered that, "Every house had a garden and chickens. . . . There were a good many cows on the [Goose] island. We fed them with slops from Schufeldt's Distillery." Complaints about loose animals led Alderman Thomas Cannon to introduce an ordinance giving the island's residents special privileges to allow their livestock to roam at will without police interference. Tenement dwellers were also the last to give up the outdated system of home work, such as the "home finishing" phase of sweatshop clothing manufacture, wherein low piecework wages and long hours meant that home and workplace were never divided. Finally, where financial resources isolated middle-class homes from workplaces with a streetcar or

M. Crowe & Son, House Raisers and Movers, advertisement, 1897. Moving a large building required precision technique on a very large scale.

Slum children, Near West Side, ca. 1900. The filthy environment of the slum street contributed to the short average lifespan of impoverished youngsters in the Hull-House neighborhood. (Jane Addams Memorial Collection, Special Collections, University Library, University of Illinois at Chicago)

Small girl and muck-laden alley, ca. 1900. An alley borders a wooden tenement whose
additions fill its lot, leaving no place for children to play except the street. (Jane Addams
Memorial Collection, Special Collections, University Library, University of Illinois at
Chicago)

Slums, alley between 900 block of Huron and Erie Streets, May 1949. Rear tenements and an outhouse stand in the shadow of a shoe factory. (Metropolitan Planning Council Records, University Library, University of Illinois at Chicago)

commuter train ride, slum dwellers were forced to limit that separation to the distance they could walk. Factories and warehouses were usually in or adjacent to poor neighborhoods, and their expansion into adjacent neighborhoods further squeezed residents into the affordable housing that was within walking distance of the plant gate. Those lucky enough not to lose their homes were always tempted by the opportunity to take in boarders.[49]

Ethnic mixing also represented the incomplete urban sorting process. The poverty of the most recently arrived immigrants left them little choice other than to take rooms in the congested polyglot portal neighborhoods of the Near Northwest and Near Southwest Sides and in the adjacent industrial districts. These areas were characterized by poverty and the presence of many ethnic groups in small clusters, none dominating and none possessing enough money or resolve to stay in the neighborhood long enough to create many social institutions of their own. The southwest portal centered on the neighborhood where Jane Addams established Hull-House in 1889 and on the Maxwell Street area to the south. Throughout her career Addams struggled with the communications problem created by the presence of twenty-three languages spoken within a few blocks of her institution. The northwest portal included the Grand-Milwaukee area not far from Graham Taylor's Chicago Commons settlement house, as well as Little Hell and Goose Island.[50]

The slum dwellers lacked the resources to isolate themselves from the outside world. Some housing even lacked doors. Noises and smells easily penetrated from the street and alley. One portion of Goose Island, for instance, became known as "Smokey Hollow" because of the constant presence of fumes from the tugboats moored nearby.[51] Nor could the poor isolate themselves from each other. Crowding left only a few square feet per person, and in the case of working men who shared quarters, alternate shifts of sleepers meant that beds never had a chance to become cool. Such close contact became an obvious cause for the spread of disease, as well as discord within the dwelling. While victims of circumstance, some tenants were lazy, had poor housekeeping habits, and were ignorant of modern methods of sanitation, garbage control, and cleanliness, which no doubt exacerbated the health dangers of the situation.[52]

The problems of the industrial slum were evident on Goose Island. When its steel manufacturing moved away to the Southeast Side, exploitive housing patterns not only followed those workers to their new location but resurfaced in the replacement industries. By the 1880s, Goose Island was becoming an especially good location for the emerging tannery trade. The processors had easy rail or water access to the hides that were being produced by the South Side packing plants. And the Michigan tree bark that was crucial in leather processing floated right to the plant door by boat. Many of the tanning companies that moved onto the island required that new employees live inside the plant grounds, often in makeshift housing for which they were charged rent. Another disadvantage became evident on the morning of August 3, 1887, when fire broke out in a planing mill and box concern on Branch Street. The flames spread to an adjacent mattress manufacturer and then to several of the small cottages and saloons intermingled with the factories.[53]

The advance of industry inevitably altered the social complexion of Goose Island. Squatter shacks gave way to small houses and wooden tenements. These structures filled with renters rather than squatters, but the greater sense of permanence did not improve the district's character. Its streets were the scene of several mob incidents during the labor upheavals of 1877, when roving crowds of strikers moved from factory to factory trying to organize a general shutdown of the city's industries. The new trade also introduced Polish residents to what had been an Irish stronghold because the latter initially refused to work in the noxious tanneries. Gradually, the two groups learned to coexist within the factories. In May and June 1882 they participated in a prolonged strike that resulted in violence against "scabs" imported from rooming houses off the island.[54]

The rest of Chicago began to associate the name of Goose Island with a generation of thugs and petty criminals who grew up there. One fictionalized account, "Judith of Goose Island," told the story of a Polish mother who saw all of her sons eventually murdered or executed. Captain Michael Schaak summarized the attitude of the Chicago police when he remarked, "Probably no place in the city has given the police force so much trouble as that muddy strip of territory." Police also realized that attempts to arrest denizens of the place often resulted in pitched battles against the whole male population. In violence, Goose Island was acting as a community in perhaps the only way it knew because it was devoid of most of the institutions that were the cornerstones of other neighborhoods—churches, schools, and retailers, for instance. Children attended the Vedder Street School on the mainland. There was no settlement house nearby. The closest churches were several blocks away. Immaculate Conception had been established on the mainland to the east on North Park Avenue in 1859 as a predominantly Irish parish. Poles attended St. John Cantius or St. Stanislaus Kostka churches to the west. The most popular social amenity on the island was its collection of tough bars.[55]

The poor had few tools with which they could cope with the situation. Extreme poverty forced people to act as individuals rather than rely on institutions. The practice of moving from one tenement to another in the constant search for someplace more livable was one form of coping. Few tenements operated with leases, while rents were often by the week, in advance. But rent increases frequently led tenants to take in boarders to share the cost, a response that only made the crowding problem worse. Most slum dwellers tolerated bad housing by being there as little as possible. Noises and smells that grew out of a lack of adequate interior space drove residents to extend their functional living space to their own roofs, nearby parks, the sidewalk in front, and other public places. They also took advantage of saloons, missions, settlement houses, and other semipublic places that were privately owned but of general public access, anywhere that might become an annex to living space. Children of the slums virtually grew up in the streets, often outside the supervision of their parents.[56]

By the 1890s, housing reformers and tenants alike realized that the roots of the problem were so complex that they had to be content with efforts to ameliorate or improve slum housing rather than eradicate it. Public bathhouses, for instance, supplied opportunities for cleanliness.[57] Public playgrounds and settlement houses provided more wholesome alternatives to the streets, saloons, and cheap theaters. (In the case of Goose Island, a new public playground that opened in 1908 closed after a year because local youth failed to attend.) In 1899 the city council established the Special Park Commission to purchase and equip small "breathing spaces" scattered through the tenement districts.[58] The Visiting Nurses Association and Infant Welfare Society visited the homes of the poor to teach sanitation and cure the sick.[59] The efforts were not always understood by those who were the intended beneficiaries. Health reformers battled tenement sweatshops, in which families sewed garments for a pittance and sent disease-laden overcoats and suits to downtown stores. But many among the poor resisted such reforms because they directly threatened a family's ability to make a living. A quarantine sign could mean complete impoverishment.[60]

When headlines failed to obliterate slums by provoking righteous indignation in the general public, and when ameliorative reforms made a bad situation only slightly more tolerable, a third approach began to gain support. By the mid-1890s, some housing reformers had shifted their faith to the model tenement. This idea, which had its origins in Europe, was based on the notion that investors might want to build rental housing for the poor and accept a modest return on their money.[61] But "philanthropy and five percent" generated far more proposals than actual dwelling units. George Pullman, the railroad-car builder, viewed his new housing development near Lake Calumet as a philanthropic business proposition, although its strict controls over tenants' social life and the bitterness generated by the 1894 strike confirmed a thin line between the model tenement and the oppressive company town.[62] Two of the small number of genuinely philanthropic projects that did materialize involved brilliant young architects. The best-known project was Francisco Terrace, built on the West Side in 1895; it gave the young Frank Lloyd Wright one of his most interesting early commissions.[63] Four years later, another young architectural genius, Dwight Perkins, designed a similar project called "The Langdon" on the Near West Side.[64] Attractive though these enterprises were on paper, investors generally found more profit in ventures other than housing the poor.

The closing years of the century brought new techniques to the old idea of swaying public opinion with information. One Northwestern University student argued that some parts of the city had population densities that he believed exceeded those of the notorious Black Hole of Calcutta.[65] In 1894, the U.S. Department of Labor conducted detailed investigations of housing and social conditions, while in the following year the resident staff working under Jane Addams published a volume entitled *Hull House Maps and Papers,* which illustrated neighborhood social conditions with large colored maps.[66] A new reform group, the Improved Housing Association, held conferences in 1897 and 1900, using scale models and photographs to illustrate the terrible conditions.[67] And in 1901 a group called the City Homes Association published a report entitled *Tenement Conditions in Chicago,* in which halftone photographs provided gruesome details that line drawings and engravings could not capture.[68]

The reform efforts shocked Chicagoans, but perhaps not as much as the revelation that taller, New York–style tenement houses were beginning to appear in Chicago. Unlike old buildings that had usually been decent at one time but later tumbled into disrepair, the new jerry-built structures were designed to be exploitive.[69] In 1902, a month of debate ended with passage of a new tenement ordinance that elevated some minimum standards. It required fireproofing, fire escapes, windows in every room, garbage-burning furnaces, and toilets in every building. Furthermore, only 65 percent of each lot (80 percent on a corner) could be covered by building.[70]

Once more, optimists predicted that Chicago's slums would disappear.[71] And once more, greedy landlords found ways to evade the regulations. Not only did the law exclude existing structures, but the understaffed and corruptible city inspectors continued to ignore hundreds of new violations.[72] Most frustrating of all was the nine-month delay that separated the introduction and the passage of the 1902 ordinance. During that time the city had issued hundreds of "old-law" building permits that contractors were able to stockpile for use years later.[73]

Dozens of studies conducted over the first three decades of the new century indicated that the slum problem continued to grow, rather than recede. Whatever relief might have been gained through the outmigration of earlier residents to the emerging bungalow belt on the city's fringe seemed more than offset by the pressure of new arrivals who took their places in the slums that encircled downtown. Race created new complications. The growing practice of segregation kept newly arrived African Americans in the worst housing of all. Racial covenants, outright refusal to provide accommodations, and direct violence drew a wall around an overcrowded district just south of the Loop.[74] At first, many of the newcomers found space in the hotels and apartment buildings that had been constructed to accommodate visitors to the World's Columbian Exposition. Constructed along major streetcar routes between the Loop and the Jackson Park fairgrounds, many of these structures had been poorly built by speculators and had sat vacant through the depression of the 1890s. They were gradually occupied by African Americans, giving a linear appearance to the segregated district that became known as the Black Belt.[75] But the migration from the South exceeded this source of space, and as the district's population grew, much of it had to be absorbed within the community. Houses and existing apartments were subdivided into rented rooms in which whole families tried to live. Makeshift kitchens became a fire hazard, while shared toilets led to sanitary problems. The same set of problems that characterized the crowded lifestyle of the old immigrant portal districts and Goose Island decades earlier replicated itself in parts of the emerging South Side ghetto: crime, unemployment, disease, and unstable residency.[76]

It was clear that there had been little progress in formulating new slum-fighting strategies. The academic discipline of urban sociology, born at the University of Chicago, brought with it intensive studies of various slum-ridden neighborhoods in 1908–10, 1923–26, and again in the early 1930s.[77] There was a long-term exhibit on the perils of the slum in the Municipal Museum that was housed in the Chicago Public Library. The City Club of Chicago sponsored a housing exposition in 1913 that repeated many of the same points made by the Improved Housing Association a decade earlier.[78] Finally, the 1920s saw a rebirth of the model tenement idea. On the North Side, the Marshall Field family built the Garden Apartments at Sedgwick and Evergreen. On the South Side, prevalent attitudes toward segregation even shaped the pattern of practical philanthropy. The Michigan Boulevard Garden Apartments, financed by Julius Rosenwald, head of Sears, Roebuck, was set aside for blacks, while a similar project financed by Benjamin Rosenthal in Chatham was white-only. None was financially successful in the long run.[79]

The great irony among these changes was what happened to Goose Island. Its image had been so cursed by 1891 that Chicago aldermen had entertained a proposal to make the "Ogden's Island" name official. By the first decades of the twentieth century, the island had become just another run-down industrial district. In 1930 one of the symbols of its past disappeared when the old Armour grain elevator burned. By then, it was clear that with only fifty families left, the city no longer regarded it as a residential neighborhood. In 1930 construction began on a city garbage incinerator plant. Municipal services had already begun to decline when the fire department withdrew the *Fire Queen* in 1924 and closed Engine Company 90 in 1932. Perhaps the final symbol of changing times was the construction of the Ogden Avenue overpass in early 1931. The elevated span carried traffic high above the island's historic soil. Yet at the same time, a more nostalgic and sanitized image of its past had displaced its reputation for crime and squalor. During the 1920s, Mayor William Dever, who had once labored in one of its tanneries, and Thomas Keane, an alderman, city collector, and council power, proclaimed themselves "sons" of the island. One reunion drew five hundred former residents back to the sod. By then, even the thugs described as so vicious in the 1890s had been reinvented as colorful characters.[80] As the prosperity of the 1920s gave way to the Great Depression, little remained of a residential nature on the island, only eight single-family homes and an equal number of duplexes in just two blocks near the center. The rest was industrial.[81]

Midway through the 1930s another solution to the city's slum problem emerged. It excited the public's imagination like no other because it was stimulated by the social legislation of the New Deal. But rather than being something new, it was really an amalgam of past solutions. It included scientific planning based on careful surveys of the facts and called itself a living model for the rest of the city to follow. It started with the spectacle of land clearance, of sweeping away old neighborhoods that had been dominated by greedy and indifferent landlords and starting over with all-new structures; old buildings that had repeatedly escaped attempts to reform the housing code would finally fall to the bulldozer. Once built, the replacement contained public health-and-welfare facilities to relieve the social as well as environmental problems of poverty, to help the family by changing the environment that surrounded it. The management, which had no interest in making profit, sponsored programs that generated a sense of community, of belonging somewhere. Yet this new housing was also intended to be no more than a temporary stop for residents on the way to homes of their own. Tenants were not expected to remain there permanently. So excited were members of the community that they lined up for blocks just to walk through models. And despite the rules that only "complete" families with good references would be accepted, the waiting lists extended for months into the future. One of the largest of the projects was planned for Little Hell, on the mainland just east of Goose Island. The name of this new project was Cabrini-Green.[82]

Once more, the optimists had spoken too soon.

Conclusion

The story of how Chicago housed its populations divides itself into obvious segments based on social class and proximity to the center of the city. But in reality, all parts of the private-sector housing market were interrelated. Dr. Egan's subdivision, the forerunner of Sam Gross's, was the first expansion of the compact village. Goose Island represented the late 1840s fringe, the depressed slum status of which remained frozen in time because its location was ideally suited to become industrial; the houses that survived that transition were fated to shelter a population marked by crime and poverty. The arrival of speedier transportation in the form of the horsecar and the steam commuter train allowed those with the money to jump over the ring of slums and seek housing opportunities based on price, amenities, and accessibility.

The operative words in describing the outward spread were "choice" and "future." Money meant being able to choose among options, most of them positive. Families with money could always decide to live in less-opulent surroundings, if they chose. But what is most significant is the orientation of the new towns toward the future. The boasting of boosters that appeared in the columns of the *Post* contest spoke of new utilities being installed, growing populations, and land contract clauses that guaranteed that neighbors would not erect a substandard house on the vacant lot next door. The fringe was also newly constructed. This meant that the decision to build housing of a particular size and sell it to a target audience gave developers the ability to shape the future character of whole sections of the city and suburban towns. The first owners also influenced the future by deciding whether to construct a custom-designed house, or, in the case of subdivisions, by choosing among the models offered. Those who bought from tract developers had the good fortune of enjoying the benefits of mass production applied to housing as well as to sofas and bicycles. Even the family whose dream home looked like every other one on the block could influence the interior and exterior appearance through landscaping and paint colors, while the way they cared for the property or conducted themselves set the moral tone of the neighborhood.

Moreover, many of the suburbs had organizations, modeled on the downtown social clubs of the elite, that offered athletics, dances, and other social events in their clubhouses. These groups not only helped to instill a sense of local patriotism and pride, but no doubt also served to socialize—if not homogenize—the newcomers so that they would "fit in." This action no doubt helped make social relations with neighbors more predictable.

Contrast that lifestyle with that of individuals at the other end of the social spectrum. A lack of money meant having to decide upon ways to survive; but the very poor had few if any choices. Although the outward expansion of the city did enlarge the inner-city housing market to some extent, the structures were hand-me-down artifacts, in many instances inhabited by several previous owners or tenants. The latest residents had no input regarding style, and many places were beyond worrying about decoration. Moreover, the slums were technological backwaters virtually disconnected from the urban utility grid. Exploitive rents made the structures too valuable to tear down, yet many buildings were hardly worth retrofitting with gas, water, sewer, and electricity. Often, the desire for such connections was thwarted by the lack of proper service, because utility companies and the city were reluctant to pour resources into neighborhoods where there would be few customers anyway.

The plight of the poor was best summarized by a *Times-Herald* reporter who ventured into the slums of "Little Hell" in early December 1895:

> How does the other half get ready for Christmas?
> Well, it doesn't get ready at all. The other half is doing very well when it can get ready for to-morrow; and then for another to-morrow; and so on for all the to-morrows as they come. The other half can make provisions for no more than one day at a time. It cannot get ready for Christmas.[83]

The backwardness of the slums—neighborhoods with no future—appeared in other areas of life. Folks there walked to work, to get food, or to get to someplace more pleasant. On the Northwest Side their tramping to and from work and the dust that it raised appeared and sounded more rural than urban. The interspersal of houses, factories, cabbage patches, and farm animals made their neighborhood far less sorted out by function. In the portal neighborhoods of the near southwest and northwest districts, the places where the newly arrived struggled to learn about city life, there was hardly even the sense of an ethnic neighborhood. The speakers of the twenty-three different languages that could be heard within a few blocks of Jane Addams's Hull-House moved so frequently that they had no interest in creating or supporting ethnic institutions.

Ultimately, the story of housing a metropolis involved two contradictory concepts that, over the decades, have been held in varying states of tension. On one hand, there was fixedness, staying in place, permanence. This applied to families such as those living along Prairie Avenue, many of whom remained for twenty or thirty years in their mansions. The contrasting force was motion, symbolized by those who decided to pull up roots and call the moving van or the house mover. Ultimately, life became a game of musical chairs; those equipped with knowledge and funds were positioned in front of the best seats when the music stopped. Those with the least money coped with what they got and waited for the next tune. Some, the homeless, got nothing.

Postscript

History survives. As a collection of physical artifacts from various ages of its past, Chicago is still home to many of the buildings that created this story. On

Hudson Street stands what is called "Policeman Bellinger's Cottage," a small house that escaped the last hours of the Great Fire. On Menominee Street between Sedgwick and Wells, one can still find two of the tiny emergency houses erected by the Chicago Relief and Aid Society in the late autumn of 1871. Sadly, many of the once-proud closer-in subdivisions in places like Lawndale themselves became part of the story of the slum.

As Chicago's inner city aged and its regional borders expanded, abandonment and demolition of older buildings gradually replaced preservation and relocation. Institutionalized in the form of urban renewal, the new scorched-earth ethic allowed the destruction and decay of many structures that in earlier years might have been moved and saved. Today, preservation most often happens when buildings have become valuable because of their location in or near gentrifying neighborhoods. A notable exception took place in 1977, when the 140-year-old Widow Clarke House, Chicago's oldest building, was moved from Forty-fifth and Wabash to Eighteenth and Indiana Avenue. The elaborate process required lifting it over the elevated structure. There was an irony involved in the journey: The old building returned to within a few hundred yards of the place from which it had been moved in 1880.

Goose Island continues to change. It became a favorite haunt of journalists in search of Chicago nostalgia, but there was progressively less of its tangible past to savor. New enterprises, such as the Greyhound Bus servicing facility and the Charles Levy Circulating Company, moved in after World War II. The tanneries have long since departed, while expanded rail yards displaced many of the stone, coal, and lumber yards. Only a small remnant of the Milwaukee Road's rail line still provides service. What is perhaps most ironic is that the future of Goose Island and Little Hell is an upscale version of their past. With the loss of factories and the workers who lived nearby, *de*-industrialization has become, in effect, *pre*-industrialization as well. Beginning in the 1970s, the trend toward gentrification began to bring higher-income families back to the convenience of the inner city. The central location has promised a future of postindustrial lofts, a far cry from the squatters' huts that once dominated the historic island.[84]

Across the river to the east, the wrecker's ball flattened the original Little Hell to make way for the Cabrini-Green public housing project in the 1950s. But the planned utopia soon became another version of Little Hell. Where the Irish, Swedes, and Italians once battled on the streets, new generations of gangbangers terrorized the thousands of decent people who were simply trying to survive. In 1995, the first of the high-rise Chicago Housing Authority buildings fell to the wrecking ball, to be replaced by new private-sector housing.

Perhaps the most ironic development in the neighborhood was the proposal early in 1997 to fill in the channel that made Goose Island an island in the first place. With the demolition of Cabrini-Green, the cost of maintaining bridges, and the rising price of land, the river will probably return to its original course.[85]

The past, it seems, is the future of the city.

PART THREE

Food

5 The Risky Business of Food

TIME and the rhythms it created were essential to the city. The railroad and internal transit systems that were its lifeblood operated according to timetables. Its workers went to and from their jobs in rush hours that were created by the need to begin and end work days in uniform fashion. School time governed the temporal rhythm of families with children. Many businesses reaped good will by placing public timepieces on streetcorners or building facades. And even when cheap "dollar watches" made possession of the correct time possible for even the working poor, city government and various churches realized their role in providing a local standard that everyone could use for synchronization. Not only were there public clocks on municipal buildings and many steeples, but city departments blasted signals and many churches rang their bells at regular intervals.[1] Time operated on larger rhythms as well. Mortgage or rent payments and bills for other necessities came due according to regular weekly or monthly schedules. Even leisure had its regular rhythm; people often read their newspapers at a regular time each day or went to the theater according to predictable schedules.

Time also dominated the story of the city's food supply. While most people knew the difference between spoiled and fresh, few understood that food had special characteristics that made its consumption potentially risky, even deadly. Because virtually everything that people ate could transmit and harbor germs, it could also spoil and give diners anything from a bellyache to a serious disease. Time thus forced urbanites to trust each other. Chicago's food industry counted on outsiders for supplies; the consumer relied on the retailer, who bought from the wholesaler; and everyone depended on the unpredictable element of the weather, which determined not only the quantity and quality of what was produced, but also how much ice was available to store it.

These dependencies complicated a basic fact: The need for a Chicagoan to find ways to cope with the food supply was even more basic than obtaining shelter.[2] One could be homeless, even for extended periods of time, but never foodless.

To Market, to Market

Despite the size and economic dominance that cities extend over their hinterland, they have always been fragile systems whose residents depended on many outsiders to supply such necessities as energy sources, building materials, and some tax revenues to operate government. Low birth rates meant that urban areas even depended on annexation, migration, and immigration to fuel their population growth. But food has always been perhaps the most critical of dependencies; no city has ever been able to grow enough to be self-sufficient. That fact was even true during Chicago's pioneer days, when Archibald Clybourn was the first to profit from that need. Soon after his arrival in 1823 he convinced the garrison at Fort Dearborn and the other residents of the tiny village that, even though they had gardens and many kept livestock, they needed a middleman to supply other foods grown by the area farmers. Clybourn's butchering business became the forerunner of the city's meat-packing plants.[3] The growing dependence on the outside became a crisis when the supply line was disrupted. When cholera afflicted Chicago in 1849, for instance, city dwellers faced food shortages when frightened farmers refused to haul their produce to town. Even city pioneers discovered that they had to place their trust in total strangers for the supply, variety, and wholesomeness of something as important as what they ate. That relationship was often marked by doubt and discord.[4]

The story of Chicago's food supplies and markets developed on two geographic levels. The first involved links with nearby farmers, whose market offerings supplemented the chickens and vegetables that many Chicagoans raised. Although there were a few privately owned meat and produce retailers, most of the trade with rural folks was disorganized and scattered at the curbside. The importation of foods from the East made up a second category. Ships from New York brought dried fruits and other nonperishable foods in barrels, which were haphazardly sold at dockside.[5]

By the early 1840s, Chicago's civic leaders began to realize that the logic of centralization—one of the primary elements of urbanization—could be applied to the marketing of foods. By 1843 an improvised market was in business near the corner of State and Lake Streets, but Chicagoans yearned to import a feature of eastern and European cities: a publicly owned market hall that would attract and house a variety of private vendors under one roof. Petitioners argued that having everything in one place gave consumers the ability to comparison shop and the city the power to regulate the dealers and banish cheaters and renegade sellers. A market hall would also result in a "great savings of time to the mechanic and the businessman in purchasing his daily supplies."[6]

In 1848 the city finally constructed its first municipal building. The two-story market hall stood in the middle of State Street, which had already been platted wider between Lake and Madison when the central area was surveyed in 1830. Although some complained that the site was not central to the population, the State Street Market became the pride of the city. The Common Council enacted elaborate regulations controlling what could and could not be sold, especially forbidding "unwholesome, or stale, or blown, plaited, raised or stuffed meat, or measly pork, or flesh of animals dead of accidents or disease." Stall renters were given a monopoly of selling within the city.[7]

The building became a testament to Chicago's desire for a center and to the logic of centralization. Its bell and weather vane became the established standards of time and wind direction. The true meridian for the city was nailed to its south wall. The second floor of the structure became Chicago's principal civic meeting place, serving as its city hall and Common Council chambers.[8]

Nothing remained stable. The State Street market stood for only a decade. By 1850 the city's population growth and dispersal into new subdivisions was beginning to generate petitions for outlying markets. Consumers on the fringe complained about the distances, and the Common Council responded by creating new halls on Market Street (now Wacker Drive); Randolph Street, just west of the river; and Michigan Street (now Hubbard), between Clark and Dearborn.[9] These thrived for more than a decade, but as the city's growing population expanded still farther outward, the difficulty of getting from here to there made it increasingly inconvenient to travel to any type of central market. Most people also lacked any kind of refrigeration, forcing them to shop frequently for perishables in warm weather or depend mainly on foods that were dried or preserved in salt. Centralized public marketing waged a losing battle against two competitors. Private shops were dispersed and could more conveniently serve their neighbors, while peddlers took the produce directly to a customer's door.[10] Some critics of the market houses also blamed their decline on disputes over official weights and measures, political problems with market masters who battled with tenants, and the strict Sunday closing laws, which were another great inconvenience to families without refrigeration. Thus, while more compact cities of the East—and even St. Louis—were able to sustain central market buildings, Chicago saw its three market halls come down, one by one. Except for a limited number of individuals who could visit the public markets in person or send servants, Chicagoans were now separated from the first point of arrival of their food supply.[11]

By the late 1860s, a second phase of market development, integration into a national network, was beginning to transform the sources of Chicago's food. The first hints of the change had been apparent for a decade. Although lake shipping was used to bring some dry foodstuffs to the city, the rapidly growing railroad network was stretching into the hinterland. Grain had arrived on the first inbound Galena and Chicago Union run in 1848, but a decade later the Illinois Central penetrated warmer southern climates to bring produce from areas with slightly longer growing seasons. Then, in 1869, a young commission merchant named Washington Porter realized the commercial opportunities presented by the completion of the transcontinental railroad. A few weeks after the driving of the golden spike, he persuaded his brother in California to pack a standard freight car with iced produce and dispatch it to Chicago. The experiment worked, and the Porters were on the way to making their home town the hub of a national food network that would transform the country's eating habits. Extensions of rail lines reached into new growing markets; in 1880, fruit grown in Florida as well as in California began to appear on Chicago tables. The shippers were quick to exploit every technological innovation. Faster locomotives hauled express fruit trains, which decreased spoilage, allowing the transport of Latin American produce from the port of New Orleans to the North. Chicago rail equipment designers improved refrigeration, which aided the fruit and vegetable industry as well as meat and fish shippers. By 1890 Porter's firm alone was handling eight thousand carloads a year, and his was only one of dozens of South Water Street wholesalers.[12]

The same new rail connections also made it possible for Chicago-area growers to sell their goods nationwide. For example, the Bowmanville area of the North Side became one of the nation's largest growers of cucumbers for pickles. In 1880 a *Tribune* reporter noted that "market-garden after market-garden appears . . . as far as the eye can reach." From "a point of advantage of Roe's Hill the land is green with upper growths of turnips, cabbages, onions, cucumbers, melons cauliflowers, etc. while here and there a blood-red patch reveals the presence of a field of beets." There were also large flower fields managed by the Budlong company, which used Chicago's rail hub to establish the city as the flower distribution center for the nation. Similar flower fields gave the southern suburban district its name, Roseland.[13]

The ability to get from here to there on the new commuter trains allowed immigrants who had been peasants in their homelands to "reverse commute" out to till these fields in the morning and to return to their inner-city homes in the evening. In 1890 the *Herald* described the scene as "the material elements that go to make up 'The Angelus.'. . . But there is no cathedral in the distance and no possibility of vespers disturbing the progress of the work." The German, Italian, Polish, and Greek workers were paid $1.25 a day for men and 90 cents for women. The newspaper article continued, "Think of the lineal descendants of Ajax or Brutus pulling beets for 90 cents a day." Truck farming was a perfect precursor of the subdivisions to come because it involved intensive cultivation and higher profits-per-acre from smaller plots of ground that were increasingly valuable because they were in the path of development.[14]

Chicago reaped other benefits from the transformation of its food sources. Not only did the seasonality of produce become less pronounced, but the generally large quantities available lowered local prices. By the end of the century Chicago's own spectacular growth had made it possible for its markets to become increasingly specialized according to the source of the food.[15] Besides the general produce market on South Water Street, a wholesale market for meat and fish developed on Fulton Street.[16] Two blocks away, West Randolph Street handled huge amounts of Chicago-grown goods to be sold wholesale to locals, primarily grocers and restaurants. That market's career as the city's official source for hay (1860–71) had endowed it with the Haymarket nickname. Most of the dealers there sold retail when asked.[17]

While Haymarket Square became best known as the site of a bloody labor riot in 1886, the farmers and buyers who regularly mingled there gave the place a unique social life and temporal rhythm. Each day's routine actually began the night before, as hundreds of wagons left truck farms within a fifteen to twenty mile radius of the city. Most tried to arrive between 7:00 and 10:00 P.M. to be in position for the next day's trading. The Dutch, Luxembourgers, and "Yankeefied" farmers who made up the bulk of the sellers clustered in their respective groups. While wives and children watched the loads, the men led the horses to nearby stables and whiled away the night in saloons. At about 4:00 A.M. the first peddlers came through in search of bargains in bruised items that could be turned over quickly, and during the next few hours a succession of restaurant and grocery owners haggled and bought. By noon, the market's legal closing hour, everyone had left rather than risk the five-dollar fine imposed by the market master. They made their way home to catch a few hours' sleep before picking and reloading to start the cycle anew. It was not an easy life, since market prices fluctuated and crops were subject to failure from disease and uncertain weather. In her 1924 novel *So Big,* Edna Ferber detailed hardships and joys in the lives of market farmers in what is now the South Side Roseland community.[18]

Reporters and tourists beat a path to the South Water Street Market because of its unique position in the national produce trade. Here was Chicago's window on exotica: miles of bananas, oranges, apples, and other colorful fruit. The noises and smells were an irresistible lure for people who had never ventured further south than Kankakee. In 1897 a *Tribune* reporter noted another unusual feature. Because of the distance from the source, some produce had to be shipped green, and it often ended up in one of the subterranean ripening cellars.

> Imagine an underground passage, about half the width of the LaSalle Street tunnel, some seven or eight feet in height, and lighted every four or five feet with gas jets. Then extend this as far as the eye can reach. On each side of the four-foot walk and suspended on strings fastened to hooks in the ceiling are glistening rows of the yellow fruit, huge bunches glowing in the various stages of maturity. . . .
>
> The heat is almost oppressive at times. One can see it shimmering and palpitating on all sides. And above it all floats the penetrating and pleasing aroma of the banana.[19]

The public was alternately fascinated and angered by the development of these markets. Farmers, who were often disappointed by the prices offered them, linked Haymarket and South Water "sharpsters" to the city's criminal element. Growers labeled any effort by dealers to form organizations for self-regulation as "price-fixing." Local farmers also grumbled at the high fee of ten cents per load at the Haymarket.[20] The market men, in turn, complained that the city did nothing about unlicensed hucksters who operated on the fringe of the produce districts, and grumbled as well about the high rents for their small stall spaces.[21] Finally, consumer complaints and newspaper exposés detailed the ways that crafty peddlers and market dealers used to cheat consumers on freshness and measurement. During the 1880s and 1890s, city government responded with laws that mandated standard bread-loaf sizes, uniform quality throughout boxes of produce, and the removal of the colored tarlatan gauze that concealed green or decaying fruit and vegetables.[22] The buying public was also incensed at soaring prices of such items as meat, which they thought should have been inexpensive because of the Chicago location of the meat-packing industry. It was easy to blame the packers and their monopolistic stranglehold over wholesale distribution, which, in turn, kept retail prices high. Few heard or understood the packers' reply that the ease of shipping products elsewhere, including overseas, drove up the demand that cost housewives the extra nickels at the butcher shop.[23]

But prices were only part of the issue. Many of the same complaints surfaced periodically during the forty years preceding World War I because consumers felt increasingly alienated and cheated when the food industry changed in ways that most of them probably did not understand. Advances in food processing and preservation, as well as the development of advertising in area newspapers and national magazines, were breaking down local barriers and creating national brands and markets. The food processors' booths at the World's Columbian Exposition, an event visited most heavily by Chicagoans, may also have intensified local enthusiasm for nationwide products. But each step in the direction of national brands was accompanied by an increase in the time and distance between the grower and the dining table. In large part this was because of improvements in packaging that allowed partial processing of such goods as cereals. While many consumers appreciated the convenience that such preparation provided, by the end of the century Chicagoans were beginning to join others across the country in a backlash against packaged foods. In 1901, *Chicago Daily News* cartoonist Luther D. Bradley summarized the exasperation of consumers in his depiction of the "Thanksgiving Day of the Future" as a feast of boxed foods with names like "Turkine," "Spudette," and "Cran-Cran." As a result, eating as many raw items as possible became a fad.[24]

The popular reaction against changes in the food industry amounted to a breakdown of trust between processor, wholesaler, retailer, and consumer. This suspicion increased and diminished in cycles; it was intense during the depression decades of the 1870s, declined somewhat during the prosperous 1880s, then resurfaced with the hard times of the 1890s and remained at a high level through the beginning of World War I. The most important general issue was adulteration. One early chorus of complaints came during the summer of 1874 when a reporter for the *Times,* Chicago's most sensationalistic paper, took samples of food purchased at leading grocery stores to a local high school's chemistry teacher. Her analysis revealed that much of it was artificially colored and contaminated with wood. Many readers were outraged by the grocers' explanation that people got adulteration because they wanted cheap prices. Later that year, the Illinois General Assembly passed the nation's first comprehensive antiadulteration law, but the definitions of the regulations were unclear and enforcement provisions too vague to halt the problem.[25] By the time a civic reform group called the Citizens Association of Chicago introduced a replacement statute in 1885, the public furor had died down and there was little interest in the matter.[26]

During the years between late 1893, when Chicago plunged into the severe national depression, and the outbreak of war in Europe in 1914, interest in food reform rebounded and remained high. Waves of anger met each revelation that adulteration, unclean preparation and sale conditions, and deceptive packaging had infiltrated virtually every area of food processing. There was ammonia in baking powder; burned peas in coffee; sawdust in flour; preservatives and other chemicals in tea, condiments, vinegar, cider, nuts, soda pop, ice cream, candy, maple sugar, honey, baked goods, and breakfast cereal; and illegal substitutions of horse meat for beef and oleo for butter. A federal investigation in 1897 revealed that a vast number of bakers ignored the 1888 city ordinance that bread be made of wholesome ingredients and sold by the avoirdupois pound.[27]

Ironically, Chicago's location directly contributed to some of its food impurity problems. Newspaper readers discovered that the increasing size of cargo and passenger ships on Lake Michigan had made it unsafe to operate the local fleet of small fishing boats on open waters. This meant that fish catches that made their way to local tables were restricted to those from the polluted waters near the Chicago shore.[28] Chicago's rail hub function created other problems. Its enormous horse market made it especially easy for unscrupulous packers to substitute horse meat for beef.[29]

More important, the city's location and access to so much produce made it the nation's food-processing center. This, in turn, meant that Chicago was the logical location for dozens of negligent and criminal factories whose practices plagued the otherwise honest food-processing industry. For instance, when farmers hundreds of miles away unpacked food cans that leaked and exploded, the problem was traced to a group of Chicago companies that had repainted thousands of over-aged and corroded tin cans and then wholesaled them to mail-order firms. Conversely, critics complained that Chicago's hub location also made it the most convenient destination for "dumped" lots of spoiled goods and diseased animals from other parts of the country.[30] While the problems were real, they were easily exaggerated. By the end of the nineteenth century there were abundant rumors and claims that "thousands" of Chicagoans were being killed annually by food additives and products contaminated by disease.[31] By the time Upton Sinclair published *The Jungle,* his novel about the Chicago stockyards, the public was so suspicious of the food-processing industry that they were willing to accept its fictional details as entirely factual.[32]

Consumers found ways to cope with the situation. One was to purchase products whose names implied quality. The Woman's Canning and Preserving Company produced such goods. It was founded in 1890 to process food under the low-temperature patent method of canning invented by a Chicagoan named Amanda T. Jones. The leaders of several women's aid charities made up the board of directors, and only women could purchase its stock, which totaled a million dollars. Its workforce, which included only one male, turned out five hundred cans of tongue, pudding, and dessert fruit at factories in Chicago and in Montello, Wisconsin. The company branched out in 1892 to create the Woman's Baking Company, advertising that "every family must have bread. And it is woman's work to supply it. . . . We will supply better—more wholesome—bread, pies, cakes, etc., for less money than the housewife can make at home. And being a woman's concern, owned and operated by women, are we unreasonable in expecting an unlimited demand for our goods?" The bakery folded in 1894, but the canning company continued in business until 1920.[33]

The second method of coping involved angry citizens using the press to lobby for additional government intervention. Chicago's health department seized and destroyed whole carloads of foodstuffs, but the level of its activity rose and fell with public emotions, and a cloud of political interference constantly compromised its credibility. The office of the Illinois State Food Inspector, created in 1899, was the most active agency, especially after 1906, when the Pure Food and Drug Act resulted in the creation of a large federal force headquartered in Chicago. The two agencies shared a whole floor of the Manhattan Building, and they investigated thousands of complaints and seized tons of mislabeled and unsafe goods each year.[34]

What consumers who knew about the conditions found most frustrating was the fact that the dispersed structure of the food trade made it difficult to avoid impure products. Although Chicagoans flocked to downtown department stores, they were not inclined to haul a pot roast and rutabaga all the way home on the streetcar. As a consequence, the city lost the central market tradition that still thrives today in Philadelphia, St. Louis, and other cities. In 1891, private investors began the final attempt at a centralized food-vending center, the Great Central Market, at the south end of the State Street bridge. It thrived for a short time, but the depression that began in 1893, the continued outward push of subdivisions, and the soaring value of downtown land put it in bankruptcy by 1896; soon afterward it was razed. The downtown of the skyscraper had little room for economic transactions that were conducted with pennies.[35]

The general structure of food retailing was instead atomized into occasional informal farmers' markets and thousands of small neighborhood stores that were often difficult to find, let alone inspect thoroughly. "Here [in Chicago] we seem to be dependent almost entirely on the corner grocery," complained one letter to the *Tribune*. "There we go each morning and try to cull from a shelf-worn, fly-specked, wilted lot of rubbish enough for the daily meals, hoping that the next day will reveal a better supply."[36]

The majority of consumers found that the most effective action they could take to protect their families was to shop more carefully. Fond personal remembrances of neighborhood grocers were probably based on positive experiences; these stores became local gathering spots, the housewives' equivalent of the saloon. The trading area of each store was small and the clientele and merchant knew not only each other but also their families. Common membership in a church parish or synagogue also reinforced a sense of trust.[37]

Tensions nonetheless did arise. Some dealers occasionally complained to the press about customers who damaged produce or stole samples. The dispersed nature of the trade made it easy for deadbeats to ingratiate themselves with a dealer, run up a bill, and disappear; the inclination of Chicagoans to move their households every few years made this kind of cheating an irresistible temptation for some. And there was occasional discord over how long stores should remain open. Customers complained that early closing and the storekeeper's Sunday off inconvenienced those with limited refrigeration.[38]

It was the poor residing in the more congested districts who doubtless encountered the greatest difficulties. One might argue that the insularity of their neighborhoods deprived them of the knowledge of the alternatives, while their poverty left them unable to afford the streetcar fares to reach them. But even if given the option, most no doubt would have been reluctant to abandon the ethnic edibles that allowed families to maintain their traditional foodways and customs.[39] This left them little choice but to patronize two types of retail food sources. One was the army of peddlers, who brought an increasing variety of foods to the doorsteps. This was especially important to families whose lack of refrigeration forced them to make purchases on a meal-by-meal basis. Housewives who also had to care for several children often had to contend with a single stove used for both cooking and heating. They depended on the street trades because they did not have to leave their homes untended. At the same time, most families also patronized neighborhood greengrocers and "dry grocers," which were located within easy walking distance. These retailers maintained an informal system of credit. Being carried "on the books" allowed poor families to weather temporary unemployment and make payments when their paychecks allowed. But neither of these food sources was noted for its cleanliness. During 1906, for instance, the city health department arrested over seventy-five fruit and vegetable peddlers for keeping their sale produce stored in the same room where they and their horses slept.[40]

Food consumption among the poor became a major concern of social reformers. Their efforts to "uplift" the home cuisine of the average Chicagoan grew out of their suspicion that the traditional foods for which the ethnic communities had such deep-seated affection provided too little nutrition at too great an expense. The food reformers called for greater variety of more skillfully prepared dishes, especially ones that were Americanized.[41] One source of homogenization among those who could read English was the so-called women's pages in the daily newspapers, which broadened considerably the trading of recipes, a custom that dated back to the 1830s. There were a few widely publicized lecture courses, including those of the Chicago Training School of Cookery, whose founder, Emma P. Ewing, complained that "too many [daughters] were taught to be ornamental." After noting that "ambition was as necessary for a woman as a man," she complained that men operated the leading laundries, became the prominent chefs, and invented the sewing machine, all women's "acknowledged branches of industry."[42] Church groups also published a number of widely read cookbooks. In an introduction to one of them, the Reverend Samuel Fallows summed up the philosophy of homogenization by claiming that "one of the chief distinctions between civilization and barbarism is the development of cookery."[43]

By the 1880s two groups led the movement to include food preparation in the public school curriculum. Various women's clubs gave the idea a strong lobbying force, while the Kitchen-Garden Association, which began its own cooking school program for young girls in church missions in 1883, provided the practical model. Chicagoans were also influenced by the success of the New England Kitchen, which targeted Boston's poor for culinary reform. All of these programs reflected a philosophy of social uplift through food. Reformers saw hunger rooted in ignorance as well as poverty and vowed to teach the future housewives of the slums how to shop and cook wisely on a limited budget. There was a temperance motive as well, since many reformers were convinced that poor cooking at home drove husbands to the free lunch counters in saloons; good home meals would keep the family together and the men out of mischief. Finally, the young women who graduated from domestic science classes also learned cooking as a marketable trade. The program's wealthy sponsors enjoyed another residual benefit in the form of a bumper crop of able domestics each year, which helped reduce the perpetual shortage of "help."[44]

One of the most important steps toward reform came in 1894, when the Retail Grocers and Butchers Association began its sponsorship of an annual Pure Food Show. A five-hundred-unit parade led thousands to cooking demonstrations, model kitchens, and displays of the many products claiming to be free from adulteration. The show's purpose was broadly educational and not aimed at any specific class. As one of its spokespeople noted, "The tenement house classes must learn that oatmeal is better and cheaper for their children than fine white bread and pastry, and best of all the luxurious classes must be taught the morality of economy and the religion of plain and simple diet." The motivation for the show was undoubtedly self-serving to some degree, because its principal sponsors were retailers who faced the daily complaints of dissatisfied customers; a more intelligent buying public would help drive unscrupulous elements from the trade. The show was also timely because consumer discontent was reaching the courts. In January 1898, the Illinois Supreme Court shifted some of the risk of liability when it ruled that the retailers, not the processors, were financially responsible for the consequences of food impurities.[45]

The middle-class families living in the dispersed neighborhoods and suburbs may have been the most fortunate group of food consumers. Although they had to depend on a more geographically scattered collection of neighborhood stores to bring goods closer to their homes, they had sufficient income to be able to choose among retailers. Their high level of literacy gave them the ability to read the many warnings contained in newspaper exposés and health department advisory bulletins. These families were also the principal beneficiaries of the new chain store form of food retailing, which began to appear in the last decade of the nineteenth century. This development promised that customers who were willing to travel a greater distance to do their shopping, as well as forgo credit and personal service, could find lower prices, more variety, and generally cleaner premises. Higher sales volume meant faster turnover and fresher goods. The idea caught on. In 1890 the Great Atlantic and Pacific Tea Company was operating five Chicago outlets, but the rival National Tea Company enjoyed the greatest expansion, growing from three stores in 1900 to forty-four in 1915. Virtually all of the National stores were located along major streets in dispersed neighborhoods and more than 3.5 miles from downtown. It was clear that the chains saw most of their customers in middle-class neighborhoods of subdivisions and suburbs. Even though the "mom-and-pop" food retailer would survive in traditional ethnic neighborhoods, the elements that would create the future supermarket were already beginning to appear.[46]

The food industry paralleled the great urban paradox of intense congestion at the city center at the same time that the fringe of development expanded wildly over the landscape. Many forms of food retailing were dispersing outward to reach customers among the subdivisions. Meanwhile, wholesalers had to find ways to cope with the fact that growth in the total volume of food consumption in the Chicago region was producing impossibly congested conditions near the markets at the center of the city. Slow-moving market-bound farm wagons disrupted commuter traffic, while South Water Street found itself severely crowded by the people and vehicles going to and from the tall buildings of the nearby Loop. Although nearly all of the rail lines had yards near downtown, these were often an hour or more away from South Water in heavy traffic. One potential solution appeared in Daniel Burnham's 1909 Plan of Chicago, which called for the produce grown in the nearby region to be transported into the city at night on the interurban and elevated transit system. Without discussing specifically where it would be relocated, Burnham also recommended removal of the unsightly old riverbank buildings of the South Water Market to make way for the double-decked boulevard that would someday be called Wacker Drive.[47]

Before any of Burnham's ideas could be implemented, soaring retail food prices led to discussion of an alternative solution. In 1913 intense lobbying by the reform-minded members of the City Club of Chicago pressured the city council to appoint a Municipal Markets Commission. In effect, the proposals it made amounted to a rejection of the economic and governmental trends of the previous decades. First, it favored a reversal of the pattern of centralization. Its investigators blamed high food costs on inefficient traffic patterns and called for the construction of municipally owned warehouse facilities and the dispersal of the wholesale markets out of their present locations. The Municipal Markets Commission also questioned the growing government hostility toward the street trades, especially when the street could serve as an employer of last resort during hard times. It suggested allowing farmers to sell produce directly to retail customers all over the city in schoolyards, in the unused space underneath elevated structures, and in other public places.[48]

The great champion of the report was Alderman William R. Rodriguez, the first person of Hispanic heritage elected to the council. A housepainter-turned-lawyer, he was first elected in 1915 as part of a bitter backlash that followed the sharp rise in unemployment and the series of strikes induced by World War I. Rodriguez came to the defense of the street trades, called himself the housewife's advocate through his proposal to regulate food prices, and put the city directly in the business of wholesaling and cold storage. Before anything could be implemented, however, the American entry into the World War and the anti-Bolshevik paranoia that engulfed the nation after 1917 made the municipal warehouse idea seem far too socialistic for most Chicagoans. The idea of a farmers' market also disappeared in the wartime frenzy, as did the political career of Rodriguez, who lost his seat in 1918.[49]

The World War only stalled the decentralization strategy of the Burnham Plan. In 1917, the Chicago Plan Commission, a nongovernmental organization created to promote Burnham's work, blamed South Water Market inefficiency for adding $5,138,400 to the "high cost of living," but it did not suggest another location for the facility. Nothing was done until 1925, when a new site was carved from one of Chicago's most notorious slums. "The Valley," which derived its name from the steep embankments of the Burlington and North Western railroads, gave way to new rows of buildings. The name "South Water Market" was transferred to a new produce complex bounded by Racine, Morgan, Fourteenth Street, and the Sixteenth Street rail embankment. It offered its 166 tenants efficiently designed space with elevators and excellent rail and street access.[50]

Thus, as the decades passed, Chicagoans constantly had to adjust to changes in their food supply. While the food hawker and the "mom-and-pop" store showed some signs of decline by the time of World War I, local shops still supplied the needs of industrial neighborhoods. Ethnic groups resisted the trend toward the consumer mass market by utilizing nearby stores to maintain the family menu. It would ultimately take a few more decades and the automobile to transform some of them into modern supermarket customers.[51]

In a century and a half, Chicagoans learned to cope with paradoxical situations that affected its food supply. The first was the fact that improved freight handling and faster trains dispatched increasing quantities of food to Chicago at higher speeds. Yet because Chicago was the nation's hub, it needed centralized yards for efficient handling of freight and the redistribution of cars to other lines. For the same reasons, food wholesaling also required centralization. Nonetheless, the result seemed to be an increase in congestion that virtually guaranteed that food shipments would be stalled once they got to the city.

There was a second paradox that grew out of the geography of food. The location of so many of the poor in the slum neighborhoods that encircled the downtown made tens of thousands of them neighbors of the South Water, Fulton, and Haymarket districts. At the same time, many of these same poor families were getting what reformers saw as inadequate diet. Contrary to the old real estate adage, location is not everything.

Finally, the element of time forced citizens to place what often amounted to an uneasy trust in the chain of supply that brought them their food. Over time, the food supply improved because of better processing and transportation technology, stricter government regulation and inspection, and more intelligent consumers who learned what to demand.

The Iceman Cometh

For almost a hundred years the iceman was a familiar sight on Chicago's streets. He stopped his wagon, which was often painted white to signify the purity of his product, to respond to signal cards in the windows of homes and shops.

South Water Street, east from Market, ca. 1890. Teamsters load and unload heavy wagons at Chicago's busy produce market, which was also accessible by ship.

Produce peddler, Near West Side, ca. 1900. The street became the market for those who found it difficult to travel to South Water Street, but public health reformers complained about the filth of the "store's floor." (Jane Addams Memorial Collection, University Library, University of Illinois at Chicago)

Maxwell Street, probably 1920s. Food vending was another function of the city's largest peddlers' market. (Jane Addams Memorial Collection, University Library, University of Illinois at Chicago)

South Side food store, 1898. The grocer extended short-term credit to customers and his store functioned as a place for neighborhood women to meet and exchange information.

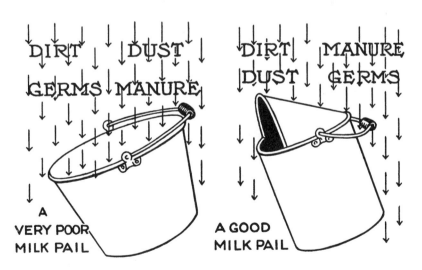

Pure milk notice, Chicago Department of Health, *Annual Reports, 1911–18*. Even illiterate farmers could understand the message of this notice sent to all who supplied milk to the city.

Giving baby-feeding instructions, Infant Welfare Society, *Annual Report, 1914.* A nurse from the society supervises a father in preparing a baby's bottle.

A family garden, ca. 1900. Families in sparsely settled outlying neighborhoods could keep large vegetable gardens and animals. Cheap glass bottles allowed them to preserve food, reducing their dependence on commercial suppliers.

• CONTENTS •

November Vines (Poem), Susan Coolidge.................. 1
Fading Leaf and Fall n Leaf (Poem), Richard Garnett... 1
The Tale of a Bag Pudding, Alice Chittenden........... 1
Balancing Accounts, Good Housekeeping................. 2
The World's Queens, No. 6, Elizabeth, of Roumania..... 3
Ballade of the Faded Field (Poem), R. B. Wilson....... 3
A Soft Answer, Helena Morrison Gates.................. 4
Thanksgiving Day in History........................... 5
A Pretty Manner, Ruth Hall........................... 5
Good Form, Eldon...................................... 5
A Pet Society Foible................................. 6
Children and Sewing, Juniata Stafford................ 6
Children's Clothing, Marion Harland.................. 7
The Golden Shoes (Poem), Selected.................... 7
Patience with the Little Ones, R. J. Burdette........ 9
To Our Readers....................................... 9
Men, Women and Money................................ 10
About Nagging, E. S. Kirkland....................... 10
From Berry to Cup................................... 11
A Real Thanksgiving, Selected....................... 12
Decorations in White and Gold....................... 13
Oriental Work, Table Scarfs, etc.................... 14
Early Winter Costumes............................... 15
Or Gin of Fashion................................... 16
The Bashful Youth (Poem)............................ 16
The Home Club, E. Conroy.......................17, 18
The Thanksgiving Turkey, E. C. Corbett.............. 19
Biscuits and Breakfasts, Selected................... 20
A Cosmopolitan Woman (Poem), S. W. Foss............. 21
Tea Table Menus, Selected........................... 22
Apples, E. C. C..................................... 22
Ye Pumpkynne Pye (Poem)............................. 23
Cranberries, Elsie Havens........................... 24
Our Servant Girl.................................... 24
    Also Choice Dinner Menus, prepared expressly for the Chi-
cago Housekeeper, and many other brief articles of Entertain-
ment and Instruction.

Cover, *Chicago Housekeeper and Ladies' Journal,* November 1888. Readers no doubt benefited from the practical articles on household management, but they may also have
dreamed of living in the Potter Palmer mansion, which adorned the magazine's cover.

The Iceman, from Sigmund Krausz, *Street-Types of Chicago* (1891). A familiar sight on Chicago streets, the iceman had to be able to handle heavy blocks.

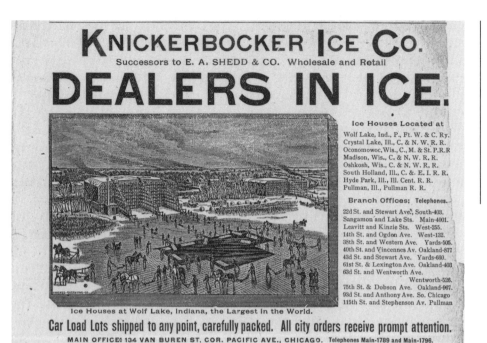

Knickerbocker Ice Company advertisement, 1895. The area's largest company owned an ice cutting and storage facility at Wolf Lake, Indiana, that met a large portion of Chicago's refrigeration needs during each summer.

After a few furious chops with his pick, he would grasp a hundred-pound block of ice between the jaws of his tongs and hoist it on his shoulder. His visits were special events for the small children who harvested the fragments he left behind. To many people, he was a personal tradesman bringing a service to the door, his flannel shirt and leather shoulder-covering symbols of trust and predictability. By bringing a physical remnant of winter during the heat of summer, he enabled city dwellers to bend the relentless cycle of seasons that shaped people's lives.[52]

The iceman was a celebrity of the streets, but for many Chicagoans he also symbolized some of the worst aspects of city life. He represented an exploitive monopoly that sold a vital commodity at an enormous profit. The ice handler was also an arbiter of family timetables and one of those who gave temporal structure to the family's week. His stops at houses and businesses followed a regular route on a predictable schedule so that housewives would know when they had to be home. This made his presence part of the give and take of urban life. Those who were fortunate enough to have an icebox faced a crisis of dependency if they missed his visit.[53]

The story of his trade was as old as the city. Alson Smith Sherman became Chicago's first ice dealer by accident. He came to town in 1836 and began work as one of Chicago's first building contractors. Three years later, when a customer could not pay a large bill, Sherman accepted a well-stocked private icehouse along the Chicago River as payment. Friends laughed at the idea. Commercial ice dealers were thought unnecessary because citizens could cut chunks from the river and store them in their own deep cellars. But Sherman's investment proved wise. In 1838 the Common Council responded to pollution fears by enacting an ordinance that required a license to cut, thus limiting access to the product by the general public.[54] The business became even more valuable as the city expanded outward. As Chicagoans found it inconvenient to go to the stream, they were increasingly willing to pay someone else for the bother of gathering, warehousing, and delivering a perishable product. Business boomed, and after only a few years of operation, Sherman erected a new brick icehouse. His position made him so well known in the community that he was elected mayor in 1844. It also made him wealthy. Five years later, he sold out to Hiram Joy and retired.[55]

The trade changed dramatically during the 1850s. The city was in the midst of a growth spurt that took its population from 30,000 to 109,000 in a decade. Fewer and fewer families were either able or inclined to cut their own ice. The major problem was the river contamination that soured the local supplies. Critics heaped blame on lake vessels that wintered in the harbor, but ironically Ellis Chesbrough's new and efficient sewer system, which discharged waste directly into the stream, solved the problem of drainage by turning the slow-moving river into an open sewer. In 1863, the obvious pollution prompted the city physician and the Common Council to ban the sale of ice cut from most parts of the stream.[56]

The solution to the problem lay in the expanding rail system, which made it possible to bring in new supplies from the clear streams and ponds in the Fox River Valley and northeast Indiana. Chicagoans now had access to more plentiful ice supplies, but consumers found that the growing distance between them and the sources drove up transportation costs and prices. At the same time, competition declined because small dealers were unable to negotiate the same favorable rates that the railroads granted high-volume shippers. Technological advances in the ice business gave an additional competitive edge to the more heavily capitalized companies, which could afford to innovate. By the late 1870s they were employing large planes (based on the same principle as a carpenter's tool) to scrape off snow and rough spots, while hand-pushed and horsedrawn plows sliced through the ice sheets. Guided by grapples and hooks, the loose blocks floated to the shore, where they were placed in heavily insulated warehouses or in caverns. Here they could survive through a hot summer. When needed, they were transported by corklined boxcars to ice depots to await retail delivery.[57]

The evolving system was a marvel in its time, but by the era of the Civil War, Chicagoans were already complaining that local monopolies charged prices that were higher than in the South.[58] The lot of the retail consumer continued to worsen in the half-century after Appomattox, in part because a pair of rapidly expanding local industries increased demand and kept ice prices high. Breweries had to chill their beer during the long fermentation process, and meat packers learned how to transform freight cars into mobile iceboxes so that Chicago meat might arrive fresh thousands of miles away. Gradually, brewers and packers bought their own ice fields, but mild winters that produced poor ice harvests forced them to purchase ice in the open market, where their demand drove up retail prices for everyone.[59]

By the late 1870s, improved transportation and an insatiable need to keep things cool forced Chicago companies to draw upon ice supplies from other states. In 1880, 1.1 million tons moved into the city by rail and by lake schooner from as far away as Green Bay, Wisconsin. The Washington Ice Company, the largest of Chicago's twenty-two firms, had icehouses on the Calumet and Fox Rivers and across the state line in Lake Geneva and Sturgeon Bay. When water pollution threatened the Knickerbocker Ice Company's large base at Wolf Lake, Indiana, the firm moved its operation to the lakes in and around Madison, Wisconsin. By 1900 it was dispatching as many as 7,000 workers, many of them drawn from seasonally idled Chicago workers, to its ice fields. At Pewaukee, in the same state, Armour built an icehouse 200 by 1,200 feet, with a storage capacity of 175,000 tons. Its rival, Swift and Company, had a facility on Lake Calumet. In claiming an ice source, all a company had to do was mark a site, protect it from competitors, and negotiate with the owners of the shoreline property for rights to erect an icehouse. In 1901, after Wisconsin legislators imposed a tax on ice cut from its waters, the state supreme court invalidated the statute, using the argument that the tax law hindered the public's use of the waters.[60]

By the end of the century, a new public-health consciousness growing out of the germ theory of disease had begun to force changes in the trade. Chicago ice companies had become dependent on Wisconsin for most of their supplies, partly because the city's board of health had started to impose tougher cleanliness standards that ice cut from Illinois and Indiana sources could not meet.[61] Wisconsin ice prices shot up, even though northern supplies were less vulnerable to the mild winters that inevitably created shortages the following summer. Limited supplies could double the retail rates. Saloonkeepers and other merchants who needed ice to stay in business grumbled about exploitation and threatened to form their own ice companies.[62] Editorials protested that the companies were making excessive profits from a product that was increasingly regarded as a basic necessity because it was used to chill meat and milk. Reformers complained that the poor could afford ice only when abundant supplies drove the price very low, which was not very often. But efforts to create a municipal ice company in 1903 failed when critics labeled it "socialistic."[63]

Chicago consumers also complained when the Knickerbocker Ice Company bought out virtually all of the independents in 1898, claiming that the simple technology of the industry made their large investments vulnerable to competition from upstarts. Knickerbocker also protested that the condition of the national economy caused its labor costs to fluctuate so wildly—depressions bringing an abundance of workers—that it needed to control its market in order to survive. The press unanimously condemned the arguments as well as the buy-outs. Politicians who were eager to gain favor with voters pushed the board of health to retaliate through more stringent inspection procedures. The board equipped roving laboratory wagons that randomly stopped ice dealers on the street and tested samples. At the same time, improvements in drinking-water quality redirected attention to the ice supply. After the new Sanitary and Ship Canal successfully reversed the river's flow on January 1, 1900, disease rates dropped. But when typhoid struck the city in 1901, it was widely believed that contaminated ice was the cause. The state food commission joined the attack, condemning Chicago ice because it was "cut from impure ponds with sewage, decayed animal and vegetable matter."[64]

By then, the ice trade was beginning to change once more, and the powerful Knickerbocker company proved vulnerable because it failed to innovate. One of its few remaining independent competitors, Consumers Ice Company, rapidly made inroads on the natural ice trade with an artificial product. For centuries, scientists had known that some chemical compounds produced a cooling effect when agitated—Benjamin Franklin had theorized that a man soaked in ether might freeze to death in a wind—but it was not until the 1870s that inventors adapted these principles to industrial use. "GIMME A PINT OF COLD," read the *Tribune* headline announcing the incorporation of one new company that manufactured ice with the use of chemical coolants. The paper went on to predict that smaller versions of the machinery might even cool a house. Large breweries began installing mechanical refrigeration in the 1880s, while a large cold-storage exhibit at the World's Columbian Exposition of 1893 demonstrated the technique to the masses, at least until its destruction in a tragic fire. Finally, after the turn of the century the monopolistic natural ice industry raised prices to the point where the machine-made product became economically competitive. Artificial ice began to demonstrate its advantages. Consumers concerned with purity considered it safer because it could be made with filtered water. Production costs shrank because making artificial ice was not as labor intensive as natural cutting and, because ice could be made on demand, it did not need to be stored from season to season. Manufacturing plants could be located in the city, so that transportation costs were minimal. Finally, the supply was much more predictable because it did not depend on the severity of the previous winter.[65]

Artificial ice all but doomed traditional harvests. By the outbreak of World War I, the more modern Consumers Ice Company had bought out Knickerbocker, which had allowed its huge ice houses on the shores of Wisconsin lakes to fall into disrepair. The only steady customers left for naturally harvested ice were the railroads, which had trouble adapting the artificial refrigeration machinery to their huge new fleets of refrigerator cars. The supplies they needed were for icing stations that were dispersed along their routes, often near lakes where the natural coolant could still be cut. And because the ice did not come into direct contact with the food they were handling, purity was of less concern.[66]

By the 1920s, a few individual consumers were finally gaining some leverage against the ice monopoly as gas and electric refrigerators started to replace the icebox. Mechanization in the kitchen began among wealthy households, who could entrust keeping their food wholesome to a grid of utility wires instead of the ice or food peddler. Besides the obvious convenience of eliminating heavy ice blocks and the drip pan, the family was also free of the iceman's schedule. But, like other forms of household technology, the new refrigeration only gradually trickled down to the poor. One investigation conducted in 1925 revealed that a fourth of the families in the Maxwell Street district did not even own an icebox, let alone a refrigerator. Like their counterparts a century earlier, the urban poor had to shop for every meal that involved perishables. While more affluent neighborhoods took electric refrigeration for granted, ice in the Maxwell Street district was still a luxury usually bought only to cool the fevered brow of a sick child.[67]

As the years passed, the iceman's tongs and the delivery signs began to appear in antique stores and junk shops. The iceboxes, which had been triumphantly hauled to the alley when the new "fridge" arrived, suffered a similar fate. Those that survived became expensive pieces of furniture. Symbols of one generation's problems have a way of becoming cherished objects to the next.

Milk Wars

Poor Mrs. O'Leary. Not only did her cow shoulder the blame for starting the Great Chicago Fire, but during the years that followed, her profession as a milk dealer also fell into disrepute. By the end of the nineteenth century, in fact, cows and what they produced had become the focus of one of the most animated and bitter struggles in Chicago's history.

Milk caused little comment during the city's first few decades. Local farmers supplied M. A. Devine, the city's first milkman, with the fresh, frothy fluid he ladled out door to door on his route around town. Chicagoans probably felt lucky that they, unlike their downstate frontier neighbors, had avoided the dreaded "milk sick," a fatal poisoning produced by tainted milk from dairy cattle that ate goldenrod and other hazardous prairie weeds. But utopia was short lived. Milk soon demonstrated its remarkable capability as a disease-growing medium, while greedy farmers and dealers helped make drinking a glass of it as hazardous in Chicago as anywhere.

The first problem arose in the backyards and barns that held the city's 10,000 head of resident cattle by the 1870s. There was little concern about the many families in the outlying districts who depended upon the output of their lovingly maintained family pets. Those animals usually had access to the requisite fresh hay and grasses. Milk became an urban hazard when demand outstripped self-sufficiency. That happened quickly, because the city's seemingly insatiable thirst outstripped its population growth. In 1871, when Chicagoans numbered about 300,000, they consumed 4.4 million gallons of milk; forty years later, with slightly more than 2 million residents, the intake topped 94.4 million gallons annually. Demand forced the milk supply network to reach out as much as a hundred miles to include not only northern Illinois but about 12,000 farms in three other states. The same twenty rail lines that hauled in vegetables, meat, and ice also brought in the product of 120,000 cows. The marketplace worked well for cowless families who purchased their milk with the knowledge of its quality and who could afford to pay as much as fifteen cents a quart for a superior product from Bowman, Wanzer, or any of the other large and reputable dairies.[68] But for others, the unregulated market meant risk. Longer distances lengthened shipping times and increased the possibility of spoilage. Dairies also collected untested milk from many sources into huge processing tanks, making it difficult to identify which producer had contaminated the whole lot. And the anonymity of the system encouraged fraud and carelessness.[69]

There was considerably more danger, however, involved in purchasing milk in the inner city. Since at least the early 1850s, ignorance of quality and the lack of choice had doomed most of Chicago's poor to exploitation. They were forced to buy from either neighborhood peddlers who ladled an inferior product at the door or from unregulated dairy stores that extended them credit. Most of these retailers relied on producers that fed their cattle a steady diet of distillery "slops" left over from whiskey manufacture. The resulting off-tasting "swill milk" that flowed from the udder also had limited nutritive value. "Whiskey is never so healthy as when it is taken directly from the distillery," advised the *Weekly Chicago Democrat,* "and if children and others are to drink it, we do not see the necessity of passing it through cows first." By 1867, when the first dairy inspections took place and the city's health department bought its first microscope, tainted milk was regarded as a central cause of an alarming death rate among children. In 1870 those under the age of five accounted for 65.8 percent of all deaths. Some parents followed the advice of physicians and resorted to condensed milk, which was reputed to be purer, but it could be contaminated when diluted with germ-laden city water.[70]

The swill-milk issue continued through the rest of the century. In March 1871, one Chicago newspaper ended its discussion of a similar problem in New York City by complaining, tongue-in-cheek, "If we are going to be a metropolis, let us have more whiskey-soaked, stump-tailed, decaying, propped-up-against-the-wall cows to give us a liquid facetiously called 'milk.'" (Yes, a swill cow's tail actually fell off.) But the problem remained widespread because, for city cows, slops were the only cheap substitute for grazing or hay. The distilleries themselves owned some of the large herds. But when health officials began to complain about swill milk, aldermen sided with the cattle owners, claiming that many were poor families that could afford no other animal feed. Even when a state statute prohibited feeding slops, the practice continued in Chicago because no one would enforce the law.[71]

By the 1860s, milk dealers had found another way to break the trust that consumers had placed in them. The widespread problems of watering and adulteration became almost universal whenever drought diminished the grasslands and reduced the supply of whole milk. Rather than raise prices and risk a consumer boycott, dairies stretched the supply. The natural tendency of cream to rise aided the cheating by allowing the dealer to remove the richest part of the milk from the can to make butter. Even a city ordinance requiring that skim milk be sold from a bright red can did not stop such practices.[72] Worse yet, some dealers stretched the product further by adding water that was often typhoid-laden and then thickening it with chalk dust, borax, or plaster to give the appearance of whole milk. One Dennis O'Rafferty described the situation in verse, which read in part:

Bedad I believe in a life of great pleasure,
To be in the milk trade, and sellin by measure
The lacteal fluid, rejuiced most discreetly
Wid wather, and thickened by chalk so completely.[73]

Uninformed consumers also purchased milk that was laced with preservatives of various kinds, a direct result of longer shipping distances and imperfect refrigeration. Formaldehyde was the most popular, although even small amounts of it killed the milk's nourishing qualities, literally starving the infants who depended on it. Large doses caused death by poisoning, even in adults.[74] Such adulterants continued to be used during the early years of the twentieth century under the trade names "Freezine" and "Milk Keep." A few dealers also tried to use hydrogen peroxide as a preservative, but health department publicity and lawsuits made this practice rare after 1910.[75]

The problems of the poor began with finding decent milk but continued with finding a way to keep it. The lack of ice boxes in tenements meant that the milk began spoiling immediately after purchase. The situation became so desperate that many families began feeding their children beer, regarding it as far safer than milk. While there were constant rumors that milk carried cholera, typhoid, and every other scourge, no one ever complained about a beer-based epidemic outbreak.[76]

The unreliability of commercial suppliers led to efforts to introduce an alternative system of distribution for the poor. In 1897, the Northwestern University Settlement opened a sterilization and pasteurization plant, selling its product at cost. Seven years later, the Chicago Woman's Club established a Children's Hospital Pure Milk Committee and began operating a plant with equipment donated by the philanthropist Nathan Strauss, who had established an extensive similar program in New York City. Soon, Chicago consumers were able to buy the pure product from thirty-three milk stations whose addresses appeared on foreign language handbills. The results of this work demonstrated that the infant death rate was clearly related to contamination, but despite favorable publicity, the higher cost per quart and limited production facilities prevented the program from making a serious reduction in the problem.[77] In 1908, physicians became involved when a division of the Chicago Medical Society took over pure milk distribution. The Pure Milk Committee, as it was called, later reorganized itself as the Infant Welfare Society and suggested breast feeding as the best solution to the infant milk crisis.[78]

All of those efforts were not enough to establish a substitute milk supply; new regulations were still badly needed. After the turn of the century, health officials began shifting their principal attention from adulteration, which continued to be a problem, to a new emphasis on the hazards of microbes. Although the work of the bacteriologists Robert Koch and Louis Pasteur had been known for two decades, practical application of their findings was another matter. To a great extent, this transition grew from the great improvement in the quality of Chicago's drinking water because of the completion of the new Sanitary and Ship Canal. When the locks were opened for the first time on January 1, 1900, the Chicago river ran backward, carrying its industrial and human contaminants toward the Illinois River and away from Lake Michigan, where the city's intake cribs were located. The quality of Chicago's water supply, which had been the principal cause of annual outbreaks of typhoid and other scourges, improved dramatically. This allowed health investigators to isolate other disease sources, including impure ice. But it was the impure milk supply that drew the most condemnation, and pasteurization that gained the greatest support as the solution to the problem.[79]

The dairy interests led the opposition, calling on paid experts who were willing to label pasteurization valueless; an industry-financed publicity campaign condemned the process as "cooking." Cheese and ice cream makers contended that it was impossible to process pasteurized milk. Farm groups intervened on the state level. The Illinois Department of Health and the Illinois State Food Commission responded to downstate political pressures and sided with the producers, breaking ranks with their counterparts in adjoining states that demanded higher standards.[80]

The issue came to a boil in 1904, when the Chicago Health Department began to order systematic inspection of all farms whose milk products entered the city. Previous visits, which had been casual and "educational," were replaced by demands to examine all dairy barns and an insistence on taking samples to test. Those who refused to cooperate faced being excluded from sales in the city. Farmers felt even more threatened when the Chicago officials also responded to yet another fear—which would later prove unfounded—that bovine tuberculosis could be spread to humans through milk.[81] In 1908, the city council took the bold step of requiring that all milk received in Chicago either be from cows tested for TB or be pasteurized. Downstate interests were furious. On March 27, 1909, members of the General Assembly denounced the Chicago law and asked that its enforcement be suspended until after a detailed investigation. City officials refused, assuming that any state study would be rigged to "prove" that pasteurization was worthless.[82] The state response came in the form of a 1911 law designed to prevent any county or city from establishing a TB test; opponents to city testing claimed that the one company that made the necessary equipment would enjoy a monopoly and that only the large dairies could afford to buy it. The antitesters managed to defeat a pasteurization ordinance in July 1912. But after a loud public outcry from protest meetings and the press, the aldermen enacted a weaker substitute on August 14. All that the Chicago health department could do was to classify the types of milk and educate consumers to choose the tested and pasteurized variety. As part of its publicity campaign, the department revealed that Illinois was becoming a dumping ground for diseased cattle from nearby states.[83]

While debate raged over the merits of TB testing, another crisis appeared with an outbreak of milk-borne typhoid in Englewood during the summer of

1911. Health department investigators traced it to the child of a downstate dairy farmer.[84] Milk delivery drivers and restaurant workers who were disease carriers reintroduced the problem several times in 1913–14, prompting officials to order that the buildings and people involved be quarantined and an alert issued to the public.[85]

Finally, in 1916, Chicago's health commissioner, Dr. John Dill Robertson, used the threat of a polio epidemic to justify an emergency order requiring the pasteurization of all milk entering Chicago. The edict was never repealed, and a decade later city officials decided to defy the state ban and openly order TB testing of all cattle producing Chicago's milk. Dairy farmers threatened an injunction, but the health commissioner proclaimed that he would go to jail in order to protect the city's children and that he would broadcast denunciations of the farmers from his cell. The downstaters backed off and scrambled to have their herds tested. Meanwhile, some suburban communities, which had been accepting milk rejected by Chicago, moved to bring their policies into compliance with those of the city and began mandatory testing. One study revealed that 80 percent of the cattle in McHenry County were tubercular.[86] But suburban progress was slow. As late as 1947 a federal study classified suburban Chicago milk as inferior and pointed out that only a dozen suburban communities even attempted to regulate their milk supplies.[87] Even though the trail from M. A. Devine to the modern dairy was not yet complete by the time of World War II, the problem of milk as a wholesale killer had passed. Every improvement along the way reduced the infant mortality rate and allowed modern generations to trust in their milk supply.

Thus, we return to Mrs. O'Leary. Her little milk business appears to have been among the healthiest, but she was still blamed for burning Chicago. It was perhaps ironic that methane from the fresh and healthy hay in her barn—or from the cattle that consumed it—may have played a part in starting the Great Fire. Had she fed her cows swill, there might not have been a conflagration.

City in a Garden

Long, hot summers and cold, dark winters do so much to shape the lives of Chicagoans. But since the city's founding, urban dwellers have used elusive days of spring to leave some mark on nature by staking their claim on a garden plot. During Chicago's infancy, women brought west with them the seeds of flowers that were unique to their native counties, and the bright blooms that appeared in front of homes served as an instant indicator of the origins of the tenant or owner. Chicago's pioneer leaders also took literally the motto on the city's seal, "Urbs in Horto." In 1847, a *Prairie Farmer* reporter's routine assignment on Chicago horticulturalists turned into a tour of the homesteads of the young town's elite. William Butler Ogden, John H. Kinzie, Justin Butterfield, George Snow, and Dr. William B. Egan all proudly displayed fruit trees and vegetable gardens. New York socialites or Boston Brahmins might have found such outdoor digging undignified, but their Chicago counterparts thought nothing of extending a muddy hand to a visitor.[88]

Through the years, gardening became more than a pastime, especially in hard economic times. Access to the soil provided a ready means of coping with the emergencies of war and depression. During the Civil War, women's organizations raised vegetables, which were canned and sent to Union troops. Individual garden plots were also a way for a city and its residents to supplement the food supply from the outside world. And each step in Chicago's outward dispersal into subdivisions and suburbs meant not only more backyards to fill with plants, but also more vacant space held for speculation, all of which was also a potential garden.[89]

Among the poor, however, gardening was sometimes necessary for daily survival, not just a form of ornamentation or a hobby. Even squatters managed to plant a few vegetables to supplement their meager meals, but those efforts were small when compared with what began during the severe depression of 1893–97, when armies of the unemployed roamed the nation in search of work. While many Americans hid behind locked doors, Mayor Hazen Pingree of Detroit suggested that the poor be allowed to plant potatoes and other vegetables in vacant city lots. The reform mayor believed that the effort would at least reduce the following year's starvation. Detroit newspapers initially laughed at the idea, calling him "King Tuber I," but the "Pingree Potato Patch" plan soon swept the nation.[90] By the spring of 1896, settlement houses and the Chicago Bureau of Charities had set aside potato patches in failed subdivisions from Englewood on the south to Forty-second Avenue on the West Side. Hull-House staff, who found a small space near their settlement building, sponsored a "People's Friendly Club" that allowed gardeners to exchange ideas year round. The plots became a popular way to cope with the problem of putting food on the table.[91]

The return of prosperity late in the decade reduced the popularity of many of the programs, but in the severe recession of 1907–9 a reform group called the City Gardens Association revived the notion of public gardening. In 1908, it cooperated with women's clubs and settlement houses in asking various industries for the use of vacant fields that factories had purchased for expansion. Among the most generous donors was International Harvester, which contributed a large plot at Thirty-first and California Avenue, now part of the site of the Criminal Courts complex. The leader of the City Gardens Association was Hull-House resident Laura Dainty Pelham. Born in Massachusetts, she had given up a stage career of two decades to join the staff of Jane Addams's famous settlement house where she directed the Hull-House Players during cold-weather months. Outdoors, Pelham worked with little publicity but great success. During the growing season she could be found directing the movement of plowing teams and seeking donations from the city's business moguls.

Pelham's favorite charity was easy to sell to philanthropists as a multifaceted reform. Gardening provided not only a source of food for the poor, she argued, but also made life in the tenement districts more tolerable. It promoted the social values of Progressive-era reform by building character among the poor. The truly indigent paid nothing, but the nominal fee charged other gardeners brought a sense of investment, as well as the use of an eighth-acre plot. Gardeners shared in a sense of America's rural past and learned the value of capitalism, since any of the produce could be sold at a profit. The operation of large plots taught the poor to respect each other's property, allowing promoters to boast that there were remarkably few reported incidents of pilfering and vandalism. Gardens drew idle men out of saloons to useful work and brought families closer together in a common project. Chicagoans of all races and nationalities turned the plots into miniature melting pots of interethnic cooperation. And even nongardeners benefited because wasted city space became beautiful, cleared of weeds and rubble at no cost to the city.[92]

The work of the City Gardens Association also proved to be an excellent preparation for the domestic mobilization of World War I. The need to feed both American troops and the citizens of war-torn European countries placed a premium on American foodstuffs. Congress shut down such "unnecessary" industries as brewing and asked civilians to economize in any way, such as recycling stale bread to extract the flour. Government agencies issued special cookbooks to teach food conservation. The gardening ethic spread nationwide under the motto "Feed Yourself." School children enlisted the aid of parents, and having a grassy backyard became tantamount to lacking patriotism.[93]

In a short time, what had been a charity for the poor became a national crusade. The War Garden Production Committee, a state agency, tried to manipulate what was grown in Illinois through its distribution of free seeds. Although many of the 238,422 Chicago gardeners in 1918 resisted such regimentation, careful record keeping showed that the state led the nation in wartime gardening. Many Chicagoans enthusiastically accepted the motto "Garden Plots to Kaiser Blot." In 1918, Illinois congressmen were also instrumental in the passage of the daylight savings time law, arguing that the extra hour of evening sunlight would allow greater after-work time for citizens to tend to their gardens.[94]

After the war, the popularity of vacant-lot gardening once again reflected swings in the health of the national economy. Huge agricultural surpluses during the 1920s drove down the price of store-bought food, while general prosperity reduced unemployment. This caused most of the plots to be abandoned, but the Great Depression brought many of them back to production. Backyard gardens supplemented relief checks, while some squatters inhabited Hoovervilles long enough to plant crops. Once more, the emphasis was on subsistence, as charities again helped the poor find vacant land to till.

With America's entry into World War II and the return of jobs at decent wages, the garden movement began once more to blossom, although more slowly than federal officials wanted. Some private companies furnished tractors that were used by the Chicago Park District plowmen who prepared the plots. Field houses and other park facilities provided meeting places for 108 neighborhood Victory Garden Clubs. Classes and demonstration gardens brought tilling to a new generation. Chicago police patrols were used to hunt packs of stray dogs. The Office of Civilian Defense promoted "Victory Gardens" as more than a citywide effort to supplement scarce food supplies. Publicity touted them as community-building "get-to-know-your-neighbor" activities. Block captains arranged carpooling to outlying plots and appointed "courts" to sort out squatter disputes. Moviegoers saw a brief but slickly done film called *City Harvest*, narrated by actor Ralph Bellamy, which emphasized the multicultural interest, as Chicagoans from many ethnic and racial groups and lifestyles came together in an annual harvest celebration. The exhortations worked; by 1943 some 145,000 Chicago gardens were producing 50,000 tons of food each harvest.[95]

Thus, throughout Chicago's history, the garden functioned as an important safety valve as well as a hobby. When food was in short supply and increasing in cost, when its quality was questioned, fresh fruits and vegetables from the garden as well as home-canned staples provided a reliable alternative to food obtained from strangers. Each decade of urban growth seemed to make dependence on faraway producers more filled with chance. Would there be shortages? Was the refrigeration reliable and the preservative healthy? Did a family have to pay the price of good nutrition to enjoy the convenience of processed foods? Growing your own presented an alternative to the hazards of depending on someone else.

And, just as they had been a century earlier, city gardens were a sure sign of spring.

Conclusion

The story of food, milk, and ice supplies involved matters of trust in a world of urban strangers. City living brought with it a dependence on the honesty and competence of others in operating a complicated system of supply. The Chicago food buyer, who was most often a woman, was at peril for deceit, unconscious errors, and the mistakes that grew out of the general public's misconceptions about sanitation and disease. But the manner in which individuals and families coped with that situation depended on a number of factors. Knowledge and the money to act accordingly was paramount; those who knew how to avoid swill milk or spoiled meat and could afford alternatives were the ones who most enjoyed the benefits of Chicago's location amidst America's agricultural bounty. And in many instances, government played the critical role of researcher, teacher, and police officer.

The element of time made food an even more important daily necessity than shelter. At worst, families could tolerate a period without shelter, but no one could survive for long without food. Each tick of the clock also increased the element of hazard from spoilage. Moreover, money meant that ice was affordable and the process of food deterioration could be delayed.

Like housing, food became a reflection of one's ethnic and social identity; what people ate, where they ate it, and with whom placed an individual in the spectrum of social classes. Food was also an element of identity; the old adage of "you are what you eat" took on new meaning in the city's ethnic mix.

Postscript

Chicago's food supply changed as the years went by. The city's food-buying habits reflected obvious trends toward nationally advertised prepackaged products, a concern with vitamins and nutrition, and other broad transformations of what and how we eat. Locally, the prosperity of the postwar years led to a decline in organized garden efforts, although gardening continued to be pursued primarily by hobbyists. Among them were the thousands of families who were part of the postwar rush to the suburbs; they turned over part of their backyards to small vegetable gardens. By the early 1970s, new opportunities also appeared in the city they left behind. Large plots of open land cleared by urban renewal became a fact of inner-city life, at the same time that new high-rise public housing units piled the poor in the air, but used only a small portion of the ground space. Many Chicagoans had already begun casual cultivation in these open spaces when the city's Department of Human Resources began an organized program in 1973. Cornstalks began to replace "KEEP OFF THE GRASS" signs. By 1978 nearly 5,600 Chicago Housing Authority residents were planting. Help from the U.S. Department of Agriculture and the University of Illinois Cooperative Extension Program supplemented the city program. Meanwhile, during the early stages of gentrification, more affluent gardeners turned out similar bumper crops in vacant lots that were later occupied with in-fill housing.[96]

Meanwhile, as the postwar years passed, Chicago retained its title as the nation's produce center. Tens of thousands of refrigerated rail cars rolled into town, many of them carrying cargo to be unloaded for regional consumption. But by the 1950s it was clear that the same decentralizing forces of transportation that had made the first municipal market building on State Street obsolete a century earlier were now eroding the efficiency of the newer South Water Market. The latter lost some traffic to large supermarket chains, which could act as their own wholesalers. But an increasing portion of the produce that had once reached Chicago by rail began to arrive in trucks. Even though the Sixteenth Street market was located not far from the intersections of four major expressways, it had been built for easy access by rail and small truck. The newer vehicles were larger and had to compete for space with others that were sent each day to make pickups for retailers and restaurants that were now increasingly dispersed into the suburbs. This resulted in the same type of inefficiency that plagued the Union Stock Yards during the last decades before it closed in 1971: a facility built for rail traffic simply could not adapt to the age of motor trucking. The congestion at South Water Market, along with aging buildings and expansion plans of the nearby University of Illinois at Chicago, brought predictions that a proud tradition and name might die or be displaced yet again. Meanwhile, by the early 1990s, the last remnants of the Haymarket had been transformed into restaurants.[97]

The great industries that supplied Chicago with food, milk, and ice left behind a few other artifacts. A marker on the side of the old Cook County Court House at Dearborn and Hubbard Streets marks the site of the North Division Market. But the most important reminder of the pioneer past is visible at the corner of State and Madison. "That Great Street" remains wider to the north of Madison than to the south, just as it was when the new State Street Market opened over 165 years ago.

For most present-day Chicagoans, the quality and quantity of food they can afford is vastly improved over what was available at the turn of the century. Retailing competition and national advances in the standard of living account for much of the change. That improvement has been reflected in storage conditions as even the poorest of families began to acquire refrigerators. The icemen and their familiar wagons gave way to delivery trucks supplying plastic bags of ice to supermarkets.[98]

But the element of risk has never fully disappeared. In 1984 several hundred Chicagoans contracted salmonella poisoning from milk sold by one of the major local supermarket chains. Subsequent investigation revealed that a mechanical flaw in processing equipment had allowed contaminated unpasteurized milk to mix with large quantities of the processed product. The dairy division of the food retailer closed permanently and the company settled hundreds of liability claims. But the event left behind a lesson: even in the modern world, vigilance against risk must be eternal.[99]

6   Eating Out

CITIES are natural collecting points for many types of minorities. We are most familiar with racial and ethnic groups. But there are countless other small segments of the population that share interests that are work-related or have to do with special skills, sexual orientation, religious beliefs, physical attributes, political ideology, cultural interests, or pastimes. The tendency for these varied minorities to gravitate toward the metropolis is related to two contradictory characteristics of cities. One is anonymity. City dwellers have the ability to disappear into the faceless crowd. Creative young people who might have been scorned and stultified by dusty country towns find in the urban masses a liberation from the prying eyes and gossip of people who insist on trying to make them conform to small-town standards of belief and conduct. Yet at the same time, the city is the place where there is recognition, where the one-in-a-thousand lover of a particular composer, believer in a nontraditional religion, or fan of a sport with few followers can locate legions of the like-minded. The larger the city, the easier it is to find both anonymity and common identity. In nineteenth-century Chicago, the presence and variety of countless minorities became, in effect, an index of how far the urbanization process had advanced.

The dining public made up one of those minorities. In many ways, food became part of everyone's singularity. We have seen how Chicago's dependence on outsiders for supplies to meet everyday household needs created risks and the need to cope, but the need to eat away from home compounded all of those problems. When Chicagoans began to commute to jobs located too far from home to eat all meals there, or when they dined out to celebrate some special event, they placed their food consumption experience—and occasionally their health—in the hands of strangers who were responsible for buying, storing, preparing, and serving the meal. Often, the success of any restaurant as an entrepreneurial venture depended not only on the quality of the food and service, but also on whether there were enough customers—minority food consumers—who shared a desire to partake of a particular cuisine at a given location. The larger and more diverse the city, the better the chance of success.

The Lobster Died in Cleveland

Although Chicago was the nation's fastest-growing metropolis in 1878, it was no culinary paradise. The *Chicago Tribune*'s Paris correspondent, who no doubt knew better, complained that it was "probably the worst off in this one essential of any great American city. . . . Chicago [has] not yet developed a restaurant where the splendid edibles of America are decently cooked and served at honorable prices." Instead, he wrote, Chicagoans preferred "jamming hot jumbles from 'lunch counters' into themselves in four minutes."[1]

The *Tribune* correspondent was right about one thing: the dining experience was a reflection of a city's maturity and stature. Contemporary Chicagoans could point with pride to the wealth and diversity of food available in their city, but the earliest dining fare grew out of the isolation of the frontier. Pioneer inns in the village and region served native fish and fowl, usually accompanied by corn dishes. Hogs were the favorite source of meat, in large part because pork was easily smoked or preserved in salt for long-term storage. Venison, processed from deer killed on the outskirts of the village, added a small measure of variety, as did fish hauled from the Chicago River. As late as 1841, hundred-pound sturgeon could still be found in the slow-flowing stream. In a gem of understatement, Joseph Balestier, a lawyer who was also Chicago's first historian, noted in 1840 that "the table had no charms for the epicure."[2]

Contact with the outside world stimulated change, beginning with a steady stream of westbound settlers who poured from the lake boats and tarried a few days before boarding wagons to the frontier. By 1847 Chicagoans had responded to the opportunity by opening twenty-five hotels in a city that numbered fewer than seventeen thousand residents, and the service at each helped fix the image of Chicago in the traveler's mind. While farmers grumbled about skimpy "shinbone steaks," one hotel dining room tried to be elegant. As noted earlier, the Lake House, originally built in 1835 as Chicago's first brick hotel, introduced such amenities as napkins and printed menus to the town. Other places boasted food "served up New York style" or dinners "with all the luxuries of the East." Thus, the status of a restaurant was based on its being as un-Chicago-like as possible.[3]

Restaurant owners tried to outdo each other by importing foods from other regions, often at great expense: oysters and clams from New England, apples from New York, oranges and lemons from New Orleans. Perhaps no event symbolized the city's effort to import exotic delicacies more than what happened in 1842. The press reported that "our epicures were thrown into intense excitement" over the effort to bring the first live New England lobster to Chicago. Despite all the strenuous efforts to run ships at full speed and change the crustacean's supply of salt water, it survived the trip only as far as Cleveland. There it had to be cooked and then shipped the rest of the way on ice.[4]

By the 1850s the growing size and sophistication of the dining clientele made it feasible to open restaurants as specialized businesses that were separate from hotels. There were coffeehouses for quick, light meals and "gentlemen's restaurants," where liquor was the main attraction. "Ice cream and eating saloons," on the other hand, were deemed safe for women and children. One of the latter establishments was operated by a Mrs. Anderson, who boasted that she "has had much experience keeping a fashionable restaurant in one of the Eastern cities." The growing competition often made decor seem as important as the food. One place claimed to have exclusive marble-topped tables, while the new lamp at the Washington, an 1849 ad proclaimed, "takes the rag off all the coffeehouse lamps in town."[5]

During the middle decades of the century the city's emerging commercial elite—perhaps reflecting its self-consciousness—began using grand, ostentatious dinners to greet visiting dignitaries and advertise its own successes. In 1855, hotel owner John B. Drake held the first of what would become the city's most famous feast, the annual game dinner. Each year Drake's cooks boiled, broiled, and roasted a veritable zoo of animals, largely representing the wildlife that once inhabited the region. By 1888 Drake was offering sixty-eight different wild game dishes to more than five hundred invited guests. The "groaning boards" and the resulting indigestion had come to symbolize the conquest of the frontier by "civilization."[6]

Dining sophistication trickled down the social scale. Many wealthy Chicagoans used the city's new rail connections to become seasoned travelers and sample the best restaurants of the nation and the world. For them, dining out became a social ritual, a form of entertainment, and a way to escape from the cares of making money. At the same time, thousands of the easterners who arrived by rail each day on their way elsewhere began to demand more sophisticated fare. The out-of-town trade was important, but local patronage was also necessary to keep any restaurant venture alive. It was not easy, however, to convince the bulk of the citizenry to support fancier local establishments. A Chicago branch of New York's famous Delmonico's was closed by the sheriff after only a few months because, it was said, practical-minded Chicagoans refused to pay high prices for food. Even before that, the disruptions of the Civil War and the Great Fire of 1871 had inhibited many attempts to bring fine dining to the city.[7]

By the late 1870s, however, the rebuilt city was entering a golden age of dining. One 1875 newspaper account placed the daily patronage of restaurants at fifty thousand—twice the per-capita rate of St. Louis, Cincinnati, or Boston—and went on to claim that the "investments and profits represented in it now aggregate from $8,000,000 to $10,000,000." Much of this growth was due to the emergence of a group of highly skilled and innovative professional chefs. While they competed for dining dollars, they also realized that their cooperative promotion of fine food could enlarge the pool of patrons. In 1877, the Meat Cooks', Pastry Cooks' and Confectioners' Cosmopolitan Society was formed to promote fine cooking; its annual banquet and food display convinced even pragmatic Chicagoans that their city need not be a backwater burg.[8]

Chicago's emergence as a railroad, commercial, and industrial giant, along with the excitement and crowds generated by the World's Columbian Exposition, also helped launch the great downtown restaurants. These establishments became symbols of the new urban civilization, much like the skyscrapers whose business activities helped fill them. What made the great ones great? Besides the food, it was atmosphere, either plain or opulent, that generated an identifiable personality for each house. Onyx, marble, electric lights, plate glass mirrors, tropical plants, paintings, mosaics, fine paneling, polished brass fittings, and electric ceiling fans drew trade to places with names as exotic as The Frogs or Milan and Company or The Peacock Cafe. These spots also became the favorite haunts of out-of-towners who wanted to gawk at notable Chicagoans and famous travelers.[9]

While all eateries were concerned about ambience, a large seating capacity and widespread name recognition allowed some places to function as department stores of dining. Only a major downtown area could attract a clientele large enough to support a restaurant the size of H. M. Kinsley's new place, which opened in 1885. It featured specialized kitchens and chefs for pastry and baking. Upstairs, there were separate rooms for ladies' and men's lunches, a "ladies and gentlemen's cafe" (bar), and private dining and banquet rooms of various sizes—all in addition to the regular dining rooms. Rector's, another large place, had five floors of cafes and dining rooms linked by elevators. Major hotels, such as the one in the Auditorium, provided duplicate luncheon and dining facilities, as well as a separate entrance, elevators, and parlor for unaccompanied women. This was the logic of urban centralization at work; many different dining demands could be met most efficiently and with greatest choice in one central location.[10]

Most other dining establishments of the late nineteenth century used their central location and the large draw provided by transportation, as well as their particular cuisines, to target smaller audiences. The "sporting crowd" (often a euphemism for gamblers) and politicians preferred Billy Boyle's Chop House or Abson's English Chop House. The latter was situated at the end of Pickwick Lane, the narrow passageway at 22 East Jackson, in a quaint little building that had reputedly survived the Great Fire. The theater crowd preferred glittery places, such as The Frogs or the more reserved Auditorium Cafe in the famous theater-hotel building. Old-timers gravitated to Chapin and Gore, where caricatures of notable Chicagoans lined the walls. Midwesterners' fascination with seafood could be satisfied at the Boston Oyster House, which finally succeeded in bringing a live lobster all the way to Chicago in 1873. The DeJonghe Hotel and Restaurant, another seafood emporium, left its permanent mark on American cuisine with a dish in which shrimp were sautéed in herbs and garlic butter; it is still known as shrimp DeJonghe.[11] Those with a taste for German fare patronized the Berghoff, which opened in 1898, while Henrici's, which began as a coffee shop in 1869, was the city's premiere Viennese restaurant.[12]

French cuisine, introduced in the 1870s, became a fad during the 1890s, according to one guidebook, because, "The attendants are polite, without ostentatious labor; the meats are good and the wines cheap . . . and the prices are always well-maintained." The *Chicago Record*'s columnist George Ade noted that Chicago had been slow to adapt to their wines, their sauces, and table d'hôte pricing. "There must have been a dozen abject failures in the ten years preceding the World's Fair," he wrote in 1894. "It was during the Fair that the tide turned. Who will ever know the full effect these visiting foreigners made on Chicago."[13]

Chicago dining was undergoing another transformation in hundreds of eateries located outside of the Loop. The growing size of immigrant enclaves not only created the market demand for many unusual ethnic ingredients sold by grocers and food peddlers, but it also fostered the creation of small restaurants and dining rooms that were often attached to saloons and coffeehouses. Milwaukee Avenue, Clark Street, Taylor Street, and every other main ethnic business thoroughfare had a few restaurants that served families in times of celebration and mourning, as well as in their search for a release from the stress of city life and work. Functioning much as saloons served working men, these spots provided a place where the native foods, drinks, music, dances, and languages were welcome. The division of many ethnic homelands into provinces led to entrepreneurial opportunities in the fragmentation of the trade into smaller, even more specialized establishments. For instance, in 1893, *L'Italia,* the local newspaper, found ten Italian restaurants "for those who want *chic* or elegance," nearly all of them featuring a different regional cuisine. During the 1890s, the variety of these institutions increased when the relatively simple ethnic structure of the earlier city—German, Irish, Scandinavian—gave way to a more complex pattern that now included many smaller groups from Asia, as well as southern and eastern Europe. In 1891 the press led verbal tours through the first Chinese restaurants, describing the cuisine and noting how patrons were expected to bus their own tables. Four years later, the influence of the World's Columbian Exposition had become clear. The *Times-Herald* described German, French, Spanish, Polish, Italian, Bohemian, and Chinese places, adding the category of "Negro" to a feature on "Chicago's Foreign Restaurants." Within the decade the list had expanded to include Greek, Turkish, Jewish, and Syrian restaurants.[14]

The 1890s also saw several prominent women enter the restaurant field after their husbands suffered financial reverses. Mrs. L. W. Haring had been known for the dinners prepared for family guests, but when her husband lost his business, she opened a tearoom. Some of the dishes came directly from her kitchen; other women in similar circumstances delivered the rest. Economic necessity brought four other housewives into the catering, tearoom, and restaurant business. One French-educated elite woman, who had "learned scientific cooking," managed to remain anonymous. "When after years of opulence," noted the *Tribune,* "a time came that she needed funds which were not forthcoming she utilized this knowledge in a way which shows what the most delicately bred women do to make ends meet should the proverbial rainy day find them unprepared."[15]

Many restaurants were little more than informal extensions of a good cook's kitchen. The lower down the economic scale, the less distinct the division between semipublic commercial spaces and the private domicile. In his "Stories of the Streets and of the Town" column, George Ade described a tiny African-American eatery called Aunt Mary's. Patrons entered the restaurant— marked only by a sign reading "Chidlins, 15 cents"—through a whitewashed basement door at the bottom of a steep flight of stairs. In the low room inside illuminated only by kerosene lamps, the proprietress served platters of hog snouts, honeycomb tripe, pig's tail, and other delicacies of the rural South to customers who occasionally included whites hungry for a taste of home. It was a social gathering place as well, as the diners lingered and chatted long after the last bone had been picked clean. Lost in the anonymity of the sparsely documented world of the urban poor, Aunt Mary may or may not have existed, but her type represented a form of survival, an independent woman who utilized rather than succumbed to the gender and racial roles assigned by society.[16]

While serious diners were attempting to cope with the diversity of Chicago cuisine, restaurateurs faced three new challenges as the twentieth century began. The root of their grief was the manner in which their desire to satisfy customers forced them to break down the narrow distinction between saloons (drinking houses that served food) and restaurants (eating houses that served liquor). The two enterprises had coexisted peacefully until reformers launched new efforts to curb the influence of the barroom on the city's social life. In 1903, the whole industry was drawn together behind the efforts of the Chicago Restaurant Keepers Association to keep local authorities from shutting their establishments on Sundays. Early the next year restaurant owners managed to persuade the Chicago City Council to extend the closing hour from midnight to 1:00 A.M.[17] Music caused another problem. Competition drove some fine dining establishments to hire orchestras, an expense that forced some old houses to close. Many patrons complained that the intrusion of music was another sign of the decline of the fine art of conversation. Yet, when the police department tried to quiet honky-tonk saloons by banning all live music performances after 11:30 P.M., influential downtown owners lobbied Mayor Carter Harrison II, who lifted the restriction.[18] In 1906, however, many restaurateurs were unable to overcome the challenge of a new $1,000 liquor license rate, which applied to them even if they only served beer or wine as a sideline. Hundreds of smaller, outlying eateries either closed, dropped wine from the menu, bribed the police, or simply hoped to evade detection. Others found a compromise by providing glassware and opening the bottles brought in by customers.[19]

Nothing, however, affected the prestige of dining establishments as much as city restaurant licensing. A new ordinance passed in 1906 was ostensibly a revenue measure, but it also reflected the same interest in consumer protection that reformed the produce markets and drove food vendors from the streets. It provided for unannounced city health department inspections along guidelines provided by the Illinois state food inspector, who had the right of access without warning. Although violations closed relatively few among the 2,500 Chicago restaurants, owners viewed it as a challenge to the sense of trust in quality and cleanliness that underlay their relationship with customers.[20]

The new regulations resulted in few visible changes, as Chicagoans and visitors alike continued to make the Loop the focus of fine dining. Although some of the old restaurants, including Kinsley's and Rector's, closed rather than comply, others took their place. The large hotels not only upgraded their restaurants, becoming a more important factor in fine dining, but they also began adding cabaret facilities when that fad hit Chicago in 1913. A couple "on the town" could thus stay in the same building for a whole evening out. At the same time, many of the downtown eating spots attained a nationwide reputation for specialized clienteles, some establishments catering to "the newspaper crowd," others to show business people, and still others to after-theater diners.[21]

By the 1920s, however, the dining habits of Chicagoans were beginning to reflect the trend toward population dispersal. The expansion of commercial activities outward from the Loop had begun to erode the status of older elite neighborhoods near the downtown; this took place just as some of the last of the generation that had built the old mansions died off. Many of the old buildings became rooming houses, but not all. "Automobile Row," the strip of dealers and garages along Michigan Avenue, had brought traffic and noise to nearby Prairie Avenue by 1920. Soon afterward a French restaurant opened in the house Marshall Field built for his sister at 1922 Calumet Avenue. On the North Side, the same transition took place on a larger scale after the new Michigan Avenue Bridge opened in 1920. Several mansions became fine restaurants, including the home of Julian Rumsey, Chicago's Civil War mayor, which ironically opened as the "Southern Tea Shop." The mansion built by dry-goods merchant John B. Farwell was taken over by Gaston Alciatore of the famous New Orleans restaurant family.[22]

The outward dispersal from the Loop, which often led to lower rents and easier access by automobile, also fueled a wave of eclecticism among restaurants. That, in turn, reinforced the growing belief that fine dining should be an unusual experience of eye-catching surroundings as well as good food. Many diners flocked to the unusual eateries of "Towertown," the area of bohemian bookstores, coffeehouses, and art galleries that stretched between the Water Tower and "Bughouse Square," the common nickname for Washington Square Park opposite the Newberry Library. Some wanted to see the artists who hung out at the Round Table Inn or the Dill Pickle on Tooker Place. Others deliberately sought cheaper places that revealed the "real Chicago," such as the Noose Coffeeshop, whose proprietor donated the last meals that were fed prisoners awaiting execution at the nearby county jail.[23]

A second trend of the 1920s, one that intensified as the Great Depression gradually bore down on the city, was the rediscovery of something Chicago had possessed for decades: a complex mix of ethnic cuisines that guidebooks had routinely ignored. Diners could move gradually toward this heritage by first patronizing what might called "tourist ethnic" houses. Like the Berghoff and other German counterparts, which had long been favorites, these were more expensive places that were often located outside of the actual ethnic neighborhoods. One guidebook described the Japanese Lunch Room in the Stevens Hotel and advised readers that the chef of Casa de Alex on East Delaware Place "knows her muttons."[24] Trusted newspaper food critics, such as John Drury and Bruce Grant, gave careful instructions about visiting Italian, Jewish, Bohemian, Polish, Scandinavian, and other cuisines, omitting only African-American cookery. Drury advised that in one Russian restaurant operated by a communist cooperative, "The foods are highly appetizing, if a bit heavy; the atmosphere comes up to expectations, and you needn't be afraid that anyone will toss a bomb."[25]

Thus, during Chicago's first century, the food habits of many of its citizens reached levels of sophistication undreamed of in the 1830s. In the city there were professional chefs, internationally famous restaurants, a flood of recipes, cooking lessons for the poor, and the recognition of ethnic heritages. Yet many people also sought "Toothpick Row," the lunchrooms near Clark and Madison, where they could find the simple dishes that Drury described as "an emerging school of American cookery."[26] That idea had gained poignant expression as early as 1912, when a *Chicago Record-Herald* editorial writer pined for the old days:

> Just how many years it has been since the last American meal was served in the "Loop" it would be hard to say, but it has been many, many, years. There was something fresh and unspoiled in the American character, a little primitive, no doubt, but appetizing and decidedly wholesome.
>
> The great point of the American meal was its candor. Food then wore no elaborate disguise and was not ashamed of its origin . . . and no glib waiter could seduce you into betraying your stomach. Everything stood or fell by its native quality. But now that the standardized menu, a mongrel product out of European ingenuity by American prodigality, has ousted the American bill of fare, you may dine from Maine to California on precisely the same stale dishes and be hungry after all.[27]

You can't please everyone.

Lunching: A Knife, a Fork, and a Clock

The event had all the elements of a page-one crime story, a tale that was becoming all too common in Chicago of 1890. A gunman named Oscar Schneider had confronted his hapless victim at noontime on Clark Street and fired pointblank at his stomach. The shot struck with a thud, but then, to everyone's surprise, it fell harmlessly to his shoe. A miracle? The lucky placement of a belt buckle? Not according to the *Chicago Mail,* which covered the story. The victim, it seems, had just finished a Chicago lunch. "The next time a man feels inclined to swear at the leaden lump in his stomach purchased in a Chicago restaurant," noted the reporter, "he will do well to remember this incident."[28]

Most lunches were far more uneventful, and, in fact, during the city's pioneer days most Chicagoans did not consider lunch to be a special meal. A few inns, such as Mark Beaubien's Sauganash near the present-day corner of Wabash and Wacker Drive, took care of the noon-hour needs of travelers, but the proximity of residence and work in the compact little town allowed locals to go home at midday. The wealthy, whose homes were in Terrace Row or other grand Michigan Avenue blocks, lived the shortest distance away. Convenience was especially important for the ethnic groups from Western Europe or Scandinavia, who regarded the noon meal as the most important of the day. Even those of modest circumstances, who then resided on the inconvenient fringe of town, could walk the mile or so home. For instance, in his description of Chicago in 1868, William Corkran, the newly arrived librarian of the historical society, told of the way clerks rushed back to their North Side boardinghouses for a quick noon meal, always fearful of being cut off from downtown by slow-moving boats that caused the swing bridge to turn.[29]

Beginning in the 1850s, however, three interconnected and simultaneous changes had begun to take place. First, in a quiet process that involved thousands of individual decisions made over the course of many years, city dwellers began to use the various kinds of city spaces in different and more specialized ways. Second, Chicago's class structure took on a geographical dimension as the city increasingly divided itself into more homogeneous areas of wealth and social standing. The amount of money each family had to spend on housing allowed it to buy or rent a portion of urban space in a district of the city that possessed a particular level of wealth. Simply put, the rich lived with the rich, the poor with the poor. Third, the early jumble of land uses in pioneer Chicago—stores next to houses next to small factories—gradually settled out into retail, wholesale, and manufacturing districts, all three of which were increasingly nonresidential and therefore distinct from areas where people lived. The increase in the population of different foreign-born groups allowed each to create and sustain its own separate neighborhood or enclave, and this sorting process fostered the development of distinct ethnic institutions and businesses, including restaurants.[30]

The daily problem of how to get from here to there was essential to this sorting process. The transformation from a city of walkers to a city of commuters not only turned pleasant boulevards into rush-hour arteries, but also promoted an outward growth of city and suburb that placed miles rather than blocks between home and work for thousands of people. Soon, only those who still lived close to their work—often workers who were too poor to move out from the shadow of factories—could ignore the nagging question of what to do for lunch. At the same time, the need for efficiency in the operation of larger factories and stores led to short and carefully timed noonday meals for employees. Chicagoans found that, while breakfast time and dinner could be extended by arising earlier or going to bed later, the meal in between was of a defined length often determined by someone else. As a result, the search for something to eat at noon became an urgent necessity. This change was complicated by the city's emergence as a rail hub, which brought in thousands of travelers each day who had to transfer between stations and wait for outbound trains. This army of nonresident noon-hour diners competed with the locals for a place in line or a seat at a downtown counter. Lunchtime became part of coping with Chicago.[31]

Henrici's Restaurant, postcard view, ca. 1910 The patrons of this famous Randolph Street eatery enjoyed German and other continental cuisine in an elegant setting. Its site is now occupied by the Daley Center.

Joy Yet Lo Chinese Restaurant advertisement, Garrick Theatre program, 1913. This Chinese restaurant overcame cultural biases and attracted middle-class and wealthy theatergoers by offering Americanized settings outside of Chinatown and even hiring a Hungarian orchestra.

"Whiskey Row," in the "Back of the Yards" neighborhood, postcard view, ca. 1900. Packinghouse workers enjoy their lunches, which they carry to work in "growlers" that also serve as pails to hold their noontime beer.

"Working Men's Kitchen," 1900. The proprietress of this lunch room could make a decent profit in the inelegant factory district setting. (Chicago Historical Society, ICHi 15113)

Burlington Diner, postcard view, probably 1950s. Many former railroad dining cars ended their careers as short-order restaurants. "The Most Beautiful Diner in Chicago" was at 4183 S. Halsted.

The elite turned the situation to their advantage. Members of private clubs were able to escape the crowds and dine amidst select company in a private space. The Chicago Club had been the first, in 1869, followed by fifteen others during the next two decades. The need to conduct business deals, discuss politics, and even launch civic reform crusades made the noon hour a major social event among the city's business leadership, most of whom were also able to determine the speed and length of their lunches. Because so many business people now lived in outlying neighborhoods and wealthy suburbs, they tended to make the most of their midday contacts. At the same time, lunch essentially became a reward for coping with the inconvenience and difficulties of the commute. Society luncheons, often conducted in connection with charitable or social events, provided similar opportunities for elite women to gather downtown.[32]

It was different for those who had to seek victuals more publicly. During the last three decades of the nineteenth century, a variety of entrepreneurs began to discover profit in providing solutions to the daily dining dilemma. The growing size of the trade tended to produce eateries that targeted specialized markets. Great downtown restaurants, including Kinsley's, Henrici's, Rector's, DeJonghe's, and the Berghoff, provided elegant midday meals. Although these were semipublic rather than private places and the cast of fellow eaters less exclusive than in clubs, these restaurants were tightly controlled spaces. The reputation and high prices kept many people away, and not everyone could get past the *maitre d'* and be served. Unlike the private clubs, even the fine restaurants were highly competitive and some dining spots had to offer novelties to draw in customers. The

Chicago Stock Exchange Restaurant, for instance, served plates of either bull or bear meat, depending on that morning's stock market trend.[33]

The vast majority of Chicagoans found lunchtime a hurried, fretful, and often joyless venture among the city's anonymous crowds. Although there had probably been precedents in older eastern cities, the mass charity feedings that followed in the wake of the Great Fire seemed to instill in Chicagoans the lesson that efficiency was far more important than comfort. Victims who had lost everything sat on hard wooden plank benches that subtly encouraged them to eat as quickly as possible. By the early 1880s there were many nickel-and-dime lunch counters where similarly uncomfortable stools guaranteed a quick turnover. In some places the utensils were chained to the counter, lest diners claim a treasure. "Ah, those Americans sitting at their lunch-counters with knife and fork," commented the essayist Max O'Reill, "it looked for all the world like 500 men playing the dulcimer." The fare was simple and often the butt of jokes. The one about making the chicken soup by letting the bird run through water was already making the rounds in 1882. One *Daily News* reporter estimated that three-fourths of the 100,000 or so citizens who ate lunch downtown had neither time nor money for anything more than a piece of pie and a cup of coffee or a glass of milk.[34]

The repetitive nature of the daily necessity produced customs and rituals. Some of the cheapest eating places sent out men clad in sandwich-board signs or black rubber all-weather suits decorated with ads for daily specials. Inside the restaurant, speed took its toll on service. Because diners expected the quick lunch to be cheaper than dinner, proprietors often had no choice but to reduce profit margins in favor of faster turnover. This, in turn, meant that the goal was the maximum profit from each seat, rather than from each diner. Patrons could select from a limited choice of entrées, which were often cooked in advance and kept warm on a steam table, while "lunch-cutters" took pride in slicing paper-thin pieces of meat with lightning speed. The rushed patrons as well as the owners who were seeking quick turnover appreciated the reduction in waiting time. Savvy owners also carefully planned the placement of tables, counters, doors, and the cash register to make most efficient use of the space, reduce lines, and make it difficult to leave without paying. Waiters recorded orders in special receipt books invented for the purpose, then employed their own cryptic language of hand signals and shouts—"Draw one in the dark" (black coffee), "slaughter in the pan" (steak), or "white wings" (poached eggs), for instance—to convey the message to the kitchen above the din of business. One restaurant's waiters had to learn twenty-five different gestures that referred to different meats and how well cooked they were ordered.[35]

The competitive nature of the lower-price houses led to the creation of the most famous of all of the lunch customs. During the early 1870s a Chicago saloonkeeper named Joseph Chesterfield Mackin began giving away a free oyster with each beer in his downtown bar. Although his original purpose had been to further his political ambitions by creating an image of generosity, Mackin had, in fact, invented Chicago's first unique contribution to national noon-hour traditions: the free lunch. To remain competitive, saloons across Chicago, and then the nation, gradually copied the idea. Some of the grander bars set out spreads fancy enough to draw the masculine trade away from the better restaurants, which countered by opening bars of their own. Both saloons and restaurants tried to draw the more affluent customers by providing small conference rooms where customers could conduct business.[36]

A much simpler fare greeted workers at bars near factories, where they already enjoyed a bargain in getting their large pails, or "growlers," filled with beer for a dime. Proprietors put out cheap meats, cold cheese, condiments, and crackers that were often meant to supplement rather than replace the lunches prepared at home and carried to work in the growler. The quality of these spreads no doubt varied, and rumors abounded that tainted meat that could not be sold to other customers ended up on the saloon sideboard.[37] By the 1890s, the success of the free lunch, in turn, began to worry temperance societies as well as restaurants. Groups like the St. Luke's Society tried to counter the saloon's offerings by establishing "penny lunch rooms," which drew thousands but failed to close down even the nearby barroom sideboards.[38]

The gender-separation of city spaces created special lunchtime problems for women of all classes who ventured out to work or shop. Because men began working away from home both in an earlier period and in much larger numbers, most lunching spaces catered primarily to males. Smoking and off-color jokes added to the masculine atmosphere of many places. Women had to seek alternatives. Those who could afford a higher tab could retreat to the better restaurants, some of which provided separate dining rooms. By the early 1890s, the major department stores had all opened eateries for the convenience of customers, most of whom were women, but these were often too expensive for female workers to patronize every day. Meanwhile, working-class women were excluded by custom from Loop saloons, while low-priced street-level alternatives to the male-dominated cheap counters were difficult to find. The Mrs. Clark Co. Lunch Room on Wabash became the most popular dining spot among women, but others either went hungry or made do with a few things brought from home.[39]

In 1897 the *Tribune* worried aloud about moral risks involved in a new alternative. "Just at the noon hour," it advised, "when the shopping girl is feeling the effects of the crushing she received at the bargain counter and is desirous of getting a bite to eat for recuperative purposes, she is more than likely nowadays to turn her steps toward the candy store or the drug store rather than in the direction of the restaurant." Cost, speedier service, and sweet tastes were the main attractions, but the paper warned of a peril: the "sherry flip," "egg punch," or "claret sangaree" contained alcohol "strong enough to answer the purpose of a mixed drink bill-of-fare for any saloon in town." Not only was the feminine customer vulnerable to harm that afternoon, but the next-day consequences included listlessness and a headache.[40]

By the early 1890s, the growing ranks of women working as low-paid store clerks and office secretaries, as well as in the printing and garment trades located on the fringes of the downtown, began to create their own dining opportunities. During the first four years of the 1890s, working women began to form clubs that provided a place to dine as well as rooms for noon-hour rest and relaxation. While many members economized by bringing lunches from home, others purchased inexpensive food provided at cost. For instance, the Woman's Exchange, which had started as a salesroom for articles made by impoverished women, had no trouble filling its dining room, which was established in 1884 on Wabash, near Madison. The Wildwood Club (1891), which was operated by alumnae of a private school, the Ursula (1891), and the Klio Association's Noon-Day Rest (1894) also provided meals. The most innovative, however, was the Ogontz Club, located in the Pontiac Building at Printer's Row. Its dining members decided to reduce the overhead and eliminate what they regarded as a demeaning task of waitressing by lining up to serve themselves as they passed a table laden with platters and dishes. Thus was born Chicago's second great gift to America's lunching traditions: the cafeteria. Soon, a Mrs. Knox, who had been manager of the Noon-Day Rest, opened a commercial version of the arrangement, while another restaurateur, who was reputedly from New Mexico, became the first in the city to borrow the Spanish word *cafeteria* to designate his new self-service restaurant.[41]

The most significant innovation to appear in the late nineteenth century was the chain operation. Owners who ran chains of restaurants realized that economies of scale in large purchases of supplies, along with instant name recognition and the saturation of downtown markets, gave them a competitive advantage over independent operations. Diners recognized that these places offered fare that was far from gourmet, but the quality and quantity of the food was fairly predictable and uniform in all of the outlets. One guidebook credited H. H. Kohlsaat, a restaurateur who also owned the *Chicago Inter-Ocean,* with inventing the cheap Chicago lunch counter, which was always located on the main floor for convenience. "You sit on a low stool, hat on, people waiting for your seat, no napkin, but quick service," it noted. The menu featured cold sandwiches, with few hot dishes and "nothing that required special preparation."[42] In the early 1890s, Kohlsaat already had seven outlets, and the Troy Lunch, three. By 1908, the ranks of the quick-lunch chains had grown to include fourteen Pittsburgh Joe, ten H. H. Kohlsaat, six Emil Reick, and five Baltimore Dairy Lunch outlets in the Loop alone. The fastest growing chain was owned by John R. Thompson, who opened his first restaurant soon after he arrived in Chicago in 1891. Using one-arm chairs for easy access to counters, standard menus, and large-scale supply purchases to maximize profit, his chain grew to eight outlets in 1900 and thirty-nine in Chicago by 1914, all but seven of them in the Loop. A similar operation, the Weeghman chain, featured a white tile decor to emphasize cleanliness, a punched-check bill to minimize confusion, and coffee served in special mugs to reduce both spilling and the number of dishes to wash.

Thousands of Chicagoans, both men and women, also bought cheap lunches on the street. Some peddlers remained in fixed locations, often on sidewalk space rented from store owners, where steady customers could easily find them. Others sold to a clientele that gathered in downtown alleys. Food vendors who pushed their carts through the streets usually followed a regular route and schedule that was attuned to the temporal rhythm of the city. Many started out the day by selling hand-held waffles to rooming-house residents who needed a quick breakfast. Then the carts moved on to the Loop, where their appearance at a regular corner and their standard fare added an element of predictability to the noon meals of "regulars." Many of the food wagons moved on to construction sites, where foremen allowed workers to take a brief afternoon break. They finally rolled around to newspaper plants and factories to serve all-night workers. The cart sellers' fare was limited to food eaten out of hand, which tested their ingenuity. To the standard sausages and sandwiches they added such items as popcorn balls, hot corn-on-the-cob, watermelon slices, and ice cream dished up on a piece of paper. Occasionally there were exciting developments, such as the tamale fad of the early 1890s. Within months of the introduction of this item there were reportedly more than three hundred *tamaleros* cruising Chicago's streets.[43]

The nighttime sandwich wagon was "considered as much of an institution in Chicago as the baked potato or fried fish stands are of English cities." The first one, which developed sometime in the early 1890s, grew out of a candymaker's failed gimmick. A vendor of sweets had a car manufactured with glass sides and a built-in stove, hoping that curbside customers would buy the candy they saw him make. When it failed, another entrepreneur spotted it parked in a rear yard, removed the glass, and gave it a fresh paint job. (Neat-looking wagons assured customers that the food was clean.) Then he took to the street. Others copied the idea, especially when the World's Columbian Exposition brought huge crowds to the city. In the years that followed, newsboys, passengers arriving on late trains, pavement-construction workers, janitors, and others who traveled the streets after dark could put as much as fifty dollars a night in the proprietor's till.[44]

Not everyone was happy with the movable feast. By the turn of the century a combination of interests had launched a campaign to drive the sidewalk and curbside food-sellers off the Loop streets. Inexpensive restaurants complained that the peddlers' free use of the streets gave them an unfair edge over those who had to pay rent or property taxes. Civic boosters objected to the noise and litter left behind on downtown sidewalks and streets. Other people complained of the disruption caused by the invasion of "lunch cars" into residential areas. The most important objection came from public-health experts, who warned that food sold outdoors was exposed to airborne disease-causing contaminants, especially clouds of dry horse manure. The result was a crackdown that by 1902 left the ranks of prepared-food vendors considerably reduced.[45]

Another tradition, the saloon lunch, came under attack from both predictable and unexpected sources. In 1903, restaurant keepers reportedly sponsored proposed anti-free-lunch legislation in Springfield. But concerns about the effect of barroom visits on workers' efficiency led mail-order mogul A. Montgomery Ward, the Chicago, Burlington, and Quincy and Chicago Great Western railroads, and other industrial managers to declare a ban on employees' lunching where liquor was served. Ward hired private detectives to follow his workers and photograph them emerging from barrooms to obtain evidence used for dismissals. The need for alternative dining facilities led to the opening of company lunchrooms, a trend that grew during the first two decades of the century.[46] In 1910, health department inspectors launched yet another attack on saloonkeepers, this time for lunches that violated health codes because of fly specks on uncovered dishes, lack of proper refrigeration, and forks used in common without being washed. In 1917 the city council, supposedly acting to reduce saloon patronage during wartime, prohibited the free lunch altogether.[47]

Finally, many noontime diners were forced to cope with mechanization. Some bar owners tried to coax a few extra coins from customers by installing coin-operated vending machines that dispensed peanuts in lieu of the friendly free lunch.[48] The most impersonal lunching place of all, the automat, made its debut in Chicago in 1917. This operation involved a large dining room, one wall of which was covered with small windowed compartments, each containing an individual dish of food. Patrons inserted either coins or tokens to open each door and take the item they wanted. They did not have to wait for a check, and there was never a dispute over the total. Although automats became popular on the East Coast, they enjoyed only moderate success competing against established lunch chains in the Windy City.[49]

Children faced the same noon-hour challenge as adults in the workplace and turned to the same alternatives. Vendors' wagons lined up in streets adjacent to schools to serve those who did not carry lunches, and the same frantic race against time recurred day after day. George Ade wrote about a virtual foot race of high schoolers, most of whom were young women, who swept toward nearby lunchrooms or to seek a shaded boulder that could serve as a table.[50]

The example of the saloon-substitute, along with the efficiency of mass-feeding made possible by chain lunch operations, inspired those who sought to combat the decades-old problem of hunger among the school-age children of the poor. The school board had established lunchrooms in a few schools as far back as 1902, but the facilities were beyond the means of most poor children and the food was described by the *Record-Herald* as "so unwholesome and unhygienic that teachers and students are suffering from gastronomic disturbances." In May 1908 the school board conducted an investigation that discovered that five thousand children arrived at school each day without breakfast and that ten thousand were "habitually hungry." However, because of the widespread belief that free lunches would be detrimental to the initiative and self-responsibility of the students and their families, the board allowed charities to operate soup lines in only two of the most impoverished schools. The answer to the dilemma came in 1910, when a group of Chicago women visited Cincinnati, where the local Council of Jewish Women had started a "Penny Lunch Center." The success of that experiment inspired the Chicago Woman's Club to undertake a similar privately financed test program in one slum school. School officials gave it credit for a sharp reduction in truancy and illness, as well as a marked improvement in classroom performance. Within three years, the Board of Education had essentially taken over the project, and by 1916 there were lunch programs in twenty-six schools, just the beginning of what would become a citywide service.[51]

Meanwhile, coping with the noon-hour frenzy meant dealing with changes brought on by World War I and evolving social patterns. Lunch places had become much more common than before. Many of the former saloons had reopened as quick sandwich outlets. The bar and foot rail were easily adapted to stand-up dining, which owners appreciated for its contribution to the fast turnover of customers. While many of the former saloons retained a masculine atmosphere, women flocked to the more feminine decor and light fare of sandwiches and salads of the tearoom. Many of these places, which were often located in low-rent spaces above the first floor in downtown shop buildings, were owned and operated by women as well.[52]

By the 1920s the school lunchroom had become a model for dining facilities offered by many private businesses. With the saloon at least officially eliminated as a competitor, many utility companies, department stores, and others opened their own employee lunchrooms. Some of them used sound systems to pipe in programs to "inform" a captive audience of employees about Americanization, wage issues, and the evils of unions.[53]

Also by the 1920s, Chicagoans had become accustomed to lunching at the drugstore lunch counter. This was the third of the city's contributions to the American lunch-hour tradition. The story dates back to 1908, not long after Charles R. Walgreen moved the family store from Dixon, Illinois, to Chicago. His wife, Myrtle, began serving sandwiches and beverages in the store as an income-producing sideline. The idea was an instant success. The substantial flow of pharmacy customers brought crowds past the lunch counter, while those who dined there often took a few moments to browse among the store's other counters.[54]

The issues of health and restaurant sanitation in Chicago had largely disappeared by the second decade of this century.[55] The inherent trust of customers in the quality of a restaurant meal helped increase the rate of dining out. The food industry could concentrate on responding to the changing social and transportation patterns of the city. Some of the cafeterias had evolved into large-scale operations that served all three daily meals to participants in the frenetic lifestyle of the Jazz Age. For instance, the Ontra Cafeteria chain had been started downtown in 1909 by Miss Mary Dutton, self-described as "a woman past fifty." Although she retained two Loop locations, during the early 1920s Dutton opened one of the largest cafeterias in America, seating 1,226, not in the Loop but in the booming Uptown neighborhood. Her business was in a logical location because it served the needs of those living in over ninety apartment hotels, as well as hundreds of leased-space apartment buildings. Most of the 400,000 Uptown-area residents were singles or childless couples who worked during the day, frequented the theaters, clubs, and dance halls at night, and took the majority of their meals outside of their living quarters.[56]

Many lunch places, chain and independent, appeared along busily traveled outlying streets. Here, a transition in ethnic ownership was already under way. By 1919, John Raklios, a Greek immigrant, had built his "luncheonette" business to nineteen outlets, no doubt providing one of the examples mentioned by the editor of a leading publication in the field: "I have been told that the greatest profits in the feeding business are made in the lunch rooms, and I find that the lunchroom business is almost entirely monopolized by Greeks. Why is it? They combine their places with soda fountains, confectionery stands, and the catch-the-nickel business. They are located mostly at or near the streetcar transfer corners. . . . Why is it that the American citizen who wants a profitable business don't [*sic*] see this opportunity as the Greeks see it?" The writer noted that a Greek-American proprietor would put in exhausting hours, save on expenses, and give customers exactly what they expected, nothing more, noting, "Apparently he is here to stay."[57]

The growth of these eateries and the public's desire for even faster service led to a new kind of food outlet that responded also to the dispersal of traffic in the new age of automobility. In 1928 the two-year-old White Tower Systems, headquartered in Milwaukee, built its first Chicago outlet. The following year, the older White Castle chain, based in Wichita, Kansas, opened its first Chicago restaurant on East Seventy-ninth Street. Both featured nickel hamburgers and limited—if any—seating in their tiny buildings.[58]

By the end of the 1930s each chapter in the story of lunchtime reflected the growing impact of geographical mobility and social diversity on dining habits. The bustling city that gave the world so many innovations in manufacturing, architecture, and literature also gave it the free lunch, the cafeteria, and the drugstore lunch counter.

And, most of what was served along the way would hardly stop a bullet.

Conclusion

Eating out has had a larger meaning than simply obtaining a good meal. It has been an index of urbanism. Unlike the farm or small town, the city had destinations of work, shopping, and leisure that were likely to be too far away for a quick return home for lunch. A place like Chicago presented many alternatives to the family meal at home. Cities are collections of choices, sometimes bewildering in their number and variety. Eating out obviously remains a more public experience than dining at home. Restaurants are semipublic places, part of a broad category of privately owned but publicly accessible spaces that included stores, saloons, and most other businesses. These have always been more numerous in cities than in small towns. Finally, eating out reflected another dimension of urbanism: depending on someone else, not just for the food itself, but also for the meal preparation, the delivery to the table, and the place where it is consumed.

The urban experience has always included dining outside of the home; the agglomeration of many people in one place can support eating places as well as a symphony orchestra. City populations have long contained those who seldom ate at home, as well as those for whom an evening out was a rare break from the daily trials and frustrations of life. Food became part of the way in which people coped with city life; the act of dining itself involved questions of choice, quality, variety, and ambience. Dining as escape often led to frustration and disappointment as well as pleasure. And at the same time, those who sold and served the food faced another set of frustrations in trying to make a profit.

The growing trend toward eating out also affected the lives of city dwellers. It tended to force a breakdown of at least some of the parochialism that accompanied ethnic and neighborhood foodways. Many workers responded by carrying a lunch bucket, which not only doubled as a growler beer pail, but also allowed a worker to carry around a bit of home, a portable social and ethnic identity. This custom worked best in a factory or shop setting, where nearby saloons catered to the particular ethnic makeup of the workforce. But lunch for many other workers was a very different experience. Female factory workers had to create alternatives to the saloon, while all of those who ended up working in the Loop discovered that the congested setting forced changes in the way they consumed the noon meal.

On another level of the dining-out experience, food was not the same as cuisine. For those who set the trends of high society in the city, what they ate, and where, became part of the process of creating images for Chicago. Food could become an indicator of style and status only where there were enough people around to care. For these individuals, food became an important part of the identity of the city as a whole, just as food had been an essential ingredient in the sense of neighborhood ethnic identity.

Postscript

The Great Depression dealt a devastating blow to all forms of the restaurant business except soup kitchens. Lunchrooms withered when nearby factories closed, while moderately priced places folded when families fragmented under the pressure of unemployment. Although the Berghoff, Henrici's, and other established institutions survived, only such special events as the Century of Progress Exposition in 1933–34 could bring back the crowds.[59] But during World War II, the trend toward eating out not only returned but accelerated. The disruption of family life and the hectic schedules of war workers left little time or inclination for many homemakers to labor for hours in the kitchen. Even though some favorite dishes were unavailable and the serving staff was occasionally inexperienced, eating in a restaurant meant avoiding the hassle of handling ration tokens and contending with shortages at the butcher shop. Large defense plants encouraged the dining-out trend by providing mammoth commissaries, while the Forum Cafeteria, Toffenetti's, and other chain eateries advertised themselves as perfect dinner-table meeting places for war-weary families.[60]

After the war, even the promise of the "kitchen of tomorrow" failed to reverse the eating-out trend. The same auto that took the family to the A&P or Jewel supermarket also stopped at the franchise food outlet. The ultimate automobile-oriented eatery was, of course, McDonald's. Although its origins lay in California, the genius of making it an American institution rested with Chicagoan Ray Kroc. A salesman for a malted-milk mixer company, he unconsciously drew upon the old formula for success that had worked for decades in the Chicago lunch business. Kroc systematized and standardized supply and production techniques, created a recognizable sign and building style, established a franchise system, and located his outlets at strategic points in traffic flows. Everyone knows that his first franchise outlet in suburban Des Plaines in 1955 not only grew into a giant chain but helped make the "burger 'n' fries" into America's standard lunch.[61]

Many of those who ate out each noon were children. In 1946 Congress passed the National School Lunch Act as a measure of "national security" to safeguard their health. The baby boom pushed the total of lunches served during the program's first decade past the 2 billion mark. Other legislation during the 1970s reflected the need to aid the poor, especially in providing breakfast and reducing the risk of malnutrition by supplying balanced meals.[62]

The rest of the restaurant business remains a mixture of old and new. Places like the Berghoff maintain the atmosphere of the nineteenth-century restaurant. Meanwhile, Greek-Americans became increasingly prominent in the economy and midpriced dining field, in some cases buying out Swedish and other ethnic restaurants. Besides the quest for healthier meals, perhaps the most significant trend especially after the 1960s was toward a broad interest in very specialized cuisines. Diners discovered that hundreds of modest neighborhood storefronts concealed the delights of dozens of ethnic groups, ultimately proving one of the principles of urbanization: Only in cities can those with highly specialized interests gather in numbers sufficient to create and sustain institutions like symphonies, libraries—and restaurants.

PART FOUR

Spare Moments

7   Reducing Risk and Taking Control

CHICAGO was a concentration of risk, a city filled with the unexpected. Sometimes it brought pleasure: a beautiful day, a wildly successful business deal, a chance meeting that turned to love. But the city could also place its citizens in a position of special vulnerability. We have already seen how a dependence on others for food, fuel, ice, and most other necessities could force Chicagoans to find substitutes or simply suffer. Similarly, Chicago presented a higher risk of accidents than did smaller towns because of its concentrations of machinery, tall places, things hanging from ropes, docks, and other opportunities for mishaps. But the crowding of the population made each urbanite vulnerable in other ways by magnifying the individual misfortune of an accident into a mass calamity that involved thousands.

Fire had been an obvious problem from the beginning. Although more substantial brick buildings gradually appeared downtown, Chicago was basically a wooden city whose buildings had often been constructed too close together. Even after the city improved its backward fire-fighting technology and upgraded its skills, it was still unsafe. During the 1860s it had added new fire engines and built one of the most sophisticated alarm systems in America, but less than a decade later, the Great Conflagration of 1871 destroyed a third of the city and left an equal portion of its population homeless. And that calamity was only the largest of a long series of blazes that shaped building codes and the ordinances governing the handling of flammable materials.[1]

Disease was the other large-scale risk factor in urban living. While the Black Hawk War of 1832 became a storied part of Illinois history, what is often forgotten is that it also brought the first major outbreak of contagious disease to the tiny village of Chicago. From that point on, the city would suffer the periodic visitation of pestilence. When cholera reappeared in 1849, its devastation forced the creation of the first orphanages and the Chicago Relief Society, which operated year round, not just in the winter. Cholera returned in 1866, striking hardest in the poorly sewered slums. The city was also subject to periodic outbreaks of typhoid, diphtheria, dysentery, and other contagions. It was fear of disease that later forced the city's leadership to approve costly measures to raise the grade of the streets, install new sewers, rebuild the water system, and reverse the flow of the river.[2]

The expansion of laws governing city life is evidence of the collective effort of Chicagoans to find ways to control the direction of their lives. As the century progressed, reformers in government and the private sector tried to shift the focus from having to cope with calamity to preventing it. One piece of evidence: the 1851 ordinance book was 256 pages long; its 1890 counterpart was 1,395 pages in length. As the decades passed, citizens found that they could no longer dispose of what they wanted when they wanted and where they wanted, whether on their own property or in the street. Fire-prevention and public-health laws and a variety of other regulatory measures were designed to reduce the risk of an accident. Workplace safety laws transformed factories from purely private places ruled entirely by their owners into a type of semipublic place in which the workers enjoyed some protection and rights. In general, the words "shall not" governed what one did in public, dictated the content of sanitary and building codes, and increasingly regulated the use of private property.[3]

Besides these public regulatory functions, there were other, individual efforts to seek a safer and healthier future. Readers turned to their favorite newspapers for columns of advice; their children read "good health" textbooks in school. Although knowledge of physiology even among the best medical minds was crude by today's standards, there was a widespread belief that exercise and the avoidance of certain unhealthy practices could help individuals contribute to improvements in their own health. These actions provided people with the means by which they could take control of their fate.

Sweating It Out: Nineteenth-Century Physical Exercise

Sometimes pride can threaten the loss of everything. An Austrian immigrant named Charles Postl learned that lesson in 1912, when he and a friend went to Milwaukee to visit Theodore Roosevelt, the Bull Moose party candidate for president, who was recovering from an assassination attempt. Postl, once a professional wrestler, had introduced the fitness-conscious Roosevelt to "scientific massage" several years earlier when "Teddy" was still in the White House, and the pair had become good friends. In 1908, Postl had established the first commercial health and fitness club in Chicago, but shortly before the Milwaukee reunion with T.R. a business partner had absconded with the firm's money. When the feisty former chief executive asked how things were going, the friend interceded for the reticent Postl and disclosed Charlie's financial crisis. Roosevelt made an unusual response. On October 22, 1912, he allowed his name to be used in a full-page advertisement for Postl's club, reportedly the first time that any living former president's picture and personal approval had ever appeared as a promotional endorsement for a commercial enterprise.[4]

Roosevelt's support undoubtedly helped Postl, but the club really survived because it fulfilled a demand. The public's perception of health had already undergone dramatic changes during the latter half of the nineteenth century. It was then that Americans, including Chicagoans, had decided that fit was better than fat.[5]

The earliest forms of vigorous exercise in Chicago had largely been extensions of the skills needed for survival on the frontier. Mass fist-fighting was regarded by many locals to be a legitimate way to break the boredom at Fort Dearborn. Informal horse racing was a popular test of equestrian skill as well as general athletic ability. Impromptu footraces, often pitting native populations against the French and American settlers, were another way to pass the time.[6] Invigorating outdoor sports also became the way many Chicagoans coped with the dull cold days of winter. During the 1830s, young men raced horses on the ice of the river. And sleighing parties—another practical necessity turned into leisure activity—became excursions into the country "to enliven the tedium of our long blockaded winters," advised the *Daily Democrat* in 1841. Other people turned to skating on frozen ponds and the river.[7]

But, as the lake boats and the railroads dissolved the city's outpost isolation, a series of gradual changes occurred in the way Chicagoans sought healthy fun, and these reflected the evolution of the young city. The first was the arrival in the early 1840s of games with more formalized rules, such as cricket and quoits.[8] This led naturally to the creation of amateur teams, which also helped overcome the lonely anonymity of the growing city. The arrival of immigrants, ever eager to introduce homeland pastimes, also hastened the development of teams. Englishmen who were members of the Chicago Wicket Club met daily on the lakefront in 1849. "In these dull [economic] times," noted the *Daily Democrat,* "the boys have plenty of leisure to amuse themselves, and the game is one of the most healthful we know of." Three years later, the same newspaper saw sports as a matter of civic boosterism and urged fans to cheer the cricket club at its Milwaukee match "and encourage them in defending the honor of the city." Cricketers honored Queen Victoria by making her birthday the traditional opening of their season.[9] Team sports continued into the winter. The city's Scottish population pursued curling and in 1860 formed the first club. "It is as innocent as it is invigorating to body and mind, and it is a pity we are not more addicted to such pastimes in this country," observed one writer.[10]

The lure of prizes and wagering begin to draw attention to the social advantages of physical prowess. Athletes were starting to become heroes. Chicago's most famous pioneer athlete was probably a free African American named Louis Isbell. Born in Kentucky in 1818, he came to Chicago twenty years later, and for the next decade he reigned as the fastest and most popular runner in the area. But even in Isbell's time, publicity and wagering were beginning to transform some almost naive feats of prowess into crowd-pleasing high-stakes spectacles. In 1847 over a thousand people watched a ten-mile contest between Isbell, an

English professional runner named Gildersleeve, and a pair of Native Americans. Smoke, a member of the Tonawanda tribe, won and Isbell finished second. But the race results would always be tainted by the charge that the heavily favored Gildersleeve had been paid five hundred dollars by gamblers to finish last. Isbell retired to establish what would be a long career as the town's favorite barber.[11]

Other athletic heroes followed, especially after the arrival of organized sports with rival teams. After 1865, for instance, baseball's growing popularity attracted enthusiastic crowds of amateur players and their fans to games held on the outskirts of town.[12] But by midcentury, money was transforming feats of fitness into professional spectacles, which, in turn, created fads. Pedestrianism, or long-distance walking against time, became the rage of the 1860s, with major contests offering purses of as much as ten thousand dollars for a thirty-day trek from Portland, Maine, to Chicago.[13]

During the mid-1840s entrepreneurs had discovered that Chicagoans were willing to pay money for the privilege of sweating in the specialized space of a commercial gymnasium. David Dicke's advertising touched a sensitive nerve. It claimed that the growing use of patent medicine for a variety of ailments indicated that the health of the townspeople must be declining and that the best way to halt the deterioration was "systematic exercise" under his expert guidance. Exercise, newspaper writers warned, was lacking in the lives of "clerks and others engaged in sedentary occupations."[14] City life was indirectly being blamed for making Chicagoans soft.

The most important catalyst for the fitness movement would continue to be amateurs, and the thousands of German immigrants who poured into Chicago after the mid-1840s would add organized enthusiasm. Many were familiar with the German theoretician Frederick Jahn, whose teaching led to the formation of Turner Societies, or *Turnverein.* These social athletic clubs promoted the idea that a healthy body was the prerequisite for a sound mind.[15] The first local branch, the Chicago *Turngemeinde,* appeared in 1852. Others were eventually established, including elaborate structures on North Wells Street and on West Diversey, which reflected the northward movement of the German community. All contained gymnasiums and swimming pools, and their teams competed in national and local meets. During the last half of the century, other nationality-oriented athletic clubs, such as the Bohemian Sokols and the Polish Falcons, met with the Turners in citywide contests that presumably allowed the groups to work out their hostilities on the playing fields rather than in the streets.[16]

Despite the anti-German nativism that exploded in the so-called Lager Beer Riot of 1855, the Turner philosophy began to have an impact on the public schools. In 1858 school board president Luther Haven introduced the idea of training bodies as well as minds. Two years later Haven's fellow board members gave in to his persistent advocacy of physical education, or "free gymnastics," as it was called, issuing orders for teachers to incorporate several daily exercise periods into classroom schedules. Those routine calisthenics continued for decades, while a debate raged about how far the activities should be extended.

In 1862 the school board took the hint from high-school students, who had built and paid for their own outdoor playing field, and constructed the first public grade school with a gymnasium. Four years later, a German-American school board member, Lorenz Brentano, pushed through approval of a gymnastics class taught by a specialized instructor, but funding disappeared after a year. It was not to return for nearly two decades.[17]

The Germans were not the only midcentury source of fitness enthusiasm. Many amateur athletic endeavors also trickled down from the wealthy. Extensive travel by Chicago's elite had brought them into contact with games throughout the world and made them innovators in several sports, which were initially meant to be enjoyed by family and a few immediate friends in a private setting. During the 1860s, they introduced bowling as a health-giving pastime, and in 1874 they organized the private Humor Club around the game.[18] A few years after the Great Fire, they began importing expensive archery equipment and in the coming years would introduce tennis and golf to Chicago.[19]

By the time of the Great Fire, fitness and exercise were beginning to evolve from an undertaking by a completely fragmented collection of enthusiasts to a multifaceted, though disjointed, movement with a philosophy and organizations to support it. Part of its growing attraction came from a new scientific interest in anthropometry, or the study of body sizes. In 1861, the need to mass-produce military uniforms led the federal government to issue guidelines for standard sizes based on the examination of recruits. With some notion of what most men of a particular height should weigh and what their average measurements were, the notions of "fat" and "thin" took on new scientific meaning. Chicagoans, like other Americans, became fascinated with measuring biceps, gauging lung capacity, and otherwise quantifying health and strength. "Every slim-waisted young man becomes at one time or another a devotee of physical culture," wrote George Ade. "He has a sudden and fierce desire to cultivate large biceps, to learn sparring and practice on the rings."[20]

Chicago manufacturers of athletic goods also helped promote the new enthusiasm, and "becoming fit" often included buying into a world of commercial products. Some of these took the form of exercise devices, such as the "Health-Lift," a graduated weight machine and exercise regimen invented in the late 1860s by a Chicagoan, Frank Reilly, M.D. Lifting weights became enough of a fad for a *Chicago Times* columnist to note wryly, "The customary salutation now, instead of 'How are you?' is 'How much do you lift?' Some young ladies . . . refuse to entertain a proposition from a young man till he has put on record his lifting capacity." Thirty years later, the Whitely Exerciser was all the rage. Usually marketed in different price brackets, such implements gave the wealthy instant class identification.[21]

Not only did such Chicago firms as John Gloy mass-produce equipment for the home exercise market, they also outfitted hundreds of gyms and clubs across the country. Much of what exercisers needed was, in fact, produced locally by companies that took advantage of the easy availability of animal hides from the Union Stock Yards. The sporting goods firm founded by the former Chicago White Stocking baseball star Albert Spalding was especially active. In

1885 it commissioned Chicago writer E. B. Warman to write a home fitness manual. That book and several competitors showed how inexpensive equipment, such as Indian clubs and pulley weights, along with jargon-free instructions and diagrams, could lead to a healthier body. In what amounted to a holistic view of health, the books quoted liberally from the Bible and famous authors to convince the reader that complete fitness also required disciplined and healthful living. Warman's suggestions included brushing the teeth, chewing food properly, and completely abstaining from tobacco and alcohol. Readers were warned to "avoid fried foods, especially meat," and to eat fresh fruits and vegetables, which were becoming more widely available thanks to the development of California agriculture and faster rail delivery. An anthropometric table allowed readers to chart their progress with confidence in scientific accuracy.[22] But even these desirable body goals changed over time. By 1894 experts could agree that "the slim, pliable muscles prevail over the bulky bound up knots that were once the athlete's pride."[23]

The manuals were aimed at both sexes because their publishers were eager to tap the growing market of female athletes. Many Chicagoans rejected the fashionable notion that women were meant to be pale, wasp-waisted, ever-fainting sylphs.[24] As early as 1870 one gym began opening its doors to women for a few hours each day. Twenty-five years later, there were at least two commercial gyms open only to women, while the YWCA was following its male counterpart in offering classes.[25] The link between exercise and culture was also evident in the work of Anna Morgan, a Chicago dramatics teacher and producer. She became well known across America for her popularization of the Delsarte system of stage training, which employed calisthenics as a technique for developing "graceful motion" in everyday life.[26]

Fitness followers often found it necessary to exert political pressure to promote their ideas. In 1885, the school board agreed to institute a free gymnastics program. Its motivations were many. There was an element of embarrassment because Chicago seemed to be falling behind other major cities in physical fitness. Turner groups also launched a substantial lobbying effort, arguing that the health of the child was paramount, that physical training was an urban substitute for the manual labor of the farm, and that Chicago's children were droopy and weak from too much study. Others claimed that rigorous gymnastics would instill discipline and train the will in boys while teaching graceful movement to girls. The program adopted in 1885 was drawn up by the Turners themselves. Eight of the group's instructors, including Jahn's grandson, taught classes under the supervision of Henry Suder, who would lead the exercises in the schools for the next thirty-seven years. But the physical training program remained controversial. Budgetary problems during the depression of the 1890s killed the program as a expendable "frill" in the primary schools, and physical training reverted back to classroom exercises. The relatively small amount of money that remained for physical education was shifted to the high schools.[27]

By the 1890s, fitness had proved itself no passing fad. There was a clear trend toward consolidation of scattered athletic interests into multifunctional organizations, much as department stores gathered a wide range of specialty shops under one roof. The elite members of the new Chicago and Illinois Athletic Clubs could afford to construct special courts for handball, squash, and racquetball, as well as gyms and pools, all contained in imposing downtown structures. Each club fielded teams in several sports that competed with their counterparts from other cities. Besides being places to meet for lunch, clubs took their athletics seriously, one of them even ousting members who boasted that they could belong without taking part in contests.[28]

Similar facilities developed for women. Some resulted from the new movement of females from the home into the workplace. In 1889, the Illinois Women's Press Club began sponsoring courses in physical culture, which included dress reform and diet, as well as exercise. More active programs followed four years later when the Chicago Business Women's Club began sponsorship of basketball teams. The club was careful to stress that "there has been no pulling of hair or scratching of faces by opposing teams. . . . It has never degenerated into anything beyond the limits of womanly decorum." In 1899 several prominent socialites formed the Chicago Women's Athletic Club. After a stormy debate over serving liquor—it was rejected—the club announced plans to construct a twelve-story building.[29]

While members of the city's elite could afford to turn to private facilities and select the people with whom they wished to sweat, Chicagoans with more enthusiasm than money could select other options. Some had to be content with private activities—climbing stairs to third-story tenements or pumping a well handle—but for others the alternative was outdoors and public. Responding to popular pressure, park administrators gave in to the demand for more play space instead of ornamental plantings. By the end of the century, the park as sylvan retreat, the "anti-city" within the city, had largely given way to what amounted to a public, outdoor version of the private athletic clubs. Like their elite counterparts downtown and the ethnic associations, the parks and the field houses that were constructed in several of them became virtual department stores of amateur athletics. Spaces with such specialized names as links, courts, ranges, fields, pits, diamonds, and tracks appeared in the larger parks.[30]

Another aspect of middle-class fitness was more commercial. The first requirement was gear. Mass production lowered the purchase price of archery, tennis, and cycling equipment to within reach. The second requirement was an alternate place to play. While the middle class lacked the wealth to create completely private facilities, they had options outside of the public parks. By 1900, several of the twenty-six golf courses in the Chicago area admitted paying guests. The small merchants, clerks, skilled mechanics, and others who made up the middle class also found themselves patronizing purely commercial venues. With that change, their athleticism became more susceptible to fads, as entrepreneurs kept remodeling facilities and introducing new activities to keep the crowds coming. During the 1870s, handball, which had first appeared in Irish saloons, became wildly popular; then it gave way to racquetball, which in turn saw its popularity slide in favor of roller skating by the early 1880s.[31]

The owners of skating rinks strived to appeal to a wealthier audience. Intoned the *Tribune* in 1880:

> The opening of the Chicago Roller-Skating Rink, corner of Michigan Avenue and Congress Street, . . . is unquestionably the most notable event in the amusement and social history of Chicago, in inaugurating in our own city on a scale of plain magnificence a social pleasure that implies a physical regeneration in its beneficent exercises, and which in London and Paris has with the aristocratic, the cultured, and the polite classes taken precedence of the ball room and left other amusements in the shade. It is the proper amusement of our intellectual social century.

Soon, there were competing rinks on the South and West Sides, and the press could note that "society" had eagerly taken up skating. The trickle-down, however, meant that many people of more modest means also embraced the pastime with similar enthusiasm. "Skating rinks seem to be cutting into the prayer meetings," grumbled the *Daily Drovers Journal*, a paper in the stock yards district. "It may be the time is coming that every prayer meeting, to be successful, will have to be provided with a roller skating attachment."[32]

By the end of the 1880s, the skates were gathering dust and a guidebook to the city could describe indoor baseball as a "Chicago invention" that "followed what became known as the 'Roller Skating Craze.'" Several skating rinks were refitted with baseball diamonds for a game similar to what would later be known as softball. A citywide organization paired teams from an "Indoor League" and a "Midwinter League." Then, in the first years of the new century, roller skating once more became all the rage. While new fads came and went, none of the earlier sports disappeared completely, much to the delight of aficionados who had their facilities to themselves.[33]

Bowling, which had once been almost entirely an outdoor sport, moved under roof in the mid-nineteenth century. In 1851 Cozzens Bowling Saloon on Randolph Street had advertised that, "Mrs. Baily, the most beautiful and graceful Female Bowler in the world[,] will be in attendance in this saloon."[34] Germans were the sport's most enthusiastic followers, organizing teams and leagues through the Turners. "Public acceptance of the game as a sport for businessmen" came about 1889, but the greatest surge of enthusiasm took place after 1895, the year the American Bowling Congress was founded in New York.[35] Within a decade there were estimated to be over thirty thousand bowlers and twelve hundred clubs in Chicago alone, a wave of interest no doubt boosted by the first national bowling tournament, held in the city in 1901. That year, the pastime was so popular that the American Bowling Congress recommended patronizing bowling alleys only three times a week, lest the bowlers' absences from home destroy the American family.[36]

The competition that often developed between commercial and public sports facilities is best illustrated by the story of where Chicago went swimming. The mid-nineteenth-century male custom of nude bathing off of the rocks along the south shoreline of Lake Michigan gave way to complaints from startled Illinois Central passengers.[37] But as the pollution that darkened the Chicago River poured into the lake, the numbers of brave swimmers declined. Much of the waterfront was devoted to industrial and transportation facilities; the rest, to erosion protection and a sanitarium in Lincoln Park. After the Great Fire, however, private entrepreneurs had begun to build piers, a half a dozen of which poked into the lake amidst private beaches. Gutchow's at the foot of Erie Street was the hit of the 1870s, but the most elaborate was Cheltenham Beach, which opened in 1885. The half-million-dollar facility featured a hundred-acre park and mile-long beach with a long pier, a beer garden, restaurants, and a resort hotel.[38] Even after winter arrived, those who had the admission fee could continue swimming. After 1877, they could retreat to their choice of commercial natatoria, the most famous of which was Kadish's indoor pool at Jackson and Michigan.[39]

As the century progressed there was a swell of complaints about the lack of public swimming facilities, especially during hot weather. In 1873 the city health department asked the Lincoln Park commissioners to build a public beach for the poor. The park board's demand that the health department pay for it virtually guaranteed that it would never be built. By the mid-1890s, the nearly completed Sanitary and Ship Canal promised to draw pollutants away from the lake, and swimmers hoped that their form of exercise would find its special space in park design. Chicago's first public beach opened in Lincoln Park in 1895, and after the turn of the century, nearly all of the scattered park districts began building outdoor pools.[40]

By the late nineteenth century, those concerned with the state of impoverished Chicagoans supported athletics and fitness as a way to overcome the social and physical disadvantages of slum life. Exercise became more than just a way to pass time or improve the mind-body relationship; it now was a part of social reform. While facilities in the larger parks might have been publicly owned and theoretically accessible to everyone, the cost of public transportation, shame over the appearance of one's clothes, and park police ever eager to enforce loitering laws acted as social filters. The poor stayed in their enclaves or ventured to one of the new small neighborhood parks that were created after the turn of the century.[41]

For the poor, the functional replacement for commercial gymnasiums and natatoria were charities. The YMCA, which had begun its work in the city in the 1850s with a primary emphasis on serving the soul and the intellect through its lectures and reading room, turned its attention to fitness. Boys' clubs and similar groups emphasized a healthy body as the foundation for moral adulthood. The settlement houses that sprang up in several slum districts added gymnasiums as necessary parts of their activities to keep children off the streets. By the 1890s, experts regarded exercise, a fit body, and the resulting sense of self-respect as important tools in the battle against delinquency.[42]

But access to fitness facilities was not always easy for minorities. African Americans, who generally faced a wall of exclusion when they tried to use many commercial amusements and accommodations, turned inward to their community in search of exercise. The black churches, which had gradually become multipurpose social centers, added gymnasiums and programs to keep local youngsters occupied and fit.[43] The Frederick Douglass Center, created in 1904, provided another alternative.[44] Then in 1911 industrialist Julius Rosenwald and community leaders responded to the plea from the African-American press and built the Wabash YMCA, which featured a fully equipped exercise program. In 1914 that institution sponsored the first all-black amateur athletic competition, a track meet held at the American Giants baseball park.[45]

Children of all economic backgrounds benefited from the school board's expansion of physical education programs for older students. In 1914, each of the city's twenty-two high-school facilities was equipped with at least one gym. By then, school superintendent Ella Flagg Young was also redirecting the program toward giving equal attention to young women. In 1910 the school board had begun hiring female physical education instructors and soon instituted a policy of building separate gymnasiums for them. On June 15, 1915, the efforts to use exercise to improve health reached a major milestone: the Illinois General Assembly finally recognized the importance of physical education in the schools by making it mandatory across the state.[46]

By the time Teddy Roosevelt saved Charlie Postl's club, Chicagoans by the thousands were already conscious of the benefits of health and exercise. They may have used Indian clubs and pulley weights instead of modern weight machines and treadmills, but the reasons for working up a sweat were the same then as now.

The Bicycle: Getting Healthy While Getting Around

Edith Ogden Harrison, Chicago's First Lady at the turn of the century, had vivid memories of her neighborhood's enthusiasm for the bicycle:

> Especially during the lovely summer evenings, before every Astor Street home on our block, one could see the trim bicycles awaiting the cessation of an early dinner for the owners inside the houses, for it was a foregone conclusion that everyone took a ride after dinner in the cool of the evening. . . .
> Almost at its very appearance, the riders numbered in the hundreds. Schools opened to teach its riding, and the traffic in this really expensive sport became a thing of wonder.[47]

Although Chicago witnessed other mass enthusiasms before and since, few could compare with the late-nineteenth-century bicycle boom. The evolution of the fad was the sum total of thousands of individual decisions, but tens of thousands took to the streets for two reasons. Some saw the two-wheeler as an important means of getting from here to there. Although its growth was chronologically parallel to that of the commuter train, the bicycle involved even more direct one-to-one contact between the individual and technology. But for most of its history, devotees of the bicycle saw it as a source of leisure and as an exercise machine that was an effective tool in the search for fitness.[48]

"Wheel mania" got off to a slow start in Chicago. The first form of the bicycle, the velocipede, appeared in the city in the late 1860s, but it was difficult to ride. Its two wheels were of equal size, but the direct attachment of the pedals to the front wheels made it difficult to gain speed. Its metal tires earned it the nickname of "boneshaker." Because of the dismal prospects for the "machine's" popularity, Chicago's Crane Brothers and Loring and Keene firms, which had been among the first to manufacture velocipedes in the United States, both returned to the plumbing supply business. They believed that the future of metal pipes lay only in carrying water.[49]

Only when the new "high-wheeler" appeared in the late 1870s did the bicycle become a hit.[50] This type remained an oddity for its first few years, its ownership largely confined to circus clowns and a few daring young men. When a few of the latter decided to form the Chicago Bicycle Club in 1878, they could find only nine riders in the city. But the new machines gradually attracted a larger following.[51] Once riders conquered the fear of the fifty-four-inch front wheel, they discovered that it was possible to reach high speeds with minimal effort. Park commissioners eventually had to ban the high-wheelers from the parks because of complaints from terrified pedestrians and carriage owners, but fast riders continued to course the 40.5 miles of boulevards that encircled the city in about five hours. Even when riding at slower speeds, the bicyclists were accused of ruining Chicago's green spaces. One park policeman blamed the wheels for bringing in so many visitors that they drove the songbirds from their habitats. All that remained were sparrows.[52]

Many Chicagoans seemed content to watch bicycle races rather than to ride one of the machines. On November 24, 1879, America's first six-day contest took place in the city, and during the next two decades the Battery D Armory, the Coliseum, and the White Stockings (now Cubs) baseball park were periodically transformed into bicycle tracks.[53] By 1885 races had become numerous enough to warrant the creation of the Chicago Bicycle Track Association, which was formed to coordinate dates and promote the pastime. Two years later, enthusiasts staged the first annual race from downtown to Pullman; the ability of this contest to attract top riders made it internationally famous. Perhaps the most ambitious undertaking of all was the 1892 Chicago–to–New York race. According to the saloonkeepers' newspaper *Mixed Drinks,* it demonstrated to the world that American affluence had not "softened the fiber or numbed the courage" of its youth. The relay teams made the 932 miles in 109 hours and 8 minutes, faster than the Pony Express.[54]

Besides entertaining thousands of spectators, bicycle races were crucial in introducing the new technology of the machines to the mass public and encouraging amateur activity. Although by 1882 there were so many riders in Lincoln Park that officials were forced to ignore their own 1879 ban, the cost of an "ordinary," as high-wheelers were known, could run into hundreds of dollars in the early 1890s. This kept membership in the cycling fraternity selective. Even though there were dozens of manufacturers, including Arnold, Schwinn and Company, making Chicago the bicycle-building capital of America, demand was so great that ownership was largely limited to those of comfortable means. Owners could separate themselves from the pack through accessories, such as a rear-view mirror, extra-bright riding lamp, or a specially designed trunk that allowed the machine to be shipped as baggage aboard a train.[55]

Perhaps the most visible impact of riders' affluence was the transformation of "wheelman's clubs" from small groups of daring tinkerers during the late 1870s into five well-funded and influential organizations in 1885. Seven years later the *Tribune* counted forty-eight clubs with six thousand members. Half of those groups owned their own posh buildings, most of which contained a gymnasium to allow members' fitness work to continue during the cold months. Dances, picnics, and even literary study groups filled the clubs' busy social schedules. The organizations also helped immigrants socialize with their countrymen. The most important activities, however, were the road outings. Although riders used the public streets and roads to travel as far as Benton Harbor, Milwaukee, or Rockford, they could be assured that their company was select. Elaborate uniforms became readily identifiable symbols for those on the road, making it unnecessary for riders to intermingle with those who could not afford to belong to a club. Within each group, members could achieve rank and status by riding a hundred miles in a day to earn a gold "century bar."[56]

The wheelmen's use of the public streets brought their organizations into political involvement and contact with nonriders in a struggle for dominance of public space. Teamsters, hack drivers, and others who used the streets to earn their livelihood were outraged when cyclists cut in front of them or ran down pedestrians. The result was a new demand for revised traffic rules that would include a ban on night riding, and for tough enforcement to meet the challenge presented by the machines. The aldermen imposed a few new laws, the most notable of which was to levy a fine on cyclists who left the scene of an accident.[57]

Wheelmen, on the other hand, argued that they were already an oppressed minority and that any new restrictions would make them even more vulnerable to shakedowns by the police. They complained that dark, deserted suburban roads often left them easy prey for robbers and they asked for more adequate police patrols. In 1886 they demanded and got a new law making it illegal to dump grass clippings or other hazardous material in the streets, and a decade later they won the right to use the pedestrian walkways of the river tunnels, because the streetcar tracks in the vehicle lanes made riding difficult.[58] They argued that if they were forced to carry running lights, then all vehicles, including teams, should be similarly equipped. Cyclists also moved into direct conflict with horse and teaming interests over street surfaces. The delicate balloon tires worked best on smooth asphalt or macadam, the material on which horses tended to slip and break legs. Equestrian advocates demanded retention of stone or brick, whose crevices provided the necessary traction.[59] Because of their mobility, bicycle riders were troubled by the multiplicity of conflicting traffic laws in the various towns and park districts through which they rode. The range of their rides transformed cyclists into lobbyists for a state highway system and uniform statewide codes fully a decade before automobilists took over the cause.[60]

The conflict over the bicycle as a means of urban exercise and mobility reached a peak in the mid-1890s, when anticycle aldermen tried to impose a high, two-dollar-per-machine tax on the two-wheelers. The severe depression

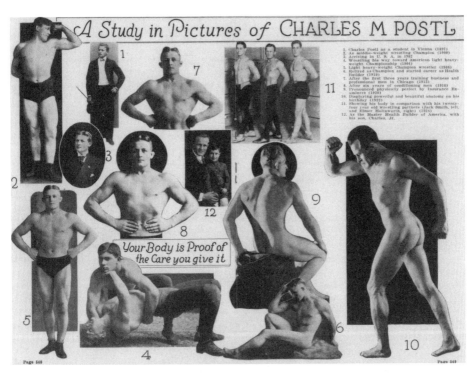

Charles M. Postl, *Postl Magazine of Pep* 2 (December 1924). The Austrian-born health club owner was one of the nation's most famous body builders.

Skating on the Midway Plaisance, postcard view, 1900. The boulevard link between Washington and Jackson Parks is still flooded each winter and opened to the public for ice skating.

Tennis Girl, from Sigmund Krausz, *Street-Types of Chicago* (1892). A proper woman dressed stylishly for her exercise.

Baseball game, Jackson Park, postcard view, early 1900s. The popularity of participatory sports forced the directors of the large Chicago parks to create ball diamonds and other open sporting spaces.

Beach scene, ca. 1898. Chicagoans regarded the private beaches and natatoria that lined parts of the southern shoreline as their "Coney Island." Factories later dominated that landscape.

ESTABLISHED BY E. J. LEHMANN, 1875.

The Fair

STATE, ADAMS AND DEARBORN STREETS.
TELEPHONE PRIVATE EXCHANGE 3

SPORTING GOODS

EVERYTHING *needed* for outdoor and indoor sports. Largest and most complete sporting goods department in the city. Qualities of the very highest grade. Prices far below those of specialty sporting goods houses.

Our 144 page sporting goods catalogue sent free upon request

The Fair advertisement, Powers' Theatre Program, May 24, 1908. Downtown department stores sold huge quantities of sporting goods to amateur athletes and fitness enthusiasts.

Facing page: Bicycle rider, ca. 1898. The "safety" bicycle, with both wheels of fairly small size, came into vogue during the 1890s and expanded the audience of wheelmen and wheelwomen.

Gymnastics class, Off-the-Street Club, probably 1910. This charity, as well as settlement houses and shelters, used athletics to combat delinquency among Chicago's impoverished youth. (Off-the-Street Club Records, University Library, University of Illinois at Chicago)

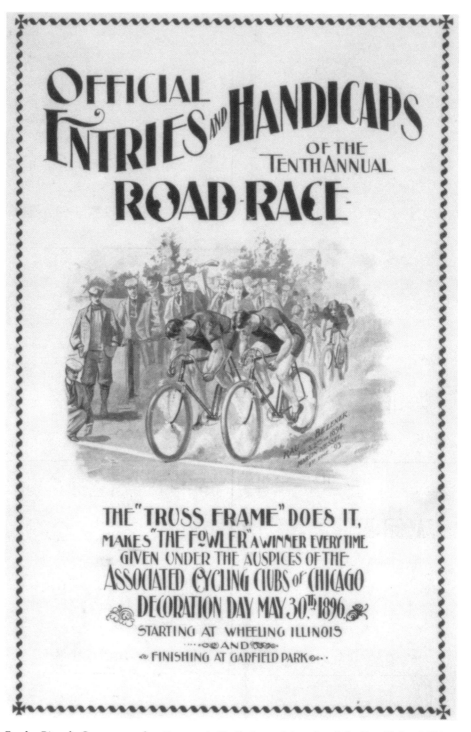

Fowler Bicycle Company advertisement, *Tenth Annual Associated Cycling Clubs of Chicago Road Race* (1896). Racing made the bicycle the center of spectator as well as participatory sports. This shows the thrilling finish of the 1894 event.

"How Refuse Tobacco Finds Its Way Back to the Market," *Chicago Tribune*, January 17, 1897. The newspaper's exposé detailed how discarded butts made their way back to fresh cigars that were purchased by the unsuspecting public.

Lucy Page Gaston emerges from a courtroom, 1910. The publicity-seeking methods of the anticigarette crusader often landed her in trouble with the law. (Chicago Historical Society, DN001988)

Unless YOU help us to
CHEAT THE STREETS*

The delinquent youngster of today will become the criminal and gangster of tomorrow . . . . . . instead of the upstanding American Citizen he might be! About one out of every twenty-nine persons in the United States is engaged in criminal careers that cost every man, woman, and child one hundred twenty dollars per year. Direct victims suffer not only a great financial loss but mental suffering as well.

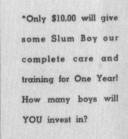

*Only $10.00 will give some Slum Boy our complete care and training for One Year! How many boys will YOU invest in?

"Cheat the Streets," Off-the-Street Club, *Annual Report, 1939*. The belief is clearly evident here: the smoking cigarette leads directly to the smoking gun. (Off-the-Street Club Records, University Library, University of Illinois at Chicago) and labor conflicts at Pullman and other local industries added to the bitterness of the debate. Supporters of the tax argued that the affluent cyclists should pay for the more expensive smooth road surfaces that they were forcing on the public. The riders, in turn, issued public reminders that a similar plan for a special tax on teaming companies had been killed by the Supreme Court because there was no provision for it in the Chicago city charter. Many riders openly declared that they would refuse to pay the tax.[61]

The antiwheel aldermen discovered that they had failed to read the social trends in cycling. Declining sales during the severe economic depression of the mid-1890s had driven the cycle manufacturers to introduce less-expensive "safety" models, which featured smaller wheels of equal size. The low price and the ease of operation caused a boom in sales that dwarfed previous efforts.[62] The *Times-Herald* reported that in June 1895 there were 40 manufacturers in Chicago alone, constructing over 144,000 units; the next year the *Journal* counted 88 companies in Chicago and claimed that two out of every three bicycles made in America came from plants within 150 miles of the city. This included the Western Wheel Works, the nation's largest. At a time when a depressed national economy meant losses in many fields, any company capable of bending steel was trying to get into the bicycle market.[63]

The resulting glut depressed prices, which made machines available to those of more modest means.[64] The new buyers may not have been as wealthy as the pioneer riders, but they continued to seek the status of belonging to a club. By 1895 there were ten thousand members organized into thirty-three Chicago cycle organizations.[65] The numbers of their votes, their campaign dollars, and their tendency to vote in a block gave them newfound power, which they were now ready to exercise at a critical time. First, they convinced the majority of the city council that Jackson Street should be declared a boulevard, which meant that it would have no streetcar tracks and would be off limits to teamsters. This was needed, they argued, because there was no other "unobstructed" street leading from the Loop to the West Side.[66] Then, in 1896, the council changed one provision of the traffic code that had often proved embarrassing for well-to-do riders: the police would no longer confiscate and hold for bail the cycle of anyone arrested for "scorching," or speeding. Formerly, red-faced society matrons and gentlemen had to suffer the indignity of a ride in the paddy wagon before they could pay their fine and claim their machines.[67]

The legislation controversy of the mid-1890s also helped launch the career of one of Chicago's most popular mayors, Edith Ogden Harrison's husband, Carter II. The son of a five-time mayor who had been assassinated in 1893, "Our Carter" started with the advantage of family name, but in 1897, at the time of his first mayoral campaign, he realized that many of the younger voters stood in awe of the athletic prowess of his opponent, a former Princeton University football lineman named John M. Harlan. Harrison quickly took up cycling, acquired a number of century bars, and had himself photographed on a bicycle for a campaign poster captioned "Not the Champion Cyclist—But the Cyclists' Champion." Although streetcar franchises and other weighty issues swayed more serious voters, Harrison later credited his victory in large part to the bicycle gimmick.[68] Once in office, Harrison rewarded his followers by blocking further wheel restriction ordinances and by building a bicycle path along Sheridan Road from Edgewater to Evanston. He also pushed a compromise dollar-per-machine tax through the city council.[69]

The new ranks of bicycle owners broadened the popularity of the machines, which, in turn, deepened their impact on society. Newspaper and magazine writers began to promote bicycle riding as a way of coping with the problems of city life. The wholesomeness of the exercise soothed frazzled city nerves and the tedium produced by the office or factory machine; the involvement of all of the family's members countered the trend toward domestic discord and divorce; and the bicycle had a benevolent effect on the young single men and women who left their furnished rooming houses to ride in the park rather than visit a saloon. The *Tribune* was happy to report that the wheel fad brought a corresponding decline in patronage at barrooms, billiard halls, and cigar stores. No one was happier about that prospect than the temperance crusader Frances Willard, herself a rider.[70]

The safety models also brought many other women into the ranks of owners. There was particular enthusiasm for the liberating impact the bicycle might have on the lives of women, but each step raised questions about violating the rules that tightly governed their behavior. One concern was health. Journalists interviewed physicians about the effect of such intense exercise and the jarring ride on women's bodies. The consensus was that moderate exertion did no harm, but it is doubtful whether any physician would have recommended emulating Miss Alice Waugh, a teacher, and Mrs. Fred McEwen, the first Chicago women to make a century run.[71]

There was also the question of the bicycle's impact on the appearance and manners of wealthier women, whose affection for the wheel forced them into new social situations. Cycling costumes were a problem because they required a tighter and more revealing fit than did ordinary street dress. Designers found tasteful compromises between modesty and necessity, but more conservative observers warned that lurking behind every accommodation of clothing to the wheel was the potential for a "scorcher's uniform" of pants and streamlined hat. One "bicycle wedding," in which the bride wore bloomers and the groom donned knickerbockers, raised many proper eyebrows.[72] Cosmetic companies were quick to introduce expensive creams to cure a flushed face caused by exercise or to soothe abrasions resulting from falls or from cinders thrown from roadways.[73]

Cyclists also challenged the traditional rules that governed behavior in public places. For instance, some experts advised that babies could be taken along wheeling. After some debate, etiquette writers decided that only in the case of an accident should a male rider address a female rider to whom he had not been formally introduced. They did believe, however, that it was proper for widows to cycle while in mourning.[74]

Many women joined the throngs of Chicagoans who turned to their wheels as a means of getting to work. In commenting on a Board of Education decision to allow female teachers to commute by bicycle, board member Alvin S. Trude made the puzzling comment, "My observation is that women who have wheels at their heels are not troubled with them in their heads."[75] In general, however, commentators stressed the benefits of trading the streetcar for a wheel. The *Journal*'s description seemed to stress it as an individualistic way of coping with the shortcomings of mass transit: "The bicycle rider is always sure of having a seat, either his saddle or the ground, and he never has to get up to offer it to a lady. He always has fresh air, and a corporation never sells standing room on his toes to other passengers at a nickel apiece. He never has to wait for a car, and never has to get out and walk, leaving his fare in the treasury of the company, when the cable breaks."[76] A Hyde Park newspaper, *South Side Sayings,* went on to claim that the lives of those who commuted to work by bicycle were generally more interesting because they were tempted to try different routes each day:

> There was the gloomy pessimist of a year ago who groaned when it was time to start to work and sighed when Sunday came, with the prospect of a whole day at home; who prophesied the spread of disease in the crowded [street] cars. . . . You may see him now, starting from home ten or fifteen minutes earlier than is necessary to take a little spin around the park. . . . You may have seen him on Sunday with acclamations, and vacation with wildest joy. Have you ever seen an enthusiastic cycler who was a pessimist as well?[77]

Parking the machines, however, became a problem. The Schiller Theater provided free checking for its patrons, and similar facilities appeared at picnic grounds, amusement parks, and other places. Some entrepreneurs learned that they could charge the wheelers enough to make a profit. Others offered service; one downtown lot near Washington Street and Fifth Avenue (Wells Street) oiled its patrons' bicycles and topped off the lamp tanks.[78]

The popularity of the wheels involved them in new forms of crime. A swindler named A. C. McCauley advertised that his Empress Bicycle Company would ship a $100 wheel for $40; those who sent in money got nothing. There were so many bicycle thefts that in December 1895 the city began to license repair shops and required mechanics to keep a register of all machines brought in to be fixed. A month later another ordinance licensed all second-hand dealers and made them register the merchandise they handled much in the manner of pawnshops. Criminals utilized bicycles to effect getaways, prompting the police department to put some of its detectives on them as well.[79]

Although the popularity of the bicycle appeared to be destined for unlimited growth, it quickly faded from vogue after the turn of the century. This disaffection was especially evident among the wealthy who had once supported cycling so eagerly. Clubs dwindled in membership and numbers, 60 percent of them closing between 1900 and 1905. Some observers claimed that the clubs had outlived their original purpose of mutual protection and legislative lobbying. The surviving organizations emphasized entertainment, rather than exercise. The large Illinois Cycling Club became the purely social Prairie State Club in 1900, then folded completely a year later. Much of the decline in support among the wealthy was due to the fact that mass production had decreased the purchase price to within reach of the working-class families, thereby diminishing the sport's exclusiveness. Fashionable magazines also began running articles stressing the contribution of cycling to the dangers of overexertion and fatigue. Meanwhile, the glutted market caused by the mass production of the safety bicycle forced most of the manufacturers to fail.[80]

By the late 1890s, Chicago's social leaders were beginning to talk about two new fads. One was the sport of golf, which, like cycling a generation earlier, thrived in an atmosphere of special clothing, exclusive clubs, and country outings. The other involved a technology that, in its simplest and earliest form, reminded many people of the daring days when cycling was young and velocipedes ruled the road. This new device was little more than a pair of bicycles attached to a platform, but it was powered by a new type of motor. It was called the automobile.[81]

Lucy Page Gaston and the Cigarette War

As soon as *Herald-Examiner* reporter Sam Blair heard who was dying, he rushed to the Hinsdale Sanitarium in the western suburbs. Chicago's attention was riveted on the spectacular trial of Leopold and Loeb, but the subject of Blair's attention had made her own headlines more than a decade earlier. The journalist expected a dressing-down from the frail sixty-four-year-old woman; he had, after all, belittled her in print some years before. Instead, he received a bit of friendly advice: quit smoking, chew gentian root. "Gentian root, remember. You spell it *g-e-n-t-i-a-n*." Those words proved to be the last public utterance of a remarkable Chicagoan, Lucy Page Gaston, long hailed as the Carrie Nation of cigarettes.[82]

Lucy Page Gaston was a rare combination of reformer and publicist. Born in Delaware, Ohio, in 1860, she was the daughter of ardent abolitionists who had turned to temperance and feminist causes after the Civil War. When her family moved to Illinois, Lucy attended the Chicago Normal School and appeared destined for the life of a small-town spinster schoolteacher. (A romance had ended, as she put it, "when I prayed it out.") She taught in Kansas and in downstate Illinois.[83]

The Gaston family, meanwhile, had moved to the unusual south suburban town of Harvey. A Chicago lumber magnate named Turlington Harvey had developed the new industrial suburb in the early 1890s. He had wisely understood the significance of a shift in the way factory machinery was powered. Since the middle of the nineteenth century most factories had employed a single large stationary steam engine, with belts and pulleys to run everything in the plant. Its water and fuel requirements usually brought a factory to the banks of a river, which provided water and access to barges of coal to feed the giant boiler. The factory also had to be as compact as possible, to minimize the wear on the belts and gears. By the 1890s the adoption of small electrical motors on each piece of machinery had begun to free factories from these site requirements. Harvey's all-electric town, which he named after himself, could accommodate the more decentralized and sprawling factories of the future. As an added attraction to companies that located there, he promised a more sober workforce by banning saloons. The Gastons were so impressed with the experiment that they moved to Harvey and made it the base of operations for their local temperance drives.[84]

By the late 1890s, Lucy's activities with the Evanston-based Woman's Christian Temperance Union consumed most of her time. She launched a magazine, the *Christian Citizen,* which flailed away at all forms of sin.[85] In 1899, however, she decided to carve a niche for herself in the fight against unhealthy vices. Her decision was logical. The WCTU had long attacked tobacco as well as alcohol. And as a teacher, Lucy had been shocked by the number of boys she had caught smoking. Now she decided to devote her life to battling tobacco, especially the cigarette.[86]

Chicago was not a promising place to fight "the weed." Tobacco leaf had traditionally been shaped into its final form near the site of consumption, often in small shops. In Chicago the tobacco business dated back to at least 1842, when the place was a village; four years later, there were six factories, and in 1859 there were twenty-one. The dawn of cheap rail transportation made it profitable to bring large casks of imported and Southern tobacco to the city for processing.[87] Some of it ended up in large establishments, such as the five-story factory of Van Etta, Friedman, and Company. Despite the wartime leaf shortages of 1861, over a hundred employees turned out a hundred barrels of fine-cut chewing tobacco a day.[88] But cigar manufacturing remained dispersed. Wholesalers delivered the leaf to colonies of Bohemian and Cuban cigar makers, who labored away in their homes and in small shops to make the deadlines for scheduled pickups. In 1873, there were already 400 such small shops in the city, and by 1888, local factories were transforming 27 million pounds of tobacco into 15.5 million cigars and 21.8 million cigarettes a year. Most of the production was concentrated in the Pilsen neighborhood, which was in the southwestern part of the crescent of slums that surrounded the Loop.[89]

Much of this enormous production was consumed locally through cigar stores, which rivaled saloons as male retreats. But despite its importance to the economy, many Chicagoans thought smoking unseemly and unhealthful. Some attacked it on religious grounds as the first step to drunkenness, a sure route to companionship with society's bad elements, and an impoverishing waste of money. Religious condemnation continued, but the ranks of smokers grew. The *Daily Democratic Press* complaining in 1855, "In spite of all the exclamation and declamation of the abstinent, in spite of all of the statistical arguments piled up against using the fragrant, delicious weed, the number of those who have tried its solacing virtues and delight in its influences, seems to be on the increase."[90]

By midcentury, issues of smoking etiquette also appeared. Although smoking in restaurants, hotels, and other semipublic places was common, its appropriateness in the horsecar was less clear. Because there were no city ordinances, the carriers made the decision about whether to permit it. Smoking had been relegated to the last rows of seats in open warm-weather cars, but even when winter brought out the enclosed equipment, it continued. In 1868 passenger complaints forced the Chicago City Railway to announce that it would eject passengers who lit cigars, but conductors did little to enforce the ban. One livid passenger complained that "ladies of sensitive nerves, or gentlemen of refined olfactories" were forced to "inhale a second-hand dose of nicotine from the lips of some perfumed dandy or the lungs of a stalwart laborer."[91] Objections by smokers and the concern over lost fares caused the carriers to reverse the policy in 1876. One angry female rider asked, "I believe the gentlemen who smoke who would vote to abolish smoking on the cars outnumber those who would vote for the privilege." The management, however, announced that it would do nothing about it.[92]

During the late nineteenth century the antitobacco arguments became more health-related and scientific, aimed at convincing smokers that they were injuring themselves. By the 1880s, there were scattered claims by local doctors that tobacco caused sore throats, dyspepsia, paralysis, and blood disorders.[93] And in 1898 the *Chicago Post* condemned tobacco as addictive and listed a vow to stop smoking among the most desirable New Year's resolutions.[94]

The most serious charges were lodged against cigarettes, or "paper pipes," which became increasingly popular through the latter decades of the century. Unlike other indulgences—fine wine or food, for instance—in which consumers tended to spend larger amounts of money on more expensive products as their taste became more refined, the cigarette transformed smoking in large part because mass machine production lowered its price dramatically and made it more widely affordable.[95] The result was an outburst of concern far more intense than that aimed at cigars or chewing tobacco. Opponents claimed that the cigarette was made from inferior filler that was often contaminated.[96] Some physicians were convinced that it caused insanity.[97]

As the decades passed, the cigarette became increasingly associated in the public mind with "fast" young men who used slang, stayed out late at night, wore flashy clothes, and sported well-trimmed mustaches. If they were wheelmen, they were invariably "scorchers." In his "Stories of the Streets and of the Town" column in the *Record,* George Ade created the recurring characters Ollie and Freddie, sophisticated young bachelors who spent their father's money for the latest clothing styles and used such expressions as "swell" and "Say, old man." Of course, they smoked cigarettes.[98]

Critics of the cigarette also argued that its low price and small size promoted its popularity among population groups not usually associated with tobacco consumption. Its short burning time seemed to complement the trend toward speed and efficiency in everyday life as well as industry. The very name "cigarette" also implied a daintiness that seemed to target women. Although many of them had smoked pipes or small cigars in the eighteenth and early nineteenth centuries, tobacco use among women was relegated to an assumption of lower-class behavior. For decades hotels and restaurants had maintained separate ladies' entrances, lobbies, dining rooms, and staircases; in part this had been a way to allow women to avoid the risk of encountering men who smoked as well as engaged in discourteous behavior. But by the late 1880s, more rebellious American women were following their avant-garde Parisian sisters and lighting up. In 1888 a reporter in search of reasons why young women took up smoking tied it to feminism, to a belief that the practice posed no health risk, and to fashion; lighting up in the bathtub, in fact, was that year's big fad. Detractors tried to tie feminine smoking to drink and other vices, and in 1896, one daring Chicago woman was arrested for smoking on the street. The debate over smoking and gender behavior would rage in newspapers and popular magazines for decades.[99]

Underage smokers constituted the second population group for whom the cigarette was ideally priced and sized. Although there were general complaints that smoking impaired growth and that children might resort to theft to obtain cigarette money, the wrath of women's organizations and youth reformers was aimed primarily at those who broke the decades-old state and local statutes outlawing tobacco sales to minors.[100] In 1890, the Illinois Woman's Alliance complained of widespread defiance.[101] The following year the Illinois Humane Society discovered a two-year-old smoker and tried unsuccessfully to have his mother jailed for contributing to his delinquency.[102]

The mid-1890s saw the beginning of a crusade aimed at banning cigarettes altogether. Reformers tried unsuccessfully to enact anticigarette legislation at each session of the Illinois General Assembly throughout the decade.[103] Such sumptuary efforts, which eventually succeeded in fourteen other states by 1921, failed in Illinois, but local reformers found more success in regulating what they viewed to be the most objectionable parts of the trade.[104] Purity was one issue. On May 28, 1894, the Chicago City Council banned the sale of "medicated cigarettes," which contained everything from sugar to belladonna, opium, and morphine. Mayor John P. Hopkins vetoed the measure because he thought sugar harmless, but the aldermen overrode his objections.[105] A few weeks later, Alderman "Bathhouse John" Coughlin introduced a bill for a $500-per-year cigarette dealers license. Drugstores, newsstands, and hundreds of other small vendors angrily signed petitions that prevented quick action on the proposal. But what really defeated it was the discovery by reporters of a fund of $50,000 of tobacco company money to be divided among those who voted no. The cigarette producers claimed that they were helplessly responding to an aldermanic extortion plot organized by Alderman John Powers. The accused lawmakers replied that the tobacco companies had approached them first. In either case, the publicity was enough to kill the bill in committee.[106]

The tobacco issue returned three years later, when *Tribune* readers were shocked to discover that the filling in many of the cheaper cigars consisted of stubs and butts that had been picked up from sidewalks and saloon floors. Armies of Italian children and elderly women sold what they had gathered for fifteen cents a basket to recyclers who cleaned away the mud and dried the shreds, which were sorted in quality and sold to cigar makers. The growing popularity of the germ theory of the origin of disease aroused the interest of the health department, but inspectors found themselves stymied by the secretive and dispersed nature of the trade.[107]

At about that same time, Alderman Coughlin reintroduced his proposal to license cigarette dealers, this time as a compromise between an open trade and a total ban. The new law, passed in April 1897, gave police leverage in prosecuting those who sold to children, while a more reasonable hundred-dollar annual license fee would help to defray the cost of the city health department's inspection of cigarettes for alien ingredients. The larger dealers rejoiced, believing that smaller competitors would be driven from business and that consumers would see the price per pack double to a dime. Opposition came from the Bohemian and Polish tobacco workers, who made 70 million of the 250 million cigarettes consumed locally each year. But those who understood how to take advantage of the anonymity of city life were not worried. As the press widely reported, few dealers ever bothered to take out the proper license because cigarette sales were so scattered and so easily concealed that the law was almost impossible to enforce.[108]

The task of overcoming either nonexistent or indifferent enforcement fell to private groups. In 1894, South Side church women formed the National Anti-Cigarette Association to promote nonsmoking through the old temperance technique of persuasion followed by a public pledge of abstinence. When that group faded, it was Lucy Page Gaston's turn.[109] In 1899, she formed the Anti-Cigarette League and began a quarter-century crusade that employed many tactics borrowed from the WCTU. Convinced that most people would respond to a moral argument backed by scientific information, she employed lectures and literature that included a monthly called *The Boy,* which brought the message to thousands of youth. She approached employers, some of whom had already begun refusing to hire smokers of any age, and convinced them to encourage minor employees to sign pledges not to smoke. She also knew that her frequent rallies would gather crowds and newspaper headlines, especially when accompanied by "The Penny Cigarette," sung by a chorus of youthful abstainers employed in department stores and telegraph offices.[110]

Gaston's anticigarette crusade struck a responsive chord among Chicagoans who worried about the future of the city's youth. Chicago had created the nation's first juvenile court in 1898, followed soon after by the founding of the Juvenile Protective Association to help administer the law, gather information, and expose dangerous conditions among the youth. In 1903 Gaston founded the Chicago Law and Order League to battle prostitution, dance halls, and other immoralities, including the sale of cigarettes.[111]

The scientific monograph, the pledge, and the emotional song were traditional temperance tools that gained some followers to her cause, but Gaston also resumed legislative lobbying in Springfield. Her goal was an Illinois anticigarette law modeled after Tennessee's strict ban. When she attacked Henry Evans, a state senator from Aurora, for burying her bills in committee, he complained that she was "making a mighty good thing" out of her crusade. The implication that she was profiting from the league brought an angry reply from Gaston that her salary often went unpaid.[112] After three unsuccessful attempts, her bill was finally enacted in an all-night end-of-term session. The first section of the law prohibited the manufacture, sale, or gift of any cigarette "containing any substance deleterious to health, including tobacco." The law also prohibited children aged seven through eighteen from smoking in public and punished anyone who sold or gave away a cigarette to a minor or allowed his or her premises to be used by smoking minors. Triumphantly, Gaston announced that her next goal would be a ban on cigarette paper and a national anticigarette law.[113]

What Gaston did not realize was that her bill contained a pair of "jokers," or hidden flaws designed to ensure that it would be nullified by the courts. Local tobacconists were quick to file suits, and two days before the ban was to go into effect, a judge ruled the first section invalid because it *prohibited* cigarettes while its titled claimed it was a bill to *regulate* them. In December 1907, the Illinois Supreme Court found that tobacco had not been found conclusively to be harmful, thus nullifying the first section of the law for a second reason.[114] Gaston had been hoodwinked, but at least the last two sections of the law stood. Ironically, she was the one who came under attack for attempting, in the words of the *Record-Herald,* "reform by stealth"; editorialists derided her efforts to reform the habits of adults, as well as those of children.[115]

Gaston also found that public smoking escaped the control of lawmakers before World War I, in large part because it was much more difficult to prove that lighting up was a direct hazard to the health of bystanders. A few scientists could claim that it injured the smoker, but no one could demonstrate it persuasively, as physicians had linked spitting and tuberculosis. Not even the city fire or building departments could regulate smoking materials for purposes of public safety.[116] Some facilities with substantial public usage, such as Chicago's elevated companies and a few restaurants, provided special segregated areas for smokers.[117] All that the press and those with offended sensibilities could do was complain about rude men who dared to smoke in church or bold women who dared smoke anywhere in public.[118]

Although forced to retire for a short time because of health problems, Lucy Gaston remained undeterred by her detractors. In 1910 she began to pursue a path that demonstrated how a reform crusade could transform itself as it expands beyond the grasp of its founder. The campaign against the "Little White Slaver," as the industrialist Henry Ford called it, branched into increasingly divergent paths. On one level, Gaston and her followers moved the crusade to the national level with the formation of the Anti-Cigarette League of America in 1910. This organization brought together activists who had already taken Gaston's message and used it to push anticigarette laws through the legislatures of twelve states, most of them in the Midwest and Great Plains.[119]

On the local level, Gaston realized that the newspapers gave free publicity through their coverage of uncommon deeds. The daily press had an insatiable appetite for the unusual, while the widespread use of halftone reproduction favored news that was also graphic. This inspired her to pursue more spectacular and attention-grabbing tactics. The theme running through most of her stunts was that of the dainty woman who kept popping up in unlikely places. In one instance she demanded that the Chicago police appoint designated anticigarette policemen, and when the department refused, she had herself appointed a special deputy.[120] Tying herself to the growing agitation against vice in the city's Levee district, she burst into Ike Bloom's and the Everleigh sisters' brothels to demand an end to smoking. Her statements to an entourage of reporters that followed her implied that tobacco was a worse sin than prostitution.[121] She lectured the Chicago Cubs on the evils of cigarettes and on how what she called the "tobacco trust" had cornered the market in "coffin nails," a term she coined and repeated so many times that it became one of her trademarks as well as part of American slang.[122] She tried to persuade Chicago aldermen to make it illegal to throw away a cigarette butt. In 1911, she caused a newsworthy flap by storming out of the Chicago Opera's performance of *The Secret of Suzanne* at the Auditorium, offended when a female lead lit up her third cigarette. (Suzanne's secret was that she smoked.) Gaston later fumed to a reporter, "Horrible. . . . It is enough to turn one forever from grand opera. An artful embellishment of a pernicious vice which should receive the stamp of disapproval from every true American woman."[123]

By 1912, Lucy Page Gaston appeared to have carried her crusade about as far as it could go. The city council had begun passing ordinances banning or segregating smoking in streetcars and a few other public and semipublic places, but fire prevention, not health or morality, was the motivation.[124] Then, on November 24, 1913, the city council unexpectedly passed an ordinance banning cigarette sales to minors under the age of twenty-one.[125] The following spring, Gaston scored another success when she persuaded officials at the juvenile court and at the Bridewell, the city jail, to send errant boys and women who smoked to a clinic that had been established by the Anti-Cigarette League. Although the treatment consisted of nothing more than spraying the throat with a solution of silver nitrate, Gaston claimed that it halted the urge to smoke.[126]

But Lucy Page Gaston's last decade was filled with disappointments. In 1919, the Chicago City Council dealt an unexpected blow. As a gesture to saloonkeepers who would be losing their livelihoods to national prohibition, the aldermen reduced the cost of a cigarette licenses issued to those holding saloon licenses.[127] Gaston's greatest problem, however, involved the way in which her headline-grabbing seemed to undermine the quiet lobbying efforts at the state level, which had stalled after 1909. During World War I, for instance, she spoke out against the charitable gesture of sending cigarettes to men in uniform. She was concerned about the young men who might become smokers; the public read her comments as antipatriotic and as mean-spirited toward the soldiers and sailors.[128]

What was even more troubling was the growing resistance to her within the Anti-Cigarette League of America itself. Internal bickering about her tactics caused her to found a secession group, the Anti-Cigarette League of the World. Expanding the scope of her organization became her way to cope with failure. She returned briefly to the headlines in 1920 when she announced her candidacy for president of the United States; the handful of votes she received in the South Dakota primary quickly scotched that idea.[129] She was in the national headlines again a year later when she sent a well-publicized letter to president-elect Warren Harding requesting that he stop smoking. His vaguely worded reply agreed with the idea of saving youth from cigarettes, but it warned that the antitobacco movement "should be free from any kind of hypocrisy or deceit on the part of those who are giving it their earnest attention." Although Harding was probably referring to Gaston's presidential bid, there was an implication of something more sinister than political competition.[130]

Gaston's problems within her organization were also mounting. She had moved her operation to Kansas around the time of the war, but broke with the Kansas Anti-Cigarette League over her tactics. Her proposal to start another magazine, which was to be called *Coffin Nails,* caused a break with the directors of the Anti-Cigarette League of America, who had grown tired of her outlandish bids for attention. In August 1921, they ousted her from the organization she had founded, claiming that their goal of "spreading scientific and other information to protect the youth from forming the cigarette habit" did not agree with her methods of "promoting prohibitory methods not approved by the board."[131]

Now living off of her savings, Lucy Page Gaston was back in the news when she blamed tobacco companies for adding what she called "furfural" to cigarettes. She claimed that it was a "colorless, aromatic, volatile compound, gradually darkening, which is formed by distilling bran, starch, sugar, etc. with sulfuric acid." It gave each smoke the "kick" of two ounces of whiskey. In other words, she was accusing tobacco companies of "spiking" tobacco with a compound that enhanced the effect of the nicotine. Her new charges attracted the financial backing of a Frenchman named Henri de Rochi but did not gain serious attention among medical researchers.

By the end of 1923, Lucy Page Gaston was beginning to face her last challenge. She had developed a soreness on the left side of her neck that had gone undiagnosed until her serious injury early the next year in a streetcar accident. Six months later she was back in Presbyterian Hospital, and in early August doctors announced that there was no hope and moved her to the suburban sanitarium. As a symbolic gesture, the Anti-Cigarette League of America took her back into the fold.[132]

Lucy Page Gaston died in Hinsdale, Illinois, on August 20, 1924, at the age of sixty-four. Although the press had predicted a large turnout for her funeral, only a few old friends attended. In the midst of the service four little children got up and pointed to her coffin, saying, "Miss Gaston, we thank you for what you have done for us." Then they recited the Clean Life Pledge, which she had written.[133] Her cremated remains were returned to Harvey.

Editorialists tried to assess her career. They could reflect fondly on her colorful antics and the seeming hopelessness of her crusade. By the time of her death, all but one of the states that had earlier banned cigarette sales had passed repeal laws; Kansas, the last, would follow in 1927. Hers had been a movement that emphasized self-control as well as morals, and writers could not escape the fact that her crusade had grown out of the same fervor that had produced two other reform victories. "The women with whom she was associated," noted the *New York Times,* "all achieved their purpose in law at least. There is prohibition and suffrage. With her there was a single idea persistent in defeat and to death."[134]

There was a sad touch of irony in the end of this story: Lucy Page Gaston died of cancer of the throat, a disease often linked to cigarette smoking.

Conclusion

The story of how and why some Chicagoans consciously tried to improve their chances of a long and healthy life has two seemingly dissimilar aspects. On one hand, aldermen sought to improve public safety and health by using their legislative powers to build public works designed to upgrade sanitation and to enact ordinances intended to keep citizens from hurting each other. But there were also things that the citizens themselves decided to do individually to aid their chances of a long, healthy life. Physical exercise in particular was an activity that could release the tensions of the city. The crowds, the noises, the tedious "sedentary occupations," and the worries about money—all could be relieved by lifting weights and pedaling a bicycle, as well as visiting a theater or a saloon. That part is obvious.

Health was a multifaceted issue. Technology and industrialization had helped create some health problems by promoting a sedentary lifestyle, particularly among the growing group of managers and office workers. The efficient transit system minimized walking; the congested downtown offered desk jobs that involved little lifting or other movement; industrial machinery not only reduced many job skills to machine-tending, but also minimized the amount of physical exertion required for a task. But technology also made the bicycle popular; it was, after all, a machine.

This story also demonstrates that healthy living had, to some extent, a social-class trickle-down element. The various athletic fads originated among the wealthy, who often imported them from outside the city, then gained popularity among the less affluent. Whether at the first health clubs or even among the Turnverein, membership was something a family could afford only after the other bills were paid. The gradual adoption of fitness activities by the parks, along with the mass production of athletic equipment, considerably widened the opportunities.

The story of healthy living also had a public-private dimension. Cleaning up the water, milk, ice, and food supplies had involved public health, an effort to reduce the common risk of city living. By contrast, bicycling, attendance at exercise clubs or school gym classes, and abstinence from smoking were individual decisions that became public matters only when they came in conflict with the interests of others: the teamsters who vied with wheelmen for control of the streets, the antifrill watchdogs of the school board budget, and those for whom tobacco represented a pleasure or a business. One person's coping invariably brought conflict with another Chicagoan's efforts to deal with city life.

Postscript

The ideal of promoting good health through fitness has survived and thrived through the century. The advertising images of Bernarr Macfadden, Charles

Atlas, and Jack La Lanne evoked sighs from those whose bulges were in the wrong places. Although traditional settlement houses have largely disappeared, the YMCA, YWCA, boys and girls clubs, and similar nonprofit places continue attracting crowds. Night basketball leagues have provided a healthy alternative to the streets for public housing residents. Chicagoans have also been able to choose among an expanding number of commercial health and fitness clubs, bowling alleys, and other places whose prosperity was diminished only by depression and war. Needless to say, the Charlie Postl Health Club prospered. It occupied the twenty-seventh floor at 188 West Randolph Street, and its founder remained in charge until his death in 1964 at the age of seventy-eight.[135]

Exercise and amateur sports in general not only survived but assumed a new importance during the Great Depression. The Chicago Recreation Commission, established to combat the tedium of the enforced idleness of unemployment, actively promoted exercise programs and amateur athletics at a time when funding cutbacks seriously affected gym classes and interscholastic athletics in the schools.[136] Meanwhile, the ethnic athletic clubs had withstood the homogenizing effect of World War I–era Americanization crusades. Nonetheless, immigration restriction and the social transitions in the neighborhoods that surrounded their clubhouses created an unstoppable downhill slide for most of them.[137]

The ideal of getting fit while getting from here to there also continued to expand through the twentieth century despite the growing popularity of the automobile. The bicycle fad among adults faded a bit after the turn of the century, as the working-class market gradually became saturated and prosperous factory workers found that they could afford a Ford almost as easily as they could buy a bike. The Great Depression decimated the ranks of the bicycle manufacturers, but Chicago's Arnold, Schwinn and Company survived to prosper by supplying the postwar baby-boomers with new models. Bicycles made a giant comeback as a health-builder in the 1970s, but by then most production had departed for foreign factories. Schwinn closed its plant doors in 1984 and its Chicago office nine years later. In 1997 the Schwinn family auctioned off its collection of bicycles that dated back to the mid-nineteenth century.[138]

Finally, Lucy Page Gaston's campaign, which seems ephemeral at first glance, has also succeeded in some ways. Her Anti-Cigarette League folded a few years after her death, but various writers, the Woman's Christian Temperance Union, and medical experts continued the attack on tobacco. Their claims gained widespread credence when Dr. Luther Terry, the Surgeon General of the United States, released a special report entitled *Smoking and Health* in 1954. By linking tobacco consumption and cancer, critics almost completely shifted the emphasis from smoking as a sin to smoking as risky behavior. Progress proved to be slow, but the cigarette industry has been under progressively intense attack for four decades. Cigarette advertising has disappeared from radio and television. And findings concerning the danger of "second-hand smoke," which largely reaffirmed Gaston's arguments, led to the outright ban of smoking from most public buildings and its segregation in others. Although teenagers continue to become smokers at alarming rates, tobacco consumption in America has ceased growing at the rapid postwar rate. And finally, seventy years after the nation's leading anticigarette crusader passed from the scene, fresh charges arose that tobacco companies spiked their product to increase its addictive characteristics; these charges, along with liability lawsuits, have left the tobacco industry on the defensive.[139]

Somewhere, Lucy Page Gaston must be happy.

8　Amusements, Crowds, and Morals

WHAT took place Back of the Yards on Saturday night? According to one report in 1910, "Dancing-dancing-dancing." Everywhere across this district of hard work and the poverty to show for it, young people and their elders got ready for an evening out: "Girls in their teens and women who do the work of men at the stockyards; girls with braids hanging down their backs and girls with towering 'rats' in their hair; men in rough clothes and men marvelously 'slicked up'; girls wearing shawls and aprons and girls in flashy silk waists; children of 3 and children of 13; girls with strong peasant features and girls whose faces have thinned considerably during their three or four years' stay in America—all dancing, dancing, dancing." Most of them were headed for one of the dance halls that three of every four saloonkeepers had opened in a rear or upstairs room. The younger men and women arrived with friends of the same gender, spending the early part of the evening looking over members of the opposite sex for potential dancing partners. A shortage of prospects might lead to a quick exit and a tour of neighborhood places that ended only when the right person and the right place had been discovered. But in all of the dance halls the evening progressed the same way: as the beer flowed, the singing and music became louder, the dancing more spirited, and the atmosphere more heavily laden with the odor of cheap tobacco and stale beer.[1]

But if dancing was "the one supreme joy of the young men and women of the dozen or more nationalities living back of the yards, . . . the soul of the community so to speak," there was an alternative for others in the form of the Davis Square Settlement House. Its parties attracted a more Americanized element, who were courteously greeted by usher-translators at the door. Those coming to the settlement dance for the first time looked around timidly at the cleanliness and size of the tastefully decorated hall, but they soon adjusted. The young women wore fashionable dresses and were addressed by name without the prefix of "Hey." The young men wore black suits and white shirts, refrained from smoking, and did not abandon their partners midfloor when the music stopped; the ice cream parlor downstairs was the sole source of refreshments. Parents often came by to watch and perform their native dances for children who looked on with admiration but preferred to be spectators. It was clear that these were the young people who had acquired American manners and ways, who aspired to work in a downtown office and perhaps live one day in a suburb. "When they do get Americanized they generally leave not only the dance hall but the neighborhood as well," noted one Americanized Slav.

These events were part of something much larger than contrasts in dancing. What Chicagoans did with their spare time reflected their way of coping with the cares of city life. It could be active or passive entertainment, free or at a price, near home or across town, something people did as individuals or part of a vast crowd. All of these possibilities represented individual decisions that had been directly affected by the forces of urbanization and the marketplace. Leisure was the great social mirror. And in many instances, Chicagoans found out that their choice of activities through which they sought an escape from their cares often created another set of headaches and problems for someone else.

Cheap Thrills: The Rise and Fall of Dime Museums

In this century, museums are institutions of solid respectability, and most strive for a reasonably clear differentiation between educational and entertainment goals. But it was not always that way. During the last half of the nineteenth century, the city's "respectable" museums—the Academy of Sciences, Chicago Historical Society, and the Academy of Design (the predecessor of the Art Institute)—had to compete with a variety of establishments and visiting attractions that combined the bizarre with the uplifting. Their rise and fall not only mark a chapter in the history of Chicago's gullibility, but also reflect larger themes of urban life.

The city's first museums, which opened in the 1840s, were little more than ephemeral displays of curios; anything that was unfamiliar, unusual in appearance, or an apparent aberration from nature was a potentially profitable asset. To some extent, that was a reflection of Chicago's size; it was too little and too isolated on the frontier to support separate institutions of "high culture" and amusement. In 1848, David Kennison, who claimed to be the last survivor of the Boston Tea Party, opened one such establishment. Reputedly 112 years old, Kennison was himself to be a star exhibit, but his backers lost much of their investment when he died that same year.[2]

As transportation conditions began to improve, operators of minor curio collections found it difficult to compete with more spectacular attractions shipped in from out-of-town. One of these was the first panorama, which claimed to be an "educational amusement" when it visited in the late 1840s. The principle was simple; the size, captivating. Giant paintings, often four hundred feet long or even larger, were unwound across a stage and rolled up on the other side. Accompanied by fanfare, narration, and music, the huge scrolls awed the thousands who paid the half-dollar admission.[3]

The panorama subjects were varied. A few, such as *Pilgrim's Progress* and *Mirror of Intemperance and Crime,* both presented in 1853, conveyed moral messages and won endorsements from churches whose ministers usually condemned commercial amusements as frivolous. But most transported their customers to another time or place through travel or history shows. The earliest, Henry Lewis's *Panorama of the Upper and Lower Mississippi,* brought huge crowds to City Hall, which the Common Council rented out because they thought the production educational. Four years later, Mathieu Arthur Andrieu created a panorama of Chicago as viewed from the top of its tallest building, the courthouse. He also took it to New York, while bringing a Gotham spectacular to Chicago. These panoramas represented more than escapist fare. By the early 1850s the railroads were enmeshing Chicago in a national network of traveling entertainers who ranged from opera singers to magicians to theatrical companies. And with that novel engagement with the outside world came a thirst for the new, whether it be cuisine (and the aforementioned lobsters) or fashion or simply information. The panorama took on the function of a painted newsreel, providing images to accompany the verbal descriptions of the life of Napoleon, the beauties of California, or John C. Frémont's travels. Timing was often critical to the shows' appeal. On May 21, 1861, advertisements announced the opening of the new panorama of the attack on Fort Sumter, only five weeks after the actual event.[4]

But by the late 1860s, the panoramas were already declining in popularity, as more sophisticated audiences were demanding to see real objects, the stranger the better. Ironically, tasteful displays of artifacts from the Chicago Academy of Sciences and the Chicago Historical Society, both founded in the mid-1850s, may have whetted the public's appetite for the bizarre.[5] For a quarter, visitors could view the treasures assembled by the city's version of P. T. Barnum, Colonel J. H. Wood, for his Chicago Museum. Like the large variety stores of that era that offered an array of wares, his establishment held more than sixty cases of birds, reptiles, insects, and objects from around the world, all arranged somewhat haphazardly. A scale model of the Parthenon stood in one room, while ship models and Daniel Boone's rifle occupied two cases. Wood was especially proud of a pair of mummies reportedly once owned by the Mormon prophet Joseph Smith. The most spectacular attraction was the "Great Zeuglo-don," a ninety-six-foot-long skeleton of a prehistoric whale. For those who doubted its authenticity, Wood employed the marketing technique widely used by the patent medicine industry and included testimonials from scientists in his catalog. Like the proprietors of many eastern "dime museums" upon which his establishment was modeled, Colonel Wood also offered a stage show with musical acts and contemporary English drama.[6]

The Great Fire of 1871 swept away Colonel Wood's museum and a few smaller rivals, as well as the collections of the academy of science and the historical society. But within a few years, Kohl and Middleton's and other dime museums were operating, albeit on a somewhat less spectacular scale.[7] Two of the most interesting places operated as sidelines to other businesses. At Clark and Center (now Armitage) stood the wedge-shaped Relic House. This saloon used displays of melted metallic remains from the Great Fire to attract customers.[8] Downtown, Charles Gunther amazed crowds in his candy store when he introduced yet another Egyptian mummy to Chicago as the princess who rescued Moses from the bulrushes. It had reportedly been removed from Thebes in 1881 and sold to Gunther by a nephew of one of the tomb robbers. As one newspaper writer described it, "And now this . . . mighty potentate's daughter bids us sit at her feet and drink her health in 5-cent soda water."[9]

Other dime museums brought in crowds by displaying "freaks." Fat-people shows were a staple, but routine. More remarkable were exhibitions of individuals like Thomas Maxwell, a twelve-year-old "street arab." When police discovered him in November 1885, they took him to two places. The first was the West Side Free Medical Dispensary, where doctors cleaned him—he had never worn underwear—and examined him. Their diagnosis: "dermatolysis," or super-elastic skin. Because of the elasticity of his scalp, it took three barbers to give him a haircut. Maxwell's second destination was Epstean's West Side Museum, where he became "Jo Jo, the Dog Faced Boy." His competitors for customer dollars included "Miss Myrtle Corbin, the Living Four-Legged Girl," "Krao, the Monkey Girl," and Fanny Mills, who wore size-thirty shoes.[10] Other places featured oddities from natural science, such as "Englehardt's Mathesoid Marionorama," which included six hundred marine objects, and "The Prince of Wales," a stuffed cetacean on a temporary visit.[11]

The popularity of the dime museum was an indication of the breadth—or shallowness—of the public's taste. It was also another example of the growing importance of a sense of place in the nineteenth-century city. This was the era when the semipublic space had special allure. The magisterial railway terminal, grand hotel, atmospheric restaurant, and eye-dazzling theater were symbols of urban growth and sophistication. When the masses wanted to play, they wanted to do so in a particular kind of place that was often escapist, such as the wide-open beach, or even ephemeral, such as the temporary circus tent. At the same time, Chicago's climate created the need for something more permanent and weather-tight. As amusements began to evolve, they became more competitive, and many of them moved into buildings designed for their distinct needs.

The appetite for vicarious travel created by the panoramas led to an ersatz "travel industry." It survived by adapting physically to changing popular tastes. During the 1880s, gigantic paintings once more became popular, but instead of being unwound across a stage, they were mounted permanently inside the perimeter walls of huge circular buildings. One of these peculiar structures stood on Michigan Avenue at Madison Street, while two rivals were erected across the street from each other on South Wabash. Their interior arrangements were similar. After paying the admission at the door, visitors walked through a long, narrow underground passageway to the center of the building; this trip not only positioned them, but the walk also adjusted their eyes to the light level of the view to come. At the end of the hallway they climbed stairs to an elevated platform in the middle of the room. Here, they had an unobstructed view of the huge mural that surrounded them. To make the scenes depicting the Great Chicago Fire or the Crucifixion even more realistic, designers blended relics and other three-dimensional reconstructions into the space that separated the bottom of the painting and the railing of the observation platform. The patron became completely enveloped in the atmosphere of the setting. The new cycloramas, as the displays were usually called, helped an older generation keep alive memories of the Civil War by depicting Bull Run, Shiloh, Chattanooga, Gettysburg, and the Monitor and the Merrimack.[12]

The cycloramas were changed periodically, and each new project brought employment to dozens of artists who were not ashamed to accept such crassly commercial work. Some painters, including the famed Chicago artists Oliver Dennett Grover and Paul Peyraud, found it an excellent training ground for mural work. Milwaukee became home to the largest group of skilled cyclorama artists, but Chicago became a major stop on a national circuit of thirty such spectacles managed by the so-called "Panorama King," Emmett McConnell of Ludlow, Kentucky.[13]

Other entrepreneurs during the 1890s tried to bring the world to Chicago in other ways. The city's spectacular growth had already begun to make it a tourist attraction in itself, but the prospect of profit from the huge crowds that were expected to journey to Chicago for the World's Columbian Exposition began to alter the local amusement scene.[14] Cycloramas had to share amusement dollars with such attractions as the old Libby Prison, which was dismantled and moved from Richmond, Virginia, to South Wabash and Fourteenth Street in Chicago. Charles Gunther and other investors added a fortresslike stone entrance and filled the old prison with hundreds of curios from the candymaker's collection. Although many of the Chicago veterans who had once been prisoners of war in the structure condemned this crass commercialization of their misery, the Libby Prison Museum opened to huge crowds.[15]

Another example of relocated history turned out to be a dismal failure from the beginning. In 1891 a group of Washington, D.C., entrepreneurs bought and dismantled the engine house from the arsenal at Harpers Ferry, West Virginia, the scene of John Brown's famous raid of 1859. This small building was transported to Chicago and reassembled inside of a larger museum of war relics, which opened with much fanfare the following spring. But, after only eleven visitors paid the fifty-cent admission during the first ten days of operation, the principal owner, an ex-congressman from Iowa, locked the door and went home.[16]

The closing of the 1893 Columbian Exposition and the severe economic depression that followed doomed many of the older amusement places. Chicagoans had precious few dollars to spend on escapist fare, ironically at a time when they perhaps needed it most. The gigantic Chicago Fire painting, which had cost $150,000 and taken eight artists a year to complete, was sold to a junk dealer several years later for two dollars. In 1897 the Panorama Building on Michigan Avenue was razed to make way for the Gage, Edson Keith, and Ascher Buildings designed by Louis Sullivan.[17] The Libby Museum operated successfully until 1898, when declining revenues forced it to close. The prison structure itself was dismantled, some of its bricks ending up in museums. The stone walls that had enclosed it were incorporated into the construction of the new Chicago Coliseum, which opened in 1900 and for the next six decades hosted local sporting events and national political conventions.[18]

The traditional dime museums survived the changes, but they were clearly dying. Kohl and Middleton had to resort to a constant stream of cat and dog shows, amateur contests, beauty contests, and "fat ladies conventions" to survive.[19] The press seldom conducted exposés of dime museums, but in one instance a paper reported that a "lion escape" staged at Kohl and Middleton's was a fraud conducted with a toothless old animal. Although an 1899 Illinois law outlawing the display of "freaks" was overturned in the courts, the publicity undoubtedly hurt some places. When Huber's, one of the smaller establishments, closed in 1900, the *Record-Herald* proclaimed that the "era of the dime museum [had] passed."[20]

Operators of dime museums and other old-style amusements had been losing revenue to competing entrepreneurs who were able to draw crowds to see the professionalization of activities that the masses already pursued. Billiards, which had become a popular participatory activity in the late 1860s, became a spectator sport when huge mirrors were suspended over the tables to reflect the action of special matches set up in hotel ballrooms.[21] Although many Chicagoans were familiar with horse racing, the throngs that attended the city's two racetracks, Garden City and Brighton, allowed promoters to offer large purses, something that attracted even larger crowds. One other large, commercial attraction of this time actually drew the condemnation of the community. In 1869 boxing ceased to exist in Illinois as a spectator sport open to legal general admission. In future years, bouts would be held either secretly or in clubs open only to members, both of which legally constituted private rather than semipublic events. Promoters found one dodge when they began opening up "club memberships" that could be had for the purchase price of a ticket.[22]

In this era of new attractions, however, nothing could match the spectacular rise of baseball. The game began to capture the public imagination soon after it was first played in Chicago in 1856. Improved railway service allowed teams to travel, and the variety of opponents helped increase interest among fans, who demanded a more honest and professional game. William A. Hulbert, a grain dealer, bought the White Stockings in 1876 and persuaded the owners of the other teams to systematize the rules and form intercity competition with a schedule of games. The result was the National League of Professional Baseball. In 1894, Charles A. Comiskey, son of an early Chicago alderman, and Byron "Ban" Johnson founded a new Western League and created a Chicago team, which adopted the modified name "White Sox" after the original White Stockings had abandoned it for the "Cubs." Finally, in 1913, a group of investors established a third baseball circuit, the Federal League. Two Chicagoans, a coal dealer named James A. Gillmore and the restaurant-chain owner Charles Weeghman, were the major backers of the Whales, the local team. Two years later, Weeghman built a new stadium, "Weeghman Park," today's Wrigley Field.[23]

Baseball created a special form of urban place. Like panorama buildings, baseball parks were monuments to Chicago's quest for leisure. Privately owned but of public access, they were examples of the semipublic space that was an essential part of city-building. The growing popularity of the game prompted the invention of a specialized building to handle large numbers of customers. Major-league baseball parks represented not only architectural innovations, they were also what might be called "crowd machines," that is, specifically designed structures that employed concrete and steel framing in new ways to provide entrance, exit, and good visibility to as large a crowd as the attraction could draw.

Ballparks were also outdoor theaters that helped to create a new type of hero whose popularity was rooted in visibility and information. Players became familiar to tens of thousands through the press, which detailed their lives on and off the ballfield. Unlike Washington or Lincoln or other political or cultural heroes whom a youth might only dream of meeting, athletic personalities were as "semipublic" as the places in which they played because they were open to anyone for an admission fee. Promoted by growing press coverage, which functioned as unpaid advertising, the commercialized baseball icon reigned supreme.[24]

Not even Colonel Wood's "Great Zeuglodon" could have competed with the legends of the diamond.

Pleasure or Peril on the Fringe: From Beer Gardens to Amusement Parks

Henry J. Kolze understood human nature. In 1885 he bought an acre of open land at Irving Park Road and Sixty-fourth Avenue and built a hotel and beer garden. Mount Olive Cemetery had just opened nearby, and he quickly realized the business opportunities it presented. Soon, funeral processions began stopping for the practical necessity of feeding and watering the horses before making their way back to the city. Kolze began offering drivers a free meal, a beer, and two cigars while their teams were being serviced; soon he was giving away as many 150 dinners a day, and his stable grew to accommodate 102 animals. Rather than sit in the carriages and wait, the mourners sought the comfortable atmosphere and good food that beckoned after the long sad drive out to Mount Olive and the solemnities of the burial. The young entrepreneur was set for life.[25]

The Kolze tavern, which continued in business until 1949, was only one of dozens of beer gardens that were once sprinkled around the city's fringe. They were there for two reasons—besides the beer and bratwurst. The first was geographical mobility, getting from here to there. Ever since the farmers began hauling grain into the city in the 1830s, there had been a substantial traffic in and out of town. Some places, like the Brighton Inn, had once been genuine inns catering to traders traveling to and from Chicago's grain and livestock markets. Others, like the Sunnyside Inn at Clark Street and Montrose, simply provided food and drink.[26]

The other reason Chicago had so many beer gardens was related to the cultural baggage of the burgeoning German population. Germans began to arrive in great numbers during the late 1840s and 1850s, bringing with them the custom of patronizing outdoor family-oriented drinking places, a very strong tradition in the old country. Since many of the German immigrants tended to live near the city's expanding fringe where land was relatively cheap, beer-garden owners had their choice of locations along roads leading from the city. By 1859, for example, Clemens and Rudd had established a place at Cottage Grove (near present-day Twenty-second Street and South Cottage Grove Avenue), while Henry Meywell's beer garden did a thriving trade near the Illinois Central tracks at Twenty-seventh Street. For those who had no other way to get there, Eisenmenger's German National Garden ran its own omnibus between the city and its grounds, which were located out on the State Street toll road. By the end of the century, a serious devotee of the hops could, in fact, drink his way around the perimeter of the city from the South Side to Lake View.[27]

The most successful beer gardens were able to blend the feeling of rural isolation from city cares with the reality of easy transportation to the heart of Chicago. By 1860, Sunday had already emerged as the busiest travel day for the horse railway companies, as whole families found amusement in visiting the lake, Union Park, or some other spot. Many riders found both urban pleasure and bucolic ambience in beer gardens that offered "shady and cool groves, green grass and gay flowers, the pleasures of good music, dancing, athletic exercise, shooting galleries, lager beer, Rhein wine and the pretzel."[28] Henry Kolze was fortunate enough to have a streetcar line terminate at his front door. In winter, it brought a steady commuter business to his indoor tavern; in summer, whole families seeking cheap Sunday entertainment rode out "to see the sights" at the end of the line. Still another category of riders ended their visits to relatives and friends at the Dunning insane asylum and almshouse with a more pleasant stop across the road at Kolze's.[29]

Other Chicagoans who owned or could rent a carriage sought out favorite rest stops during Sunday sojourns into the city's hinterlands. During the 1890s it became a fad for groups of a dozen or more to hire large "Tally-Ho" coaches for short excursions. And when bicycles were all the rage during the closing three decades of the century, expeditions of wheelmen made certain places their unofficial headquarters. Chicago's commuter railroads also aggressively sought weekend business for the dozens of picnic groves that were within a few hours of the city. Perhaps inspired by Sam Gross and the other real estate subdividers, the carriers could utilize suburban equipment that might otherwise be idle. And finally, several entrepreneurs shared Henry Kolze's secret and opened establishments near cemeteries, which were then far out in the country. The business generated by mourners was steady and predictable. In one unusual case, a German immigrant named Ferdinand Haase transformed his farm on the banks of the Des Plaines River into a picnic park, which became especially popular after the North Western railroad built a spur to its door. In the early 1870s, however, Haase sold the land to form Concordia and Waldheim Cemeteries.[30]

Beer gardens also became important bastions of ethnicity, especially during the late nineteenth century. Poetry readings, dramatic presentations, and folk dancing were common supplements to vocal and instrumental music. Various organizations also rented the gardens for fund-raising parties, which helped to finance old folk's homes, hospitals, charities, and other institutions. For decades, the names of Colehour's and Excelsior Park appeared on handbills and newspaper ads promoting fun-filled philanthropy. Ogden's Grove, at Clybourn and Willow, also advertised in such labor periodicals as the *Eight-Hour Herald,* noting that it was "Union throughout: Union Cigars, Union Help, Union Music, Union Beer."[31]

Competition transformed the beer garden, especially after improvements in public transit—from horsecar to cable car to electric trolley to the elevated—allowed successful entrepreneurs to draw from a wider geographical area. This extended the choices available to patrons, but it also compelled proprietors to add sidelight attractions. Bands became orchestras, and indoor winter gardens were built to overcome the problem of inclement weather. The Bismarck Garden at Halsted, Broadway, and Grace Streets played on the reputation of the hotel of the same name, both of which were owned by Karl Eitel. At Irving Park Road and Sixty-fourth (now Narragansett), the Kolze family added acetylene gas lights to become the area's most notable nighttime beer garden; playful patrons quickly dubbed it "Kolze's Electric Park," a name the owners soon adopted. Down in south Chicago, Colehour's added boxing matches. Fischer's Garden, at Diversey and Sheridan Road, boasted a long pier that extended into the lake.[32]

The cost of adding cultural come-ons could be prohibitive, even if they brought in a better class of clientele. In 1875, for instance, Philip Henrici opened the Lincoln Pavilion at Clark and Grant Place, a fancy beer garden with entertainment provided by a forty-piece orchestra. But expenses drove Henrici to give up the place three years later. "The attraction drew society," he complained, "but a beer garden must be run for the masses." Henrici then turned his attention to the restaurant that made his family name famous to generations of Chicagoans.[33]

Four decades later, Edward Waller Jr. learned a similar lesson. His Sans Souci, which had operated at Sixtieth and Cottage Grove under previous owners, had been highly successful as a middlebrow place, with a ballroom, roller rink, and a tall sightseeing tower. But in 1914 Waller decided to reach for the monied market and commissioned Frank Lloyd Wright to design a large complex that included a restaurant, ballroom, and outdoor dining. For his new Midway Gardens, Waller brought an expensive orchestra and even ballet. But not all Chicagoans were ready to hoist their steins to Anna Pavlova; the enterprise folded after two seasons, even before the architectural detail was complete, and it was sold to a brewer who reopened it as the less pretentious Edelweiss Gardens.[34]

The story of Sharpshooter's Park is a capsule history of the way in which competition transformed the beer garden business. In 1879, the North Chicago Shutzen Verein bought a large plot of land at present-day Western and Belmont for a rifle range. Members of the group had once belonged to the Jaeger Corps, a unit of crack German riflemen. A city crackdown on the display and use of weapons following the 1877 railway strike violence prompted a move just outside the city limit. The new acreage also contained large picnic areas for members' families, and many in the group were content to keep it private. But they were outnumbered, and a bandstand, dance pavilion, seating area, and booths selling a variety of food swallowed up the park's open spaces.[35]

Traditional beer gardens proved to be endangered for another reason. Temperance organizations condemned them as particularly pernicious drinking spots because so many families attended and exposed their children to beer. The idea of the Continental Sunday, including drinking and other secular pursuits, angered conservative Protestants, who were unable to pressure the city to enforce Sabbath closing laws. Another type of opposition came from residents who had purchased homes near Chicago's ring of large public parks and boulevards. They were upset when the peace and tranquility of their neighborhoods, already threatened by soaring park attendance, were shattered by noises from beer gardens that had been located to take advantage of the pedestrian traffic. The Downer and Bemis Brewing Company lost a sizable investment because neighborhood opposition drove its Tivoli Gardens out of business.[36]

No beer garden symbolized the fragile nature of the business as clearly as the one that became associated with the largest and most famous object on display at the World's Columbian Exposition. George Ferris's giant invention was actually very simple, little more than a huge bicycle wheel, 250 feet in diameter and suspended between two enormous piers sunk deep into the ground. But the size of the Ferris wheel defied all superlatives of the day. The axle, 32 inches in diameter and 45 feet long, was the largest hollow metal rod ever cast. The spokes were nearly 3 inches thick, and each of the 36 cars comfortably held 40 people. In one record-setting day, a total of 35,000 patrons (1,768 in one trip) paid fifty cents each to take the twenty-minute one-revolution ride. During its Chicago run, the wheel revolved 10,000 times and carried 1.4 million riders.[37]

When the exposition closed, Ferris and his investors faced the serious question of what to do with the wheel. Although its gross earnings had been large, the high costs of fabricating it in Pittsburgh, shipping it to Chicago, and erecting it on the Midway of the the fairgrounds had left only a small profit. The size of the investment precluded junking it. Since no immediate decision could be reached, the wheel was left standing through the winter of 1893–94, a sad reminder of the exposition euphoria. During the following spring, hundreds of workers began the task of constructing a huge timber framework within which the various iron members were numbered, disassembled, and lowered to the ground. Wagons carried the parts to dozens of flatcars parked at a Sixty-first Street siding of the Illinois Central Railroad.[38]

The dismantling followed an announcement that the wheel would be moved to New York City in five thirty-car trains. It was to be part of an "Old Vienna" beer garden and amusement park, which was to open in the late summer of 1894 at Broadway and Thirty-seventh in Manhattan. When that plan fell through, sites at Coney Island and, later, London, England, were proposed. But the months passed, and a summertime opening became impossible because of the lengthy rebuilding time.[39] Another winter arrived, and the machinery sat deserted at the Woodlawn railroad siding. Early in 1895, Ferris and his investors found a site for the wheel through a new secret partner, but neither realized the troubles their business deal would bring.

The new chapter of the saga started on the morning of February 25, 1895, when the Ferris Wheel Company took out a building permit for a powerhouse at 1272–1306 (later renumbered 2619–2665) North Clark. Reporters learned that Ferris's new associate was Charles T. Yerkes, the streetcar monopolist who was one of the most hated men in Chicago. The location of their new enterprise was perfect: only two blocks from Lincoln Park and adjacent to one of Yerkes's most heavily traveled trolley lines. The plans included a spectacular roof garden, designed by architect Jarvis Hunt, as well as a restaurant at the level of the wheel's hub, 130 feet in the air. Other amusement rides and a beer garden would also be crowded into the grounds, and hundreds of lights would make it a prime nighttime attraction.[40]

While the investors dreamed of profit, nearby residential property owners fumed that the wheel was "undesirable industrialism invading residential districts." Fifty of them stormed into the office of Mayor George B. Swift demanding a halt to the construction. The city corporation counsel declared that he did not know whether or not the wheel was technically a building, which would require a building permit. Swift interpreted that opinion as giving him the power to deny approval. The Ferris Wheel Company filed suit to force the granting of the permit, and when a local judge ruled in favor of the Ferris interests, construction began despite the mayor's announcement that he would appeal the case.[41]

The local property owners quickly pursued two other tactics, including an effort to create a local-option district that would take in the proposed Ferris Wheel Park. This followed the lead of many other Chicago neighborhoods whose aldermen had driven out saloons with ordinances requiring the consent of property owners within a specific district before a liquor license application could be processed. Many affluent residential voting precincts had already used the tactic to chase saloons out of substantial portions of outlying wards. The wheel's opponents hoped that the potential loss of liquor sales revenue would cause the developers to look elsewhere. One embarrassing revelation came from the proceedings: One of the leading "dry" activists was Francis J. Dewes, whose magnificent mansion stood at Wrightwood and Hamden Court, just down the street from the wheel site. Dewes, however, was also a brewer with considerable interest in dozens of saloons and was, himself, fighting local-option battles in other neighborhoods. The Ferris Wheel Company also disclosed that the attorney for the property owners was Harry Rubens, who served as legal counsel for the city's saloonkeepers' association. Despite that exposure of apparent hypocrisy on the part of Dewes, the city council approved the local option district, and the wheel's owners found themselves in court challenging the denial of a liquor license.[42]

The other strategy employed by the property owners came to light on April 28, 1895, when the city council passed a law requiring a fifty-dollar-a-day license on any form of commercial amusement located within fifteen hundred feet of a public park. Ferris's group correctly predicted that their challenge of the license fee would succeed. But even though that matter was still pending and a strike by structural iron workers slowed the reassembly of the wheel, the backers decided to proceed with construction during the summer of 1895. The wheel rims were in place by the end of August and the cars attached by mid-September. A few small side-show amusements moved into the grounds, but by then the season was nearly over, leaving the towering contraption idle for another winter.[43]

By the following spring, the central attraction of the little amusement park was operating, but the lack of a liquor license stalled the plans for a roof garden. In October 1895, the Illinois Appellate Court found in the amusement company's favor and the following spring friends of Yerkes in the city council pushed through an ordinance that would have exempted the park from the local option district. Mayor George Swift vetoed it. The final blow came on June 23, 1896, when the Illinois Supreme Court reversed the appellate decision and upheld the license ban.[44] By then, the wheel was already losing money. The nation was two years into a severe depression, and too few Chicagoans were willing to part with a half-dollar for a ride, the same price it had been during the prosperous exposition days. The company stopped paying its bills in mid-1896, and by the time that George Ferris died of tuberculosis in November that year, his giant invention had passed into receivership.[45]

The Ferris wheel remained in limited operation on Clark Street for four more years. The return of national prosperity in 1898 brought some optimism. But by 1900, the wheel had accumulated a debt of $400,000, and dissolution proceedings in June of that year brought an end to the second sad chapter of its life. What had once been the center of world attention passed into the hands of a junk dealer for a mere $1,800, far less than even the labor costs involved in removing it. Once more, it lay in pieces.[46]

The Ferris wheel failed on the North Side not only because of neighborhood opposition, but also because of changes in entertainment economics and tastes. It had to compete with other amusement spots that were inspired by the success of the wheel's original home, the Midway of the World's Columbian Exposition. This strip of rides and reproductions of foreign villages was laid out along the Midway Plaisance, which had been part of the original 1869 park plan. Added almost as an afterthought to the fair, the Midway proved to be an enormous attraction and a popular counterbalance to the more serious cultural pursuits in Jackson Park and the exploitive cheap amusements that were located off the fairgrounds. The Midway mixed together anthropological exhibits in the form of reconstructed foreign villages, as well as animal shows, an ice slide, and Little Egypt doing her exotic dance. In some ways, the Midway became to the world's fair what the Levee district was to vice, an area where commercialized amusement was allowed to take place but under some control and within a restricted geographical area.[47]

The enormous popularity of the Midway demonstrated anew that people were willing to pay to be amused. Mechanical rides such as the Ferris wheel provided an opportunity for more than just passive fun; being spun around required more involvement than sitting in a theater seat—and it was more thrilling. The small amusement park called Sans Souci had actually opened just before the fair at Sixtieth Street and Cottage Grove (the eventual site of Midway Gardens), but other entrepreneurs began issuing new plans and soliciting investors soon after the big exposition closed. One group wanted to build a gigantic tower on the lakefront; another, an exact reproduction of the Midway on the West Side.[48] But because of the depression, only a few scaled-down enterprises were ever built. There was a short-lived Electric Park at Elston, California, and Western,[49] but the most successful was The Chutes, built in 1894 by a famous swimmer named Paul Boynton. Water flowed down tall inclines, carrying with it small boats filled with people. "The sensations are not easily described, as the entire trip of 700 feet is accomplished in something over ten seconds," wrote columnist George Ade. "There is a confused sensation of flying lights, band music and everyone shouting—you among the others." There was also a small zoo that allowed visitors to touch and ride camels and other exotic animals. After two successful seasons on Stony Island, the operation was rebuilt on the West Side at Jackson and Kedzie with the addition of a water-wheel mill and roller coaster to draw in the revenue.[50]

Amusement parks evolved into their final form between 1904 and 1908. There was a short-lived Luna Park, built in 1907 at Fifty-second and Halsted; the following year it fell into the hands of the notorious gambler James O'Leary, the son of Mrs. O'Leary of the Great Fire fame. He replaced it in 1912 with a large food-market hall.[51] The most famous parks, however, were Riverview, White City, and Forest Park. These institutions bore some resemblance to the old picnic parks in their casual outdoor atmosphere and their beer gardens and picnic grounds, but they were far more complex. The oldest, Riverview at Western and Belmont, evolved out of Sharpshooter's Park. By the turn of the century, the owners had added roller skating and a growing list of mechanical rides, including a roller coaster and chutes. There was a dancing pavilion and a stage for vaudeville acts. Political groups rented the place, and such luminaries as William McKinley, William Jennings Bryan, and Theodore Roosevelt addressed rallies there.[52]

While Riverview served the North Side, South Siders had White City, which opened in 1906. Billed as the largest amusement park in America, it was built on land owned by the meat packer J. Ogden Armour along the Sixty-third Street leg of the South Side Elevated, or "Alley El." It incorporated The Chutes and added a roller coaster and other rides that jolted the senses, while a quarter-million lights made it eye dazzling after dark.[53] In 1908, a third competitor, Forest Park, opened after the owner of a picnic ground in west suburban Harlem arranged for a trolley company to provide service to a new amusement park he was building. It had the usual roller coaster and chutes, and the "Pneumatic Tube," which combined the attractions of a haunted house and a "tunnel of love." Ironically, it was located not far from where Ferdinand Haase had opened his park-turned-cemetery more than a half-century earlier.[54]

The amusement park provided escapism, a way to cope with city life, but the social and economic factors that created it forced many Chicago families to deal with new issues. For the adult amusement consumer, leisure was a matter of finding time and money and choosing where to spend them. Parents faced more serious questions. Amusement parks tempted children to travel beyond the watchful eyes of the neighborhood into a world of anonymity and potential peril. There were new physical dangers. Each season, an average of one or two customers who had not absorbed the safety discipline fell to their deaths from rides or were otherwise injured in the major parks. In May 1910, for instance, twenty-six people were injured at Riverview, and the following September one woman was killed.[55]

The major parks had opened during the years when the issue of social purity was at the center of an intense debate. The city was preoccupied with the issues of prostitution, the survival of the "red-light" Levee district, and the abduction of young rural women and girls into what was called the white slave trade. Critics pointed out that youngsters traveling on their own had to run a gauntlet of temptation just to get into the parks. Near the entrances there were clusters of saloons, "stalls," and other liquor sellers who developed a reputation for selling to minors.[56] What went on in the parks themselves presented another problem. It was easy for thousands of parents to regard the gaudy sights, raucous sounds, and pungent smells as little more than parts of a stationary carnival operated by suspicious people. Church groups had already led the opposition to the construction of Forest Park, which was built in a town that already contained several tranquil cemeteries.[57]

But the loudest complaint about amusement parks came from the Chicago Law and Order League. Founded in 1903 by the anticigarette crusader Lucy Page Gaston, it first battled the tradition of wide-open vice within the Levee, lobbied for film censorship and anti-tobacco laws, and tried to eliminate the dance hall. In 1909, it took on the amusement parks. League investigators complained that the shows were vile, that women associated with them paraded around in indecently tight pants, that the barkers' spiels were foul, that some performers had such titillating names as the "bare bronze beauty," and that some of the entertainers were female impersonators. On top of that, the various games of skill induced children to gamble. The league demanded that the parks be shut; the police made threats; the shows stayed open.[58]

Meanwhile, the new competition from amusement parks was forcing traditional beer gardens to change. The venerable institutions had thrived because of a certain amount of geographical mobility, which was limited by the slow pace of the bicycle, carriage, or lumbering streetcar. But as the years of the new century began to pass by, the era of the elevated railway, the speedy electric interurban, and the automobile began to broaden the ability of the average family to move about the city when and where it wanted. This newfound freedom not only allowed families to live in distant subdivisions, but also enabled them to find new leisure sites within the region. This mobility had a profound impact on the way people spent weekends and warm summer evenings. Ultimately, traditional beer gardens were the losers in the process. Once isolated, quiet, and simple in their operation, they now faced well-financed competition for a less-than-secure grip on a potentially greater group of customers, a market that consisted of strangers instead of neighbors. That change, in turn, forced beer gardens to become multifunctional to survive. Vaudeville, floor shows, and public dancing transformed some places into outdoor cabarets. Others lost their weekend clientele to the automobile. Families went out for a spin instead of a stube, while automobile drivers were encouraged not to drink at all. Most traditional beer gardens were too specialized and financially weak to survive the transition.[59]

America's entry into World War I was yet another blow. In an excess of patriotic fervor, all things German fell under the suspicion of disloyalty. The Eitel family responded by renaming their place Marigold Gardens (their Bismarck Hotel temporarily became the Randolph).[60] Prohibition was, of course, the fatal blow to many places. The Sieben family, which had been in business since 1876, found itself tangled up with illegal brewing and bootleg wars.[61]

Prohibition also claimed the Midway Gardens. In a sad example of adaptive reuse, Wright's magnificent buildings became a roller-skating rink before falling to a wrecker's ball to make way for a filling station. "It is better so," noted Wright, who preferred demolition to disfigurement. "In the wilderness of smoky dens, car tracks, and drugstores is there no place for a rendezvous such as its backers knew Chicago needed and believed Chicago wanted?" Apparently, there was not.[62]

And what happened to the Kolze Family? Henry J.'s Electric Park not only prospered, but its popularity propelled him into a political career during the first two decades of the century. As a Cook County commissioner, he brought new roads and sewers to his neighborhood. He also supervised construction of the eastern half of the City-County Building; a bronze plaque next to the door bears his name. Even though the Dunning insane asylum–poor farm across the street continued to generate traffic, Kolze was concerned that its presence depressed property values. He sponsored the legislation that closed it in 1912 and he moved some of its functions to Oak Forest. Henry J. Kolze died in 1926, but his wife and children continued to operate the Electric Park for another twenty-three years. His great idea of 1885 demonstrated how well he understood human nature.[63]

Tripping the Light Fantastic

Charles Fenno Hoffman was amazed at what he saw. It was New Year's Eve 1833, and his determination to sample the social life of the frontier had just brought him to Chicago. Still wearing his dusty traveling clothes, he followed his hosts to a frame house where the unfinished second floor had been decorated with pine boughs and flags for the occasion. A three-piece band, consisting of a black violin player, a bass drummer from Fort Dearborn, and another man who played both the flute and the triangle, provided the accompaniment for dozens of dancers. What astounded the eastern visitor most was the intermixture of people: soldiers with civilians, and the social leadership with the less wealthy. "In one quarter," he wrote, "the high-laced buttons of a linsey-woolsey coat would be *dos à dos* to the elegantly turned shoulders of a delicate-looking Southern girl; in another, a pair of Cinderella-like slippers would *chassez*

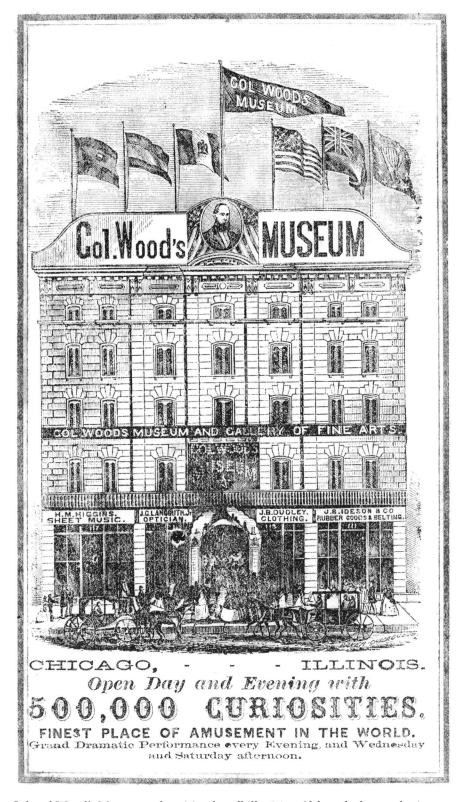

Colonel Wood's Museum, advertising handbill, 1860s. Although the emphasis was on the bizarre, the dime museum attempted to bring as many kinds of amusement as possible under one roof.

COMPLIMENTS OF LONDON DIME MUSEE, (INC.)

THE ORIGINAL WORLDS FAIR MIDWAY DANCERS

London Dime Musee, advertising card, early 1900s. This popular downtown spot exploited popular memories of the World's Columbian Exposition.

Edelweiss Garden entrance, ca. 1898. This Bavarian-style beer garden catered mostly to families from the more affluent neighborhoods near Hyde Park.

SUNNYSIDE PARK

S. FREUDENBERG, Prop'r.

CLARK STREET AND MONTROSE BLVD.

The Finest Resort for Cyclers in the City.

Meals Served at all Hours.

Eight Acres of Shady Grounds.   Thirty Private Dining-rooms, with Cuisine,
Wines and Liquors Unsurpassed.

CONCERT BY
ROSENBECKER'S ORCHESTRA   EVERY EVENING

And Matinees Saturday and Sunday Afternoons.

Sunnyside Inn advertisement, *Tenth Annual Associated Cycling Clubs of Chicago Road Race*
(1896). The old establishment, which had once catered to travelers, later was surrounded by residential neighborhoods and found a new clientele among cyclists.

Ferris wheel, ca. 1898. Once the center of attraction at the World's Columbian Exposition of 1893, "the big wheel," as it was popularly known, moved for a few seasons to the North Side neighborhood at Clark and Wrightwood Streets.

Bismarck Garden handbill, early 1900s. There was a lot more than beer at beer gardens. The dancer's bare feet, revealing costume, and seductive poses rankled ministers and moral reformers.

Marigold Gardens advertisement, 1929. Opened in 1918, the Marigold, at the Broadway-Grace-Halsted intersection, offered sophisticated dancing that was appropriate for pre-Depression prosperity.

Aragon Ballroom, postcard view, probably 1940s. The Aragon, at Broadway and Lawrence, along with its South Side counterpart, the Trianon, allowed patrons a few hours of affordable escapism in a place much more elegant than most of them normally enjoyed.

cross with a brace of thick-soled brogans, in making which, one of the lost feet of the Colossus of Rhodes may have served for a last."[64] But the event that Hoffman witnessed was more than an evening of fun. The pastime of dancing was also an important reflection of larger social trends in Chicago. It told volumes about the meaning of economic class, perceptions of social space of the city, and the relationships between parents and their children.

The prairie party that Hoffman attended was one of pioneer Chicago's ways of coping with both the isolation and narrow recreational opportunities on the undeveloped frontier and the shortage of women. Throughout those early days people were willing to travel many miles through the snow just to join in the revelry, with Chicagoans exchanging party visits with residents of Naperville and Warrenville, which were thirty miles away.[65] The sponsors were often the young bachelors of the town, who really wanted to see whether any of the farmers who had moved into the region had attractive daughters. Spontaneity gave way to planning. By 1839, once-a-week wintertime assemblies had evolved into events formally known as the "Bachelors' Assembly Balls," as well as quadrille parties featuring the popular three-quarter-time square dance.[66] With the creation of the volunteer fire companies during the late 1830s and 1840s, however, the organizers gained a more benevolent motive. Besides giving the firemen— or "extinguishers," as the *Weekly Chicago Democrat* called them—a chance to dress in formal uniforms and show off for the benefit of their ladies, these parties raised as much as four hundred dollars for the benefit of disabled firemen, widows, and orphans.[67]

Most of the early dances took place in private homes and the South Market Hall, but the growing size and sophistication of the city, as well as the growing popularity of dancing, forced changes. The same direct rail links to the East that exposed Chicagoans to fine dining also led to the demand for more sophisticated places to dance. In 1852 a new generation of facilities began with the opening of Melodeon Hall, a building measuring 30 by 65 feet. Gas lights, then a novelty, shined from three chandeliers, and cushioned crimson cloth adorned the side walls. But the most unusual feature was the ceiling, described by the *Weekly Chicago Democrat* as a full "17 feet between the joists." It was "arched and provided with unique additions to give better effect to the music—these consist of bottles holding about ten gallons each, which are fixed above the ceiling out of sight, with the necks down and mouths open. These it is said to increase the vibration and give better tone qualities." A "professor of dancing" was in charge. Irving Hall, which opened the following year, was even larger and more spectacular, with dressing rooms to allow a change to street clothes and stuffed sofas around the perimeter of the 3,400-square-foot room.[68]

Most Chicagoans were no doubt impressed by these advances, but some religious leaders regarded the new halls as little more than gilded hells. Even the parties with worthy fund-raising goals drew the wrath of those who objected that merely holding hands was a sinful form of bodily contact because there was no way to control who touched whom. (The predictability of formal dance cards would eventually remove some of the dangerous spontaneity.) They also complained that the public nature of many parties too often allowed entrance to undesirables who might be drunk or have lascivious motives. A religious paper, *The Watchman of the Prairie,* complained that any social gathering should have at least one constructive purpose, such as enlightening conversation or healthful exercise, but "whatever brings men together in masses, without setting some good before them, corrupts them." The paper especially condemned the new fad of dancing aboard lake excursion steamers because it took young people far away from community observation. True Christians, added the *Northwestern Christian Advocate,* had neither the time to spend on such idleness, nor the money to divert from true charity.[69]

Despite the divided opinion about the social value of dance, the growing popularity of dancing made its mastery a social necessity for many Chicagoans. But many worried that their clumsiness or their ignorance of the latest steps might lead to ostracism and loneliness. The solution came in the form of professional instruction. As early as 1834 out-of-town dance teachers began including Chicago on regular seasonal circuits, and by the end of the decade there was healthy competition among several resident instructors. James A. Marshall, for instance, invited potential pupils to a one-dollar sample evening of dance at the New York House, hoping to sign them up for three months of weekly lessons for ten dollars. During the 1840s many of the schools added juvenile classes. In 1850, "A. Woods" boasted that he had traveled East to learn "the latest style of dancing, waltzing, and galopading . . . together with . . . the new and improved polka, Schottisch, Redowa, Chacuca, German Celarious, Two and Four Step Waltzes, also the German Cotillion."[70]

By midcentury, the quest for expertise and the interest in eastern fads indicated that dancing was ready to move into its next phase, which emphasized the social class distinctions that were growing in the city. During the early 1860s the most popular dancing schools were located downtown. Mirasole's at 214 (now 219 South) Wabash lost many of its pupils to J. Edwin Martine, who opened his first place in 1860 at Dearborn and Wabash. Seven years later, two of Martine's best pupils, then instructors, Augustus E. Bornique and his wife, opened their first academy, also downtown, "for [the] thorough and scientific instruction in the Art of Dancing."[71]

Martine and Bornique quickly realized that their most profitable markets lay closer to where the wealthier families lived. In 1865 Martine moved to Ohio Street, where his new hall boasted of a solid black walnut interior. Four years later he moved to a larger place with a $1,000 chandelier. Soon, he added a West Side branch on Ada Street, between Washington and Madison, to serve the fashionable neighborhood around Union Park. It featured two 50' × 100' rooms, the downstairs for banquets and the upstairs for dancing. Not to be outdone, in 1869 the Borniques opened a grand hall "fitted up in a style the most *recherché*" at Halsted and Adams. Soon afterward they opened a branch on Twenty-fourth Street near Prairie Avenue's elite, moving again in 1883 to a new hall designed by Burnham and Root. The latter, a Queen Anne–style structure that cost over $90,000, was decorated throughout with a cherry wood and light olive decor.[72]

The outward move of Bornique and Martine was both a cause and an effect of the growing popularity of dancing among Chicago's wealthier families. The new facilities were closer to the mansion districts, with Bornique's in particular becoming an important institution in the Prairie Avenue neighborhood. It was convenient for the privileged to send their children to learn the poise and grace—Bornique's called it "an absence of rusticity"—from the dance master. The lavish facilities were also accessible for those whose houses did not contain a ballroom, a feature that gradually disappeared when the elite and near-elite began building row houses to accommodate narrow city lots and soaring land prices.[73]

Dancing reflected the desire for predictability in the lifestyles of the elite. Their social calendar included a standard array of charity balls and other social events, at which the dance card established the schedule for the whole evening.[74] But the growing cosmopolitanism of the city's first families created a problem. Travel to the East Coast and abroad became increasingly common as the century progressed, and Chicagoans, who already suffered because of the brash and crude image of their city, wanted to be sure that they could intermingle without calling attention to themselves. They wanted to try new dance steps without falling prey to a chaos of fads. The answer came in the form of the American Association of Professional Dancing Instructors, whose seventy national members included Martine and Bornique. The group, formed in 1879 and headquartered in New York, met twice at the beginning of the fall dancing season to discuss mutual problems and decide which of last year's dances had lost popularity. They also passed judgment on new steps proposed by members, which were put to an elaborate dance trial and a secret ballot. Of course, millions of dancers across the country would determine whether the Minnehaha or some other step would be a hit or a flop, but the approved list allowed elites in major cities across the country to be familiar with a standard repertoire of dances. Needless to say, the arrangement virtually ensured profit for the businesses of Bornique and Martine. Ultimately, as one newspaper writer put it, the new dance "will percolate, drop by drop, to the lower stratum of the social fabric—until at last the mere common people, the numberless crowds of dancers for dancing's sake, will be initiated into the mysteries of the novel rite."[75]

Each step down the social scale meant a progressive decline of the kind of privacy and predictability in social relations that marked the lives of the wealthiest families.[76] Both Bornique and Martine had separate classes for the upwardly mobile middle class, who sought opportunities to show off their dancing skills. While these gatherings were considerably less private than were those of the elite, the participants did benefit from the selective screening. The schools also sponsored large parties for all of their pupils, who were able to bring their lady and gentleman friends and to socialize with new friends they had made in class. Although Bornique encouraged this stratum of his trade, he was somewhat condescending in his comment that the bourgeois's thinner rugs allowed them to glide along the floor with greater ease than the elite, who were hindered by their thick carpets.[77] Bornique also encountered one unexpected problem that appeared when he ventured outside of the city's elite circles. In 1882 he found himself publicly accused of anti-Semitism after he refused to allow a Jewish family to join one of the classes. He responded that his other pupils would not have tolerated a "mixed" group, but that he would be happy to teach an all-Jewish class. The family went to the newspaper instead, but the issue quickly disappeared from the press.[78]

The more that dances were open to the public, the more they seemed to attract those in the lower echelons of respectability. The charity fund-raising event was a favorite among ethnic groups, and the dance became a vehicle for such efforts. The nineteenth century was the great age of institution building, and all across the city Chicagoans strived to establish hospitals, orphanages, old-folks homes, and other institutions, as well as collect money for the poor. Fund raising was sporadic, even haphazard, and thus very dependent on special events such as dances, which, through admission fees and the sale of food and beverages, provided a painless way to raise money. Labor unions realized that social events outside the workplace not only built up funds to finance strikes and help injured coworkers, but also generated a sense of solidarity. Everyone was happy. Dancers could keep their weekend evenings filled, bonds were formed among coworkers, dollars poured into the coffers of worthy causes, and the owners of the several large halls in the city had a booming business. The evidence of newspaper stories indicates that the overwhelming majority of these events were attended by whole families and were free from the disorder of drunkenness, fighting, or sexual misconduct. Those who were squeamish about the company of strangers stayed away.[79]

Dancing at this level of society also demonstrated a spontaneity that was usually absent among the elite. There were events associated with occupational groups, such as the annual Custom Tailors Ball, and even more informal evenings. In 1889, for instance, young clerks and upwardly mobile mechanics and their dates formed a number of informal neighborhood dancing groups and began boasting about their waltzing skills. Soon, Schoenhofen Hall was the scene of a contest among the "Blue Island Avenue Bon-Tons," the "Commercial Pleasure Club (Fourteenth Ward)," and the "Elite Pleasure Club of Larabee Street." In awarding the championship to a couple from the Commercial Club, the awards committee decreed, "Waltzin's waltzin' an' hoppin' ain't waltzin'. Ye can pivot or ye can walk; but when ye go to hoppin' then yer in the soup."[80]

At the bottom of the ladder of respectability were the public dance halls, which began to appear as early as the 1840s. These were semipublic places, privately owned commercial enterprises that were generally open to all. Many Chicagoans believed that this lack of customer selectivity contributed to the problems they caused. News accounts of these dives constantly stressed the social and ethnic variety among the lowlife that gathered there. "The sailor leaves his vessel at the dock, the canal-boatmen, the low lounger, the pimp, the green countrymen, giddy among the license that surrounds him, are sure to be there," noted the *Tribune* in 1861. "The half grown girl a few years since a rag picker, now out at service, the housemaids and domestics from citizens' families, the Bridgets and Margarets, on leave for the evening, 'jist to see a cousin,' or 'jist at a little dance,' are their partners for the evening." By then, the dance hall had become an important conduit of customers into the city's vice structure.[81]

As the years passed, most Chicagoans were probably confident in the prevailing municipal strategy of coping with vice, the segregation of inevitable sin into specific districts. Although never an official policy, police tolerated "the Sands," the tough Irish squatter district on the north bank of the river, until Mayor "Long John" Wentworth closed it down in 1857. Then came "the Patch" and associated areas to the southwest of the downtown, which thrived until they were replaced early in the 1880s by the Levee, the most famous red-light district, which was located just to the south edge of downtown. In its 1890s heyday, the Levee reputedly had a population of ten thousand—as large as that of a medium-sized downstate town. And the variety of activities available in that district—narcotics dealing, pornography, massage parlors, gambling, tough dance halls, as well as prostitution of every imaginable form—allowed it to function as a centralized department store of vice. The ability to get from here to there created the vice district, but for most Chicagoans, its most important function was to isolate their families in safe zones of purity.[82]

The dancing issue was becoming entangled in much larger issues of behavior and morals that were rooted in the geographical mobility and anonymity that urban life fostered. The improved ability to get from one place to another enabled citizens to put distance between their homes and their vices. Ultimately, the reputation of the place where people did the two-step would come under the influence of institutions that had nothing to do with dancing. By the turn of the century the same new extensions of the elevated and new streetcar routes that made it possible for amusement parks to draw customers from miles away opened new questions within families about how far young people should be allowed to venture on their own. Thousands of people, many of them unsupervised youngsters, discovered that one way of coping with city life was to "catch an el" to travel what were often long distances across town to pay an admission fee to a private entrepreneur to be amused. Ideally, these amusements not only relieved the tensions of everyday life and work, but their semipublic nature was supposed to provide a measure of safety. Theoretically, the purchase of a ticket would exclude "riffraff" of the street, but it also would ensure that those who entered agreed to abide by "house rules," a semiformal code of conduct. It was assumed that unruly behavior would lead to ejection.

But many parents, social reformers, ministers, and others worried about the consequences of underage patrons' joining the anonymous crowd, where they might be exposed to harm. Danger could take several forms. Few people thought much of the physical peril, however, until December 30, 1903, when a flame from a defective stage lamp touched off a curtain at one of the downtown's newest theater, the Iroquois. Eddie Foy Jr. was starring in *Mr. Bluebeard,* and the holiday crowd contained hundreds of children. In the ensuing panic, patrons rushed against exit doors only to find some of them locked and others inoperable because they opened inward. As the building filled with flames and dense smoke, the struggling humanity crushed those unfortunate enough to be closest to the doors and trampled those who had fallen under foot. The horrible event transpired in only minutes, too little time for the fire department and rescuers to save many lives. The final death toll reached 571. After the Iroquois Theater fire, revisions of building codes across the nation mandated outward-opening exit doors and outlawed any locking device that could not be opened from the inside.[83]

Most people assumed that city government could enact and enforce building code reforms that would alleviate physical hazards, but legislating morality was another matter. Many citizens had felt that the saloon—privately owned but of public access—had long been out of control. Respectable people would not set foot inside, while it was widely believed that the police who entered probably did so to drink rather than to patrol. There had been a longstanding problem with children either drinking or entering barrooms to fill beer pails, which they delivered to factory workers. Some juveniles used saloons as headquarters for youth gangs or for fencing stolen merchandise.[84]

After 1900, a growing concern with the problem of urban prostitution swept America. A sophisticated antivice publicity crusade began to erode support for the longstanding idea of a segregated "red-light" district, claiming that it represented tacit government support for immorality. Confident that prostitution could be eradicated, vice reformers no longer accepted geographical compromises. One of their most effective tools was the "seduction story" that they circulated. Chicago's rail hub function made it the center of national rings of "white slavers" that abducted young women from one part of the nation for sale to vice bondage in another region. These reports increased parental fears about several other kinds of semipublic amusement spots, including the large amusement parks.[85] A Chicago congressman, Adolph J. Sabath, led an effort by federal authorities to regulate Lake Michigan cruise ships and patrol them for violations of moral conduct. Some parents even accused the large department stores of allowing disreputable characters to prowl their waiting rooms.[86]

Many reformers and parents became increasingly concerned about the way in which turn-of-the-century technology was beginning to transform the world of indoor popular amusement. The first nickelodeon, which opened on Milwaukee Avenue in 1901, was the forerunner of a flood of such enterprises that numbered 606 in 1913. The early movies lacked color and had short running times and jerky motion, but they still seemed more realistic than the unrolling canvas panorama or motionless cyclorama.[87] The nickelodeon also seemed to combine all of the worst fears of parents about semipublic amusements. The earliest movie houses were little more than storefronts crudely fitted with folding chairs. Initial licensing laws grew out of concerns about the safe handling of the highly flammable nitrate film so near the open arc lamps of the projectors. But by 1906 the nickelodeon boom was on. Antidelinquency groups such as the Juvenile Protective Association, formed four years earlier to help administer new juvenile court law, expressed increased anxiety over moral perils. Theaters were dark, poorly monitored, and open to the smallest children. Moreover, the films themselves were often deemed questionable. The first production with a local setting, *How They Treat Strangers in Chicago* (1902), showed a country bumpkin whose sojourn in Chicago streets is cut short by thugs who rob and beat him unconscious. A cop wanders by, turns the hick over, checks for anything the thieves might have missed, and then saunters off screen, a shocking lesson, many thought, in why authority deserved little respect.[88]

The reform groups responded to the situation by pressuring the Chicago City Council to enact the nation's first movie censorship law, in 1907. It gave police the power to review and reject anything showing nudity or sexual innu-endo, but violence was not subject to the censor's scissors. In its 1911 investi-gation, the Juvenile Protective Association noted:

> The pictures not only showed crime of all kinds, but scenes of brutality
> and revenge calculated to arouse coarse and brutal emotions. One set of
> pictures, for instance, would show Indians on the warpath. It would detail
> with great accuracy the torturing and burning and horrible scenes atten-
> dant upon massacre. Another set, called "The Gypsies' Revenge," represent-
> ed a band of gypsies robbing a man and then, because he resisted, binding
> him and hanging him by a rope over a precipice. As the picture showed
> vividly the body dangling between heaven and earth and being plucked at
> by vultures, the shudder of horror which passed over the audience was
> quite obvious. Another set of films was called "The School Children's
> Strike." It showed a school principal reprimanding a pupil, who, in revenge,
> organized all the other children in the school into a revolt. They all went
> on strike, seized all the furniture in the school room, piled it in the mid-
> dle of the floor and set it on fire. This was continued until the building was
> a heap of ashes.[89]

The amusement park, the ice cream parlor, the lake cruise ship, the nickel-odeon, and other transformations of commercialized leisure helped create the tense atmosphere that extended to the dance hall during the first years of the new century. At first, the issue was purely economic. Saloonkeepers began to realize that the upstairs or adjacent hall rooms could be used more profitably for dancing than for weddings and union meetings. Carpenters hammered to-gether cheap bandstands, and signmakers turned out attractive displays that touted the new places. Gaudy cardboard "bills," which dotted neighborhood lamp posts, especially near schools, advertised contest prizes and special eve-nings of barefoot dancing. Wily proprietors removed drinking fountains and invited underage imbibers to the connecting barroom. No one bragged about the chandeliers when dim lighting was an important feature of the place. Nor did anyone boast about the quality of music, which was so poor that in 1902 the better dance musicians complained that they were being undercut by infe-rior bands that played for less in this new variety of dive.[90]

The dance hall fad was the universal nightmare-come-true that seemed to justify the religious critics' warnings about the sinfulness of all dancing. As in the nickelodeon, the darkness of the dancing place compounded the major problem with its semipublic nature: there was no screening of its clientele. Anyone who paid admission and behaved properly—there were varying inter-pretations of propriety—was welcome. This included lowlifes such as brothel recruiters. They reportedly cruised the dance floor in search of potential vic-tims, who, after losing their innocence in a nearby rooming house, might be too ashamed to return home.[91] Public discussion of the problem reached its first peak in 1905 with the suicide of a teenager, Mabel Wright, in the American Dance Hall on Thirty-third Street. In the wake of that event, proprietors began to employ off-duty policemen to ensure compliance with the law, but critics complained that the officers were too often asleep, away from their posts, or oblivious of what was happening a few feet away.[92]

The dance hall issue moved to page one of the press, where it remained for a decade. Antidelinquency reformers complained loudly and applied public pressure, which traveled upward through the chain of police command and then to the mayors. Only during Mayor Edward F. Dunne's two-year term, 1905–7, was there any real effort to revoke the liquor licenses of those who sold to minors, but the situation was beyond the control of the chief executive. For decades, saloon regulations ensuring a closing hour, Sabbath observance, and the exclusion of minors had been almost universally ignored. Public lawbreaking of this type had provoked an occasional angry sermon or condemnation from prohibitionists, but Chicagoans had developed a tolerance for infractions that seemed trivial compared with "real" crimes of violence. A charge of selling to minors had traditionally referred to dispensing a pail of beer to a youth in a working-class neighborhood who purchased it for his or her parent. The policeman on the beat, whether paid to look the other way or not, routinely ignored what went on inside the barroom unless there was a complaint of violence or theft. But now it was the more affluent families with children sheltered in outlying neighborhoods who felt threatened and helpless. When pressure became too great for officials to ignore, an occasional raid and license revocation temporarily quieted critics but solved no problems.[93]

By 1905 the growing public pressure to curb liquor sales at parties created a fear among ethnic communities that their traditional fund-raising fests might be outlawed along with the sleazy dances. The answer was ethnic unity. A politically ambitious Bohemian immigrant named Anton Cermak formed the United Societies for Local Self-Government, a federation of ethnic societies that totaled over 100,000 members. Two years after it was founded in 1904, the group pushed through the city council an ordinance creating a new and inexpensive one-night liquor license that organizations could purchase for specific dances. The "special bar permit" law also helped the proprietors of rental halls, whose primary business was in weekend charity dances. These individuals were able to avoid buying a regular saloon license, which cost $500 until it was raised to $1,000 in 1906. Critics of the special bar permit law, led by Hyde Park alderman Charles Merriam, were outraged and pointed out that owners of disreputable dance halls, whose busiest nights were also on weekends, merely created fictitious social clubs to take out the cheaper license. Moreover, the one-night permits lacked the 1:00 A.M. closing provision found in regular barroom licenses, thus allowing the revelry to proceed nonstop into the following day. The aldermen refused to change the permit law and would not even pass an ordinance prohibiting the sale of liquor to minors in dance halls, when it was presented to them twice during Mayor Dunne's term. Finally, on April 18, 1907, the Illinois General Assembly enacted a statewide ban on underage drinking, but the Chicago police were not eager to attempt enforcement. The city council also refused to consider laws prohibiting public dance halls in unsanitary basements and in the upper floors of wooden firetraps.[94]

The issue disappeared from front pages during 1908 and 1909, in large part because the passage of the 1907 local option law had allowed nearly all of the outlying middle-class neighborhoods to vote themselves dry. Parents felt a bit more comfortable knowing that at least the tough dance halls could not appear down the street from their homes. But the Juvenile Protective Association soon shook the city from its apathy. The JPA conducted extensive investigations during 1910 and 1911. It found that 86,000 young Chicagoans could be found in dance halls on some evenings, compared with 32,000 in nickelodeons, which shared the peril of dim lighting and an unselected patronage. The JPA's reports, with such titles as *Our Most Popular Recreation Controlled by the Liquor Interests,* condemned the dance halls for their proximity to immoral lodging houses, tolerance of profanity, poor fire protection and ventilation, toilet rooms that were accessible only through the barroom, and dancing that included "open embracing."[95]

Masquerades and "fancy dress balls" were an especially serious problem because they allowed patrons to conceal their identities and were an excuse to wear indecent costumes and to abandon respectable behavior. Some of these were no doubt inspired by the famous First Ward Ball, held each year by denizens of the Levee. Prostitutes, pimps, gamblers, thieves, narcotics dealers, and other shady characters donned their version of formal attire and engaged in a night of drunken revelry.[96]

The press enjoyed describing the First Ward Ball as a bizarre digression from the usual news, but this brazen parody of the gatherings of the elite signaled a decline in respect for the social and moral leadership of Chicago's leading families. Some things had remained essentially unchanged since the last century. The children of privilege still went to Bornique's or Martine's for training in ballroom steps, and the national association of dancing instructors still decided which dances would be fashionable. The wealthy still attended charity balls and other exclusive parties. Perhaps the greatest change was the introduction of country clubs during the 1890s as a more bucolic setting for the social season, which extended further into warm weather.[97]

But as the dance hall controversy progressed, news stories and editorials began to complain that the dancing practices of the "better" level of society were beginning to legitimate the bad behavior among the less respectable elements. For instance, in 1900, just as the dance hall issue first appeared, an anonymous letter appeared in the Oak Park newspaper complaining that the "bowery dance" had invaded the youth parties of the prestigious Oak Park Club. "Some football crank must have devised that hold," the writer grumbled. "The girl has scarcely any option in the matter. She must come and recline on Willie's bosom, and, to tell the truth, she rather likes it. Their heads snuggle down over each other's shoulders in the most confiding fashion." After 1900 there arose a growing number of charges that wealthy parents seemed ignorant of the fad of "slumming." Their thrill-seeking children secretly ventured into some of the city's toughest vice spots, where they exposed themselves to physical and social dangers. Occasional newspaper accounts of the practice doubtless led to morning-after confrontations between the teenagers and their worried parents. By the first decades of the new century, the cordon of respectability that separated the world of dancing among the elite from that involving society's dregs had begun to erode through direct contact.[98]

By 1910 the traditional world of dancing was beset by another crisis: the adult elite's declining willingness to conform to a standard set of acceptable dances. During their June 1912 meetings, members of the national dance instructors association agreed to resist pressure to teach the "Grizzly Bear, Bunny Hug, Turkey Trot, and similar dances." In October of that year, they jointly vowed that ragtime music, which they denounced as leading to the downfall of girls, would never be heard in their halls.[99] The dance teachers also resisted the invasion of the tango in 1913, but it was clear that they no longer acted as the arbiters of taste. The new Latin dance was so popular that society women held "tango teas" and rushed out to buy specially designed dance clothing and large, gaudy "tango jewelry." Other Chicagoans were not amused, leading the city council to adopt a resolution on October 6, 1913, which denounced "the Tango and similar dances" that had trickled down from the parties of the wealthy to the public dance hall level.[100]

Social class relationships also permeated the heated issue of cafe dancing. On July 30, 1913, the city council passed an ordinance outlawing it in restaurants. Opponents charged that the dance hall interests were behind the measure, but the aldermen resisted efforts to modify it.[101] Finally, the owners of some of the city's finest hotels decided to challenge the law in court. On the night of January 15, 1913, they summoned the police to the Blackstone, where officers took a lone dancing couple into custody. The Drake Hotel Corporation, its owners, went to court. In March a circuit court judge threw out the ordinance, but the city appealed; on June 22, 1916, the Illinois Supreme Court overturned the law. Hotel attorney Levy Mayer exclaimed, "We contended that the right to dance was as sacred as the right to pray and that the city council could no more prohibit the one than the other." The justices agreed, noting that as long as the cafes did not charge admission to dance, it would be an invasion of any couple's privacy to tell them what they could or could not do. The decision was especially significant because for the first time a semipublic business whose clientele was drawn from among affluent locals as well as travelers went to court to allow dancing in public.[102] This case, along with the dance masters' loss of control over what steps would be fashionable, signaled the demise of the nineteenth-century hierarchy that set apart the elite and subjected it to a prescribed style of dancing.

For many sensitive Chicagoans dancing represented society out of control. At about the time the Drake case was reaching a final decision, the issue was being publicly tied to the rise of cabarets. Many saloonkeepers were adding bandstands to transform their places into nightclubs. The morality of the music, as well as the relaxation of restrictions on the contact between patrons and entertainers, increased the concern over intimate dancing. Reformers pleaded in vain for new laws at the same meeting in which aldermen discussed censorship of a movie called *The Little Girl Next Door* because its plot revolved around a seduction.[103]

The dance hall issue would continue on for several more years, with settlement houses and even the city itself attempting to lure patrons away from the tougher commercial dance floors by providing a more wholesome substitute.

Louise deKoven Bowen and the Juvenile Protective Association worked with the Dance Hall and Ballroom Managers' Association to eliminate most of the smaller halls. The JPA furnished chaperones who were paid by the management of the larger ones.[104] There was also a short-lived effort to operate a municipal dance hall. This evolved into city-sponsorship of dances at Dreamland, one of the big commercial halls at Van Buren and Paulina on the West Side. Some of these affairs drew more than seven thousand young people.[105] But some observers questioned whether settlement houses, schools, and other governmental agencies should be sponsoring purified dances when so many citizens objected to dances of all types.[106]

During the 1920s, the gulf between "good" and "bad" dancing widened. Some dance and motion picture venues reached heightened levels of respectability through the creation of posh new facilities. Like the Chicago, Nortown, Central Park, and other great "popcorn palace" theaters, the new Aragon and Trianon Ballrooms provided semipublic facilities that were as grand as anything the wealthy of yesteryear had seen. These new halls were larger, their interior designs more elaborate, and their orchestras more famous than anything the city had ever witnessed. The atmosphere was that of the glamorous nightclub or restaurant, rather than that of the dance hall. But most important of all, like the amusement parks or the magnificent theaters built during the same decade, they could draw a highly varied audience from many miles around.[107]

But the Jazz Age also brought new challenges to old morals. There was the "Shimmy," invented by Chicagoan Gilda Gray and denounced by the last of the old dancing masters.[108] The post–World War I era also saw a vast expansion of the phenomenon of the "taxi dance hall." In these gaudy businesses, often located on the perimeter of downtown, a male customer could buy the partnership and companionship of a young woman at the rate of a dime a dance. The taxi dance hall had few defenders. At best, the purchase of conversation and contact seemed to bespeak the desperate loneliness created by the anonymity of city life. It was part of a lifestyle that also included the cheap diner and the furnished room or efficiency apartment. At worst, it was a musical house of assignation in which the customer selected the evening's partner-in-vice.[109]

There were many ways to spend Saturday night.

Conclusion

Civil War–era Chicagoans who wanted to unwind after a tough work week could choose among participatory sports, a few theaters, and dime museums. Their turn-of-the-century counterparts, especially if they had some discretionary money to spend, found an array of choices that became more complex and bewildering as the years passed. It was not unusual to resort to newspaper listings to get a grasp on the selection. Little wonder that many people simply settled for the neighborhood saloon.

There are many ways to view what happened to amusements during the intervening years. The growth and increasing complexity of the city and its institutions obviously accounts for the quantity of change, but there were qualitative differences as well. For instance, the spectacular dime museums of the midcentury had become weak survivors forty years later. What accounts for changes in a city's taste in amusement? Perhaps rising levels of education and sophistication doomed the public's willingness to be fooled—what the historian Neil Harris has called the "operational aesthetic"—by the inheritors of P. T. Barnum.[110]

But dime museums also were squeezed by two seemingly contradictory economic trends that were reshaping urban entertainment. The first involved the same pattern of specialization and consolidation that redefined retail merchandising. As the city grew, the chaotic general store of pioneer Chicago became the more specialized clothing or furniture store or even the emporium that sold only children's apparel or stoves. The move toward specialization transformed virtually every other area of retailing. The same thing happened to late-nineteenth-century arenas of commercial amusement; they prospered, proliferated, and in time became more specialized because the rapidly growing urban population provided enough customers to pay the bills and generate profit. For example, early Chicago playhouses had attempted to serve all types of audiences with stock company productions. But the theaters that replaced those that burned in the Great Fire seemed to be less willing to accommodate a wide spectrum of offerings, instead appealing to particular types of clientele. A few concentrated on serious drama while others turned to earthy burlesque. By the 1890s, uncultivated musical and comedy acts traveled the nation in vaudeville circuits. Still other venues, whose original owners may have held high hopes for acclaim, declined into sleazy "concert saloons," which attracted Chicago lowlife and out-of-town patrons with striptease shows, gambling, prostitution, and other imaginative vices. It was often necessary for residents and visitors alike to consult a city guidebook to avoid stumbling into one of Chicago's less-desirable theaters. But dime museums, by contrast, remained in their mid-nineteenth-century form, predictable in their appeal to a wide range of curiosity seekers, both local and out-of-town. Because they were assemblages of items that were too small and unspectacular to draw crowds on their own, they had only limited ability to specialize any further. As a consequence, their audiences remained diffuse and could never be carefully targeted. Even baseball, which on the surface seems a more simplistic activity than a dime museum, drew from a wide spectrum of fans.[111]

The amusement parks were everything the dime museums were not, and in many ways they were the ultimate urban entertainment enterprise. First, they made maximum use of the emerging transit system. Forest Park, White City, and Riverview were part of the same trend toward geographical mobility—getting from here to there—that created the rush hour, the subdivision, and the outlying business district. The complex of streetcar lines reached into every residential neighborhood and funneled passengers onto elevated lines. The latter, in turn, not only enabled the amusement enterprises to draw customers from wide sections of the city, but also allowed their grounds to be located on the fringes of the city, where speculative land was cheap. It was no coincidence that the major investors in the parks included transit companies, who enjoyed yet another advantage in the utilization of their rolling stock and power generation equipment on weekends. Had there not been any place to go, the generators, streetcars, and tracks would have been an economic drain rather than weekend profitmakers.[112]

The second way in which amusement parks were archetypal urban institutions involved the city as maker of centralized places, a gatherer of functions. These extravaganzas were to leisure what department stores were to shopping, what large factories were to manufacturing, what Hull-House and other social settlements were to welfare, what the World's Columbian Exposition was to artifacts of human progress, and what urban newspapers were to contemporary information. All of these aimed to gather in one place a collection of activities that would function more efficiently together or would appeal to a wide variety of interests. And all of them achieved their greatest success—could only achieve such heights of success—in cities. For example, amusement parks were collections of varied rides, spectacles, games, and illusions. The parks' "Midway" sections absorbed the freaks and oddities of the dime museums. Their musical, dancing, and stage shows had wide appeal. White City could advertise in 1908 that it was "the only place in Chicago where you can sit and dine and at the same time enjoy a high class vaudeville show." And improvements in transportation made it possible for this to happen on the fringe rather than the center of town.[113]

Finally and perhaps most important of all, the amusements of the city were a reaffirmation of the culture of the crowd and the congested city. Like restaurants that appealed to particular tastes, the giant new metropolis attracted sufficient numbers of people to support any specialized pastime. The search for the common denominator brought not only the largest profits but also the largest following. Perhaps only citizens with a completely cheerless temperament or those whose desperate poverty never allowed them the luxury of thinking of anything but survival may have missed the escapist joy of discussing the progress of a ball team or "taking in the sights" at a theater or dime museum.

Coping never had it so good.

Postscript

Nineteen sixty-seven was a sad year for Chicagoans who remembered summers as they used to be. At Belmont and Western Avenues, Riverview Park closed for good, leaving the sounds and smells of that aging fantasy land mere memories. Meanwhile, in the 1400 block of North Larabee, the Sieben brewery and beer garden—with its red brick walls, leaded casement windows, and elderly waiters bearing trays loaded with a dozen or more steins—also shut down. And at Sixteenth and Wabash another Chicago institution was in its last years. The old Chicago Coliseum stood virtually abandoned, some of its windows missing, its paint peeling; the building that had housed every Republican National Convention from 1904 to 1932 looked desperately for anyone who would rent it. These three Chicago institutions, different though they were, shared more than a common year of demise. They owed their existence to the pastime of gawking at oddities in dime museums and drinking beer outdoors. How they evolved in different directions is a story that reflects the changing tastes and economics of leisure-time Chicago.[114]

After the Ferris wheel was dismantled on Clark Street, its saga had one final chapter. Instead of converting it hastily to scrap, the junk dealer who bought it carefully followed the dismantling plan that had been used in 1894. Once more, the parts ended up on flatcars, where they sat on a siding for a few more years before making one final trip. New owners obtained permission to erect the big wheel in St. Louis on the grounds of the Louisiana Purchase Exposition of 1904. It was reassembled for the last time in that city's Forest Park, but by then it had lost its drawing power. It seldom appeared in either the promotional literature or the guidebooks for the St. Louis fair, and the new owners were barely able to pay for the fuel for its steam engine. When the exposition closed, they simply abandoned it. While St. Louis officials busily restored the surrounding park to its natural landscape, nearby residents complained about the creaking, rusty eyesore. The end came on May 11, 1906, when a dynamite charge brought it down with a crash. More explosions reduced the rubble to small chunks. Although later legends maintained that graceful arched bridges in the Midwest were built from parts of its rim, nothing was actually salvaged.[115] Its former site on Clark Street became a streetcar barn.

The later years were also unkind to amusement parks, which were hard to maintain and vulnerable to economic and meteorological factors that affected attendance. Shaky finances closed Forest Park in 1922. The last building connected with White City, which went bankrupt in 1933, was an old skating rink that burned in November 1959. After Riverview Park closed, its site became a district police headquarters, the campus of DeVry Technical Institute, and a shopping mall. Its carousel was eventually moved to the Six Flags over Atlanta amusement park in Georgia, where it still operates.[116]

A few of the old beer gardens survived, including Wozniak's Casino on Blue Island Avenue. But in 1950 Kolze's Electric Park and adjoining inn were leveled and the land sold to the Chicago Park District to create Merrimac Park. The Marigold Gardens lasted through the decade, mainly because of the boxing and wrestling matches that were televised from there by the DuMont network. (*Wrestling from Marigold,* with Jack Brickhouse at the microphone, was a staple of weekend viewing during television's infancy.) Finally, in 1963, the property was sold to a church.[117]

Dancing survived, of course. During the Depression years dance marathons became pitiful spectacles in which desperate couples pushed their endurance to the limit in quest of prizes.[118] The World War II years brought back the more pleasant idea of dancing as a release from tensions, a way to cope with the world. The North Shore Line interurban trains that passed through Great Lakes Naval Training Center stopped near the Aragon, and thousands of sailors and their dates crowded the place on weekends to do the jitterbug.[119] The Aragon later underwent many transitions. The 1950s saw Lawrence Welk use it as the main venue in his rise to stardom; Liberace played frequent concerts there as well. Later, Latin American rhythms and hard rock concerts have allowed it to stay open, a bit worse for the wear, but a durable artifact of an age of simple pleasures. The Trianon remained profitable until the late 1950s but was torn down in 1967. Meanwhile, Martine's and Bornique's survived well past the era of the elite dancing academy, the former into the Depression and the latter until 1953, an odd reminder of another age.[120]

Few remnants of Chicago's early mass amusements have survived. Some of the enormous stones that once formed the entrance of the Coliseum, which was razed in 1983, remained in place for another decade at Fourteenth and Wabash, but they are now gone.[121] There are a few surviving panorama paintings; a smaller version of the *Battle of Gettysburg* still brings in tourist dollars near that historic battleground in Pennsylvania, and in 1966 a North Carolina man reportedly rescued the larger Gettysburg painting from a Chicago warehouse. The abandoned engine house in which John Brown made his final stand fell into disrepair before the World's Columbian Exposition closed in 1893. The small brick building was threatened with demolition, but Ida B. Wells, John Jones, Ferdinand Barnett, and other prominent Chicago African-Americans raised much of the money to move this historic monument of the antislavery struggle back to West Virginia, where today it is an important attraction in the Harpers Ferry National Historic Monument.[122]

Much of Charles Gunther's famous collection of curios ended up being divided in the 1920s between the Chicago Historical Society and the Field Museum of Natural History, which retained the princess mummy. But locked away in the collections of the historical society are a pair of Gunther's items that still evoke the sense of mystery and wonder that brought the multitudes through the turnstile more than a century ago: the fleece described in "Mary Had a Little Lamb," as well as another item labeled "The Skin of the Serpent that Tempted Adam and Eve."[123]

PART FIVE

Hard Work

9   Chicago Is Work

FOR many of Chicago's workers, life was a problem within a problem. Not only did they have to contend with finding food and shelter, sometimes on a day-by-day basis, but they were also burdened by the sad fact that their material possessions were so meager. The immigrant trunk that they lugged to each new home was usually packed with cheap items that were only of sentimental value. Their living space was rented; their furniture was minimal; their everyday clothes were little more than rags and a bank account was only a dream. Their only resource of any real value was the labor they could furnish to someone else. Hard work and ambition were their primary assets.

While large numbers of Chicago's workers were able to secure long-term employment with companies that appreciated their skills and loyalty, the unpredictable nature of urban life made finding a steady source of income more difficult for others. Workers confronted a high risk of failure on two levels. First, they were minuscule constituents in a large labor market that was controlled by forces they often did not understand. In part, this was because many came from rural backgrounds that better equipped them to face the past than the future. The life of the typical Chicago worker changed dramatically during the nineteenth century as the local economy rapidly developed from that of a maritime trading city to one of an industrial metropolis. This brought a shift from skilled to machine labor, from the small workplace downstairs or near home to a large factory that often required a lengthy daily commute, from sales involving local markets to global balances of supply and demand, and, finally, from a world of animal and water power in stone and wooden workplaces to one of steam and electric energy in giant factories of steel, cement, and bricks.[1]

On this level, the seasonality and dependence on agricultural markets that marked the yearly cycles in the early Chicago economy gave way to unforeseen crises of the industrial age. The prosperity of individual families fell prey to national fluctuations in unemployment and business cycles; the better years always tempted Chicagoans to forget the lean ones. Industrialization drew workers into a national labor pool that became increasingly mobile as the railroad network proliferated. Workforce portability tended to undercut the independence of workers because at any time competitors could come from another part of the United States or from the pool of immigrants to flood the local market. Conversely, Chicagoans sometimes found that they, too, had to become mobile and take to the rails when opportunity seemed greater elsewhere.[2]

But there was a more personal dimension to this story. The individual worker, as part of a local workforce, could become frustrated at his or her status. Ultimate financial success or failure could be seen in the quality of a family's shelter and clothing, what food was put on the table, and what kinds of amusements the family could afford. Eviction and homelessness placed its plight on public display. It was on this level that the worker struggled every day to make ends meet. Where persons of greater financial resources could dip into private savings when needed, the poor had to depend on others: a credit extension at the food store, a visit to the pawnshop or loan shark, or outright begging and welfare.

On this second level, the worker also encountered the unforeseen in the form of accidents. Factory owners may have thought of risk only in terms of venture capital, expansion plans, and a competitive market, but it had another meaning for those who entered their gates. Workplace reform was a discovery process wherein knowledge of what was harmful ran years behind the invention of new industrial processes and machinery. Without the employees knowing it, the factory became a testing ground to learn the effects of caustic acids, lead arsenate, lead oxide, airborne fibers, livestock diseases, and moving machinery of many types. Industrial hazards multiplied the inherent dangers of fire, traffic, poorly ventilated buildings, and other problems that the city and its crowding had already created.[3]

For all the negatives, however, workers could think of themselves as more than statistics. At times, they could experience a sense of efficacy, that is, a feeling that they could guide their own destinies. Sometimes this involved the search for a new job or the decision to go into business for themselves. It also included efforts, sometimes successful, to join together to form unions.

Looking for "Mr. Watstodoe": Employment Agencies and Fraud, 1844–1915

The story in *L'Italia* of February 16, 1895, contained a desperate message. Two hundred Italian immigrant workers had been recruited for heavy manual construction labor in the Pacific Northwest. Their trip out there had been in boxcars, and living conditions in the camp had been uncomfortable at best. But now the contractor had disappeared without paying them, and they were stranded with only reluctant local charity in the form of beans and potato flour to keep them from starvation. Contributions from Chicagoans paid for their tickets home. Similar cases of immigrant exploitation, most often at the hands of countrymen, dot the ethnic press of the late-nineteenth- and early-twentieth-century city, extreme examples of the larger problem of finding a job. The rapid growth of Chicago and the city's emergence as a transportation hub created enormous opportunities for exploitation and a growing demand for change.[4]

"Intelligence offices," as employment agencies were then known, were a fairly insignificant factor in pioneer Chicago's labor market. In a village society most information about jobs passed informally in conversations. But even in a small town, the agency was one of the most important forms of information. There was only one such service in 1844, operated by J. W. Norris in conjunction with his publication of a city directory. With his "Corrected Register of the Inhabitants," a constantly updated list of where everyone lived and worked, he could offer information about the occupational and residential stability of any potential employer or employee. This was an asset in a town whose eight thousand residents included many drifters. The following year, one local newspaper advised, "Persons wanting employment, or those wanting help in their families, will do well to call and leave their names and wants at our . . . office."[5] Norris and his eventual competitors appear to have worked primarily with the skilled and domestic sectors of the employment market. Laborers with little more than a strong back to offer in exchange for a paycheck were largely left to search the scattered newspaper notices, the other principal source of job "intelligence," to seek information from countrymen and relatives, or to stand at the employer's door and hope.

By the mid-1850s the Common Council had begun to enact regulations on what was becoming a more competitive trade. In 1856 it defined the nature of the business and excluded nonresidents, apparently to reduce the possibility of fraud. The license law created a steady stream of petitions from widows, the physically handicapped, and others who claimed that they could not afford the fifty-dollar fee. Ironically, being employed was itself a reason to go into business finding jobs for others, because it was a service occupation that required little physical mobility. A "Mrs. McGinn"—"she being destitute and unable to support herself by any other means"—got a free license, but Mrs. Mary Jane Bates was not as fortunate. The latter, who claimed that she had placed more than seven hundred servants, petitioned that her husband's illness had left her broke. But the alderman refused to believe her story after her competitors claimed that it was a lie to evade fee payment. The following year she tried again, petitioning that her business had been hurt by the influx of immigrant women and the vigorous efforts of charitable institutions to place indigent females in jobs. Once more, her petition failed.[6]

The chances of success in finding employment were in part determined by Chicago's economic relationship with the nation. Since the economy of the early city was based largely on the handling and processing of agricultural commodities, many workers arrived and departed with the planting and harvesting cycles. Until rail links to the East were regularized in the mid-1850s, Chicago was virtually cut off from the outside world after the lake freeze interrupted the shipping season. While winter took some city dwellers to midwestern lakes to cut ice for refrigeration, it brought far larger crowds of unemployed farm workers and sailors to Chicago.[7] "Our city is full of laborers out of employ," complained the *Daily Democrat* in 1851, "and their sufferings will be very severe between this and Spring. . . . Pity the Poor and give them work!"[8] When warm weather returned, many agricultural workers migrated to the country, but other job seekers took their places. The latter included the young men who had spent the winter attending commercial colleges and now clutched freshly minted diplomas. Meanwhile, every improvement in cross-country transportation increased the mobility of those hunting work and enmeshed Chicago further in a national labor market that was driven by cycles of prosperity and depression. During boom construction times of the mid-1840s, for instance, the Illinois and Michigan Canal and plank-road building projects absorbed many of the unskilled.[9] Soon after the canal opened in 1848, the city saw an influx of unemployed St. Louisans.[10] Wartime labor scarcity also affected the market. For instance, in 1863 the Union Pacific Railroad advertised in Chicago newspapers for a thousand men to help construct the transcontinental railway; inducements included a homestead and exemption from the draft.[11]

In other years, workers were caught in the contractions of the economy, a problem often complicated by the misfortune of arriving in Chicago just as the boom turned to bust, as it did during the national depression that began in 1857.[12] The Civil War caused a severe economic slump at first, followed by a manufacturing boom. But the end of the conflict brought a flood of returning soldiers who competed with people already holding jobs and with the large pool of war widows.[13] During the resulting unemployment crisis, estimates of the idle ran into the tens of thousands, and the desperate pleas issued by the Young Men's Christian Association (YMCA) Relief Committee did little good. The Chicago Relief and Aid Society hoped to reduce the number of city job seekers by aiming a plea toward farmers who might house and feed whole families in exchange for their labor. When prosperity returned during the late 1860s, it came primarily to skilled mechanics and others who built steam engines and farm machinery. Others were left jobless.[14] In 1872, the enormous influx of those seeking opportunities in the post-Fire rebuilding of Chicago was just one indication of the potential size of the railborne workforce.[15]

The disruption of the postbellum years produced the first large wave of incidents of employment agency fraud, and the army of unskilled workers, both men and women, who sought out-of-town jobs became its earliest victims. The expanding railway network made relocation easier and swelled their numbers into a mobile army of unemployed that seemed capable of overrunning places where openings were rumored to be plentiful. In 1866 the *Tribune* exposed the first major scams, which took advantage of the opportunities for northerners in the Reconstruction South. In one scheme, sixty carpenters paid their own transportation costs to Memphis, plus two dollars each in advance to the Chicago agent; no carpentry jobs were waiting at the other end. Others were fortunate to use legitimate job-finding services. By 1870 many of the unemployed were headed south because they were directed there by the employment bureaus of the YMCA and the Chicago Relief and Aid Society. Some joined the opportunistic band of northerners popularly labeled "carpetbaggers," while others saw the South as a place to buy inexpensive farms, sometimes as part of cooperative colonization societies of the type that sprang up in Arkansas.[16] Similarly, officials in western states issued glowing invitations to laborers to build the railroads, transform forests into lumber, and construct the cities of that region.[17]

Much of that migratory labor settled permanently in Chicago, where some came to grief. About 1870 one young bank clerk had left his home in England to seek his fortune in America. After failing to find work in New York, he had gone out to Chicago. The failure to find work had forced him to sell his clothes, watch, and books to survive for a few weeks in a boardinghouse. He later recalled:

> I went from store to store, begging for work, and found none. . . . Driven to desperation I went to the employment bureau of the Young Men's Christian Association, and stated my case as also the condition I was reduced to. You will not believe it Sir, but they treated me almost as badly as the others, expressing doubts as to an honest young man not being able to find work. I told them that I had offered to put in coal, but had been refused that. They told me they would try and help me, and asked me to call again. Day after day I called, and each time I was told they had nothing for me. I asked for bread, they told me I must apply at the Relief Society. I went there and was told that they would have first to enquire into my affairs. I went back to the Association and was turned off, and told to trust in Jesus. With that insolent mockery ringing in my ears, I walked the streets, till I was arrested.

The man became a burglar and footpad, or mugger, until he was caught and beaten by a police officer. When William Corkran, librarian of the Chicago Historical Society, found him in the Bridewell city jail, the unfortunate man was near death from his injuries.[18]

While others were perhaps not as unlucky, they, too, had been lured to the fast-growing city by the hope of jobs. Their growing numbers and their credulity about the poorly regulated intelligence offices frequently brought them to grief. City directories listed a dozen legitimate intelligence offices and employment agencies in 1866, but others came and went without leaving permanent record of their names. One scheme victimized employers by taking advantage of the perpetual shortage of domestic servants. A crooked agency charged local housewives fifty to seventy-five cents each to send over a new servant, who had been instructed to find fault with the employer or the house and quit after only a few hours on the job. Each replacement, who used the same scam, required an additional fee. A year later, the *Tribune* warned readers that its pages were being used to defraud the unsuspecting job applicants who were being asked to pay an agent fifty cents to cover the cost of an ad promising high-paying jobs. After hundreds of people had been duped, the crooks had fled town.[19]

This type of fraud was new to Chicago, but it quickly caught on. The early schemes utilized most of the essential features of the swindles that would be carried on for decades afterward. The Chicago press reported dozens of employment agency frauds before 1900, and the success of all of them was based on the anonymity of urban society. The victims of this vicious form of fraud were most often trusting people who believed the promises of strangers and had no way of knowing the criminal's true identity or reputation. Nineteenth-century Americans had great difficulty coming to grips with "appearances" in the growing anonymity of American society. Whom did you trust? Someone who dressed well? Or spoke well?[20] Chicago's rapid growth and its function as a rail hub made it ideal for cons, because at any one time there were tens of thousands of strangers in town to conduct legitimate business, change trains, or shop. The rare instances when victims recognized the swindlers resulted in chases through the city streets and occasional thrashings by angry mobs.[21]

The second characteristic of the successful intelligence office scam was its veneer of respectability. Con artists realized that this could be achieved in a downtown office. Victims found it hard to believe that crooked operations could be headquartered in an impressive Loop skyscraper. Newspaper advertising was also important in establishing credibility, because it was easy to assume that the press would not accept fraudulent ads. Impressive corporate names, often including "and Company," were also important. For instance, the "Chicago Guarantee and Reference Company," which operated in September 1892, victimized men and women searching for desirable clerical positions. Often, the con would also claim to be a "special agent" of a railway or contractor to give his operation a ring of authority.[22]

Good appearances helped establish the victim's confidence—the root of the terms "confidence game" and "con artist." The requirement of a fee payment in advance was a new gimmick that appeared in the early 1890s, especially during the severe depression that began just as the World's Columbian Exposition was closing. Hundreds of world's fair workers stranded in Chicago were the saddest victims of this ploy. Having to pay a fee made the client feel that he or she was the untrustworthy party. Virtually every one of the complaints that surfaced in the press contained a common pattern: unsuspecting people paid money in advance to learn about jobs that did not exist when they got there. The amounts charged were usually between two dollars and five dollars, not huge, but great when they were the victim's last dollars. Too often, those who had been duped regarded their losses as either too embarrassing to report to the police or too insignificant to be worth the effort. Although the fees were normally half of what legitimate agencies charged, they quickly added up to large profits. The advanced payment system also enabled crooks to collect money and depart before the discovery of the crime. When caught, they often claimed that they had merely collected a fee in exchange for providing leads based on what they honestly thought was the true job situation.[23]

Many of the victims were immigrants who had made the mistake of trusting someone from their native land.[24] That problem had existed indirectly as early as 1847, when a New York labor contractor brought over the group of impoverished Irish workers who would later inhabit the notorious Goose Island. Later, the postbellum rail construction boom brought a dozen Scandinavian labor agencies to recruit workers in the Swedish neighborhoods of the North Side. Some even placed "runners" at the depots to greet trainloads of immigrants with grand promises of high-paying jobs. The agencies were often working under legitimate contracts to supply specific numbers of workers, but they resorted to any means to fill their quotas. Wages, in turn, were paid to the men through the contractors, who deducted inflated living expenses and ticket fares to railhead camps.[25]

The best-known and perhaps most vicious of the labor agency problems involved the *padrone,* or "boss," who preyed on the Italian immigrants who began displacing the Scandinavians in rail construction during the 1880s. This system combined the worst forms of exploitation, the theft of wages through overcharges for "services," and a nearly complete domination over the timid and naive immigrants. The padrone served as the single intermediary between the worker and American society, controlling where the men lived, what they ate, what clothes they wore, what tools they used, and what they knew of their new land. In exchange for the unquestioning trust of their "friend," the men suffered abject poverty despite their hard work and the loneliness of the separation from their families.[26]

On occasion, the workers found themselves far from home and abandoned by the labor contractor. Once the fees had been collected, the agent often dispatched the men to far distant places. In the bitterly cold January of 1886, one dupe was told to report to a rail construction project a hundred miles away. Finding no job there, he had no choice but to walk back to Chicago, pawning his watch and overcoat along the way for food and lodging. Other scams took job seekers to Nebraska, Dakota, and Buffalo, New York. The distance factor profoundly affected immigrants, who made up a large portion of the legitimate rail construction crews and thus were more credulous when presented with scams that involved travel.[27] These victims appear to have been ignorant of an 1869 state law that gave workers a lien on a railway for six months' wages in the event they fell victim to any labor contractor who defaulted on his obligation.[28]

Distance, anonymity, and the rails also drew victims to the city. The extension of the railroad into the hinterlands provided the element of distance that was often critical to the success of the recruiting scams that targeted immigrants and native-born alike. Depressions and other major fluctuations in the labor market increased the flow of suckers. Some Chicagoans advertised in small-town newspapers to attract victims, who were often ambitious young people who saw limited opportunity in country towns or farms.[29] During the early 1890s, for instance, the promise of jobs constructing and operating the World's Columbian Exposition unleashed a large wave of rural laborers. Hundreds of them fell victim to Marce de Claremont, a well-known French con man, who lured midwesterners to Chicago by advertising in the rural press, then took their money and fled.[30]

Women were especially vulnerable to sharpsters who took advantage of the naiveté of what the *Tribune* called "Helpless Young Women," who had been sheltered from the "man's world" outside of the home. As early as the late 1860s there were reports of young women who answered want ads promising high wages for easy work but found themselves trapped as inmates in brothels. The sensationalist book entitled *Chicago after Dark* (1868) warned that the rural or immigrant innocents who found themselves fired from respectable families sank so far in self-esteem that they were easy prey for blandishments from a potential employer who was really a brothel madam. Some rural newspapers refused to carry advertising designed to lure young people to the city, but in 1894 a *Tribune* columnist noted that each year the paper received hundreds of inquiries from young country women regarding their prospects for success in the city. After advising them to stay where they were, the writer recounted the pitfalls of city life. A woman with limited resources would end up in a third-rate rooming house or worse. Pulchritude meant that "she will have to carry herself like snow on high hills to avoid contamination." But if she happened to be "homely," the doors of opportunity "are firmly closed against her."[31]

Women found ways to avoid the employment agency trap. One was to track down jobs from want ads, but that was time consuming when living expenses were fast eroding a meager savings fund. It could also be frustrating and potentially dangerous, as the press demonstrated during the late 1880s when they assigned reporters to pose as job seekers. The *Times*'s "Nell Nelson," whose sensationalist articles were collected in a book entitled *The White Slave Girls of Chicago*, told her readers of wages far below the advertised rates and escapes from attempted seductions. At about the same time, the *Tribune*'s "Nora Marks" series recounted long hours waiting for job prospects, as well as bias based on appearance and ethnicity. Both described cunning cons perpetrated by phony "schools" that took hard-earned tuition money and disappeared before providing any instruction. Other job applicants were forced to purchase "work materials" that always cost more than they produced in profit. Finally, many of those who did get employment were subjected to long hours without rest, poor ventilation and lighting, fire danger, and other types of inhumane working conditions.[32]

The pattern of employment agency fraud remained generally consistent between 1866 and 1900. The only significant changes were a gradual increase in the amount of the fee and the appearance of more organized rings by the 1890s. While most of the intelligence agency crooks appear to have been independent operators, others were part of multiple outlets. This not only enhanced the air of legitimacy, but also allowed the rotation of personnel to other locations where they were less likely to be recognized by past victims. One such group was rumored to have made over $10,000 in two months.[33] Another sophisticated scheme linked agents who clustered along Canal Street with cohorts among the foremen at the ten construction companies digging the Sanitary and Ship Canal. In January 1894, one James Eggen reportedly bilked over two thousand men by collecting $3 from each as an advance fee before sending them to find "Mr. Watstodoe" ("What's to do") at the canal. Other victims were charged an additional $2 for transportation to the work sites and another $2 for a "commission" to work, then fired after a few hours' labor in order to make room for others. One victim recovered none of his $7.34, which included the wages due him.[34]

The severely depressed economy of the middle of the last decade of the century, however, not only increased the number of cons, but also generated a strong demand for reform. What had been so distressing to the newspapers, the legitimate agencies, and the police had been the ease with which the con artists escaped prosecution. Frequently, those who were apprehended could point to office signs or to the proverbial fine print on contracts the victims signed, both of which stated clearly that there was no absolute promise of work and that the agent was merely selling what he believed to be information about job openings. The X-mark left by those unable to provide a signature rendered them vulnerable to fraudulent contracts. Because of that loophole, few wrongdoers were successfully prosecuted under the city's vaguely worded 1856, 1882, and 1883 laws that licensed the business.[35]

Some workers coped with the situation by avoiding the crooked downtown agencies in favor of less formal "hiring halls" that were often operated in conjunction with saloons. By mutual custom, employers and potential workers patronized particular bars where those "without a position" were welcome to spend idle hours, provided of course that they purchased drinks. These arrangements had the obvious potential for abuse, especially when hiring was slow and the few coins in the pockets of workers ended up in the hands of the barkeep. After several hours of waiting and drinking, some customers found themselves too inebriated to work.[36] In the transient districts on the north, west, and south fringes of the downtown there were earlier versions of today's day labor agencies that listed short-term jobs on sidewalk blackboards and chose workers from among the crowd of those who showed up at dawn. These agents supplied groups of laborers to employers and extracted their extortionate fees as a percentage of the wages they distributed to the men.[37]

The crookedness of the few damaged the legitimate bureaus, which made up the great majority. Many of the honest firms remained in business for decades because their clients had more marketable skills that brought them better-paying jobs and also possessed the prudence necessary to avoid being exploited and trapped. But even the most respectable places were hurt by the scams that siphoned off fees that would have resulted in genuine jobs for the customers. It was the bad publicity generated by the few that reduced public confidence in all job-seeking firms.[38]

What was to be done? Reformers in the ethnic communities could not rely on the power of newspaper exposés, which had little effect.[39] Others saw hope in what they called "moral substitutes," the notion of replacing "vicious" institutions with honest alternatives that were meant to drive crooked operations out of business. Various charitable organizations tried to combat abuses by providing alternatives to the cons. The YMCA's labor bureau, begun during the 1860s, was overwhelmed by the number of job seekers. Other groups targeted women, who generally did not provide direct competition in the male labor market. As early as the late 1860s, the Ladies' Christian Union enjoyed some success aiding women who had lost their wartime positions in clothing manufacture. Later, the YWCA took on the task of helping a more general population of unemployed women, while other organizations concentrated on specific groups. The Woman's Christian Temperance Union, the Woman's Alliance, and various women's clubs also provided successful referral services.[40]

The idea was also tried and tested among ethnic groups. Since midcentury, Scandinavian and German emigrant aid societies had enjoyed some success in placing countrymen fortunate enough to seek their services, and by the beginning of the 1900s every major group supported some sort of charitable agency. No immigrant group wanted to be accused of flooding the city with their jobless.[41]

The same principle could be found at work within the late-nineteenth-century African-American community, where the institutional church came to the rescue. These multifunctional entities combined worship with social clubs, political halls, kindergartens, reading rooms, penny savings banks, gymnasiums, and other activities we now call "human services." They also directly aided the African American's search for a job. Day nurseries and cooking instruction enabled mothers to find domestic work, while church employment bureaus secured positions for both men and women. Membership in a congregation itself became a character reference of sorts for men and women who had great difficulty battling discrimination. Years later, even after the Chicago Urban League took over some of this job-finding assistance, black ministers continued to be labor agents for their flocks.[42]

The idea of moral substitutes grew in popularity during the severe depression of the 1890s, but the struggle between unions and management complicated the issue. In February 1894, the Central Relief Association, a division of the newly formed Civic Federation of Chicago, opened a "free employment bureau" at its Loop office. In less than a month, it had over two thousand workers on its books, but unions soon complained that the registry was in reality a central information file that allowed employers to avoid hiring those known to be union activists.[43]

On the opposite end of the labor spectrum, settlement houses followed the lead of Jane Addams and opened employment bureaus. Their impact seems to have been localized in their neighborhoods. The most important limitation to the job placement efforts of Hull-House in particular was the frequent connection of the settlement movement to labor organizing activities. Antiunion employers looked elsewhere.[44]

The trade unions themselves emerged as another alternative to employment agency exploitation. The Building Trades Council and Carpenters' Union, for example, established a bureau at 167 (now 180 West) Washington Street in 1891. Workers could use comfortable lounge rooms on the upper floor of the building, and neither they nor the employers were charged a fee for the service. Other unions and occupational organizations, such as the National Association of Women Stenographers, had similar arrangements. More than a decade later, the Women's Trade Union League responded to an influx of young Scandinavian immigrant women by finding jobs for 313 of them. But, ideal as these services were, they did little to alleviate the problem because they dealt only with organized workers, who constituted a small percentage of the workforce. Employers who wanted nonunion workers of course avoided these facilities.

Critics complained that the unions sometimes used newspaper ads for their "employment agencies" as little more than a means to lure the unemployed to recruiting rallies at the same addresses.[45]

While substitutes allowed many job seekers to avoid exploitation, other interests argued that the final route of redress was an appeal to government. If licensing and policing proved ineffective in Chicago, hope shifted to Springfield. Here the greatest expectations were directed toward an idea first implemented in 1890, when the state of Ohio established a free employment agency service. The corrective features of the plan were obvious. The exploitive profit incentive was gone, as was any tendency to support or undermine organized unions. The prospective employer and employee would both benefit from the larger pool of applicants and jobs that such a program could generate. Most important of all, the success of the state employment bureau was expected to drive the dishonest private agencies out of business.[46]

The opposition to the state plan was vocal and well organized around the central argument that it provided unfair and "socialistic" competition for legitimate private agencies. Others in the Illinois legislature objected to the cost of operating offices. Nonetheless, the plan gained favor through the depression of the 1890s. When the Chicago City Council inexplicably repealed the existing licensing ordinance in 1896 without replacing it, not only were private employment agencies in the city now without any regulation, but officials did not even know how many there were.[47]

Another impetus for reform came from the intensifying attack on organized vice and the white slave trade that began at the decade's close. Chicago was becoming sensitive to the fact that its central location made it the recruiting and exchange center for a national network of brothel recruiters, some of whom used employment agencies to lure victims. Reform was further stimulated in 1898 by the specter of veterans from the popular Spanish-American War flooding the labor market and falling victim to abuse.[48] By the following year the Illinois General Assembly could no longer withstand the pressure to establish a no-fee state employment agency.

The new 1899 law seemed almost utopian to its backers. Three free, nonpolitical, and carefully run offices were to be established in Chicago to match applicants with employers. The district managers were authorized to take out newspaper ads listing the skills of their applicants, but they were prohibited from disclosing the identities of the job seekers to any business involved in a strike. The new law placed private agencies under state licensing, charging a $200 a year fee and demanding a $1,000 performance bond.[49]

Jane Addams and other proponents applauded the new law as the beginning of the end for the exploitive employment agency. During its first full year of operation the system successfully placed 31,218 of the 37,285 applicants for employment.[50] But optimism soon turned into frustration. Private agencies sued, targeting the law's failure to specify that violation of the regulations could lead to their revocation. Although some points of the licensing provision survived a court challenge, the lack of funding for enforcement left that section of the bill useless. Less than half of the private firms even bothered to take out the licenses.[51] Another court challenge in 1903 effectively destroyed the whole law when the Illinois Supreme Court decided that the free offices had no right to deny access to applicant files to the owners of businesses closed by strikes.[52]

Within days of the 1903 court decision the General Assembly passed a revised act. Once more it gave the state the power to license the private offices, but now it established a maximum fee that had to be returned to the job applicant if no position had been found within thirty days. All employment agencies also had to retain records, which were open to state inspection, although charities were specifically exempted. The increasing concern about the safety of young working women was evident in the provision prohibiting any referrals to immoral resorts. Finally, the free offices established under the 1899 act were retained.[53]

Even this new law proved to be disappointing, in large part because of imprecise definitions of key terms. In a detailed report entitled "The Chicago Employment Agency and the Immigrant Worker," the social welfare expert Grace Abbott of the League for the Protection of Immigrants described abuses that had changed little from those of decades earlier. Innocent and trusting workers were overcharged in their application fees and dispatched to nonexistent jobs by private agencies that failed to keep records and often operated without proper licenses. Given the choice, immigrant workers made proportionately little use of the free employment service, in large part because the private agencies seemed to have greater success in getting them jobs and the neighborhood job brokers spoke their native tongue. A total of 110 of the 289 agencies in Chicago focused their business on immigrants. Employers also preferred dealing with the private agencies, with whom they were able to strike more favorable bargains for groups of laborers. But the unemployed who sought more-skilled positions regarded the state offices as little more than charities that were to be avoided by those with self-respect. As a result, instead of reducing the influence and numbers of private offices, state regulation may actually have contributed to an increase.[54]

In the midst of the investigations, vice-reform advocates utilized stories about the entrapment of innocent immigrant and rural women, occasionally at the hands of fraudulent labor agencies.[55] But the main issues were economic. Grace Abbott joined in 1909 with representatives of the Illinois Bureau of Labor Statistics and the legitimate private employment agencies to draft yet another revision of the law regulating for-profit job bureaus. Its provisions closed many of the loopholes that had been opened by imprecise definition and covered in detail every aspect of the business, prompting the chief inspector of employment offices to commend the law for bringing "a wonderful change in the conduct of these concerns." But even the 1909 reform failed to correct all of the abuses, which many regarded as inevitable in an immigrant labor market that saw over 250,000 foreign-born workers sent out from the city to build America's rail system.[56]

Despite the decades of talk and reforms, amazingly little had actually changed by 1910. Newspaper want-ads, information received from friends and relatives, and perseverance at the factory hiring office still accounted for a large share of the jobs obtained. But when the City Club of Chicago, a prestigious reform organization, conducted an investigation, it found major flaws in the six principal nonprint sources of employment information that most workers utilized. The first source was the charitable institution. While the bureau operated by the Chicago Woman's Club was apparently popular, a proportionately small number of job seekers sought the services of the nonprofit agencies because of the high fees that some, most notably the YMCA, charged.[57]

Some job seekers had already been venting their disappointment in the charitable groups in noisy demonstrations. One protest at the employment office at the B'nai B'rith Free Employment Bureau brought a charge from the *Daily Jewish Courier* that often an employer who realized that an applicant was not suitable would say that the position had been filled. "The bitter applicant returns to the employment bureau and wants to know why this job did not materialize—on his way he has been building sand castles in the air—he pictured himself coming home from work and telling his family of his job and that they will not suffer hunger any more, and all of his hopes are nothing, and the one to blame for that is the manager of the bureau."[58]

The City Club investigation also noted that the experience of the fairly large group who went to commercial agencies, the second major source, depended on the job seekers' social class. The reform investigators discovered that the honest commercial agencies handled most of the newly created skilled jobs with a minimum of complaint. Rapid technological change had opened up job opportunities for machinists, electricians, draftsmen, designers, and others, who were also wise enough to avoid exploitation. But the plight of the unskilled remained essentially unchanged. Many continued to be fleeced by less-reputable agencies that were neither required to supply information about the exact nature of the job, nor forced to return fees when jobs proved nonexistent. The club's best legal opinion was that the constitutional guarantee of the right of private contract would likely limit future reform.[59] Some workers had to frequent certain saloons that doubled as hiring halls, the third source of job leads; their proprietors were exempted from licensing because they did not charge a fee, but it was an unwritten rule that the job seeker was expected to patronize the bar frequently during the day.[60]

Although utilized by over fifty thousand job seekers a year, the fourth major job source, the Illinois Free Employment Office system, often produced disappointment. The City Club found that the system was hampered not only by its small advertising budget, but also by its division into branch offices. Originally intended as a convenience that would reduce job seekers' travel times from home, this administrative dispersal left applicants at each branch unaware of work opportunities recorded elsewhere in the system. Agency officials bristled at the thought of reorganization. One of them also complained that they were forced to deal with "the driftwood of our population, having no settled habitation." He was referring to the difficulties involved in conveying job information to the unemployed who not only lacked telephones, but whose constant moving meant that they had no permanent mailing address as well. Only lucky coincidence brought many job applicants to the employment office on the days when calls for workers arrived. State officials also revealed that they were being asked by prison officials to handle increasing numbers of parolees. The implication of the "driftwood" description was clear to the City Club: the job markets handled by the state offices were limited to the poor. The club recommended that the consolidation of the state agency could even become the basis of what amounted to a citywide department store of job intelligence, a centralized operation that could respond to opportunities in the new industries that required special skills.[61]

Another portion of the job seekers turned to labor unions, which constituted the fifth job source. Although useful in coordinating strikes, the citywide Chicago Federation of Labor did not function as the multifunctional clearing house that it might have been. Virtually all of the forty-two labor organizations that replied to the City Club's questionnaire admitted that they had no formal employment departments. Union business agents often handled the task, but further investigation revealed this presented a great opportunity for "favoritism, arbitrariness and petty grafting." Unions were also hampered by the increasingly specialized nature of the skilled crafts; employers needing butchers did not contact the sheet-metal workers, for instance. There was also the implication that it was in the union's best interest to limit the supply of workers in order to bolster wages of those who already had jobs.[62]

Unions were also ineffective against what the City Club described as a rising tide of employers' organizations, the sixth job source. Newspaper publishers, laundry operators, and garment manufacturers had joined forces to create centralized information files on workers in each trade. While the announced purpose of the files was to prevent incompetents fired in one place from obtaining employment in another, the real reason was to ensure, as a club investigator put it, "an inoffensive labor supply." That meant nonunion workers. Only during extreme labor shortages would the garment manufacturers, for instance, bend their rule and hire someone not cleared by their labor exchange; but even then the applicant would have to sign a union resignation form to go to work. When the City Club asked John T. Wigmore, dean of the Northwestern University Law School, whether this conduct constituted illegal "blacklisting," he could reply only that the situation in Illinois was still "an open one."[63]

The City Club investigators also recommended that more attention be focused on the city's position in the national flow of labor. In 1912 a University of Chicago sociologist, Charles R. Henderson, suggested the creation of a "municipal labor exchange" that would aid mainly the large number of transient agricultural workers who continued to become stranded each winter in Chicago. No agency was ever created, but before he abandoned the issue, Henderson had announced that any effort to improve conditions in Chicago would likely fail because a successful program would simply attract more applicants. Only a coordinated chain of labor agencies in a number of cities would be able to handle the tides of job seekers.[64]

The City Club work and the Henderson recommendations did result in two more investigations of employment practices that were part of a growing problem of joblessness after the outbreak of war in Europe. The report of the Mayor's

Pullman Company workers, illustration from *The Story of Pullman* (1890). The rush of workers at shift changes demonstrated how the factory regulated time for the working class.

Sweatshop inspection, 1903. A look of fear and dismay sweeps the faces of young girls caught in an unexpected examination of the clothing manufacturer where they worked. (Chicago Historical Society, DN001246)

White Slave Girls of Chicago, cover of reprint, probably 1910s. Originally published in 1888, this exposé of women's employment conditions remained a compelling document many years later.

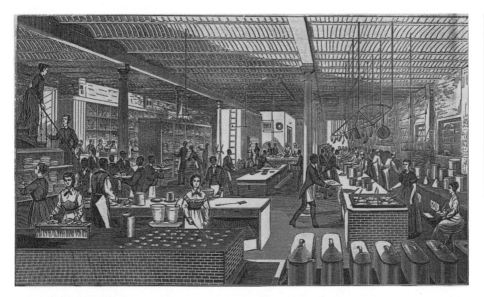

Palmer House kitchen, from *Seven Days in Chicago* (1878). African-American waiters pick up orders for the hotel's busy dining rooms, considered among the best in the city. Many of the other kitchen employees were women.

Waitresses' strike, June 1903. While waitresses went on strike to achieve better pay and working conditions, these restaurant customers took to the kitchen to serve themselves. (Chicago Historical Society, DN000639)

Municipal Markets Commission reiterated much of the club's findings, but went on to emphasize that finding a job was really a matter of risking the loss of time while acting on information that declined in value as the minutes and hours ticked away. It also suggested the pre-Keynesian idea that government should reduce public works expenditures during prosperity and spend the surplus monies during hard times. Finally, it advocated lowering the license fee as a way of opening up street peddling as an employment of last resort. The markets commission's findings largely paralleled those in a more detailed report of the Mayor's Commission on Unemployment, released nine months earlier.[65]

In early 1915 the newly created Chicago Department of Public Welfare conducted its own investigation of the employment problem, the third in two years. Its report recommended that the state employment bureau be merged into a locally controlled municipal labor exchange and that workers be able to buy into a system of unemployment insurance. The welfare department also disclosed that it had established a "preferential employment system," which encouraged giving Chicago workers with families access to information about job prospects before it was distributed to out-of-towners.[66] The report went on to detail results of interviews with 1,137 former clients of Chicago's 307 licensed employment agencies. The old abuses were still there. Agents collected fees from unskilled immigrant labor in the city and shipped the men to distant locations, where the jobs proved to be short term. Young women who went to the domestic help agencies along Milwaukee Avenue usually spent thirty days waiting and then chasing jobs that did not exist before losing their application fees. Those who did find work too frequently ended up laboring in cheap restaurants at less than promised wages.[67]

By the time America entered World War I in 1917 the problems of finding work had at least stabilized, and wartime prosperity closed some of the ethnic charities.[68] The abuses could never be completely eradicated in a large and anonymous city, particularly one whose railroad hub made it the point of confluence of mobile strangers. The most important new factor was the migration of African Americans from southern oppression to northern jobs. Although major industries such as meat packing and steel were eager to hire anyone who showed up at their gates, hopeful workers in other fields turned to the newly founded Chicago Urban League or learned about jobs through traditional information networks or family, friends, and neighbors from their old home towns. There was also a concentration of black-owned private agencies along South State Street.[69]

During the years that followed, opportunities ebbed and flowed with the national economy, comfortable during the first world conflict, dismal during the "depression" of 1919–20, prosperous again during the 1920s.[70] But prospects for employment were already beginning to deteriorate rapidly on both the national and local levels by 1928, when the growing numbers of job seekers portended an economic downturn that was beginning long before the stock market crash. By the mid-1930s, government public works projects were the employers of last resort. But for many families, the loss of a job put the former breadwinner on the road, often separated from the family by hundreds of miles. Men, women, and children by the thousands lost the security of a home and hopped freight trains—at best in search of any kind of employment anywhere, at worst in an effort to lose themselves in the rhythmic noise and swirling dust of the distant journey. But what was perhaps the most tragic aspect of their situation was the sad similarity between their experience and that of those Italian-American workers of 1895, who found themselves broke, out of work, and stranded far from home.[71]

"Commanders of the Dining Room": Race and Restaurant Waiters, 1850–1900

The black faces stare out from old photographs and engravings. The men wear starched white coats, and their rigid, almost military bearing lends an air of efficiency, manners, and obedience. One can almost hear them: "Your order, sir?" "Yes, sir, right away." Who they were and what they did are nearly forgotten now, though the ranks of African-American servers in Chicago numbered perhaps a thousand strong at the turn of the century. Theirs is the story of the efforts to use unionization to cope with the city and with working conditions in large restaurants, among the most urban of institutions. It is also a sad example of how racial division hampered those efforts.

Many historians have recounted the development of labor in Chicago. The relative newness of a city whose factories were the largest, most technologically advanced, and most impersonally organized of any in the country helped make its strikes particularly violent. Many Americans regarded what happened in Chicago as a frightening indication of where the rest of the nation was heading. The absence of a tradition of labor-management relations and the variety of its industries made a bad situation worse. The violent railway strikes of 1877, the infamous Haymarket riot of 1886, the Pullman strike of 1894, the 1937 Memorial Day massacre of the Republic Steel strike—all were milestones in efforts by workers to use their unified force to balance or combat the organized economic power of capital. Historians have chronicled union efforts in such widely diverse labor groups as packing-house workers, carpenters, and clothing workers, as well as unionization drives among women. But only a few studies have dealt with African Americans, most of them concerning the Pullman porters. However, the manner in which racial divisions thwarted worker unity is particularly well demonstrated by the plight of the men and women who worked as waiters.

The story began in the middle of the nineteenth century, when African Americans, who made up about 2 percent of Chicago's population, had already begun to concentrate in what we now call the service sector of the economy. Louis Isbell, for instance, arrived in the city in 1839 and established a barbershop whose customers included the city's emerging business elite.[72] The tailoring skills of John Jones, a free black who arrived in 1845, attracted a clientele substantial enough to make him one of the wealthier men in town, with assets of over $100,000 at the time of the Great Fire. He used his position in society to become the spokesman for his race in the city and to persuade white Chicagoans to support antislavery movements; when he took his place on the Cook County Board, he became the first African American to hold elective office in Illinois.[73] Other blacks worked in the hotel and restaurant business and included the chef of the Lake House, the city's fanciest dining room during the 1830s and 1840s. Contrasts in the rate of financial success in the service trades among blacks is most clearly seen in the stories of two men who shared the nickname "Uncle Dan." One, whose last name is not known, was a whitewasher. Born in 1810, he had purchased his freedom in Virginia and arrived in Chicago in the mid-1850s. After earning a barely comfortable living for half a century, by the late 1880s he lost his whitewashing trade to competitors who introduced the new mineral housepaints that were more colorful and permanent. The other "Uncle Dan," Daniel Scott, arrived in the city in 1872 and immediately joined with his brothers in opening a saloon. He used the profit from that venture to buy an interest in a cartage company, which he later owned outright. When he died in 1895, his estate was said to be worth $100,000.[74]

Emancipation brought an influx of service labor to Chicago in the form of freed people who had been servants on plantations and in Southern cities. The story of Thomas L. Johnson was typical. He had spent his first twenty-eight years as a slave in Virginia, where he had taught himself to read and write. When his services were not needed in his master's house, he was "hired out" to work in a seaside hotel. After the war, he and thousands of other house slaves—as opposed to the less-privileged field hands—took their domestic skills north. Johnson moved to New York, and then to a Rhode Island resort. Here, his knowledge of restaurant operations captured the attention of the vacationing Chicago restaurateur H. M. Kinsley, who immediately offered him a job. Johnson started as a dishwasher at Kinsley's, which became one of America's most elegant dining establishments, in 1866. Within a few years, he had climbed through the serving ranks to become the headwaiter. Only a few years out of slavery, Thomas L. Johnson was greeting the Marshall Fields, the George Pullmans, and others among Chicago's commercial and industrial elite. Although Johnson later left the restaurant business to pursue a successful career as an evangelist, his restaurant career continued to be cited as an example of what care and determined effort could bring in the field.[75]

During the postbellum decades, the ranks of African-American waiters in Chicago began to grow. The city's emergence as a rail, convention, and hotel center fueled the rapid expansion of large, fancy eateries, whose owners were anxious to secure the skills of hospitality and service nurtured in the South. The continuing migration of ex-slaves, moreover, assured a large pool of talent at low wages.[76] But any expectation on the part of management that servers would remain servile began to evaporate in the 1870s, when scattered walkouts erupted over depression-era pay reductions that drove the average of $27 to $30 per month down to $18 to $20. Poor treatment by obnoxious white headwaiters, as well as the length and timing of the employees' dinner hour, triggered other walkouts. In 1876 the Palmer House tried to force its service employees to use an alley entrance; the black waiters initially refused. "The dark-haired gentry took umbrage at this for awhile," noted the *Tribune,* "and a number stood on their dignity and walked off; but nearly all concluded to take the back alley next time they came in."[77]

By the end of the decade, both management and workers of all races were moving toward organization. In April 1877 the new Hotel Keepers' Association of Chicago established not only uniform wage levels, but also a central file to which each member was bound to send the name of every discharged employee. This shared knowledge allowed members to avoid hiring the incompetents as well as "troublemakers." The association also promised to hold firm at the $15–$20 wage level, even though St. Louis waiters were reportedly in the city trying to encourage a strike.[78] None materialized that year. In September 1878, however, about fifty men formed a new German Waiters' Association; its primary purpose was to function as a mutual benevolent insurance association and employment agency. An "American Waiters' Association" popped into existence in December 1879. The *Tribune,* which emphasized that violent "carving scrapes are by no means unusual occurrences in the profession," played down the potential of the latter group as a strike organizer, focusing instead on the membership's demand for status and respect by customers: "Of grievances they have many, but the principal one is that those upon whom they wait day by day seem to insist upon calling them 'soup' and 'hashslingers,' to which they decidedly object."[79]

Waitresses in the trade provided little challenge to their male counterparts at first. Although it was not unusual for women to work in family restaurants and saloons, the first notable employment of female servers came during the early 1870s, when saloons of questionable character hired what were called "pretty waiter girls." Their job was to encourage the male clients to purchase more drinks, although much of the community viewed them as little more than prostitutes. The cloud of suspicion surrounding females who served male customers survived for nearly two decades, with employment of waitresses largely limited to the dining rooms of a few outlying hotels or in food facilities that catered to women. Females were assumed to be more easily forced to work at lower wages and were slower to form unions. Their labor actions were confined to brief, barely organized walkouts. As a consequence, they presented no real competition to the black waiters.[80]

During the 1880s several factors began to reshape the status and organization of waiters. First, there was the ongoing problem of image. The press generally treated the waiters with some measure of contempt, publishing feature articles that spoke of a particular ethnic or racial group's supposedly inborn abilities or inclination to serve other people. African Americans constantly faced racist assumptions about their fitness and status. The proprietor of one Chicago hotel told a *Tribune* reporter, "Colored men are the best waiters by nature, and are peculiarly adapted to servitude" because they are "not ambitious." He went on to claim that blacks would work only at a first-class hotel and restaurant because it imparted "a certain degree of responsibility" and gave them status within their communities. If no "public" jobs were available at that level, they went into "private service" with elite families. Only whites would lower themselves to work in cheap second-class places, which usually refused to hire African Americans.[81]

Self-respect was an important issue. Waiters, black and white alike, implored fellow unionists to spurn such nicknames as "biscuit pushers." There was also the matter of tipping. Many servers considered it as an insult; they regarded accepting tips as a form of begging that undermined any effort to add dignity to the occupation of serving food to another person. But many restaurant owners encouraged "feeing," as tipping was known, as an ensurance of efficient service because it transformed the waiters or waitresses into quasi-entrepreneurs whose incomes depended on how hard they worked rather than on a standard wage. Tips were a substitute for wages that restaurant owners did not have to pay. They assumed that the quest for gratuities would create a competition among the waiting staff that would help undermine any organization efforts.[82]

The serving staffs retaliated in the battle for status by developing a type of language that helped give the restaurant a unique character among semipublic places. Waiters—like "shoeshine boys," taxi drivers, and others in service occupations who came into contact with the public—were able to communicate through the use of slang and signals. On the surface, this patter often involved staccato monosyllabic words that could clearly convey orders over the din of clattering plates and metal pans and improve efficiency during busy periods. But words and gestures also allowed employees to communicate unflattering comments about their bosses and customers. Outsiders were reportedly left to ask, "Is this a lunatic asylum or the Board of Trade?"[83]

Black waiters faced a critical issue during the 1880s: Their race denied them service in the same places where they worked. There was a sharp increase in the number of complaints about the denial of access to public accommodations, particularly after the U.S. Supreme Court struck down civil rights legislation in October 1884. Although the Illinois General Assembly passed new legislation the following June, promising "full and equal enjoyment of the accommodations, advantages, facilities and privileges of inns, restaurants, eating houses," a flood of successful court suits demonstrated that blacks were sometimes forced to ride in freight elevators, told that theatrical performances were sold out when they were not, or denied hotel rooms.[84] In restaurants, they either were left unserved or were grossly overcharged for spoiled or cold food.[85] Overt discrimination made it particularly difficult for black waiters, who were placed in the awkward position of being unable to serve people of their own race in the same manner as others. W. Willis Howe, a manager of the Palmer House, explained to a reporter, "If a colored man comes to the [Palmer] house we put him in a room by himself, and when he enters the dining room the head waiter seats him at a table by himself and sees that he keeps it to himself. . . . Naturally, if colored people began coming to the hotel in great numbers we should have to find the means to stop it—it would kill our trade."[86]

By late in the 1880s it was clear that the issues of respect and image that had dominated the world of labor in previous decades were gradually giving way to more directly economic issues that were being pressed by more highly organized groups. In part, this was a reaction to the changing nature of the larger restaurants. As Chicagoans developed more sophisticated tastes and demanded higher levels of service, restaurants responded by combining the efficiencies of department stores and factories. First, they divided the lunch, barroom, coffee shop, and banquet functions from the rest of the house. Then they broke food preparation and service into specialized jobs, which were arranged in an elaborate hierarchy of status and pay. The Lexington Hotel at Michigan Avenue and Twenty-third Street, for instance, employed fifty waiters divided into ten levels of rank. The "Head," a college-educated African American, made one hundred dollars a month. The scale descended through the "Second Lieutenant" and "Third Man." There was a specialist in desserts and another who doled out bread and butter pats all day, and down at the bottom of the ranks was the lowly water boy, whose monthly pay was only ten dollars.[87]

Job security was another critical issue in a quasi-industrial situation. Owners routinely responded to slack times by reducing their staff size with little or no notice. This meant that some waiters in effect worked on a day-to-day basis. The long hours, which often resulted in seven-day work weeks, became even more burdensome because of split shifts, which left workers with nothing to do during the unpaid midday breaks that were sandwiched between hectic noon and dinner hours. Many others worked only part-time shifts at a pay level far below that of regular employees. This unpredictability made it difficult for them to enjoy stable family lives.[88]

Waiters were increasingly distressed about the factory-like discipline that grew out of the need for efficiency. Many owners charged exorbitant fees for breakage—twenty-five cents for a butter dish that cost a penny, for instance—and the laundering of aprons. Some required waiters to provide large amounts of their own cash for change. Managers also deducted arbitrarily inflated penalties for customer complaints, despite the fact that the public nature of the waiters' work made them vulnerable to the whims of patrons. Because the servers were the ones who had to deal directly with cranky diners, they shouldered the blame for such kitchen foul-ups as cold, spoiled, or poorly prepared food.[89] Some restaurants refused to grant promised pay rates, offering instead meals that were often scraps culled from patrons' plates. Occasionally, managers complained that revenues were down and lowered the pay scale without warning.[90]

The role of the headwaiter was often the focus of other disputes. At his best, he was the self-proclaimed "Commander of the Dining Room," holding one of the most prestigious jobs in his community. Years later a black physician remembered that headwaiters who came into contact with wealthy whites were able to "acquire the manners, polish, and social graces attendant to upper class behavior. This meant that . . . head waiters were at the top of society. They almost dictated social customs. A man prided himself on being Mr. So and So's valet. Next to the head waiters were the [railway] porters, and then came the barbers."[91] One headwaiter at a North Side club reportedly received free use of a cottage owned by his employer and was able to save enough money to make payments on a 268-acre Georgia farm and a retirement house in Atlanta.[92]

Within the restaurant, the headwaiter held a position of special trust. At his best, his duties included recognizing and greeting distinguished patrons, resolving real and imagined grievances among customers, and ensuring the smooth operation of waiters under his control. Many headwaiters, both black and white, had many years of experience in famous eateries and regarded themselves as superior to common servers. But at his worst, the headwaiter could be a parasite who extracted bribes in exchange for jobs and demanded a share of the tips. He could force a waiter to buy uniforms from a particular dealer who returned a kickback.[93]

The fact that black waiters hated to work for white headwaiters, whose racism occasionally led to a walkout by an entire staff, reflected the local labor pattern in general. The 1880s saw sharp racial and ethnic divisions among the ranks of many categories of Chicago workers. Among whites there was an increasing belief that every African American who migrated to Chicago was at least a job competitor, if not a potential strikebreaker. Labor disorders, often involving small-scale violence, broke out during strikes among seamen (1880), stevedores (1881, 1892), grain-trimmers (1888), lumberyard workers (1887), coalyard workers (1879), and the stockyards (1886). In each case, the presence of black workers quickly became the central issue of the labor action, regardless of the original sources of each dispute.[94]

The traditional presence of people of all backgrounds on the waiting staffs may well have made racial and ethnic divisions among the ranks of the restaurant trade develop more quickly. Caucasians, who comprised about half of the ranks of waiters, split into English-speaking and Teutonic groups. The latter, who worked almost entirely in German restaurants, remained distrustful of the others throughout the rest of the century and demanded freedom of negotiation independent of any of the other waiters' groups.[95] The first overt signs of racial division among the other labor organizations within the serving trade appeared in February 1884, when the White Waiters' Assembly announced its formation. Germans were welcome; blacks, who constituted half of the city's waiters, were not.[96]

The African Americans responded to white unionization in two ways. First, some among their ranks developed greater loyalty toward a few restaurants than toward others, depending on their treatment. For instance, black waiters had enjoyed the best wages and working conditions at the chain of low-priced lunch places owned by H. H. Kohlsatt. The German-born restaurateur had also contributed generously to charities in the African-American community. He was the major benefactor of the Colored Men's Library Association, a reading room that was especially popular among the upwardly mobile waiters.[97] It was clear that the black waiters would respond to unionization by whites on a restaurant-by-restaurant basis. The blacks' other independent action was to unionize themselves. The first thrust came under the auspices of the Knights of Labor, the large national movement that used union organization as the base for massive national social reform.[98] In late 1886, J. Ross Fitzgerald, a New York organizer for the Knights, came to Chicago and created the William Lloyd Garrison Colored Waiters Local Assembly 8286. Some 400 African-American waiters and porters joined, though only 120 participated fully in the Friday-night meetings and picnics. According to the *Chicago Times,* the union "braced up the colored waiters considerably" and gave them "confidence with themselves."[99] The Knights of Labor, however, began to decline. Its seemingly imprecise goals of social change made it more difficult for some workers to appreciate its economic goals, while others were uncomfortable with its biracial makeup. Unfair blame for involvement in the Haymarket Riot of May 4, 1886, also tainted its efforts.[100]

There was one partial victory. On May 1, 1887, white waiters employed by three major downtown restaurants suddenly walked out at the busiest part of the dinner hour. They demanded the slightly higher pay usually given those whose waiting tasks included shucking the seafood. Although the management of one of the struck eateries, Race Brothers, hired a nonunion white crew, the other two, the Chicago Oyster House and Rector's, hired nonorganized African Americans in the place of the whites. The division between the races opened quickly and publicly, with the White Waiters' Assembly warning its "colored brethren," as the *Daily News* put it, "to the effect that there would be a war to the knife" if strike-breaking continued. Some of the struck restaurants settled under union terms, but the 1887 May Day strikes established a precedent: For decades to come, restaurateurs would segregate their staffs and threaten complete replacement of one group by the other as a way of countering demands for increased wages.[101]

By the end of 1888, it was clear that the Knights was disintegrating. Some dissident African-American waiters had seceded from the Garrison local to create a separate Charles Sumner Waiters' Union, while white locals also fragmented. On January 3, 1889, a group of German waiters, cooks, and bartenders formed the Culinary Alliance, an interracial alliance of eight independent unions, in an effort to end the disunity. Its young organizer, W. C. Pomeroy, had already attained a national reputation for organizing the waiters in major hotels and restaurants in St. Louis.[102]

The first test of the Culinary Alliance came on May 5, 1890, against Kinsley's elegant eatery. At a prearranged signal, the African-American servers marched through the dinner-hour crowd to the street, leaving behind patrons who fumed at the long waits and the inept emergency replacements who spilled coffee and misdirected the food orders. After a while, several well-dressed businessmen who were regular customers got up from their favorite tables, strolled into the kitchen, cooked their own meals, and carried them back to the dining room. But curiosity soon turned into bitterness, with talk of most of the 1,800 black waiters in Chicago becoming part of the movement.[103]

The Culinary Alliance knew how to run a job action. It assessed all members a dollar for a strike fund and established an employment bureau that could provide skilled workers to any establishment with little notice. The alliance also demanded a review when any member was dismissed, and it worked out contract offers that spelled out more precise time and pay schedules. Most important, it recognized the role of railroads in the struggle. The alliance realized that the owners were likely to import strikebreakers and enlisted the aid of porters and dining car crews to discourage any Chicago-bound passenger who looked as if he might be a waiter; the union also established lookouts at railway depots. Flying bricks greeted "scabs" who showed up at Kinsley's back door. Finally the press disclosed a Culinary Alliance plan to fill the Kinsley's staff with union men posing as strikebreakers, who would walk out in unison during the busiest serving hour.[104]

The labor action divided the African-American community, though most likely not into even parts. The strike became the topic of discussion in churches, and the Fisk Jubilee Singers made a special trip to the city to lend musical support.[105] But W. W. "Clambake" Rodley, the city's only black caterer, opposed the strike because, as he put it, "My people have a monopoly on the waiter business in this country. It is about all they can do. I'd hate to see them thrown out of it." His large staff of employees backed their boss.[106]

The major restaurant owners, meanwhile, promised to make concessions on tardiness and breakage rules, provided that they did not have to sign a union contract, and all except Kinsley reopened within a day or two with union help. While most proprietors were resigned to riding out the problem, some quietly tried to undermine faith in the Culinary Alliance by circulating leaflets accusing its leadership of malfeasance.[107]

Toward the end of the month, however, the strike began to stall. It was clear that the owners were successfully importing out-of-town replacements by meeting the inbound trains at suburban stops. The newcomers were promised wages higher than union scale in exchange for a no-union pledge. One by one, the union crews found themselves on the street. Most distressing of all, proprietors played off white workers against African Americans.[108] With a facade of cheery confidence, the Culinary Alliance tried to prevent defeat by enlarging the walkout to include private downtown clubs, but here it ran into even more determined and vocal opposition. The business elite felt a more personal anger when labor agitation threatened their private lunching spots, as well as the more public restaurants. By early June, the strike fervor was beginning to ooze away. When the club effort failed, the union tried to organize hotel dining rooms.[109] That proved most disastrous of all because the proprietors could readily shift compliant and unorganized housekeeping staffs into dining room jobs. The press, unsympathetic to the walkout from the beginning, praised the manner in which replacements of all types were nearly as competent as the strikers.[110]

By early summer 1890, however, the issue was no longer the success of the strike but the survival of the Culinary Alliance itself. The results of the job actions had been disappointingly mixed. While some owners agreed to union terms, most negotiated individual settlements with their former employees. But the fact that whites replaced striking blacks, and vice versa, caused the demise of the interracial Culinary Alliance: German-speaking waiters, English-speaking whites, and African Americans went their separate ways, agreeing to aid each other but shunning any further formal cooperation.[111] That division caused the failure of scattered walkouts that took place over the next two years, especially during the 1892 Democratic National Convention. These work stoppages did, however, bring one antiscab innovation: sympathetic cooks aided the strikers by handing red-hot plates to unsuspecting strikebreakers, who dropped them and were fired.[112]

By the early 1890s the stigma of the "pretty waiter girls" had disappeared and more women were seeking positions in the trade. Waitresses were introduced as downtown strikebreakers, which further complicated the efforts to organize the serving trade. One incident in particular may have drawn the attention of management. Just as the Culinary Alliance was collapsing, the Woman's Christian Temperance Union reduced wages by a third at the restaurant it ran in its Loop skyscraper. The waitress meekly accepted the cuts, and six months later one of them became the subject of a *Tribune* feature on the destitute families who came to the Harrison Street police station for relief.[113] It was clear, however, that the women would soon shed their docile image. By early 1892 the waitresses were themselves on strike against several small hotels and Henrici's, the popular German restaurant in the Loop. On May 14, 1893, four hundred of them organized the Waiter Girl's Union No. 1.[114]

Meanwhile, by the time plans were formulated for the 1893 World's Columbian Exposition, both black and white male waiters were employing different and separate organizing strategies. The African Americans formed the National Hotel and Restaurant Employees' Alliance, whose branches in several states tried to prevent members from coming to Chicago. It was clear that this tactic kept competition for jobs from escalating. The alliance then carried on a series of successful strikes against individual restaurants that were vulnerable because they did not want to lose the lucrative exposition patronage. Wage issues triggered most of the walkouts, but in a few places, the waiters struck over demands that they shave their mustaches.[115] Meanwhile, the white American Waiters' Association accused the black union of using civil rights public accommodation laws to oust white waiters. Blacks who were refused service by white restaurant crews would file lawsuits claiming violation of public accommodation statutes. While these actions were probably motivated by the real problem of growing racial segregation in Chicago and other northern cities, white waiters condemned them as only tactics to grab jobs.[116]

As the end of the century approached, however, many black waiters clearly saw themselves as part of a declining trade. A proliferation of employment bureaus, schools, and self-improvement clubs attempted to make the "ebony-hued knights of the soup," as the *Times* called them, more attractive to employers. One local man, Winfield Cozart, wrote a 115-page manual on the "science" of waiting.[117] The African Americans who had risen to the level of headwaiter felt especially vulnerable. They had long regarded themselves as an elite whose members had been robbed of the success they might have attained in business or the profession because of discrimination. In September 1899, fifty of them gathered in Chicago to form the Head and Second Waiters National Benefit Association. Although the group's principal purposes were to provide benevolent burial insurance and to form a school to educate waiters, it was clear that status and opportunity were the central concerns. The members of the group wanted to improve the station of their profession by recruiting more young black college graduates. Moreover, by denouncing unions as coercive, they were doubtless trying to improve their own prospects by aligning with the owners.[118]

During the first decade of the new century the pattern established in the wake of the 1890 strike continued: smaller, racial- and gender-exclusive unions conducted a series of short-lived and ineffective strikes against individual restaurants. The only major action came during the summer of 1903, when declining wages prompted walkouts by the African Americans against twenty-six hotels and fifty-eight restaurants. But while white waiters allowed state arbitrators to settle their differences when they struck, the blacks felt unfairly treated and continued to strike. Even the veneer of unity broke down when many of the black waiters were replaced by white waitresses.[119]

One of the clearest signs of the declining status of the work was the way certain saloons gradually took over the function of the union hiring hall. When the City Club of Chicago conducted an exhaustive study of employment conditions in 1910, the most plaintive cry for reform came from waiters. No union was powerful enough to compete with a group of saloons that had become hiring halls for cooks, pastry chefs, stewards, servers, and even headwaiters.[120]

By the turn of the century, it was also clear that the ranks of the African-American waiters were declining proportionately. Although census classifications combined servants and waiters into one category in 1900 and 1910, the returns showed the waiting force to be 38.7 percent black in 1900, but only 30.9 percent in 1910; there was a rebound to 33.7 percent in 1920, undoubtedly due to the enlargement of the community after the Great Migration and a relative gain because of the downturn in immigration. Why the decline early in the century? Some observers blamed the weakness of their national union and the ease with which they could be replaced by white women in the serving trade. Some owners fabricated the excuse that à la carte menus were too "complicated" for the blacks. National trade journals, supposedly rising to the waiters' defense, repeated racist stereotypes, among them that African Americans were "born servants." The *Chicago Chronicle* countered that young black men were not entering the serving trade precisely because they did not consider themselves "born servants." The lure of the status and steady employment of the Pullman car, job openings in meat packing and other industries, and opportunities in more skilled professions and businesses also siphoned talent away from waiting tables.[121]

And so we return to the men in the photographs, to those determined faces above the starched jackets. Their legacy was pride.

Conclusion

Getting a job could be one of the most difficult aspects of coping with city life. In part, the problem grew out of the variety of places in which to search. The newspapers were a critical source of leads, as was a tip from a friend or relative, or the good fortune of inquiring at the employment office just as a position opened. To a great extent, there was a resemblance between this process and finding a place to live. Both involved movement from an uncertain world of drift and insecurity to one of fixedness and at least the illusion of permanence. Securing a "position" that was vacant was like finding a vacant flat or house.

Like the search for housing, the story of seeking employment involved the interplay of three factors in the urban marketplace. The first was information about a job vacancy, the knowledge of the name and address of someone who needed an employee and, conversely, the identity of someone who needed a job. The latter was easily obtained when job seekers were lined up at the factory gate, but at other times companies were willing to pay employment agencies for that data. Sometimes the information came from a network of family, friends, neighbors, or fellow parishioners. House and flat listings worked in a similar fashion. Often, information about vacancies was abundant and easily accessible, but sometimes it was necessary for landlords and tenants to find each other through rental agencies, which functioned for a fee much like their "intelligence office" counterparts.

The second factor was time. As in the search for a house or flat to rent, knowledge about the potential job or employee was valuable only when no competitors knew about it; the more widely shared the "hot prospect," the greater chance that someone equally qualified could snap it up. Every day that passed tended to lower the value of that information, much in the way that food or milk spoiled or a newspaper lost its value the next day. When there were thousands of unskilled involved, there was the ever-present danger that the wage would be driven downward; labor shortages had the opposite effect. Similarly, when the demand for housing was overwhelming, the buyer/renter got little for the money.

Ironically, the third factor, that of the risk involved in this situation, came from the unknown and the unknowable. How many immigrant arrivals were there from Europe? How would weather conditions affect the construction season? What upturns and downtowns could be expected from the national economy? All of these elements added to the instability and prospects for employment, just as they affected the demand for housing. The poorer the family, the more likely it was that they would be touched by these unknown factors.

The situation was made even worse by another set of risks that grew from misplaced trust in an anonymous society. Because cities were crowds of strangers, they were concentrations of hazards. Employment agencies were usually properly run and delivered what was promised to both employer and employee, but there was always the danger that the name selected from a phone book or overheard at a saloon could bring only grief. The dispersed and almost secretive nature of the enterprise contributed to the potential for abuse. The apparent indifference of authorities to the plight of victims drove the lucky ones to turn inward to their communities for help from charities and churches. Others became perpetual prey and lacked any real means of fighting back. To some extent, the same was true of the housing market. Poverty and a lack of understanding about how the market worked helped perpetuate poor living conditions.

While there were few ways in which the poor could unite—except through the political process, which will be described later—they could attempt to pool their labor. The story of unionization efforts among African-American waiters involved out-of-town competition for relatively scarce jobs, but this was just one factor in a complicated issue. This occupational group represented only a small portion of those who attempted to find power through organization, but over the years they all found themselves thwarted for the same reasons. First, the subdivision of their work into routine tasks that required relatively little skill to master left them vulnerable to replacement by someone who would settle for less money. Efforts to organize were further thwarted by a pair of factors. One was the divided nature of the workplace. Unlike large factories, such as McCormick Reaper, or the railroads, where strategically placed disruptions could stop an entire operation, most restaurants were relatively small work units that competed with each other and were scattered throughout the city. A work stoppage at one house did not close down the rest. Furthermore, the specialized hierarchical nature of the restaurant as a workplace tended to set different ranks and pay levels against each other. The lead waiter might constantly wonder whether the bread-and-butter server really was after his job.

The most important factors, however, were race and gender. Restaurant owners quickly discovered that African Americans and whites distrusted each other, especially in an urban society where minorities daily encountered discrimination in housing and public accommodations. It became easy to play one group off against the other, and when that failed to work, they introduced competition from waitresses.

Perhaps the most subtle issue was that of self-respect in the service sector. The waiters as a whole, but especially the African Americans among them, were almost desperately trying to imbue their work with dignity as well as to find a decent wage. Being a headwaiter brought with it not only status within the black community, but also an earned trust from the white restaurant owners. The racial divisions that destroyed unionization efforts also diminished that status.

Postscript

There was another chapter to the story of African-American waiters. On October 13, 1937, black workers at the Palmer House and the Sherman House formed the Federated Hotel Waiters and Hotel Attendants of Chicago. Although all of its charter members eventually lost their jobs, the group gained recognition two years later as Local 356 of the Hotel and Bartenders International Union. This was the same year they signed a contract with the two downtown hotels where the movement started. Meanwhile, an organizer named Levert "St. Louis" Kelly formed a separate Bartenders, Cooks, Waiters, and Waitresses Union in the South Side cocktail lounges and small restaurants. The two black unions merged in 1954, but the most important event took place eight years later when that group merged with Local 25 of the Hotel and Bartenders International Union. It was integrated, thus ending decades of racial divisions. Finally, the spirit of the Culinary Alliance returned, although most servers remained unorganized because of scattered workplaces and the ease with which workers could be replaced.[122]

After the Great Depression, the way in which Chicagoans searched for employment continued to mirror the larger social trends of America. When unemployment fell to about 1 percent during World War II, labor shortages became so severe that corporate canvassers went door-to-door trying to persuade housewives to join the workforce. The postwar readjustment led to two decades of manufacturing prosperity and labor shortages in the city. The old expression from the 1950s, "If you can't get a job in Chicago, you can't get one anywhere," reflected not only the optimism of the time, but also the diversity of a local economy that needed every level and type of job skill.[123]

As industrial job losses after 1960 climbed toward nearly a million in the city alone, something more closely resembling the turn-of-the-century "intelligence office" hierarchy emerged once more. At the top, reputable agencies dealing with the skilled-service sector matched employers and applicants in a private setting. Each step down the skill and income ranks saw increasing risk of fraud from unscrupulous operators, as well as a more public job search. Instead of having a private interview, applicants sat in large waiting rooms until their names were announced or saw their identities become anonymous numbers at the state employment office. At the bottom, Skid Row—and later Uptown—the day-labor agencies scrawled notices on sidewalk blackboards, gathering today's "driftwood."

In more recent years, the "downsizing" of places employing middle-class workers has introduced them to the insecurity once reserved for the armies of the unskilled. The old risks are not entirely gone.

10   Getting Ahead on Your Own

HERB PERRY is a Chicago success story. In 1990 he was jobless and virtually broke when he decided to seek his fortune in the streets. He might easily have ended up on welfare, but he saw an entrepreneurial niche that needed filling. He bought an old bicycle, attached a castoff supermarket cart behind it, and began selling a variety of goods on the streets. None of the combs, shower caps, underwear, rubber sandals, or other items was expensive, but his mobile business brought in enough money to survive and to allow him to restock his wares. He soon began adding carts, until his rolling "store" totaled six. He exchanged the original wheels for larger ones to navigate the potholes and curbs of the streets near the North and Central Avenues district where he lives and sells. The addition of vertical racks of merchandise fluttering in the breeze gave his rig the appearance of a parade, as he jostled his way through traffic.[1]

Perry had discovered that the small size of his mobile store gave him the ability to go directly to the customer, rather than vice versa, much as the iceman, the milkman, and even the physician of the nineteenth century took their wares and expertise on the road. But his story reflects another aspect of coping with urban life: the determination to get ahead by using selected opportunities in the urban environment that might contribute to individual economic mobility. Because it also indicates a decision to shape one's own future, to cope in an active rather than just reactive way, it implies more than just entrepreneurship.

The Curbstone Economy: The Peddler's Life

An enquiry into the rise and decline of the street trades is more than a venture into nostalgia. Peddling was the central economic institution for vast numbers of Chicagoans in many neighborhoods. It was a means of independent action, a strategy for economic survival. It also provided an important example of how thousands of people coped with the problem of finding a job in the city without falling victim to employment agency cons, unfair industrial hiring practices, exclusion from certain unions, union busting, and other problems.[2]

Street peddling provided an instructive contrast to the usual notion that only unity brought survival. Although unorganized, poor, and seemingly powerless, these sidewalk salespersons survived best by doing the exact opposite of joining together in a union. They "atomized" into a pool of individual economic competitors who employed their own wits, knowledge, and hard work to survive. Most ended up in the street trades by choice, but when times got very bad, the pavement could always become an employer of last resort, a final "safety net," to use our contemporary term.

Traders could not have existed without free access to the public spaces in which they began plying their trade. During the city's earliest years, the best opportunities lay in supplying everyday necessities on a door-to-door basis. Archibald Clybourn, the founder of the city's packing industry, sold meat to families in this manner. Other vendors profited from the growing problem of well-water pollution by filling carts with clean lake water and ladling it out to customers along a regular retail route.[3] But new opportunities arose when improvements in water transportation and the new railroads began to erode Chicago's isolation. During the 1840s, when the population grew from about four thousand to thirty thousand, itinerant salespersons from other parts of the country began stopping on their way through the young town to sell a variety of new products to the locals. In 1848 one dealer reportedly offered everything "from the 'genuine razor strop' to the 'infallible grease remover and clothes renovator.'"[4]

The growing complexity of urban life and the evolution of the city's streets contributed to the expansion and diversity in the ranks of the curbstone entrepreneurs. One category of activity concerned getting either people or merchandise from here to there. The burgeoning Civil War rail traffic introduced "hotel runners" to carry travelers' suitcases for the short distance between the depots and nearby lodging. At first, a few semidestitute drifters began providing the service, but soon large crowds of runners began greeting the arriving trains. For decades to come, most would be hard-working porters, although the opportunities for robbery also attracted a disreputable group who gave many out-of-towners a painful introduction to the Garden City.[5] The physical growth of the city increased the distances traveled; this not only put passengers in the seats of the omnibuses, but also created opportunities for another form of street trade, the cabdriver. Finally, the thirst for information generated by the war and the growth of the reading public enlarged the newspaper audience, but the outward expansion of the city put blocks, then miles, between the news office and the reader. Newsboys not only hawked headlines downtown, but also brought them into the neighborhoods.[6]

The four decades that followed the Civil War were the heyday of the peddler. Chicago's streets provided selling space for as many as thirty thousand tradesmen, their ranks swollen by immigrants eager to make their way in a new land. The street trades were an ideal introduction to the economic system. The capital needed to establish a business was minimal, just enough pennies to buy a stack of newspapers or to stock a cart or a box supported by a strap around the neck. Often, two or more traders would share a cart that could be kept in operation virtually around the clock. Widows and single women could join the ranks, and it was not unusual to see children trailing behind their mothers and the family cart. The simplicity of their transactions meant that they could get by with only a few words of English or the predominant language of the neighborhood they wished to serve. Skill was learned in the street through successes and disappointments and measured by the daily intake of coins; it had nothing to do with a diploma. Others, who had been in the city longer and who knew about the rigid discipline, poor wages, and unsafe working conditions of the factory, were attracted to the freedom of the trader's self-scheduled routine and the possibilities of profit.[7]

The variety of street trades was enormous. In one category Chicago functioned as a headquarters for an army of individuals who fanned out across the midwestern countryside selling portable goods not readily available from local merchants. Many went to places like the Peddlers' Supply Company at Canal and Liberty Streets to "equip their pack." This was perhaps the most strenuous type of peddling because of the mileage between customers and the loneliness of the road, but also because during the late nineteenth century it became less profitable. The improved delivery of goods ordered from mail-order catalogs undercut the business, while local merchants pushed hostile licensing laws through state legislatures. The more sophisticated peddlers were a primordial form of the traveling salesmen who made the sale and arranged the orders, leaving the shipping to someone else.[8]

Most street traders never ventured from the city. As word of promising activities and profitable routes spread through the neighborhoods, families introduced newly arrived relatives to the trade. Because the variety of items was too great for any one peddler to handle, ethnic specialties gradually developed. Italians and Greeks, for instance, dominated the fresh produce trade, eventually becoming predominant in the wholesale end of the business as well.[9] Other ethnic groups created their own niches. Germans were prominent in mobile fix-it services. Many of them sharpened scissors; others went door-to-door offering to repair anything in the house.[10] Jews established themselves mainly in the trade of recycling used clothing, rag, and junk. Their regular routes took them through Chicago's better neighborhoods, where they hauled away castoffs. They could resell some clothing to other individuals, but they would always sell rags to paper manufacturers. On occasion, the daily search through the streets would yield some salable metal, but the staple of the trade in the late nineteenth century was the glass bottle, the new packaging form that was returnable for a deposit or resale. One individual established a highly successful milk bottle exchange, which purchased the valuable glass containers from junk pickers and then resold them to the dairies whose names were printed on them.[11]

The street trades were a crucial avenue of social mobility, but they also eased the burden of feeding tenement families. By the 1870s, Chicago's slum districts had begun to spread beyond easy walking distance of the produce markets of Randolph Street. A nickel streetcar ride—with no free transfers—was an expensive venture for those with incomes of a few dollars a week; many others were sensitive about their appearance and never ventured to the major shopping districts. Yet the homemaker of the tenements had to shop every day because of the lack of refrigeration. Nearby groceries were either expensive or under investigation for filth; their only attraction was credit sales. The mobile vendor proved to be a convenient alternative. He scouted the city wholesale markets for bargains, often buying produce that was discounted below normal wholesale because it was slightly damaged or too ripe. The quick turnover of goods on his cart and his flexible prices allowed him to move his merchandise before it spoiled. The slum dweller appreciated the convenience of buying food cheaply right at the door.[12] As both an occupation and a source of essential goods, peddling became one of the most valuable neighborhood institutions.

Although many peddlers dreamed of one day operating in a permanent indoor location, often they were content to begin by pushing fast-food carts. Those early versions of "meals-on-wheels" appeared near factory entrances, construction sites, and shopping districts. A few sandwich and popcorn vendors talked their way past sympathetic conductors onto streetcars and commuter trains. By the 1890s dozens of purveyors of ice cream and roasted chestnuts brought their version of technology to the street by building their own portable coolers and heaters. *Chicago Record* columnist George Ade noted that the hot-corn peddlers were invariably surrounded by a crowd that included the "bootblack, the cabman, the sport and the swell [who] . . . may be seen under the flaming gasoline lamps gnawing away at the succulent ear."[13] One enterprising cook even established a "breakfast wagon," which he drove through neighborhoods inhabited by middle-class single people. They were happy to buy a quick stand-up breakfast of pancakes and eggs.[14]

The most colorful denizens of the street were the mobile music makers, many of them from the ranks of the blind. The mass production of small crank organs and cheap musical instruments had enabled whole families of street musicians to create small orchestras. Although many people thought of them as no more than noisy beggars, some of Chicago's four hundred organ grinders reputedly made eight to ten dollars per day, far more than was earned by laborers or in any of the occupations traditionally pursued by the handicapped. The dean of the blind street organists, Giovanni Mazzo, made enough to purchase three West Side tenements. Accompanied by a paid chaperone, he began his day outside of Holy Family church on Twelfth Street, then proceeded to the Loop in the early afternoon. His corner at State and Van Buren Street was ideal because he caught department store shoppers, the theater crowds, and "country people" on their way to see the lake. Despite the complaints about the cacophony, most organ grinders chose their sentimental tunes with care and practiced them.[15]

To some observers, the peddler seemed to be a casual ambler, but success in the street trades depended on more than simply luck or being able to get from here to there. It also required a thoroughgoing knowledge of crowds and neighborhoods, as well as the temporal rhythms of it all. This vital information added an element of predictability to peddlers' relationships with their suppliers and customers. The traders generally divided into two groups. The first, like Mazzo, let the crowd do the walking and encountered the moving streams of customers on the street. Flower peddlers, for instance, stationed themselves outside department stores, so that they could attract the attention of the middle-class women shoppers who would pass by the cartloads of blooms. Toy sellers were positioned nearby, where they played on the guilt of middle-class matrons who had forgotten to purchase something for their children. Others sold gum and songbooks outside theaters. Umbrella vendors magically appeared on rainy days, crowding around the entrances to better stores and restaurants where customers who had clothing good enough to protect were happy for the opportunity to spend fifty cents.[16] Even the fakir, the colorful character who sold gadgets, knew where to find crowds of awe-struck children and gullible adults. In 1890, one real estate dealer revealed his formula for predicting whether a particular location would be successful for business purposes: He looked for Italian fruit vendors' stands. "These men never stay where they can make no sales," he told a *Post* reporter. "If one of these fellows stays three days in succession on a corner it is sure to be a good business corner."[17]

The second group of peddlers supplied the mobility by following regular door-to-door routes that had been developed over years of trial and error. One sampling of these itinerant salespersons included, besides the usual fix-it specialist, a photographer, a professional cockroach exterminator, a professional entertainer for children's parties, a coat-of-arms seller, a metal polisher, a seat-caning expert, and instructors offering to teach housewives how to braid their hair or bake the latest-style cake. Another specialist roamed the suburbs selling every type of glue a household might need; still another went from office to office downtown selling men's tailored clothes for one dollar a week.[18]

The work of many street traders frequently took them out of their own neighborhoods. For some like Fred Lundin, who had arrived as a penniless Swedish immigrant child, the experience was enlightening. He began peddling "Juniper Ade," a combination patent medicine–temperance drink, from the back of a wagon. The intimate knowledge of the city, its people, and their needs and aspirations that he gained at curb level became more important than formal schooling as he rose through the ranks of Republican party politics to become one of the state's most powerful politicians. "Bathhouse John" Coughlin, Michael "Hinky Dink" Kenna, and other ward boss politicians put in similar apprenticeships as newsboys and bootblacks. Later, a Bohemian-born kindling-wood peddler named Anton Cermak would use his curbstone education in creating the Democratic party machine that would rule the city and county from 1931 until the late 1970s. Cermak himself served as mayor from 1931 until his assassination two years later.[19]

But travel abroad in the city, as well as in a familiar neighborhood street, had its hazards. The newsboy was frequently young and defenseless. The small and often ramshackle peddlers' carts were vulnerable when they got in the way of larger vehicles. And the pursuit of pennies and nickels often took the street merchant down alleys and avenues where deep puddles concealed nails and other dangerous objects. The poverty that many had to show for their efforts forced them to work year round, including bitterly cold days and nights. Hucksters who ventured into parts of the city dominated by ethnic groups other than their own could be attacked by gangs of neighborhood youth, who regarded "foreign" street traders as "fair game" for violence as well as pranks. In one particularly vicious incident a group of between fifty and one hundred Polish youths looted dozens of stands along Milwaukee Avenue, leaving two Italian vendors seriously injured.[20]

Peddlers also encountered problems when their routes penetrated the social-class lines of neighborhoods. As cities grew, they became more segregated not only according to income, ethnicity, and housing type, but also by the amount of privacy afforded by a particular lifestyle. In tenement districts the separation between the public space of the street and sidewalk and the private space of the home was already diffuse and unclear in many ways. Families in overcrowded buildings shared hallways and toilet facilities, and summer heat drove them to seek relief by sleeping on the roof, the fire escape, or the sidewalk. Children played on the streets. In these areas the peddlers were just another part of the streetscape. But in middle- and upper-class neighborhoods, where fences and yards surrounded single-family homes, peddlers were often accused of violating privacy in two ways. The first was their contribution to the general problem of street noise. Much of the urban din was regarded as inevitable: the steel flanges of streetcar wheel grinding against rails, hooves pounding on stone pavements, and the sound of factories that gave employment, for instance. The sounds, however, were not uniformly distributed. People who ventured to the Loop were prepared for an assault on their senses. But just as the city separated itself by social class, economic land-use, and ethnicity, so too did many Chicagoans think that noise should not only be reduced in general, but also kept out of places and periods of the night where it was an intrusive nuisance. Out in the residential neighborhoods the shouts of newsboys that broke the early morning quiet, the blare of the hurdy-gurdy, and the various chants and clanging of bells associated with a particular type of street trade aroused angry responses. Even in more modest neighborhoods, where peddlers were a necessity, the loudest complaints came from night-shift workers who were trying to sleep during the day and from the mothers of small babies. In March 1897 the Common Council tried to quiet criticism—and neighborhood noise—by enacting a law prohibiting whistles, and it followed that with a law banning bells larger than four inches. But the problem lay clearly with enforcement of the laws already on the books. The peddlers complained that the only real result was an increase in their vulnerability to shakedown by police officers.[21]

In 1906 the police department began one of its periodic crackdowns on noise, but this time there were unexpected consequences. When officers began arresting the peddlers who shouted, the persistent salespersons changed their strategies by opening the front gate, marching up a private sidewalk, and ringing the doorbell and pounding on windows and doors. This distressed householders, who felt not only invaded but also more personally threatened by the people they had previously encountered only at a distance. The "foreign" and frequently unkempt appearance of many peddlers, as well as their apparent freedom from timeclocks and industrial discipline, caused many to be classified with the growing army of aggressive tramps and hoboes that had begun to appear in America during the depression of the 1870s. These wanderers often went door to door in fringe neighborhoods and asked for food in exchange for light labor. Not knowing whether the stranger on the porch was asking for a handout or selling a featherduster, many upstanding homeowners confused the two types of "invasions." Thus, only a few days after the enforcement started, the same Chicagoans who had complained about noise decided that they preferred the shouts from the streets to the knock at the door. Intensive lobbying pressured the police chief to reverse the policy.[22]

The door-to-door peddler also forced the householder to balance philanthropic tendencies against the desire for privacy, one of the conflicts of coping that city life often produced. In 1890 the Chicago correspondent to *The Dawn,* a Boston socialist publication, had noted:

> Does the busy city matron ever stop to think what it means when she runs to the door a dozen times in a busy day to answer an agent's appeal? It is impossible to buy a tenth of what they have to sell; she had stored away brooms because she could not turn off the blind boy; . . . the old woman with lace she made has been asked to rest, and the "lady of the house" has voiced her regret because she is unable to buy; then come bananas, pictures, matches, and rugs. Oh, the motley procession!
>
> But there is no rest and she begins to be indignant. Has she no right to plan her own time? Is she to have no privacy in her own house? Now here is the answer—this importunity means that these "disinherited classes" are in the life and death struggle; every ring at that bell by one who sells something says; "Give me the chance to *live!*"

One woman coped with fending off the unwelcome intrusion; the other saw in that intrusion an attempt to survive.[23]

Many people resented the peddlers because they seemed to violate society's schedules, timeclocks, and other temporal conventions. The fact that many curbstone merchants were Jewish and made sales on the Christian Sabbath irritated not only religious conservatives but also the merchants who by custom and occasional law had to remain closed. The city council banned all Sabbath shouts and noisemaking in 1883, and in 1898 it made citizenship a requirement to get a license, but many nativists were dissatisfied.[24]

At the same time, the anonymity of the city and the itinerant nature of the business fed rumors of shady practices and quick escapes from misdeed. It was easy to complain that peddlers could get away with using short-weight scales or undersized containers to cheat customers because city inspectors could not find them to test for accuracy.[25] Early consumer advocates complained that the street vendors charged extortionate prices for coal purchased in small quantities, all that the poor could afford or could store. Health reformers accused the peddlers of cheating those who depended upon them most by selling spoiled produce concealed under colored mesh or top layers of fresh fruit.[26] And store-keepers protested that street traders routinely failed to take out licenses and paid no property taxes, while at the same time enjoying police protection and benefiting from every improvement in paving or lighting that was provided by taxpayers. The implication was that impermanence brought with it an unwarranted immunity from civic responsibility. Thus, to many hostile observers, the peddler was to retailing what the con artist was to crime and the homeless person was to real estate: a rootless individual who survived by stealth.[27]

There were also vague suspicions and widespread uneasiness about the children in the street trades. The Italian-American press could condemn some of its community's parents who had reportedly trained their youngsters to beg as a source of family income. But the Newsboys and Bootblacks Home, founded in 1868, was shown to be a haven for dozens—some reported hundreds—of abandoned non-Italian children who had turned to the curbstone economy as a last resort. The least society could do was provide them with food and shelter. The public reacted to the "newsies" with a combination of pity and fear. One newspaper column spoke admiringly about one youth who was wise enough to offer German-language papers on trains headed into German neighborhoods. Yet the same writer could paint a pathetic word portrait of a very small youngster whose exhaustion and force of habit made him continue to shout the headlines long after he had sold his last paper.[28]

Consistent and vociferous opposition to the noisy vendors came from shop owners who complained to the city council that the leather-lunged competitors on the sidewalks outside made it impossible to conduct business inside. The battle went on for decades. Every time the store owners won a legislative victory, the peddlers formed a temporary organization and lobbied sympathetic aldermen to pressure city officials to ignore its enforcement. An 1883 ordinance limited the hours and locations of vocal advertising, but it proved difficult to enforce because of efforts of the Peddlers and Canvassers Protective Association. In 1890, grocers began an intensive lobbying effort to force the city council to raise the annual peddler's license from $5 to $50, but they managed to get only a revised noise ordinance and a $10 license. An ad-hoc 1,700-member Peddlers Protective Association persuaded sympathetic aldermen to repeal the "anti-hollering" part of the ordinance.[29]

In time it became clear that the battle lines were not always clearly drawn. Over the years some merchants who owned buildings or operated indoor businesses had come to believe that peddlers were an inevitability and had begun renting sidewalk space to them, much to the chagrin of neighboring business people who were upset at the competition. Those arrangements brought up the question of whether rents should not go to the municipal government, the true owner of the sidewalks.[30] In 1902 and again in 1906, business owners cited all of these problems and launched unsuccessful lobbying campaigns to force the city council to outlaw the vendors from the Loop area.[31]

After the turn of the century, many Chicagoans viewed the army of peddlers as an anachronism, an unwanted reminder of a bygone age. Those who understood the germ theory of disease voiced new concerns about municipal

Youthful Peddler, from Sigmund Krausz, *The Street-Types of Chicago* (1891). Peddling allowed those with minimal capital to create a business supplying easily carried goods door-to-door.

Scissors Grinder, from Sigmund Krausz, *The Street-Types of Chicago* (1891). Before the widespread use of automobiles and throwaway goods, consumers appreciated service trades that came to the home rather than requiring customers to travel to a business.

Ragpickers, from Sigmund Krausz, *The Street-Types of Chicago* (1891). Nineteenth-century recycling included the collection of discarded cloth for paper making, upholstery stuffing, and other uses.

Maxwell Street, 1930s. In 1913 this street was designated the official peddlers' market, a function it retained until 1994. (Marcy-Newberry Records, University Library, University of Illinois at Chicago)

Adult education class, Medill High School, 1919. Night school became especially important for immigrants learning English in response to the intensely nativist atmosphere of the World War I era. (Chicago Historical Society, ICHi 01489)

cleanliness and complained that it was dangerous to push uncovered carts through streets coated with manure on wet days and wreathed in clouds of powdered horse droppings when it was dry. Health officials were also concerned with the problem of overnight storage of edible wares under unsanitary conditions.[32] Peddling seemed to thrive on one aspect of city life that made all other citizens angry: the inefficiency of public spaces. Their activity was part of an intensive use of those spaces. Slowdowns in street and sidewalk traffic made it easier to attract the attention of customers. Critics also blamed the street traders for littering and for blocking traffic on purpose.[33]

The automobile generated a new demand for more freely flowing traffic, for getting from here to there more efficiently. Because the new vehicles moved along more quickly than a pedestrian or horse-drawn buggy, they demanded the undivided attention of the driver; the peddler could be a dangerous distraction. The car, which also isolated its riders from direct contact with the street, sealed the fate of the curbstone traders, who were left in a cloud of exhaust. In the end, civic aesthetics proved even more important than angry merchants in convincing most Chicagoans and their lawmakers that peddlers were unpleasant vestiges of an unprogressive past. Civic boosters had already been battling for years to remove anything unsightly or inefficient from Chicago's streets when Daniel Burnham and his assistant Edward H. Bennett unveiled their dramatic Plan of Chicago in 1909; peddlers were notably absent from the depictions of streetlife in the future city.[34]

The street trades were clearly on the decline before World War I. By 1913, opponents had launched what appeared to be a successful campaign to banish the carts altogether. Only an economic slump saved the peddlers from legislated extinction. The following year, a special commission appointed by Mayor Carter Harrison II advised that the best way to reduce unemployment rolls was to encourage the poor to find something to sell and to allow them to take to the streets with carts.[35]

At the same time, the city council at the end of 1912 declared Maxwell Street the official outdoor retail emporium. Peddlers from all over the city were shunted to the old Jewish-Bohemian market area, while Randolph and South Water Streets were preserved for the wholesale produce trade.[36] For the next eighty-two years this outdoor emporium created a unique city space that concentrated capitalism in its purest form. It was the Marshall Field of the masses. Hundreds of vendors vied for a prime spot on the curb or in one of the booths that lined the sidewalks outside the small stores. Over the years, many penniless immigrants started there but ended their days living in the comfort of suburbia.[37]

In many ways Maxwell Street was really an anachronism from the beginning. Its dealers and customers were often dressed in the garb of their homelands. But most of all, the disorganized offerings of produce, clothing, and furnishings—cheap enough to be within the budgets of the poor—along with an odd assortment of used, recycled, and stolen merchandise, sat in a jumble of carts, stands, and wagons. At a time when most retailing had evolved into specialty shops or had been consolidated in logically arranged department stores, Maxwell Street resembled the hasty dockside selling customs of the 1840s. At the same time, the mud and manure of the physical setting and the lack of inspection of foodstuffs were a health reformer's nightmare, a throwback to an age before the world understood the germ theory of disease. Thus the poor who patronized Maxwell Street, whose housing lacked most modern amenities and whose poverty forced them to employ shoe leather as the means of transportation, were also consumers in a marketplace of the past.

Burning the Midnight Oil: Night Schools

On a cold February evening in 1910 most Chicagoans were at home with their families, having dinner or reading the newspapers. Others toiled at night jobs, or perhaps ventured out to a dance hall or to take in a show at a Randolph Street theater. But at the Dante School on Desplaines Street, at the Jones School on Harrison, or at any of thirty-one elementary and twenty-two high schools across the city, over twenty-one thousand night-school pupils were hard at work. They were a diverse lot that included older immigrants struggling to master English, elderly African Americans finally getting a chance to learn how to read and write, women taking home-economics courses to improve their households, and ambitious young men and women trying to absorb the "high tech" of their era: office machines, telephone "instruments," automobiles, and electrical equipment. Their ages ranged from fourteen to eighty-five, and they came from forty-four nations, but they were all part of one of Chicago's greatest achievements, mass education through night schools.[38]

The beginning of the night-school movement was not very promising. It took half a dozen years of editorial prodding before the city's first evening school opened in January 1856. Even then, it was only a semester-long experiment run by volunteers in the meeting hall of the municipal market building. Although two hundred students enrolled and seventy-five of them learned to read through these classes, there were no funds in the school budget to develop the program.[39] The idea lay idle another six years through economic depression and recovery before fears of what the press labeled a large mass of ignorant working youth prompted education officials to open Dearborn School every evening. Males could take a few rudimentary courses on Mondays, Wednesdays, and Fridays, while females attended on Tuesdays, Thursdays, and Saturdays. To avoid conflict with curfew laws, applicants had to be at least twelve years old, and, most important, they had to demonstrate that they were unable to attend day classes. Despite the obvious limit on the participants' weekend free time, enrollment grew from a hundred pupils in 1862 to more than four thousand in 1870.[40]

Chicago's night schools were not without their problems and detractors, however. A direct subsidy from the city council financed the program, but in 1863 the city comptroller, a Democrat, denounced the expenditure as illegal. The Republican *Tribune* answered that the opposing party was merely afraid that education would shift the masses of voters away from the Democratic fold.[41] Other critics complained that a combination of accessible night schools and weak child-labor laws would encourage parents to force their children into the daytime workforce.[42] The most critical issue may have been poor attendance rates. When asked to explain why daily absentee rates frequently soared over 75 percent of the enrollees, school officials answered that students were often detained at work, lured away by amusements, or driven to walk the streets in search of employment during depressions.[43]

The evening schools limped through the last three decades of the nineteenth century, victims of frequent budget cuts and official indifference. On four occasions fiscal problems caused yearlong cancellations of classes, and enrollment failed to keep pace with the mushrooming growth of the city.[44] In 1886 the *Tribune* labeled the program a "decided failure" and complained of abysmal attendance, lack of supervision, and low-quality teaching. The caliber of the instruction was an especially critical issue, because officials had created a separate and reputedly inferior night faculty made up of political hacks and inexperienced young law and medical students who needed the income. Teachers had neither skills nor long-term commitment to the classroom.[45]

Problems with the distribution of programs also plagued the system. In July 1889, Chicago annexed 125 square miles of surrounding suburban territory, much of it made up of middle-class subdivisions. The Board of Education responded to political pressure from the aldermen representing the new Chicagoans, many of whom had supported joining the city because of its superior educational resources. As a result, school officials made the mistake of diverting precious resources to the fringe even though classes offered in outlying schools were lightly patronized. While outlying classes were largely empty, inner-city night pupils found themselves crowded into packed classrooms in ancient buildings, some of which were still illuminated by old oil lamps instead of gas or electricity. As it was with their housing, the poor had to contend with technologically obsolete hand-me-downs.[46]

Late-nineteenth-century school administrators also failed to understand that thousands of night-school pupils viewed education as a tool of social mobility. Many enrollees quickly dropped out because the poorly planned curriculum merely repeated a limited set of basic courses each term. There was no grading of skills to reveal stages of achievement, and students were deprived of a sense of advancing toward a goal in the form of a diploma.[47] Thus, while New York, Boston, and other major cities were proud of the success of their public night schools, the Chicago program was losing ground.[48]

Other types of evening education filled the gap. Some were private and designed to turn a modest profit. In 1894, for instance, Mrs. Julia Cole, an Art Institute graduate who had worked on the Woman's Building at the world's fair, opened the Chicago Evening School of Design. Its classes, which began late enough to allow the women who attended to travel from outlying areas, covered all aspects of design. Meanwhile, Chicago's settlement houses began to establish their own evening classes in citizenship, English, and vocational skills. The YMCA was another major source of education for those outside the public school system. In 1893, it began expanding its programs to appeal not only to the newly arrived immigrants, but also to more advanced college prep and technical students. The "Y" even operated evening classes in the summertime.[49]

The reformation in public evening education came in 1901, when schools superintendent Edwin Cooley closed the program for a year to reorganize it completely. He revoked all of the old night-school teaching certificates and required applicants to hold the same qualifications as the day staff. Then he reduced the number of sites from thirty-four to twenty-one, concentrating efforts in the districts where the demand was greatest. He added new vocational and home-economics classes. Advanced registration and a small deposit of one dollar, refundable after a minimum 75 percent attendance rate, dramatically reduced absenteeism. Definite course plans that were clearly outlined in advance, along with the incentive of earning a diploma, also helped resuscitate the dying system.[50]

Cooley and his successors realized that the vast majority of students were recently arrived immigrants whose first goal was to learn enough English to function in society. Though most came to their first class with an interpreter, the majority were eventually able to read newspapers and job applications. "Ambition," noted one writer, "accounts for the full classes of the evening school." Chicago's 13,000 night students included "500 fruit-vendors, 175 hand-organ men, 40 street cleaners." A tenth of the student ranks were women and girls. "Of the thirteen hundred [female] pupils in different evening schools, few intend to use the knowledge gained for anything outside their homes," the same writer continued, "yet there is an addition to the earning power of the family." The knowledge of sewing, canning, and baking could allow the family to save money by reducing dependence on outsiders.[51]

The scene the students created became the recurring subject of newspaper and magazine features. Reporters delighted in quoting from the fractured English of their term papers and describing how the night pupils overfilled the small desks occupied in the daytime by children.[52] Although there was a romanticized notion of an ethnic melting pot in every room, Cooley's reorganized system now separated the groups according to nationality to reduce ethnic hostilities as well as the confusion of languages. Classes were established for every group requesting it.[53] Because each group could look upon a particular classroom as its own space on a given night, many newcomers lost their reluctance to participate. The variety of pupils from forty-four nationalities was endless—"around the world at Jones School," as one feature described it. Enrollment soared from 8,680 in 1900 to 13,027 in 1903, 17,295 in 1907, and 38,000 in 1914. In 1912, 75 percent of the students in night schools at the elementary level and 23 percent of nighttime high-school pupils were foreign born. Schools held at settlement houses enjoyed a similar increase in popularity, with twenty sites in operation by 1909.[54]

As the night schools grew, their purpose and clientele began to change. In 1913, a new mandatory school attendance law, which limited the number of hours youngsters could work, began to shift many of the youngest pupils back to daytime classes. Great improvements in the public and parochial school systems extended the normal course of education through high school. The First World War, which broke out in Europe in 1914, interrupted the flow of immigrants who had in the past gone directly into the night classes. After America entered the conflict in 1917, those already in America were pressured to become citizens as soon as possible. Americanization became the overriding purpose of the immigrant English classes. The stream of immigrants resumed after the war, but the 1924 immigration restriction act essentially cut off the flow of incoming foreign-born enrollees.[55]

The revived night-school system kept its attendance high despite the reduction of the foreign born by keeping pace with the demand for more advanced courses. Shifting opportunities in the employment market and the 1913 mandatory attendance law, as well as the greater prosperity of much of the working class, meant that children were less often forced to leave school in order to contribute to the family income. By World War I, the common goal of most students was to reach beyond the traditional eighth-grade termination to a high school diploma. The Board of Education had responded with a massive program to erect new buildings to accommodate the upper grades, and in 1921, after the delay of wartime, it also began to introduce a "complete standard evening high school" program.[56] By the end of the 1920s, a night pupil could finish secondary school at any one of six sites scattered across the city.[57]

During the Great Depression, the purpose of night schools began to shift once more. While many night-school students were still in search of a rudimentary education, more than half already held high school diplomas. Now, many of the enrollees were seeking "adult education," a popular catchword of the

1930s. Some interpreted this to mean a more enriching way to cope with the enforced idleness that came from underemployment. Others saw it as a way to upgrade their schooling and credentials in hopes of finding some type of employment. The system responded by providing such courses as radio script writing, clothing design, air conditioning, and other contemporary interests.[58] In 1938 three evening programs also opened on junior college campuses, thus expanding availability to the post-high-school level.[59]

And despite the end of immigration, the foreign born continued to seek training in English. The humorist Leo Rosten, who taught night classes to support himself while a graduate student at the University of Chicago, drew upon his experience in a Depression-era classroom to create his popular *The Education of H*Y*M*A*N K*A*P*L*A*N,* published in 1937.[60]

World War II proved to be the night school's finest hour. Chicago's rail hub location and its industrial diversity quickly pushed the region to a position of leadership in war production of all types. While Chicago had an abundance of idle workers, most did not have the skills needed for defense plant work. The city needed to train huge numbers of skilled workers for metal working, electronics, pharmaceuticals, and other fields. The night-school program responded by reinventing itself once more, this time with a new emphasis on technical subjects. Whole shops had to be re-equipped as quickly as possible. Most high schools began operating on a twenty-four-hour basis. The youngsters occupied the facilities during the normal school hours, but beginning in the late afternoon the first of two additional shifts of adults arrived for classes. The second of these was usually departing the buildings just as the first teenagers were arriving in the early morning.[61]

When the victory celebrations died down and the soldiers came home, the night schools were ready for another task. The Depression had forced many young people out of school and into the workforce; others were so ashamed of their tattered clothing that they had never attended. Then came World War II. Many young men dropped out of high school. Some had lied about their age to join the military; others had found the lure of a job and money irresistible after so many years of hardship. In either case, thousands realized that the opportunities for advanced training and higher education so widely promised by the GI Bill, as well as a job in the booming postwar economy, would require a high school diploma after all.[62] Many were concerned that they were too old to fit into the daytime school population or had jobs and families to support. Night classes in a wide variety of topics became important ways for them to catch up to opportunity.

The lights were still on for them.

Conclusion

The night-school pupil and the peddler were both examples of people who tried to be independent actors in a world where corporations, laws, and social class often constrained opportunity and individual action. Even among those whom we describe as oppressed, the response was not entirely passive.

Peddlers also demonstrated that one person's survival was another's problem. The peddler had to be noisy when much of the city wanted it quiet. The peddler had to get in the way to be seen when many Chicagoans were complaining about how hard it was to get from here to there. The peddler was intrusive when those with more comfortable means wanted to shield themselves from the unpleasantness of urban life. Like the homeless or the transient tenement-dweller, the peddler's impermanence clouded his identity and made him a pariah. The peddler was everything the city was, amidst people who wanted to make Chicago what it wasn't: an uncomplicated, serene, and orderly place.

Yet as part of the growing urban economy, peddlers became enmeshed in an important economic transformation: the evolving relationship between the point of sale and the point of delivery. During the nineteenth century the balance was clearly in favor of those who took the service to the customer. Milkmen, icemen, and coal haulers delivered their products to the door. The piano teacher came to the home of the pupil. And department store customers routinely had their purchases delivered, especially after telephone sales and charge accounts made shopping at home easy. At a time when the average family owned neither an auto nor a horse, those selling a service were usually expected to furnish the transportation.

The peddler's fate underscored the distinction between the public streets, curbstones, sidewalks that were their selling floor and the semipublic world of the store. The proprietor of the latter not only enjoyed such benefits of permanency as exclusive access to a space and being identified in the public mind with a particular location. The shopkeeper also benefited from the security of being able to exclude those deemed undesirable, at least within the limits of public accommodation laws. The peddler, on the other hand, had far smaller expenses and took advantage of the inherent rootlessness to place his or her cart in the best location to troll the fickle flow of customers; but the price was often insecurity and danger.

The school brought knowledge and skill to the neighborhood in a similarly decentralized fashion. In many ways, the experience of the night-school students reflected the expectations of their younger counterparts. First, both groups passed through periods when the system in which they participated made little effort to differentiate among its students, either in age or in interests. High schools and graded instructional levels did not appear until the mid-1850s, about the same time as the first evening experiment. For decades after that, the system was slow to acknowledge the demand for vocational-technical or office skills classes; only gradually, during the last decades of the nineteenth century, did the neighborhood school become part of a complex system. By the time that Edwin Cooley reorganized the evening classes, the public schools had already begun to emerge as a multifunctional centralized institution that served a number of differing constituencies and did so with increased effectiveness. There was still a classical program to prepare graduates for college, but there were also a separate vocational school, a wide collection of classes in foreign languages, a division that dealt with delinquents, and other programs to serve special needs. The school nurse became a first line of defense against childhood health problems, and by 1915 schools were neighborhood social centers and the source of breakfast and lunchtime nutrition for their neediest pupils. Thus, in the larger context, the evening scholars were customers in a department store of offerings that functioned much like the settlement house, amusement park, city newspaper, or any one of the other complex multifunctional institutions fostered by urban growth.

Postscript

The night-school idea that was launched more than a hundred years ago is still alive, but in different forms. In 1973, the cash-strapped Chicago Board of Education turned the evening high-school program over to the City Colleges of Chicago, which operated the Graduate Equivalency Degree (GED) and other instructional programs designed to allow those who left school early to obtain a diploma. Twenty years later, the junior colleges lost interest in the initiative, complaining that such rudimentary classes were a waste of its faculty's talents. In the spring of 1995, the City Colleges Board decided to drop the night-school program altogether, thus ending an institution of assimilation that dated back 140 years.[63] The principle survives, however. Settlement houses, which supplemented the school programs decades ago, still provide critical classes in English for newcomers. Junior colleges reach into their surrounding communities, while the radio receiver and television screen of public broadcasting long ago replaced the classroom lamp for many scholars. Various schools and colleges and exchange organizations have sold adults on the idea that continuing education can be more than vocational training; it can be fun.

The peddlers are still there, too. They work Chicago's streets—newspaper vendors on major corners, souvenir dealers outside sporting events, occasional produce sellers, a few scissors grinders, and others. In the summer the noise from the ice cream truck's loudspeakers can drown out a conversation a block away. Sometimes the junk scavenger can be heard poring through the trash in the alley in search of aluminum cans and other resalable items. Coffee trucks may be found at most suburban commuter stations and flower sellers still use many major intersections as their shops.

Conditions among peddlers have changed. One of the great transformations of the mid-twentieth century and beyond was the shift of responsibility for transportation from the seller to the buyer. When we pick up a quart of milk or a bag of ice at a grocery store on the way home from a doctor's appointment, we are demonstrating that fact. Cheap refrigerators and hand-me-down automobiles have also undercut the demand for the peddler's services by giving the mobility to shop to all but the most desperately poor.

The ranks of the street vendors have diminished and they are more likely to be African American or Hispanic, rather than Jewish, Italian, or Greek. And the "Fuller Brush Man" and "Avon Lady"—and even the electronic version, the telephone solicitor—have softened the distinction between the peddler and the sales representative.[64]

Over the years, welfare programs have largely displaced the notion of the streets as the true "safety net" of society. No event symbolized the decline of peddling as much as the closing and demolition of the Maxwell Street Market in late 1995. The remaining traders were shunted to a new and "improved" area a few blocks away.[65] But these manifestations of progress can also be illusory. All signs indicate that for hundreds of Chicagoans the streets still represent an alternative to disappearing factory work, dead-end service jobs, or the welfare rolls.

Just ask Herb Perry.

PART SIX

Avoiding Disaster

11 Time, Risk, and Family Finances

ON the afternoon of August 6, 1906, the terrible news swept through the tenements of the Northwest Side. Women screamed in disbelief, left their children with neighbors, and ran as fast as they could down Milwaukee Avenue, their babushkas bobbing and their long dresses flowing behind them. Tears streamed down their faces. Their husbands were at work, and it was left up to the wives, mothers, and sisters to salvage the family assets. They joined the throng, already twenty-deep by midafternoon, that surrounded the wedge-shaped building, only to be pushed back by a cordon of police officers. The Milwaukee Avenue State Bank had failed, and the only people permitted inside were those renting safety deposit boxes. Some of the latter crammed everything they could in pockets and skirts—coins, dollar bills, family relics, and anything else deemed precious—and headed for the door as if escaping. Others looked confidently into their boxes and replaced them before leaving. Those with bank deposits, however, could only stand in the street. They were among the twenty-two thousand working-class Poles and Scandinavians who had entrusted their money to a place they had regarded as secure, almost sacred.[1]

The shock continued. That evening a *Tribune* reporter found two young women standing outside the bank's doors in the rain. Nellie Novak, a widow, had worked in a tobacco factory until tuberculosis put her in Presbyterian Hospital; when she came out several weeks later, all she had left in the world was $350 in the bank. After her stepfather heard about its failure, he threw her worldly goods on the curb. Margaret Johnson had started the day with $850. "I felt secure against the cold and hunger with this, but now its gone," she moaned, as she explained that her landlady had evicted her from her boardinghouse. Both women were now homeless and broke. Many of those who joined the three-block-long line that formed in the morning were equally desperate.

Its neighbors had long called the place the "Stensland Bank," after its founder, Paul O. Stensland. He was a Norwegian immigrant who had arrived just before the Great Fire of 1871, but his now-perfect English concealed his origins. Everyone seemed to know his story. Twenty-one years earlier he had been a small struggling grocer, but a fire gutted his store. He had then entered the real estate business and made a fortune selling lots and small houses to land-hungry immigrants who were flocking to the northwest edge of town. As his personal wealth grew—it included $600,000 in real estate alone by 1906—he had involved himself in many community activities. He took on a founding role in Mount Olive Cemetery, worked with several charitable societies, and assumed leadership in financing both the statue of Leif Eriksson in Humboldt Park and the transatlantic voyage of a reproduction Viking ship to the 1893 World's Columbian Exposition. His friend Mayor Carter Harrison II had appointed him to the Chicago Board of Education. He had also quietly begun buying shares in a small bank, until he became the dominant investor and took over its management himself. The bank thrived, in part because his reputation had long helped ease the fears of non-Scandinavian depositors.[2]

No one suspected what Stensland and his cashier, Henry W. Hering, had been doing until the bank's sudden insolvency revealed that something in excess of a million dollars—a fourth of the bank's assets—was missing. Bank examiners later found that for at least thirteen years Stensland had used depositors' money to grant bogus loans and mortgages to himself and his real estate company, that bonds given as collateral had been changed to his personal accounts, and that customer accounts and the bank's working cash fund had been systematically looted of money. Stensland had used some of the money to carry on a lavish lifestyle for a mistress and himself; Hering had been a regular at the racetracks. As the discovery of their misdeeds loomed, both fled town. Hering was arrested after only three days, but Stensland remained a fugitive for nearly a month. "King Paul," as the newspapers called him, was finally caught in Tangier with twelve thousand dollars in cash. The sultan agreed to his extradition. Upon arriving back in Chicago on September 26, he pleaded guilty, as did Hering a few weeks later. Both received long sentences at the state prison in Joliet.

The collapse of the Milwaukee Avenue State Bank left a trail of tragedy. Ultimately, most of its trustees were implicated in the schemes, and most lost all of their assets to financial liabilities and fines. Then there were the deaths. Within a few hours of the closing one depositor had dropped dead of a heart attack, while another had taken his life when he learned that the funds of a charitable organization that had been entrusted to him were gone as well. A few days later Frank Kowalski, a teller who was not immediately implicated in the wrongdoing, shot himself after suffering the taunts of his neighbors. Over the next few weeks there were other reports of suicides, heart attacks, and people driven to insanity by the collapse.

Depositors of the Milwaukee Avenue collapse were lucky; they got back over forty cents of each dollar. Their experience, however, was by no means unique. In an age of "wildcatting," it was easy to establish a private bank. Select a name that evoked feelings of reliability, rent a storefront space, print the necessary forms, buy a second-hand safe, take out a state charter, and you were in business. As long as more money kept flowing in as deposits and loan payments than flowed out as withdrawals, interest, and loans, it was easy to show a profit. Many of the new banks were legitimate and provided a neighborhood or an ethnic group with an enormous sense of pride. The North Western Trust and Savings Bank was Polish. Such family names as Wiersema (Dutch), Skala, Papanek (Bohemian), Schiff, and Greenebaum (Jewish) appeared at the top of other banks' letterheads. Asset requirements were negligible, and audits were cursory. But trouble could come in several forms that usually related to what was done with deposits. Poorly chosen loans could become nightmares of default, while rumors could touch off panics, or "runs," when depositors demanded more in withdrawals than there was in the cash reserves. Other banks were simply not well managed. It was not unusual to have two or three close in a year; eight of them shut down in a single day, June 5, 1893. It would take decades of failures before legislators finally forged a combination of federal and state laws that established effective regulation.[3]

In the meantime, the nature of the city and its neighborhoods contributed to the problem. Although Chicago was becoming a giant among cities, wildcat banking often thrived because of the insularity of its ethnic enclaves. Working-class immigrants, who frequently lacked sophistication and knowledge of the world beyond the few city blocks that surrounded them, thought in terms of smallness: the neighborhood grocer, the nearby school, a factory job a walking commute away, and the police precinct house down the street. As part of their ability to cope, they sought refuge and help in their neighborhood churches, which were often islands of language, custom, and ethnicity in a vast urban sea. The "bigtime" was what took place along major streets like Milwaukee Avenue, while the Loop was a seldom-visited dream. In this world, which one writer called "Dinner Pail Avenue," the small-scale private banker could use his community reputation and powers of personal persuasion to carve out a business that thrived on parochialism.[4]

The existence of wildcat banks, as well as more substantial institutions, also revealed much about what the depositors thought of life. Thrift reflected a strong sense of confidence in the future. Like the great industrialists who sought production quotas or the reformers who pursued a vision of political honesty and social justice, those who carried lunch pails and scrubbed kitchen floors also pursued clear goals and found places to set aside cash to ensure reaching them. Steamship agents kept accounts that accumulated toward the purchase of tickets to bring loved ones to America. Building and loan societies served the similar function toward the goal of a house. Settlement houses also introduced "penny savings" programs to encourage payday thrift. A citywide Penny Savings Society, established in June 1897, collected $208,533 through more than two hundred stations during its first six years. In 1903 it began "home collection" for those who were unable to get out or, in the words of a charities newsletter, were among "the naturally thriftless and those who lack initiative or are ignorant of, or indifferent to the opportunities open to them."[5] For many, the ultimate purpose of a savings account was a more secure old age and eventually a proper wake and a burial in a "nice" casket with silver handles rather than in a pauper's grave, even when the price was extravagant.

The insecurity of the institutions in which the poor entrusted their money motivated the federal government to develop a substitute. Beginning in the early 1890s Victor F. Lawson, the editor of the *Chicago Daily News,* began a campaign for the creation of a postal savings bank similar to that established in England. The principle was simple. Account holders could go to any post office to purchase stamps for as little as two cents apiece, and when a sufficient number accumulated, they could be traded in for a certificate of deposit. Although Lawson lobbied in every Congress for the plan, it was the failure of the Milwaukee Avenue State Bank that brought the avid support of ethnic organizations, especially the Turner athletic societies. The movement soon became national, and when President William Howard Taft signed the bill into law, he sent the pen to Lawson.[6] The Chicago branch opened at the main post office on August 1, 1911, and its hours were soon extended far into the evening to accommodate "the foreigners and others whose hours of employment keep them busy all day." Within four months of the opening, local deposits had reached $577,842 out of $15 million nationally.[7]

Those who had the money did indeed save what they could, but it was not always enough. At the center of the issue was the interplay of time and risk. The traditional wisdom had long defined thrift as the postponement of the instant gratification of spending in order to set aside money for the future. Not only would purchases ultimately be wiser and cheaper, but a bank account would provide protection against the certainty of minimal or nonexistent pensions, as well as the possibility of emergencies. But time was the constant enemy of those with little money or few investments. Providing the essentials of life on a minimal income left them with a painfully slow savings rate. Intermittent employment, which was often terminated without warning, was another obstacle to thrift.[8]

This lesson was not lost on the twenty-two thousand depositors of the Milwaukee Avenue State Bank, many of whom realized that they, like Nellie Novak and Margaret Johnson, could easily be left just a paycheck or two away from poverty. But as their sad story demonstrates, the problem of penury was often rooted in not just the source and amount of one's assets, but how they were handled and by whom. In the end, it was a question of trust that was often tragically misplaced.

The Perils of Payday

The events were repeated all too often in turn-of-the-century Chicago. J.W.A. (we do not know his real name) had worked as a typesetter in a suburban printing office. When he quit, he went to his employer to collect his wages, but he was told to come again another day. The same thing happened a few days later. Since J.W.A. lived in the city with his aged mother, his several failures to secure payment were frustrating and expensive. In desperation, he went to a charity known as the Bureau of Justice, which initiated a successful lawsuit on his behalf. Finally, as the former employer's equipment was about to be hauled away to satisfy J.W.A.'s judgment, the company paid its debt to him.[9]

Payday was normally a cause of minor celebration and a source of good feeling that came with money in one's pocket, but it also could be the beginning of a nightmare. Three related problems grew out of the rituals of payday. One was the manner, time, and method of payment. The second involved claims against employers for back wages. The third was the trap of consumer debt that led to garnishment and, ultimately, to the loan shark who preyed on those who were most vulnerable.

During much of the nineteenth century, the pay process was a relatively simple cash transaction. Because there were very few banks outside of the central business area, employees simply took home pay envelopes. But during the severe depression that began in 1873 and brought many firms to bankruptcy, many employees discovered that their wage claims could legally be ignored. In 1878, a force of workers brandishing clubs refused to allow the new owners of a Goose Island brickyard to take possession until the wages due them were paid. The police had to be called to disperse them.[10] Nine years later, the Illinois General Assembly responded to public pressure and gave wages legal preference over other claims against a bankrupt business.[11]

Meanwhile, workers like J.W.A. encountered occasional employers who knew that their employees had little recourse in wage-collection cases. The small size of most claims, the cost and trouble of hiring a lawyer, and the likelihood of losing the case in a biased justice-of-the peace court all promoted employer dishonesty.[12] Workers who wanted to avoid the stigma of seeking charity could also call upon several commercial wage-collection agencies that performed the same service for a fee.[13] Beginning in the 1880s, a series of charities—the Protective Agency for Women and Children (1887), the Bureau of Justice (1888), and the labor-union-supported Wage Workers' Free Collection Bureau (1891)—settled claims by providing attorneys and threatening to expose seemingly respectable business owners. The Protective Agency, which called the technique "whitemailing," was especially sensitive to the plight of women in the courts. Opposition lawyers in wage-claim cases commonly prejudiced juries and judges by implying that the female plaintiffs were immoral. "After due consideration," noted one newspaper writer, "it was decided that there was no reason why, in the matter of legal rights, the character of a woman should be considered when a man's is not." In its first four years the Protective Agency for Women and Children handled 3,300 cases, but it collected only $8,582.50 for its clients.[14]

Through these years Chicagoans debated the related questions of how, where, and with what frequency workers should be paid. In most places, employees received envelopes of cash at the end of the work week, usually Friday night or Saturday.[15] But the growth of the city and the complexities of businesses made the once-simple task more complicated. When city employees who labored in the neighborhoods complained about having to travel downtown each week to collect wages, the public works department introduced an innovation: a mobile pay wagon, the forerunner of today's armored truck, which dispersed envelopes of cash at twenty scattered locations.[16] The introduction of paychecks during the last fifteen years of the century solved the employers' problem of moving and holding large amount of currency. In 1898, for instance, the Chicago and North Western Railway was greatly relieved when it could replace the pay car that had always been vulnerable to robbery as it was hauled from one location to another.[17]

The change to checks, however, led to a new problem: workers now had to find places that would cash them. Companies that provided that service found themselves once again holding large amounts of cash. But the lack of banks in many neighborhoods (and the occasional desire of workers to conceal the actual size of their income from their spouses) meant that the check and its owner often ended up in saloons, which were only too happy to accommodate customers. Large barrooms, which were often financed by brewing companies, became regular stops on armored-express routes and the special targets of hold-up artists. Temperance workers were appalled at how easily an obligatory glass of beer to thank the barkeep could result in an evening of carousing and a customer's going home with empty pockets. Labor unions even complained that, instead of paying workers individually, some employers dropped off lump sums of cash with the saloonkeepers to be distributed in exchange for a "service fee" in drinks.[18] By the 1890s, some companies that opened cashiers windows to cash paychecks also forbade employees from frequenting bars.

There was also the question of how often the worker should be paid. Time was once again a critical factor. Employers claimed that they needed at least a few days to process time cards, but some workers argued that bookkeeping need not take weeks and that less-frequent and delayed paydays provided what amounted to interest-free loans to employers. In 1891 the Illinois General Assembly stepped into the issue with legislation making weekly payment the standard in most industries. By contrast, others argued that biweekly or monthly pay periods had the positive effect of promoting savings by keeping the money out of the hands of spendthrifts as long as possible.[19]

While the debate about collecting wages raged, the last decades of the century also saw a distressing increase in problems that linked the spending habits of workers and their perilous paydays. These sad stories usually began with installment purchases. The forces of necessity and whim were important causes of the problem, but there was also the question of the buyer's attitude toward time and his or her future. Optimism about the amount of money they would make motivated the poor to go into debt in order to put some time between immediate use and eventual payment. Consumer credit had become very popular by the mid-1870s, many decades before modern "plastic."[20] For a housewife or a single woman, for instance, the purchase of a sewing machine could not only save money on future clothing expenditures, but also provide a source of income through sewing in a factory or at home. Few had the funds for such a large cash purchase.[21] It other cases, the need was furniture or pots and pans or a stove or a baby carriage. Even the more expensive items of personal clothing, such as a suit or a heavy winter overcoat, were also available for a few dimes a week. Sometimes it was something as seemingly frivolous as a watch or a cheap ring, but it could also be food at a neighborhood grocer or meat market or even the false teeth necessary to eat it.[22]

For the middle class, the purchase of a piano was the sign of respectability and refinement, its arrival a public event in the neighborhood. In 1874, mothers and fathers balanced the outlay of twenty to thirty dollars per month for a Kimball piano against the savings in entertainment costs, as well as the enhancement of their sons' and daughters' popularity if they learned how to hammer out the latest tune.[23]

It was easy to fall into debt. All that was needed was proof of a job and perhaps a listing in a city directory. The stores that sold "on time" advertised widely and made expensive purchases more tempting. They were conveniently positioned at major transportation hubs, such as Lincoln-Belmont-Ashland or Sixty-third and Halsted. Passengers waiting at these corners for streetcars might be lured by the display windows of merchandise and signs promising low payments, while others took note of the convenience of being able to make the payments on the way home, before the money could be spent on less-necessary temptations.[24]

In any case, it was easy to buy too much, or to assume that one's income would be steady, or to forget about the risk of losing one's job before the payments were completed. At that point, both time and public exposure became the enemies. The first sign of trouble was the appearance of the bill collector. Most collection agencies carried out the honest occupation of pursuing deadbeats. Americans then lacked the type of paper identities on file that we have today. A *Lakeside Directory* listing could refer to someone else, and a letter from an employer could be faked. Before the telephone grew popular in the late 1880s, credit verification was difficult. The anonymity of the city and the ease of circulation in and out of town made it easy for criminals to purchase merchandise and then disappear. Many business operators became more reluctant to grant credit after 1874 when the Illinois General Assembly established a rule that those filing to collect through the courts had to wait until the following term to pursue the suit. In response, one Chicagoan began publishing a "deadbeats list" of names gathered from boardinghouses and retailers.[25] By the 1880s, debt-collection agencies found themselves in trouble for violating postal laws protecting the privacy of addressees. One bill collector was arrested for sending a card marked "Call at once at our office and pay your grocery bill." The courts decided that because neighbors often handled each other's mail, they were given an opportunity to read the message side of a card and spread gossip about the addressee. Another collection agent got around that limitation by parking his wagon in front of the residence of a debtor. The tall gold letters on the side read "BAD DEBTS ARE COLLECTED—WE VISIT DEADBEATS ONLY."[26]

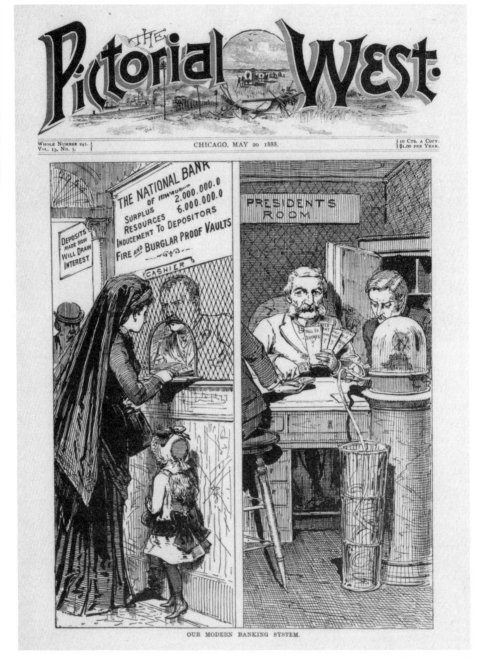

"Our Modern Banking System," *Pictorial West,* May 20, 1888. Insecurity and fraud riddled the banking system, according to popular image. Widows risked and suffered; bank presidents profited. (Chicago Historical Society, ICHi 27259)

Home clothing manufacture, ca. 1915. The purchase of a sewing machine allowed women to support their families, but the transaction was one of the leading causes of consumer debt problems among the poor. (Chicago Historical Society, ICHi 03911)

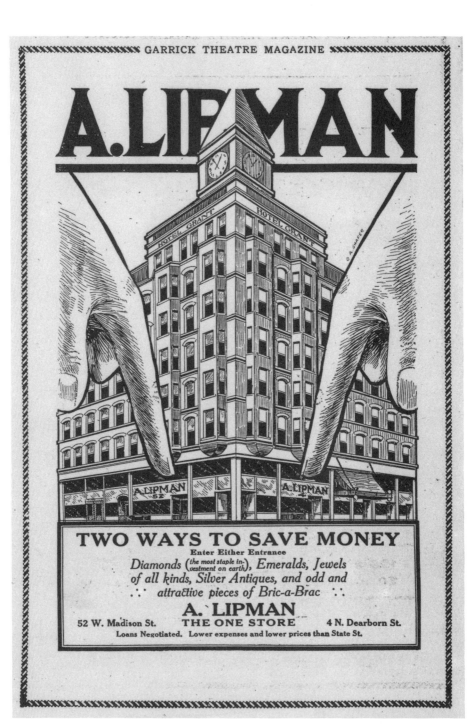

Diamond broker advertisement, Garrick Theatre Program, 1911. Pawn brokers catering to a better clientele omitted the common name for their trade.

Payroll office, Kirk's Soap Company, 1904. Until the introduction of checking accounts, companies paid the workers weekly in cash, a factor that reformers complained led to the temptation to spend rather than save. (Chicago Historical Society, ICHi 00483)

The next step toward financial oblivion was garnishment, the legal action that gave the creditor prior claim to what was in the pay envelope. Before 1872, anyone who was owed money could force an employer to hand over all of an employee's wages until a judgment was satisfied. But a state law passed in that year gave some relief by sheltering twenty-five dollars per month from garnishment. Three years later, companies that owed workers back wages were forbidden from garnishing, and in 1879 the amount protected was raised to fifty dollars.[27] But even with this protection from legitimate garnishment claims, workers were still liable to fall prey to fraud. In 1884 and again a decade later, the press described how con artists conspired with unscrupulous suburban justices of the peace to file fake claims against Chicagoans, who would then have to travel many miles to defend themselves. Those who did not, lost their money.[28] During the depression of the 1890s, the power shifted against the debtors and the labor unions that lobbied on their behalf. A new garnishment law, which was passed in 1897 in response to pressure from grocers and other creditors, reduced the exemption to only eight dollars a week, leaving many families once more vulnerable. It took several years before the higher level of exemption was regained.[29]

What could debtors do? The legal aid societies were able to extricate some clients from installment contracts that were grossly exploitive. But in moments of quiet desperation, thousands sought short-term loans "to make ends meet." On occasion, ethnic organizations came to the rescue; the Woman's Loan Committee of the Associated Jewish Charities, for instance, was making over four hundred loans a year by 1908, most of them to peddlers and factory workers.[30] But most cash-strapped Chicagoans found that they had few legal ways to borrow money. Illinois usury laws allowed only a small legitimate margin of profit on unsecured loans, and many borrowers owned no real estate on which they could seek help from a bank. Some hauled prized possessions to pawnshops (a process described later in this book), but many turned to loan sharks in the form of "salary loan companies." Concentrated in the Loop and near major factories, these firms legally "purchased" a portion of the customer's next paycheck in exchange for ready cash. This loophole allowed the sharks to escape prosecution for usury while charging whatever interest rates the market would bear. Most important, their victims were afraid to complain to their bosses out of fear that they would lose their jobs or face some sort of violence at the hands of the shark.[31]

In 1900 reform groups and the press launched a crusade against loan sharking, and two years later Judge Murray F. Tuley decreed that wage assignment as security for a loan was also illegal. But both practices continued. The press disclosed that one lender, the Chicago Credit Company, not only operated inside City Hall but used government clerks to drum up business among municipal employees, as well as to deduct payments from their salaries. Its influence was particularly strong within the police force, where fifteen hundred officers were reputedly on its books and Chief Joseph Kipley gave his approval. Loan sharks reportedly sold copies of police examinations and used their influence to rescue the jobs of officers suspended from the force. The problem was so widespread among city employees that the city electrician switched the pay schedule of his employees from monthly to biweekly in an effort to help them make it between paychecks without resorting to a loan broker. These revelations led to some relief in the courts, where Judge Edward F. Dunne nullified the assignment of wages before they were earned because it was a form of "wage slavery," but Dunne was only one judge.[32]

Despite the court cases and the publicity, the loan sharks seemed invincible. An investigation in 1908 found that there were 125 such offices in the city, with 70,000 regular customers and a combined capital of $3.5 million. Monthly interest ranged from $12 to $20.[33] By 1910, the *Tribune* had crowned Frank Jay Mackey "King of the Usurers." Arriving in Chicago from Wisconsin in 1882, he found that the reputation of his business prevented his breaking into local high society, so he and his wife let subordinates handle the everyday affairs and moved first to New York and then across the Atlantic. Ranking among the wealthiest Americans living in England, Mackey ran operations that took in $400,000 a year from Chicago, enough for the lavish entertaining needed to become good friends of Edward VII and Queen Alexandra.[34] Meanwhile, his customers dug themselves deeper into debt. In 1912, the story surfaced of a Milwaukee Road locomotive engineer who sued for a restraining order against two loan companies. He had borrowed $800, paid back $3,900, but was still in debt for the next ten years.[35]

Reformers attacked on two fronts. The efforts to kill the loan shark through legislation grew out of recommendations made in 1910 by a committee of the

City Club of Chicago. It proposed laws establishing a maximum interest rate for salary loans, regulating wage assignments, and licensing operators in the field. By 1917, wartime inflation had increased the plight of the poor. The Legal Aid Society, formed in 1905 by the merger of the Protective Agency for Women and Children and the Bureau of Justice, undertook lobbying efforts in Springfield and succeeded in shaming the General Assembly into action. It passed a law requiring loan offices to register and limit interest charged on loans of $300 or less to 3.5 percent a month.[36]

The second tactic was the creation of functional substitutes that were designed to drive the miscreants from the scene by providing an honest service at a cheaper cost. This approach was inspired by the work of the Associated Jewish Charities, which had begun loaning money to peddlers. Noticing that the ranks of street traders always seemed to expand when seasonal employment disappeared, it began issuing loans of up to $250 to carry families through the "slack season" layoffs. It also provided aid to merchants to meet their financial obligations when customers who were on strike could not pay their bills.[37] In 1913 the Illinois General Assembly passed a law facilitating the organization of similar charities. The next year the Industrial Club of Chicago created the First State Industrial Wage Loan Society. Sixty bankers and heads of department stores, railroads, and factories subscribed $50,000 to a fund to create what became known as the Poor Man's Bank. By 1917 it was making nearly three hundred loans a month, as well as helping debtors settle disputes with salary loan sharks.[38] The most important achievement was the 1925 law that created credit unions, which allowed those working in the same factory or living within a community to deposit money and borrow at rates that were not to exceed 1 percent per month.[39]

The debates over payday and its perils continued into this century, long after the once-cherished pianos and parlor suites had worn out and the last paywagons had lumbered into history. Check cashing in saloons died temporarily during Prohibition, while the prosperous 1920s spawned a growing number of neighborhood and suburban banks that absorbed much of the payroll business. But the Great Depression closed so many of these institutions that a new kind of payday entrepreneur was born. In the summer of 1932, the first three currency exchanges opened in the city. Within a decade, there were 475, cashing $5 million in paychecks each week. The exchanges, which rapidly consolidated into chains, had credit arrangements with banks to cover payday transactions.[40] The Illinois ban on branch banking allowed currency exchanges to flourish even after the return of prosperity, and in many poor neighborhoods they stayed on when many other financial institutions left for suburbia.

"The Graveyard of Hopes": The Pawnshop

Consider the pawnshop. Like the transient tenement poor and the street peddlers who were often its customers, its financial assets distinctly lacked fixedness. To its enemies, it was a flagrant exploiter of the impoverished, a usurious vulture that preyed on the most vulnerable. But to its legions of defenders, it was the poor man's last hope, a necessary service for those ignored by the banking system. Regardless of which image seems more credible, it is hard to deny that the shop with the three golden balls over the door was—and still is—an important and colorful part of Chicago's story.

Pawning, the centuries-old practice of extending a loan of money on the security of valuables,[41] first appeared in Chicago during the early 1850s, a decade of spectacular population growth. In 1853, an English-born carriage builder named James Launder took out the first license, and by mid-decade four competitors had entered the field. The trade was concentrated in "the Patch," the tough, predominantly Irish district of cheap saloons, brothels, and slums southwest of downtown. The neighborhood's unsavory reputation no doubt contributed to the police department's suspicion that pawnbrokers were little more than legitimate fences for burglars and other thieves.[42] The business became known by the company it kept, and in 1856 the aldermen altered the city code to require a five-hundred-dollar bond from each broker. Every transaction was to be recorded in a book always kept accessible to the police.[43]

The pawnshop found its reputation tarnished by a small percentage of its ranks. Because it dealt in the quick purchase and sale of valuables as well as junk and was frequently open late, "when honest men and women should be in their homes," the pawnshop remained under the suspicion that it fenced stolen goods.[44] The problem of reputation began just after the Civil War, when a great increase in the number of gangs of street children who lived off the proceeds of thievery resulted in the passage of an 1866 city ordinance prohibiting pawn transactions with minors.[45] The code was later tightened, requiring that a detailed report of all goods taken in pawn be filed each morning with the police.[46] By 1880 a special pawnshop division of the city detective bureau began comparing these reports with lists of stolen merchandise.[47] The Tribune, which dismissed the pawnshop as a "school for thieves," claimed that pawners falsified the descriptions of articles in their daily lists submitted to the police. It also complained that the growing ranks of loan brokers were largely supported by wholesale theft from the thousands of freight cars that passed through the nation's rail hub each week.[48] The paper also went on to describe what it called collusion on the part of corrupt judges who refused to issue search warrants and allied politicians who steered police away from proper inspection.[49]

There is little evidence that more than a few pawnshops were ever involved in crime. The vast majority simply provided a convenient way for thousands of Chicagoans to make ends meet each month and a desirable alternative to the loan shark. Pawnshops were remarkably versatile institutions, adaptable to use by many social classes. At the top of the status ladder were the "diamond brokers," "loan brokers," or "private bankers" who catered to a fairly wealthy clientele. Customers were assured privacy, so that nosy reporters would not discover that a leading family had fallen temporarily on hard times. In one instance worthy of an O. Henry story, a husband and wife, not knowing that they were in adjoining booths, pawned expensive gifts they had exchanged with each other only hours earlier. According to newspaper reports, gambling debts, narcotics, payments to psychics, and other secret cash needs brought the rich to the pawner's desk. And those who were a little unsure about their economic future were advised to resist the temptation to engrave initials and inscriptions on jewelry and other items of precious metal because it might reduce their resale value.[50]

At a somewhat lower level were the shops that serviced the lower middle class. Many of the customers—often young, single, and poorly paid—lived in the rooming houses that lined Clark and other streets north of the river.[51] The effort to keep up the appearance of respectability and prosperity on a small salary often left them with the choice of skipping meals, seeking a loan shark, or visiting a pawnbroker with Grandma's wedding ring. "Going to see my uncle" became a popular euphemism, a form of secret slang that concealed the true purpose of the trip from the uninitiated.[52] In one case, a young man pawned his best suit every Monday morning, only to claim it again each Saturday evening for use on Sunday. This went on for years, until the suit finally wore out.[53]

Many of the customers of this level of shop were only passing through the city. Some travelers who intended to change trains found themselves short of funds for the continuing ticket. The proximity of pawnshops to the railway stations was no accident.[54] Actors and actresses were another mobile group whose unpredictable employment pattern frequently prompted the need for quick cash. It was not unusual for a thespian to pawn something during one stage tour and claim it months later while passing through as part of another production.[55]

Some of these shops also catered to gamblers, and some pawnbrokers stretched advertising banners on gaming room walls. Where else could a player cover a temporary shortage due to bad luck and then go back to claim the valuables after a hot hand? The gamblers' expensive watches, diamond stickpins, and gold belt buckles were more than gaudy ornaments of a "fast" lifestyle. They also functioned as a practical investment reserve that could be turned into ready cash in minutes; the more expensive the jewelry, the larger the "portable account." In the districts where gaming was common, a single watch might pass across the broker's desk several times in a day, along with countless hard-luck stories of fixed horse races and loaded dice.[56]

The very poor made up the saddest class of customers. In 1864 the *Tribune* labeled the shop of the impoverished "a condensed chronicle of the miseries of a city . . . the graveyard of hopes, of aspirations, of domestic happiness," a characterization that passing years failed to change.[57] Many decades later, the same description applied. A "blushing damsel, for the moment penniless," someone in need of a drink, and immigrant families down to their last coins— all frequented the pawners that were at first concentrated in the rundown skidrow and vice districts on the fringes of downtown. By 1910 shops were also found in the emerging African-American neighborhoods of the Near South Side. This level of pawnshop was identifiable by the crude sign out front and the cheap merchandise crossing the counters. Much of it was old clothing and shoes and other items of negligible value that gave the pawner a symbiotic relationship with the junkshop: the customer brought the goods to the three golden balls, but the junk dealer had to take to the streets to buy the same type of castoff merchandise.[58]

There was a cyclical nature to the pawnshop trade. Each Christmas season saw a sad procession of customers desperately trying to scrape together a small bit of cash for children's gifts, while the return of spring brought an influx of the previous winter's heavy garments. The larger cycles of periodic downturns in the economy filled the pawnshop shelves with mechanics' tools and other items refused by "chattel-mortgage" companies that made loans on furniture and other household goods. Always evident were many pathetically personal items, such as children's toys "hocked" for a penny or two by their tiny owners, as well as wooden legs and artificial eyes. Napoleonic medals and Russian silver belt buckles attracted collectors, some of whom specialized in European curios pawned by immigrants. No questions were ever asked by purchasers or borrowers, and pawnshops on this level frequently dealt with cheap handguns.[59]

By century's end, pawning had become a large business, with sixty-seven licensed shops and perhaps two hundred others pursuing the trade in the guise of second-hand stores. One estimate set the number of watches hocked each day in Chicago at 800 and the monthly total of all items at nearly 125,000.[60] While even the most avid critics agreed that something like the pawnshop was necessary for the survival of the poor, what troubled them most was the interest charged on the loans. In 1883 the legal limit of 3 percent per month was established, but the actual rate often reached 10 percent. Pawners found it easy to evade the law by "purchasing" an item with a promise to "sell" it back at the same price, plus interest. When caught, many pawnbrokers simply pleaded ignorance of the law. There were reports in the 1880s that brokers tried to "freeze out" their brethren who charged more than 120 percent a year, but the dispersed nature of the trade and the desire for anonymity among many of its customers made it virtually impossible for the police to monitor all of the items transferred in thousands of transactions.[61]

The severe depression of the mid-1890s, which put many of the middle-class as well as the poor at the mercy of the unscrupulous among the pawners, catalyzed the strongest antipawning sentiment. The police department created a separate pawnshop bureau and intensified inspections, while the definition of the trade was widened to include "private bankers" and others catering to wealthier clients.[62] Most important, reformers also decided to establish a less predatory substitute. During the 1890s the Civic Federation publicized the fact that there were numerous philanthropic pawn operations around the world, including the *monts-de-piété* in France and Belgium, the Royal Pawn Office in Berlin, and the *Assistanthuset* of Copenhagen. In the United States, charitable pawnshop substitutes had already been established in Boston in 1859 and again in 1888, as well as in New York City, Buffalo, Baltimore, Providence, and Worcester, Massachusetts.[63]

The Chicago equivalent took the form of a private corporation, the First State Pawners Society, founded by 1899 by John V. Farwell, a philanthropist and dry-goods merchant, and other members of the Merchants Club. It was designed to turn a small profit on a $50,000 investment. Under Farwell's close supervision, it made 286,276 loans for $5,781,962.25—an average of just under $15 per transaction—during its first decade and was able to reduce its interest from 1.5 percent to just 1 percent a month. But even then, it failed to drive out its competition, and in 1949 it converted from a philanthropic to a private business.[64]

The pawnshop business remained basically unchanged over the decades. In 1918 the Municipal Reference Library found that over half of the sixty-two shops had been in business for at least a decade, fourteen of them for twenty-five years or more. Moreover, the police department credited the pawners with helping authorities apprehend 208 criminals in one year.[65] Pawners survived the prosperous 1920s, but found themselves flooded with merchandise during the Great Depression. Few people redeemed their tickets during those desperate years, limiting the amount of money the pawners had available to loan. During World War II they did a heavy business for several reasons. Many pessimistic servicemen who were about to be shipped out to the front turned all their belongings into cash, which they distributed to friends and relatives. At the same time, many defense workers heeded the rumors and warnings about curtailed wartime production of domestic goods and bought everything they could afford during the first few weeks of the conflict. When the predicted shortages of everything from wristwatches to radios appeared, they converted these items into ready cash at pawnshops, which gained sudden popularity.[66]

Thus, a century after the first pawnshops appeared, they were providing the essential service to those in need. Pawning allowed customers to convert material assets of many different types into cash without the bother of selling items themselves. But most important of all, because it handed over instant cash, the pawnshop provided the illusion, at least, of being a service operating on one of the few precious occasions when time seemed to be on the side of the poor. The price, however, was high interest rates.

Conclusion

The immigrant bank, the loan shark, the savings-and-loan association, the penny-savings plans, and the pawnshop all represented responses to the working-class crisis of finding ways to stretch limited assets across time. What has become known as "fringe banking" was a supply-and-demand story for those whose needs were underserved by traditional banking interests. Although we cannot pinpoint the exact rationale, it is likely that major banking investors seldom ventured into neighborhoods because they thought there was little profit to be made from large numbers of small transactions among immigrants who placed more trust in their countrymen than in strangers. At the same time, laws prohibiting branch banking barred established institutions from reaching out to communities even if they had been inclined to do so. The basic cause of the woes besetting the poor was rooted in the low incomes they could earn in factories and on their own. Exhortations to set aside and save meant little when the money coming into the family barely covered basic immediate needs of food, shelter, transportation, and clothing. But even among those who had saved as a hedge against disaster, ignorance on the part of the victims, a lack of proper banking regulation, and the absence of alternatives meant exposure to the risk of personal financial calamity.

Time played an important role in making ends meet. It always favored those with money set aside; the passing days and months brought interest payments, a self-accelerating movement toward the accumulation of wealth. Debt twisted time so that it worked in the opposite direction. The loan-shark trap was only an extreme instance of the way tens of thousands of people accumulated an increasing amount of debt in their efforts to enjoy the products of modern economic society. Even though a late wage payment or unemployment created by a national economic downturn caused their predicament, the debt-ridden poor also faced classification as "unworthy poor" when it came to the distribution of charity.

If there was an irony to the situation it was that those at the very bottom of the economic scale, the homeless beggars, were the cruelest victims of the city's movement, spatial divisions, and temporal rhythm. They lacked even the minimal assets to participate in the city's fringe economic system at all. No one trusted them with a loan because they lacked the requisite fixedness of an address and a job. And for them, savings lasted only long enough to secure their next meal.

Postscript

For most Chicagoans, the reforms and lessons of the past have eliminated the perils of payday for most people. The creation of the Federal Reserve system in 1913 stabilized banking, although the "runs" on the banks early in 1933 left many middle-class families in the same situation in which the Stensland depositors had found themselves twenty-seven years earlier. Most had little idea how much shared risk there was in entrusting their savings to others. Depression-era banking reforms, however, restored most depositors' confidence. In recent decades, many of the most flagrant payroll abuses have been eliminated. But the words "garnishment" and "wage assignment" still linger in hiring halls, and there are occasional exposés about excessive currency exchange fees. The 1960 suicide of a Chicagoan who had fallen hopelessly behind in payments and compound interest led to a crusade by attorney Mark Satter against "easy credit" furniture and appliance stores.[67]

Loan sharks and "juice" loan operations still provide quick profit, but now it accrues to the organized crime interests that seized control. Charitable complaint-and-inquiry services still report stories of employees' attempts to collect back wages owed them. The money that makes it to the savings account is safer. Regulation enacted during the Great Depression improved the reliability of thrift institutions, but not completely. Scandals surrounding the failure of savings and loan associations during the 1960s still generate pain, while the collapse of deregulated institutions during more recent decades brought back fears reminiscent of the Stensland failure.

Meanwhile, the postwar years saw the beginning of a tailspin for pawnshops. There were 85 of them in Chicago in 1948, 56 in 1960, 26 in 1970, and 15 in 1985. Why the decline? One chronic problem was location. Before the 1960s many shops operated among their customers in poor neighborhoods of the South and West Sides. During the riots of that decade, these shops were among the targets of looters. This made it difficult for them to obtain insurance, while strict zoning laws largely limited their relocation to districts that were targeted for urban renewal. Several moved into an informal pawnshop district on State Street, south of Van Buren, but that was leveled in 1983.[68]

The pawnshop was always a small business trying to survive in an age of chain stores and retailing giants. Its ranks dwindled in part because the owners' children opted for other professions, while the high startup investment— probably $250,000—limited newcomers to the field. "Easy credit" stores, gold and silver purchasers, and especially unsecured credit cards have nibbled away at the business. At the same time, the influx of inexpensive foreign-made watches and radios cheapened the value of many of the items crossing the counter. Though less a target of the reformer's wrath than it was a century ago, the pawnshop became endangered, and its survival less certain with each passing year during the 1970s and 1980s.[69]

The obituaries for the pawnshop proved to be premature, however. During the late 1980s the ranks grew dramatically, reaching over fifty in the city in 1996. Why the turnaround? A new generation of entrepreneurs discovered that image was important. Exactly half of the businesses do not have the word "pawn" in their names, preferring such terms as "broker" or "exchange."[70] Some cleaned up their facilities, tried to cooperate with the police in tracking stolen merchandise, and moved to outlying neighborhoods or suburbs in pursuit of more affluent customers who needed quick cash. Others stayed with the traditional trade among the poor who were shut out of modern credit sources.[71]

12   The Institutional Trap

FINDING a home or a job or securing food for the day could be an individual or family experience. But many of the daily challenges of urban life required Chicagoans to look to each other and pool their resources, whether ample or meager, to create social structures that would help them cope with city life. The group experience was molded in myriad settings, ranging from clubs to neighborhoods to labor unions to mutual aid societies to churches and synagogues. Regardless of the makeup or formality of the context, members found support in such benefits as financial subsidy, friendship in an anonymous city, and comfort during personal crisis. A century ago few people understood the principle of synergism—that interrelationships within an enterprise can yield a sum that is greater than its constituent parts—but a vague hope for something like it underlay many group efforts.

Such experiences gave members a perspective on where they fit into the life of Chicago, an outlook that ranged from the constricted and parochial to the citywide and visionary. This was as true of the elite as of the other social classes. Families and individuals with substantial economic resources supported an extensive network of charitable fund-raising activities, cultural institutions, and social organizations. Their world was voluntary and defined by listing in the *Blue Book*. Their clubs were part of their social identities. These organizations not only provided a wide set of choices, but also oriented them toward a concern with citywide or even regional needs and issues. The private clubs drew their membership from a wide scattering of tonier neighborhoods and suburbs. They were places where men of substance lunched or exercised, but they also fostered political action. The wealthiest business owners were frequently upset over the direction of city politics and were convinced that local government was little more than a wasteful instrument to redistribute their tax dollars to the undeserving. In response they formed a series of political reform groups, including the Citizens Association (1874), Union League Club (1880), Civic Federation (1894), Municipal Voters League (1896), City Club (1902), and Better Government Association (1902). Each group utilized slightly different methods, and most shared an interest in humanitarian reform, but they all pursued the goal of a graft-free, efficient, minimalist city administration that was honestly elected. In their view, government should share their citywide viewpoint and operate with some measure of uniform standards across Chicago, regardless of the power of local political bosses.[1]

The organizational world of elite women was similarly voluntary and selective. These women created some purely social organizations, but many of those with a philanthropic conscience also championed citywide civic reform causes. The Chicago Woman's Club, Women's City Club, and similar groups tackled such questions as air pollution, infant mortality, juvenile delinquency, prostitution, and conditions for women prisoners. Like their male counterparts, they held a view of the city and its needs that extended far beyond Prairie Avenue and Astor Street.[2]

Each step down the social ladder brought a somewhat less cosmopolitan relationship with the rest of the city. The middle class, who bought the more expensive Sam Gross houses or who rode the Ravenswood el, may have been priced out of the world of elite Chicago, but they still shopped at Field's or Carson's in the Loop and otherwise traveled outside of their communities for work and entertainment. The focus of much of their social life, however, was more localized. The 1890s saw the creation of a number of outlying clubs whose members were residents of specific neighborhoods and suburbs. Their clubhouses, like their elite downtown counterparts, were the scene of holiday dances, bowling and billiard tournaments, amateur theater productions, and other social events.[3] In the middle-class communities bicycle clubs abounded, and churches were gathering places for socializing as well as worship. On a less formal scale, schools and local food or confection shops provided other points of social contact with familiar people. Political involvement in the outlying districts was usually carried out through a neighborhood improvement association that badgered aldermen about city services in their immediate locale.[4]

The lower rungs of the social ladder provided yet another view of the relationship between the family and the city as a whole. Not only were Chicago's working classes often poor, but they were also more ethnically diverse, and where they lived was often separated from other parts of the city by railroad embankments, factories, and the river. As a consequence, their vision was parochially focused on neighborhood institutions that were essential to their day-to-day ability to cope with the world. Although some ethnic institutions such as newspapers were citywide, most concentrated on the neighborhood and were much more localized than those patronized by the wealthy. Sometimes they were small businesses, which were in many ways the backbone of immigrant communities. The neighborhood merchant serviced the demand for ethnically oriented food, clothing, reading material, or even, in the case of the saloon and the dance hall, companionship. The local midwife was there at birth; the undertaker prepared the deceased for burial. The vast majority of savings and loan associations served similarly narrow clienteles.

Churches, which were often elaborate symbols of a community's pride, also provided emotional, financial, and informational support for their congregations. The memorial books and histories that eventually poured forth at centennials and other anniversaries were evidence of the manner in which members of churches and synagogues had traditionally pulled together to cope with Chicago. Religious activities, whether through synagogues, a patchwork of several hundred Protestant congregations, or the St. Vincent de Paul Society of the Catholic Church, took the generalized form of what became known as the institutional church, which often included job-finding services, day care, provision of food and coal, and other practical aids. Even when funds came from wealthy donors, it was the local institution that usually distributed the direct aid.[5]

Similarly, settlement houses reinforced the notion that the neighborhood was the essential building block of the city. Jane Addams's Hull-House, Chicago Commons, the University of Chicago and Northwestern University settlement houses, as well as the forty-six smaller ones in operation by 1920, provided a veritable department store of activities to people in their immediate areas. These ranged from job training to recreation, folk presentations, health care, and the arts. Thus, except for those who had to commute to a distant factory or to peddle, many of Chicago's ethnic communities were large enough to meet most everyday needs within a few blocks of home. A trip to some place like the Loop or even one of the larger city parks was a special occasion, not a regular event.[6]

Politics was part of a strategy of neighborhood survival. Chicago's division into thirty-five wards, often formed by such natural boundaries as the river and the railway embankments, promoted parochialism. Its ethnic diversity reinforced it. On Goose Island, for instance, the community was separated from the larger Irish district, which gradually moved down the South Branch of the river, but it was solidly Democratic. For years, stories circulated about how Kilgubbin Irish would intimidate voters at the North Side polling place located at Wells and Kinzie Streets. All of this was made easier because politics so easily became a part of one's public identity. Before the secret, or Australian, ballot became law in Illinois in 1892, casting a vote was a public act that could place a citizen in jeopardy because he had to request a paper ballot by the name of each candidate he supported and place each one in a box.

Finally, on a more personal level, the politics of dependency was part of everyday survival for many of the poor. The local politician, especially on the aldermanic level, could supply many of the things that the poor needed to cope with the risks of everyday life. Someone of "inflooence," as the press called it, could help a constituent in three basic ways. One was most obvious: using his access to government jobs and contracts. At his peak, Alderman John "Johnny de Pow" Powers of the West Side's Nineteenth Ward reportedly had as many as a third of his voting constituents on the payroll. Contracts for many materials and services remained in the private sector, providing an opportunity to reward or punish.[7]

A second source of an alderman's clout was his ability to use governmental power to apply pressure or punish. An alert alderman knew how to direct a swarm of harassing inspectors or order a street torn up in a strategic place to bring private citizens and businesses into line. He could use that power on behalf of his constituents to negotiate bills with grocers and even undertakers. The third power source was the politician's access to knowledge. In our contemporary "information society" we might forget that, even for citizens a century ago, life involved the intake and use of an enormous and bewildering quantity of information. The local politician often knew how to fill in strategic gaps about such things as where to obtain living quarters or how to get help from charity. Getting a job through him meant being able to bypass the employment agency and the hiring hall. Saloonkeepers, grocers, undertakers, and similar neighborhood business operators enjoyed the special political advantage of being at the center of information of this sort in the nonliterate communities.[8]

Most working-class families were self-sufficient, but they were vulnerable to the calamities of illness, injury, and loss of employment. Each step down the social ladder brought with it a greater dependence on outside help. Near the bottom this took the form of charitable activities that were progressively more unstructured and narrow in geographical focus. This perspective of life was clearly evident among the most desperate of tenement districts, where language barriers, the lack of a streetcar fare, or the shame of one's appearance trapped people in their immediate surroundings. This was especially the case during winter, when the want of sufficient outerwear confined them indoors. When the *Tribune*'s ace reporter Nora Marks visited the slums of the West Side during the bitter winter of 1888–89, her descriptions of the suffering emphasized what other newspaper writers had noticed: how the poor neighbors substituted, shared, and set priorities for what few resources they had. Some decisions were easier: A baby's socks took the place of shoes, and a husband and wife apportioned use of a single pair of boots according to which of them had a better chance of getting a job that day. The decision to use Christmas toy money to buy medicine was more emotional and difficult. People also survived because the networks that helped the poor to cope reached outside of their families. Everywhere she went, Marks found that neighbors and friends shared their meager supplies of coal and cabbage according to need and looked in on those who were aged or infirm.[9]

But for a few thousand others, life's challenges were beyond individuals' abilities to cope on their own. Whether through bad luck, accident, disease, improvidence, misdeed by their own hand, the economic climate, or some other sad event, they found themselves slipping into some form of public dependency. Only a helpful politician or perhaps charity or handouts from friends prevented the dismal downhill slide from the loan shark to the unemployment line to the pawnshop to the institutional traps of the county hospital, the poor house, or jail. For those who could not avoid it, there was little that resembled what we now refer to as the "safety net" to keep them out of the places from which there was often no return.

Perhaps the most ironically cruel part of it all was that the increasingly parochial experience of the descent into poverty led many Chicagoans to one ultimate destination: a nightmare of public institutions in which one's neighborhood background, former status in the community, and even ethnic identity meant little at all. Those whose poverty had often kept their neighborhood experience narrow now had no choice but to experience the harshest form of cosmopolitanism, living among a diversity of people who were also trapped in an institution.

Jekyll and Hyde on Harrison Street: Cook County Hospital's First Century

The burning question has lingered in Chicago for decades: What is to be done with Cook County Hospital? Should a new building rise on the present site? Should the central facility be closed and its functions dispersed? Or should the institution be abolished altogether, with government paying for the care of public patients in clinics and private hospitals? Those timeless and timely questions echo the concerns that have plagued the great gray warehouse of suffering for nearly all of the century and a half that the sick poor have turned to local government as the healer of last resort. For many of its thousands of patients, it was a doorway of healing; but to others, it was a frightening trap from which many feared they might never be freed.[10]

"County," as it is often known, had its roots in two early-nineteenth-century institutions that were designed to quarantine both medical and social problems. One was the almshouse, a shelter-turned-prison, which grew out of the county's legal responsibility to care for its paupers. (Chicago's Dunning will be described later.) The other was the city-run pesthouse, a number of which were set up to isolate the ill and dying from the rest of the population during the periodic epidemics that swept Chicago. These developed from the city government's legal obligation to ensure the public's health.

The horror of epidemics had been part of Chicago's past since 1832. These scourges originated outside of the city, whose emergence as a transportation hub increased the uncertainty of when pestilence would strike and how serious the affliction would be. Cholera had arrived at Fort Dearborn in 1832 along with the first steam-propelled ship, which carried troops led by General Winfield Scott who had been dispatched to fight Chief Black Hawk in western Illinois. One out of every five people on board the vessel died, and virtually all of the permanent residents of the village of Chicago fled when the fort was turned into a temporary hospital. The disease died out in the cold weather, but in 1834 a form of malaria called "canal cholera" infested the camps of Irish workers digging the Illinois and Michigan Canal. Each summer for the rest of the century saw intermittent outbreaks of typhoid, cholera, and other fevers transmitted primarily by poor sanitary practices. The belief that epidemics originated among the poor, who were also the most seriously afflicted, created in the public mind a negative association of the indigent with disease.[11]

With nothing but vague theories about why epidemics appeared periodically, physicians and politicians could do little except recommend spreading lime in the streets, burning sulphur, and trying to isolate the afflicted. In 1843 the city built a pesthouse where today's North Avenue meets the lakeshore. It burned two years later but had to be rebuilt because of the large number of scarlet fever and smallpox cases. It was in this atmosphere of emergency that city officials decided that it would be cheaper and more efficient to create a permanent medical institution.[12] In 1847, they appropriated $846 and converted a section of a North Side warehouse to general hospital purposes. The city paid for the building and the staff; the county bought the supplies. But Tippecanoe Hall, as it was known, proved inadequate from the beginning. Less than nine months after the hospital opened, the *Weekly Democrat* complained that from seventy to a hundred patients were crammed into a space that was too small. Moreover, patients with various diseases were mixed rather than isolated, and "the aroma was pungent and particularly unpleasant."[13]

The most devastating cholera epidemic arrived in 1849 as a indirect result of the opening of the Illinois and Michigan Canal the previous year. Although city leaders were forewarned of disease outbreaks to the south, they refused to close off trade because doing so might precipitate economic hardship. Instead, they allowed the canal boats to dock, among them the *John Drew* from New Orleans. Its captain and several passengers were afflicted, and as the scourge spread across the town, 687 people died within a few months; an additional 1,257 succumbed to cholera during the next three years. After the first season, so many children were left parentless that the informal adoption process broke down, prompting Protestants and Catholics to establish orphanages. Meanwhile, in the fall of 1850, Dr. Nathan Smith Davis, the founder of the American Medical Association, and his fellow instructors at the Rush Medical College decided to create the first private hospital, the Illinois General Hospital of the Lakes. The following year Davis used the admission fees from his popular health lecture series to rent a portion of the Lake House Hotel. Although patients were expected to pay for at least their room and board, the Illinois General Charter allowed the city and county to place its pauper cases there. Even then, the shortage of operating funds caused Davis and his board members, all staunch Protestants, to call upon the Roman Catholic Sisters of Mercy to provide the nursing staff. By 1851 the religious order had taken over operation of the hospital, which moved two years later into the Tippecanoe building and reorganized itself as Mercy Hospital. It retained its affiliation with Rush Medical College.[14]

The hospital situation changed rapidly during the turbulent 1850s, a decade when Chicago's population grew from 29,000 to over 100,000 and the city emerged as an important rail hub. County government assumed responsibility for sick paupers; in January 1851 it transferred care of some of its indigent patients to Mercy Hospital, at a cost of three dollars a week, an arrangement that would continue until 1863. Meanwhile, the city of Chicago continued to fulfill its obligation to provide isolation facilities during epidemics. Cholera suddenly appeared in all parts of the city in October 1852, killing 630. Smallpox took over as the main epidemic threat in 1853, killing 1,424 the following year, but cholera returned in 1854–55. Because these annual epidemics, which killed between 1 and 2 percent of the population, remained seasonal and were mainly concentrated among the poor, a temporary "shanty hospital" and another city pesthouse along the lakeshore housed victims of the summer scourges.[15]

In November 1854 the two levels of government sought more permanent solutions. Cook County decided that it would be cheaper to operate its own facility and took over the city's lakeshore pesthouse building for its noncontagious pauper cases. At the same time, Chicago officials made plans to build a permanent city hospital building to handle epidemic cases. The first step was the acquisition of the land at Eighteenth and Arnold (now LaSalle) in 1853, but use of the site as a temporary pesthouse delayed construction. The new building was finally completed in 1856–57. It was grand; its fate, however, was unexpected. When a wave of annual epidemics subsided during the late 1850s, the city faced the question of whether or not to admit noncontagious cases, which were outside of its charter responsibilities. The ranks of these nonepidemic patients were growing because more people were surviving chronic diseases and others required treatment after losing limbs in canal boat and railroad accidents.[16]

Before any admissions decision could be made, however, a bitter debate erupted over treatment techniques. Physicians who employed conventional methods quarreled with the followers of homeopathy, a somewhat faddish new treatment system that claimed that disease could be cured by introducing substances that induced similar symptoms. Homeopathy had become popular enough to support a new Hahnemann Medical College, named after Samuel Hahnemann, the European founder of the medical sect. Some 40 percent of all homeopaths in the world were located in the Chicago area. The equal numerical division of the city board of health into "regular" and "irregular" camps gave each faction an opportunity to veto its opponents' professional appointments. The resulting standoff not only left the hospital unopened and vacant for two years, but it also resulted in the disbanding of the board of health.[17]

A second split further complicated the situation. In 1859, Dr. Nathan Smith Davis and his allies withdrew from the Rush Medical College in a dispute over the length of the medical course. The Davis group established a new Chicago Medical College, taking the affiliation with Mercy Hospital with them. The remaining Rush faculty took advantage of the opportunity by renting the empty city hospital building for use as a second private hospital that competed with Mercy. Then the Rush group persuaded the county commissioners to send the indigent to them for a fee.[18]

Chicago's strange hospital situation unraveled during the Civil War. The Rush arrangement quickly soured when unexpectedly high operating expenses brought its hospital to the financial brink in 1863. At the same time the U.S. Army used a legal loophole to force the city to lease its building for use as a military eye and ear infirmary for the remainder of the war. Finally, that same year, the pressure to transform the old city cemetery grounds into Lincoln Park forced Cook County to abandon its little lakeshore pesthouse building and establish a hospital at its poorhouse facility at Dunning in suburban Jefferson Township. Chicagoans were stunned. A city of two hundred thousand was suddenly left with neither a public hospital nor any way to guarantee care in private facilities outside of Mercy Hospital.[19] The need became even more obvious when declining sanitation standards in the crowded wartime city brought outbreaks of typhoid, scarlet fever, smallpox, dysentery, and measles; there were 947 smallpox cases in 1863 alone. But, as military needs decreased at the end of the war, the army provided a solution to the crisis by agreeing to sublet the Eighteenth Street facility to the county. Early in 1866 a permanent Cook County Hospital finally went into operation.[20]

The last third of the nineteenth century saw a shift in health-care needs among the poor. The era of seasonal epidemics gradually subsided. Cholera struck again in 1866 and 1873, but the death toll was relatively small. There was a brief smallpox outbreak in 1893, but few were afflicted. Improvements in national communications and reporting procedures, as well as rigid employment of quarantines at international ports, helped prevent "scares" from developing into epidemics. By the early 1890s, the germ theory of disease became popularly known and sanitary habits improved among everyday citizens, which also contributed to the decline in epidemics. Moreover, the growing problem of pneumonia caused a shift toward higher death rates in winter, which helped even out seasonal mortality cycles.[21] Rates of water-borne disease also fell gradually because drinking-water supplies improved with the capping of private wells, which had often been located dangerously close to outhouses. The new water tower and intake crib system, which went into service in 1869, also helped improve conditions, as did a drive to improve drinking water for the World's Columbian Exposition. On January 1, 1900, the new Sanitary and Ship Canal opened and forced the flow of the polluted river backward, away from the lake; within a few years the summer scourge had virtually disappeared.[22]

The decline in warm-weather epidemics by the end of the century meant that Cook County Hospital gradually settled down to a more predictable flow of chronic care and accident cases. Industrial injuries accounted for a growing portion of the admissions. The rapid expansion of both the size and quantity of factories brought with it management personnel and workers who had only limited experience with unfamiliar and dangerous equipment and chemicals. Chicago's position as the "high-tech" capital of its day meant that its workforce was especially vulnerable to injury from the newest machinery and experimental processing techniques. The result was a sharp increase in accidents resulting in burns and crushing injuries of limbs. Sadly, Chicago would become the nation's prosthetics capital.[23]

While all of these changes altered the source of many of the hospital's admissions, most other problems remained the same. The clientele was still largely too poor to pay for care. And the chief issues that faced County Hospital during the last third of the century continued to involve inadequate physical facilities, political interference, and a negative image. A new wing, added in 1870, was quickly outgrown, and the place had become, in the words of one angry citizen, "a great, shameful, blistering, festering, rotten, vermin-haunted, crazy old rookery." In 1874 the county board decided to close the facility on Eighteenth Street and build anew on the square block bounded by Harrison, Lincoln (now Wolcott), Polk, and Wood Streets. Although there were charges of corruption surrounding the land acquisition, the West Side location was purposely chosen to balance the siting of the county courthouse downtown in the South Division and the county jail at Hubbard and Dearborn on the North Side. The first hospital building opened at Harrison Street in 1876.[24]

It quickly became a colossus. Like the department store, Cook County Hospital became a multifunctional center that was intended to serve many needs and constituencies under one roof. During the next thirty-five years, the growing complexity of public medical care resulted in major building additions devoted to hospital administration, maternity care, pediatrics, and patients with tuberculosis and other contagious diseases. The county morgue was also there, a fact that did not help the image of the place. In its growth, Cook County Hospital mirrored the growth of the industrial city. And like the factory, another large and centralized urban facility that was emerging at the same time, County became known for the impersonal and sometimes brutal goal of efficiency in trying to transform the raw materials of illness into the finished product of health. That target remained elusive. Many poor Chicagoans with special needs lived and died unserved, while the institution's size only increased the opportunity for inefficiency and malfeasance. And even the frequent expansions never seemed to keep pace with the health needs of America's fastest growing city.

The subsequent overcrowding and mismanagement contributed to the curious Jekyll-and-Hyde image that would plague the institution throughout its history. On the one hand, there were great achievements. Close ties with Rush Medical College provided the county hospital with a steady supply of interns, whose encounters with a wide variety of illnesses and injuries came to be regarded as valuable training.[25] Moreover, the medical staff included such giants of the profession as Dr. Christian Fenger, who brought Joseph Lister's ideas about antiseptic techniques to Chicago, and the world-renowned Dr. Nicholas Senn, author of twenty-three books on surgery. And the facilities constructed during the 1880s were regarded at the time as among the best designed in the United States.[26]

But it was Cook County Hospital's problems that largely determined its image. One large central public hospital stood amidst a city whose subdivisions were sprawling rapidly outward. In part, its reputation remained rooted in the debate about what Chicagoans thought was the proper location for health-care delivery. Much of the citizenry continued to associate public institutions of healing with poorhouses and pesthouses for the dying. The private residence continued to be the site of most medical care for those who could afford to summon a doctor, in large part because hospitals could offer little in the way of equipment or technique that a physician did not have in his office or even carry in his bag. The growing popularity of the telephone after its introduction in 1878 contributed to further dispersal by making it easier to summon help. The Chicago Medical Society lobbied for lower phone rates as a way for members to build their practices. Even the availability of emergency transportation strengthened dispersal; police patrol wagons regularly took all but the most seriously injured accident victims either home or to apothecary shops, where pharmacists dispensed pain killers.[27]

Those among the middle and upper classes who did patronize hospitals could make a consumer's choice that was denied the poor. Chicago's size meant that it could support specialized institutions. Patients with funds could select among small private facilities operated by physicians (Garfield Park) or religious groups (Mercy, Presbyterian, Michael Reese, Mt. Sinai). They might opt for ones catering to certain races (Provident) or to specialized groups such as alcoholics (Martha Washington) or teetotalers (Temperance) or women (Woman's—later, Mary Thompson) or children (Maurice Porter, now Children's Memorial) or immigrants—Norwegian American, Swedish American, German, Mary of Nazareth (Polish), Michael Reese and Mt. Sinai (Jewish). Specific charities also supported nonpaying admissions to most of these facilities.

Most care among the poor was similarly dispersed. The home bedroom was the domain of the midwife, who attended the vast majority of births, while only life-threatening medical crises could usually frighten poor families into summoning a physician. The most popular alternatives were several dispensaries that were operated by medical schools, hospitals, and independent charities. These were early versions of today's outpatient clinics and they allayed some of the antimedical fears of the poor, who were free to go home after treatment. Central Free Dispensary, which stood adjacent to Cook County Hospital, received a fifth of its operating budget from county government. It alone recorded 446,445 patient visits between 1867 and 1891, refusing to treat only 632 applicants. In addition, Central Free staff members contributed to the further decentralization of treatment by making 83,383 home visits during that twenty-five-year period.[28] The Visiting Nurses Association, which went into operation in 1883, also helped perpetuate dispersal by calling on the homes of the poor to give care, comfort, and advice, as well as vaccinations and eye tests.[29]

At the same time, sensational exposés fed the belief that the giant Cook County Hospital was the worst place to find treatment. In 1876, for instance, one former patient filled the first one and a half pages of the *Tribune* with detailed charges. The food served at virtually all meals consisted of watered-down soups and milk, moldy bread, and a meat substance so tough that it earned the in-house name of "B.A.," for blacksmith's apron. Doctors, who were described as "largely students," prescribed essentially the same medicine for all ailments and took what seemed to be sadistic satisfaction at seeing patients retch after overdoses. Medical instruments, urinals, hospital gowns, and bedding passed from patient to patient without proper washing or sterilization. Although the building was new, it had already become filthy, while a faulty heating and ventilation system subjected patients to great temperature differences when they were herded from their rooms to the dining hall and back again. The incompetent warden, who had been a politically ambitious iron puddler only three years earlier, had appointed his seventeen-year-old daughter as the hospital's head of housekeeping. Informants and reporters also complained that the nurses were women of loose morals and "tramps that steal the patients' food."[30] The latter charges led directly to the organization of the Illinois Training School for Nurses in 1880 and the subsequent requirement of professional training for the nursing staff. The school's founders included Dr. Sarah Hackett Stevenson, one of the city's most prominent physicians.[31]

The nursing school was the most positive development in a situation that otherwise deteriorated during the last part of the nineteenth century. The roots of the hospital's problems lay in a combination of partisan politics and the administrative complexity of a large urban institution. Rapid growth provided layers of bureaucracy, which made it easier to conceal the unbridled thievery among government officials that tainted the postbellum decades. The crooked "wardens," or business managers who headed the hospital, were party hacks who drained its coffers. Two were indicted. One of them, William J. McGarigle, fled to Canada to escape embezzlement charges, but he later returned and was convicted.[32] Doctors, including the distinguished Dr. Christian Fenger, had to buy their appointments with secret bribes.[33] In 1899, there were further charges that hospital employees were secretly paid to call personal injury lawyers before treating the patients.[34] Critics also alleged that political influence outweighed test scores in obtaining the coveted internships. But a major grand jury investigation two years later uncovered more reason for praise than blame and concluded that political interference prevailed mainly on lower-level unskilled jobs.[35]

This was little consolation for patients who had to face an unpleasant stay. There were endless waits for service that was often indifferent. Reporters and state inspectors revealed that patients often slept on improvised beds directly on the floors, which were permanently used as "spittoons" and were seldom cleaned. Stench lingered because fresh-air ducts constantly malfunctioned. Food and sanitary conditions improved only long enough to pass supposedly surprise inspections that had been advertised well in advance. By 1892, contagion-spreading conditions had proliferated to the point that, in the case of an outbreak of diphtheria, "Many who came in to be cured of one disease contracted another."[36]

By the turn of the century, many of the hospital's problems could once more be blamed on an antiquated and undersized physical plant. Basements and attics that had never been intended for patient care were remodeled into wards.[37] In 1910, living conditions for the interns had become crude enough to precipitate a strike.[38] Few people questioned the need for a new structure, but political infighting broke out in the Cook County Board over such questions as whether several dispersed hospitals should replace the large central facility. The director of at least one private hospital believed that a new building was unnecessary because the county could place patients in other institutions closer to their homes, pay their bills, and still save money. Some Chicago politicians thought that the city, rather than the county, should build and maintain the new facility.[39]

In the midst of this debate, epidemics of scarlet fever and diphtheria decimated the nursing staff and led to further exposés.[40] Investigations focused on the county board president, Peter Bartzen, who had taken office in 1910. He was blamed for reducing the nursing ranks to only half of the needed size, diverting the funds to expand the army of laborers who could vote. (Illinois women did not obtain local suffrage until 1913.)[41] Even after Bartzen was defeated for reelection in 1912, "Bartzenism," as the newspapers called it, influenced the county board. For two years board commissioners withheld payments to the Illinois Training School for Nurses, which provided much of the staff, in a crude effort to drive the institution out of business and replace it with an alternative run by political hacks. Public opinion finally forced the board to back down.[42] There were also charges of mismanagement arising from the fact that the new main building constructed under Bartzen cost $4,600 per bed, while the new psychopathic hospital erected by his successor was built for $2,100 per bed.[43]

The new buildings and a more efficient administration quieted most criticism for the next few decades, as did the boastful confidence that somehow bigger meant better. By 1927 the complex had grown to ten acres and the 3,200-bed capacity had made it the largest public hospital in the world. In January of that year, the millionth patient passed through its doors, and annual admissions exceeded 40,000.[44] Chicagoans pointed with pride to County as one of the anchors of what was emerging as the nation's largest concentration of healing facilities.

Chicago's Living Hell: "You're Going to Dunning"

For many generations of Chicago children, bad behavior came to a halt with a stern warning: "Be careful, or you're going to Dunning." The prospect sent shivers down the spines of youngsters, who regarded it the most dreaded place imaginable. New York had its Bellevue and London its Bedlam, but in Chicago it was Dunning that evoked images of gloomy institutional walls, the cries of the insane, and the hopeless poor peering from its windows.

Aid to the indigent had always followed two courses. Chicagoans who had lost regular employment, visited the pawnshop and perhaps the loan shark, lost their health at Cook County Hospital, or even spent some time in jail still had a layer of private charities to cushion their fall. That story had begun in 1850, when the tragedy of dependency left in the wake of the previous year's cholera epidemic resulted in the creation of the city's first full-time charity, the Chicago Relief Society. It distributed food baskets and firewood, along with lectures on the virtues of self-sufficiency. As the decades passed, charities tried to become more "scientific" in determining who should receive help. Sorting the worthy from the unworthy became an obsession. Charities also became more specialized in their functions. Some were settlement houses, which operated as multifunctional and permanently fixed neighborhood centers, essentially department stores of reform. Others processed applications from downtown offices. One 1891 directory listed 133 charities that combated a wide spectrum of physical, moral, social, legal, and economic problems that afflicted the poor.

But those who were beyond that kind of help ended up behind the sad walls of Chicago's cruelest place. Its story began long before there was a Dunning.

When Cook County government was organized in 1831, one of its duties was to provide for those who could not live independently because of insanity or physical disabilities. The many needs of nonresidents, mainly newly arrived immigrants or travelers trapped because of accident or illness, generated a resistance against helping the poor. The *Daily American* blamed the Irish construction gangs building the Illinois and Michigan Canal for providing the bulk of the paupers. Various residency requirements, as well as rules that demanded that relatives provide support, all proved unenforceable.[45]

Stuck with its new burden, Cook County government faced a choice of three alternatives. Initially, the county opted for the alternative of literally farming out its paupers. It paid local agriculturalists to house and feed extra "family members," much as modern foster care operates. This practice continued until 1848, when county officials finally decided that the money, in the words of the *Daily Journal,* was "squandered [because] fraud will creep in when the eye of watchfulness is withdrawn."[46]

Over the decades to come, county government remained generally hostile to the principle of the second option, "outdoor relief," which allowed recipients of a public dole to live in their homes. Most people viewed this type of support as the proper responsibility of church groups and charities, although some government funding continued sporadically throughout the county's history. But even when government inspectors visited recipients, opponents fretted that the dole aided the undeserving because it did not provide what many thought to be proper supervision. Later exposés revealed that the greater fraud was carried out by the private companies that supplied spoiled food and underweight coal deliveries.[47]

The county was at the same time pursuing a third and cheaper option. This was "indoor relief" in the form of an institution to house its social burden. The first poorhouse, constructed in the early 1830s, was no more than a humble shelter next to the animal "estray" in the courthouse square. Inmates had to endure the taunts of children and the pain of seeing their names published in the newspapers.[48] When county officials realized that the poorhouse was an unsightly intrusion on the public square, they built a new one on 160 acres of lakefront land five miles south of the city. The farm was productive. In 1848 its major crop was potatoes, which were no doubt welcome among the Irish clientele whose relatives back in the old country were suffering that year from the devastating famine. But the building was inadequate, and conditions gradually degenerated. In February 1853, the county grand jury complained about overcrowding and poor ventilation, but it was especially shocked at the "rooms for the insane," which were "lamentably inadequate for their accommodation." In the fall of 1854 the old poorhouse became a death house when dozens of newly arrived Swedish and German immigrants who were dying of cholera spent their last hours crowded into its tiny rooms.[49]

By this time, a replacement was nearing completion. In 1852, the county purchased an eighty-acre plot nine miles from the center of town from a farmer named David Dunning. Because the location was nearly three miles from the nearest railway, the price was low and the isolation was exactly what the county commissioners wanted.[50] The site, which retained the Dunning name, would provide not only a bucolic atmosphere far from the evil temptations of the city but also enough agricultural land to allow the institution to save taxpayers' money by growing most of its own food. And so, on December 14, 1854, twenty-seven women, twenty-five men, and twenty-four children made the long journey by wagon to the new three-story brick building in the country. They were pleasantly surprised when families from surrounding farms threw a merry housewarming party for their new neighbors.[51]

Dunning represented an optimistic social philosophy that was popular across America during the middle decades of the nineteenth century. Its basic tenet was that the physical separation of criminals, paupers, orphans, alcoholics, and the insane from the rest of society provided the best setting in which to treat their problems. Appropriate institutions could offer expertise and resources that were lacking in family homes. Thus, orphanages began protecting children from the homelessness of the street, while inebriate asylums provided the firm guidance needed by the chronically intoxicated, penitentiaries emphasized rehabilitation over punishment, and lunatic asylums allowed the quiet isolation necessary to cure troubled minds.[52] In the case of paupers, almshouses such as Dunning were regarded as superior to outdoor relief. The institutional setting would provide an opportunity to teach self-sufficiency and the work ethic to the perpetually poor, while administering strong doses of moral instruction to them as well. At the same time, taxpayers who did not accept the notion of uplift and improvement could be satisfied that a stay in Dunning amounted to incarceration. The new site also helped reduce the everyday public visibility of people that Chicagoans did not want to encounter. Over the decades, pesthouses, prisons, garbage dumps, and dog pounds, as well as such unpleasant industries as stockyards and rendering works, had been exiled from town. Dunning would similarly suburbanize the social problem of beggars, transients, and the homeless out of sight.[53]

Dunning's failure, however, was virtually assured by the manner in which it was established and operated. The first and most enduring problem was that it was forced to divide its funding to provide for the care of the mad as well as the poor. Cook County residents who could not afford private treatment were unwilling to see insane relatives taken hundreds of miles away to the state-run institution at Jacksonville. In response to the demands for something closer, the county constructed a separate 40-by-100-foot wing at Dunning for those classified as the insane poor. They were confined to 7-by-8-foot cells behind heavy iron doors, their special medical needs left untreated and their food and clothing limited to barely enough to allow survival in the unheated building.

Meanwhile, the county encountered loud complaints that the well-heated rooms and the good and plentiful food in the poorhouse part of the facility might be better than many taxpayers enjoyed. The response was to make the paupers uncomfortable, in order to discourage applications from unworthy idlers. There may also have been a nativist motive, since the inmates were overwhelmingly foreign born; in 1858, for instance, there were only nine "Americans" among the 186 residents. In either case, life was not easy. Staff members

The County Hospital Group, *Rand-McNally's Birds-Eye Views of Chicago* (1888). The clustering of charities, schools, hospitals, and other medical facilities around Cook County Hospital was an excellent example of the logic of concentration. The area was once a working-class residential neighborhood. Key: (1) Cook County Hospital; (2) Chicago Post Graduate Medical School and Hospital; (3) West Division High School; (4) College of Physicians and Surgeons; (5) Congress Hall; (6) Illinois Training School for Nurses; (7) Marquette School Buildings; (8) Presbyterian Hospital; (9) Rush Medical College; (10) Chicago College of Dental Surgery; (11) Laboratory of Rush Medical College; (12) Chicago Homeopathic Medical College; (13) The Woman's College.

Cook County Insane Asylum, 1880s. Institutional monotony and large size added to the miseries of this Dunning facility.

Dunning entry gate, ca. 1910. A guard stands in the forbidding portal at Chicago's most feared address.

Dunning and its farms, 1908. The farm fields surrounding the institution were meant to contribute to its financial self-sufficiency, but the crops seldom offset more than a small portion of the operating costs. (Chicago Historical Society, DN006806)

Harrison Street Police Station lockup, 1895. Located in the Levee vice district, this was one of the busiest feeders for the Bridewell. (Kellogg Collection, Michigan Historical Collection, Bentley Historical Library, University of Michigan)

Recreation grounds for women, Chicago House of Correction, *Annual Report, 1907.* In 1907, a tenth of the inmates who served time in the Bridewell were female.

Solitary cells, *The House of Correction of the City of Chicago, World's Fair Edition* (1933). The most troublesome of the Bridewell's guests ended up here.

stole food supplies and inmates' personal belongings. One scandal that emerged in 1857 revealed that the chief physician exhumed freshly buried corpses of inmates under cover of night, then reburied the coffins filled with rocks. The bodies were concealed in barrels, which were shipped to medical colleges for a payment of twenty dollars each. All the while, the press complained about the "vast amount of idle and unproductive muscle" there and demanded that poorhouse labor be farmed out to the highest bidder.[54]

The industrial boom of the Civil War brought low unemployment and high wages. Initially, the existence of Dunning provided the county board with an excuse to cut back on the dole. The threat of confinement was used against those falsifying applications for outdoor relief. But as the war progressed, the county resumed the practice of handing out bread and coal to maimed veterans, widows, and children left orphaned by the conflict, the same groups that overwhelmed officials with pleas for admission to Dunning. The war also left in its wake many elderly mothers whose deceased sons had once cared for them at home. The aged who could afford the entry fee moved to the Old Ladies' Home, founded in 1863, but the others ended up at Dunning.[55]

The overflow crowd at the poorhouse broke down efforts to classify and separate elderly, infant, and sick inmates, but most tragic of all was the mixing of insane patients with the general population. The construction of a new Cook County Insane Asylum on the grounds in 1870 officially separated the dependent and insane populations, and several subsequent additions solved the space problem. The new facility complied with institutional practices found across the nation, which meant that it consisted of little more than large ward rooms equipped with restraints. As the cries of the mad echoed across the neighboring farmlands, Dunning became synonymous with the shame of poverty and the hopelessness of mental illness. The local press reinforced the negative images with sensational stories that emphasized the bizarre. In 1874, for instance, the directors tried a new therapeutic approach by opening an amusement room, but a *Tribune* reporter's visit there focused only on the delusions he witnessed at an inmates' ball, where the "Queen of Sheeba" danced with "Bismarck," "Pope Pius IX," and "a member of the Board of Trade."[56]

The same reporter also visited the almshouse, by then renamed the Cook County Infirmary. This account, like those that followed visits by other journalists, was designed to shock readers in a stomach-wrenching way. The smell was described as overwhelming, and the food inedible. "Coffee," for instance, was a solution boiled from burnt bread, peas, and chicory; and breakfast consisted of stale bread dipped in spoiled syrup that had been confiscated from food shops by the city's health department. The colorful report carefully noted the overcrowding, the flophouse atmosphere of the men's department, and the vermin crawling everywhere. The elderly were mixed with unruly children; the terminally ill and the well slept side by side in dormitory wards that afforded no privacy. An 1875 exposé conducted by Dr. J. S. Jewell, a prominent Chicago physician, added credibility to the charges of widespread mistreatment, malnutrition, and intoxication among staff and inmates alike.[57]

Throughout these exposés, writers called attention to the mixture of groups of people within the institution who were increasingly separated from each other in the outside world. For instance, the financially successful and even the thrifty working person could use the purchase of a house to escape the dangers and evils of the slums. Immigrant groups could move from the richly varied portal neighborhoods of the Near Northwest and Southwest Sides to more homogeneous enclaves where they could built ethnically based institutions and raise families. Society could even isolate prostitution into the segregated Levee district. But at Dunning, those inmates who still had any modesty, self-control, or self-respect found themselves trapped. They suffered the most because they were not able to defend themselves from the invasive nature of the place. They could plan no strategy of survival except perhaps to dream of escape.

Early in the 1880s, Cook County officials attempted to improve Dunning's reputation with a massive building program that relieved the overcrowding for a few years. The change reflected professional trends in the field of institutional design. The large dormitories gave way to smaller cottages for patients, a veranda for sitting outdoors, and, on the administration building, an impressive Gothic facade that attempted to project a new image of respectability. During the mid-1880s it renamed itself the "Cook County Infirmary" instead of "almshouse" or "poorhouse." And, perhaps in the belief that too much isolation had fueled the ugly rumors, the county persuaded the Milwaukee Road to construct a new railway spur and depot. Soon, the cheap land and good transportation sparked the development of a nearby community that included the Kolze Electric Park.[58] Annexation to Chicago in 1890 eventually brought city water service that replaced the inadequate wells that had created sanitary and fire hazards.

But even this physical renaissance could not silence the critics. State charity officials openly attacked the management for the lack of trained medical personnel. The press picked up the story of one unmarried Norwegian immigrant woman who died after giving birth to a fifteen-pound baby; the immediate cause of death was an incorrect prescription made by an inexperienced doctor.[59] There was also the problem of the inevitable mixing of the two types of inmate populations. Sometimes this grew out of accidental misclassification, but it also resulted from the use of poorhouse residents to perform housekeeping tasks among their insane neighbors.[60]

County officials also did not know what to do with children. Although male and female inmates were separated, even if they were married, there were several births each year in the institution. Other youngsters continued to arrive with their parents. There had been talk of removing the children, especially after it was revealed that they had been receiving little or no education. Heads of orphanages and adoption agencies complained about the adverse impact of the environment on children, but the state refused to remove them from their institutionalized parents.[61]

The Chicago Woman's Club, the Citizens Association, and the Chicago Medical Society unearthed the most serious scandals beginning in the mid-1880s. They discovered that incompetent management had inflated costs to twice those of comparable institutions. The management received kickbacks from crooked suppliers who delivered rancid butter, spoiled meat, and rotten produce.[62] Before 1882 the budgets of the insane and poorhouse divisions were mixed together, and it took another three years before the two units had separate directors. In 1886, a former medical director, Dr. J. G. Kiernan, gave the most damning evidence before a special state investigation of the Dunning insane asylum. He testified that staff members, virtually all of whom gained appointments because of political connections rather than expertise, were often intoxicated and insubordinate. They routinely gave doses of sedatives that were strong enough to kill.[63] Some patients, both sane and mad, wandered about with keys and frequently walked away. Attendants still robbed helpless inmates of their property, while reports of body selling resurfaced.[64] The most controversial charges grew out of the beating death of an insane-asylum inmate named John Burns three years later. But when the grand jury interrogated suspects, they included not only the abusive attendants who were indicted, but also Kiernan, who had been reappointed to his old job. Despite efforts of the doctor's political enemies to implicate him, he escaped indictment and suffered only the loss of his position. The jury found the attendants innocent and condemned conditions that were so overcrowded that no individuals could be blamed.[65]

The 1890s saw no end to the controversies. The announcement by the county board that it was actively looking for land on the North Shore for a new insane-asylum site brought a flood of opposing petitions from that area. Instead, the board decided to build new cottages at Dunning to relieve the overcrowding, while the families of many inmates obtained court orders to remove their loved ones to the more humane state institutions.[66] But institutional apologists maintained that the congestion was merely seasonal because, in the words of the superintendent, "Whiskey brings most of them, and in winter particularly they vibrate between the Bridewell [prison], Clark Street lodging houses, and our place."[67] Other controversies swirled around the mistreatment of detainees at the Cook County Detention Hospital, where those suspected of being insane were held before commitment hearings. There was also a widespread fear that Dunning's concentration of the sick poor was harboring an incipient smallpox epidemic during 1893–94.[68]

The effect of the policies, headlines, and debates was to dehumanize the inmates. When poorhouse officials introduced a plan for mandatory rug weaving, sewing, and broom making, no one criticized the inmates' lack of choice; instead, labor unions complained that the institution provided unfair competition for able working men. There were further allegations that resident labor was being used by private building and decorating contractors on the grounds without compensation.[69] And a particularly macabre scandal returned when it was discovered that medical schools were still buying the bodies of deceased inmates. In at least two instances, horrified relatives rescued corpses from dissecting tables. Rather than deny the allegations, Dunning officials explained that the county had legal claim to the remains because tax funds had fed and clothed the inmates in life.[70]

The new century brought few changes at first, but three factors eventually forced reforms. The first and most important, which led to the demise of Dunning, was the action of the state in exercising its superior power over local governments. The county board had begun discussing the transfer of the insane-asylum part of Dunning over to state control as early as 1904, but nothing was done until the county was ready to start operations at Oak Forest. In 1911, the General Assembly and the Cook County Board agreed to the change. This action finally divided the facilities for the poor, which remained under county authority, from those for the mad. As the sun set on June 30, 1912, Dunning officially closed, reopening the next day as Chicago State Hospital. It later became the Chicago-Read Mental Health Center, a place that would have its own troubled history.[71]

The second factor was the emergence of a more scientific and humane approach to dealing with both the insane and the poor. Mental health programs, psychiatric evaluation, professional social work, and the case-study method of charity all helped to make the asylum an anachronism. The third was the growing public hostility to the belief that isolation aided the healing of people with problems. Endless scandals and the failure to demonstrate positive results made almost every type of institution vulnerable to critics, especially when tax dollars operated it. Thus, over the next several decades, probation and parole lowered the number of inmates at penitentiaries, foster homes and adoption replaced most orphanages, and, in 1934, Alcoholics Anonymous began to take care of many of the inebriates who might have ended up in hospitals. Eventually, halfway houses and the unfortunate policy of "dumping" reduced the populations at mental institutions. Outdoor relief through private charities, as well as public welfare payments, made the Dunning almshouse unnecessary.

When county officials began planning a new complex of institutions at Oak Forest in 1905, it was agreed that only the most helpless pauper cases should be admitted.[72]

But in the folklore of Chicago, there still remains the ultimate threat to an unruly child, "Be careful, or you're going to Dunning."

A Trip to the Bridewell

"The Bridewell." It is as much a part of Chicago's lexicon as the "gangway" and the "Gold Coast." For more than sixteen decades Chicago's city prison symbolized failure and frustration. As a place of incarceration for minor offenders—the others went to Cook County Jail—it was a slippery spot on which the unwary could fall. Homelessness or a drunken spree to forget one's problems could lead one step further down the road to hopeless dependency. Yet at the same time, the jail's forbidding stone buildings embodied what Chicagoans sometimes thought of themselves and their city.

The Bridewell name was generic. In 1555, King Edward VI transformed a castle at St. Bride's Well in London into a workhouse for short-term incarceration, creating the widely adopted sobriquet. Chicago's first Bridewell was more humble, a log cabin that literally replaced a pigpen on the town square. It was thought adequate for a precocious hamlet of the 1830s and 1840s, and, from the beginning, Chicagoans established a pattern of ignoring the jail's problems until they became a threat to decent folk.[73] By 1849 the once-sturdy oak building had decayed so badly that escapes were common and Mayor James Woodworth admitted that he was releasing prisoners early to relieve overcrowding. In 1850, the jail was filthy and without heat in two of its three rooms, and a grand jury called it a "public nuisance."[74]

After another year of complaints, the city erected a new Bridewell, this one in the tough district of brothels and saloons that had developed at the southwest outskirts of the city at Polk and Wells Streets. The 100-by-24-foot structure could hold two hundred prisoners in fifty cells, while three acres of grounds around it gave an air of spaciousness behind a fence ten feet high.[75] By the end of the 1850s, however, Chicago again faced a jail crisis. The city's population nearly quadrupled during the decade, bringing with it a natural increase in the number of miscreants. At the same time, the creation of a rail network fanning out from the city attracted not only drifters, but also more sophisticated professional criminals who used Chicago as a headquarters for intercity careers.[76]

Changes in the criminal justice system, however, were most critical in crowding the Bridewell. Because the railroad made it so easy to leave town, judges increasingly exercised their power to hold witnesses in custody to ensure that they would be around to testify.[77] At the same time, when the rapid growth of the city brought a parallel increase in wrongdoing, the cheapest way to expand the court system was to add justices of the peace to handle less serious cases. Often untrained in the law, "j.p.'s" drew their salaries from the fines they assessed. This led to the temptation to assess expensive penalties for misdemeanors. All that cash-strapped defendants could do was to exercise their option to "work out" their punishment at fifty cents a day. Often, their families would present petitions of hardship to win early release.[78]

By the early 1860s, the impoverished prisoners had grown numerous enough to fill the Bridewell and to force the city to press an old armory into service to accommodate the crowd.[79] Moreover, vagrants, prostitutes, drunks, and other "revolvers," or repeat customers, were indiscriminately mixed with respectable witnesses and terrified first-time offenders, much as similar groups had been mingled at Dunning.[80] By 1865, conditions had become intolerable; when representatives of the New York Prison Association visited the Bridewell, they condemned its overcrowding, rotten wood, vermin, and sickening smells as among the worst in the nation.[81]

Despite the criticism, city administrations did little for the next four years beyond improving the housekeeping.[82] In 1869 the Common Council finally authorized the purchase of fifty-eight acres at Twenty-sixth Street and California Avenue to build a new facility. It was an ideal site, isolated from the city and its "decent people" and endowed with a large clay deposit that could be worked by the inmates to make bricks. During the summer of 1871, the notorious "Black Maria," or jail van, began what would be a forty-year career of carrying the "roomers" to their new home. With a capacity of eight hundred, the facility was little more than half filled on an average day, and boastful Chicago could now claim that it had the most modern jail in America.[83]

The spirit of civic pride brought with it the willingness to experiment with reform. In a symbolic break with the past, the Bridewell was renamed the House of Correction, and the members of a new Board of Inspectors announced their determination to follow the model of Dunning and make the institution self-supporting. The inspectors believed that work would be an uplifting and corrective alternative to the traditional enforced idleness; taxpayers had always approved anything that would reduce costs and make life more strenuous for the inmates. Back in 1850, Mayor Walter Gurnee had instituted a chain gang for street work, and for decades prisoners had been employed making brooms and bricks and caning chairs.[84] But the new city jail sought to establish work contracts with private companies, whose supervisors ran the prison shops. Almost everyone seemed to gain from this arrangement: the prisoners learned a skill; the Bridewell gained income; and the contractors got cheap labor. The only parties left out—the labor unions—were outraged and applied pressure to the city council. In 1884, the aldermen passed a resolution condemning the practice of prison labor as injurious to law-abiding workers. The work, however, never constituted much of a threat to laborers on the outside. After the new 1870 state constitution mandated a two-dollar-per-day rate for working off fines, the turnover of the inmate population became so rapid that it was not worth training them to do any type of skilled work. Contractors complained that it was too much trouble hauling goods to and from the jail's isolated location, while the financial crisis caused by the Great Fire of 1871 diverted funds away from constructing most of the buildings that were to house the workshops. Instead, prison workers ended up manufacturing inmate uniforms and linens, as well as maintaining the facilities.[85]

During the 1880s, the Board of Inspectors could probably claim that its institution was one of America's best-maintained city jails. A major addition was completed in 1886 and facilities were kept clean. Incoming prisoners were efficiently processed. They were given uniforms that replaced those that had been made of large patches; earlier, escapees had discovered how to sew matching pieces together to resemble street clothing, something that was much harder to do with the new stripes.[86] Unlike state prisons or the Cook County Jail, a sister institution holding more serious offenders, the Bridewell enforced stiff discipline. There was a no-talking rule, and inmates walked single file, in lock step, each with one hand on the person in front. Those who broke the rules were handcuffed to their cell doors in a standing position. Women, who made up nearly half of the inmate population, were kept in a separate wing, where they slept in a dormitory rather than in cells. There was also a concerted effort to isolate the hardened women of the streets from first-time offenders.[87]

As the years passed, the House of Correction increasingly functioned as hospital and home for the desperate. According to the medical director, those who rode in the Black Maria mixed with "all the alcoholics, drug habitués, epileptics, chronic incurables, cripples, blind and helpless beggars, cranks, perverts, and general mental and moral defectives who require special medical and surgical attention."[88] As many as a third of all entering inmates required some type of care. Police justices lacked the power to sentence the insane to the Dunning asylum and the most helpless to the Dunning almshouse; they found it easiest to pack defendants away to the city jail.[89] People whose minds were troubled—but not too troubled—ended up behind bars. Judges also sentenced virtually all "street drunks" to the House of Correction, even though a portion of city liquor license revenues went to support the private Washingtonian Home for inebriates. Cook County Hospital refused to admit alcohol or narcotics cases, leaving the Bridewell infirmary as the only place where many of the middle class as well as the poor could seek aid in their battles with alcoholism and other health problems. Some inmates stayed as long as a month after the expiration of their sentences so that they could complete their treatment. Perhaps as a symbol of the Bridewell's function as a "dumping ground" for people who seemed to fit nowhere else, the city also built a contagious disease hospital, garbage crematory, storage warehouses, and dog pound on its grounds.[90]

The most serious obstacle in combating the inmates' medical and social problems was the revolving-door nature of the place. The Bridewell's superintendent explained that his population increased in times of prosperity because money led to "excesses," which led people into "trouble." Depressions made people value each dollar earned.[91] Because its inmates had committed minor infractions of city ordinances, the Bridewell's sentences were much shorter than those at the county jail next door or the state prisons at Alton and Joliet. This canceled any benefit that might have been gained by isolation from society. At the same time, the families of prisoners were frequently successful in seeking mayoral pardons. It was not unusual to find spouses and children camped outside the mayor's office rehearsing their pleas. Nor was it rare for local politicians and even the governor to intervene on behalf of loyal supporters. Mayors justified absolutions of this type by claiming that the offenders would be less likely to get into trouble again because so many people would be watching them. But political opponents, as well as many law-abiding citizens and those who wanted the criminal justice system to perform as the law prescribed, vehemently condemned the frequent clemency. In reality, pardons also served to weed out the least-serious offenders to reduce severe overcrowding. New cell houses constructed in 1897, 1904, and 1908 temporarily reduced crowding, but they also quickly filled.[92]

Youthful inmates, some only six and seven years old, had long been the object of special concern. Many children were picked up on vagrancy, petty theft, and assault charges, misdeeds that experts blamed on everything from the decline of the apprenticeship system to parental abuse to the social disorganization that resulted from immigrant adjustment in a new land. No one could agree on what to do with them. Some critics claimed that education only made those who were criminally inclined even more dangerous. Many convicted delinquents received quick pardons out of fear that mixing them in the general Bridewell population would only provide advanced training in crime. The House of Correction superintendents themselves openly wished that their youthful "guests" were elsewhere. "Institutional life is machine life," complained one warden, who wanted all juveniles "placed out" in private homes, much as the earliest poor had been dispersed. That solution was not politically practical, but it was possible to isolate the juvenile population within the institution. The first important reform was the creation of the John Worthy School. In 1894 the Board of Education began providing instruction to boys in a chapel. Two years later, the school board constructed a separate John Worthy building on the grounds and in 1897 the city council finally appropriated funds to erect a separate cell house adjoining the school to accommodate inmates under the age of sixteen. In 1899, when Illinois became the first state in the nation to create a Juvenile Court, Chicago's facility was ready to receive the wayward youth. A few years later, however, Bridewell officials were lobbying for the removal of all juveniles to the new state reform school for boys at St. Charles.[93]

There were other signs of a more humane treatment of adult Bridewell inmates during the new century. The lock step disappeared in 1901, as did the ball and chain, and the striped uniforms gave way to ones made out of "blue jean material." Baseball and movies relieved the tedium, and, in 1918, the city purchased a farm in Willow Springs to make the prison's food production more self-sufficient.[94] In 1915, the Bridewell and the Municipal Court created a psychopathic laboratory to examine criminals and to study what were believed to be genetic and social reasons for their behavior.[95]

But even though the half-century following the creation of the House of Correction had changed the physical appearance and programs, "the Bridewell," as it remained in popular memory, was still a sad collection point for a motley assembly of prostitutes, petty criminals, transients, street drunks, and others among society's outcasts.

Conclusion

The institutions described in this chapter were alien to the vast majority of Chicagoans. When those citizens needed medical care, a doctor visited their homes or they sought care in the public hospitals operated by charitable or religious institutions. For the poor who mistrusted County, there were numerous dispensaries that administered inoculations, set bones, and prescribed medicines without the dread of hospital admission.[96] For most Chicagoans, crime was something that perhaps enlivened the conversation at the breakfast table. The closest thing to Dunning that all but a few hundred Chicagoans encountered was the admonition about the consequences of bad conduct or perhaps a view of its fearsome entrance from Kolze's Electric Park. But for those who could cope the least well with life, these institutions were familiar destinations.

Dunning and the Bridewell, along with Cook County Hospital, represented both the best and the worst of the urban process. As noted earlier, cities were, after all, made up of hundreds of different kinds of minorities. Some were ethnic and racial and took visible form as neighborhoods; whether they were there voluntarily or trapped by segregation, this type of minority status was obvious. But other kinds of urban minorities were less visible or geographically distinct, especially those interested in particular pastimes or arts, those who possessed certain skills, those who worshiped in their own way. They may not have constituted a large portion of the population—that fact made them minorities—but in an urban setting like Chicago their numbers were large enough that they formed organizations, churches, labor groups, lodges, clubs, teams, and almost any other collective entity. Chicago, like any other city, became a complex network of neighborhoods and communities.

But the same process also created concentrations of others deemed to be society's problems, including the sick poor, people with physical problems, and those unable to resist whatever made them petty criminals. Even if these groups had never gravitated to the city—and there is no hard evidence that they did—their random appearance in the population would have generated numbers sufficient enough to force local government to face the "problem" they posed. In this way, their perpetually dependent status transformed these groups into involuntary minority communities. At the same time, their concentration in a particular location turned each institution into a sad type of neighborhood. This was especially true at Dunning, where the period of residence often lasted a number of years.

The three institutions that served these populations were, in theory at least, never meant to be what they became. At their best, they were intended to be caring refuges from a cruel world where those who had fallen by the way could regain their ability to function independently. Even the old Bridewell changed its name to reflect the goal of correction as well as punishment.

There were several reasons why these institutions strayed from the course. The anonymity that was inherent in their large size and multiplicity of functions opened the door to mismanagement. Similar problems could be found on any level of government, as well as in private industry. Administrators and staff who dealt first-hand with the everyday maintenance of these institutional residents and patients reflected the prejudices of the city as a whole. The managements of all three institutions and the members of the Chicago City Council and the Cook County Board, which financed them, also faced a general public that demanded that the institutional setting be equated with punishment. This was probably a majority opinion. No one who was in any way supported by public funds was ever to be more comfortable than the worst-off self-supporting individual. Cook County Hospital was never to be as caring and efficient as its private counterparts; the same was to be true of the Cook County Insane Asylum. The poorhouse and the Bridewell spoke for themselves. The reputations of the institutions as traps were meant to be devices to keep down the size of their populations.

Postscript

The passing decades were not kind to the institutions that housed the poor. After the construction of the new Cook County Jail and Criminal Courts Building nearby in 1929, the Bridewell remained essentially unchanged for the next twenty-five years. Despite a revision of the municipal code that provided for payment of fines in installments, the House of Correction remained a revolving door where the poor worked off fines and served minor sentences. The handicapped, the aged, and the derelict, all of whom belonged in other institutions, still made up a large portion of the jail population. "Where else will they go?" asked an exasperated judge in 1960.[97] The physical condition of the buildings also deteriorated. The former clay pit, which had been deepened into a stone quarry in 1901, became a garbage dump. The old buildings crumbled. Superintendent Frank Sain upgraded youth facilities and remodeled the hospital, but he also convinced Mayor Martin Kennelly that a crisis was coming. The bleak report of the Mayor's Commission on the House of Correction persuaded Chicago voters to approve a $4 million bond issue.[98] By 1960, thanks to another bond issue pushed through by Mayor Richard J. Daley, two new cellblocks and a new Cermak Memorial Hospital had been added. But lice, insane inmates, and accusations of poor administration remained grist for investigative reporters whose exposés would produce waves of denials, charges of cover-up, temporary reforms, and reversions to previous conditions.[99]

During the early 1960s, rumors began circulating that the Bridewell would be merged into the Cook County Jail. Sheriff Richard Ogilvie endorsed the idea. But when the necessary legislation neared passage in the Republican-dominated General Assembly, Mayor Richard J. Daley balked. Complaining that the consolidation plan constituted a "gift" of city facilities to the county without compensation, he announced plans to sell the farms to the Chicago Dwellings Association (CDA), a government agency that would erect low-income housing on the site. On June 24, 1969, the city accepted the CDA bid and down payment. The new town for the poor was never constructed, and the CDA quietly sold the valuable land back to the city, which then resold it to developers in 1979.[100] Meanwhile, on January 1, 1970, the long-anticipated merger took place, and the former Chicago House of Correction became part of the Cook County Department of Corrections. But despite these administrative changes, the nickname and the reputation of the old Bridewell survive in the collective memory of Chicagoans.[101]

As the decades passed, the idea of the poorhouse faded away. Outdoor relief displaced its indoor counterpart, with the possible exception of public housing. Government obligation to treat dependent groups within institutional settings shrank to cover only the sick, the criminal, and the criminally insane. Chicago-Read lost much of its inmate population to deinstitutionalization, but the name of Dunning survives in a comfortable neighborhood of neatly kept houses and an official city "community area" that surrounds it. Meanwhile, the sad past continues to haunt. In 1989 a developer was beginning to excavate part of the vacant Chicago-Read grounds for a new shopping center when construction crews unearthed large numbers of human bones. In the middle of prime real estate stood an unmarked and forgotten cemetery in use for sixty years and containing as many as three thousand graves. Many no doubt held the last mortal remnants of the unfortunates who once peered out from Dunning's windows and suffered its indignities.[102]

Meanwhile, Cook County Hospital had struggled with the problem of contrasting images when the rosy confidence of the 1920s gave way to the stark reality of the Great Depression. Because the newly unemployed could not afford alternatives, they joined the permanently poor in crowding Cook County Hospital as the healer of last resort. In the midst of the overcrowding, the rumors of incompetence started anew. In 1935, the American Medical Association lifted its accreditation of the internship program, citing inadequate training. Two years later, renewed complaints about political interference from the Democratic machine led to a major investigation and a shakeup of hospital leadership.[103] Yet, amidst these scandals, the positive aspect of the image also grew: in 1937 Cook County Hospital created the world's first blood bank, inventing a system that has saved millions of lives since.[104]

The years following World War II brought remodeling and expansion that somewhat relieved the problem of overcrowding, but the age of the main County Hospital structure and the rapid growth in the number of indigent patients brought about the beginning of another crisis.[105] Two new factors shaped the hospital's direction. First, an increasing portion of the sick poor were African Americans, who could not gain admittance to most other facilities. Second, there was the expansion of Chicago's vast slum district and its accompanying social problems. Increasing numbers of the poor were no longer within a mile or two of County Hospital; the Woodlawn neighborhood was seven miles away through heavy city traffic. In 1956 the Welfare Council of Metropolitan Chicago proposed construction of a South Side branch hospital instead of a further expansion on the existing site. After two years of debate that resembled the discussions of 1912, the county board rejected the idea of decentralization, but it also failed to build a new central facility.[106]

Funding cutbacks during the early 1960s brought staff reductions and deferred maintenance that once more threatened the hospital's accreditation.[107] A new generation of reporters posed as patients to write exposés that could have been published a century earlier: they told of peeling paint, lapses in sanitation, the misery of overcrowding, and a harried and seemingly indifferent staff.[108] A special commission appointed in 1967–68 by Governor Richard Ogilvie called conditions "intolerable" and again recommended decentralization. In reply, staff physicians complained of interference by politicians who were most interested in filling the roster with unnecessary jobholders.[109] With its accreditation again jeopardized during the late 1960s, County Hospital, at one point, could attract only 60 percent of the interns it needed.[110] The creation of a County Hospitals, Health, and Allied Medical Programs Governing Commission in 1969 reduced the county board's political control,[111] but the following year a stand-off between it and the county board forced the hospital to turn away patients and threaten total shutdown.[112]

Of the three institutions that ensnared Chicagoans, only Cook County Hospital survives, but its history has continued to haunt the place. The old problems remained unsolved through the 1980s and into the 1990s. Physical facilities continued to deteriorate. In April 1990 and again during the following January, the hospital temporarily lost its accreditation because of building-code violations.[113] But every dollar spent on the old building evoked complaints of waste from those who wanted to replace it on its present site.[114] One controversial 1989 plan called for the county to take over the nearby University of Illinois Hospital building, with that institution's medical school affiliating with Michael Reese Hospital, located several miles away, as its teaching hospital. The awkward plan proved unpopular on all sides.[115]

Other schemes called for the hospital to disperse its functions into smaller facilities in the community. But unlike in the mid-1920s, when there were 110 hospitals (only 38 of them for-profit) scattered across Chicago, the ranks have thinned considerably. Cutbacks in federal aid, a decrease in insured patients, the rise of for-profit health-care corporations—all have prompted the demise of such storied institutions as Henrotin, Illinois Central, Augustana, Mary Thompson, Cabrini, and Cuneo. Like the closing of stores, schools, and churches, the loss of hospitals has been part of the wave of deinstitutionalization that has devastated inner-city neighborhoods.

The bankruptcy and closing of Provident Hospital in September 1988 especially complicated the issue. Once the pride of the city's African-American community and a symbol of its institutional independence, Provident financially overextended itself at a time when federal support for its indigent patients declined and operating costs soared.[116] When the U.S. Department of Housing and Urban Development seized the structure and turned it over to Cook County government, everyone expected it would be quickly reopened as a satellite replacement for County Hospital. What followed instead was nearly five years of remodeling and the continued full-capacity operation of the old building, which most of the poor continued to prefer. In May 1994, the Provident Pavilion reported using an average of only 56 percent of its beds. Meanwhile, in 1995, county and state officials announced plans for a $542 million replacement for the central facility, the largest public works project in the county's history.[117]

Personnel issues have also revived memories of century-old debates. The hospital was unable to find enough pharmacists to fill the positions of nearly a third of those who quit rather than work seventy hours a week. Nurses walked off the job on October 28, 1976, and did not return until December 12.[118] The press called for more cooperation from local medical schools to ensure sufficient numbers of residents and interns. At the same time, the hospital's staff members have expressed their dismay over the way that inadequate funding for personnel and supplies, self-engorging bureaucracy, and lack of public respect have long squelched their desire and impeded their capacity to deliver competent and humane health services.[119]

The last three decades have seen a revival of the newspaper cliché portraying County Hospital as a "patient" about to "die." Assigning the blame for its problems is as much the grist of politics in the 1990s as it was more than a century ago. But now there is a major change in the larger contexts in which institutions operate. The hospital, the poorhouse, and the Bridewell represented responses to problems that took place in an era when industrial cities and the national economy were both growing rapidly. In recent years, federal funding in the form of hospital grants, Medicare, and Medicaid eased the burden of the poor, but those sources now face even more skeptical questioning by those advocating a scaling back of the notion of the safety net. Yet, amidst the crises, Cook County Hospital has adapted itself to fit a pair of growing needs that developed in a troubled city. It not only opened one of the nation's first gunshot trauma units (described by the press as the "MASH of the West Side") but it also developed a burn unit that ranks among the nation's best.[120] Because it is the hospital of last resort, it also cares for AIDS patients who have exhausted their resources and have nowhere else to turn.[121]

The problems of the sad old "gray lady" have remained the same—past, present, and future. But, despite the hospital's crises, the victims of modern society's urban ills can find caring help in an institution that a century earlier served those afflicted with cholera, smallpox, and typhoid.

Jekyll and Hyde still live on Harrison Street.

Conclusion:
Coping with Urban Life

ITS formal name was the High Bridge, and when it was dedicated in Lincoln Park in 1894, it was the pride of Chicago. Although it crossed only a narrow portion of a lagoon, park commissioners had decided to keep alive the spirit of the Ferris wheel at the World's Columbian Exposition by building a span that was spectacular rather than utilitarian. Visitors were invited to enjoy the healthful exercise of climbing the stairs for a panoramic view of the North Side from seventy-five feet up, the highest publicly accessible point in the city. Those who were frightened at the thought of soaring so high could stand around its base and admire the intricate patterns of its ironwork arches. But within a few years of its opening, the bridge was beginning to attract unwanted visitors: those bent on taking their own lives. Chicagoans disappointed in love, in trouble in their businesses, facing the disclosure of some embarrassment, or suicidal for some undefinable reason leaped to their deaths with an alarming frequency that at one point reached almost once a month. The next day's papers would routinely speculate about some deep secret, and those who read the details while sipping their morning coffee could shake their heads at the tragedy of another sad casualty in the war of urban existence.[1]

The park commissioners responded in the only way they could: by increasing security. At first, they augmented park police patrols in the area and after nightfall locked the gates in the fences that then surrounded the park. When that failed to stop the problem, they placed a guard on the structure itself, at first only at night and then around the clock. They considered extending nets beneath the span to catch the jumpers. But even then, the ingenuity of troubled minds prevailed, and bodies continued to plunge toward the water or ice below at an alarming pace. Some even chose to end it all with a gunshot while standing on the span. Chicagoans began referring to the structure as "Suicide Bridge," the name even appearing on macabre souvenir postcards that tourists mailed to relatives back home. The commissioners resisted the idea of razing it while it was still structurally sound, but finally on November 1, 1919, the American House Wrecking Company began the process of dismantling it. After that, firearms, poison, or jumping into the lake or river—the river near Goose Island became a popular place—would have to suffice for the job of self-destruction.[2]

The sad history of Suicide Bridge was an indication that some Chicagoans could no longer deal with their life situations. But, compared with the millions attracted to the growing metropolis, the small numbers who chose to end it all were really proof that most people, no matter how desperate their circumstances, managed to find a way to cope with life in the city and the situation in which it put them.

The Challenge of Chicago

But why was there an endless need for Chicago's people to cope? Why did city life often seem so cruel? It is an easy but superficial response to blame the struggle of the poor on social-class exploitation. Certainly it is clear that money bought the privacy and knowledge that allowed the wealthy to insulate themselves from the unpleasantries of city life. Historians have demonstrated that, despite their philanthropies, many among the rich held most of the poor in contempt. But a social-class interpretation of the situation is far too simplistic.

Lincoln Park High Bridge, postcard view, 1895. As the years passed, this graceful structure assumed a gloomy reputation as the scene of many suicides.

It does not allow for the great variation in the ways in which people within each social class faced urban challenges. Why did some impoverished immigrants attend night school to better themselves, for instance? Why did the need to find strategies of survival often pit poor against poor and make them responsible for the misery of others of the same class. Those near the bottom of society often exploited, cheated, discriminated against, and committed crimes against each other. Wealth and class are clearly part of the story, but not all of it. There are several independent factors that play at least as important a role as the amount of money or influence a family or individual might have possessed.

First, to a great extent, the problems of daily life and the strategies to survive it grew from the urbanization process itself. Historians and sociologists who have studied the phenomenon have often disagreed about what this process was, but they concur that it has always involved much more than simply gathering people together in one place. Life in a city of two million was more complex than it was in a town of two thousand. The most obvious consequence of urban growth was crowding, which took both public and private forms. For most of the nineteenth century, Chicago attracted each week as many as two thousand more people than left it. Its housing stock and its borders, however, did not always expand at the same pace, and those of limited means found themselves crammed into fetid slums. Space was the most elastic part of a family's, or individual's, economic life. If income fell, it was easier to move into cheaper quarters or even to the streets than it was to stop eating. Life in such circumscribed private spaces brought a much higher risk of dying in a tenement fire, contracting disease, or ending up in the institutional trap.

By contrast, wealth ensured the ability to withdraw to a series of institutions and places that insulated the few from the many. Those with money coped with urban life by becoming part of Chicago yet being able to withdraw from it. Lunch at the private club, a box at the opera, the carriage ride through crowded streets, a visit from the tailor for a fitting—all were part of the lifestyle of those who lived in the city but were in command of how and where they came in contact with fellow Chicagoans and the urban environment. Each step down the social scale meant a greater loss of that control. The middle-class suburbanite could at least withdraw to his or her subdivision, but the homeless had very little choice of company or location.

The urbanization process also resulted in highly public forms of crowding. The legal complexities of condemnation and the cost of property acquisition made it difficult to broaden the city's public streets. Chicagoans realized that much of the congestion that made the streets nearly impassible and dangerous was inevitable, but they tried to overcome the problem through new technologies, especially transit innovation and the creation of new layers of the city. Often, however, these solutions themselves became problems. Many Chicagoans came to realize that one person's means of coping with the city created new problems for others. For example, the automobile, the bicycle, and the commuter train gave new mobility and speed to one group at the expense of pedestrians and residents of neighborhoods and towns along transportation routes. The same principle applied to various forms of leisure; one person's enjoyment of tobacco or an excursion to a beer garden or an amusement park sparked a reaction of moral concern among another group. Even peddling, which to the poor was a last-resort source of income and sustenance, was to others a preventable and environmentally disruptive private invasion of public space. In other words, one Chicagoan's means of survival was another's nuisance.

Ironically, amidst the congestion, distance itself became an independent element in the story of coping with city life. The urbanization process included what seemed to be the related yet apparently opposite trend of dispersal. Because Chicago was not as compact a place as older cities in the East, destinations were often beyond an easy walk. This made getting from here to there a chronic problem of everyday life for almost everyone. Distance not only pushed investors and city government into speedier but more expensive transit technologies; it also became a complicating factor in household moves. Distance from home translated into anonymity, contributing to the anxiety of parents when their children used the transit system to escape to amusement parks and other faraway attractions. It was a special burden for the poor; the price of a streetcar ride often determined how much distance a worker could place between the place of employment and the family. The long journey from home increased the dangers faced by street vendors and made it easier for fraudulent employment agencies and payday scams to succeed. Distance also presented a mixed blessing for those of greater means. It allowed commuters to escape most of the hazards of inner-city disease, while bicycle riders pursued the goal of a "century bar" ride of a hundred miles. But distance also increased the potential dangers of the daily railway commute or the likelihood of an auto accident. Distance even played a special role in the quality of everyone's food. It limited the number of customers served by Chicago's failing public market houses, and the ever-growing distance between home and work transformed lunch from a family meal into an away-from-home experience in a semipublic place. The greater the distance from which a restaurant could draw customers, the more famous it was. But for the poor, distance limited the choice in food suppliers to shops nearby and to peddlers who came to their door.

Distance was inextricably related to another variable in the process of coping with city life: the element of time. As urbanization continued, Chicagoans became increasingly conscious of the ways in which their lives were forced into synchronous rhythm with each other. Those who worked outside of the household recorded their arrival and departure from work, sometimes on a time clock. Their noon-hour meal often became a frenzied feeding. Then they faced a twice-daily rush hour. The amount of commuting time available and the cost helped determine the commuting distance; a half hour and twenty cents on a commuting train would put many more miles between home and work than the same number of minutes and a nickel on a streetcar.

On their way home, thousands of Chicagoans stopped to make time payments on a new parlor suite, an automobile, or a house. Being able to put money aside for the proverbial "rainy day" meant being able to control the timing of expenditures to take advantage of sales. Perhaps as they gazed from the streetcar windows, their thoughts turned to regret about living payday-to-payday.

Time always seemed to work against Chicagoans who were poor. The number of weeks they had been on the dole might determine how long they could expect charity. If they had some possession in the pawnshop or owed money to a loanshark, time meant fast-accumulating interest. Their poverty also virtually assured that they were consuming food and milk that was much closer to the end of its shelf life than were the products sold to the middle- and upper-class.

Urban time was marked by two interrelated characteristics. The first was its ability to increase or diminish the worth of things. Wise investments and bank accounts became more valuable as the days passed. But time had the opposite impact on many forms of information. Those who were dissatisfied with their jobs faced that fact. Like the sought-after newspaper that lay valueless in the gutter the next day, a want-ad or "hot tip" about an employment prospect depreciated by the hour.

Second, cities also operated on larger temporal cycles. Saturday night meant dancing for as many people as Sunday meant church. Fixed paydays, as well as a half-day or full day off, established the weekly rhythm of the city. Other cycles were annual. Moving day rolled around with relentless predictability, as did the heat of the summer. Some families planned a warm-weather getaway, if not to the beach, at least to the amusement park. Others had little choice but to contemplate the increased price of ice and the greater likelihood that the milk they bought would be spoiled or laced with preservatives. Each summer and winter brought extremes in temperature that caused widespread suffering among those who could not afford to escape; all that tenement dwellers could do was to spend their nonworking hours on sidewalks and stoops, in parks and other public places. For peddlers who sold frozen treats, summer meant prosperity. The onset of winter signaled the annual build-up of coal supplies in the subdivision or suburban basement, while for the poor, who could not afford to store things for a future time, it initiated the women's work of securing small scraps of wood or clumps of coal that had fallen from railway cars.

Time and distance were also part of a larger urban-rural relationship. Although cities exercised economic domination over their regions, urbanization also forced city residents to rely on those who lived outside their borders. On a day-to-day basis, Chicago's food, milk, and ice came from out-of-state sources. The chance of finding a job fluctuated with the demand for a local industry's goods in the national market, as well as with the numbers of potentially competing workers who stepped off arriving trains. The waiters of the Culinary Alliance realized this, as did padrones and those who operated employment agencies. The availability of housing also depended on how many of these strangers stayed, became Chicagoans, and entered the demand side of the market equation. Food prices were similarly affected. Thus, as the city grew, it became part of many different national systems and networks, each of which contributed to opportunities for growth and to crises of dependence and vulnerability at home.

The urbanization process also resulted in the collection and creation of minorities, not just ethnic and racial groups but also clusters of individuals possessing particular attitudes or interests or even wanting to purchase a particular item. The gathering of these people in a city fostered a process that can best be described as synergistic because the sum of their efforts was ultimately greater than the contribution of the individual parts. City dwellers faced an astounding variety of choices. On any given day Chicago could support entities as diverse as competing picture-frame stores, neighborhood whist clubs, and more than half a dozen major downtown men's clubs; none of these could have survived for very long in a smaller city. Geographical mobility became absolutely essential in fostering this process by making it easier for communities of interest to congregate. By conquering distance, the streetcar and the commuter train created the fancy downtown restaurants, as well as the amusement parks.

Obviously, income levels controlled the number and kinds of choices that were open to any individual or family. For the very poor, the options were most often related to everyday survival and the avoidance of hazards. Even those of humble income could choose among peddlers or food shops, saloons or settlement houses. The higher the Chicagoan was on the social scale, the more these choices related to discretionary expenditures such as those for amusements, athletic facilities, or restaurants.

The City as a Collection of Risks

The issue of risk surrounds us in very subtle ways. It is as old as humankind. At the close of the twentieth century, however, problems such as trying to avoid an epidemic or computing actuarial tables has given way to something much more pervasive. The possibility of illness is at the heart of the tobacco consumption and "healthy eating" issues, while the possibility of contamination breeds suspicion of our food supply. Those advocating an increase in the speed limit have to confront those who fear soaring highway accident rates. Our health insurance debate intensifies; the cost of care is ballooning out of control at precisely the time when the ranks of older people who will need more of it have begun to grow. Our overworked term "safety net" itself conjures images of the risk of fall. The *Journal of Risk Management* reveals a serious scholarly commitment to finding ways to reduce the burden of insuring against future loss in a myriad of forms. And the government that funds research in many of these areas is itself increasingly supported by revenues from gambling, which is a form of risk-taking.

To a great extent, the story of coping with everyday life in Chicago is a tale of risk. While the city concentrated the positive qualities of life, such as achieving prosperity, finding love, and stimulating the mind, it also increased many opportunities for loss, peril, and disappointment. Contemporary city living is fraught with the potential for crime, technological disaster, and other menaces, yet urban survival was much more difficult a century ago. Epidemics, industrial accidents, and street perils made being a Chicagoan much more hazardous then. But other risks, though subtle, were no less substantial. These risks stemmed from three sources.

The first was technology. Cities like Chicago depended on new forms of technology, which were on the whole enormously beneficial, yet the introduction of these advances sometimes brought hazard and grief. The commuter express, the elevator car, the el train, the electric streetcar, and the skyscraper all presented danger from fire, dismemberment, electrocution, or other forms of injury.

Technology played an important role in Chicagoans' ability to cope. Elevators, skyscrapers, and public transit created downtown congestion, while at the same time the addition of modern lighting, telegraph and telephone wires, specially designed vehicles, and buried utilities transformed streets into corridors of technology. Sidewalks sprouted not only the posts to hold up the wires, but also police and fire alarm boxes and "iron newsboys," or newspaper vending machines. Streets choked on their own activities. But it was nearly impossible to regulate the access of one group or another to them. In this situation, technology enabled politicians to avoid making hard decisions that might be highly unpopular. The battles between teamsters, bicyclists, and automobile owners over just a few streets demonstrates how much bitterness a political decision might have aroused. Instead, the easiest response was to capitalize on technology and create another layer of transportation in the form of the elevated and the tunnel.

While some Chicagoans were clearly modernizers who eagerly embraced change, others were stuck in a world of old technologies. Ironically, living in a place like Chicago could be a risky venture for the poor because of inadequate levels of science and technology in the areas where they lived and worked. Accidents, fires, epidemics, and other calamitous events might have happened on the farm or in the village, but when they happened in the city, the concentration of interdependent people made the impact that much worse. The poor especially suffered, not only because their neighborhoods were the most crowded, but also because they had inherited the technologically obsolete city that the middle- and upper-classes had abandoned. Deficient heating and lighting systems in their homes resulted in fires. Inadequate water and sewage technologies in their streets contributed to the spread of disease. Moreover, the most poorly paid workers were engaged in the most dangerous occupations, such as working on the killing floor of the packinghouse, toiling in steel-making jobs nearest the furnace, and pulling coupling pins in a rail-switching yard. Immigrants were often the most ill-equipped to cope with such problems; they were unfamiliar with life in a nation that placed a premium on innovation. Their lack of the wherewithal of survival, such as education, money, or fixedness in society, often led to insecurity and family catastrophe.

The second source of risk was the obvious one of crowding. Disease, fire, and violent crime, for instance, spread quickly through fetid slums. The downtown throngs, meanwhile, increased the danger of being knocked down on the sidewalk, getting tangled in the doors of an elevated train, or being run over by a wagon or automobile. Crowded apartments, smoke-filled factories, and stuffy offices represented other threats to the public health through their stifling atmosphere.

The third source of risk was the anonymity that came with city growth. Success in coping with Chicago became increasingly dependent on information that the citizen did not learn from firsthand experience. One might get a tip about a job or an available house on the other side of town from secondary and even tertiary sources instead of directly from family and close friends. Incomplete information about people, places, and things made choices more difficult and sometimes more dangerous. Urbanization forced people to trust strangers, and the resulting misplaced confidence in someone else presented a constant problem for city-dwellers. Middle- and upper-class Chicagoans were able to find reliable sources of survival information that reduced the risks of city living. Their reading of the daily papers and the endless exposés published there alerted them to such potential problems as food dangers and employment cons. The impoverished suffered the most, however, because they had to rely on information of the poorest quality. The peddler who misrepresented the purity of milk or food, the employment agent who lied about a job lead, the banker who quietly looted depositors' accounts, the employer who refused to pay workers, the household mover who suddenly demanded an extra payment to unpack a family's goods from the van—all left behind trails of anger, frustration, and loss for their victims.

Risk avoidance was also an integral part of the search for the right subdivision, a process that created neighborhoods and whole suburbs based on class as well as ethnicity and race. In turn, the measure of homogeneity that existed within a neighborhood brought with it the fear of outside invasion—that a life's investment in a house might be lost because of the arrival of someone or something that was unwanted. Crossing borders became an especially touchy issue. Peddlers wandered too far into hostile neighborhoods, old houses were moved where they were not wanted, apartment buildings sprang up among detached houses, factories opened in residential districts, and beer gardens survived where incoming neighbors wanted them removed. Community reactions to such transgressions took many forms over the years. The neighbors' nosy inspection of the furniture being unloaded from a moving van was an important assessment of where the area was heading. Conflict over racial and ethnic borders could easily lead to violence. Most often, residents turned to their aldermen, who were able to exert their influence over building permits and utilities to control the situation. Various forms of local option, which gave householders control over saloon license location, dried up two-thirds of the city more than a decade before Prohibition. Finally, in 1923, a new zoning law defined the types of economic land uses and confined them to zones so that they could invade each other only with the approval of a government agency.

The Multifunctional Place

The urbanization process combined the factors of distance, time, risk, and the creation of minorities to foster the growth of characteristic institutions. In many ways, the triumph of the nineteenth-century urbanization process was the formation of the complex organizations that attempted to serve many audiences and functions under one roof. Just as the factory brought many manufacturing processes together, so, too, did other urban places. Most were semipublic, that is, they were privately owned but of public access; they could not have functioned without the latter. In one way or another, they were intended to help reduce the risks of urban life. The specialized dining facilities in the large restaurants served breakfast and lunch eaters, as well as evening diners, but also provided special facilities to accommodate unaccompanied women. Hotels did the same, most of them offering women separate staircases to prevent the risk of encountering a male who might be smoking or engaging in uncouth behavior. The department store replicated an entire downtown of retail shops and services so that customers could reduce the need to face the unpleasantries and dangers of the street. Its counterpart, the mail-order catalog, provided a parallel service for those located miles away, but they became successful only after rural customers were convinced that the company could be trusted. The modern amusement parks, especially White City, Riverview, and Forest Park, responded to the different ways in which Chicagoans sought emotional release and an escape from daily burdens by assembling dozens of highly varied attractions. The railway station served as a grand point of entry or departure, but its services also made it unnecessary for many passengers changing trains to leave the building and venture into the dangerous city. The school system broadened the definition of education, while becoming a primary welfare institution for the children of the poor; instruction in vocational education, civics, and domestic science all had the underlying motive of reducing society's risk of collapse from unemployment, radical labor discontent, and family disorganization. Night school was a response to a demand from a group outside the normal synchrony of education. In their efforts to define and combat many of the same sources of poverty, the settlement house and the institutional church grew into a complex of activities. The daily newspaper united a diverse collection of readers and at least exposed them to knowledge in fields that might not immediately interest them; it also informed the public about impure food, workplace dangers, and other risks. Finally, the large public hospital reflected the growing specialization of the medical field, as well as its professionalization; it faced the monumental task of convincing the poor that admission reduced rather than increased the risk of death from injury or disease.

As diverse as they were, these institutions were not only intrinsic parts of big-city life, but they were also celebrations of the logic of centralization. This amounted to a belief that the reduction of the physical distance between related activities was intrinsically good, even when those who used the new central institutions had to travel greater distances. Many of these activities were concentrated in the Loop district, which itself operated like a multifunctional machine, with specific streets and blocks given over to financial pursuits, entertainment, newspaper publishing, shopping, cultural events, and other grouped activities. The city, county, and state government activities headquartered there reflected a trend toward performing new services through an increasingly complex bureaucracy. When Chicagoans of previous decades looked for efficiency and bottom-line costs, they assumed that bigger was better. Every improvement in public transportation extended the geographical area and the populations that could be served, while every advance in communications seemed to encourage complexity. But, as the story of Cook County Hospital reveals, size did not necessarily ensure smooth operation or humane achievement of goals.

This centralization seems perhaps outdated today. Out-sourcing is a euphemism for dismantling factories and dispersing in-house workers. Department stores have declined in favor of specialty shops gathered in shopping centers that are far less complex or efficient. Only one-half of the 1920s Union Station survives to service a dwindling fleet of Amtrak trains. Daily newspapers have lost out to specialty publications and a "narrow-casted" electronic media. The settlement house and the institutional church in their diminished forms are less tied to a particular location. The amusement park idea survives in suburban Gurnee, but it thrives as a regional rather than a city institution. During the 1990s the most firmly held notions of uniform central administration in the schools gave way to some extent to the concept of control by neighborhood councils. City government has increasingly "privatized" its functions and become a check writer rather than a provider of services. And even the Loop itself has lost most of its retailing functions during the last two decades. Two major parcels of State Street land, one of them virtually an entire square block, have been vacant for a decade, something that would have been labeled economic lunacy a century ago. Any discussion of these changes must come back to a basic unraveling of the old logic and a substitution of decentralization. "Big" is assumed to mean inefficient and oppressive.

Coping with Chicago

It is clear that city life required day-to-day strategies for survival, and that the ability to formulate them contributed to the success or failure of an individual, a family, or even a community. Many of those strategies were almost unthinking responses to individual situations, such as trying one food vendor instead of another or borrowing from relatives to stay out the clutches of a pawnbroker. By contrast, many situations prompted collective responses, such as the formation of reform organizations that attempted to correct problems through government intervention and other planned strategies. Boycotts, city council ordinances, and the federal Pure Food and Drug Law were measures taken on behalf of large groups of anonymous sufferers.

In general, coping with Chicago took several basic forms. One was escape, to disengage oneself from the city and its cares. A relatively small number chose the tragic means of suicide or less drastic escape through inebriation. More commonly, diversion took the form of the visit to the sylvan retreat of the large city park, the frenetic activity of the amusement park, the unifying crowd of the baseball game, or the more active sports and exercises; all provided cheap, convenient, and safe escapes. Chicagoans with the means to do so could depart from the city altogether, either to suburban sanctuaries or, in the case of the elite of 1897, to the more pleasantly situated second homes elsewhere.

A second reaction was tolerance. There is no precise way to measure its extent because the evidence remains somewhat impressionistic and the definition of the term itself varied from person to person. Nonetheless, quiet suffering was undoubtedly the most common reaction of all. Many urbanites, especially newly arrived immigrants, could convince themselves that conditions were not all that bad. Columnist George Ade, for instance, described how the horrible slums seen from the city's elevated trains contained many poor people who seemed contented at their lot in life because it was better than that which they had fled. In another variation thousands of young women tolerated unpleasant factory conditions because they felt certain that their eventual marriage would remove them to a better life. Other Chicagoans turned to their church parishes or inward to their religious beliefs to give them the emotional strength to tolerate their problems.

A third general form of coping involved adaptation, as city dwellers conquered and even thrived in situations they knew they could not change. This mode included the actions of the immigrant who took advantage of night school or who exploited an economic niche and peddled something no one else provided. In this manner, much of what we call entrepreneurship was a form of coping. Although illegal or immoral, most forms of economic crime also represented a means of coping. People who saw opportunities worth taking, whether they were exercising informed judgment in selecting produce or questioning letter carriers to learn of the best apartment vacancies, could also claim small victories over the difficulties urban life presented them.

Even those who lacked the money and education to escape disease and disorder by moving to the city's fringe or who were unprepared to make wise consumer decisions often demonstrated a remarkable resilience. The poor survived by making use of seemingly contradictory coping tactics. They either joined in union efforts or pooled their resources in other ways; at the same time, they often acted in an individualistic and competitive fashion by taking to the streets as peddlers, by "harvesting" the city of coal that had fallen off railway cars, or by rooting through garbage boxes. If successful, they moved upward and outward, perhaps to a new subdivision; but they also often attempted to make their traditional environment portable, by moving their old houses to new neighborhoods or even simply by carrying their lunches to work.

Many Chicagoans pursued a fourth course and sought to correct a problem rather than alter their own behavior. They might rebel as individuals, writing angry letters to newspaper editors, refusing to pay fares for the privilege of hanging onto the sides of overcrowded streetcars, or, if they were property owners, carrying out vigilante repairs to defective streets adjacent to their land. But this form of coping also included organized reformers of many stripes. Their reaction began with the realization that something needed changing, but it escalated to a sense that something could be done. Food quality, transit discomforts, and slum conditions were just three of many of the targets of their reform efforts. Sometimes the thrust for change remained in the private sector, among the charities and settlement houses that first noticed and publicized the problems. But the reform of such large-scale problems as impure food, unfair employment practices, and slum housing usually evolved into some form of government intervention in the form of ordinances and inspections.

Information was critical to all of these means of coping. Reformers circulated ideas around a national and international network of journals, organizations, and correspondents. Laws and regulations first formulated in one part of the country sprang up elsewhere. On a much smaller scale, informal networks of families, neighbors, and friends passed on news of jobs or warnings about an unreliable butcher shop or how to get around on the el. The broadening base of information taught Chicagoans to live with technology. As autos became more numerous they killed fewer people not only because they were better constructed, but also because the general level of driving and pedestrian skills among the populace increased. The same was true of electrical wires over streets, as well as safety aboard trains and at crossings. Knowledge was the first step to successful coping.

It is essential to emphasize that most of the challenges described here are much less difficult now for the majority of people than they were in earlier decades. There are several reasons for this. First of all, most of what is described in this book took place during the years between 1850 and 1920. These were the decades of Chicago's enormous growth, a period when the comfort and well-being of the poor were likely to be ignored when they got in the way of the move toward economic and physical development. In the decades following 1920, Chicago, like most places in America, became much more humane. While growth remained the goal, there was new consideration of the "means" to that goal, that is, the general well-being of the populace. New protective laws, government aid programs, concerns about the environment and public health, and the realization by most businesses that workers were assets rather than enemies—all contributed to the trend toward diverting some of the emphasis away from growth and toward protecting people.

Through all of this there is a more remarkable thread that ties together these diverse stories: the greater the risk, the more harsh the adversity, and the more substantial the challenge, the more durable Chicagoans became.

Notes

Abbreviations

AABN	*American Architect and Building News*
AR	*Annual Report*
CA	*Chicago American*
CC	*Chicago Chronicle*
CCCD	Chicago Common Council Documents
CCCP	Chicago City Council, *Proceedings*
CD	*Chicago Democrat*
CDA	*Chicago Daily American*
CDD	*Chicago Daily Democrat*
CDDP	*Chicago Daily Democratic Press*
CDJ	*Chicago Daily Journal*
CDN	*Chicago Daily News*
CG	*Chicago Globe*
CH	*Chicago Herald*
CHi	*Chicago History*
CHS	Chicago Historical Society
CI-O	*Chicago Inter-Ocean*
CJ	*Chicago Journal*
CM	*Chicago Mail*
CP	*Chicago Post*
CPM	*Chicago Post and Mail*
CPT	*Chicago Press and Tribune*
CR	*Chicago Record*
CR-H	*Chicago Record-Herald*
CS	*Chicago Sun*
CS-T	*Chicago Sun-Times*

CT-H	*Chicago Times-Herald*
CTi	*Chicago Times*
CTo	*Chicago Today*
CTr	*Chicago Tribune*
DCA	*Daily Chicago American*
Econ	*Economist*
IRAD	Illinois Regional Archives Depository
ISA	Illinois State Archives
JISHS	*Journal of the Illinois State Historical Society*
LDC	*Lakeside Directory of Chicago*
NEIU	Northeastern Illinois University
NU	Northwestern University
NYT	*New York Times*
REBJ	*Real Estate and Building Journal*
UC	University of Chicago
UIC	University of Illinois at Chicago
WCD	*Weekly Chicago Democrat*

Introduction

1. Most recently, see Donald Miller, *City of the Century: The Epic of Chicago and the Making of America* (New York: Simon and Schuster, 1996).

Chapter 1: Coping with a New Sense of Place

1. *CTr*, Dec. 26, 1897.

2. The classic studies are: Homer Hoyt, *One Hundred Years of Land Values in the City of Chicago* (Chicago: University of Chicago Press, 1933); Earl Shepard Johnson, "The Natural History of the Central Business District with Particular Reference to Chicago" (Ph.D. diss., University of Chicago, 1941); and Harold M. Mayer and Richard C. Wade, *Chicago: Growth of a Metropolis* (Chicago: University of Chicago Press, 1969).

3. I was the first to state the concept of the semipublic space, in "The Saloon and the Public City: Chicago and Boston, 1880–1920" (Ph.D. diss., University of Chicago, 1975), and in "Whose City? Public and Private Spaces in Nineteenth-Century Chicago," *CHi* 12 (Spring 1983): 2–17, and "Whose City? Part Two," ibid. (Summer 1983): 2–23. The idea appeared later as a theme in Steven A. Riess, *City Games: The Evolution of American Urban Society and the Rise of Sports* (Urbana: University of Illinois Press, 1989).

4. *CH*, Jan. 30, 1887; Bessie Louise Pierce, *A History of Chicago* (New York: Knopf, 1937), 1:46.

5. Docs. 1833/154–59, 165, 171; 1835/165, 175–89, 190–95, 197, 201, 203–6, 209–10, 214–23, 227, 229, 232, 234, 236, both in CCCD Collection, IRAD, NEIU.

6. Ibid., 1837/282, 285, 375, 413; 1838/694; 1842/1411. On problems of Mark Beaubien, who was forced to move a building, see Jacqueline Peterson, "The Founding Fathers: The Absorption of French-Indian Chicago, 1816–1837," in *Ethnic Chicago: A Multi-Cultural Portrait,* ed. Melvin G. Holli and Peter D'A. Jones, 4th ed. (Grand Rapids: Eerdmans, 1995), 50.

7. The most perceptive new study of street space is Clay McShane, *Down the Asphalt Path: The Automobile and the American City* (New York: Columbia University Press, 1994); the most useful sources on this topic are G. Koehler, "Annals of Health and Sanitation in Chicago," in Chicago Department of Health, *Report and Handbook of the Department of Health, 1911–18,* 1461–1524 (the quotation in the paragraph is from p. 1467), and Constance Bell Webb, *A History of Contagious Disease Care in Chicago before the Great Fire* (Chicago: University of Chicago Press, 1940), 31–32, 39–40.

8. Docs. 1837/393, 410; 1838/528; 1839/738; 1840/884, CCCD Collection, IRAD, NEIU; *CA*, Sept. 10, 1836, Apr. 13, 1839, Feb. 20, 1841; *CD*, Sept. 12, 1836, Aug. 24, 1842.

9. Docs. 1840/943, 957, 959; 1844/2168, CCCD Collection, IRAD, NEIU; *CD*, Aug. 17, 1836, Nov. 20, 1844. For a history of early paving, see Chicago Department of Public Works, *AR, 1882*, 32–41.

10. Chicago Department of Public Works, *AR, 1882*, 41–42; doc. 1843/775, 181, CCCD Collection, IRAD, NEIU.

11. *CD*, June 18, 1834; the principle of limited or extended responsibility for local government is the central theme of Robin Einhorn, *Property Rules: Political Economy in Chicago, 1833–1872* (Chicago: University of Chicago Press, 1991).

12. Erne Rene Frueh, "Retail Merchandising in Chicago, 1833–48," *JISHS* 32 (June 1939): 149–72.

13. *CD*, Oct. 28, 1845, May 24, 1852; *CTr*, Dec. 4, 1865; "Chicago Reminiscences," *Bonfort's Wine and Spirit Circular* 67 (Mar. 10, 1907): 512–18.

14. "John Ellis Clark, Chicago's Old Town Crier," unidentified clipping, c. 1901, Clipping File, CHS.

15. A. T. Andreas, *History of Chicago*, 3 vols. (Chicago: A. T. Andreas, 1885), 2:90, describes the arrival of the first fire engine, Feb. 5, 1858; on Independence Day fireworks, *CDD*, June 29, 1849, June 26, 1850, June 25, 1852, July 6, 1855.

16. Petitions on behalf of Schoneker contained many names from the German community; see, for example, docs. 1837/288, 1838/667, 1839/874, CCCD Collection, IRAD, NEIU.

17. Bessie L. Pierce, *A History of Chicago* (New York: Knopf, 1940), 2:5.

18. "The Crossing Sweeper" (Chicago: Root and Cady, 1868) is a maudlin tune about street children of the era; there are many sidewalk complaints in the pre-Fire Common Council documents, CCCD Collection, IRAD, NEIU. See also, *CDD*, July 25, 1850; *CDDP*, Apr. 16, 1855; *CPT*, Mar. 29, 1859.

19. *CD*, Oct. 7, 1835; "The 'Nicholson Pavement,'" *Ballou's Pictorial Drawing-Room Companion* 17 (Oct. 15, 1859): 253; "Nicholson Paving Blocks," unidentified clipping, c. 1910, Clipping File, CHS; *Wooden Pavements: Their Utility in Streets of Larger Cities* (Chicago: Northwestern Stafford Paving Co., 1869); Joseph Matousek, "History of the Development of Chicago Pavements" (M.S. thesis, University of Illinois, 1905), 1; *American Builder* 1 (Apr. 1869): 110–11; ibid. (Aug. 1869): 163–64; *AABN* 4 (Sept. 28, 1878): 110–11.

20. Louis Cain, *Sanitation Strategy for a Lakefront Metropolis* (DeKalb: Northern Illinois University Press, 1978), 20–36; "Up from the Mud: An Account of How Chicago's Streets and Buildings Were Raised," mimeographed report carried out under Works Progress Administration, 1941, CHS; see also the twenty-two part series "Chicago Sewage" in *Sanitary News* 1 (Apr. 15, 1883): 137–38, through ibid. 3 (Mar. 15, 1884): 122.

21. *CDJ*, Oct. 20, 1849, May 28, July 31, Aug. 26, Sept. 5, 6, 1850; *CDD*, Sept. 5, 6, 9, 1850, Jan. 16, 1851; *WCD*, Sept. 7, 1850; *CDDP*, July 1, 1854.

22. *Rules and Ordinances of the Department of Electricity of the City of Chicago* (Chicago: Halliday Witherspoon, 1900), 91–105; J. P. Barrett, *Electricity at the World's Columbian Exposition* (Chicago: R. R. Donnelley, 1894), 351–65; undated *CI-O* clipping, Harpel Scrapbook, H2S4–5, pp. 155–56, CHS.

23. Pierce, *History of Chicago*, 2:321–22; there are dozens of pre-Fire bridge references in CCCD Collection, IRAD, NEIU.

24. Chicago Board of Public Works, *AR, 1865*, 27, *AR, 1866*, 34, *AR, 1869*, 3.

25. Advertisement for expertise in docs. 54/55 0498A, 1053A, 1426A, CCCD Collection, IRAD, NEIU; *History of the Chicago River Tunnel at Washington Street* (Chicago: J. M. Wing, 1869). On the tunnels in general, see *CH*, June 20, 1886, and William Artingstall, "Chicago River Tunnels—Their History and Method of Construction," *Journal of the Western Society of Engineers* 16 (Nov. 1911): 869–921.

26. *CTi*, Feb. 2, May 13, 1870; *CJ*, Mar. 5, Apr. 15, 1870; *CTr*, Feb. 24, 1870, May 5, 1871.

27. Statistics from *CDD*, June 21, 1851; ibid., Feb. 20, 21, 25, June 29, 1852; *WCD*, June 25, 1853; *CDDP*, Sept. 1, 1854; *CTr*, Apr. 4, 1861.

28. *CTr*, June 30, 1861, Jan. 14, Sept. 30, 1862.

29. *CM*, May 18, 1871; *CI-O*, Oct. 26, 1900. On Dexter Park, *CJ*, Nov. 29, 1897; *CDN*, Jan. 29, 1900.

30. *CDDP*, Aug. 1, 1855 (quote). On equestrianism, *CDD*, Sept. 30, 1851; *CDDP*, Nov. 18, 1856. On later schools and shows, *CTr*, Oct. 22, 1863, Jan. 30, 1866, Jan. 15, Sept. 6, 1868, Aug. 28, Oct. 23, 1870, May 3, June 7, 1896; *CR-H*, Sept. 10, 1905, June 26, 1910.

31. R. David Weber, "Rationalizers and Reformers: Chicago Local Transportation in the Nineteenth Century" (Ph.D. diss., University of Wisconsin, 1971), 10–16, 75–77.

32. On frequent replacement of horses on car lines, *CTi*, Feb. 2, 1874, and Weber, "Rationalizers and Reformers," 83–84.

33. Weber, "Rationalizers and Reformers," 86–89.

34. Ibid., 84–85.

35. *CJ*, May 17, 1859.

36. *Laws and Ordinances Governing the City of Chicago, 1873*, 130–35, 137–46.

37. Franc Wilkie, *Walks about Chicago and Army and Miscellaneous Sketches* (Chicago: Kenney and Sumner, 1869), 9–10.

38. Carter H. Harrison, *Stormy Years: The Autobiography of Carter H. Harrison* (Indianapolis: Bobbs-Merrill, 1935), 18–20.

39. Wilkie, *Walks about Chicago*, 10.

40. Perry R. Duis and Glen E. Holt, "Kate O'Leary's Sad Burden," *Chicago* 27 (Oct. 1978): 220–22, 224.

41. *Laws and Ordinances Governing the City of Chicago, 1890*, 580, 589.

42. Andreas, *History of Chicago*, 2:83, 85.

43. *CTr*, July 29, 1863, Aug. 7, 1865.

44. *CDD*, Feb. 17, 1849 (quote). There are other examples in almost every newspaper, but see especially ibid., Jan. 6, 1849; *WCD*, Mar. 6, 1858; *CPT*, Aug. 6, 1858; *CTr*, Dec. 25, 1864, Feb. 20, 1866.

45. *CD*, Oct. 27, 1846; *CDD*, Mar. 1, July 17, 19, 1849; *CTr*, Feb. 15, 1853, Aug. 12, 1857, July 10, 1861, Jan. 13, 1863.

46. See *CD*, Feb. 7, 1847, for example.

47. *Tricks and Traps of Chicago* (New York: Dinsmore, 1859); *Chicago after Dark* (Chicago: Western News Co., 1868).

48. *CD*, July 15, 1840 (quote); see also, *CDA*, July 13, 1840.

49. Andreas, *History of Chicago*, 2:83–90. John J. Flinn, *History of the Chicago Police from the Earliest Settlement of the Community to the Present Time* (Chicago: W. B. Conkey, 1887), is a detailed uninterpretive account. The most perceptive work remains David R. Johnson, *Policing the Urban Underworld: The Impact of Crime on the Development of the American Police, 1800–1887* (Philadelphia: Temple University Press, 1979).

50. *CTr*, May 27, 1888; *Marquis' Handbook of Chicago* (Chicago: A. N. Marquis, 1885), 73–75.

51. On early church bells, *CD*, Oct. 5, 1845; on municipal clocks, *CTr*, July 3, 1865, Mar. 3, 1870, Jan. 4, July 4, 1871.

52. *CD*, Aug. 5, 1835 (on John Marshall); *CDD*, July 15, 18, 20, 26, 1850 (on Zachary Taylor); ibid., June 30, July 12, 1852 (on Henry Clay); ibid., Nov. 25. 1852 (on Daniel Webster); *CTr*, Apr. 16–20, May 2, 3, 1865 (on Lincoln, who had delivered the Taylor Eulogy in Chicago fifteen years earlier).

53. *Illustrated Chicago News* 1 (May 8, 1868): 34; *CTi*, Dec. 25, 1872; *CPM*, July 27, 1875; *CTr*, Oct. 1, 1879, Jan. 4, 1913; *Rights of Labor* 7 (Mar. 4, 1893): 5.

54. Illinois, *Laws, 1869*, 114–17; see especially Virginia Marciniak, *The Illinois Humane Society, 1869 to 1979* (River Forest, Ill.: Rosary College, 1981), as well as the *AR*s of the organization, which changed its name from the Illinois Society for the Prevention of Cruelty to Animals to the Illinois Humane Society in 1871. On the society's horse ambulance,

see also *CTr*, Dec. 6, 1881. On its fountain, see *CJ*, Sept. 23, 1877; *CTr*, Nov. 27, 1881; and *Newsboys Appeal* 1 (Nov. 1878): 5. On the other anticruelty work of the society, see *CTi*, Mar. 23, 1871, Sept. 20, 1872; *CTr*, Oct. 26, 1872, May 22, Dec. 14, 1873, Feb. 13, 1881, May 5, 1894; *CR-H*, June 5, 1904.

55. Gerald Carson, "In Chicago, Cruelty and Kindness to Animals," *CHi* 3 (Win. 1974–75): 151–58; *CR*, Oct. 16, 1900; *CR-H*, June 5, 1904, May 6, 1906, Jan. 11, 1907; *CTr*, Jan. 4, 12, 1913; Chicago Work Horse Parade Association, *Second Annual Parade, May 30, 1911.*

56. Anthony Platt, *The Child Savers: The Invention of Delinquency* (Chicago: University of Chicago Press, 1969), employs the model.

57. Weber, "Rationalizers and Reformers," 77–82.

58. *CTr*, Feb. 23, 1853 (quote).

59. Daniel Bluestone, *Constructing Chicago* (New Haven: Yale University Press, 1991), deals with the ethos of Chicago's early public buildings and parks; see also Perry R. Duis, "Yesterday's City: Dearborn Park," *CHi* 15 (Winter, 1986–87): 66–69, and Galen Cranz, "Models for Park Usage: Ideology and the Development of Chicago's Public Parks" (Ph.D. diss., University of Chicago, 1971), 11–69.

60. Glen E. Holt, "Private Plans for Public Places: The Origins of Chicago's Park System, 1850–1875," *CHi* 8 (Fall 1979): 173–84.

61. Carl Abbott, "The Location of Railroad Passenger Depots in Chicago and St. Louis," *Bulletin of the Railroad and Locomotive Historical Society* 120 (Apr. 1969): 31–47; George H. Douglas, *Rail City: Chicago USA* (San Diego: Howell-North Books, 1981), 1–59 (this is a popular account); *CTr*, Aug. 13, 1866.

62. *CDD*, Dec. 14, 1850 (quote).

63. *CTi*, Dec. 27, 1891.

64. Ibid.

65. *CTi*, Feb. 25, 1880; *CDN*, Mar. 20, 1900; *CM*, June 28, 1895; *CTr*, Feb. 4, 1894, May 17, 1902.

66. On early livery stables, *CDD*, Jan. 3, 1849, Ledger, 1841, Sauganash Hotel Ms., CHS; *Official Directory of the Carriage and Wagon Manufacturers Association of Chicago, 1900* (Chicago, 1900), 41–55, 57; Chicago Work Horse Parade Association, *Second Annual Parade, May 30, 1911,* passim, for ads. On horse-related industries, see *Lakeside Directory of Chicago, 1895,* 245, 325, 398; *CDN*, Jan. 30, 1895; two undated pamphlets entitled *Chicago Horse Shoe Company* and the "Horseshoeing" Scrapbook, CHS.

67. *CTi*, May 26, 1871.

68. *CI-O*, Sept. 1, 1876.

69. *CCCP*, Nov. 30, 1885, 279; Chicago Real Estate Board, *Call Board Bulletin* 6 (Sept. 1892): 30; *Econ* 13 (Feb. 16, 1895): 183; *CP*, May 13, 14, 1896; *CTr*, May 13–16, 1896.

70. *Journal of the Western Society of Engineers* 21 (Mar. 1916): 265.

71. *CTi*, Nov. 5–21, 1872; Chicago Board of Health, *AR, 1870–73*, 45–47; Adoniram Johnson, "History and Course of the Epizootic among Horses upon the North American Continent in 1872–73," in American Public Health Association, *Reports and Papers, 1873*, 88–109; *CI-O*, Oct. 7, 1875.

72. Weber, "Rationalizers and Reformers," 92–95.

73. Ibid., 93.

74. Ibid., 125–27.

75. Ibid.

76. Ibid., 100–102.

77. Ibid., 105–6.

78. Ibid., 103–4, 106–9.

79. Flinn, *History of the Chicago Police*, 397–411, on the patrol wagon. Jack Rittenhouse, *American Horse-Drawn Vehicles* (New York: Bonanza Books, 1948), 54–99, and R. F. Karlovits, *This Was Trucking* (New York: Bonanza Books, 1966), are useful accounts.

80. *Municipal Code of Chicago, 1881,* 357; Citizens Association of Chicago, *AR, 1882,* 11, *AR, 1885,* 16, *AR, 1886,* 15–16, *AR, 1887,* 18 (on fast driving, specifically).

81. Citizens Association of Chicago, *AR, 1877*, 12, *AR, 1878*, 6–8, *AR, 1879*, 13–15, *AR, 1880*, 7–10, 16–19, *AR, 1881*, 6–13, *AR, 1883*, 8–17.

82. Andreas, *History of Chicago*, 3:600–603, describes the evolution of express companies. For an illustration of a blackboard used as a call box, see Forrest Crissey, *Brink's Incorporated: The Romance of Moving Money* (Chicago: Library of Institutional Biography, 1934), 17.

83. John R. Commons, "Types of American Labor Organizations—The Teamsters of Chicago," *Quarterly Journal of Economics* 19 (May 1905): 400–433.

84. *CDN*, Jan. 4, Feb. 19, Aug. 3, 16, 24, 30, 31, 1906; *CR-H*, Jan. 13, Feb. 16, Aug. 16, 18, 24, 1906; *CTr*, Aug. 5, 31, 1906; *CP*, Nov. 19, 1906.

85. Delos F. Wilcox, *Municipal Franchises* (Chicago: University of Chicago Press, 1910), 1:1–31, 73–99.

86. Robert Woodbury, "William Kent: Progressive Gadfly" (Ph.D. diss., Yale University, 1967), 80–164, gives a sample of the atmosphere, which is discussed in general in Glen E. Holt, "The Changing Perceptions of Urban Pathology: An Essay on the Development of Mass Transit in the United States," in *Cities in American History*, ed. Kenneth T. Jackson and Stanley Schultz (New York: Knopf, 1972), 324–43.

87. The Yerkes story is told in Weber, "Rationalizers and Reformers," 225–354.

88. Sidney I. Roberts, "Businessmen in Revolt: Chicago, 1874–1900" (Ph.D. diss., Northwestern University, 1960), 183–238.

89. *CJ*, Mar. 1, 1890; Artingstall, "Chicago River Tunnels," 869–921.

90. *CDN*, May 4, 1892.

91. *CTr*, May 29, 1881, reported that 54,612 evening commuters left the Loop through tunnels or over bridges to the North or West Sides alone, with 26,950 on foot and the rest in 497 horsecars and 3,839 vehicles; August Gatzert, *Limitation of Building Heights in the City of Chicago* [Chicago, 1913], n.p. (quote).

92. *CTr*, June 5, 1906; Raymond M. McClellan, "Underground Chicago," *Morrison's Chicago Weekly* 2 (Apr. 13, 1909): 16–17.

93. The logic of centralization is the theme of Perry R. Duis, "The Shaping of Chicago," in *AIA Guide to Chicago*, ed. Alice Sinkevitch (New York: Harcourt Brace, 1993), 3–24.

94. *CP*, Dec. 22, 1899 (quote).

95. *CTi*, Dec. 11, 1870, June 10, 1871; *CTr*, Jan. 24, 1880, Jan. 12, 1884, Aug. 14, 1891, Nov. 25, Dec. 14, 1894.

96. "Report on Minors Employed as Messengers by the Chicago Telegraph Company," Mar. 10, 1914, Juvenile Protective Association Papers, Special Collections, UIC.

97. Angus Hibbard, *Hello-Goodbye: My Story of Telephone Pioneering* (Chicago: McClurg, 1941), 179–95; Herbert N. Casson, *The History of the Telephone* (Chicago: McClurg, 1910), 135–40.

98. *CTr*, July 1, 1883, Dec. 24, 28, 1886.

99. Bruce Moffat, *The "L": The Development of Chicago's Rapid Transit System, 1888–1932*, Bulletin 131 (Chicago: Central Electric Railfans, 1995), 14–19

100. *CTi*, Jan. 5, Dec. 14, 1892; *CP*, Jan. 13, 1894; *Econ*, 10 (Dec. 9, 1893): 609; ibid. 11 (Jan. 20, 1894): 68–70; ibid. 11 (Jan. 27, 1894): 95; ibid. 12 (Dec. 15, 1895): 659; ibid. 13 (Jan. 19, 1895): 73; ibid. 29 (Mar. 28, 1903): 413–14.

101. *CR-H*, May 2, 1901.

102. For example, *AABN* 8 (Aug. 14, 1880): 73; ibid. 9 (June 25, 1881): 301–2; ibid. 11 (June 3, 1882): 253; unidentified clippings, Zebina Eastman Scrapbooks, CHS; "The Hannah Railway" (1888), a handbill reproduced in Perry R. Duis, "Whose City? Part Two," *CHi* 12 (Summer 1983): 14; Moffat, *The "L*," 9–10, 55–56.

103. Weber, "Rationalizers and Reformers," 90–91; Moffat, *The "L*," 22–36.

104. Moffat, *The "L*," 166–85.

105. *CJ*, Aug. 28, 1894.

106. Moffat, *The "L*," 31, 38.

107. Woodbury, "William Kent," 80–106; Roberts, "Businessmen in Revolt," 183–238;

Paul F. Barrett, *The Automobile and Urban Transit: The Formation of Public Policy in Chicago, 1900–1930* (Philadelphia: Temple University Press, 1983), 16–21.

108. Charles K. Mohler, *Report on the Union Elevated Railroad of Chicago* (Chicago: By the author, 1907).

109. Elevated cars fell on June 20, 1896, Apr. 7, 1908, and Jan. 8, 1913, with no loss of life (Moffat, *The "L,"* 42, 77, 109); however, thirteen were killed when cars fell in the Loop during rush hour in Feb. 1977. Barrett, *Automobile and Urban Transit,* 10–12, describes an el fatality and the public reaction.

110. *Rules and Ordinances of the Department of Electricity,* 109–18.

111. Bruce Moffat, *Forty Feet Below: The Story of Chicago's Freight Tunnels* (Glendale, Calif.: Interurban Press, 1982); *Lifting the Lid in the Loop: Forty Feet Under* (Chicago: Chicago Tunnel Co., 1915); *The Chicago Freight Tunnels* (Chicago: Chicago Tunnel Terminal Corp., [1928]); Chicago, Commissioner of Public Works, *Report on the Tunnels of the Illinois Tunnel Company* (Chicago: City of Chicago, 1905), 1–14; George W. Jackson, "Freight Tunnels in Chicago," *The Independent* 57 (Nov. 3, 1904): 1018–22; *Rules and Ordinances of the Department of Electricity,* 199–207.

112. The railroad plan is described in *CTr,* June 26, 1881; on the newspaper tubes, see Horace Thompson Carpenter, "The Associated Press," *The Midland Monthly* 4 (Oct. 1895): 302–5; *CTr,* Jan. 18, 1979.

113. Charles U. Gordon, *Reports on Pneumatic Tube Service* (Chicago: Postmaster of Chicago, 1898); Carl Scheele, *A Short History of the Mail Service* (Washington, D.C.: Smithsonian Institution Press, 1970), 131–35.

114. Glen E. Holt, "Will Chicago's Itinerant City Hall Be Moved Once More?" *CHi* 6 (Fall 1977): 155–66.

115. See Carl Condit, *The Chicago School of Architecture: A History of Commercial and Public Buildings in the Chicago Area, 1875–1925* (Chicago: University of Chicago Press, 1964), on the commercial orientation of Chicago architectural talent.

116. *The Palmer House Illustrated* (Chicago: J. M. Wing, 1876), 12 (quote); "The Grand Pacific Hotel," *Chicago* 3 (Dec. 1874): 130–31; *The Leland Hotel Illustrated* (Chicago: n.p., n.d.); *CTr,* Nov. 9, 1873, Feb. 2, 1874; *CDN,* Jan 7, 1884, Mar. 30, 1888.

117. On Chicago department stores in general, see Lloyd Wendt and Herman Kogan, *Give the Lady What She Wants: The Story of Marshall Field and Company* (Indianapolis: Bobbs-Merrill, 1952); Joseph Siry, *Carson Pirie Scott: Louis Sullivan and the Chicago Department Store* (Chicago: University of Chicago Press, 1988); Neil Harris, "Shopping—Chicago Style," in *Chicago Architecture, 1872–1922,* ed. John Zukowsky (Munich: Prestel Verlag, 1987), 137–56.

118. *CTr,* June 15, 1877.

119. Douglas, *Rail City,* 32–37, 95–148.

120. E. S. Hand, *Auditorium* (Chicago: E. S. Hand, 1890), 25 (quote).

121. Dankmar Adler, "The Chicago Auditorium," *Architectural Record* 1 (Apr.–June 1892): 416–34; clippings, Harpel Scrapbook, S4-11, pp. 260–63, and S4-13, pp. 32–33, CHS.

122. Walter A. Wycoff, *The Workers: The West* (New York: Charles Scribner's Sons, 1898), 1–287, relates numerous instances of being denied entry to various stores, hotels, restaurants, and other businesses because of his unkempt appearance; Chicago Police Department annual reports regularly listed out-of-town fugitives apprehended, many at railway stations.

123. On the saloon in general, see Duis, *The Saloon.*

124. Perry Duis, "Yesterday's City: Elevators," *CHi* 16 (Summer 1987): 64–72.

125. Earl R. Beckner, *A History of Labor Legislation in Illinois* (Chicago: University of Chicago Press, 1929), 223–82.

126. On the trolley's replacing horses, see *CTr,* Oct. 7, 1894; *CJ,* June 5, 1895; *CP,* May 16, 1895.

127. "Pneumatic Tube Service," typescript, CHS.

128. "Close the LaSalle Street Tunnel," unidentified clipping, Clipping File, CHS; on the Van Buren tunnel, *CDN,* Aug. 31, 1938; on the Washington Street tunnel, see Chica-

go Department of Public Works, Division of Bridges and Viaducts, "History of the Washington Street Tunnel," typescript, CHS, and *CDN*, Feb. 5, 1954.

129. Moffat, *Forty Feet Below*, 55–71.

130. *CDN*, Aug. 3, 1940; A. A. Dornfeld, *"Hello Sweetheart, Get Me Rewrite!" The Story of the City News Bureau* (Chicago: Academy Chicago, 1983), 61.

131. David H. Cherry, "When Private Went Public" (M.A. thesis, University of Illinois at Chicago, 1992), tells the story of transit, from 1925 to the creation of the Chicago Transit Authority in 1946.

Chapter 2: Counting Minutes and Miles

1. *CTr*, Feb. 9, 10, 1890. Most accounts give the time of death as after midnight, but the official date of death is February 8, or before midnight. The floor plan and other details of the Snell house are given in "Residence of A. J. Snell, Esq., Chicago," *The American Builder and Journal of Art* 3 (May 1870): 106–7.

2. *CTr*, Feb. 9–14, 1890.

3. Details from file, "Snell, A. J.," Clipping File, CHS, and especially *CTr*, Feb. 9, Nov. 6, 1913, and *CDN*, May 20, 1944; on a Tascott sighting, *CTr*, July 1, 1888.

4. Carl Abbott, "The Plank Road Enthusiasm in the Antebellum Midwest," *Indiana Magazine of History* 67 (June 1971): 95–116.

5. Some newspaper accounts gave the date of purchase as 1865, but Snell v. City of Chicago, 133 Ill. 14 (1890), gives it as August 6, 1870.

6. *CTr*, May 1, 3, 6, 7, 15, 17, 1890. Alfred Bull, *The Township of Jefferson and "Dinner Pail Avenue"* (Chicago: Alfred Bull, 1911), 44, has an illustration of the burned gates. In 1894, the U.S. Supreme Court reaffirmed the Illinois decision; this is described in *CTr*, Mar. 6, 1894.

7. *CJ*, Feb. 2, 1886.

8. Robert J. Casey and W. A. S. Douglas, *Pioneer Railroad: The Story of the Chicago and North Western System* (New York: Whittlesey House, 1948), 276–77; *WCD*, Dec. 1, 1849; *CDDP*, June 10, 1854; *CTr*, Jan. 27, 1883. On the general background of the railroad, see H. Roger Grant, *The North Western: A History of the Chicago and North Western System* (DeKalb: Northern Illinois University Press, 1996).

9. Andreas, *History of Chicago*, 1:255; *CPT*, Dec. 16, 1858, Apr. 9, July 20, 1859; *CDDP*, Sept. 4, 1856; *CM*, Jan. 26, 1871.

10. *CTr*, May 18, 1884, Aug. 5, 1894; Bion J. Arnold, *Report on the Re-arrangement and Development of the Steam Railroad Terminals of the City of Chicago* (Chicago: Citizens' Terminal Plan Committee of Chicago, 1913), 236. Locomotive power limitations meant short trains averaging only 4.3 cars each.

11. *CI-O*, Mar. 14, 23, Apr. 25, 1876.

12. Ibid., Mar. 14, 1876.

13. *CTi*, Jan. 17, 1871; *CM*, Jan. 26, 1871; *CTr*, June 13, 1877.

14. *CTr*, Jan. 7, 1883.

15. Ibid., Jan. 5, 1888.

16. Ibid., Jan. 7, 1883.

17. Ibid. (both quotes); baggage discontinuance described in ibid., June 24, 1881.

18. *CTi*, June 22, 1870; *CM*, Jan. 31, Mar. 31, 1871; *CPM*, Jan. 5, 1875.

19. *CTr*, Apr. 8, 1877; *CTi*, Apr. 13, 1877; Illinois, *Laws, 1877*, July 1, 1877, 65. On litigation in Lake View, *CTr*, Jan. 8, Feb. 1, 1888, Feb. 16, Mar. 9, 11, 14, 1890; *Railway Age* 15 (Apr. 5, 1890): 232.

20. *CP*, Jan. 1, 1878; *CTr*, Aug. 2, 3, Sept. 16, 1881.

21. *CTr*, Oct. 5, 1881, Aug. 25, Sept. 17, 1882, Feb. 10, Mar. 1, Dec. 30, 1883.

22. *CTr*, Jan. 8, Feb. 1, 1888, Feb. 16, Mar. 9, 11, 14, 1890; *Railroad Gazette* 15 (Apr. 5, 1890): 232. Ultimately, the Evanston Division of the Milwaukee Road was divided into two parts. The portion south of Lawrence Avenue remained a grade-level freight-only line that served light industry along its route. It is no longer used, though portions of its track

are still extant. The grade of the section north of Lawrence Avenue was elevated and in 1908 it became part of the Northwestern Elevated Railway. It is presently the portion of the Howard and Evanston routes of the Chicago Transit Authority from Lawrence Avenue to Linden Street in Wilmette. *Railroad Gazette* 13 (Aug. 31, 1900): 159; Moffat, *The "L,"* 206, 208-14.

23. *CTi*, Feb. 16, 1892, Feb. 24, 1893; *CP*, Sept. 22, 1892; *The Vanguard*, Jan. 1, 7, 21, 1893; *CR*, Jan. 2, 1896; *CTr*, Apr. 30, 1897; *Railway Age* 26 (Dec. 2, 1898): 872.

24. *CTr*, Jan. 7, 1883.

25. *CPM*, Mar. 16, 1876; *Skandinaven*, May 11, 1883; a more favorable view of Illinois Central service is *CTr*, Dec. 19, 1880.

26. George Ade, "The Search for 'Mother's Cooking,'" *CR*, Mar. 8, 1894, and idem, "The Suburban Resident," ibid., July 24, 1894; Casey and Douglas, *Pioneer Railroad*, 277; unidentified clipping, "Pouring into Chicago," Harpel Scrapbook, HS4-13, p. 70, CHS.

27. *Chicago Illustrated Journal* 1 (Mar. 1873): 56.

28. *Railroad Gazette* 14 (Jan. 27, 1882): 53; *Railway Review* 30 (Mar. 15, 1890): 152. However, the *Railway Review* 31 (Feb. 21, 1891): 121-22, noted the counterargument that the suburban railways lacked the money-losing diners, lounge cars, sleeping cars, baggage operations, "foreign" ticket commissions, advertising, and station expenses.

29. *CJ*, Sept. 22, 1877, Mar. 17, 1880; *CTr*, July 10, 1879, May 13, 14, 1880, July 19, 1881.

30. *CI-O*, Sept. 25, 1897; *CP*, Apr. 9, 1895. On the example of C&NW and the narrow gauge Chicago-Maywood steam dummy, *CI-O*, Aug. 4, 1874; *CTr*, Apr. 4, 1881; *CTi*, Oct. 2, 1881; *CR*, Dec. 5, 1895. On the Rock Island–C&NP competition, *CT-H*, June 9, July 14, 1896.

31. *CTr*, July 11, 1895, Mar. 27, 1897; *CT-H*, Nov. 25, 1895.

32. *CR*, Aug. 3, 1900.

33. Editors of *Automobile Quarterly, The American Car since 1775* (L. Scott Brady-E. P. Dutton, 1971), 48-49, 64-67.

34. Charles B. King, *A Golden Anniversary, 1895-1945: Personal Sidelights of America's First Auto Race* (New York: Charles B. King, 1945); *CT-H*, Nov. 29-30, 1895; George S. May, "The Thanksgiving Day Race of 1895," *CHi* 11 (Fall-Winter 1983): 175-83.

35. On 1901 auto show, "Auto Show Sets New Precedent," *Fort Dearborn Magazine* 1 (Feb. 1920): 12-13. There were several claimants to the title of "first auto show." On subsequent shows, see *CJ*, Jan. 7, Sept. 25, 1899; *CTr*, Sept. 26, 1899, Feb. 19, 1950; *CI-O*, Sept. 26, 1899, Sept. 18, 1900; *CR-H*, Mar. 2, 1902, Feb. 14, 1903, Feb. 7, 1904, Feb. 2, 1906, Feb. 5, 1910.

36. On Charles Coey, unidentified clipping, Nov. 15, 1953, Clipping File, CHS; *CR-H* July 4, 1906; *Charles A. Coey School of Motoring* (n.p., n.d.).

37. *CR-H*, July 30, 1903.

38. Barrett, *Automobile and Urban Transit*, 58-61; McShane, *Down the Asphalt Path*, 31-33.

39. *CI-O*, Sept. 7, 1900; *CR-H*, Apr. 6, 1912; Chicago Board of Operators of Automobiles, *AR, 1900*, 10; see also, Virginia Scharff, *Taking the Wheel: Women and the Coming of the Motor Age* (New York: Free Press, 1991).

40. *Chicago* 1 (Sept. 1899): 1; *CR-H*, Nov. 28, 1901.

41. Chicago Department of Health, *AR, 1900*, lists 5,122 dead horses picked up; the numbers over the next fifteen years fluctuate between a low of 4,157 in 1905 and a high of 8,083 in 1914.

42. *CTr*, June 11, 1899.

43. "Editorial: Sanitation in Public Conveyances," *Chicago Medical Record* 1 (Mar. 1891): 67-68, notes that a density of 64 people in a 1,500-square-foot trolley car provided less that 25 square feet per person, in addition to the problems of contagion and dust in the upholstery.

44. *CTr*, June 11, 1899; *CDN*, Jan. 4, 1900; *CR*, Mar. 7, 1901.

45. *CHi* 2 (Winter 1949-50): 170; *Motor Age* 1 (Dec. 28, 1899): 317-18.

46. John Harvey Kellogg, "Dangers in Gasoline," Michigan Board of Health, *AR, 1887*, 24-28.

47. On calls for licensing, *CP,* June 28, 1899; *CDN,* July 1, 1899. *CI-O,* Apr. 11, 1900, says the first auto fatality was Richard Kinney.

48. *CCCP,* July 6, 1899, 944–47.

49. *Illinois Staats-Zeitung,* Feb. 10, 1900; *Joliet Daily Republican,* Oct. 30, 1900; *CI-O,* Feb. 17, 1900.

50. *CR-H,* May 16, 1902.

51. Ibid., Dec. 9–11, 1902.

52. *CCCP,* May 25, 1903, 321–22, Jan. 18, 1904, 2043; *CTr,* May 28, 1903.

53. *CR-H,* Dec. 10–11, 1902 (quotes).

54. Ibid., Apr. 17, 1903.

55. *CTr,* July 30, 1903; *CR-H,* July 30, Sept. 20, 1903; for the larger context of Chicago v. Banker, 112 Ill. App. 94., see McShane, *Down the Asphalt Path,* 118–19.

56. *CR-H,* May 28, 1903.

57. *CCCP,* July 11, 1904, 922–26

58. *CR-H,* Oct. 9, 1904.

59. Ibid., Oct. 19, 1904 (quote).

60. On the Farson chase, ibid., Oct. 19, 22, 1904.

61. *CTr,* Aug. 25, 1906, cited in Barrett, *Automobile and Urban Transit,* 60.

62. *CI-O,* Apr. 11, 1900; Frederick S. Crum, "Street Traffic Accidents," *Journal of the American Statistical Association,* n.s. 103 (Sept. 1913): 473–528; Horace Secrist, "Automobile, Motor Truck, and Motor-Cycle Accidents in Chicago," ibid. 16 (Dec. 1919): 512–32.

63. *CR-H,* June 12, 1905.

64. Ibid., Oct. 19, 1905.

65. Ibid., Oct. 19, 25–27, 1905.

66. Ibid., Oct. 25, 1905; *CTr,* Oct. 19, 1905.

67. *CR-H,* Aug. 18, 1906.

68. *CCCP,* Feb. 3, 1908, 3829–30.

69. Ibid., Dec. 18, 1911, 2053–54, acknowledges the state's right to license, but asks that the license fee be collected only on change of ownership, not annually. The state ignored the request. *CCCP,* May 20, 1912, 380–81, abolishes the city's Board of Public Vehicle Registry and turns over the task to police.

70. *CCCP,* Apr. 26, 1915, reproduces corporation counsel opinion on effect of the ruling, City of Lincoln v. Dehner (#9972).

71. In 1907, car owners numbered 3,733, versus 77,141 horses, according to Chicago, Department of Public Works, *AR, 1907,* 404–7.

72. *CCCP,* Nov. 11, 1911.

73. *CTr,* July 16, 1914; *Popular Mechanics* 20 (Oct. 1913): 559.

74. James A. Durkin, *The Auto Bandits of Chicago* (Chicago: Charles C. Thompson Co., 1913); there are also many other auto-related robberies, reported with great detail in *CR-H,* beginning in late August 1912.

75. *CJ,* May 8, 15, Dec. 31, 1895.

76. Ibid., Jan. 28, 1899.

77. *CT-H,* Nov. 2, 1894; *CI-O,* Aug. 14, 1899; *Evanston Index,* Aug. 24, 1912.

78. Chicago Department of Public Works, *AR, 1907,* 404, put the number at 77,141 horses, and reported also that there were 61,392 horsedrawn vehicles and 3,733 horseless vehicles.

79. *CR-H,* July 22, 1910.

80. *Proof for City Transportation Users Covering the Economy of the Short Haul* (Chicago: Horse Association of America, 1920), one of a number of pamphlets in CHS; Horse Association of America, *Proceedings of the First Annual Meeting, December 1, 1920.*

81. *CS-T,* Oct. 1, 1983.

82. Unidentified stories in file, "Snell, A. J.," Clipping File, CHS; *CTr,* June 9, 1943; *CDN,* May 20, 1944; *CS,* May 25, 1944.

Chapter 3: Housing Strategies

1. *CP*, Aug. 18, 21, 22, Sept. 30, 1890.

2. Standard works on local land development and suburbanization include: Ann Durkin Keating, *Building Chicago: Suburban Developers and the Creation of a Divided Metropolis* (Columbus: Ohio State University Press, 1988); Michael Ebner, *Creating Chicago's North Shore: A Suburban History* (Chicago: University of Chicago Press, 1988); Hoyt, *One Hundred Years of Land Values in Chicago;* Carl Abbott, "'Necessary Adjuncts to Its Growth': The Railroad Suburbs of Chicago, 1854–75," *JISHS* 73 (Summer 1980): 117–31. The national context is best found in Kenneth T. Jackson, *Crabgrass Frontier: The Suburbanization of the United States* (New York: Oxford University Press, 1985).

3. Walker Field, "A Reexamination into the Invention of the Balloon Frame," *Journal of the Society of Architectural Historians* 4 (Oct. 1942): 3–29, argues that Augustine Taylor, the first builder in Chicago, may have invented the balloon frame; see also Paul E. Sprague, "Chicago Balloon Frame: The Evolution during the Nineteenth Century of George W. Snow's System for Erecting Light Frame Buildings from Dimension Lumber and Machine-made Nails," in *The Technology of Historic American Buildings: Studies of the Materials, Craft Processes, and Mechanization of Building Construction,* ed. H. Ward Jandl (Washington, D.C.: Foundation for Preservation Technology for the Association for Preservation Technology, 1983), 35–61.

4. *CC*, May 16, 1897.

5. *Tricks and Traps of Chicago,* 43.

6. *CP*, Sept 16, 1890; *CDN*, Sept. 27, Oct. 8, 1890; *CH*, Sept. 28, 1890. Some of these institutions are discussed in chapter 11.

7. *Out of Town: Being a Descriptive, Historical and Statistical Account of the Suburban Towns and Residences of Chicago* (Chicago: Western News Co., 1869).

8. *CDDP*, July 6, 14, 21, 25, 27, Sept. 17, 19, Oct. 23, 25, 1855; U.S. Works Progress Administration, *Historical Register of the Twenty-Two Superseded Park Districts* (Chicago: Chicago Park District and the Works Progress Administration, 1941), 576–78.

9. Illinois, *Laws, 1869,* 1:342, 358–66, 368; *CTr*, Jan. 13, 19, 21, 25, 26, Feb. 2, 7, 9, 10, 13, 24, 28, Mar. 9, 10, 16–20, 22–24, 1869; *The Parks and Property Interests of the City of Chicago* (Chicago: Western News Co., 1869).

10. Chicago Building and Loan Association, *Statistical and Historical Review of Chicago* (Chicago: City Directory Publishing House, 1869), 65–90.

11. On Highland Park see Ebner, *Creating Chicago's North Shore,* 36–37. On Irving Park see *CDDP*, Aug. 4, Oct. 12, 1855; *CTr*, Apr. 22, 1868; *CP*, Sept. 5, 1890.

12. *Facts about Maywood* (Chicago: Proviso Land Association, n.d.); *A Home in Maywood* (Chicago: Proviso Land Association, n.d.); *Maywood and Its Homes* (Maywood: Village of Maywood, 1904).

13. Nicholas Sommers, *The Historic Homes of Wicker Park: A Tour Guide and Sampler* (Chicago: Old Wicker Park Committee, 1978).

14. *CTr*, Apr. 15, 1884.

15. Ibid., Mar. 25, 1900, Mar. 4, 1904.

16. Walter Creese, *The Crowning of the American Landscape: Eight Great Spaces and Their Buildings* (Princeton: Princeton University Press, 1985), 219–40; *Riverside: A Village in a Park* (Riverside, Ill.: Frederick Law Olmsted Society of Riverside, 1970); *American Builder* 1 (Dec. 1869): 228–29; Illinois, *Laws, 1869,* 2:483; *CTr*, Oct. 25, Dec. 6, 1868, Aug. 4, 1871, Feb. 25, 1900.

17. Keating, *Building Chicago,* 74–77; Ebner, *Creating Chicago's North Shore,* 21–42; *CJ*, May 18, 1895; on Bowmanville, a good example of a development with pre-installed amenities, see *CDDP*, Sept. 11, 1855.

18. "Riverside," *Chicago* 2 (Sept. 1871): 238–39.

19. *CP*, Aug. 21, 1890 (quote); ibid., Sept. 4, 8, 10, 12, 16, 26, 1890; Ebner, *Creating Chicago's North Shore,* 54–57.

20. On Edgewater, *CP*, Oct. 4, 7, 12, 1897. On Kenilworth, *CJ*, Sept. 25, 1890; the Kenilworth script logo can be found today on the Metra depot sign. On Downers Grove ad, *CJ*, Oct. 9, 1890.

21. *CP*, Aug. 27, 1890 (Oak Park quote); ibid., Sept. 18, 1890 (Hinsdale quote).

22. Ibid., Aug. 25, 1890 (Evanston quote); ibid., Aug. 27, 1890 (Oak Park quote); on clubs, for example, *CTr*, Feb. 8, 1892.

23. *CP*, Sept. 18, 1890 (quote).

24. On hotels, see Creese, *Crowning of the American Landscape*, 232–35; *Our Suburbs* (Chicago: Blue Island Land and Building Co., 1873), 26–28; *CTr*, Apr. 22, 1868. On summertime enjoyment of suburban living, *CDDP*, Nov. 22, 1854, Nov. 6, 1855; *CPT*, July 20, 1859.

25. On Glen Ellyn, see *CJ*, Sept. 10, 1890; on the Maywood tower, see *Maywood and Its Homes*, 2–4.

26. *Biographical Dictionary and Portrait Galley of Representative Men of Chicago* (Chicago: American Biographical Publishing Co., 1892), 78. Perry R. Duis and Glen E. Holt, "Little Boxes, Big Fortunes," *Chicago* 26 (Nov. 1977): 114–16, 118, was the first modern piece on Gross. The best and most complete recent work on Gross is Emily Clark and Patrick Ashley, "The Merchant Prince of Cornville," *CHi* 21 (Dec. 1992): 4–19.

27. *CTr*, Jan. 22, 1951.

28. S. E. Gross, *Tenth Annual Catalog* (Chicago, 1891), 4–20; on West Grossdale, *CJ*, May 18, 1895, and June 15, 1897; on Hollywood, *CP*, Jan. 27, 1894; *CTi*, Mar. 2, 1894, quotes Gross on Chicago's becoming "a city of houses" and his claim that he had built over seven thousand houses during the previous twelve years.

29. *CTr*, Mar. 1, 1889, discusses Gross's popularity among socialists.

30. Gross's magic worked until the recession of 1907–9 wiped out his five-million-dollar fortune and left him bankrupt. He died a few years later in Michigan (Clark, "The Merchant Prince of Cornville," 18–19). *CTr*, May 26, 1907, describes his flight from process servers.

31. *CG*, Sept. 25, 1890; on McElroy and Kenny, see *CJ*, Oct. 14, 1890; on Englewood on the Hill, *CJ*, July 31, 1890; on McLean, Bierbach, *CP*, Aug. 30, 1890; on Edison Park, *CP*, June 6, 1890; on Gross's Dauphin Park, *CP*, Aug. 29, 1890; on Grossdale, *CP*, Nov. 15, 1890; S. M. Bloss ad appears in *CJ*, Sept. 21, 1890.

32. On Homewood, Canfield, and Turner Park, see A. T. Andreas, *History of Cook County* (Chicago: A. T. Andreas, 1884), 501, 880, 866, respectively; on Riverside, *CP*, Aug. 29, 1890; on the fire at Moreland, which is today part of Austin, *CTr*, May 9–12, 1889.

33. Vivien Palmer Neighborhood Scrapbooks, History of Ravenswood, docs. 22–34, CHS.

34. Duis, *The Saloon*, 213–18.

35. U.S. Bureau of the Census, *Twelfth Census, 1900*, Populations, II, part 2, table 89, clxi–clxiv.

36. George W. Hilton and John F. Due, *The Electric Interurban Railways in America* (Stanford, Calif.: Stanford University Press, 1960), 335–38; on the Illinois Central, *Greater Chicago Magazine* 1 (Aug. 1926), passim. (The suburb of Markham was named for Charles H. Markham, president of the Illinois Central.) On the CA&E and building, ibid. 2 (Dec. 1927): 25, and ibid. 4 (Apr. 1929): 9; on Westchester, ibid. 1 (Oct. 1926): 1, 16–18.

37. United States Bureau of Public Roads and the Cook County Highway Department, *Report of a Study of Highway Traffic and the Highway System of Cook County, Illinois* (Chicago: Cook County Highway Department, 1925), 9–17. *Greater Chicago Magazine* published numerous articles throughout the late 1920s on the subject of highways and housing, but see especially 2 (Oct. 1927): 20, 26, 28, on Avondale Avenue; ibid. 3 (Aug. 1928): 21, on Butterfield Road; and ibid. 3 (Nov. 1928): 11, on North Avenue.

38. *CDN*, Apr. 7, Nov. 3, 1923, May 17, 24, 1924, on golf; on English-style architecture, see articles, ads for Brannigar Brothers' Ivanhoe, *Greater Chicago Magazine* 1 (Apr.–May 1926); on English cottage architecture in suburbia, see ibid. 3 (Aug. 1928): 4, regarding Flossmoor Terrace, and ibid. 2 (Dec. 1927): 12, regarding Midlothian.

39. Daniel J. Prosser, "Chicago and the Bungalow Boom of the 1920s," *CHi* 10 (Summer 1981): 86–95.

40. *Western Citizen,* Apr. 13, 1847 (quote). On New York's moving day, see Kenneth Jackson, ed., *The Encyclopedia of New York City* (New Haven: Yale University Press, 1995), 778–79.

41. *CDD,* Aug. 4, 1849, describes the impact of that year's cholera epidemic on moving patterns.

42. *Econ* 3 (Mar. 21, 1914): 588; *CTr,* Mar. 15, 1861 (quote).

43. On Mayor John Wentworth as permanent hotel resident, *CTi,* Feb. 15, 1874. On residential hotels in general, see Steven M. Davis, "Of the Class Denominated Princely," *CHi* 11 (Spring 1982): 26–36.

44. William Corkran, "Chicago and the Chicago Historical Society," typescript, 45–46, William Corkran MS, CHS. Corkran's career is described in Paul Angle, *The Chicago Historical Society: An Unconventional Chronicle* (Chicago: Rand, McNally, 1956), 37–43.

45. Corkran, "Chicago and the Chicago Historical Society," 59–63.

46. On Prairie Avenue, *CTr,* Jan. 9, Oct. 30, 1898; Robert Pruter, "The Prairie Avenue Section of Chicago: The History and Examination of Its Decline" (M.A. thesis, Roosevelt University, 1976), 44–47. On the Perry Smith residence, unidentified clipping, "Lodgings in a Palace," June 16, 1895, Harpel Scrapbook, S4-3, pp. 169–70, CHS. On the decline of Ashland Avenue, *CDN,* May 12, 1923.

47. George Ade, "The Barclay Lawn Party," in *George Ade, Chicago Stories,* ed. Franklin Meine (1941; rpt., Chicago: Henry Regnery Co., 1963), 195–200; Ade's article originally appeared in the *CR,* July 15, 1896.

48. *CTr,* Dec. 4, 1865, Sept. 19, 1886; Henry Villard, *Memoirs of Henry Villard,* vol. 1 (Boston: Houghton Mifflin, 1904), 23–24; Isaac E. Adams, *Life of Emery A. Storrs* (Chicago: G. L. Howe, 1886), 87–89 (which reprints Storrs's humorous article, "A Chapter on Boarding Houses," from November 1861); George Ade, "His Experience with a Superior Woman," *CR,* Sept. 28, 1894, and "Tale of a Folding Bed," ibid., Feb. 11, 1899.

49. Harvey Zorbaugh, *The Gold Coast and the Slum* (Chicago: University of Chicago Press, 1929), 69–86, remains the classic description of the lonely "dwellers of the furnished room." One good eviction story appears in *CTr,* Feb. 21, 1890.

50. Joanne Meyerowitz, *Women Adrift: Independent Wage Earners in Chicago, 1880–1930* (Chicago: University of Chicago Press, 1988), 70–79, discusses their housing problem.

51. *CTr,* Sept. 1, 4, 8, 14, 16, 17, 21, 1873, Nov. 6, 10, 1883; Duis, *The Saloon,* 192–95.

52. Eleanor Association, "Eleanor Club Five Special: Our First Thirty Years," typescript, CHS; Meyerowitz, *Women Adrift,* 47, 97; *CTr,* May 16, June 15, 1914, Jan. 21, 1915.

53. George Ade, "His Day to Be Miserable," *CR,* Nov. 29, 1894.

54. On the search for a rental house, see *CPT,* Mar. 18, 1859; *CTr,* Apr. 27, 1873, Jan. 3, 1875.

55. *CTr,* Jan. 10, 1875.

56. James B. Runnion, "Our City Homes—What They Are and What They Should Be," *American Builder* 1 (Oct. 1869): 184–86, and idem, "Ideal and Real Homes," ibid. (Dec. 1869): 215–16; *CP,* Oct. 12, 1895, on the move from a boardinghouse to a flat; Duis, *The Saloon,* 205–6; on the apartment in general, C. William Westfall, "From Homes to Towers: A Century of Chicago's Best Hotels and Tall Apartment Buildings," in Zukowsky, *Chicago Architecture, 1872–1922,* 266–89.

57. *CTr,* Jan. 6, 1884.

58. George Ade, "As to Janitor Service," *CR,* Aug. 18, 1898 (quote); *CR-H,* May 17, 1902.

59. *CTr,* Jan 6, 1884; on the fire hazard of flats in general, ibid., Mar. 16, 1883.

60. *CP,* May 1, 1890 (Franklin quote); *CR-H,* Apr. 23, 27, 1909.

61. *CTr,* May 1, 1874, Apr. 30, 1876 (quotes); Edgewater Improvement Association *Bulletin,* Dec. 3, 1910, n.p., Chicago Improvement Association Collection, UC (Edgewater quote); on radicalism, Ira Brown, "Amelioration of Industrial and Middle Classes," in *CTr,* Aug. 4, 1875; on destruction of neighborhoods by apartment dwellers, *CR-H,* May 29, 1904.

62. *CTr*, May 4, 1873, Apr. 30, 1876, May 2, 1888.

63. Frances Glessner, "The Story of a House," typescript prepared by Chicago Architecture Foundation based on the Glessner family journals, CHS; household gods mentioned in *CTr*, Apr. 27, 1873, Apr. 30, 1876.

64. The case is described in George Ade, "The Little Yachts at Van Buren Street," *CR*, Sept. 12, 1894.

65. On dodging debt, *CTr*, May 1, 1874. On landlord organizations, *CTi*, Jan. 18, 1883; *CTr*, May 3, 1896.

66. Duis, *The Saloon*, 120–21.

67. Quotes, in order, from *Daily Drover's Journal*, May 2, 4, 1883, and *CTr*, May 2, 1888.

68. *CTr*, May 27, 1873.

69. Ibid., May 2, 1880 (quote). Other stories, ibid., May 4, 1873; ibid., May 2, 1897; *CP*, May 1, 1896.

70. *CTr*, May 4, 1873, May 1, 1874.

71. Marshall Kirkman, *The Science of Railways* (New York and Chicago: World Railway Publishing Co., 1895), 3:163.

72. *CP*, May 1, 1890, May 1, 1896; *CR-H*, Apr. 30, 1903.

73. *CR-H*, Apr. 23, 27, May 1, 1909, Apr. 18, 28, 29, May 2, 1910.

74. On the amount of household goods in storage, see *The Advance* 59 (May 5, 1910): 549.

75. Martin H. Kennelly, "It All Comes Out on Moving Day," *American Magazine* 112 (Oct. 1931): 60–61, 170, 172. On Kennelly's moving-company career, Perry R. Duis and Glen E. Holt, "The Real Legacy of 'Poor Martin' Kennelly," *Chicago* 27 (July 1978): 162–65; Peter O'Malley, "Mayor Martin H. Kennelly: A Political Biography" (Ph.D. diss., University of Illinois at Chicago, 1980), chap. 1. On his civic image, Arnold Hirsch, "Martin H. Kennelly: The Mugwump and the Machine," in *The Mayors: The Chicago Political Tradition*, rev. ed., ed. Paul M. Green and Melvin G. Holli (Carbondale: Southern Illinois University Press, 1995), 126–43.

76. *CTr*, Mar. 29, 1903.

77. *The Advance* 61 (Mar. 23, 1911): 357.

78. Prosser, "Chicago and the Bungalow Boom," 86–95.

79. *CTr*, May 3, 1920, May 1–5, 7, 8, 10–13, 1921, May 2, 1922.

80. Kennelly, "It All Comes Out on Moving Day," 172.

81. William H. Whyte, *The Organization Man* (New York: Simon and Schuster, 1956); Jane Jacobs, *The Death and Life of the Great American Cities* (New York: Random House, 1961).

Chapter 4: Living in the Inherited City

1. *CTr*, Mar. 4, 1894.

2. *Industrial Chicago: The Building Interests* (Chicago: Goodspeed, 1891), 233–34.

3. *CDJ*, Apr. 24, 1845 (quote); *CDA*, July 9, 1837; doc. 1846/3462, CCCD Collection, IRAD, NEIU.

4. Cain, *Sanitation Strategy*, 20–36; *Industrial Chicago: The Building Interests*, 234–35.

5. Chester Tupper appears in Robert Fergus, *Fergus' Directory of the City of Chicago, 1839* (Chicago: Fergus Printing Co., 1876), 33, while Simmeon appears in later directories; *CDDP*, June 19, July 9, 23, 1856; *CTr*, Feb. 17, 1857; *CPT*, Mar. 29, Apr. 2, 1860; Ellis S. Chesbrough Scrapbook, CHS.

6. *Prairie Farmer* 20 (Sept. 28, 1867): 193 (quote); *Building Materials and Ready Made Houses* (Chicago: Lyman Bridges, 1870); *CTr*, Aug. 7, 1866, Jan. 16, 1872; *CTi*, Apr. 28, 1883; *Chicago Commerce, Manufactures, Banking, and Transportation Facilities* (Chicago: S. Ferd. Howe and Co., 1884), 180–82.

7. Christine Rosen, *The Limits of Power: Great Fires and the Process of City Growth in America* (Cambridge: Cambridge University Press, 1986), 98–101.

8. *CTi*, June 11, 1871, Dec. 14, 1872.

9. *CDN,* Dec. 6, 1902 (quote); other examples, *CTr,* Sept. 14, 1891, *CDN,* May 27, 1891.

10. *CTr,* Apr. 23, 1871; *Chicago Dispatch,* June 28, 1893.

11. *CTr,* July 7, 1886; undated *CH,* July 1889, clipping, Harpel Scrapbook, H2S4-16, pp. 129-31, CHS; *Industrial Chicago: The Building Interests,* 234.

12. Chicago Department of Public Works, *ARs,* 1883-1908, give statistics on numbers of permits.

13. Undated *CH,* July 1889 clipping, Harpel Scrapbook, H2S4-16, pp. 129-31, CHS; *Industrial Chicago: The Building Interests,* 235-36; *CTr,* Dec. 19, 1892.

14. *CJ,* Mar. 6, 25, 1891.

15. *H. Sheeler Company* (n.p., n.d.); [Harvey Sheeler], *Modern House Moving and Shoring* (Chicago, [1896]), pamphlets, CHS.

16. Original Ashland Block described and illustrated in *Land-Owner* 4 (Aug. 1872): 125, 130; *CI-O,* Oct. 29, 1892; *REBJ* 39 (Jan. 6, 1906): 5; Frank A. Randall, *History of the Development of Building Construction in Chicago* (Urbana: University of Illinois Press, 1949), 131, 136; *Rand, McNally and Company's Bird's-Eye Views and Guide to Chicago* (Chicago: Rand, McNally, 1898), 89-90, 116-17, 136; unidentified clipping, "Ashland Block Must Go," Harpel Scrapbook, H2S4-15, p. 53, CHS.

17. In 1896 the aldermen passed a law allowing house movers to cut the wires that had not been relocated by their owners (the utility companies or the city), who then shouldered the responsibility for reattachment. Mayor George Swift vetoed the bill. *CCCP,* May 25, 1896, 282, June 1, 1896, 304.

18. *CJ,* Mar. 7, 8, 1895; *Illinois Staats-Zeitung,* June 23, 1887; on moving houses by river, *CI-O,* July 22, 1891, *CT-H,* Mar. 28, 1895, *CJ,* Mar. 27, 1895.

19. Rev. Msgr. Harry C. Koenig, *A History of the Parishes of the Archdiocese of Chicago,* (Chicago: The Archdiocese of Chicago, 1980), 1:285, 704.

20. *Industrial Chicago: The Building Interests,* 66 (quote).

21. The best general source on the island up to the Depression is Charles S. Winslow, "Historic Goose Island," typescript, 1931, CHS; see also *CDN,* Mar. 26, 1930, Oct. 21, 1938, Nov. 11, 1962.

22. *CTr,* Apr. 12, 1886; *CDN,* June 22, 1939; Winslow, "Historic Goose Island," 4-5.

23. Winslow, "Historic Goose Island," 6-10.

24. Vivien Palmer, "Study of the Development of Chicago's Northside," typescript, 1932, CHS, 63-65.

25. *CTr,* Apr. 12, 1886.

26. *CDDP,* May 28, 1855.

27. Ibid. (quote); *CTr,* Mar. 1, 1861, July 29, 1863, Aug. 7, 1865; Wilbur F. Storey to Mr. Olinger, Nov. 24, 1871, Miscellaneous Ms. Collection, CHS.

28. Quote on "Paddies," William Butler Ogden to Henry Lanabee, Mar. 6, 1838, Letterbooks, I, 117, Ogden Papers, CHS. On the Ogden Canal, *Illinois Staats-Zeitung,* Mar. 13, 1871; *CJ,* Aug. 29, 1872; Winslow, "Historic Goose Island," 11-12.

29. Keith McClellan, "A History of Chicago's Industrial Development," in Center for Urban Studies, University of Chicago, *Mid-Chicago Economic Development Study* (Chicago: Mayor's Committee for Economic and Cultural Development, 1966), 3:3-7; Charles Cleaver, *Reminiscences of Chicago during the Forties and Fifties* (Chicago: Lakeside Press, 1913), 59-64.

30. *Illustrated History of Chicago* (Chicago: Chicago Herald and Examiner, 1887), 47, 69; Charles Longenecker, "A Pioneer Plant Both in Time and in Practice," *Blast Furnace and Steel Plant* 23 (Aug. 1938): 6.

31. *CT-H,* Dec. 8, 1895; Winslow, "Historic Goose Island," 13-14; nineteenth-century writers applied the term "Little Hell" to the district between Larabee Street and the river, areas near the gas plant, including Goose Island. June Sawyers, *Chicago Chronicles* (Chicago: Loyola University Press, 1996), uses the term only in reference to the island, reflecting an error probably generated by *CTr,* Oct. 20, 1929.

32. *CTr,* Mar. 19, Aug. 22, 1866.

33. *CDD,* Nov. 11, 1852.

34. William K. Beatty, "When Cholera Scourged Chicago," *CH* 11 (Spring 1982): 2–13; on the early housing problem in general, Edith Abbott, *The Tenements of Chicago, 1908–1935* (Chicago: University of Chicago Press, 1936), 8–11.

35. U.S. Immigration Commission, U.S. Senate, 61st Congress, 2d Sess. (1910), Sen. Doc. 338, Part I, p. 249; Robert Hunter, *Tenement Conditions in Chicago* (Chicago: City Homes Association, 1901), 14–24; Abbott, *Tenements of Chicago, 1908–1935,* 190–97.

36. Hunter, *Tenement Conditions in Chicago,* 24–43.

37. Winslow, "Historic Goose Island," 14, 22.

38. Frances Embree, "Housing of the Poor in Chicago," *Journal of Political Economy* 8 (June 1900): 357; *CTr,* Nov. 16, 1871, Jan. 7, 1872, May 18, 1873; Karen Sawislak, *Smoldering City: Chicagoans and the Great Fire, 1871–74* (Chicago: University of Chicago Press, 1995), 81, 94–95, 180–82; Arthur Kinzie, "Fire Statement," typescript, CHS; "Judge Lambert Tree [Fire] Narrative," typescript, CHS.

39. Sawislak, *Smoldering City,* 121–62; Rosen, *Limits of Power,* 95–108.

40. Winslow, "Historic Goose Island," 15–17, 18–26; *CP,* May 10, 1897.

41. Winslow, "Historic Goose Island," 41–42; *CTr,* Aug. 4, 1887.

42. Winslow, "Historic Goose Island," 32–36; *CTr,* Dec. 19, 1897.

43. *CCCP,* Mar. 16, 1874, 131, Apr. 2, 1874, 147, Apr. 20, 1874, 183, June 15, 1875, 231; Illinois, *Laws, 1881,* 155; *CTi,* July 10, 1881; *CTr,* July 10, 1881, Sept. 12, 1884; Citizens Association of Chicago, *AR, 1883,* 28–29, *AR, 1887,* 14–15, *AR, 1888,* 28–29.

44. Chicago Department of Health, *AR, 1881–82,* 30, 47, *AR, 1885,* 78. *Chicago Tribune* reporters accompanied tenement inspectors on their rounds, as described periodically beginning July 1880; see also that paper, Apr. 10, Aug. 7, 1881, Oct. 21, 1882, Feb. 16, June 12, July 8, 1883; see also the series entitled "How the Poor Live," *CDN,* Jan. 4, 12, 14, 21, 30, Feb. 2, 9, 23, 1884; *CTi,* Apr. 7, May 17, 1892. On alcoholism and slums, *CTr,* Oct. 11, 1873; *The Curse of Chicago* (n.p., [1882]), a pamphlet at CHS; and Duis, *The Saloon,* 93–95, 107–10.

45. "Plumbing in Chicago," *Sanitary News* 14 (Sept. 28, 1889): 261; "Class Plumbing," ibid. 15 (Apr. 12, 1890): 589–90; *CTr,* Feb. 20, 1881, Nov. 11, 1883.

46. *CP,* Dec. 10, 1896; "The Housing Problem of Chicago from a Sanitary Standpoint," Chicago, Department of Health, *Monthly Bulletin* 7 (Oct. 1900): [1–4]. On gas, Winslow, "Historic Goose Island," 44; *CTr,* Jan. 25, 1880.

47. *CTr,* Apr. 10, June 11, 1881

48. McClellan, "History of Chicago's Industrial Development," 3:1–70.

49. *CTi,* Nov. 15, 1891; Alderman Thomas Keane, in Winslow, "Historic Goose Island," 54–55 (quote on farm animals); Hunter, *Tenement Conditions in Chicago,* 60–71.

50. Graham Taylor, *Chicago Commons through Forty Years* (Chicago: Chicago Commons Association, 1936), 46–51; Graham Taylor, *Pioneering on Social Frontiers* (Chicago: University of Chicago Press, 1930), 187–202.

51. Duis, *The Saloon,* 94–95; Chicago, Special Park Commission, "Report on Sites and Needs, October 25, 1902," typescript, UC.

52. *CTr,* Dec. 4, 1875, May 9, 1895; *CP,* Jan. 5, 1900.

53. On Goose Island tanneries and on tannery housing, *CP,* May 10, 1897; on fire, *CTr,* Aug. 4, 1887.

54. Winslow, "Historic Goose Island," 23–25.

55. An example of crime, *CTr,* Aug. 18, 1870; "Judith of Goose Island" story, ibid., Nov. 14, 1899; *CTi,* Nov. 15, 1891 (Schaak quote); on churches, Koenig, *History of the Parishes,* 1:434–38, 487–91, 2:887–94.

56. Duis, *The Saloon,* 4–6.

57. *CTr,* Aug. 11, 1906; Marilyn Williams, *Washing "The Great Unwashed": Public Baths in Urban America, 1840–1920* (Columbus: Ohio State University Press, 1991), 82–95.

58. Dominic A. Pacyga, "Parks for the People," in *A Breath of Fresh Air: Chicago's Neighborhood Parks of the Progressive Era,* ed. Constant Gordon and Kathy Husey-Arnsten (Chicago: Chicago Public Library and Chicago Park District, 1989), 15–20.

59. On this topic see Helen F. Lyon, "The History of Public Health Nursing in Chicago, 1883-1920" (M.A. thesis, University of Chicago, 1947).

60. *CTr*, Dec. 4, 1875; "The Sweating System in Chicago," in Illinois Bureau of Labor Statistics, *Seventh Biennial Report, 1892,* 355-43, is an exhaustive analysis.

61. *AABN* 2 (Jan. 20, 1877): 19-21, ibid. 2 (Aug. 25, 1877): 269-70, ibid. 5 (Jan. 4, 1879): 6, ibid. 7 (Apr. 17, 1879): 116-17; *American Builder* 1 (Nov. 1869): 210.

62. U.S. Commissioner of Labor, *Eighth Special Report: The Housing of Working People* (1895), 329-32; Richard T. Ely, "Pullman: A Social Study," *Harper's Monthly* 70 (Feb. 1885): 452-66; Stanley Buder, *Pullman: An Experiment in Industrial Order and Community Planning, 1880-1930* (New York: Oxford University Press, 1967); William H. Carwardine, *The Pullman Strike* (Chicago: Charles H. Kerr and Co., 1894); Almont Lindsay, *The Pullman Strike: The Story of a Unique Experiment and of a Great Labor Upheaval* (Chicago: University of Chicago Press, 1942), 38-89; Mrs. Duane Doty, *The Town of Pullman* (Pullman, Ill.: T. P. Struhsacker, 1893); Frances Embree, "The Housing of the Poor, with Special Reference to Conditions in Chicago," Northwestern University, Seminar in Political Science, 5 (1896), 94-98, NU.

63. Devereaux Bowly, *The Poorhouse: Subsidized Housing in Chicago, 1895-1976* (Carbondale: Southern Illinois University Press, 1978), 1-4.

64. Embree, "Housing of the Poor in Chicago," 370-73; *CP*, May 3, 1899.

65. George T. Nesmith, "The Housing of the Wage-earners of the Sixteenth Ward of the City of Chicago" (Thesis, Northwestern University, 1900).

66. Residents of Hull-House, *Hull-House Maps and Papers* (New York: Macmillan, 1895).

67. Improved Housing Association Papers, Special Collections, University of Illinois at Chicago; *Chicago Commons* 1 (Jan. 1897): 1; ibid. 1 (Feb. 1897): 1; *CP*, Feb. 3, 1897; *CJ*, Mar. 23, 1900; *CTr*, Nov. 7, 1899; *CDN*, Mar. 14, 1900; *Ec* 23 (Mar. 17, 1900): 323; *The Advance* 33 (Feb. 25, 1897): 239.

68. Hunter, *Tenement Conditions in Chicago;* Robert Hunter, "Chicago Housing Conditions," typescript [1905], in "Chicago Housing Conditions, 1897-1910," George Hooker Collection, UC; *CR*, Nov. 21, 1900, Feb. 16, 1901, May 30, June 1, 3, 9, 1901; *CP*, Dec. 10, 1896, notes that the health department saw the halftone illustration as an important publicity tool.

69. Hunter, *Tenement Conditions in Chicago,* 43-52.

70. *Argument of Cyrus Bentley, Esq. in Behalf of the Tenement House Ordinance Introduced by Alderman Mavor Before the City Council at its Regular Meeting April 28, 1902* (Chicago: n.p., 1902); *Econ* 27 (May 3, 1902): 571; *CTr*, Apr. 29, June 3, 10, 1902; *CR*, May 14, June 3, 1902; *CI-O*, May 31, 1902; *CCCP*, Dec. 22, 1902, 1653-64.

71. *CR-H*, Dec. 10, 1902.

72. *CTr*, Feb. 10, 11, 1903.

73. *Econ* 29 (Jan. 17, 1903): 80

74. Allan H. Spear, *Black Chicago: The Making of a Negro Ghetto, 1890-1920* (Chicago: University of Chicago Press, 1967), 129-222; James R. Grossman, *Land of Hope: Chicago, Black Southerners, and the Great Migration* (Chicago: University of Chicago Press, 1989), passim; William M. Tuttle, *Race Riot: Chicago in the Red Summer of 1919* (New York: Atheneum, 1972), 74-107.

75. Perry R. Duis and Glen E. Holt, "Chicago As It Was: Checking In at the Fair," *Chicago* 31 (July 1982): 84-86.

76. Alice Quan Rood, "A Study of Housing Conditions in One of the Negro Districts of Chicago" (M.A. thesis, University of Chicago, 1924).

77. The early studies appeared in *American Journal of Sociology,* vols. 16-21; the later ones remain unpublished M.A. theses. A complete list of both groups appears in Abbott, *Tenements of Chicago, 1908-1935,* 76-77n.5.

78. Alfred B. Yeomans, *City Residential Land Development: Studies in Planning, Competitive Plans for Subdividing a Typical Quarter Section of Land in the Outskirts of Chicago* (Chicago: University of Chicago Press, 1916).

79. *Five Year Report of the Michigan Boulevard Garden Apartment Building Corporation* (Chicago, 1935); Rose Alschuler, "A Nursery School that Functions in a Housing Project: Michigan Boulevard Garden Apartments Nursery School," Feb. 1935, typescript, Rose Alschuler Papers, UIC; Thomas L. Philpott, *The Slum and the Ghetto: Neighborhood Deterioration and Middle-Class Reform, Chicago, 1880–1930* (New York: Oxford University Press, 1978), 209–43.

80. On renaming efforts, *CTi*, Nov. 15, 1891, *CH*, Nov. 24, 1891; Winslow, "Historic Goose Island," 41–45; John R. Schmidt, *"The Mayor Who Cleaned Up Chicago": A Political Biography of William E. Dever* (DeKalb: Northern Illinois University Press, 1989), 12–13; nostalgic view, *CTr*, Oct. 20, 1929, Oct. 21, 1938, *CDN*, Mar. 26, 1930, Oct. 21, 1938, June 22, 1939, Nov. 10, 1962.

81. Chicago Plan Commission, *Chicago Land Use Survey: Residential Chicago* (Chicago: City of Chicago, 1942), 41, 51, 61, 71, 81, 101, 111, 121, 131, 151; idem, *Chicago Land Use Survey: Land Use in Chicago* (Chicago: City of Chicago, 1942), 154–55.

82. Bowly, *The Poorhouse*, 17–33, 35–37, 79, 116–19, 203–5; the Frances Cabrini Homes was later expanded to include the William Green Homes to make Cabrini-Green.

83. *CT-H*, Dec. 8, 1895.

84. *CTr*, Mar. 10, 15, Apr. 2, 1996.

85. *CS-T*, Mar. 10, 1997.

Chapter 5: The Risky Business of Food

1. *CTr*, July 3, 1865, Mar. 3, 1870, Jan. 4, June 4, 1871.

2. Barbara G. Shortridge and James R. Shortridge, "Cultural Geography of American Foodways: An Annotated Bibliography," *Journal of Cultural History* 15 (Spring–Summer 1995): 79–108, provides excellent access to the growing literature on food.

3. *Encyclopedia of Biography of Illinois* (Chicago: Century, 1894), 2:128–33.

4. *CDD*, June 7, 1849.

5. Ibid., Jan. 9, June 7, Aug. 10, 17, 1849.

6. Doc. 1845/2789 (quote); see also doc. 1846/2948; both in CCCD Collection, IRAD, NEIU.

7. Doc. 48/4909 (quote); see also, docs. 48/4174, 5055; 49/5054, 5145, 5673; all in CCCD Collection, IRAD, NEIU.

8. Docs. 48/4971, 4989; 49/5146, 5372; 50/5094, 6131, 6353, 6366; all in CCCD Collection, IRAD, NEIU.

9. *CDD*, Jan. 3, 24, 1849, Oct. 7, 1851, May 26, 1852; *CDJ*, Nov. 13, 18, 1850, Aug. 10, 1851, Mar. 9, Apr. 15, 1852, May 2, 1853; docs. 50/6070, and 52/295, 623, 863, 1638, 1649, all in CCCD Collection, IRAD, NEIU.

10. *The Grayland Market: Its Object, Location and Advantages* (Chicago: n.p. [1910]).

11. *CDDP*, Dec. 31, 1855; *CDD*, Aug. 28, 1860; *CTi*, Nov. 3, Dec. 12, 1872; on the eastern market tradition, Thomas DeVoe, *The Market Assistant* (New York: Hurd and Houghton, 1867), and J. W. Sullivan, *Markets for the People: The Consumer's Part* (New York: Macmillan, 1913).

12. *CP*, Oct. 20, 1870, May 9, 27, 1890; *CTr*, Dec. 27, 1896, Apr. 11, 1897, Dec. 31, 1898; Siegfried Gideon, *Mechanization Takes Command* (New York: Oxford University Press, 1948), 222–23.

13. *CTr*, Sept. 6, 1880.

14. *CR*, Sept. 14, 1890 (quote).

15. *Chicago City Manual, 1912* (Chicago: City of Chicago, 1912), 69–75; *CR-H*, Oct. 10, 1905.

16. Fulton Street, partially identified clip, *CI-O*, July 21, 189?, CHS.

17. *Econ* 37 (Feb. 2, 1907): 272; *CP*, Aug. 29, 1896; *CJ*, Aug. 21, 1899.

18. Edna Ferber, *So Big* (New York: Grosset and Dunlap, 1924), 175ff., describes the Haymarket; George Ade, "With the Market-Gardeners," *CR*, May 9, 1894, reprinted in Meine, *George Ade*, 55–60; *CTr*, Apr. 11, 1897.

19. *CTr*, Feb. 7, 1897 (quote); see also, ibid., Apr. 1, 1914.

20. On farmers, *CP*, Aug. 15, 1897; *Ec* 44 (Oct. 29, 1910): 718; *CR-H*, Nov. 22, 1905. On dealers and price-fixing, *CTr*, Apr. 15, 1868, June 13, 14, 1906. On weights, *CDDP*, Feb. 15, 1854; *CTr*, Feb. 14, 1861, May 20, 1867, Apr. 4, 1871.

21. *CM*, June 15, 1871; *CP*, Nov. 10, 1891; *CTr*, Nov. 11, 1894; *CT-H*, June 6, 1895; *CJ*, Apr. 10, 1896.

22. On bread weights, *CTr*, Apr. 29, May 2, 7, 12, 17, 18, 24, 27–29, 1877. On fruits, Illinois, *Laws, 1872*, 218; *Laws, 1875*, 43; *CTr*, May 21, 28, 31, 1877, Feb. 19, 1878, Aug. 7, 1878, Sept. 1, 1880, Aug. 16, 1882.

23. *CTr*, Sept. 24, 1882, Jan. 13, 1895.

24. Richard O. Cummings, *The American and His Food* (Chicago: University of Chicago Press, 1940), 106; Harvey Levenstein, *Revolution at the Table: The Transformation of the American Diet* (New York: Oxford University Press, 1988), 30–43; Bradley cartoon reproduced in *Ideas for Refreshment Rooms* (Chicago: Hotel Monthly Press, 1923), 348–49; raw food fad, *CR*, Sept. 19, 20, 1900. One of the food fads involved cereals, the story of which centers on the Kellogg brothers of Battle Creek; see Richard W. Schwarz, "John Harvey Kellogg: Health Reformer" (Ph.D. diss., University of Michigan, 1964).

25. *CTr*, July 4, 1874, *CTi*, July 11, 1874.

26. *CTr*, June 24, 1882, May 25, 28, Dec. 19, 1884; *Daily Drovers Journal*, Jan. 19, 1883; *CTi*, Feb. 11, 1883; Citizens Association of Chicago, *AR, 1885*, 8–9; *CDN*, Mar. 28, Apr. 12, 1888.

27. The references to specific problems regarding food would fill a book by themselves, but the best summaries are in the annual reports of the Chicago Department of Health and the Illinois Food Commissioner; bread is discussed in *CTr*, Jan. 10, 1897.

28. *CT-H*, May 11, 1895; *CR*, May 1, 1900. On political corruption and fish inspection, *CTr*, May 25, 27, 1904; *CP*, May 27, 1904.

29. *CR*, Sept. 28, 1894; *CH*, Aug. 17, 1895; *CTr*, Feb. 4, 1896; *CR-H*, Feb. 12, 14, 1902.

30. Early reports about swelled canned goods are in *CTr*, Apr. 29, May 5, 1888; Chicago Department of Health, *AR, 1906*, 4; Illinois Food Commissioner, *AR, 1908*, 184, *AR, 1910*, 268, *AR, 1915*, 7.

31. *American Artisan* 37 (Apr. 1, 1899): 13; ibid. (May 20, 1899): 12; *CR-H*, Jan. 30, 1906; Illinois Food Commissioner, *AR, 1910*, 266–67.

32. Edward F. Keuchel, "Chemicals and Meat: The Embalmed Beef Scandal of the Spanish-American War," *Bulletin of the History of Medicine* 48 (Summer 1974): 249–64. Louise C. Wade, "Hell Hath No Fury Like a General Scorned: Nelson A. Miles, the Pullman Strike, and the Beef Scandal of 1898," *Illinois History Journal* 59 (Autumn 1986): 162–84, and idem, *Chicago's Pride: The Stockyards, Packingtown, and Environs in the Nineteenth Century* (Urbana: University of Illinois Press, 1987), are both revisionist attempts to demonstrate the inaccuracies of Sinclair. See also, Dominic A. Pacyga, *Polish Immigrants and Industrial Chicago: Workers on the South Side, 1880–1922* (Columbus: Ohio State University Press, 1991), 165–66.

33. *CT*, Feb. 14, 1892 (quote, ad). Other information on Woman's Baking Company in ibid., Nov. 11, 1891; *CTr*, Nov. 15, 1891, Sept. 20, 1892; *CJ*, May 11, 1892; *CP*, Aug. 9, 1894. On the canning company, Illinois Bureau of Labor Statistics, *Biennial R, 1892*, 154–55; *CP*, Aug. 28, 1890; *CI-O*, Apr. 2, 1891; *CTr*, Feb. 14, July 12, 1892, Feb. 11, 15, 1894. On Jones, a prolific inventor who lived 1835-1914, see Autumn Stanley, *Mothers and Daughters of Invention: Notes for a Revised History of Technology* (Metuchen, N.J.: Scarecrow Press, 1993), 93, which notes that the Woman's Canning Company operated until 1920.

34. Ruth E. Parsons, "The Department of Health of the City of Chicago, 1894-1914" (Ph.D. diss., University of Chicago, 1939), 43–67, is a useful, though uncritical, summary of its food inspection activities; on the opening of the state office, *CTr*, Feb. 16, 1900.

35. *The Graphic* [Chicago] 5 (Nov. 14, 1891): 314, 325; *Econ* 16 (Aug. 15, 1896): 16.

36. *CT*, Sept. 21, 1883 (quote); see also, ibid., Oct. 19, 1886, and *CP*, Oct. 11, 1890.

37. Brother Thomas M. Mulkerins, *Holy Family Parish, Chicago: Priests and People* (Chicago: Holy Family Parish History Commission, Universal Press, 1923), 884–85, 934–43, contains excellent block-by-block descriptions of neighborhood stores.

38. *CTr,* Jan. 15, 1884, May 4, 1889, Jan. 24, 1900.

39. The best general works on foodways and customs include Alan Kraut, "Ethnic Foodways: The Significance of Food and the Designation of Cultural Boundaries between Immigrant Groups in the U.S.," *Journal of American Culture* 2 (Fall 1979): 409-20, and Harvey Levenstein, "The American Response to Italian Food, 1880-1930," *Food and Foodways* 1 (1985): 1-23.

40. Robert Slayton, *Back of the Yards: The Making of a Local Democracy* (Chicago: University of Chicago Press, 1986), 34, 36, 65-69, 76-79; *CT-H,* Dec. 8, 1895; *CTr,* Apr. 11, 1897.

41. W. O. Atwater and A. P. Bryant, "Dietary Studies in Chicago in 1895 and 1896," in U.S. Department of Agriculture, Office of Experiment Stations, *Bulletin No. 55* (Washington, 1898).

42. *CTr,* May 27, 1881 (quotes); the contents of the lectures appear in the *CTr* throughout the month.

43. *Good Living and How to Secure It* (Chicago: Ladies of the St. Paul's Reformed Episcopal Church, 1890), Introduction, n.p. (quote); Mrs. Harriet J. Willard, *First Book of the Art of Cookery: For Industrial Schools and for Homes* (Chicago: Sherwood, 1886); Carrie V. Shuman, comp., *Favorite Dishes: A Columbian Autograph Souvenir Cookery Book* (Chicago: R. R. Donnelley, 1893).

44. Chicago Kitchen-Garden Association, *AR, 1890-91; CTr,* Nov. 7, 1883, Jan. 15, 1898; *CR,* Nov. 10, 1900.

45. *CTr,* Oct. 2, 1894 (quote); *CJ,* Mar. 4, 1895; *Illinois Staats-Zeitung,* Oct. 12, 1896; *CR-H,* Nov. 17, Dec. 7, 1901.

46. *LDC, 1890,* 881; *LDC, 1900,* 1382; *LDC, 1915,* 1184; Ray Westerfield, "The Rise of the Chain Store," *Current History* 35 (Dec. 1931): 359-66.

47. Charles Moore, ed., *Plan of Chicago . . . by Daniel H. Burnham and Edward H. Bennett, Architects* (Chicago: Commercial Club, 1909), 68; *CR-H,* Nov. 1, 1910; *CTr,* Apr. 1, 1914; *Econ* 44 (Nov. 5, 1910): 748.

48. City Club of Chicago, Civic Committee, vol. 8, Minutes of the Committee on Purveying the City's Food, May 29, 1913, p. 292, City Club Papers, CHS. On the Municipal Markets Commission, *CTr,* Jan. 8, Feb. 13, Apr. 28, Sept. 1, 4, 25, 26, 29, Oct. 1, 5, 1914; *Report of the Municipal Markets Commission of the City of Chicago* (Chicago: City of Chicago, 1914).

49. On Rodriguez, see Perry R. Duis and Glen E. Holt, "Chicago's First Hispanic Alderman," *Chicago* 30 (Nov. 1981): 144-47. Rodriguez was born in Naperville, Illinois, in 1879, the son of a Spanish immigrant.

50. *Reclaim South Water Street for All the People* (Chicago: Chicago Plan Commission, 1917).

51. Lizabeth Cohen, *Making a New Deal: Industrial Workers in Chicago, 1919-39* (New York: Cambridge University Press, 1990), 106-13.

52. Carl Sandburg, "Ice Handler," in *Chicago Poems* (New York: Henry Holt, 1916), 45, presents an excellent image.

53. Henry Hall, "The Ice Industry of the United States," U.S. Bureau of the Census, *Tenth Census of the United States,* 1880, xxii:1-42.

54. Doc. 1838/0544A (1838), CCCD Collection, IRAD, NEIU.

55. *CTr,* Aug. 19, 1903.

56. Docs. 53-54/1359A; 54-55/1554A, CCCD Collection, IRAD, NEIU. See also *CTr,* Feb. 10, 1863; *CCCP,* Jan. 2, 1865.

57. *How to Harvest Ice* (Hudson, N.Y.: Gifford-Wood, 1912); *American Builder* 1 (Dec. 1869): 233.

58. *CPT,* Feb. 5, 1859; *CTr,* Feb. 27, 1861; Chicago Ice Co., *Charter and By-Laws,* 1863, incorporated Feb. 22, 1861; on ice exports to South via canal, *CDD,* Oct. 10, 1851; on ice monopoly during Civil War, *CTr,* June 14, July 15, 1861.

59. On general increase in consumption, *CTr,* July 8, 1863; on brewers, ibid., Oct. 14, 1878, Jan. 24, 1882. On packers and railway refrigerator, J. Ogden Armour, *The Packers,*

the Private Car Lines, and the People (Philadelphia: Henry Altemus Co., 1906), 15–66; *CTi,* Jan. 3, 1874; *CJ,* Dec. 29, 1878; *CI-O,* Sept. 28, 1890; *Chicago: The Marvelous City of the West* (Chicago: Flinn and Sheppard, 1891), 356. On Chicago retail consumption compared with that of other cities, *CTr,* Mar. 2, 1883.

60. Lee Lawrence, "The Wisconsin Ice Trade," *Wisconsin Magazine of History* 48 (Summer 1965): 257–67; *CTr,* Oct. 2, 1880, Jan. 2, 1900; Rossmiller v. State, 114 Wisc. 169 (1901).

61. *Sanitary News* 7 (Feb. 27, 1886): 169; *CI-O,* Aug. 20, 1895; *CT-H,* May 26, 1896; Chicago Department of Health, *AR, 1897–98,* 144; Illinois Food Commissioner, *AR, 1901,* 8, 20–21; *CR-H,* Aug. 18, 19, 1901, Aug. 9, 1904.

62. *CTr,* May 17, 21, 1865; *CJ,* Jan. 6, 7, 25, 1876, Dec. 14, 1886; *CR-H,* July 11, 13, 15–19, 1903, May 11, 1906; Duis, *The Saloon,* 56.

63. *CI-O,* July 14, 1903; on later efforts to create a municipal ice house, see *CR-H,* Jan. 18, 1905, Jan. 29, 1912.

64. Lawrence, "Wisconsin Ice Trade," 264–65; *CR-H,* May 6, 1906; *Econ* 38 (Sept. 28, 1907): 492–93; Illinois Food Commissioner, *AR, 1901,* 8 (quote).

65. *CTr,* Jan. 18, 1888 (quote); "Brevities: Making Ice by Steam," *Putnam's Magazine* 6 (Aug. 1870): 226–28; *Half-Century's Progress of the City of Chicago* (Chicago: International Publishing Co., 1887), 84, 268; *Western Brewer* 4 (Apr. 15, 1879): 297; ibid. 4 (Dec. 15, 1881): 1614; *CTr,* Sept. 4, 1881, June 26, 1890; *CP,* Jan. 7, 1899.

66. Lawrence, "Wisconsin Ice Trade," 266–67; on regulation of ice trade during the war, Marguerite Jenison, *The Wartime Organization of Illinois,* vol. 5 in *Illinois in the World War,* ed. Theodore Calvin Pease (Springfield: Illinois State Historical Library, 1923), 229.

67. Elsie Wolcott, *Use of Ice in Families with Children* (Chicago: Department of Public Welfare, 1925).

68. "History and Business of Bowman Dairy Company," Bowman Dairy Corporation Papers, CHS; in the same collection, see also "Beginnings of Pasteurization in Illinois," *Bulletin of the Dairy Research Bureau* 19 (May 1, 1940): 49; ibid. 19 (May 8, 1940): 53; ibid. (May 15, 1940): 57. On Wanzer, see any Chicago newspaper for Jan. 6–7, 1906.

69. Joe Follmar, "The C & N.W.'s Milk Cars," *North Western Lines* 12 (Fall 1985): 32–35, which reprints "Milk for the Million," which first appeared in *CH,* June 29, 1890.

70. *WCD,* Apr. 30, 1853 (quote); Chicago Normal School, *The Fight for Life in Chicago* (Chicago: Board of Education, 1901), 20–21; Chicago Medical Society, *Proceedings, 1867,* 23–25.

71. *CM,* May 17, 1871 (quote); see also ibid., Apr. 28, May 5, June 14, 1871; *CTr,* Dec. 14, 1884.

72. *CTr,* Sept. 2, 4, 1879, Mar 23, July 1, 1880.

73. *American Builder* 1 (Aug. 1869): 164 (quote); the complete poem has seven stanzas. On chalk used in adulteration, see *CJ,* Mar. 12, 1877, Feb. 24, 1879; *CP,* June 20, 1877; *Dr. R. U. Piper's Report on Diseased Milk* (Chicago: n.p., 1879).

74. Illinois Food Commissioner, *AR, 1901,* 4; *CTr,* May 24, 1900; *CR,* July 18, 1900; *CR-H,* July 13, 14, 28, 1901, July 27–28, 1906.

75. Illinois Food Commissioner, *AR, 1906,* 76, 131; Chicago Department of Health, *AR, 1906,* 55–56; *Milkine: Nature's Ideal Nourishment* (n.p., n.d.), CHS.

76. Karel Ficek, "Milk: A Type of Study in Social Control" (M.A. thesis, University of Chicago, 1935), 68–108; *The Neighbor* 1 (June 1900): 1–2; *CR-H,* May 20, 1903, Feb. 21, Apr. 12, 1908; *CI-O,* Dec. 29, 1907.

77. Chicago Department of Health, *State of Chicago's Health,* June 27, 1903, n.p. On Chicago Woman's Club, *CR-H,* May 26, 1903, May 28, 1908; the New York model is described in Patricia Mooney Melvin, "Milk to Motherhood: The New York Milk Commission and the Beginning of Well-Child Programs," *Mid-America* 65 (Oct. 1983): 111–36; "*Latte Puro pei Bambini,*" undated handbill, Chicago Commons Scrapbook, Graham Taylor Papers, Newberry Library, Chicago.

78. *CR-H,* Dec. 20, 1908, Jan. 21, Nov. 22, 1909.

79. Isaac Rawlings, *The Rise and Fall of Disease in Illinois* (Springfield: State Department of Public Health, 1927), 2:338–39, 375, 388.

80. Chicago Department of Health, *ARs, 1911–18*, 853, 890–93.

81. *CR-H,* July 26, 1904; Illinois Food Commissioner, *AR, 1905,* 175; *Chicago City Manual, 1912* (Chicago: City of Chicago, 1912), 182–95.

82. *CCCP,* July 13, 1908, 1183; *CR-H,* Apr. 17, 30, May 1, 2, June 6, 1908, Mar. 30, Apr. 1, 3, 23, 1909.

83. *CR-H,* June 19, 1911, July 23, 24, Aug. 15, 1912; Chicago Department of Health, *ARs, 1911–18,* 853–59; *CCCP,* Jan 2, 1912, 2264, Aug. 14, 1912, 1702–9.

84. "Beginnings of Pasteurization in Illinois," *Bulletin of the Dairy Research Bureau* 19 (May 15, 1940): 57.

85. Ibid.

86. Chicago Department of Health, *ARs, 1911–18,* 853.

87. *The Chicago-Cook County Health Survey* (New York: Columbia University Press, 1949), 237–46.

88. Emily Saterlee, "Narrative of a Journey from Raymertown, N.Y. to Chicago, 1836–37," typescript, 10–11, CHS (on eastern flowers); *Prairie Farmer* 7 (Sept. 1847): 276–77; ibid. (Oct. 1847): 307–8. On early garden clubs, see ibid., n.s. 4 (July 7, 1859): 9; ibid., n.s. 5 (Feb. 16, 1860): 103; *CD,* July 6, 1847.

89. Theodore J. Karamanski, *Rally 'Round the Flag: Chicago and the Civil War* (Chicago: Nelson-Hall, 1993), 127.

90. Melvin G. Holli, *Reform in Detroit* (New York: Oxford University Press, 1967), 70–72; for support for the idea from the Cook County Board president, D. D. Healy, *Official Messages to the Board of Cook County Commissioners, 1894–1898* (Chicago: J. M. W. Jones Stationery and Printing Co., 1898), 192–93.

91. *Chicago* 1 (Apr. 1870): 12–13; Laura Dainty Pelham, "The City Garden Association," *Survey* 50 (June 19, 1909): 423–25; obituary for Pelham in *CTr,* Jan. 23, 1924.

92. *Co-operation* 1 (Jan. 12, 1901): 5; ibid. (Jan. 19, 1901): 3–5; *Chicago Commerce* 5 (Nov. 5, 1909): 13–15; Henry W. Koehler, "Vacant Lot Gardening in Chicago," *Physical Culture* 12 (Aug. 1910): 173–75; *CR-H,* May 8, 1912; *CTr,* Apr. 4, 1910, Apr. 12, 1915.

93. Jenison, *Wartime Organization of Illinois,* 224–55; J. Seymour Currey, *Illinois Activities in the World War* (Chicago: Thomas B. Poole Co., 1921), 3:798–800, 804–6.

94. [Illinois] *State Council of Defense News* 1 (Dec. 28, 1917): 1; ibid. (Mar. 1, 1918): 2; ibid. (Mar. 15, 1918): 2; ibid. (Mar. 22, 1918): 3; ibid. (Mar. 29, 1918): 3; ibid. (Apr. 5, 1918): 1; ibid. (Apr. 26, 1918): 3; ibid. (May 10, 1918): 3; ibid. (June 7, 1918): 2; ibid. (June 14, 1918): 1; ibid. 3 (July 18, 1919): 2.

95. Mary Watters, *Illinois in the Second World War* (Springfield: Illinois State Historical Library, 1951), 1:278–92; Perry R. Duis and Scott LaFrance, *We've Got a Job to Do: Chicagoans and World War II* (Chicago: Chicago Historical Society, 1992), 19, 45–46, 57.

96. *CS-T,* Apr. 29, July 25, 1976; *CTr,* Apr. 18, July 29, 1976, Mar 17, 1977, June 22, 1978, May 5, 1980; *Chicago Defender,* May 1, 1978; *NYT,* June 22, 1977.

97. *CS-T,* Dec. 30, 1984, June 5, 1988, Dec. 10, 1989, May 28, 1992; *CTr,* Aug. 27, 1980, Jan. 26, 1981.

98. Dick Frye, "The Iceman Surviveth," *CTr Magazine,* Sept. 2, 1973, 28–30.

99. *CTr,* Apr. 2–7, 9, 10, 12–26, 28–29, May 2–4, 7–9, 12–16, 21, 26, 29, June 7, 10–12, 14, 20, 25–28, July 5, 20, 23, 24, 27, Aug. 1, 7, 10, Sept. 15, Oct. 27, 1985.

Chapter 6: The Lobster Died in Cleveland

1. Quoted in *Hotel World* 7 (Aug. 10, 1878): 4.

2. Joseph Balestier, *The Annals of Chicago: A Lecture Delivered before the Chicago Lyceum, January 21, 1840,* Fergus Historical Series, no. 1 (Chicago: Fergus Printing Co., 1876), 33 (quote); Edward Everett Dale, "The Food of the Frontier," *JISHS* 4 (Mar. 1947): 38–61; unidentified clipping on Green Tree Inn, Aug. 2, 1891, Harpel Scrapbook, S4-15, pp. 88–89, CHS.

3. Quotes on the East, *CDDP*, July 7, 1855, and *CDA*, Apr. 29, 1839; on menu, Foster House, Feb. 24, 1856, CHS; on Lake House, Arnold Shircliffe, "The Fascinating History of Early Chicago Restaurants," in Chicago Restaurant Association, *Buyer's Guide, 1945* (Chicago: Chicago Restaurant Association, 1945), 27, 29.

4. *CDA*, May 5, 1842, quoted in Cummings, *The American and His Food*, 59–60.

5. *CDDP*, July 7, 1855 (quote about Mrs. Anderson); *CDD*, May 26, 1849 (quote about coffeehouse lamps). On coffeehouses, ice cream, and eating saloons, see *CDA*, Apr. 9, 1841; *CDD*, Jan. 1, 1849; *CDD*, Jan. 1, June 23, 1849, Sept. 3, 1852; *CDDP*, Nov. 20, 1854, Oct. 30, 1855.

6. *CDN*, Apr. 26, 1888; *CTr*, Nov. 22, 1885, Nov. 19, 1888.

7. *CTr*, Mar. 7, 1871, June 16, 1872, Jan. 10, 1873, Apr. 7, 1874, Feb. 7, 1875; *CI-O*, Jan. 8, 1873; *CTi*, Feb. 8, 1874.

8. *CTr*, Feb. 7, 1875 (quote); *Hotel World* 7 (Dec. 7, 1878): 1; *CTr*, June 16, 1872, Jan. 10, 1873, Apr. 7, 1874, Feb. 7, 1875.

9. *CTr*, June 16, 1872, Jan. 10, 1873, Feb. 7, 1875, Feb. 18, Dec. 18, 1893; *CJ*, Apr. 22, 1924. In George Ade, "They Had Met Once Before," *CR*, Sept. 4, 1895, a fictional out-of-towner wants to visit only restaurants with mirrors.

10. On Kinsley's, *H. M. Kinsley, Caterer, Season of 1885–'86*, pamphlet in CHS; *CR-H*, Feb. 19, 1905; *Restaurant Bulletin* 2 (Feb. 1905): 28–29. On Rector's, [Charles H. Hermann], *Recollections of Life and Doings in Chicago* (Chicago: Normandie House Publisher, 1945), 59–60; Frederick E. Coyne, *In Reminiscence* (Chicago: Privately printed, 1941), 22–23; George Rector, *The Girl from Rector's* (New York: Doubleday, Page, 1927), 22–25. On the Auditorium, Hand, *Auditorium*, 65–67, 70–72, 74, 82.

11. On great restaurants in general, *CTr*, Dec. 18, 1892; on Billy Boyle's and Abson's, *CDN*, Nov. 7, 1953 (the Abson's building, which is thought to have been part of the family homestead of Illinois's Depression-era governor, Henry Horner, was still standing in 1997); on Chapin and Gore, Duis, *The Saloon*, 28–29, 68; on the Boston Oyster House, *Chicago Commerce* 17 (Jan. 7, 1922): 18; on the DeJonghe brothers, *CTr*, July 11, 1911, Nov. 13, 1938.

12. On the Berghoff, Duis, *The Saloon*, 186; *CTr*, June 19, 1950; *CTr Magazine*, Sept. 10, 1872.

13. Quote on French food, *Rand, McNally and Company's Bird's-Eye Views*, 69; quote from George Ade, "Since the Frenchmen Came," *CR*, Feb. 21, 1894, reprinted in Meine, *George Ade*, 12.

14. On early German cooks and restaurants, Emil Dietzsch, *Chicago's Deutsche Manner* (Chicago: Max Stern und Fred Kressmann, 1885), 31–32. On Italian eating places, *L'Italia*, July 8, 1893. On Chinese, *CI-O*, Sept. 27, 1891; *CTr*, Jan 24, 1891, June 26, 1892, Sept. 27, 1903; *CT-H*, Sept. 22, 1895.

15. *CTr*, Apr. 8, 1894 (quote).

16. George Ade, "A Plantation Dinner at Aunt Mary's," *CR*, Nov. 12, 1894.

17. *Restaurant Bulletin* 1 (Mar. 1904): 9; ibid. 2 (Jan. 1905): 22–23.

18. *Hotel World* 54 (Feb. 15, 1902): 16; *Restaurant Bulletin* 1 (Dec. 1903): 9; ibid. (Aug. 1904): 16; ibid. 2 (Mar. 1905): 12; ibid. (Aug. 1905): 17.

19. Duis, *The Saloon*, 259–60; on evasion by Chinese restaurants, *Champion of Fair Play* 36 (Feb. 3, 1912): 5; ibid. 42 (June 13, 1914): 4; People v. King Chow Lo, 174 Ill. App. 96 (1912).

20. *Restaurant Bulletin* 1 (Mar. 1904): 18–19; ibid. (July 1904): 16–17; ibid. (Sept. 1904): 11; Chicago Department of Health, *AR, 1906*, 6–7, 181–85; *CR-H*, Feb. 6, May 8, Aug. 15, Oct. 21, 1906.

21. *Restaurant Bulletin* 1 (May 1904): 19; ibid. 2 (Feb. 1905): 28–29; Duis, *The Saloon*, 293–94; on the restaurant scene in general, Morrison Wood, "A Half Century of the Culinary Arts in Chicago," *CHi* 2 (Spring 1972): 18–25.

22. Sinkevitch, *AIA Guide to Chicago*, 127.

23. John Drury, *Dining in Chicago* (New York: John Day, 1931), 181.

24. Alfred Granger, *Chicago Welcomes You* (Chicago: A. Kroch, 1933), 187 (quote).

25. John Drury, "Dining 'Around the World' in Chicago," in *Chicago's Progress: A Review of the World's Fair City,* ed. Glen A. Bishop and Paul T. Gilbert (Chicago: Bishop Publishing Co., 1933), 98.

26. Ibid., 99.

27. *CR-H,* Oct. 14, 1912 (quote).

28. *CM,* Mar. 13, 1890 (quote).

29. Corkran, "Chicago and the Chicago Historical Society," 48–49; *Bonfort's Wine & Spirit Circular* 67 (Mar. 10, 1907): 512–18; Balestier, *The Annals of Chicago,* 33; *CDA,* Dec. 30, 1840; *CD,* Oct. 28, 1845.

30. Hoyt, *One Hundred Years of Land Values in Chicago,* 53–128.

31. *CTr,* Feb. 7, 1875, Dec. 18, 1892.

32. *The Chicago Clubs Illustrated* (Chicago: Lanward Publishing Co., 1888); for an example of society luncheons, *CTr,* Mar. 6, 1910.

33. Changes in restaurants in general, Levenstein, *Revolution at the Table,* 185–95; on Chicago changes, *CTr,* Mar 7, 1871, Feb. 7, 1875, Dec. 18, 1892; *CTi,* Feb. 8, 1874; on Berghoff, *CTr,* Sept 10, 1972; on Kinsley's, *CR-H,* Feb. 19, 1905, and *Restaurant Bulletin* 2 (Feb. 1905): 28–29; on Henrici's, *CR-H,* Jan. 26, 1906.

34. *Rand, McNally and Company's Bird's-Eye Views,* 71 (quote); Frank McElwain, "The Saloon Question in Chicago from a Financial, Administrative, and Political Standpoint," Northwestern University, Seminar in Political Science, 3 (1895), 52–60, NU; *CTr,* Mar. 7, 1871, Feb. 7, 1875, Oct. 15, 1883, Dec. 18, 1892; *CDN,* Mar. 1, 1884; *Moran's Dictionary of Chicago* (Chicago: George E. Moran, 1894), 132–33.

35. *CTr,* Dec. 18, 1892 (quote); "The Chicago Bar," *American Architect* 89 (June 2, 1906): 183–85; *CTr,* June 19, 1881, May 4, 1888, Nov. 20, 1894, Mar. 6, 1903. C. A. Patterson, ed., *The Lunch Room as Money Maker* (Chicago: Patterson Publishing Co., 1921), is an important compilation of articles emphasizing efficiency and profit. See also George Ade, "Sign Language in a Restaurant," *CR,* Aug. 11, 1894. Robin Leidner, *Fast Food, Fast Talk: Service Work and the Routinization of Everyday Life* (Berkeley: University of California Press, 1993), describes the modern equivalent of early lunch operations.

36. Royal Melendy, "The Saloon in Chicago, II," *American Journal of Sociology* 6 (Jan. 1901): 454; an ad for Hough's Old Tree House, *CDD,* Feb. 27, 1860, offering "Free lunch served from 10 to half-past 12 every night," suggests that Mackin may have adapted someone else's idea for drumming up late-night trade.

37. Duis, *The Saloon,* 52–56, 185–87; on unwholesome food, *CP,* Feb. 14, 1894.

38. *Co-Operation* 1 (Jan. 19, 1901): 8; ibid. (Oct. 5, 1901): 5–6.

39. The Fair Store (1885) and Field's (1890) had the earliest tearooms for women; Robert Twyman, *History of Marshall Field & Company, 1852–1906* (Philadelphia: University of Pennsylvania Press, 1954), 125–26; Siry, *Carson, Pirie, Scott,* 216–18; *Restaurant Bulletin* 1 (Oct. 1904): 24; *Ideas for Refreshment Rooms,* 38–40, 100–110, 165, 291. *CTr,* Apr. 8, 1894, describes Mrs. Clark.

40. *CTr,* Jan. 17, 1897 (quotes).

41. On the general difficulty of lunch hours, Nell Nelson, *The White Slave Girls of Chicago* (Chicago: Barkley Publishing Co., 1888), 17, 75; "Origins of the Cafeteria—The Institution," *Journal of Home Economics* 17 (July 1925): 390–93; "Origins of the Cafeteria—The Name," ibid., 393; Edith Brown Kirkwood, "The Business Woman's Lunch," *Good Housekeeping* 52 (May 1911): 555–59. On the Ursula, Katherine Head, "A Lunch Club," *The Outlook* 57 (Apr. 7, 1894): 628–89. On the Ogontz Association, *CDN,* July 28, 1891; "The Ogontz Association," *The Graphic* [Chicago], n.s. 5 (Aug. 8, 1891): 96; *Noon-Day Rest* (Chicago: Klio Association, 1905). On the women's lunch phenomenon in general, *CTi,* Jan. 21, 1894; *CT-H,* Oct. 6, 1895; *CTr,* July 24, 1892, Apr. 29, May 2, 1894.

42. *Rand, McNally and Company's Bird's-Eye Views,* 75 (first quote); this edition of the guide obviously reprinted one from 1893. "Feeding the Nooners," *Ideas for Refreshment Rooms,* 156 (second quote). On Kohlsaat, see also [Charles H. Hermann], *Recollections of Life and Doings in Chicago,* 59–60, 64–65, and *Restaurant Bulletin* 1 (Mar. 1904): 13.

43. *CH,* July 14, 1895; Sigmund Krausz, *Street Types of American Cities* (Chicago: Werner Co., 1892), 90–91. George Ade, "Buying Matinee Tickets," *CR,* Aug. 18, 1894; idem, "Sidewalk Merchants and Their Wares," ibid. Sept. 13, 1894, is reprinted in Meine, *George Ade,* 109–13.

44. *CTr,* Apr. 15, 1894 (quote).

45. *CDN,* Mar. 14, 1900.

46. *CTr,* Mar. 6, 1903; *Among Ourselves* 3 (Nov. 1906): 72, on Montgomery Ward.

47. Duis, *The Saloon,* 296–97; *CCCP,* May 5, 1913, 321, Apr. 12, 1915, 4416–17, June 21, 1915, 802–3, May 21, 1917, 319–20, June 11, 1917, 544.

48. *CG,* Sept. 2, 1891; *Champion of Fair Play* 42 (Feb. 6, 1915): 1.

49. "Feeding the Nooners," *Ideas for Refreshment Rooms,* 156–57; "Automatic Idea in Restaurants," *Restaurant Bulletin* 1 (Oct. 1904): 15–17, describes the automat's Swedish origins; *Econ* 57 (Mar. 17, 1917): 587.

50. George Ade, "The High School's Noonday Half-Hour," *CR,* Sept. 20, 1894, describes the scene near the West Division High School.

51. *CR,* Jan. 1, 1898; *CR-H,* Mar 17, 1902, Nov. 12, 1904, Oct. 2, 3, 7, 27, 1908, Feb. 9, Nov. 10, 1910, Apr. 28, 1912; *CTr,* Feb. 16, 1915; Chicago Board of Education, *AR, 1910–11,* 129–30, *AR, 1912–13,* 209, *AR, 1915–16,* 90–121.

52. *Ideas for Refreshment Rooms,* 38–41, 100–110.

53. Ibid., 115, 159–62, 172–73; on propaganda "broadcasts," *CDN,* Aug. 21, 1924.

54. On Walgreen, Jerome H. Kerwin, "Charles R. Walgreen," *Dictionary of American Biography* (New York: Charles Scribner's Sons, 1951), vol. 22, 688; *CA,* Apr. 25, 1958.

55. One exception was a pamphlet, Pasquale Russo, *Twelve O'Clock Lunch* (Chicago: Pasquale Russo, 1923), a pro-union exposé of unsanitary conditions in downtown restaurants.

56. *Ontra Magazine* 1 (Apr. 1924): 2–11; *Ideas for Refreshment Rooms,* 208–9 (on Ontra); ibid., 145–47, 155, 250, on other cafeterias.

57. *Ideas for Refreshment Rooms,* 116 (quote); John Raklios, "How I Built a Restaurant Business," *American Restaurant* (Dec. 1919): 19, cited in Levenstein, *Revolution at the Table,* 186.

58. Paul Hirshorn and Steven Izenour, *White Towers* (Cambridge, Mass.: MIT Press, 1979), 1–24, 61; on White Castle, *CS-T,* Oct. 9, 1977; April Ozak, "Burger of the Bombed," *Chicago Reader,* Nov. 30, 1979.

59. Drury, *Dining in Chicago,* passim.

60. Duis and LaFrance, *We've Got a Job to Do,* 24.

61. See Max Boas and Steve Chain, *Big Mac: The Unauthorized Story of McDonald's* (New York: Dutton, 1976).

62. Naperville, Ill., *Sun,* Aug. 30, 1996.

Chapter 7: Reducing Risk and Taking Control

1. James S. McQuade, *A Synoptical History of the Chicago Fire Department* (Chicago: Benevolent Association of the Paid Fire Department of Chicago, 1908).

2. Webb, *History of Contagious Disease Care,* and Rawlings, *Rise and Fall of Disease in Illinois,* are the best general sources for the history of epidemics.

3. *Revised Charter and Ordinances of the City of Chicago* (Chicago: Daily Democrat Office, 1851); *Laws and Ordinances as in Force April 2, 1890.*

4. *CDN,* Apr. 12, 1958; *CTr,* Aug. 27, 1961.

5. This story deals primarily with exercise, as opposed to sporting events, which involved competition and more rigid rules. On urban sport, see Riess, *City Games.* On exercise and health in general during this time period, see Harvey Green, *Fit for America: Health, Fitness, Sport and American Society* (New York: Pantheon Books, 1986); James C. Whorton, *Crusaders for Fitness: The History of American Health Reformers* (Princeton: Princeton University Press, 1982), 92–131; John Rickard Betts, "American Medical

Thought on Exercise as the Road to Health, 1820–1860," *Bulletin of the History of Medicine* 45 (Mar. 1971): 138–52; D. A. Sargent, "Physical Training," *Proceeds of the American Public Health Association* 9 (1883): 116–28; J. Madison Watson, "Physical Training," ibid., 129–36. On Chicago, Gerald Gems, "Sport and Culture Formation in Chicago, 1890–1940" (Ph.D. diss., University of Maryland, 1989).

6. "Sports of Early Days," unidentified clipping, 1890, Harpel Scrapbook, H2S4-12, p. 75, CHS.

7. *CDD*, Jan. 22, 1841 (quote). On sleighing, ibid., Oct. 19, 1847; William Butler Ogden to Dr. Nelson K. Wheeler, Jan. 11, 1841, Letterbooks, III, 130, Ogden Papers, CHS. On horse races, Charles Fenno Hoffman, *A Winter in the West,* quoted in Viola Van Zee, "The Role of Recreation in Chicago from 1803 to 1848 as Revealed in Literature Available in the Metropolitan Area" (Ph.D. diss., Northwestern University, 1942), 62, which describes incident of Jan. 10, 1834. On early ice skating, *CTr,* Jan. 31, 1868.

8. The first cricket match is recorded in *CDA,* Sept. 2, 1840; see also, ibid., Aug. 24, Sept. 25, 1840, Sept. 13, 1841, and *CTr,* Aug. 5, 1868.

9. *CDD,* Apr. 2, 1849 (first quote), Oct. 16, 1852 (second quote); see also ibid., Sept. 23, 1852, Sept. 1, Oct. 18, 1856, May 24, 1861.

10. *CDDP,* Jan. 6, 1857 (quote); see also, *CTr,* Dec. 11, 1860, Jan. 18, 1861.

11. *CD,* Nov. 16, 1847; *CP,* Apr. 23, 1896.

12. Stephen Freedman, "The Baseball Fad in Chicago, 1865–1870: An Exploration of the Role of Sport in the Nineteenth Century City," *Journal of Sport History* 5 (Summer 1978): 42–64. Federal Writers Project (Illinois), *Baseball in Early Chicago* (Chicago: McClurg, 1939), gives a popular account.

13. Charles Latrobe, *The Rambler in North America: MDCCCXXXII–MDCCCXXXIII* (London: R. B. Seeley and W. Burnside, 1836), 2:209; *CDD,* Oct. 5, 1858; *CTr,* Nov. 30, 1867, Jan. 3, 5, 1868.

14. *CTr,* Apr. 26, 1862 (quote); Dicke's gym advertised in *CDJ,* Mar. 3, 1845.

15. Henry Metzner, *A Brief History of the North American Gymnastic Union* (Indianapolis: North American Gymnastic Union, 1911); Fred E. Leonard, *Pioneers of Modern Physical Training,* 2d ed. (New York: Association Press, 1915), 103–18.

16. *CP,* Jan. 7, 1896; *CTr,* Dec. 18, 1892; Rudolf A. Hofmeister, *The Germans of Chicago* (Champaign: Stipes Publishing Co., 1976). Thirty thousand Turners showed up at one Physical Culture Exhibition, according to *CR-H,* June 18, 1906. See also Riess, *City Games,* 23, 96–99, for general background on the Turners.

17. Wilma Jane Pesavento, "A Historical Study of the Development of Physical Education in the Chicago Public Schools, 1860 to 1965" (Ph.D. diss., Northwestern University, 1966), 9–22.

18. *CR-H,* Nov. 27, 1904.

19. *Hotel World* 7 (Aug. 10, 1878): 17; ibid. (Aug. 24, 1878): 3; ibid. (Aug. 31, 1878): 4.

20. George Ade, "Going Out between the Acts," *CR,* Aug. 7, 1894 (quote); Daniel J. Boorstin, *The Americans: The Democratic Experience* (New York: Random House, 1973), 188–89; *Physical Culture: A Manual of Home Exercise* (Chicago: A. G. Spalding and Bros., 1892), 52–53.

21. "Poliuto," *CTi,* June 7, 1868 (quote); *The Health Lift: Theory and Practice* (Chicago: Frank W. Reilly, M.D., 1869); *Who Patronizes the Health-Lift?* (Chicago: n.p., n.d.); *The Whitely Exerciser* (Chicago: n.p., [c. 1900]); the exercise equipment phenomenon is generally described in Stephen Hardy, "'Adopted by All the Leading Clubs': Sporting Goods and the Shaping of Leisure, 1800–1900," in *For Fun and Profit: The Transformation of Leisure into Consumption,* ed. Richard Butsch (Philadelphia: Temple University Press, 1990), 71–101.

22. *Physical Culture: A Manual of Home Exercise,* 40; Hardy, "'Adopted by All the Leading Clubs,'" 49 (quote); Peter Levine, *A. G. Spalding and the Rise of Baseball* (New York: Oxford University Press, 1985), 78–89.

23. *CTr,* Oct. 28, 1894.

24. *CDN,* Nov. 30, 1891.

25. *CTr*, Dec. 4, 1870, May 24, 1896. On the YWCA, ibid., Jan. 28, 1868, Apr. 19, 1896; *CT-H*, Nov. 29, 1896; *CR*, Mar. 15, 1901. The papers of the Chicago YWCA are in Special Collections, UIC.

26. Anna Morgan, *An Hour with Delsarte: A Study of Expression* (Boston: Lee and Shepard, 1889).

27. Pesavento, "A Historical Study," 22–44.

28. *CTr*, Feb. 23, 1894; John Hipwell, "The Chicago Athletic Club," *Outing* 33 (Nov. 1898): 145–52; *CR*, Oct. 15, 1900; the whole issue of *The Cherry Circle* 15 (Mar. 1909), is devoted to the history of the Chicago Athletic Club.

29. *CR-H*, May 10, 1903 (quote). See also, ibid., July 26, 1904; *The Gymnasium* 1 (Dec. 1889): 1; *CP*, Aug. 20, Sept. 17, 1898.

30. On climbing and pumping, George Ade, "Hot Weather Athletics," *CR*, July 30, 1894. The present-day Chicago Park District was not created until 1934; the annual reports of the Lincoln Park, West Parks, and South Parks districts provide copious detail. See also, U.S. Works Progress Administration, *Historical Register of the Twenty-Two Superceded Parks Districts,* which describes the evolution of physical facilities in detail, and Cranz, "Models for Park Usage," 59–69; Marian Osborn, "The Development of Recreation in the South Park System of Chicago" (M.A. thesis, University of Chicago, 1928), 43–46.

31. *CTi*, Jan. 14, 1881; *CR-H*, May 1, 1910.

32. *CTr*, Nov. 7, 1880, and *Chicago Daily Drovers Journal,* Mar. 2, 1885 (quotes). See also, *CTr*, Sept. 19, 1880, May 18, Oct. 2, 1884, Jan. 9, 1886; *CTi*, Jan 23, 1881; *CJ*, Dec. 18, 1883; *CI-O*, Apr. 20, 1884.

33. *The Standard Guide to Chicago for the Year 1891* (Chicago: Flinn and Sheppard, 1891), 209 (quote).

34. *CDD*, Apr. 16, 1851 (quote).

35. *CR-H*, Nov. 27, 1904 (quote); on Germanic influence, *CTr*, Feb. 18, 1894.

36. *CR-H*, Nov. 27, 1904, Mar. 3, 1912.

37. *Abendpost,* July 29, 1892.

38. *Illinois Staats-Zeitung,* July 17, 1871; *CJ*, July 4, 1885.

39. *Pomeroy's Democrat,* Aug. 11, 1877; *CTr*, Aug. 3, 1879, Aug. 31, Sept. 11, 1883; *CJ*, Sept. 11, 1883.

40. I. J. Bryan, *Report of the Commissioners and History of Lincoln Park, 1899* (Chicago: Commissioners of Lincoln Park, 1899), 110.

41. Pacyga, "Parks for the People," 15–19; U.S. Works Progress Administration, *Historical Register,* includes detailed accounts of many former properties of the Special Parks system.

42. Some type of exercise or fitness program in a gymnasium could be found in virtually every one of the thirty-one Chicago institutions described in Robert A. Woods and Albert J. Kennedy, *Handbook of Settlements* (New York: Charities Publication Committee, 1911), 37–80; *CTr*, Mar. 14, 1886, gives a good description of YMCA facilities.

43. Richard R. Wright Jr., "The Negro in Chicago," *The Southern Workman* 35 (Oct. 1906): 563–64; Junius B. Wood, *The Negro in Chicago* (Chicago: Chicago Daily News, 1916), 9, 19.

44. Woods and Kennedy, *Handbook of Settlements,* 50–51. The smaller Charles Sumner Settlement on the West Side was apparently too small for a gym; see ibid., 39–40.

45. *CR-H*, Apr. 17, 1910; Jan. 26, 1911; *CTr*, June 14, 1914; Booker T. Washington, "A Remarkable Triple Alliance: How a Jew Is Helping the Negro through the Y.M.C.A.," *Outlook* 108 (Oct. 28, 1914): 485–92; Wabash YMCA Papers, Special Collections, UIC.

46. Pesavento, "A Historical Study," 46–112.

47. "Bicycles and Billiards," typescript, Carter Harrison Papers, Newberry Library, Chicago.

48. On the cycling enthusiasm in general, see "The World Awheel," *Munsey's Magazine* 15 (May 1896): 130–59; Mary Ann Parker, "The Bicycle in American History" (M.A. thesis, University of Illinois, 1947).

49. *CJ*, Jan. 23, 1875; *CTr*, Nov. 7, 1885, Apr. 14, 1889; Parker, "Bicycle in American History," 1–55.

50. *Railway Age* 2 (Jan. 11, 1877): 601.

51. *CTr*, Nov. 7, 1885.

52. *CTi*, Oct. 29, 1879; Bryan, *Report of the Commissioners and History of Lincoln Park*, 48–50; *CTr*, May 11, 1890, May 2, 1897.

53. Ibid., Nov. 22–24, 1879, Jan. 2, Feb. 23, May 22, 27, Dec. 30, 1883, Aug. 7, 1887, May 16, 1889, Jan. 31, 1890. On professional bicycle-racing handicappers, *CP*, May 9, 1896.

54. *Mixed Drinks*, June 22, 1892 (quote); on the Bicycle Track Association, *CTr*, Nov. 7, 1885; on the Pullman Race, *CC*, July 6, 1897, and *CTr*, May 31, 1892; on the Chicago–New York race, ibid., Apr. 10, 1892; on Ralph Temple, "the World's Champion Cyclist" and winner of the race to New York, ibid., May 6, 1890.

55. *CTr*, Feb. 20, 1893, May 2, 1897; John Moses and Joseph Kirkland, *History of Chicago* (Chicago: Munsell, 1895), 1:429; *CJ*, Apr. 11, 1895; *CT-H*, June 2, 1895, Jan. 1, 1896; Helen Sikuta, "Loring & Keene: Manufacturers of Bicycles Made in Chicago," typescript, Index of American Design, n.d., CHS; *CR*, Aug. 16, 1894, Mar. 8, 1895; "History of Ignaz Schwinn," *Bicycling* 2 (Aug. 1946): 10.

56. *CTr*, Jan. 12, 1887, Jan. 31, 1890, Apr. 10, 1892, May 17, 1896; Hermes Bicycle Club, *By-Laws* (1883), CHS; on ethnic clubs, *Svornost*, May 20, 1891, and *Skandinaven*, Jan. 12, 1893.

57. *Cycling Record Book: Season 1898* (Chicago: Siegel, Cooper, 1898), 3; *CR-H*, Apr. 15, 16, 1901; *CTi*, July 10, 1881, Jan. 12, 1882; *Svenska Tribunen*, July 16, 1879. On the ordinance, *CR*, Nov. 23, 1897; *CCCP*, Nov. 23, 1897, 897.

58. *Cycling Record Book*, 13–16; on grass ordinance, *CC*, May 12, 1886; on tunnels, *CR*, Apr. 23, 1896.

59. On asphalt in general, *CTr*, Apr. 22, 1898; *CJ*, Apr. 26, 1899.

60. On state highway system, *Cycling Record Book*, 9, 11, and *CTr*, Apr. 28, 1896; on lamps, *CC*, Oct. 2, 1897.

61. *CJ*, Feb. 14–25, 1895; *CCCP*, July 6, 1899, 982, July 12, 1897, 612–14; Collins v. Chicago, 175 Ill. 445 (1897).

62. *CTr*, Oct. 1, 1893.

63. *CT-H*, June 2, 1895, Jan. 1, 5, 1896; *CJ*, Jan. 9, 11, 1896.

64. *CT-H*, July 4, 1897.

65. *CTr*, Apr. 28, May 17, 1896.

66. *Cycling Record Book*, 3, 5; *CTr*, Apr. 28, May 4, 5, 1896.

67. *CTr*, July 21, 23, 1896; *CC*, July 22, 23, 1896; *CCCP*, July 23, 1896, 759–61.

68. Harrison, *Stormy Years*, 105–6.

69. *CI-O*, July 14, 1897; *CT-H*, Aug. 2, 3, 1897.

70. *CTr*, May 7, 1896; *Chicago South Side Sayings*, May 16, 1896.

71. *CTr*, Sept. 25, 1891, May 15, July 22, 1894.

72. On wealthy female cyclists, George Ade, "The Challenge of the Trotter," *CR*, Aug. 22, 1894; *CJ*, Aug. 20, 1895.

73. *CP*, Aug. 20, 1890.

74. On babies, *CP*, May 27, 1896; on widows, *CTr*, May 24, 1896.

75. *CTr*, June 15, 1895.

76. *CJ*, Apr. 11, 1895.

77. *Chicago South Side Sayings*, May 16, 1896.

78. George Ade, "Buying Matinee Tickets," *CR*, Aug. 18, 1894; *Eight-Hour Herald*, May 7, 1896, Apr. 27, 1897.

79. *CTr*, Oct. 24, 1897; *CJ*, Jan. 10, 1896, Feb. 10, 1896; *CT-H*, Dec. 28, 1895; *Illinois Staats-Zeitung*, Dec. 21, 1895.

80. *CR*, Jan. 24, Aug. 22, 1900, Feb. 8, 1901. On the decline of manufacturers, *American Artisan* 32 (Oct. 3, 1896): 25; *CTr*, Dec. 31, 1898; *CDN*, Sept. 17, 1902; *CR-H*, Jan. 1, 1903.

81. *CTr*, Apr. 12, May 3, 1896; *CR-H*, Dec. 13, 1901; *American Artisan* 28 (Dec. 22, 1894): 36; ibid. 30 (Oct. 26, 1895): 22; "Country Club Life in Chicago," *Harpers Weekly* 40 (Aug. 1, 1896): 761–62.

82. *Chicago Herald-Examiner,* Aug. 21, 1924.

83. Ibid.; *CTr,* Aug. 21, 1924; *CDN,* Aug. 20, 1924.

84. *History: The City of Harvey, 1890–1962* (Harvey, Ill.: First National Bank, 1962), 34–36; on the background of Harvey, James Gilbert, *Perfect Cities: Chicago's Utopias of 1893* (Chicago: University of Chicago Press, 1991), 192–98.

85. *CDN,* Oct. 15, 1890, June 13, 1891.

86. There are antitobacco references throughout the *Union Signal,* the WCTU publication; see also Frances Willard's letter relating Yale University's findings on smoking and athletics, *The Gymnasium* 2 (Aug. 1891): 10.

87. *CDA,* Jan. 27, 1842; *CDJ,* Dec. 10, 1847, July 1, 1848; *Industrial Chicago: Vol. 3, The Manufacturing Interests,* 585; *CDD,* Jan. 31, 1849; *WCD,* Oct. 15, 1859.

88. *CTr,* Sept. 11, 1861.

89. On the industry in Chicago, see undated clipping, "Tobacco," in Elias Colbert "Chicago in 1862" scrapbook, n.p., CHS; *CTr,* Jan. 1, 1875, Jan. 1, Sept. 21, 1880, Jan. 2, 1888, Jan. 1, Nov. 24, 1894, Jan. 1, 1895; *CR,* Feb. 22, 1895; *CT-H,* June 5, 1897; *Western Manufacturer* 6 (Jan. 15, 1879): 909; *Lumberman's Gazette* 3 (Nov. 1873): 145, 147. On the cigar makers, *CDN,* Feb. 19, 1903.

90. *CDDP,* May 10, 1855 (quote); on morality and smoking, *Watchman of the Prairies* Jan. 18, 1848, Sept. 11, 1849; *North-Western Christian Advocate,* Jan. 12, Feb. 2, May 11, 1853; *The New Covenant,* May 3, 1862. John C. Burnham, *Bad Habits: Drinking, Smoking, Taking Drugs, Gambling, Sexual Misbehavior, and Swearing in American History* (New York: New York University Press, 1993), 86–11, skillfully places the general antitobacco issue in a larger context.

91. *CTr,* May 4, 1873 (quote).

92. Ibid., Aug. 23, 1876 (quote). See also, ibid., Aug. 24, 1876; *The Advance,* Aug. 18, 1870.

93. *CJ,* Dec. 12, 1885; *CDN,* Mar. 8, Apr. 1, 1890.

94. *CP,* Jan. 8, 1898.

95. Jane Webb Smith, *Smoke Signals: Cigarettes, Advertising, and the American Way of Life* (Richmond, Va.: Valentine Museum, 1990); Robert Sobel, *They Satisfy: The Cigarette in American Life* (New York: Anchor, 1977).

96. *CJ,* Jan. 10, 1881.

97. *CT-H,* Mar. 27, 1895; *CI-O,* Feb. 6, 1896; *CDN,* Apr. 26, 1890.

98. George Ade, "Ollie and Freddie," *CR,* June 13, 1896; "Ollie's Meeting with Beatrice," June 27, 1896.

99. An informed early history of the general topic can be found in Jack J. Gottsegen, *Tobacco: A Study of Its Consumption in the United States* (New York: Pitman Publishing Corp., 1940). On smoking in Chicago, *Elite* 11 (Feb. 3, 1894): n.p, *The Advance* 51 (Jan. 5, 1911): 3; *Morrison's Chicago Weekly* 1 (Feb. 9, 1911): 14; *CTr,* Jan. 1, 1888, Dec. 4, 1898, Feb. 8, 1915; *CR-H,* Mar. 22, 1906, Oct. 19, 1910.

100. *Temperance Lesson Manual* 2 (Oct. 1886), passim.

101. *CDN,* Jan. 3, 1890.

102. Ibid., Aug. 14, 17, 22, Sept. 1, 1891.

103. *CTi,* Apr. 20, 1891; *CJ,* Feb. 6, Apr. 22, 23, 1895; *CTr,* May 1, 1897.

104. Gottsegen, *Tobacco,* 154, lists the sumptuary efforts and the dates at which all were eventually repealed.

105. *CTr,* May 29, June 4, 5, 9, 1894; *CJ,* May 29, 1894; *CP,* June 5, 1894.

106. *CTr,* Dec. 23, 1894.

107. Ibid., Jan. 17, 1897.

108. Ibid., Nov. 27, Dec. 9, 1894, Apr. 9, 30, May 1, 1897, Feb. 3, Mar. 15, 1898; *CJ,* Apr. 22, 1895, Mar. 2, 3, 1897; *CP,* Feb. 16, Mar. 2. 1897, Aug. 2, 1898; *CDN,* Oct. 23, 1899; *CT-*

H, Mar. 1, 8, May 9, Aug. 27, Nov. 3, Dec. 7, 1897; *CI-O,* Apr. 30, 1897; *CR,* Oct. 25, 1898, Apr. 16, 1900.

109. *CP,* May 28, 1903, Mar. 30, 1904.

110. *CTr,* June 11, 12, 18, July 2, 1894; *CP,* June 26, 1894; *CT-H,* May 23, 1899; *CR-H,* Apr. 7, 1901, Jan. 10, Apr. 3, 5, 1903; two issues of *The Boy* 2 (Jan. 15, 1901) and 7 (Apr. 1908) survive at the CHS; "Public School Pupils and Tobacco," *The Light* 23 (July–Aug. 1920): 47–50.

111. *A Quarter Century of War on Vice in the City of Chicago* (Chicago: Hyde Park Protective Association and the Chicago Law and Order League, 1918), 7; the league was formed in response to efforts to extend saloon closing hours from midnight to 2 A.M.

112. *CR-H,* Oct. 17, 1903 (quote); see also, ibid., Oct. 17, 1903.

113. Illinois, *Laws, 1907,* 265; *CR-H,* June 21, 1907; *CI-O,* June 25, 1907.

114. *CI-O,* June 26, 29, July 1, 3, Aug. 2, 1907.

115. Ibid., July 1, 1907 (quote).

116. Ibid., May 11, 1907, Mar. 2, 3, 1908.

117. *CR-H,* July 4, 1908, Feb. 25, Apr. 27, 1909.

118. Ibid., May 11, Nov. 14, 1908, Feb. 16, 1909.

119. The states included Arkansas (1907), Indiana (1905), Kansas (1909), Minnesota (1909), Nebraska (1905), Oklahoma (1901), South Dakota (1909), Washington (1909), Wisconsin (1905); three states enacted laws before Gaston's crusade began: Iowa (1896), North Dakota (1895), Tennessee (1897) (Gottsegen, *Tobacco,* 154).

120. *CTr,* Aug. 21, 1924.

121. On Ike Bloom's, *CR-H,* Mar. 4, 1907; on Gaston at the Everleigh Club, Emmet Dedmon, *Fabulous Chicago* (New York: Random House, 1953), 268. Reportedly, Lucy told Minna Everleigh, "There is something you must do. You alone can stop your girls from going straight to the devil. You must make them stop smoking cigarettes."

122. *CR-H,* Feb. 19, 1912.

123. Dedmon, *Fabulous Chicago,* 308 (quote); Edward C. Moore, *Forty Years of Opera in Chicago* (New York: Horace Liveright, 1930), 93–94.

124. *Railway Age Gazette* 46 (Mar. 5, 1909): 441; *CR-H,* Apr. 9, 1910, Jan. 6, 1912.

125. *CCCP,* Nov. 24, 1913, 2748.

126. *NYT,* Mar. 14, 1914.

127. *CCCP,* Feb. 10, 1919, 1627–28.

128. *CTr,* Aug. 21, 1924.

129. *NYT,* Jan. 10, 12, 1920.

130. Ibid., Jan. 17, 1921.

131. Ibid., Aug. 27, 1921 (quote); see also, ibid., Jan. 24, 25, 1921.

132. Ibid., Jan 21, Aug. 2, 3, 16, 21–23, 1924; *CTr,* Aug. 21, 23, 1924.

133. *NYT,* Aug. 22, 23, 1924.

134. Ibid., Aug. 23, 1924 (quote).

135. *CDN,* Jan. 18, 1964.

136. Elizabeth Halsey, *The Development of Public Recreation in Metropolitan Chicago* (Chicago: Chicago Recreation Commission, 1940), 80–84, 120–21; Chicago Recreation Commission, *First AR, 1935.*

137. *CTr,* Feb. 27, 1937; *CDN,* May 3, 1937; *North Loop News,* Feb. 25, 1937.

138. *CTr,* June 9, 1977, Sept. 15, Oct. 26, 29, 1980, Feb. 2, 1981, Sept. 28, 1982, July 8, 1983; plant closing, ibid., Oct. 26, 1984; on later takeovers, ibid., Dec. 24, 1989, Aug. 6, 9, 1991; on bankruptcy, ibid., Oct. 8, 9, Nov. 7, 1992; on later takeover, sale, and office closing, ibid., Dec. 8, 10, 19, 1992, Jan. 1–3, 20, 23, Mar. 4, June 7, 1993; *CS-T,* Feb. 16, 1997.

139. Allan Brandt, "The Cigarette, Risk, and American Culture," *Daedalus* 119 (Fall 1990): 155–76; John C. Burnham, "American Physicians and Tobacco Use: Two Surgeons General," *Bulletin of the History of Medicine* 63 (Spring 1989): 1–31; Richard Kluger, *Ashes to Ashes: America's Hundred Year Cigarette War, the Public Health and the Unabashed Triumph of Philip Morris* (New York: Knopf, 1996).

1. The quotations in this paragraph and the following one are from a magazine feature, *CTr,* Feb. 6, 1910.

2. *CJ,* Nov. 6, 8, 1848, Jan. 1, 1849, July 24, 1850; on Western Museum, ibid., Nov. 5, 1844, July 16, Aug. 21, 1846, Oct. 6, 19, 1847.

3. Joseph E. Arrington, "The Story of Stockwell's Panorama," *Minnesota History* 33 (Aug. 1953): 284–90; the works included "Panorama of the Mexican Battles," *CJ,* Oct 19, 1847.

4. *CDD,* May 3, 14, 1850, Aug. 7, 1860; *CDDP,* June 27, 1855. Andrieu's *Panorama of Chicago* described in *CDDP,* Sept. 23, 27, 30, Oct. 1, 4, 7, 13–15, 17–20, 1853. Other works included *Harris' Mississippi River Panorama, CDD,* Oct. 17, 18, 25, 1849; *The Funeral of Napoleon, CDD,* Feb. 20, Mar. 9, 1850; *The Conflagration of Moscow, CDD,* Aug. 29, Sept. 2, 1850; *Pantopticon of India and the Sepoy Rebellion, CDD,* Aug. 7, 1860; *Diorama of the Bombardment of Fort Sumter, CTr,* May 21, Dec. 5, 1861; *Mirror of Intemperance and Crime* in *Western Democratic Review* 1 (Jan. 1854): 87.

5. On the Chicago Academy of Sciences, Ronald Vasile, "The Early Career of Robert Kennicott," *Illinois History Journal* 87 (Autumn 1994): 150–70. Angle's *The Chicago Historical Society* remains the only account of that institution.

6. *CJ,* Nov. 5, 1844, July 16, Aug. 21, 1846, Oct. 6, 19, 1847.

7. On Kohl and Middleton, *CTr,* Mar. 18, June 17, 1883; *CDN,* June 12, 1883; *CG,* Apr. 13, 1891; *CJ,* Feb. 9, 1895; *Moran's Dictionary of Chicago,* 143.

8. *History of Chicago and Souvenir of the Liquor Interests* (Chicago: Belgravia, 1891), 169; the competitive business environment is described in Duis, *The Saloon,* 67–73.

9. Unidentified clipping, July 1887, Harpel Scrapbook, S4–7, p. 126, CHS (quote); on Gunther, Clement Silvestro, "The Candy Man's Mixed Bag," *CHi,* n.s. 2 (Fall 1972): 86–99.

10. *CTr,* Dec. 27, 1884, Nov. 5, 1885, Mar. 14, 1886, Mar. 23, 1890; George Ade, "The Wonders of a Dime Museum," *CR,* Mar. 28, 1894.

11. *CTi,* Dec. 24, 1880; *CTr,* Jan 9, Sept. 27, 1881, July 2, 1882.

12. On the cyclorama entitled General Grant's World Tour, *Svenska Tribunen,* June 17, 1885; on *Jerusalem on the Day of the Crucifixion,* see two undated pamphlets of that title, CHS; on the Chicago Fire, *Sanitary News* 10 (Oct. 1, 1887): 258, and *Inland Printer* 10 (Jan. 1893): 317–21. On Civil War battles, *CTr,* Mar. 4, 1881, Nov. 18, 28, 1883, Dec. 28, 1884, Oct. 4, 1885, Jan. 10, Feb. 24, Apr. 13, 1886, May 1, 1887; *CH,* Jan. 31, 1886; *Manual of the Battle of Shiloh* (Chicago: A. T. Andreas, 1885).

13. *CTr,* June 25, 1942; *CDN,* May 27, 1948; Esther Sparks, "A Biographical Dictionary of Painters and Sculptors in Illinois" (Ph.D. diss., Northwestern University, 1971), 407; *The Panorama Painters and Their Work* (Milwaukee: Milwaukee County History Center, 1969), 1–8.

14. Guidebooks, such as *Rand, McNally's Birds-Eye Views of Chicago,* describe nonfair amusements in detail.

15. *CDN,* Feb. 5, 7, 29, Oct. 3, Mar. 1, 1888, Sept. 22, 1889; clippings, Harpel Scrapbook, H2–S4, vol. 11: pp. 185–87, 190–93, vol. 12: 155–56, CHS.

16. *The Graphic* [Chicago] 6 (Jan. 9, 1892): 22; "John Brown's Fort," typescript, CHS; *CTr,* Feb. 4, 1894, Apr. 1, 1895.

17. Randall, *History of the Development of Building Construction in Chicago,* 146.

18. *CTr,* Apr. 19, 1913; on rebuilding Libby Prison as the Coliseum, *CJ,* Mar. 28, 1899.

19. *CDN,* June 23, 1883; *CTr,* Oct. 22, 1882, Mar. 18, May 6, June 3–4, 17, 1883, Mar. 8, 10, 1885.

20. *CR-H,* Aug. 14, 1900 (quote); Illinois, *Laws, 1899,* 124; *Laws and Ordinances . . . 1890,* 2205; *CP,* Jan. 27, 1900; on the sleazy conditions in dime museums, "Investigation of the Ethical Sub-Committee of the Committee of Fifty, Chicago Commons, Royal Melendy, Sept. 15, 1899," typescript, box 1899–1903, Graham Taylor Papers, New-

berry Library, Chicago. The general problem of lurid exhibitions is the subject of Robert Bogdan, *Freak Show: Oddities for Amusement and Profit* (Chicago: University of Chicago Press, 1988).

21. M. A. Lane, "In a Chicago Pool Room," *Harper's Weekly* 36 (Sept. 10, 1892): 878, 880; *CTr,* Jan 26, 1873, Jan. 18, 1874; *CH,* May 9, 1892.

22. On horse tracks, *CJ,* Aug. 25, 1879; on boxing, Illinois, *Laws, 1869,* 309 (on ban), and *CTr,* Oct. 19, 1873, Apr. 8, Dec. 20, 1882, May 21, 22, 1883, Mar. 3, 1885; on arguments against racetrack gambling, Citizens Association of Chicago, *AR, 1886,* 11–12.

23. Harold Seymour, *Baseball: The Early Years* (New York: Oxford University Press, 1960), 77–91, 311–15; idem, *Baseball: The Golden Years* (New York: Oxford University Press, 1971), 200–201, 215–16; Steven Riess, *Touching Base: Professional Baseball in the Progressive Era* (Westport, Conn.: Greenwood Press, 1980), 85–87, 98–100.

24. David Q. Voight, *America through Baseball* (Chicago: Nelson-Hall, 1976), treats baseball and its heroes generally.

25. Scrapbook, Henry Kolze Family Papers, Special Collections, UIC.

26. Unidentified clipping, Nov. 14, 1895, Harpel Scrapbook, H2S4-16, pp. 318–19, CHS; Frederick Francis Cook, *Bygone Days in Chicago* (Chicago: McClurg, 1910), 144–49.

27. *CDD,* July 16, 1851, Aug. 15, 1859; *CTr,* Aug. 21, 1866; *Workingman's Advocate* 5 (July 17, 1869): 3.

28. *CDD,* June 11, 1860 (quote).

29. *North Shore News,* July 22, 1949, in Kolze scrapbook, UIC.

30. *Tally-Ho: Coaching through Chicago's Parks and Boulevards* (Chicago: J. P. Craig, 1888), n.p., was a photographic souvenir of what tally-ho passengers saw; *Chicago Directory of Picnic Grounds and Public Halls* (Chicago: Stromberg, Allen, and Co., 1899) lists twenty-seven picnic grounds, most of them within forty miles of the city; a fictional trip is the subject of George Ade, "Mr. Norris Goes to a Picnic," *CR,* June 14, 1895; on Haase, *Forest Park Review,* Nov. 19, 1926.

31. Ogden's Grove ad, *Eight-Hour Herald,* July 30, 1896 (quote); on Colehour's, *CTr,* June 20, 1882; on Excelsior Park, *Chicago Federalist,* July 15, 1899.

32. On Bismarck Garden, *CTr,* May 2, 1937, Oct. 10, 1950, June 7, 1954; Vivien Palmer Scrapbooks, III, Lake View Document #14, 1, CHS. On Fischer's Garden, see ibid., p. 12. On Kolze's Electric Park, see clips, Kolze family scrapbook, UIC: *CTr,* Jan. 3, 1883; *Abendpost,* July 7, 1924; *North Shore News,* July 22, Nov. 11, 1949; *CS-T,* May 11, Nov. 6, 1949.

33. Unidentified clipping, May 20, 1888, Harpel Scrapbook, H2S4-12, CHS (quote).

34. *CDN,* Oct. 10, 1929, Dec. 8, 1948; *Midway Gardens* (undated pamphlet, CHS); the project is described in most biographies of Wright, including Robert Twombley, *Frank Lloyd Wright: An Interpretive Biography* (New York: Harper and Row, 1973), 121–26. For a detailed treatment of Midway Gardens, see Paul Kruty, *Frank Lloyd Wright and Midway Gardens* (Urbana: University of Illinois Press, 1998).

35. "Sharpshooter's Park," typescript, CHS; *CTr,* Aug. 22, 1873, Aug. 17, 1879; *CR-H,* Sept. 14, 1910.

36. *CR,* June 9, 1900; *Chicago's Dark Places* (Chicago: Craig Press and Women's Christian Temperance Union, 1891) 52; Royal Melendy, "The Saloon in Chicago, I," *American Journal of Sociology* 6 (Nov. 1900): 303; idem, "The Saloon in Chicago, II," 448; on the struggle between beer gardens and residents near Humboldt and Wicker Parks, *CTr,* Mar. 3, 10, 1878. On Tivoli Gardens, *Western Brewer* 2 (May 15, 1877): 161; ibid. (Apr. 15, 1877): 297; ibid. 4 (Feb. 15, 1879): 130.

37. Pat Meehan, "The Big Wheel" *U.B.C.* [University of British Columbia] *Engineer* 5 (1965): 28–32, is useful but contains errors in dates; *The Ferris Wheel Souvenir* (n.p., [1893]), pamphlet, CHS; *Scientific American* 49 (July 1, 1893): 1; *CTr,* June 18, 22, 1893; Norman D. Anderson, *Ferris Wheels: An Illustrated History* (Bowling Green, Ohio: Bowling Green University Popular Press, 1992), 43–85. The last mentioned is the best account.

38. *Eight-Hour Herald,* May 25, 1894.

39. Ibid.; *CTr,* Apr. 7, 1894.

40. *CP*, Feb. 26, 1895; *CJ*, Feb. 26, 1895.

41. *CJ*, Feb. 28, Mar. 6, 12, 1895; *Econ* 13 (Mar. 2, 1895): 240; ibid. 13 (Mar. 16, 1895): 302; *CH*, Feb. 28, 1895.

42. *CH*, Feb. 28, 1895; *CCCP*, Mar. 8, 1895, 2747; *CJ*, Mar. 23, 26, Apr. 30, 1895; *CP*, Mar. 26, 1895; People ex. rel. v. Swift 60 Ill. App. 395 (1895).

43. *CI-O*, June 6, 26, 1895; *CTr*, July 2, 3, 23, 24, 1895; *CDN*, Oct. 31, 1895; *Mida's Criterion* 11 (Aug. 1, 1895): 84

44. *CDN*, Oct. 31, 1895, May 13, 1896; *CC*, June 9, 1896; Swift v. People, ex. rel. Ferris Wheel Company 162 Ill. 534 (1896).

45. *CDN*, Nov. 9, 1896.

46. *CTr*, Apr. 2, 1900

47. David F. Burg, *Chicago's White City of 1893* (Lexington: University of Kentucky Press, 1976), 216–25; Robert Rydell, *All the World's a Fair: Visions of Empire at America's International Expositions, 1876–1916* (Chicago: University of Chicago Press, 1984), 38–71.

48. On the tower proposal, *CP*, July 1, 1895; *CT-H*, June 22, 1897. On the West Side park, *Econ* 17 (May 22, 1897): 560.

49. On Electric Park, *Econ* 15 (Apr. 25, 1896): 510; *CTr*, July 15, 1896; *CI-O*, July 19, 1896; *Eight-Hour Herald*, June 29, 1897.

50. George Ade, "About 'Shooting the Chutes,'" *CR*, July 5, 1894 (quote); *CJ*, May 11, 1895; *CR-H*, July 22, 1906.

51. *CDN*, May 24, 1908, and unidentified clips, in file, "O'Leary, James," Clipping File, CHS.

52. Chuck Wlodarczyk, *Riverview: Gone but Not Forgotten, 1904–1967* (Chicago: Riverview Publications, 1977), and clipping file, CHS.

53. Perry R. Duis and Glen E. Holt, "Bright Lights, Hard Times," *Chicago* 27 (Aug. 1978): 176–79; *CR-H*, May 27, 1905.

54. *Forest Park Review*, June 14, 1956; *Champion of Fair Play* 31 (Jan. 18, 1908): 4; ibid. 32 (Sept. 23, 1909): 5; *CTr*, Jan. 19, 1908; *Broad-Axe*, Jan. 25, 1908.

55. *CR-H*, July 2, 1905, July 4, 1906, June 20, 1908, May 24, 1910; *CTr*, Sept. 4, 1910.

56. A brothel across from White City is noted in *A Quarter of a Century of War on Vice in the City of Chicago*, 5. On moral conditions near Riverview, see Albert Webster, "The Relation of the Saloon to Juvenile Delinquency" (B.A. thesis, University of Chicago, 1912), 8.

57. *CR-H*, Oct. 10, 16, 1907, Jan. 20, 22, Feb. 7, 19, 24, 25, 1908.

58. Ibid., June 1, 27, 30, July 7, 8–13, 20, Aug. 4–6, 13, 18, 1909.

59. *North Shore News*, July 22, 1949.

60. Research note, "Kretchmer's Summer Garden," Clipping File, CHS.

61. *CTr*, Oct. 28, 1983 on Sieben's; on World War I and Bismarck/Marigold, Melvin G. Holli, "The Great War Sinks Chicago's German *Kultur*," in Melvin G. Holli and Peter D'A. Jones, *Ethnic Chicago: A Multi-Cultural Portrait*, rev. ed. (Grand Rapids: Eerdmans, 1984), 508.

62. *CDN*, Oct. 10, 1929.

63. *North Shore News*, July 22, 1949, clipping in Kolze Scrapbook, UIC.

64. Charles Fenno Hoffman, *A Winter in the West*, quoted in Bessie Louise Pierce, *As Others See Chicago* (Chicago: University of Chicago Press, 1933), 71–74.

65. *CD*, Sept. 26, 1838, Jan. 1, 1845; *CA*, Feb. 19, 1842.

66. John Lewis Peyton, *Over the Alleghenies and Across the Prairies*, 2d ed. (London: Simpkin, Marshall, 1870), 349–51; *DCA*, Dec. 21, 1839; *CDJ*, Feb. 20, 1847; Van Zee, "The Role of Recreation in Chicago," 261.

67. *WCD*, Jan. 26, 1847; *CDD*, Dec. 25, 1847; *CJ*, Dec. 31, 1847, Jan. 3, 1848. Most dance sponsors expected 100 to 150 people to attend, as suggested by printers' records, for example, Calhoun Account Book, 1831–41, for Dec. 17, 1833, and *Chicago American* day book (job printing), Feb. 6, May 31, 1838, CHS.

68. *WCD*, Oct. 11, 1851 (quote); on Irving Hall, *CDDP*, Nov. 22, 1852; on a third facility, Metropolitan Hall, *CPT*, Oct. 28, 1858.

69. *Watchman of the Prairies,* Feb. 26, 1850 (quote). On lake steamers, ibid., Mar. 19, 1850; see also, ibid., Jan. 8, Mar. 5, 1850. On idleness, *Northwestern Christian Advocate,* Jan. 12, 1853; other religion-based comments on dancing appeared in *The Advance,* May 12, 1870, and *Interior,* Sept. 21, 1871.

70. *CDD,* Sept. 18, 1851 (quote); on Woods, see also *CDDP,* Oct. 6, 1852; on out-of-town teachers, *CD,* Nov. 19, 1834, Dec. 10, 1836; on Marshall, *CD,* Nov. 19, 1834, and *CA,* Jan. 12, 15, 1842, Nov. 2, 1847.

71. Engraved announcement, Aug. 1867, in Bornique Scrapbook, vol. 1, CHS (quote); on Mirasole, *CDD,* Jan. 5, 1860; on Martine, *CTr,* Oct. 13, 1861.

72. Unidentified clippings, Bornique Scrapbook, vol. 1, CHS (quote on Bornique's 1869 hall). On Bornique's, see annual announcements dated, 1874, 1875, 1877–78, 1885–86, 1893–94, 1901–2, 1917, as well as Bornique Scrapbooks, 3 vols., CHS, and *CTi,* Oct. 8, 1882. On Martine, *CTr,* Feb. 17, 1866, Sept. 26, 1868, as well as advertising pamphlets, all entitled *Martine's Academy* and dated 1878, 1887, 1902–3, CHS.

73. *CP,* Sept. 24, 1894 (quote); *CTr,* Oct. 7, 1883, Dec. 29, 1909.

74. Charity balls were regularly described in the daily press.

75. "Choose Partners All," unidentified clipping, Bornique Scrapbook, vol. 3, 71, CHS (quote); see also, "Choose Partners," ibid., vol. 2, 71; Bornique introduced the "Minnehaha" (c. 1890).

76. "Mrs. M. Field's Mikado Ball for Son's Seventeenth Birthday," unidentified clipping, Bornique Scrapbook, vol. 2, 29, CHS.

77. *CDN* (eve. ed.), Sept. 28, 1888.

78. Ibid., Oct. 25, 1882.

79. *CTr,* May 3, 1884, Jan. 8, 1888, among many regular examples of charity balls mentioned in the press.

80. Ibid., Jan. 13, 1889 (quote); on Custom Tailors Ball, first organized in 1869, ibid., May 3, 1888; George Ade describes the vain effort of an outsider woman to enter the fictional Balmoral Pleasure Club dance, in "Fred Had Met Her Before," *CR,* Sept. 20, 1895.

81. *CTr,* July 2, 1861.

82. *CI-O,* Mar. 25, 1876; Duis, *The Saloon,* 253–58.

83. On the opening of the new Iroquois, *CR-H,* Nov. 8, 22, 1903; on the disaster, ibid., and every local paper, Jan. 1–20, July 7, 13, 1904, also *CTr,* Mar. 31, 1904. Marshall Everett, *The Great Chicago Theater Disaster* (Chicago: Publishers Union of America, 1904), is a popular account.

84. Duis, *The Saloon,* 225–40.

85. Louise deKoven Bowen, *The Road to Destruction Made Easy in Chicago* (Chicago: Juvenile Protective Association, 1916), passim.

86. On lake boats, *Champion of Fair Play* 37 (June 28, 1913): 4, and *American Issue* 8 (Aug. 23, 1912): 4. On department stores, Juvenile Protective Association, *Semi-AR, June 1, 1909,* 13–14, *Semi-AR, April 23, 1909,* 4, *AR, 1910,* 19.

87. Kathleen D. McCarthy, "Nickel Vice and Virtue: Movie Censorship in Chicago, 1907–1915," *Journal of Popular Film* 5 (1976): 37–56; Frederic Gordon, "The Movies in Chicago: Early Growth and the Rise of Censorship," unpublished paper, UC, 1968; *Report of the Chicago Motion Picture Commission* (Chicago: City of Chicago, 1920).

88. Lois Kate Halley, "A Study of Motion Pictures in Chicago as a Medium of Communication" (M.A. thesis, University of Chicago, 1924); George Mitchell, "The Image of the City in the American Film" (Ph.D. diss., University of Chicago, 1971), 26.

89. Louise deKoven Bowen, *Five and Ten Cent Theaters: Two Investigations by the Juvenile Protective Association, 1909 and 1911* (Chicago: Juvenile Protective Association, 1911), reprinted in *Speeches, Address, and Letters of Louise deKoven Bowen* (Ann Arbor: Edwards Brothers, 1937), 1:138–43.

90. Louise deKoven Bowen, *Our Most Popular Recreation Controlled by the Liquor Interests* (Chicago: Juvenile Protective Association, 1912); "The Public Dance Hall and Its Relation to Vice," anonymous typescript, 1912, Juvenile Protective Association Papers, Special Collections, UIC.

91. H. W. Lytle and John Dillon, *From Dance Hall to White Slavery* (Chicago: Charles C. Thompson, 1912), is a typical antivice condemnation of dance halls.

92. *CR-H*, Jan. 9, 16–17, 19–26, 28, 30, Mar. 1, 2, 1905.

93. Duis, *The Saloon*, 101–5.

94. Ibid., 258. On Apr. 18, 1907, the General Assembly enacted a statewide ban on admission of minors to dance halls where alcohol was served (Illinois, *Laws, 1907*, 305).

95. Louise deKoven Bowen, *Our Most Popular Recreation Controlled by the Liquor Interests: A Study of Public Dance Halls*, passim.

96. Lloyd Wendt and Herman Kogan, *Lords of the Levee: The Story of Bathhouse John and Hinky Dink* (Indianapolis: Bobbs-Merrill, 1943), 153–58, 268–81, 288–89; Richard T. Griffin, "Sin Drenched Revels at the Infamous First Ward Ball," *Smithsonian* 7 (Nov. 1976): 52–61; Chicago Law and Order League, *Summarized Report, 1909–10*, 4.

97. *CR-H*, Feb. 8, 1903; *CDN*, Apr. 16, 1930.

98. *CTr*, Jan. 14, 1900, Aug. 11, 1914; the most perceptive description of this phenomenon in another city is Lewis Erenberg, *Steppin' Out: New York Nightlife and the Transformation of American Culture, 1890–1930* (New York: Greenwood Press, 1981).

99. *CTr*, June 10–11, 1912; *CR-H*, Oct. 14, 1912.

100. *CCCP*, Oct. 6, 1913, 2168, Oct. 15, 1913, 2194; *CTr*, Jan. 7, 1914.

101. *CCCP*, July 30, 1913, 1988–89, Oct. 26, 1914, 1883, Nov. 18, 1914, 2042.

102. *CTr*, Nov. 16, Dec. 9, 1914, Jan. 14, Mar. 18, 1915, June 23, 1916; City of Chicago v. Drake Hotel Co., 274 Ill. 408 (1916).

103. *CCCP*, June 12, 1916, 634–35, 641–42, June 19, 1916, 738–42; on the *Little Girl Next Door* issue, ibid., June 12, 1916, 635–41.

104. "President's Address to the Juvenile Protective Association [Jan., 1925]," in Louise deKoven Bowen, *Speeches, Addresses, and Letters of Louise deKoven Bowen*, 2:748, 798.

105. *CCCP*, Mar. 9, 1914, 4207–12, June 21, 1915, 778–79; *CTr*, Nov. 15, Dec. 3–5, 1915.

106. *CR-H*, Jan. 16, 21, Feb. 2, 1912, Jan. 16, Oct. 20, 1914.

107. Nancy Banks, "The World's Most Beautiful Ballrooms," *CHi*, n.s. 2 (Fall–Winter 1973): 206–15. On the later fate of the Trianon (razed in 1967) and the still-operating Aragon, *CS*, Aug. 9, 1946; *CTr*, Feb. 18, 1950, Jan. 2, 1967; *CDN*, Oct. 11, 1952; *CS-T*, Jan. 13, 1978.

108. *CA*, Nov. 2, 1957; *CTr*, Jan. 29, 1984.

109. Paul G. Cressey, *The Taxi-Dance Hall: A Sociological Study in Commercialized Recreation and City Life* (Chicago: University of Chicago Press, 1932); Robert McIntosh, "Ten Cents a Dance," typescript student paper, 1933, Louis Wirth Papers, UC; on the background of recreation and its customers, see Cohen, *Making a New Deal*, 145–47.

110. Neil Harris, *Humbug: The Art of P. T. Barnum* (Boston: Little, Brown, 1973).

111. On types of theaters, see *Rand, McNally's Birds-Eye Views*, 78–92; Riess, *Touching Base*, 85–87, 97–100.

112. Barrett, *Automobile and Urban Transit*, 109, 162, notes the decline in weekend passenger traffic as a major factor in driving transit lines into bankruptcy. Some loss was due to a trend toward a shortened work week that eliminated Saturday travel, but the loss of riders to traditional nonwork, weekend destinations was also a factor.

113. *CR-H*, May 17, 1908.

114. *Chicago* 1 (July 1954): 22–27.

115. *CTr*, May 12, 1906.

116. On Forest Park, *CTr*, Aug. 2, 1979, and *Forest Park Review*, June 14, 1956; on White City, *CA*, Dec. 5, 1959; on Riverview, *CTo*, Jan. 12, 1973, and *CTr Magazine*, May 16, 1976.

117. On Kolze, *CTr*, Jan. 3, 1983. On Marigold, *World Famous Marigold Gardens: Buildings and Grounds Now Offered for Sale* (1948), pamphlet in CHS Library; *CTr*, Apr. 4, 1963; *CDN*, Apr. 25, 1964. Wozniak's Casino, condemned as unsafe for public use, made one last appearance in the 1991 Hollywood movie *Backdraft*.

118. *CTr*, Jan. 30–31, 1931, Feb. 27, 1970, Dec. 4, 1983.

119. *CS-T*, Oct. 4, 1970; *CTr*, July 8, 1984; Duis and LaFrance, *We've Got a Job to Do*, 108–9.

120. On the Trianon, *CTr*, Feb. 18, 1950, Jan. 2, 1967; *CDN*, Oct. 11, 1952; *S-T*, Jan. 13, 1968. On the Aragon, *Chicago Reader*, July 14, 1972, Nov. 28, 1980; *S-T*, June 22, 1980. J. E. Bornique died Nov. 19, 1920.

121. On the Coliseum, which stood vacant for years before its demolition, *CTr*, Jan. 3-5, 1954.

122. *This Week Magazine*, Mar. 13, 1966.

123. Silvestro, "The Candy Man's Mixed Bag"; letter about the fate of the mummy, Adria Katz, Field Museum, Chicago, to author, Oct. 5, 1977.

Chapter 9: Chicago Is Work

1. *CTi*, Apr. 6, 1890; *CTr*, Dec. 27, 1896.

2. Sawislak, *Smoldering City*, 163-216; *CTi*, Aug. 1, 9, 1893; *CP*, Jan. 16, 1894; *Eight-Hour Herald*, Feb. 23, 1897; *CI-O*, May 28, 1899.

3. Beckner, *History of Labor Legislation*, 223-82.

4. *L'Italia*, Feb. 16, 1895.

5. *CJ*, Jan. 25, 1845 (quote); *Directory of Chicago* (Chicago: J. W. Norris, 1845), 65.

6. Doc. 56/57 1638 (quote); see also docs. 56/57 673, 1466, 1525; 58/59 465; 59/60 180, all at CCCD Collection, IRAD, NEIU.

7. *CDD*, June 19, 1849, which advised that "cities are no places for those who have been brought up to an agricultural life"; *WCD*, May 1, 1858.

8. *CDD*, Dec. 6, 1851.

9. J. V. Vanderpool to Col. W. H. Swift, Feb. 28, 1848, Swift Papers, CHS; *CDD*, June 19, 1849.

10. *CDD*, May 26, 1849.

11. *CTr*, Sept. 17, 1863.

12. *CDDP*, Mar. 12, Oct. 19, 1857, describe arrivals during that depression.

13. *CTi*, Mar. 26, May 5, 13, June 28, 1870.

14. *CTr*, July 15, 1861, describes five hundred people applying for one post office position; on returning vets, ibid., Sept. 25, Dec. 11, 1865, Aug. 20, Dec. 2, 1866.

15. *CP*, Dec. 7, 1870; Sawislak, *Smoldering City*, 163-216.

16. On the YMCA, *CJ*, Jan. 8, 17, 27, Feb. 9, 12, 14, 15, 1870; *CTi*, Jan. 18, 1870; *CP*, Jan. 21, 31, Feb. 21, 1870; on the Arkansas colony, ibid., May 26, 1870.

17. *CTr*, Aug. 17, 1875.

18. Corkran MS, 165-66, CHS.

19. *Chicago City Directory, 1865-66* (Chicago: C. W. Bailey, 1865), 777; *Directory of Chicago, 1865-66* (Chicago: Halpin, 1865); comments on naiveté of workers; *CTr*, Jan. 22, 1866, Jan. 31, 1867.

20. Karen Haltunen, *Confidence Men and Painted Women: A Study of Middle-Class Culture in America, 1830-1870* (New Haven: Yale University Press, 1982), 35.

21. *CT-H*, Dec. 22, 1898.

22. *CDN*, Sept. 24, 1892.

23. *CJ*, Oct. 1, 1886; *CDN*, Sept. 24, 1892; Illinois Bureau of Labor Statistics, *AR, 1898*, 134; *Chicago Dispatch*, Nov. 7, 1893; *CTr*, Jan. 6, 1894; *CP*, Aug. 21, 1894.

24. On ethnic employment in general, Grace Abbott, *The Immigrant and the Community* (New York: The Century Co., 1907), 201, 203, 219; idem, "The Chicago Employment Agency and the Immigrant Worker," *American Journal of Sociology* 14 (Nov. 1908): 289-305.

25. *CDDP*, Nov. 12, 1857; *CTr*, June 4, 1894, Jan. 7, 1896; *CH*, June 30, 1894; *CT-H*, June 4, 1894; *Dziennik Chicagoski*, Dec. 30, 1893; *Denni Hlasatel*, June 29, 1905; *Narod Polski*, Nov. 8, 1911.

26. Humbert Nelli, *The Italians in Chicago, 1880-1930: A Study in Ethnic Mobility* (New York: Oxford University Press, 1970), 56-66; Rudolph J. Vecoli, "Chicago's Italians Prior to World War I: A Study of Their Social and Economic Adjustment" (Ph.D. diss., University of Wisconsin, 1963), 235-78; *L'Italia*, May 9, Dec. 1, 15, 1895, June 20, Sept. 5, 1897,

May 4, 1901; U.S. Commissioner of Labor, *Ninth Special Report: The Italians in Chicago. A Social and Economic Study* (1897), 49–50.

27. *CTr*, Jan. 21, 1886, Feb. 2, 1889, Nov. 1, 1894; *CDN*, Sept. 10, 1895.

28. Illinois, *Laws, 1869,* 255–58.

29. For advertisements, see, for example, *Hillsboro* [Illinois] *Journal,* May 8, 1891, and *Mendota Reporter,* May 6, 1893.

30. Wycoff, *The Workers,* 247–87, describes work on the fair from the viewpoint of itinerant labor. On Claremont, *Lee County Times,* May 26, 1893; *CTi,* May 20, 1893; *Knox County Republican,* May 31, 1893.

31. *CTr,* Mar. 2, 1894 (quote); on "Helpless Young Women," ibid., Aug. 19, 1888; for an example of reported brothel recruiting, *CTi,* Mar. 22, 1870. For other stories, ibid., Nov. 24, Dec. 29, 1883, Apr. 11, 1886; *CDN,* Apr. 30, 1892; *Chicago after Dark,* 77–82. Some historians have tended to discount the validity of many white slave allegations, believing them to have been manufactured by reformers: Mary deYoung, "Help, I'm Being Held Captive! The White Slave Fairy Tale of the Progressive Era," *Journal of American Culture* 6 (1983): 96–99, and David J. Langum, *Crossing over the Line: Legislating Morality and the Mann Act* (Chicago: University of Chicago Press, 1994).

32. *CTr,* Mar. 13, 1898; Nelson, *White Slave Girls of Chicago,* reprints a scathing series that appeared in the *CTi;* Francis Lederer, "Nora Marks, Investigative Reporter," *JISHS* 68 (Sept. 1975): 306–18, and idem, "Nora Marks—Reinvestigated" ibid. 73 (Spring 1980): 61–64, recounts the story of one reporter who specialized in this type of story. The Nora Marks articles appeared in *CTr,* Aug. 31, Sept. 1–9, 1888. *CTi,* Aug. 5, 1893, describes a fraudulent telegraphy school for women, while *CTr,* Aug. 8, 1895, uncovers a scam in which women purchased expensive embroidery material and then had their payments refused for shoddy work; an inquiring reporter feature appeared in ibid., Mar. 13, 1898.

33. *CP,* May 19, 1893; *Chicago Dispatch,* Aug. 2, 1893.

34. *CTr,* Jan. 10, 1894; *CTi,* Jan. 10, 1894; *Illinois Staats-Zeitung,* Jan. 10, 1894; *CH,* Feb. 9, 1894; *Eight-Hour Herald* 3 (Mar. 25, 1894): 6.

35. *CTr,* Jan. 6, 1894, for the story of a worker cheated by the fine print in a contract.

36. Duis, *The Saloon,* 180–81; City Club of Chicago, Civic Committee, Minutes, vol. 5, 1910–11, "Committee on Labor Conditions," 398–550, City Club Papers, CHS; "The 'Vampire' Employment Saloons," *Survey* 23 (Jan. 8, 1910): 491–92.

37. *CTr,* Nov. 30, 1893, Jan. 14, 1894.

38. Ibid., Jan 6, 1894

39. Vecoli, "Chicago's Italians," 249–51, reprints an excellent example of an exposé; see also, *CJ,* Apr. 22, 1899, and *Union Label Bulletin* [Chicago], Apr. 29, 1899.

40. *CTr,* Sept. 25, 1865, June 27, 1868, Aug. 1, 1868.

41. Ibid., Feb. 18, 1895, on Italian Institute of Chicago. On Swedish employment charities, see *Svenska Nyheter,* May 12, June 9, 1903, May 4, 10, 1905; *Svenska Kuriren,* Feb. 9, 1907; *Svenska Tribunen-Nyheter,* Mar. 9, 1909. On Jewish groups, see *Reform Advocate,* Feb. 19, 1898; *Courier,* Nov. 29, 1907. On Danish employment charities, see *Revyen,* Dec. 14, 1912. On German efforts, see *Chicagoer Arbeiter-Zeitung,* July 1, 1881. On Norwegian-Danish agencies, see *Skandinaven,* Sept. 13, 1903, Apr. 24, Aug. 16, 1907, Jan. 17, 1911, Aug. 10, 1912. On non-ethnic citywide efforts, see Immigrants Protective League, *AR, 1909–10,* 21, and *AR, 1913–14,* 15.

42. Fannie Barrier Williams, "Social Bonds in the 'Black Belt' of Chicago: Negro Organizations and the New Spirit Pervading Them," *Charities* 15 (Oct. 7, 1905): 41–42; Wright, "The Negro in Chicago," 563–64.

43. *CTi,* Feb. 26, 1894; *CTr,* Mar. 11, 1894.

44. Jane Addams, *Twenty Years at Hull-House* (New York: Macmillan, 1910), 219–30. On job-finding for women, *CTi,* Mar. 26, May 5, 13, June 28, 1870; *CP,* Dec. 7, 1870; *CTr,* Feb. 3, 1871, Oct. 30, 1873, Sept. 25, 1894; *CH,* Jan. 7, 1894; *CI-O,* Oct. 6, 1894, Mar. 3, 1897; *Illinois Staats-Zeitung,* Feb. 16, 1897; *CDN,* Feb. 15, 1897.

45. *Eight-Hour Herald,* Feb. 25, 1894; *American Federationist,* July 15, 1894; *CI-O,* Oct.

11, 1891; *Denni Hlasatel,* Mar. 3, 1892; *CJ,* Dec. 22, 1892; *CTr,* June 22, 1893, Feb. 25, 1894; *CR-H,* Dec. 21, 1907.

46. Beckner, *History of Labor Legislation,* 387–92.

47. Ibid., 392–93; Illinois, Bureau of Labor Statistics, *Report, 1898,* 137–38.

48. *CI-O,* Nov. 20, 1898; *Illinois Staats-Zeitung,* Nov. 8, 1898.

49. Illinois, *Laws, 1899,* 268; Beckner, *History of Labor Legislation,* 389–92; *CT-H,* Mar. 23, July 13, 1899; *CTr,* Apr. 15, Aug. 1, 5, 6, 1899; *CI-O,* July 9, 25, Aug. 1, 6, 1899; *CP,* July 29, Aug. 1, 1899; *CJ,* Aug. 1, 10, 1899; *CDN,* Aug. 6, 1899; *CR,* Aug. 2, 6, 1899.

50. *CJ,* Aug. 15, 1899; *CI-O,* Aug. 16, Oct. 29, 1899; *CT-H,* Aug. 21, 1899; *CTr,* Aug. 23, 1899; *CP,* Sept. 26, 1899; *CR,* Oct. 27, 1899; Illinois Free Employment Bureau, *First AR, 1899.*

51. *CDN,* Nov. 22, 24, 1900; *CR,* Aug. 18, 19, 1899; *CI-O,* Dec. 23, 1900; *CJ,* Feb. 26, 1900.

52. Mathews v. People, 202 Ill. 389 (1903); *CDN,* Dec. 10, 1899; *Railway Age* 35 (May 1, 1903): 185; *CR,* Apr. 25, 26, 1903.

53. Illinois, *Laws, 1903,* 194.

54. Abbott, "Chicago Employment Agency," 289–305; a hint of what she would find surfaced in a state hearing the previous year, reported in *CTr,* Apr. 25, 1908.

55. On morals and events leading to the Mann Act in general, Langum, *Crossing over the Line;* Mark Connelly, *The Response to Prostitution in the Progressive Era* (Chapel Hill: University of North Carolina Press, 1980); and David Pivar, *Purity Crusade: Sexual Morality and Social Control* (Westport, Conn.: Greenwood Press, 1973). See also J. H. Greer, M.D., *The Social Evil: Its Cause, Effect and Cure* (Chicago: By the author, 1911), 51–64.

56. Abbott, "Chicago Employment Agency," 303–5.

57. On the Chicago Woman's Club, *CTr,* Nov. 25, 28, Dec. 1, 6, 9, 1914, Jan. 13, Mar. 6, 10, 1915; see also City Club of Chicago, Civic Committee, Minutes, vol. 5, part 2, 441–44, City Club Papers, CHS.

58. *Daily Jewish Courier,* Jan. 9, 1914.

59. City Club of Chicago, Civic Committee, Minutes, vol. 5, part 2, 440, 507–8, 525–26, City Club Papers, CHS.

60. Ibid., 432–38, 445–46, 538.

61. Ibid., 509 (quote); see also, ibid., 477–87, 496–98, 507–11, 526–27, 531–35.

62. Ibid., 520 (quote); see also, ibid., 511–22.

63. Ibid., 489 (quote); see also, ibid., 489–94

64. *CR-H,* Feb. 27, Mar. 31, Apr. 2, 1912; Henderson's role in general is delineated in Steven J. Diner, *A City and Its Universities: Public Policy in Chicago, 1892–1919* (Chapel Hill: University of North Carolina Press, 1980), 137, 140–48.

65. *Report of the Municipal Markets Commission,* 23–26, 32–34, 51–52; *Report of the Mayor's Commission on Unemployment* (Chicago: City of Chicago, 1914).

66. *CR-H,* Feb. 27, Mar. 31, Apr. 2, 1912; Chicago Department of Welfare, *First Semi-AR, 1915,* 15–28.

67. Chicago Department of Welfare, *First Semi-AR, 1915,* 32–40.

68. *Skandinaven,* Sept. 17, 1917.

69. Arvarh E. Strickland, *History of the Chicago Urban League* (Urbana: University of Illinois Press, 1966), 48–49; Grossman, *Land of Hope,* 185–88, is a particularly excellent analysis of job seeking by African Americans during the Great Migration.

70. *CTr,* Jan. 17, Feb. 28, 1914.

71. Nels Anderson, *Men on the Move* (Chicago: University of Chicago Press, 1940).

72. *CP,* Apr. 23, 1896.

73. *CTr,* Jan. 2, 1874, Mar. 12, 1875, May 22, 1879 (obituary).

74. *CDN,* May 15, 1888; on Daniel Scott, unidentified clipping, July 1895, Harpel Scrapbook, S4-3, p. 366, CHS.

75. Unidentified clipping, Dec. 1887, Harpel Scrapbook, S4-7, pp. 334–35, CHS.

76. *CTr,* Feb. 26, 1866, contains an ad that specifies a black cook in preference to an Irish one.

77. Ibid., May 20, 1876 (quote). Other labor stories, *CTi,* May 10, 1871, Mar. 4, 1874; *CI-O,* Feb. 20, 1875; *CJ,* Feb. 19, 1875.

78. *CI-O,* Apr. 2, 1877; *CP,* Apr. 30, 1877.

79. *CTr,* Mar. 28, 1886, on "Hurlers of Edibles."

80. *CTi,* Mar. 14, May 8, 9, 29, 1874; *CTr,* Apr. 15, May 11, 1873; *CJ,* Apr. 18, 1874.

81. *CTr,* Nov. 4, 1883, Mar. 28, 1886 (quotes).

82. Ibid., May 11, 1888.

83. George Ade, "Sign Language in a Restaurant," *CP,* Aug. 11, 1894 (quote); *CTr,* Mar. 28, 1886; *CP,* May 17, 1897; *CR-H,* Feb. 21, 1909.

84. Illinois, *Laws, 1885,* 64. It was approved June 10, 1885, and went into effect July 1.

85. *CTr,* Aug. 28, 1887, Mar. 16, Apr. 24, 1888, Feb. 10, 1890, July 19, 1891, Feb. 1, 1893; *CDN,* Feb. 8, 1888.

86. *CTr,* Oct. 21, 1883 (quote).

87. Richard R. Wright Jr., "The Industrial Condition of Negroes in Chicago" (M.A. thesis, University of Chicago, 1901), 21–22.

88. *CTr,* May 11, 1888.

89. *Hotel World* 6 (Feb. 16, 1878): 1; *CTr,* Nov. 4, 1883.

90. *CTr,* May 11, 1888.

91. Estelle Hill Scott, *Occupational Changes among Negroes in Chicago* (Chicago: Works Progress Administration, 1939), 41, 88 (quotes).

92. Wright, "Industrial Condition of Negroes," 22.

93. *Hotel World* 6 (Mar. 2, 1878): 1, complains about head waiters, as do *CTr,* May 11, 1888, *CP,* May 1, 1890, *CI-O,* Aug. 12, 1892.

94. On the seamen and stevedores, *CTr,* Apr. 29, 1880, Aug. 4, 1881, Apr. 18, 21, 1892; *CTi,* Apr. 6; *CI-O,* June 16, 1892. On grain-trimmers, *CTr,* Oct. 1, 1888; on lumber workers, *CJ,* June 17, 1887; on coalyard workers, *CTr,* Aug. 25, 1879; on packinghouse workers, *CJ,* Nov. 20, 1886. On the issue of race and labor in Illinois in general, see John H. Keiser, "Black Strikebreakers in Illinois, 1865–1900," *JISHS* 65 (Autumn 1972): 313–26; on the question of race and labor unity, see Eric Arnesen, "Following the Color Line of Labor: Black Workers and the Labor Movement before 1930," *Radical History Review* 55 (Winter 1993): 53–87, and idem, "The African-American Working Class in the Jim Crow Era," *International Labor and Working-Class History* 41 (Spring 1992): 58–75.

95. *Illinois Staats-Zeitung,* Sept. 20, 1879; *Die Abendpost,* Jan. 10, Mar. 12, 1880; *CTr,* Sept. 20, 1879.

96. *CTr,* Feb. 25, 1884.

97. Ibid., May 2, Dec. 4, 11, 1887.

98. Gerald Grob, "The Knights of Labor and the Trade Union," *Journal of Economic History* 18 (June 1958): 176–92, and idem, "Organized Labor and the Negro Workers, 1865–1900," *Labor History* 1 (Spring 1960): 164–76; Sidney H. Kessler, "The Organization of Negroes and the Knights of Labor," *Journal of Negro History* 37 (July 1952): 248–76.

99. *CTi,* Aug. 22, 1888.

100. Philip S. Foner, *Organized Labor and the Black Worker* (New York: Praeger, 1974), 47–63.

101. *CDN,* May 6, 1887 (quote); *CTr,* May 3, 7, 1887; *CH,* May 3, 1887; *CDN,* May 2, 6, 1887.

102. *The Freeman* [Indianapolis], May 31, 1890, reprinted in Philip S. Foner and Ronald L. Lewis, *The Black Worker during the Era of the Knights of Labor,* vol. 3 of *The Black Worker: A Documentary History from Colonial Times to the Present* (Philadelphia: Temple University Press, 1978), 406–10.

103. The strike was front-page news for most of its duration and was covered in de-

tail in all of the papers; see especially, *CP,* May 5–8, 1890, *CTr,* May 6–8, 1890, *CTi,* May 6–8, 1890; *St. Paul Appeal,* May 10, 1890.

104. *CTi,* May 7–9, 1890; *CP,* May 9, 1890; *CM,* May 9, 1890.

105. *CTi,* May 19, 23, 1890; *CP,* May 20, 1890.

106. *CDN,* May 26, 1890; *CTi,* May 17–18, 1890.

107. *CTi,* May 15, 17, 1890; *Illinois Staats-Zeitung,* May 15, 16, 1890.

108. *CP,* May 19, 1890; *CTi,* May 18–23, 1890.

109. *CTi,* May 23–June 4, 1890; *CP,* May 23–39, 1890.

110. *CP,* June 28, 1890.

111. *CG,* May 29, 30, June 2, 3, 6, 9, 10, 12, 1890; *CDN,* June 4–6, 11, 1890; *CH,* June 10–12, 1890; *Rights of Labor* 6 (June 14, 1890): 8; ibid. (June 28, 1890): 8.

112. *CTr,* June 19, 1892.

113. The WCTU badly overextended its finances by building the Women's Temple Building, which it eventually lost in bankruptcy. See *CG,* Aug. 2, 1890; *CM,* July 29, 1890; *CTr,* Feb. 3, 1891; *CP,* June 17, 1892.

114. *CTr,* May 15, 1891, Aug. 12, 1892; *CI-O,* May 15, 1891, Mar. 4, 1892; *CTi,* Oct. 3, 1891. On the union, ibid., May 13, 1893; *CDN,* May 14, 1893; *CR,* May 14, 1893; *CTr,* May 17, 1893. In 1914 a strike of waitresses at Henrici's Restaurant drew national attention; see Howard B. Myers, "The Policing of Labor Disputes in Chicago" (Ph.D. diss., University of Chicago, 1929), 747–71. The classic sociological study of later conditions is Francis Donovan, *The Woman Who Waits* (Boston: R. G. Badger, 1920); for a modern view, see Dorothy Sue Cobble, *Dishing It Out: Waitresses and Their Unions in the Twentieth Century* (Urbana: University of Illinois Press, 1991), 1–85, which is particularly excellent on waitressing.

115. *CTr,* Dec. 20, 1892, May 5, 8, 10, 19, 22, June 4, 20, 1893; *CDN,* Mar. 29, Apr. 10, May 10, Sept. 18, 1893; *CTi,* Apr. 30, May 1, 2, 3, 5–7, 13, 21, 22, June 1, 1893.

116. *CJ,* Feb. 3, 1893; examples of real discrimination cases were reported in *CDN,* Sept. 11, July 16, 1891, Oct. 22, 1895. One incident involved placing a screen around the table of Booker T. Washington (ibid., Aug. 3, 1900).

117. *CTi,* May 6, 1893 (quote), in reference to an Evanston strike broken when university students were recruited as replacements; *CTr,* July 9, Dec. 20, 1892, Feb. 10, 1893; *CP,* Aug. 13, 1897 (reprinting *New York Sun*), Jan. 5, 1900; Winfield Cozart, *A Technical Treatise on Dining Room Service: The Waiter's Manual* (Chicago: Hotel World, 1898); [John B. Goins], "The American Colored Waiter," *Hotel Monthly* 9 (Apr. 1901): 26–27, ibid. (June 1901): 21–22; H. Pettigrew, "Advice to Colored Waiters," *Hotel World* 54 (Jan. 4, 1902): 28–29.

118. [E. C. Maccannon], *Commanders of the Dining Room: Biographic Sketches and Portraits of Successful Head Waiters* (New York: Gwendolyn Publishing Co., 1904), 9–19.

119. *CTr,* Jan. 7, Feb. 12, May 18–27, 1903; *CDN,* May 18, 20, 21, June 12, 13, 18, 24–27, 1903; *CR-H,* May 27, June 5, 13–16, 26, 27, 1903.

120. City Club of Chicago, Civic Committee, Minutes, vol. 5, 432–38, 445–46, 538, City Club Papers, CHS.

121. *CC* article reprinted as "Negroes as Waiters," *Restaurant Bulletin* 2 (Apr. 1905): 26–27 (quote); J. P. Mitchell, "Colored Waiters Are Best," *Hotel World* 54 (Feb. 1, 1902): 26–27; "Observations of a Traveling Man," ibid., 15; "Why He Is Losing Ground," ibid. (Mar. 1, 1902): 26–27.

122. [Maida Springer Kemp], *Negro Pioneers in the Chicago Labor Movement* (Chicago: A. Philip Randolph Institute, Midwest Office, [c. 1970]), n.p.

123. Duis and LaFrance, *We've Got a Job to Do,* 115–21.

Chapter 10: Getting Ahead on Your Own

1. *CTr,* Jan. 29, 1995; Perry also appeared on news segments of CLTV, a Chicago-area cable news service, and on "Wild Chicago," WTTW.

2. The numbers are difficult to estimate because few peddlers bothered to take out a license. *CJ*, Apr. 23, 1885, set the number at 2,800, while the *CP*, May 15, 1894, estimated 9,000.

3. *DCA*, Aug. 19, 1839; Cleaver, *Reminiscences*, 46–47; Elizabeth Furbeck Porter, "Personal Reminiscences of Pioneer Life," manuscript, CHS.

4. *CDD*, May 30, 1848.

5. *CDJ*, Apr. 16, 1845; *CA*, Aug. 16, 1841; *Laws and Ordinances, 1873*, 103–5, indicates that porters were licensed as early as 1866. The law required them to wear a numbered badge and forbade "any misrepresentation or evil practice toward any emigrant or other person" (sec. 6); a general description of porters can be found in *CTr*, July 14, 1883.

6. *Chicago American* day book, pp. 155, 202, CHS, lists carriers; *Tri-Weekly Chicago Tribune*, Feb. 1, 1865; *CTr*, Dec. 31, 1852; Feb. 12, 1867; "Newsboys and Bootblacks Home," *Illustrated Chicago News* 1 (June 6, 1868): 104, 109.

7. Alfred R. Schumann, *No Peddlers Allowed* (Appleton, Wis.: C. C. Nelson, 1948), is an excellent general account.

8. *CTi*, Feb. 26, 1874; Schumann, *No Peddlers Allowed*, 33–56, tells the story of Solomon Levitan, who worked as a pack peddler out of Chicago and later became state treasurer of Wisconsin. The national story of the pack peddlers can be found in J. R. Dolan, *The Yankee Peddlers of Early America* (New York: Bramhall House, 1964); Richardson Wright, *Hawkers and Walkers in Early America* (Philadelphia: J. P. Lippincott, 1927); and W. Lee Provol, *The Pack Peddler* (Philadelphia: John C. Winston Co., 1937).

9. On Italians, *L'Italia*, Sept. 28, 29, 1895, and *CTr*, Nov. 12, 1888. On Greeks, Grace Abbott, "A Study of the Greeks of Chicago," *American Journal of Sociology* 15 (Nov. 1909): 389–90; *CTi*, May 1, 1892; *Greek Star*, Oct. 8, 1908. On food vending in general, Padraic Burke, "Rolling Carts and Songs of Plenty: The Urban Food Vendor," *Journal of American Culture* 2 (Fall 1979): 480–87.

10. Gertrude Savage, "The Scissors Grinder," *Arena* 9 (Jan. 1894): 253–60, is a general account.

11. Schumann, *No Peddlers Allowed*, 1–56; Associated Jewish Charities, *AR, 1908–09*, 130–31, *AR, 1909–1910*, 144–45, *AR, 1910–11*, 129–30; Carolyn Eastwood, "A Study of the Regulation of Chicago's Street Vendors" (Ph.D. diss., University of Illinois at Chicago, 1988); "Memorandum, Dec. 10, 1917," p. 15, Bowman Dairy Company Papers, CHS.

12. *CJ*, June 21, 1895.

13. George Ade, "Buying Matinee Tickets," *CR*, Aug. 18, 1894 (quote). On sandwiches and food carts in general, *CH*, May 26, 1888; *CTr*, Dec. 1, 1883; *CI-O*, July 8, 1896. On tamales, *CH*, July 14, 1892; *CTi*, Mar. 27, 1892. On hickory nuts and peanuts, *CTr*, Dec. 9, 1880, Nov. 9, 1883, May 4, 1888.

14. *CR-H*, July 21, 1894.

15. *L'Italia*, Sept. 10, 24, 1887, Aug. 1, 11, 18, 1888; Residents of Hull-House, *Hull-House Maps and Papers*, 138–39; Henry Krausz, *Street Types of Chicago* (Chicago: Max Stern and Co., 1892), 11–12, 24–25, 26, 32; feature on Mazzo in *CTr*, May 19, 1907.

16. *CP*, Sept. 23, 1890.

17. Ibid., Sept. 23, 1890 (quote); *Chicago Evening News*, Mar. 16, 1892; *CTr*, Feb. 4, 1894; *CT-H*, Dec. 26, 1895; *CR-H*, Dec. 20, 1910; John McGovern, "A Fakir," in Krausz, *Street Types of Chicago*, 27.

18. George Ade, "Queer Ways of Making a Living," *CP*, Aug. 28, 1894, and idem, "The Four Places in a Row," ibid., Oct. 9, 1895; on suit salesman, *CTr*, Apr. 1, 1906.

19. Wendt and Kogan, *Lords of the Levee*, 15, 73–74; idem, *Big Bill of Chicago* (Indianapolis: Bobbs-Merrill, 1953), 47–49, 81–83; Alex Gottfried, *Boss Cermak of Chicago: A Study of Political Leadership* (Seattle: University of Washington Press, 1962), 17.

20. For examples of peddler hardship stories, see *CJ*, Jan. 19, 1893; *CH*, Aug. 28, 1893; *CTi*, Aug. 29, 1893; Eastwood, "A Study of the Regulation of Chicago's Street Vendors," 37–39.

21. *CTi*, Aug. 23, 1880, Nov. 7, 1891; *CR*, Sept. 9, 1899. On nuisances in general, ibid.,

Oct. 11, 1898; *CJ*, Feb. 19, 1896; *CDN*, Sept. 10, 1892, Apr. 18, 1900; George Ade, "Some Singular Misconceptions," *CP*, July 25, 1894; *CCCP*, Mar. 29, 1897, 1932, Jan. 24, 1898, 1516–17.

22. *CR-H*, June 27, July 6, 1906.

23. *The Dawn* (Dec. 18, 1890): 11.

24. *CCCP*, June 25, 1883, 48–49; *CP*, Sept. 4, 1891.

25. Eastwood, "A Study of the Regulation of Chicago's Street Vendors," 55–56.

26. *CDN*, June 17, 1892.

27. *CTr*, Feb. 7, 1876, May 20, 1893; *CTi*, Oct. 4, 1881.

28. *L'Italia*, Oct. 1, 1890, July 25, 1891, Jan. 23, Mar. 5, Dec. 17, 1892; *CTr*, Jan. 19, 1874, Feb. 8, 1883; George Ade, "They Had Met Once Before," *CR*, Sept. 4, 1895, and idem, "Having a Man's Night of It," ibid., Oct. 4, 1895. See also David Wishnant, "Selling the Gospel News, Or, The Strange Career of Jimmy Brown the Newsboy," *Journal of Social History* 5 (Spring 1972): 269–309.

29. *CTi*, Aug. 20, 1875, Oct. 4, 1881, Nov. 7, 1891; *CTr*, Aug. 23, 1880, Apr. 23, June 2, 1891; *CDN*, May 17, 1884, Mar. 19, 1892; *CM*, Mar. 12, 1890, June 2, 1891; *CP*, Sept. 4, Nov. 5, 1891; *CR-H*, June 7, July 1, 1906.

30. *CTr*, May 31, 1894; *CT-H*, July 26, 1895; *CJ*, Feb. 5, 10, 1896, Aug. 10, 1899; *CI-O*, Feb. 18, 1896; *CC*, July 27, 28, 1904, Mar. 2, 1907; *CR-H*, Aug. 19, Nov. 21, 1905, Feb. 21, 1906, Mar. 2, 1907, Jan. 16, 30, 1912.

31. *CC*, Jan 9, Feb. 1, 7, 20, 1902; *CTr*, Feb. 6, 19, 20, 1902; *CDN*, Feb. 18, 1902; *CP*, June 1, Aug. 4, 1906.

32. *CP*, Aug. 18, 1893.

33. *CTi*, June 8, 1883; *Harper's Weekly* 46 (Feb. 22, 1902): 227.

34. Moore, *Plan of Chicago*, plates 107, 112, 115, 117, 128.

35. *Report of the Mayor's Market Commission*, 51–52.

36. *CCCP*, July 22, 1912, 1659, revised June 2, 1913, 784–85. On background of Maxwell Street, *CTr*, Sept. 20, 1896, Dec. 5, 1897; *CT-H*, July 28, 1895.

37. The story of Maxwell Street is told with great feeling in Ira Berkow, *Maxwell Street: Survival in a Bazaar* (Garden City: Doubleday, 1977).

38. *CTr*, Feb. 16, 1910.

39. Chicago, Superintendent of Education, *Annual Report, 1856–57*, 53–55; doc. 1865/66, 1625, CCCD Collection, IRAD, NEIU.

40. Chicago Board of Education, *AR, 1859–60*, 40–41, *AR, 1861*, 35, *AR, 1862*, 10–11; *CTr*, Jan. 5, Nov. 6, 1863.

41. *CTr*, Dec. 2, 1863, Jan. 1, 1864; Chicago Board of Education, *AR, 1863*, 15, 25, *AR, 1864*, 39, 41.

42. Chicago Board of Education, *AR, 1866–67*, 100–102, *AR, 1870–71*, 130–32.

43. Ibid., *AR, 1866–67*, 89–90; *CTr*, Oct. 25, 1866; doc. 1867/68, 0113A, CCCD Collection, IRAD, NEIU.

44. Chicago Board of Education *AR, 1872*, 128–29, *AR, 1876–77*, 21, *AR, 1880–81*, 50, 120, *AR, 1901–02*, 15.

45. *CTr*, Sept. 26, 1886.

46. Chicago Board of Education, *AR, 1887–88*, 117, *AR, 1889–90*, 156–67.

47. Ibid., *AR, 1868–69*, 117; *CTr*, Mar. 28, 1886; *CP*, Nov. 4, 11, 1895.

48. *Report of the Educational Commission of the City of Chicago* (Chicago, 1898), 147–51; Chicago Board of Education, *AR, 1886–87*, 136–41.

49. *CTr*, Apr. 22, 1894; Louise C. Wade, *Graham Taylor: Pioneer for Social Justice, 1851–1938* (Chicago: University of Chicago Press, 1964), 124–25; *Immigration* 2 (May 1910): 42. On the YMCA, see Frederick R. Dunn, "The Central Y.M.C.A. Schools of Chicago" (Ph.D. diss., University of Chicago, 1940), 82–95; Emmett Dedmon, *Great Enterprises: 100 Years of the Y.M.C.A. in Metropolitan Chicago* (Chicago: Rand McNally, 1957), 118–19.

50. *CR-H*, Oct. 3, 4, 1901, Jan. 9, 14, 1902. On tax suit, ibid., Sept. 2, 11–18, Oct. 1–3, 30, 1902; Chicago Board of Education, *AR, 1902–03*, 65–74.

51. Adele Marie Shaw, "Evening Schools for Foreigners," *World's Work* 9 (Jan. 1905): 5738 (quotes); Chicago Board of Education, *AR, 188-82,* 102-6, *AR, 1883-84,* 122-28, *AR, 1885-86,* 136-42, *AR, 1887-88,* 123-24, *AR, 1894-95,* 172-87; *L'Italia,* Sept. 15-16, 1894, Nov. 25, 1899.

52. *CI-O,* Oct. 9, 1892; *CTr,* Oct. 1, 1893.

53. Shaw, "Evening Schools for Foreigners," 5738, comments that different nationalities "often sit side by side in the class that struggles 'for spik the Englis,'" but most of the illustrations show classes of only one nationality.

54. Charles Meggan, "Teaching English in Evening School," *Educational Bi-Monthly* 3 (Oct. 1, 1908): 49-55; ethnic enrollments from Chicago Board of Education are reported in the board's annual reports and in Florence J. Chaney, "The Social and Educational Protection of the Immigrant Girl in Chicago" (M.A. thesis, University of Chicago, 1912), 39-41; *Immigration* 1 (June 1909): 17; ibid. 4 (May 1912): 58.

55. Chicago Board of Education, *AR, 1914-15,* 97-99, *AR, 1917-18,* 217-21, *AR, 1918-19,* 7-8; Taylor, *Chicago Commons through Forty Years,* 220-21, 237-47; *Free Evening Schools, Americanization Classes* (Chicago: Chicago Board of Education, 1921).

56. Englewood High School was the first. Chicago Board of Education, *AR, 1921-22,* 26; *Free Evening Schools: Circular of Information* (Chicago: Board of Education, 1921).

57. High-school enrollment increased fivefold, 1905-26. Mary Herrick, *The Chicago Schools: A Social and Political Portrait* (Beverly Hills, Calif.: Sage Publications, 1971), 178.

58. Chicago Board of Education, *AR, 1924-25,* 121-23, *AR, 1936-37,* 185-215; Milo H. Stewart and D. H. Eikenberry, "Secondary Education in Chicago," *Report of the Survey of the Schools of Chicago* (New York: Teachers College, Columbia University, 1932), 2:232-37.

59. Chicago Board of Education, *AR, 1938-39,* 227-42.

60. Leonard Q. Ross [Leo Rosten], *The Education of H*Y*M*A*N K*A*P*L*A*N* (New York: Harcourt, Brace, and World, 1937); see also Rosten's obituary, *NYT,* Feb. 20, 1997.

61. *CTr,* Jan. 1, 4, 1942; *War Production Training in the Chicago Public Schools* (Chicago: Chicago Board of Education, n.d.), passim.

62. *CDN,* May 21, 22, June 2, 1943, May 4, Nov. 12, 1944, Mar. 22, 1945.

63. *CS-T,* Apr. 7, 1995.

64. The most perceptive recent studies, besides Eastwood, "A Study of the Regulation of Chicago's Street Vendors," are Alfonso Morales, "Making Money at the Market: The Social and Economic Logic of Informal Markets" (Ph.D. diss., Northwestern University, 1993), idem, *Institutionalizing Informal Economic Resources: The Case of Property in Chicago's Maxwell Street Market* (Chicago: American Bar Foundation, 1991), and idem, *Tax Problems of New Immigrants: Merchants of Chicago's Maxwell Street Market* (Chicago: American Bar Foundation, 1991).

65. *CTr,* Oct. 27, 1993, Mar. 27, Aug. 29, 1994, Sept. 4, 1995.

Chapter 11: Time, Risk, and Family Finances

1. The failure occupied much of the first and second pages of all of the Chicago newspapers beginning with afternoon editions of August 6. See *CTr,* Aug. 7–Sept. 30, 1906.

2. Odd S. Lovoll, *A Century of Urban Life: The Norwegians in Chicago before 1930* (Northfield, Minn.: Norwegian-American Historical Association, 1988), 140, 186, 196-98, 211, 212, 241.

3. There is no excellent book on ethnic banking in Chicago, but see Francis M. Huston, *Financing an Empire: History of Banking in Illinois* (Chicago: S. J. Clarke, 1926), 4:87-88, 120-26, 164-65, 175-76, 211-13; on ethnic banking in general, "Immigrant Banks," *Immigration* 2 (Nov. 1910): 140-49; failures are recorded in *CTr,* Sept. 2, 1888, June 7-8, 1893, Jan. 8, 1897.

4. Bull, *The Township of Jefferson and "Dinner Pail Avenue,"* 43; Louis Schick, *Chicago and Environs* (Chicago: Louis Schick, 1891), 115.

5. *CT-H,* June 18, 1897; *Co-operation* 3 (June 13, 1903): 185-86, ibid. 4 (Mar. 5, 1904): 77.

6. *The Advance* 24 (Aug. 5, 1897): 164; *CR-H*, Aug. 23, 24, 30, 1906; *New World*, Sept. 22, 1906.

7. *The Advance* 52 (Aug. 10, 1911): 164 (quote); ibid. (July 13, 1911): 36–37; *CR-H*, Mar. 7, June 10, 27, 28, July 8, 9, 19, Dec. 26, 28, 1910, Jan. 5, Nov. 1, 1912; *Pratt's Digest of National Banking Laws, 1917* (Washington, D.C.: A. S. Pratt, 1917), 388–401.

8. Mary Willcox Brown, *The Development of Thrift* (New York: Macmillan, 1899), 1–31, makes numerous references to time.

9. Bureau of Justice *AR, 1889–90*, 20.

10. *CJ*, Jan. 12, 1878.

11. Illinois, *Laws, 1887*, 308.

12. *Twentieth Century*, Oct. 16, 1890, 14.

13. In *CDN*, Apr. 1, 1898, want ads, for instance, list "National Claims and Adjustment Bureau" and "Poor People's Legal Assistance Bureau."

14. Protective Agency for Women and Children, *AR, 1888*, 19–20 (whitemailing quote); *CP*, July 18, 1890 (second quote). See also *CJ*, Jan. 31, 1887; *CTr*, Mar. 4, 1894. On Bureau of Justice, *The Advance* 27 (May 4, 1893): 347. On the Wage Workers Collection Bureau, *CTi*, Sept. 27, 1891.

15. Some 57 percent of companies surveyed in 1918 still paid workers in cash. *Questionaire Digest on Methods of Wage Payment* (Chicago: Western Efficiency Society, 1918), 14.

16. *CI-O*, Nov. 28, 1891; Chicago Department of Public Works, *AR, 1888*, 77–78.

17. *CT-H*, Oct. 7, 1898.

18. Duis, *The Saloon*, 43, 181–82.

19. *CJ*, Mar. 30, 1885.

20. *CTr*, Jan. 11, 1874; though geographically specific in its discussion, there is an excellent summary of the issue in Lendol Glen Calder, "Financing the American Dream: Debt, Credit, and the Making of a Consumer Society, 1890–1940" (Ph.D. diss., University of Chicago, 1993).

21. *CTi*, Feb. 6, 1879.

22. *CTr*, Jan. 11, 1874, Apr. 19, 1896.

23. Craig H. Roell, *The Piano in America, 1890–1940* (Chapel Hill: University of North Carolina Press, 1989), 23, 31, 206–11; *Workingman's Advocate*, June 13, 1874.

24. Malcolm Proudfoot, "The Major Outlying Business Centers of Chicago" (Ph.D. diss., University of Chicago, 1936), 162–91.

25. *CTr*, Jan. 8, 11, 29, 1874.

26. *Illinois Staats-Zeitung*, Aug. 29, 1887; *CH*, July 3, 1888.

27. Beckner, *History of Labor Legislation*, 102–32, is the best general discussion of wage legislation; Illinois, *Laws, 1871–72*, 465, *Laws, 1879*, 175.

28. Citizens League of Chicago, *AR, 1880*, 22; *CTr*, Mar. 27, 1884, Apr. 1, 1894.

29. *Eight-Hour Herald*, Mar. 25, 1894; *CH*, Feb. 13, 1895; *Illinois Staats-Zeitung*, Apr. 28, 1895; *CJ*, Apr. 29, 1895; Illinois, *Laws, 1897*, 231, *Laws, 1901*, 214, *Laws, 1923*, 413–14, *Laws, 1925*, 427.

30. Associated Jewish Charities, *AR, 1908–09*, 130–31.

31. The outstanding work on the subject of loan sharking is Mark H. Haller and John Alviti, "Loansharking in American Cities: Historical Analysis of a Marginal Enterprise," *American Journal of Legal History* 21 (Apr. 1977): 125–56.

32. *CR*, Nov. 1, 2, 6, 9, 10, 15, 16, 1900; *CR-H*, Apr. 28, 1901, Nov. 13, 1902; *CI-O*, July 18, 1900.

33. "To Control Loan Sharks in Illinois," *Charities and the Commons* 21 (Dec. 12, 1908): 407–8.

34. *CTr*, Mar. 13, 1910.

35. *CR-H*, Feb. 28, 1912.

36. *Morrison's Chicago Weekly* 1 (Jan. 5, 1911): 6; ibid. (Jan. 26, 1911): 6; "Report of the

Subcommittee on the Loan Shark Evil," Civic Committee, Minutes, vol. 5, City Club Papers, CHS; Illinois, *Laws, 1917*, 553, upheld in People v. Stokes, 281 Ill. 159 (1917).

37. Associated Jewish Charities, *AR, 1908–09*, 130–31, *AR, 1909–10*, 144–45, *AR, 1910–11*, 129–30, *AR, 1911–12*, 141–42, *AR, 1912–13*, 138–39, *AR, 1913–14*, 182, *AR, 1914–15*, 170.

38. Illinois *Laws, 1913*, 199; Stanley R. Osborn, "The Good Loan Shark," *Chamberlin's* 14 (Apr. 1917): 7–8.

39. Osborn, "The Good Loan Shark," 7–8; Illinois, *Laws, 1925*, 255.

40. *CS*, Dec. 20, 1942; *Chicago Tribune Magazine*, Dec. 18, 1960; *CS-T*, Dec. 5, 1976.

41. The classic early study is Samuel Levine, *The Business of Pawnbroking* (New York: D. Halpern, 1913); an excellent recent examination is John P. Caskey, *Fringe Banking: Check-Cashing Outlets, Pawnshops, and the Poor* (New York: Russell Sage Foundation, 1994).

42. First regulatory ordinance, *Revised Charter and Ordinances of the City of Chicago*, 176; on Launder, see Edward H. Hall, *Hall and Smith City Directory 1853–54* (Chicago: Robert Fergus, 1853), 113. Edward H. Hall, *Hall's Chicago City Directory, 1855–56* (Chicago: Robert Fergus, 1855), 187, lists Patrick and James Carey, and Ellen Cunningham on Wells Street. The first non-Irish name, Abraham Lipman, appears in *Chicago Business Directory for 1864–65* (Chicago: W. S. Spencer, 1864), 174.

43. *Charter and Ordinances of the City of Chicago* (Chicago: D. B. Cooke and Co., 1856), 330–32.

44. *CH*, Feb. 20, 1893 (quote).

45. *Laws and Ordinances of the City of Chicago, 1866*, 299–301.

46. *Municipal Code of Chicago, 1881*, 393–95.

47. *CP*, July 16, 1895.

48. *CTr*, editorial, Dec. 4, 1883; see also, ibid., Mar. 20, 1883. On freight car thefts, ibid., Feb. 4, 1883.

49. Ibid., Feb. 4, Mar. 20, 1883, reiterating the earlier charge in *CI-O*, Oct. 9, 1878.

50. *CTr*, Dec. 16, 1882; *CDN*, Oct. 31, 1896; *CP*, Dec. 7, 1894, notes that "loan brokers" to the wealthy still had to take out a pawnbroker's license. George Ade, "The Gold Star Set with Diamonds," *CR*, Dec. 13, 1894, describes the fate of a Cook County Commissioner's badge.

51. *CTr*, Dec. 16, 1882.

52. *CDN*, Dec. 8, 1891; *CTr*, Apr. 1, 1883; pawning slang is discussed in *Moran's Dictionary of Chicago* [1894], 162, the identical text of which appears in the same publisher's 1910 edition, 183–84.

53. *CP*, July 6, 1895.

54. *CTr*, Oct. 4, 1903.

55. Ibid.

56. *CTr*, Dec. 16, 1882; *CDN*, Oct. 31, 1896.

57. *CTi*, June 27, 1864.

58. *CTr*, Dec. 16, 1882, *CH*, Oct. 24, 1886; *Lakeside Directory of Chicago, 1910*, 1660.

59. *CTr*, Dec. 16, 1882; *CH*, Oct. 24, 1886, Jan. 10, Dec. 19, 1897; George Ade, "Chattel Mortgage Methods in Chicago," *CR*, July 14, 1894.

60. *CP*, July 16, 1895; W. R. Patterson, "Pawnbroking in Europe and the United States," U.S. Department of Labor, *Bulletin*, no. 21 (Mar. 1899): 274.

61. *CTr*, Mar. 21, Apr. 1, 1883; ibid., Jan. 19, 1877, reports a bill in General Assembly to limit maximum interest to 3 percent per month.

62. Ibid., June 13, Dec. 7, 1894; *CP*, Dec. 7, 1894.

63. *CTr*, Apr. 1, 1883, June 9, Oct. 31, Nov. 1, 1899; Patterson, "Pawnbroking in Europe and the United States," 173–310; *CJ*, Jan. 14, Feb. 27, 1895, Dec. 2, 1899; *Illinois Staats-Zeitung*, Jan. 14, 1899; *CP*, Feb. 7, 1899.

64. *CT-H*, May 24, 1899; First State Pawners Society, *ARs*, 1899–1949.

65. "Analysis and Summary of Replies Received from Sixty-six Pawnbrokers Relative to Sundry Inquiries Contained in a Questionnaire of the Committee of License of the

Chicago City Council Including Information Pertaining to Capital Invested, Sales, Payrolls, Rentals, Gross Income, Dividends and Personal Property Taxes Paid in 1917," typescript, Apr. 1918, 1–11, Municipal Reference Library, Chicago.

66. *CTr,* June 5, 1944.

67. *CDN,* June 29, July 1, 1961; *CS-T,* Aug. 3, 1961; *CA,* Jan. 15, 1962; *Focus/Midwest* (July 1963): 12–13; *Chicago Courier,* Jan. 6, 1962.

68. *CDN,* June 12, 1957, Feb. 28, 1970; *CTr,* Jan. 15, 1968; *CS-T,* Feb. 20, 1972.

69. *Chicago Ilini,* Nov. 22, 1982; *CS-T,* Jan. 16, 1983.

70. *Ameritech Chicago Consumer Yellow Pages, 1995-96,* 1141–52.

71. *CTr,* Dec. 10, 1985, Jan. 13, 29, 1987, Dec. 20, 1989, Aug. 14, Oct. 21, Nov. 19, 1990, Aug. 14, 1991, Mar. 1, June 11, 1992, May 8, June 11, Sept. 5, 1995, July 10, 1996. On tighter police regulation see ibid., Feb. 27, Apr. 24, 1997.

Chapter 12: The Institutional Trap

1. Mark Haller, "Police Reform in Chicago," *American Behavioral Scientist* 13 (May–Aug 1970): 649–66; Michael P. McCarthy, "Businessmen and Professional Reform, 1887–1920: The Chicago Experience" (Ph.D. diss., Northwestern University, 1970); Roberts, "Businessmen in Revolt."

2. Dorothy Powers, "The Chicago Woman's Club" (M.A. thesis, University of Chicago, 1939); Frederick C. Jaher, *The Urban Establishment: Upper Strata in Boston, New York, Charleston, and Chicago* (Urbana: University of Illinois Press, 1982).

3. On club houses, see, for example, *CTr,* Dec. 8, 1892 (the Morton Park Club), ibid., Dec. 15, 1892 (the Edgewater Club).

4. Amilee Hofer, *Neighborhood Improvement In and About Chicago* (Chicago: Chicago Woman's Club, [1909]); Edwin D. Jackson, *The Northwest Federation of Improvement Clubs, 1914-1947: A History* (Chicago: Northwest Federation of Improvement Clubs, 1947).

5. Charles Shanabruch, "The Catholic Church's Role in the Americanization of Chicago's Immigrants: 1833-1928" (Ph.D. diss., University of Chicago, 1975), 330–70; Rev. Daniel T. McGolgan, *A Century of Charity: The First One Hundred Years of the Society of St. Vincent DePaul in the United States,* 2 vols. (Milwaukee: Bruce Publishing Co., 1951), 1:485–514, 2:486–87, 508; Elizabeth E. Wade, "Social Aspects of the Work of Protestant Missions and Institutional Churches among Certain Foreign People of Chicago" (M.A. thesis, University of Chicago, 1926); *Twenty-Five Years of Blessing: Historical Sketch of the Chicago Hebrew Mission, 1887-1912* (Chicago: Chicago Hebrew Mission, 1912).

6. Woods and Kennedy, *Handbook of Settlements,* 37–80.

7. Humbert Nelli, "John Powers and the Italians: Politics in a Chicago Ward, 1896–1921," *Journal of American History* 57 (June 1970): 67–84.

8. Duis, *The Saloon,* 126–28.

9. *CTr,* Dec. 19–24, 1888.

10. On the general history of the hospital, William E. Quine, "Early History of Cook County Hospital to 1870," *Bulletin of the Society of Medical History of Chicago* 1 (Oct. 1911): 15–21, and Enid R. Rich, "The Cook County Hospital" (M.A. thesis, University of Chicago, 1927); G. Koehler, "Annals of Health and Sanitation in Chicago," 1461–1524, remains remarkably useful; Thomas N. Bonner, *Medicine in Chicago: 1850-1950* (Madison: American History Research Center, 1957), 62–64, 161–65, puts the institution in general context; *CTr,* Mar. 30, 1997, is a recent assessment.

11. Webb, *History of Contagious Disease Care.*

12. *CA,* Jan. 28, 1837; *CJ,* Apr. 29, 1845; *CD,* Feb. 24, Dec. 8, 1846.

13. *WCD,* Dec. 28, 1847.

14. Illinois, *Laws, 1849,* 40; Koehler, "Annals of Health and Sanitation in Chicago," 1475; *History of Medicine and Surgery and Physicians and Surgeons of Chicago* (Chicago: Biographical Publishing Corporation, 1922), 48–50, 235–36; Andreas, *History of Cook County,* 597.

15. Rush Medical College, *Fifth Annual Catalog, 1847–48*, 3–4; James W. Norris, *Norris Directory of Chicago, 1847–48* (Chicago: J. H. Kedzie, 1847), 97; James Nevin Hyde, *Early Medical Chicago* (Chicago: Fergus, 1879), 42–43; *CD*, Apr. 6, 1847; *CDJ*, Feb. 24, Mar. 15, 1848, June 26, 1850.

16. Chicago Board of Health, *Biennial Report, 1867–69*, 32, 39, 43; on question of admitting noncontagious cases, Hyde, *Early Medical Chicago*, 51–54.

17. The board was reestablished in 1876. *CPT,* Aug. 15, 1859; *Chicago City Directory, 1862–63* (Chicago: T. H. Halpin, 1982), xxxv.

18. *CDD*, Sept. 6, 1860; *CTr*, May 8, 1862.

19. Hyde, *Early Medical Chicago*, 51–54; *CTr*, June 9, Nov. 13, 1865; *Chicago City Directory for the Year 1864–65* (Chicago: John Baily, 1864), appendix, xxviii.

20. *CTr*, Jan. 8, 15, Mar. 8, 1866, Jan. 1, 1867.

21. Rawlings, *Rise and Fall of Disease in Illinois*, 1:35–86, 101–15, 304–95.

22. Ibid., 2:261.

23. Alice Hamilton, *Exploring the Dangerous Trades* (Boston: Little, Brown, 1943), is the autobiography of the physician, long affiliated with Hull-House, who was most responsible for identifying workplace hazards during the period from the mid-1890s through World War I. On industrial health in general, see Henry B. Selleck, *Occupational Health in America* (Detroit: Wayne State University Press, 1962), 34–53.

24. *CTr*, Jan. 17, 1870 (quotation); information about the county hospital in this paragraph and the following one comes from Henry M. Lyman, "A Bit of the History of the Cook County Hospital," typescript, CHS, copied from *Bulletin of the Society of Medical History of Chicago* 1 (Oct. 1910): 8–12, 25–36.

25. Jim Bowman, *Good Medicine: The First 150 Years of Rush–Presbyterian–St. Lukes Medical Center* (Chicago: Chicago Review Press, 1978), 1–37.

26. *CTi,* Dec. 11, 1880; Illinois State Commissioner of Public Charities, *Biennial R, 1878,* 229, *Biennial R, 1880,* 316–19.

27. Chicago Medical Society, Directors' Minutes, meeting of Oct. 15, 1888, vol. 9, 96, Jan. 21, 1889, vol. 9, 117–18, June 17, 1907, vol. 17, n.p., Oct. 9, 1906, vol. 20, n.p., Nov. 13, 1906, vol. 20, n.p., Nov. 9, 1907, vol. 20, n.p., Apr. 12, 1910, vol. 23, n.p., CHS; Chicago Police Department, *ARs* list calls taking victims to their homes.

28. On the national trends in the general image of hospitals, Morris J. Vogel, *The Invention of the Modern Hospital: Boston, 1870–1930* (Chicago: University of Chicago Press, 1980), 9–14, and Charles Rosenberg, "Social Class and Medical Care in Nineteenth-Century America: The Rise and Fall of the Dispensary," *Journal of the History of Medicine and Allied Sciences* 29 (Jan. 1974): 32–54. On local dispensaries, *Handbook of Chicago Charities* (Chicago: Illinois Conference of Charities and Corrections, 1892), 6, 18–19, 22–23, 34–36, 39, 94, 117, 161–63; Paul A. Buelow, "The Dispensary Comes to Chicago: Health Care and the Poor before 1920" (Ph.D. diss., University of Illinois at Chicago, 1997).

29. Perry R. Duis and Glen E. Holt, "Chicago As It Was: Angels of Mercy," *Chicago* 28 (May 1979): 198–201; Lyon, "History of Public Health Nursing."

30. *CTr*, Nov. 22, 27, 1876; *CP*, June 1, 4, 1878.

31. Henrietta Frank, "Woman's Achievements: Development of Trained Nurses," *Fine Arts Journal* 18 (June 1907):n.p.; Grace Fay Schryver, *A History of the Illinois Training School for Nurses, 1880–1929* (Chicago: Board of Directors of the Illinois Training School for Nurses, 1930), 1–17; Helena F. Richter, *A Nurse's Journal* (Chicago: S. I. Bradbury, 1884), is a guidebook for nurses written by an early ITSN graduate.

32. Richard Lindberg, *Chicago Ragtime: Another Look at Chicago, 1880–1920* (South Bend: Icarus, 1985), 45–73, gives a delightful popular account of McGarigle's adventures.

33. *CTr*, July 28, 1890, May 23, 1891; James Brown, *History of Public Assistance in Chicago, 1833 to 1893* (Chicago: University of Chicago Press, 1941), 149–59; Residents of Hull-House, *Hull-House Maps and Papers,* 154; the charges continued in *CR-H,* Nov. 27, 30, 1904, Apr. 17, 1906.

34. *CP,* Apr. 29, 1899.

35. *CT-H,* May 9, 1901; *CTr,* June 4, 1901; *CR-H,* Apr. 12, 20, 21, 23, 26, 28, May 11, 12, 1901.

36. llinois, Board of State Commissioners of Public Charities, *Biennial R, 1892,* 138 (quote). Conditions also described in *Biennial R, 1888,* 94, and Residents of Hull-House, *Hull-House Maps and Papers,* 154.

37. *CR-H,* June 15, Sept. 21, 22, 1910, Feb. 23, 1912; *The Advance* 61 (Feb. 23, 1911): 240.

38. *CR-H,* Nov. 5, 6, 1910, Feb. 17, 18, 1911.

39. Cook County Board of Commissioners, *Proceedings, Oct. 27, 1911,* 1422; *CR-H,* Dec. 15, 1910, on the single site-dispersal issue.

40. *CR-H,* Mar. 12–14, 16, 1912.

41. Ibid., Sept. 2, Oct. 10, 1912.

42. Ibid., Nov. 29, 1912; *CTr,* May 14, 17, 18, 21, June 10, 11, July 3, 1914; Schryver, *History of the Illinois Training School for Nurses,* 98–105.

43. *CTr,* Mar. 19, July 3, 1914; *Survey* 32 (Aug. 15, 1914): 496.

44. *CTr,* Apr. 7, 1927; Cook County, Charity Service Reports, Hospital Warden, *AR, 1916,* 185–207, *AR, 1917,* 233–61, *AR, 1918,* 21–24, 153–67, *AR, 1919,* 159–83, *AR, 1920,* 26–28, 177–89, *AR, 1921,* 161–80, *AR, 1922,* 17–18, 146–58, *AR, 1923,* 226–38, *AR, 1924,* 109–24, *AR, 1925,* 23–28, *AR, 1926,* 31–37, *AR, 1927,* 25–35.

45. *CDA,* Sept. 25, 1839, Oct. 30, 1841.

46. *CDJ,* Jan. 6, 1848 (quote); Illinois *Revised Statutes, 1846,* 797–99, contains the placing-out provisions.

47. Sophonisba Breckinridge, *The Illinois Poor Law and Its Administration* (Chicago: University of Chicago Press, 1939), 3–45.

48. Henry H. Hurlbut, *Chicago Antiquities* (Chicago: By the Author, 1881), 575–76, notes that the victim of an unsuccessful amputation was taken to a poorhouse on the Court-House Square in 1838 and that the building was sold and moved away in 1840.

49. *CDD,* Dec. 22, 1847, Jan. 5, 1848, Dec. 10, 14, 1850, Feb. 15, 1851; *CDJ,* Dec. 29, 1847, Jan. 6, Feb. 24, 1848, Mar. 13, 1849; *Gem of the Prairie,* Jan. 8, Sept. 15, 1848; *CT,* Jan 19, 1853; *WCD,* Feb. 19, 1853.

50. Brown, *History of Public Assistance,* 18–23; obituary of David Dunning, *CTr,* July 13, 1901.

51. *CDDP,* Dec. 11, 1854.

52. David Rothman, *The Discovery of the Asylum: Social Order and Disorder in the New Republic* (Boston: Little, Brown, 1971), provides the best general explanation.

53. On question of indoor and outdoor relief, *Gem of the Prairie,* Jan. 8, 1848, Apr. 12, 1851; *CD,* Jan. 5, 1848; *CDJ,* Mar. 10, Dec. 12, 1858, Dec. 8, 1859.

54. *WCD,* Jan. 9, 1860 (quote); ibid., June 13, 1857 (corpse scandal). For general description, see ibid., Dec. 16, 1854; *DCA,* Dec. 11, 1854, Feb. 13, 1855; *CDDP,* Dec. 8, 1856; *CPT,* Sept. 15, 1858; *CTr,* Dec. 8, 1860, June 11, 1861.

55. Cecelia Hilliard, *Providing a Home: A History of the Old People's Home of Chicago* (Chicago: Old People's Home of Chicago, 1983); Arthur E. Anderson, "The Institutional Path of Old Age in Chicago, 1870–1912" (Ph.D. diss., University of Virginia, 1983), 42–78.

56. *CTr,* Feb. 24, 1874; another exposé is in ibid., Jan. 2, 1874.

57. On the almshouse exposé, see *CTr,* Feb. 22, 1874; *CPM,* Jan. 25, Feb. 1, 1876; *CP,* Apr. 8, 1878, reports results of investigation exonerating the insane-asylum staff.

58. *CDN,* Jan. 25, 1884; *CTr,* July 28, 1889.

59. *CTr,* May 6, 1888.

60. Illinois State Commissioner of Public Charities, *Special Report of an Investigation of the Management of the Cook County Hospital for the Insane* (1886), 3–19; Illinois State Board of Charities and Corrections, *Biennial Report, 1881,* 223, *Biennial Report, 1883,* 243, *Biennial Report, 1886,* 188–19, *Biennial Report, 1888,* 93; *CTr,* Nov. 19, 1885, Apr. 30, 1889; Citizens Association of Chicago, *AR, 1886,* 6, *AR, 1889,* 21.

61. *CTr,* Jan. 19, 1895.

62. Ibid., July 10, 19, 1889; *CP*, Feb. 13, 1897; there are many newspaper articles about conditions at Dunning in the Charles Ambler–Citizens Association Scrapbooks, vols. 79–81, CHS.

63. Illinois State Commission of Public Charities, *Special Report of an Investigation of the Management of the Cook County Hospital for the Insane* (Springfield, 1885), 3–19; *CTr*, Nov. 19, 1885, Feb. 26, 1888, May 5, 1889, Mar. 7, 1894; Katherine Reed, "The Cook County Hospital for the Insane," *The Graphic* [Chicago] 8 (Feb. 18, 1893): 122–23, and idem, "A Day at the Poorhouse," ibid. 7 (Sept. 24, 1892): 224–25.

64. *CTi*, Dec. 29, 1883, on body snatching; *CTr*, May 22, June 20, July 13, 19, 21, 1889, detail one particularly brutal case in which the attendants were later exonerated.

65. *CTr*, Apr. 30, May 5, 22, July 10, 13, 19, 21, 1889.

66. *CDN*, Jan 29, Feb. 4–6, 11, 18, 21, Mar. 4, 5, 13, 27, 1890; Illinois Board of State Commissioners of Public Charities, *Biennial R, 1892*, 36–37, 137.

67. Katherine Reed, "A Day at the Poorhouse," *The Graphic* [Chicago] 7 (Sept. 24, 1894): 224–25 (quote).

68. Cook County Board of Commissioners, *Proceedings*, Apr. 2, 1894, 390; *CTr*, Mar. 3, 1894; *CP*, June 29, 1895.

69. *CTr*, Aug. 13, 1891, Oct. 30, 1894, Sept. 2, 1895; *Illinois Staats-Zeitung*, Oct. 18, 1894.

70. *CJ*, Mar. 27, 1891.

71. *CR-H*, Apr. 12, 1912; Johnson, *Growth of Cook County*, 271; Illinois Board of Administration, *AR, 1912*, 931–76.

72. Charles B. Johnson, *Growth of Cook County* (Chicago: Board of Commissioners of Cook County, 1960), 1:261–65.

73. Andreas, *History of Chicago*, 1:175; *CD*, Oct. 6, 1846.

74. *CD*, Sept. 7, Aug. 10, 1847; *CDJ*, Mar. 18, 1849, Feb. 19, 1850.

75. *CDJ*, June 19–22, Aug. 31, 1850, Jan. 3, 1851, Mar. 19, July 17, 1852; *CDD*, Oct. 30, 1852, Feb. 27, 1860; *CDDP*, Feb. 1, 12, 1853.

76. *CTr*, June 28, Oct. 1, 1861.

77. Ibid., May 30, 1861.

78. See, for instance, doc. 56/57 1449, 1640, 1662, 1663, 1706, 1942, CCCD Collection, IRAD, NEIU; *CDDP*, Mar. 16, Aug. 23, 1854, Mar. 11, 1857; *CTr*, Nov. 20, 1861.

79. *CTr*, Mar. 20, 1861.

80. Unidentified clipping, "City Bridewell," in Elias Colbert "Chicago in 1862" Scrapbook, n.p., CHS; on vagrants, Illinois, *Laws, 1863*, 40.

81. *CTr*, Sept. 16, 1863, Aug. 14, 1865.

82. Ibid., June 11, 1867, Mar. 19, 1868, Jan. 5, Feb. 16, 1870.

83. Ibid., July 22, Aug. 14, 1870, Jan. 17, 1873, June 22, 1874; *CTi*, Dec. 11, 1871, Jan. 15, 1874.

84. G. A. Claussenius, *The House of Correction of the City of Chicago: A Retrospect, 1871–1921* (Chicago: City of Chicago, 1921), 10–11; *CDD*, Feb. 27, 1851; *CDDP*, Apr. 15, 1858.

85. *CTi*, Mar. 3, 5, 15, 1872; *CTr*, Feb. 2, July 29, 1884, Feb. 1, 1886; Illinois, *Laws, 1879*, 70–71.

86. Chicago House of Correction, *AR, 1886*, 3–4.

87. On women, Chicago House of Correction, *AR, 1891*, 5; *CTr*, Jan. 4, 1885.

88. Chicago House of Correction, *AR, 1910*, 37.

89. Ibid., *AR, 1878*, 8–10, *AR, 1880*, 7.

90. Ibid., *AR, 1892*, 4–5.

91. Ibid., *AR, 1874*, 20–21.

92. *CTr*, June 20, 1857, July 31, 1869, Jan. 11, 25, 1870; Chicago House of Correction, *AR, 1876*, 12–16, *AR, 1885*, 18.

93. Classenius, *House of Correction*, 11–12, 13–16, 22–23 (cell house).

94. Ibid., 29 (lock step), 59–60 (baseball and movies), 36–37 (Willow Springs).

95. Ibid., 44.

96. *CTr*, June 1, 1890, describes various institutions; Buelow, "The Dispensary Comes to Chicago," 400–14, lists 131 dispensaries operating between 1843 and 1918.

97. *CDN*, Sept. 8, 1960 (quote).

98. Ibid., Sept. 12, 1960.

99. *CDN*, Sept 8–10, 12–14, 30, 1960, Mar. 1, 1961, Mar. 2, 1962; *CA*, Apr. 19, 1962, Dec. 6, 1967; *CTr*, May 13, Dec. 18, 1962.

100. *CS-T*, Apr. 18, 1969, July 5, 1970, Aug. 19, 1971; *CTr*, June 24, 1969, May 25, 1975, Dec. 7, 12, 1979; *CTo*, June 24, 1969; *CDN*, Feb. 5, 1970, Mar. 22, 1973.

101. *CTo*, Jan. 1, 23, Mar. 11. 1970.

102. *CTr*, May 6, 1989, July 9, 1990, June 10, Dec. 2, 1994, Dec. 22, 1995.

103. Petra Dahl, "Cook County Hospital Reorganization Plan," reprinted from *Bulletin of Medical Women's Club of Chicago*, Apr. 1931; *CTr*, Nov. 18, 1939.

104. *CDN*, Feb. 22, 1939, Aug. 2, 1941; *CTr*, Feb. 26, 1935.

105. On the problem in general, *CDN*, Dec. 27, 1948, Jan. 3, 1949, Sept. 28, 1950, Apr. 24, 1953; *The Chicago–Cook County Health Survey*, 1083, 1087, 1118.

106. *CS-T*, Apr. 25, 1956; Chicago Urban League, "A Commentary on the Improvement of Cook County Hospital with Recommendation," Apr. 1957, and Welfare Council of Metropolitan Chicago, "Location of a South Side Branch of Cook County Hospital," Feb. 1957, typescripts, both at CHS.

107. *CDN*, Dec. 11, 1962; *CS-T*, Jan. 31, Feb. 5, 14, Dec. 13, 1963; *CA*, Feb. 1, 3, Nov. 16, 26, 1963; *CTr*, July 21, 1964; *Medical World News*, Aug. 28, 1964, 62–63.

108. *CDN*, Mar. 5, 6, 8, Apr. 21, 1962, Feb. 14, Apr. 13, 1963; *CA*, Oct. 4, 1960; *CTr*, Mar. 19, 20, 1961, Jan. 29, Feb. 1, 1968; *CS-T*, Nov. 10, 22, 1967.

109. *CTr*, Dec. 15, 1967; *CS-T*, Jan. 19, 1968.

110. *CTr*, July 7, Dec. 22, 1968, Mar. 14, 1969; *CS-T*, Mar. 15, 1969.

111. *CS-T*, Mar. 20, Apr. 20, 1969; *CA*, Mar. 20, Apr. 25, July 24, 1969; *CTr*, Mar. 23, Aug. 19, 1969.

112. *CTr*, Jan. 26, May 16, 19, 20, July 26, 1970; *CDN*, Mar. 13, 19, Apr. 17, May 20, 28, 1970; *CTo*, Feb. 22, 25, Mar. 19, 1970; *CS-T*, May 30, July 29, 1970; see also, Illinois Legislative Investigating Commission, *Report on Cook County Hospital*, 1972.

113. *CTr*, Apr. 21, 1990, Jan. 21, 23, 27, Feb. 6, 8, Apr. 30, 1991.

114. Ibid., Nov. 15, 22, 1989, Jan. 9, Mar. 9, 30, 1990, Jan. 5, Oct. 1, Dec. 10, 1993, Mar. 22, 25, May 17, June 2, 1994; the issue of historic preservation of the old building also briefly entered the picture, ibid., Oct. 6, 1994.

115. Ibid., Jan. 11, 12, 22, 31, Feb. 2, Apr. 11, May 12–14, June 2, 4, 16, 18–20, 22, 23, 28, July 2, 3, 10, Aug. 5, 11, Sept. 29, 1989.

116. Ibid., July 30, Sept. 15, 1988.

117. Ibid., Mar. 23, 25, 1989, Jan. 11, 19, Feb. 6, 7, 9, 12, May 9, 16, July 18, 22, Aug. 22–25, Sept. 18, 1990, Mar. 1, 6, May 1, June 20, 25, 1991, Oct. 29, 1992, Aug. 3, 17, 18, 1993, May 6, 8, 1994. The facility reopened as the Provident Pavilion of Cook County Hospital in August 1993.

118. On pharmacists, ibid., May 22, 1990, and on nurses, ibid., Oct. 28–30, Nov. 2–19, 22–30, Dec. 7–12, 1976; ibid., Sept. 29, 1990, reports a work slowdown.

119. Ibid., Oct. 31, 1990; Sydney Lewis, *Hospital: An Oral History of Cook County Hospital* (New York: The New Press, 1994), is an excellent inside account from the medical staff.

120. *CTr*, Feb. 3, 1993 (quote); *CTo*, May 5, 1971; *CTr*, Mar. 23, 1966; *Look Magazine*, May 18, 1971, 25–33.

121. *CTr*, Dec. 28, 29, 1989, Apr. 27, 1990, Mar. 28, 1991.

Conclusion

1. *CTr*, July 22, 1898.

2. *CA*, Apr. 7, 1963, Clipping File, CHS.

Selected Bibliography

Challenging Chicago grew out of many sources, the most important of which were articles and features gleaned from thirty years of research in Chicago's newspapers and magazines. Although not without their biases and errors, writers of long ago generally did an excellent job of providing the various segments of the reading public with a wealth of detail about people who were different from themselves. The writers' natural curiosity and excitement about the phenomenon of city living is especially obvious in the thousands of Sunday features about Chicago's social life. The *Tribune, Herald, Journal, Record-Herald,* and *Post* did the best job of describing the everyday details of city life; even the *Times,* the *Mail,* and the *Dispatch,* which were early Chicago's equivalent of today's supermarket tabloid, occasionally rose to excellence.

The endnotes of this work function as a detailed index of where to go to find more information about any subject, especially in the numerous manuscript collections consulted. The following is a list of the secondary books that were most important for this work and are most accessible for the general reader.

Abbott, Edith. *The Tenements of Chicago, 1908–1935.* Chicago: University of Chicago Press, 1936.

Andreas, Alfred T. *History of Chicago.* 3 vols. Chicago: A. T. Andreas, 1884, 1885, 1886.

Barrett, James R. *Work and Community in the Jungle: Chicago's Packinghouse Workers, 1894–1922.* Urbana: University of Illinois Press, 1987.

Barrett, Paul F. *The Automobile and Urban Transit: The Formation of Public Policy in Chicago, 1900–1930.* Philadelphia: Temple University Press, 1983.

Beckner, Earl R. *A History of Labor Legislation in Illinois.* Chicago: University of Chicago Press, 1929.

Bluestone, Daniel. *Constructing Chicago.* New Haven: Yale University Press, 1991.

Bowly, Devereaux. *The Poorhouse: Subsidized Housing in Chicago, 1895–1976.* Carbondale: Southern Illinois University Press, 1978.

Brown, James. *History of Public Assistance in Chicago, 1833 to 1893*. Chicago: University of Chicago Press, 1941.

Cain, Louis. *Sanitation Strategy for a Lakefront Metropolis*. DeKalb: Northern Illinois University Press, 1978.

Cohen, Lizabeth. *Making a New Deal: Industrial Workers in Chicago, 1919–39*. New York: Cambridge University Press, 1990.

Condit, Carl. *The Chicago School of Architecture: A History of Commercial and Public Building in the Chicago Area, 1875–1925*. Chicago: University of Chicago Press, 1964.

Douglas, George H. *Rail City: Chicago, U.S.A.* San Diego: Howell-North Books, 1981.

Duis, Perry R. *The Saloon: Public Drinking in Chicago and Boston, 1880–1920*. Urbana: University of Illinois Press, 1983.

———. "The Shaping of Chicago." In *AIA Guide to Chicago*, edited by Alice Sinkevitch, 3–24. New York: Harcourt Brace, 1993.

Duis, Perry R., and Scott LaFrance. *We've Got a Job to Do: Chicagoans and World War II*. Chicago: Chicago Historical Society, 1992.

Ebner, Michael. *Creating Chicago's North Shore: A Suburban History*. Chicago: University of Chicago Press, 1988.

Einhorn, Robin. *Property Rules: Political Economy in Chicago, 1833–1872*. Chicago: University of Chicago Press, 1991.

Gilbert, James. *Perfect Cities: Chicago's Utopias of 1893*. Chicago: University of Chicago Press, 1991.

Grossman, James R. *Land of Hope: Chicago, Black Southerners, and the Great Migration*. Chicago: University of Chicago Press, 1989.

Holli, Melvin G., and Peter D'A. Jones. *Ethnic Chicago: A Multi-Cultural Portrait*. 4th ed. Grand Rapids: Eerdmans, 1995.

Hoyt, Homer. *One Hundred Years of Land Values in the City of Chicago*. Chicago: University of Chicago Press, 1933.

Jaher, Frederic C. *The Urban Establishment: Upper Strata in Boston, New York, Charleston, and Chicago*. Urbana: University of Illinois Press, 1982.

Karamanski, Theodore J. *Rally 'Round the Flag: Chicago and the Civil War*. Chicago: Nelson-Hall, 1993.

Keating, Ann Durkin. *Building Chicago: Suburban Developers and the Creation of a Divided Metropolis*. Columbus: Ohio State University Press. 1988.

Lewis, Sydney. *Hospital: An Oral History of Cook County Hospital*. New York: The New Press, 1994.

Lovoll, Odd. *A Century of Urban Life: The Norwegians in Chicago Before 1930*. Northfield, Minn.: Norwegian-American Historical Association, 1988.

Mayer, Harold M., and Richard C. Wade. *Chicago: Growth of a Metropolis*. Chicago: University of Chicago Press, 1969.

McShane, Clay. *Down the Asphalt Path: The Automobile and the American City*. New York: Columbia University Press, 1994.

Meine, Franklin, ed. *George Ade, Chicago Stories*. 1941. Reprint. Chicago: Henry Regnery Company, 1963.

Meyerowitz, Joan. *Women Adrift: Independent Wage Earners in Chicago, 1880–1930*. Chicago: University of Chicago Press, 1988.

Moffat, Bruce. *Forty Feet Below: The Story of Chicago's Freight Tunnels*. Glendale, Calif.: Interurban Press, 1982.

———. *"The L": The Development of Chicago's Rapid Transit System*. Bulletin 131. Chicago: Central Electric Railfans, 1995.

Nelli, Humbert. *The Italians in Chicago, 1880–1930: A Study in Ethnic Mobility*. New York: Oxford University Press, 1970.

Pacyga, Dominic A. *Polish Immigrants and Industrial Chicago: Workers on the South Side, 1880–1922*. Columbus: Ohio State University Press, 1991.

Pierce, Bessie Louise. *A History of Chicago.* 3 vols. New York: Knopf, 1937, 1940, 1957.

Randall, Frank A. *History of the Development of Building Construction in Chicago.* Urbana: University of Illinois Press, 1949.

Riess, Steven A. *City Games: The Evolution of American Urban Society and the Rise of Sports.* Urbana: University of Illinois Press, 1989.

Rosen, Christine. *The Limits of Power: Great Fires and the Process of City Growth in America.* New York: Cambridge University Press, 1986.

Sawislak, Karen. *Smoldering City: Chicagoans and the Great Fire, 1871–74.* Chicago: University of Chicago Press, 1995.

Slayton, Robert. *Back of the Yards: The Making of a Local Democracy.* Chicago: University of Chicago Press, 1986.

Spear, Allan H. *Black Chicago: The Making of a Negro Ghetto, 1890–1920.* Chicago: University of Chicago Press, 1967.

Wade, Louise. *Chicago's Pride: The Stockyards, Packingtown, and Environs in the Nineteenth Century.* Urbana: University of Illinois Press, 1987.

Webb, Constance Bell. *A History of Contagious Disease Care in Chicago before the Great Fire.* Chicago: University of Chicago Press, 1940.

Westfall, C. William. "From Homes to Towers: A Century of Chicago's Best Hotels and Tall Apartment Buildings." In *Chicago Architecture, 1872–1922,* edited by John Zukowsky, 266–89. Munich: Prestel-Verlag, 1987.

Zorbaugh, Harvey. *The Gold Coast and the Slum.* Chicago: University of Chicago Press, 1929.

Index

Abbott, Grace, 254
Academy of Design, 205
Accidents: at amusement parks, 217; with automobiles, 56; on the elevated, 33; industrial, 323; railroad, 48, 62–63; street, 49; workplace, 244
Addams, Jane, 4, 103, 252, 253. *See also* Hull-House
Ade, George: on the Chutes, 216; on cigarettes, 195; on janitors, 84; on neighborhood decline, 82; on peddlers, 277; on physical culture, 173; on restaurants, 149; on school lunch, 161
African Americans: athletes, 171–72; churches and employment, 252; John Ellis Clark, 6; as early musicians, 218; and fitness, 177; and hospital care, 343; John Brown exhibit, 239; John Jones, 261–62; and labor organizations, 261–70, 272; and migration, 260, 266, 270; and pawnshops, 311; public accommodations law, 264; in restaurants, 150, 152, 268; W. W. "Clambake" Rodley, 268; and slums, 106; "Uncle Dan," 262; as waiters, 259; whitewasher, 262. *See also* Chicago Urban League; Waiters; Wells, Ida B.; Women
Aged persons: Civil War and, 333
Alcohol: and athletics clubs, 175; and fitness, 174; and lunch, 157–58
Alcoholics Anonymous, 336
"Alley El," 32; and White City, 216

Allied Van Lines, 87
American Express Company, 25
American House Wrecking Company, 348
American Storage Battery Company, 50
American Medical Association: and Cook County Hospital, 343
American Tube Service Company, 34
Amusement parks, 216–18, 236–37; the Chutes, 216; Ferris Wheel Park, 214, 222; Forest Park, 216–17, 238; Riverview Park, 216–17, 237, 238; Sans Souci, 216; Sharpshooter's Park, 212–13, 216; White City Amusement Park, 216–18
Amusements, 204–39; and morals, 216–17
Anderson, Mrs.: ice cream saloon, 147
Andrieu, Mathieu A., 206
Animals, farm: in city, 135, near downtown, 12; on West Side, 12
Anthropometry, 173–74
Anti-Cigarette League of America, 197, 198, 199, 202. *See also* Gaston, Lucy Page
Anti-Cigarette League of the World, 199
Anti-city, theme of: parks and, 175. *See also* Semipublic places
Anti-cruelty Society, 14
Apartments:
—evolution of, 83–84
—lifestyle and dance halls, 235
—model tenements, by name: Field Garden Apartments, 107; Francisco Terrace, 105;

Langdon, 105; Michigan Boulevard Apartments, 107
—by name: Beaurivage, 84; Pattington, 80
—stigmatized, 84–85
—Uptown neighborhood and, 162
Armour, J. O.: and White City, 216
Armour, Philip D.: grain elevators, 97
Armour and Company: ice house, 133
Ascher Building, 208
Ashland Avenue district, 70
Ashland Blocks, I and II: moving, 92
Associated Cycling Clubs of Chicago, 186
Associated Jewish Charities, 308, 309
Astor Street district, 178
Athletic equipment, 175, 175–77, 184; exercise and sporting goods, 173–74. *See also* Bicycles
Atlas, Charles, 201–2
Auditorium: building, 37–38; hotel, 55, 148
Automobile Row: and Prairie Avenue, 151
Automobiles: and alcohol, 58; and amusement parks, 217–18; and apartments, 80; bicycles replaced by, 193; commuting by, 50, 60; country excursions, 53; electric, 54; as environmentally beneficial, 51; and government boundaries, 58; impact of, 60–61; licensing of, 56, 57, 58; parking, 59; and peddlers, 286; racing, 50; shows, 50, 54; speeding, 50, 56–58; subdivisions and, 77; and urban congestion, 51, 53

Bachelors: and rooming houses, 81–83
Back of the Yards neighborhood, 204
Balloon-frame construction, 68, 90, 369n.3
Ballrooms: Aragon Ballroom, 224, 235, 238; Trianon Ballroom, 235, 239
Banker, A. C.: as speeder, 57
Banks: currency exchanges, 309; ethnic, 299; failures, 297–300; fringe banking, 313; and paychecks, 302; wildcat, 304
Barnum, P. T., 206, 236
Bartzen, Peter: and Cook County Hospital, 326–27
Baseball, 183
—parks: Chicago American Giants, 178; indoor games, 176; as semipublic places, 210; Weeghman Park, 209; White Stockings Park, converted for bicycle races, 179; Wrigley Field, 209
—professionalization into leagues, 209–10
—teams: Chicago Cubs, 199, 209; Chicago Whales, 209; White Sox, 209; White Stockings, 209
Bath houses: public, 104–5
Battery D Armory, 179
Beaches, 183; Cheltenham Beach, 177; commercial, 177; Gutchow's Beach, 177
Beaubien, Mark, 152

Beer gardens, 43, 210–18
—amusement parks and, 217–18
—bicycles and, 211
—decline of, 217–18
—by name: Bismarck Gardens, 223; Brighton Inn, 210; Cheltenham Beach, 177; Clemens and Rudd, 211; Colehour's, 211; Edelweiss Gardens, 212, 220; Eisenmenger's German Gardens, 211; Excelsior Park, 211; Kolze's Electric Park, 212, 216, 238, 334; Lincoln Pavilion, 212; Marigold Gardens, 224, 238; Midway Gardens, 212, 218; Ogden's Grove, 211; Sieben Beer Garden, 218, 237; Sunnyside Inn, 210, Sunnyside Park, 221; Tivoli, 213; Wozniak's Casino, 213, 238, 393n.117
—origins of, 210
Bellamy, Ralph, 141–42
Bennett, Edward H., 286
Benton Harbor, Mich.: bicycle excursion to, 180
Bicycles: 184, 185, 186; accessories for, 179; Arnold, Schwinn and Company, 202; as athletic equipment, 178–80; and automobile, 50; and beer garden, 211; clubs, 179–80, 190–93; commuting by, 191–92; Crane Brothers, 179; crime and, 192; Great Depression and, 202; inns and, 221; Loring and Keene, 179; manufacturing, 179, 202; parking, 192; races, 179, 186; velocipede, 178
Billiards, 209
Black Hawk War, 320
"Black Maria," 27
Blair, Sam, 193
Bloom, Ike, 198–99
Boardinghouses, 81–83, 103; and lunch, 153; and pawnshop, 311
Bohemianism, 151
Bohemians, in Chicago: and athletics, 172; tobacco manufacture and, 194, 197
Boston: and food reform, 122; restaurant patronage, 147
Bowen, Louise deKoven, 235. *See also* Juvenile Protective Association
Bowman Dairy Company, 136
Bowmanville neighborhood: truck gardens, 116
Boxing, 209
The Boy, 197
Boyington, W. W., 69
Boynton, Paul, 216
Bracken, Julia, 51
Bradley, Luther, 118
Brentano, Lorenz, 173
Brickhouse, Jack, 238
Bridewell (House of Correction), 332; becomes House of Correction, 338; condi-

tions in, 338–39; and Cook County Jail, 339, 342; and Dunning, 336, 339; inmate's story, 247; modern, 342; name origin, 337; smoking clinic, 199; and urban fringe, 68; and youth, 340

Bridges, "Major" Lyman: as producer of prefabricated houses, 90

Bridges, 8, 22; and lunchtime traffic, 153; moved, 92

Brighton racetrack, 209

Brookfield (suburb), 67

Brown, John, 208; Harper's Ferry Engine House, 239

Building and loan societies, 69; and destabilizing neighborhoods, 87; modern scandal of, 314

Building materials, 96–97, 99, 101

Bughouse Square (Washington Square Park), 151

Bureau of Justice, 301, 309

Burnham, Daniel, 123, 286; and house moving, 92

Burns, John: murdered at Dunning, 335

Businessmen: and Loop elevated, 33

Butterfield, Justin: as gardener, 139

Cabaret: rise of, 234

Cable car, 18, 20, 26

Cabs: accidents, 56; automobile, 50; bicycles and, 180; and crime, 13; evolution of, 27

California: and Chicago food supply, 116

Canfield (suburb), 73

Cannon, Thomas, 99

Capone, Al, 59

Carriage and Wagon Manufacturers Association of Chicago, 17

Cemeteries:
—and beer gardens, 210, 211
—grave robbing in, 333, 336
—by name: City, 322–23; Concordia, 211; Dunning, 343; Mount Olive, 210, 298; Rose Hill, 69; Waldheim, 211

Centralization: and amusements, 207, 209, 215, 217–18, 236–37; and charities, 327; and Cook County Hospital, 324, 330; and food markets, 114–24; logic of, 355–56; and Maxwell Street Market, 287; and multifunctional organizations, 174–75; and night school, 292–93; and power sources, 26; and public institutions, 341–42; and restaurants, 148, 264–65; and semipublic places, 354–56; theme of, 351–52, 354–56; trend against, 356; and vice, 228–29

Century of Progress Exposition, 164

Cermak, Anton, 232; as peddler, 278

Chain store trend. See Food; Lunch

Charities: Central Free Dispensary, 325;

Chicago Bureau of Charities, 140; fundraising dances, 225, 228; gardens and philanthropy, 140–41; loan aid, 307–9; medical at Bridewell, 339; and pawnshops, 312; scientific, 327; West Side Free Medical Dispensary, 207. See also Poor persons; Settlement houses; Welfare; specific groups by name

Charles Levy Circulating Company, 110

Charles Postl Health Club, 202

Chesbrough, Ellis, 7–8, 132

"Cheyenne" neighborhood, 94

Chicago: motto of, 139; image and public spaces of, 12–13; plat survey of 1830, 4–5

Chicago Academy of Sciences, 205, 206

Chicago after Dark, 13, 250

Chicago and Milwaukee Railroad: and Chittenden, 69; Evanston Division, 60, 366–67n.22. See also Chicago, Milwaukee, St. Paul, and Pacific Railroad

Chicago and North Western Railroad, 44; commuter trains, 45, 46, 47, 53, 62; depot, 37, 40, 92; and Irving (suburb), 69; pay car, 302

Chicago and Pacific Railroad: and Goose Island, 97

Chicago and South Side Rapid Transit Railroad, 32

Chicago Athletic Club, 175

Chicago Auto Club, 57

Chicago Automobile Show, 50

Chicago Bicycle Club, 179

Chicago Bicycle Track Association, 179

Chicago Board of Education: and bicycles, 191–92; cooking classes, 121–22; lunch provisions of, 161, 162; and physical education in schools, 172–73, 174, 178; Paul Stensland, 298. See also Exercise; Night schools; Sports

Chicago Building and Loan Association, 69, 76

Chicago, Burlington, and Quincy Railroad: commuter trains, 62; and temperance, 160

Chicago Business Women's Club, 175

Chicago Chronicle: on African-American waiters, 270

Chicago, City of:
—annexation to, 288; and Dunning, 334
—Board of Examiners of Operators of Automobiles, 56
—city cemetery, 322
—City Council, 28; aldermen provide social services, 318–19; and bicycle regulation, 180, 190–91; and Bridewell, 338, 341–42; and dancing, 234; licenses amusements, 214–15; licenses automobiles, 58–59; and local option laws, 214; and milk inspection, 138; and movie

censorship, 230–31; and night schools, 288–89; and railroad speed, 46; regulates employment agencies, 253; regulates house moving, 91; regulates pawnshops, 310; regulates peddlers, 279, 281; regulates tobacco, 196, 199; and restaurant regulation, 150–51; and saloon lunch, 161. *See also* Markets; Streets
—city hospital, 322
—Common Council, 338; and highway regulation, 27–28; and ice supply regulation, 132; and market regulation, 115; ordinances of, general, 170; regulates employment offices, 245; and river tunnels, 9; and sidewalks, 5; traffic laws passed by, 11. *See also* Markets; Streets
—Department of Human Resources: promotes gardens, 143
—Department of Public Welfare: employment agency investigation, 260
—Health Department, 56; and food inspection, 121, 161; ice inspection, 134; milk inspection, 127, 136–38; and moving day, 86; and peddlers, 281, 286; and refuse tobacco, 196; and slum housing inspection, 97–98
—mayors: and Bridewell pardons, 339–400; Commission on Unemployment, 260; Municipal Markets Commission, 123, 260
—Municipal Museum, 106–7
—Municipal Reference Library, 313
—pesthouses, 321–22
—Police Department: and bicyclists, 180; and Harrison Street lockup, 332; liquor law enforcement by, 232; as loan shark victims, 308; mounted patrols by, 62; off-duty at dance halls, 232; and patrol wagon invention, 27; and pawnshops, 310; and peddlers, 279; and street conditions, 13–14; transports accident victims, 325
Chicago City Railway, 15; and smoking, 195–95
Chicago Coliseum, 209; bicycle races at, 179; closing of, 237–38; horse shows at, 61; stone walls of, 239
Chicago Credit Company, 60
Chicago Daily American: on the Illinois and Michigan Canal, 328
Chicago Daily Democrat: on depots, 16; on slums, 95–96; on sports, 171; on street crime, 13; on unemployment, 246
Chicago Daily Democratic Press: on horses, 10; on smoking, 10
Chicago Daily Drovers Journal: on skating, 176
Chicago Daily Journal: on aid to the poor, 328
Chicago Daily News: on African-American

waiters, 267; on lunch, 157; and postal savings banks, 300; and processed food, 118
Chicago Dwellings Association: and House of Corrections Oak Forest site, 342
Chicago Evening School of Design, 289
Chicago Gas Light and Coke Company, 8
Chicago Great Western Railroad: and employee temperance, 160
Chicago Herald: on truck gardens, 116
Chicago Herald-Examiner: on Lucy Page Gaston, 193
Chicago Historical Society, 205, 206; William Corkran and, 81; Gunther Collection, 239
Chicago Horse Show, 21
Chicago Housekeeper and Ladies Journal, 129
Chicago Housing Authority, 110; Cabrini-Green public housing, 108, 110; and garden plots, 143
Chicago Illustrated Journal: on commuting, 48
Chicago Inter-Ocean: and H. H. Kohlsaat, 159; and Charles T. Yerkes, 29
Chicago Journal: on bicycles, 190, 192; on house moving, 90
Chicago Law and Order League: and amusement parks, 217; and Lucy Page Gaston, 197
Chicago L'Italia: on stranded workers, 244–45
Chicago Mail: on Chicago lunches, 152
Chicago Medical College, 322
Chicago Medical Society, 137; and Dunning, 335; and telephones, 324–25
Chicago, Milwaukee, St. Paul, and Pacific Railroad: and Dunning, 334
Chicago Motor Club, 56, 57
Chicago Opera Company, 199
Chicago Park District: formed, 57, 385n.30; and gardens, 141
Chicago Post: on cabs, 31; on housing conditions, 98–99; on peddlers, 278; on smoking, 195; "suburban ballot" of, 67; on Wilmette, 71
Chicago Post Office: and postal savings plan, 300
Chicago Public Library: Chicago Municipal Museum at, 106–7
Chicago Real Estate Board: on moving day, 87
Chicago Record: on food peddlers, 277
Chicago Record-Herald: on automobiles, 57, 58, 59; on dime museums, 209; on restaurants, 152; on school lunches, 161; on tobacco, 198
Chicago Recreation Commission, 200
Chicago Relief and Aid Society: and housing, 110; and unemployment, 246, 247

Chicago Relief Society, 170
Chicago Restaurant Keepers Association, 150
Chicago River, 22, 23; and fish, 146; and Goose Island, 93–99, 103–10; ice cut from, 132; and land traffic, 30; swimming in, 176–77; unpleasantries, 11
Chicago, Rock Island, and Pacific Railroad, 16; commuting on, 48–49, 85; depot, 24
Chicago Surface Lines, 40
Chicago Times: on African-American waiters, 267, 269; and Nell Nelson, 250, 258; on temperance, 18; on weight lifting, 173; on working women, 250, 258
Chicago Times-Herald: on bicycle manufacturing, 190; on ethnic restaurants, 149; on "Little Hell," 109; sponsors automobile race, 50
Chicago Training School of Cookery, 121
Chicago Transit Authority, 40–41; and Evanston commuter line, 366–67n.22
Chicago Tribune: on African-American waiters, 262–63, 263, 263–64; on banks, 297–98; on bicycle clubs, 180; on commuting, 46, 47; on Cook County Hospital, 325; on dance halls, 228; on depots, 37; on Dunning, 334; on employment agencies, 246–47, 247, 249–50; on loan banks, 308; on moving by streetcar, 85; on night schools, 288; Nora Marks features, 250, 319; on parks, 15; on pawnshop, 310–11; publishes letter concerning food, 120; on refuse tobacco, 187, 196; on restaurants, 146; on roller skating, 176; on South Water Market, 117; on tenant deadbeats, 85; on truck gardens, 116; on waitresses, 269; on wealthy and environment, 3; on West Side slums, 319; on women restaurateurs, 149; on women's lunch, 158; on working women, 83
Chicago *Turngemeinde*, 172
Chicago Urban League, 252, 260
Chicago Wicket Club, 171
Chicago Wide Tire Association, 28
Chicago Woman's Club, 137; and Dunning scandals, 335; employment bureau of, 255; and lunch, 161
Chicago Women's Athletic Club, 175
Chicago Zoave Prize Band, 73
Children. *See* Youth
Children's Hospital Pure Milk Committee, 137
Chinese in Chicago. *See* Restaurants
Christian Citizen, 194
Churches, 89, 104; African-American, 252; as communities, 318; establish orphanages, 321; and gymnasiums, 177; and hospitals, 321; missions and cooking, 122; oppose amusement park, 217; as semipublic places, 39; suburban, 70–71. *See also by name*
Cigarettes. *See* Tobacco
Cincinnati: restaurant patronage in, 147; school lunch idea from, 161
Citizens Association of Chicago: and Dunning, 335; and food quality, 119; and slums, 98; and traffic regulation, 27–28
Citizens Protective Association, 15
City Club of Chicago: food cost investigation, 123; investigates employment agencies, 255–56; and loan sharks, 308–9; waiters' employment agency, 270
City Colleges of Chicago: and night schools, 293
City Gardens Association, 140–41
City Harvest (film), 141
City Homes Association, 105
City News Bureau: and pneumatic tubes, 40
City Press Association, 34
Civic Federation of Chicago: employment agency, 252; and pawnshops, 312
Civil War: cycloramas of battles, 208; and Dunning, 333; and gardening, 140; and hospital, 322–23; hotel runners during, 275; and river tunnels, 9; and unemployment, 246
Clarendon Hills (suburb): design of, 70
Clark, John Ellis: town crier, 6
Clarkdale (suburb), 73
Clarke, Widow, house of, 110
Cleaver, Charles: soap manufacturing, 95
Cleveland, H. W. S.: and suburbs, 70
Clubs: elite and lunch, 156; suburban and risk, 71–72. *See also* Elite
Clybourn, Archibald: meat vendor, 114, 275
Coey, Charles: and Coey-Mitchell automobile, 50
Coffin Nails, 200
Cole, Julia, 289
Comiskey, Charles, 209
Commercial Club, 228
Commonwealth Edison Company, 40
Commuting. *See* Automobiles; Railroads; Vehicles
Complex organization, theme of. *See* Centralization
"Conley's Patch," neighborhood, 94
Consumers Ice Company, 134
Cook County Board: and Bridewell, 341–42; and Cook County Hospital, 326; John Jones on, 262; Oak Forest institutions, 336
Cook County Detention Hospital, 336
Cook County Hospital, 320–27, 330; and Bridewell, 339; established, 323; and

Great Depression, 343; image of, 323; medical achievements of, 343; modern incarnation of, 343–34; reputation of, 325–27
Cook County Infirmary, 334
Cook County Insane Asylum, 330, 333; and urban fringe, 68
Cook County Jail: and Bridewell, 339
Cooley, Edwin: and night schools, 289
Coping: with amusement parks and children, 217; and amusements, 205, 229, 235; with boredom and isolation, 225; with city life in general, 348–58; defined, and forms of, 356–58; with dining conditions, 163–64; with disease, 170; with food markets and supplies, 119–24, 140; and geographical distance, 350; and house moving, 81, 91; with housing conditions, 104, 108–9; information and, 358; with lunch, 153, 161; organized forms of, 14–15; peddling as form of, 274–75; with public transit, 38; by sharing, 319; slang as form of, 157; and social class, 316–20; with street dangers, 49, 60–61; and technology, 349–50; and time, 350; with urban growth, 349; with vice, 228–29. See also Accidents; Food; Loan sharks; Pawnshops; Poor persons; Semipublic space; Slums; Streets
Corbin, Myrtle: as "Living Four-legged Girl," 207
Corkran, William, 81, 153, 247
Coughlin, "Bathhouse John": as peddler, 278; and tobacco regulation, 196–97
Country clubs, 50, 233
County Hospitals, Health, and Allied Medical Programs Governing Commission, 344
Cozzens Bowling Saloon, 176
Credit: consumer purchases on, 302–3, 314–15; debt collection, 303; for retail food purchase, 121. See also Loan sharks; Pawnshops
Crime: and automobiles, 59; execution as a public event, 13; street, 12–13. See also Prostitution
Cruise ships: and vice, 230
Cubans in Chicago: cigar manufacturing by, 194
Cudahy Packing Company, 97
Currency exchanges, 309
Cyclorama, 207–8; of Crucifixion, 208; of Great Fire, 208; and movies, 230

Daley, Richard J.: and Bridewell, 341
Daley, Richard M.: and streetcars, 41
Dance halls: American Dance Hall, 231; Dreamland, 235; evolution of, 231; and Mabel Wright, 231; "taxi dance hall," 235. See also Dancing

Dancing: 204–5
—instruction: American Association of Professional Dancing Instructors, 227, 234; Augustus Bornique, 226–27, 233, 239; James A. Marshall, 226; L. Edwin Martine, 226–27, 233, 239; Mirasole's, 226
—modern, 238–39
—moral objection to, 225–26
—steps: popular, 234
—venues: Bachelors' Assembly Balls, 225; cafe dancing, 234; charity balls, 228; Irving Hall, 225; Schoenhofen Hall, 228
—see also Dance halls
Danes in Chicago. See Scandinavians in Chicago
Darrow, Clarence, 44
Davis, Dr. Nathan Smith: and early hospitals, 321; establishes Chicago Medical College, 322
The Dawn: on peddling, 280
Delsarte system, 174
Democratic National Convention of 1892, 268
Department stores: downtown congestion and, 30; postfire, 36; and vice, 230. See also Semipublic space
Detroit: gardening in, 140
Dever, William, 107
Devine, M. A.: first milkman, 135, 139
DeVry Technical Institute, 238
Dewes, Francis J., 214
Dexter Park Pavilion, 9
Dicke, David: gymnasium, 172
The Dill Pickle, 151
Dime museums: 205–10, 219
—attendance: decline of, 209, 236; popularity indicated by, 207
—attractions: "Jo Jo, the Dog-faced Boy," 207; David Kennison, 205; "Krao, the Monkey Girl," 207; mummies, 207
—by name: Chicago Museum, 206; Colonel Wood's Museum, 219; Englehardt's Mathesoid Marionorama, 207; Epstean's West Side Museum, 207; Huber's Dime Museum, 209; Kohl and Middleton, 207, 209; Libby Prison, 208, 208–9; London Dime Museum, 220
Disabled persons: and employment office license, 245; as street musicians, 277
Disease, 169–70
—epidemics, 98, 326–27; Civil War and, 323; germ theory of, 323, 324; and hospital origins, 32–21; and streetcars, 367n.43
—by name: cholera, 114, 320–22, 328; malaria, 73; "milk sick," 135; smallpox, 336; tuberculosis, 138–39; typhoid, 136–37, 138–39
Dispensaries. See Charities

Douglas, Stephen A.: and Paul Cornell, 69
Dowie, Rev. John Alexander: and Ashland Block I, 92
Downer and Bemis Brewing Company, 213
Downers Grove (suburb), 71, 73
Drake, John B., 147
Dreiser, Theodore, 29
Drury, John, 152
DuMont Television Network, 238
Dunne, Edward F., 28, 308; and automobile licensing, 58; and liquor licenses, 231
Dunning (Cook County Institutions, poorhouse and insane asylum): asylum ideology, 329; county hospital at, 322–23; David Dunning farm, 328; Dunning neighborhood, 211, 218, 343; image of, 327, 329–30, 331, 333–34; poorhouse inmate conditions, 327–29, 331, 333–36
Duryea, J. Frank, 50
Dutch in Chicago: as market farmers, 117

Economic depressions:
—and Bridewell, 339
—of the 1890s: bank failures, 299; and bicycles, 190; and employment agency reform, 251; and food, 119; and pawnshops, 312
—see also Great Depression
Eddy, Arthur J., 56
Edgewater neighborhood, 78; apartments in, 84; bicycle path in, 191; as suburb, 71
Edison Park neighborhood: as suburb, 71, 73
Edson Keith Building, 208
The Education of H*Y*M*A*N K*A*P*L*A*N, 291
Egan, Dr. William B.: as gardener, 139. See also Real estate: developers and developments
Eight-Hour Herald: and beer garden ads, 212
Eitel family: and World War I, 218
Eleanor Club: single women at, 83
Electricity: dangerous wires, 27; as power for elevated, 33; in suburbs, 71
Elevated railway, 24, 32–33
—impact: on amusement parks, 216–17; on apartments, 80; on house moving, 92; on markets, 123; on subdivisions, 74
—operations: compete with rail commuting, 48–49; electrification of, 33; el longevity, 40
—riding conditions: safety, 33; and smoking, 198
Elevators: and housing, 81–82. See also Skyscrapers
Elite:
—amusements: bicycles, 190, 191, 192–93; dancing, 226–27, 233, 234; sports, 173
—automobiles, 50–51, 56–57, 58

—clubs, 317; athletic clubs for, 175; and labor disputes, 268; and political reform, 316–17
—dining: and African-American waiters, 262; and lunch, 153, 156
—housing, 9; developers and, 69; early housing of, 94; geographical mobility and, 61
—lifestyle: environment and, 60; isolation from city unpleasantness, 3, 348–49; servants, 263–64
—neighborhoods, 316–17; Astor Street, 178; decline of Prairie Avenue, 82, 151
Employment agencies, 244–56, 260–61; Central Relief Association, 252; and charitable reforms, 251–53; for day labor, 251; fraud and regulation of, 245, 246–55, 260; labor unions as, 252–53, 256; the padrone and, 249; peddling as way to avoid, 274–75, 287; and stranded workers, 244–45
Englewood neighborhood: and typhoid from milk, 138–39
Environment: 3, 5, 35. See also Anti-city, theme of; Noise; Public space; Smoke
Epidemics. See Disease
Erring Woman's Refuge: and urban fringe, 68
Ethnicity: Americanization, 204–5, 289; banking and, 298–99; beer gardens and, 211, 212–13; and charities, 252, 307–8, 329–30; and education, 289–90, 291; and employment, 245; and food, 149, 164; and modern peddlers, 293; and neighborhoods, 317–18; and temperance, 232; See also Markets; Neighborhoods; Peddlers; and ethnic groups by name
Evans, Henry, 197
Evanston (suburb), 71–72; bicycle path to, 191; Woods Electric automobile, 54. See also Chicago and Milwaukee Railroad; Commuting
Everleigh sisters, 198
Ewing, Emma P., 121
Exercise: bicycles and, 178–80, 185–86, 190–93; and physical culture, 170–71, 173

Fads: dancing, 227, 231–32; 235; equestrianism, 9–10; smoking, 196. See also Sports; Time
Falcons: Polish athletics, 172
Families: in boardinghouses, 81, 83; moving and, 84. See also Food; Housing; Women; Youth
Farmers: and beer gardens, 210; market complaints, 117–18
Farson, John, 58
Farwell, John V., 151, 312–13
Fenger, Dr. Christian, 324, 326
Ferber, Edna, 117

Ferris wheel: destruction of, 213–15, 238; and George W. G. Ferris, 213–14, 215; in Ferris Wheel Park, 214, 222; production company, 213–15; and World's Columbian Exposition, 213

Field, Marshall: house converted to restaurant, 151

Fire: Iroquois Theater, 229–30; movie film hazards, 230. *See also* Great Fire of 1871

Fire Queen, 107

First Presbyterian Church, 89

First State Industrial Wage Loan Society, 309

First State Pawners Society, 312–13

First Ward Ball, 233

Fisk Jubilee Singers, 268

Food: chain stores, 122–23; cookbooks, 121; diet and exercise, 174; at Dunning, 329, 334, 335; ethnicity and, 142; fish, 119; and gardening, 139–42; Latin American sources, 116; municipal warehouse proposal, 123–24; peddling, 276–77, 277, 280–81; prepared, 277; prices, 118; processed, 118–24; quality and freshness, 117–24, 119, 280–81; retailing, 114–24, 127; and time, 113–14; trends, 142–44; wholesale markets, 114–24, 125. *See also* Lunch; Restaurants

Foot races, 171–72

Ford, Henry, 198

Fort Dearborn, 218; and cholera, 320; food at, 114; massacre, 6

Foy, Eddie, Jr., 229

Franchises: utility, 28–29; transit, 49

"Freezine," 137

Fringe districts: annexation and night schools, 289; Bridewell and, 338, 339; isolation of unpleasant urban institutions, 329; and truck gardens, 116. *See also* Dunning

Fullerton Avenue: toll gate, 52

"Furfural," 200

Gage Building, 208

Galena and Chicago Union Railroad, 16; commuters, 45; and food, 115

Gamblers: and pawnshops, 311

Garden City racetrack, 209

Gardens, 15, 128, 139–42, 143

Gas lighting, 95, 99; and dancing, 225. *See also* Goose Island; Little Hell

Gaston, Lucy Page, 188, 193–201, 217

Gatzert, August, 30

Gentian root, 193

Geographical mobility:
—amusements and: amusement parks, 215–18, 236; and dance schools, 226–27
—children and, 216–17
—distances and contradictions in, 87–88, 350

—elite and, 61

—and food: dining, 163–64; preparation, 145–46; and lunch, 153, 156, 163

—labor: labor force and market, 244, 245–47; state employment office and, 255–56, 256–57; transient labor, 273; unemployed, 260–61; waiters, 263

—peddlers and, 281

—the poor, 93–99, 103–4; and medical care, 343; and slums, 106, 108

—social class and, 60–61, 334

—*see also* African Americans; Labor: supply; Moving day

Germans in Chicago: aid societies of, 252; and beer gardens, 210–11; and bowling, 176; and cholera, 328; and fitness, 172–73; housing of, 96–97; Jaeger Corps, 212–13; North Chicago Shutzen Verein, 212; as peddlers, 276; as truck gardeners, 116; and World War I, 218

GI Bill: and night schools, 291

Glen Ellyn (suburb), 72, 73; Glen Ellyn Hotel and Springs Company, 72; Lake Ellyn, 72

Gloy, John, 173

Golf, 175; and elite, 173; replaces bicycling, 193

Goose Island, 103–10; early history of, 93–96; and politics, 318; suicides at, 348

Grand Crossing neighborhood, 70

Grant, Bruce, 152

Grant, Ulysses S., 14

Gray, Gilda, 235

Great Atlantic and Pacific Tea Company, 122

Great Depression, 314; and bicycles, 202; and Cook County Hospital, 343; and currency exchanges, 309; and gardens, 141; and Goose Island, 107–8; and moving day, 87, 88; and night school, 290–91; and pawnshops, 313; and recreation, 202; and restaurants, 151–52, 164; unemployment during, 260–61; and waiters, 272. *See also* Economic depressions

Great Fire of 1871, 169; and amusements, 206–7, 236; and Bridewell, 338; cause of, 139; house moving and, 90; housing and, 82, 110; lunch customs and, 157; postfire rebuilding and labor, 246; restaurants and, 147, 148; and slums, 96–97

"Great Zeuglodon," 206

Greeks in Chicago: as peddlers, 276; and truck gardens, 116. *See also* Restaurants

Greyhound Bus Lines: Goose Island facility, 110; terminal, 92

Grossdale (suburb), 67

Grover, Oliver Dennett, 208

Gunther, Charles, 207; collection, 239; Libby Prison Museum and, 208

Gurnee, Walter, 338

Gymnasiums, 175; in Turner societies, 172
Gymnastics, 185

Haase, Ferdinand, 211, 216
Hahnemann, Dr. Samuel, 322
Haines, John C., 13
Hannah Railway, 32
Harlan, John M., 190
Harpers Ferry arsenal, 208
Harris, Neil, 236
Harrison, Carter II: and automobiles, 56–57; and bicycles, 178, 190–91; and early West Side, 12; and peddlers, 287; and restaurant music, 150; and Paul Stensland, 298
Harrison, Edith Ogden (Mrs. Carter II): and bicycles, 178, 190
Harvey, Turlington, 193–94
Harvey (suburb), 193–94
Haven, Luther, 172
Health: of commuters, 51; concepts of good, 201; education in, 170; and personal fitness, 171–86, 190–93. See also Chicago, City of: health department; Chicago Board of Education; Disease; Exercise; Food
Henderson, Charles R., 256–57
Hering, Henry W., 298
Heroes, sports, 210
Highland Park (suburb): Highland Park Land Company, 69; Woods Electric automobile, 54
Hinsdale (suburb), 72
Hoffman, Charles Fenno, 218–19
Homeopathy: hospitals and, 322
Homewood (suburb), 73
Hopkins, John P., 196
Horse Association of America, 61
Horsecars: end of, 39–40; passenger conditions, 15; smoking on, 194–95. See also Public space; Streetcars; Streets
Horses: and automobile, 49, 51; decline of, 61–62; and the Epizootic, 18; market, 9; racing of, 209; related industries, 17–18; show, 21; and social status, 9–10; and streets, 17–18, 51, 59. See also Horsecars; Omnibus; Public space; Streetcars; Streets
Hospitals: Cermak Memorial, 342; Illinois General Hospital of the Lakes, 321; Mercy, 321, 323; neighborhood, closing of, 344; Provident, 344; and social class, 324–25; specialization, 325; Tippecanoe Hall, 321. See also Cook County Hospital; Dunning
Hotels:
—dancing at, 234
—evolution of: early, 6; Great Fire and, 36; inns and beer gardens, 210; railroads and, 16–17

—by name: Drake Hotel, 234; Grand Pacific, 16–17, 36; Hotel Imperial, 92; Lake House, 146, 321; Lexington Hotel, 265; Palmer House, 16, 36, 272, 259, 264; Sauganash Inn, 152; Sherman House, 272; Tremont Hotel, 36
—as restaurant, 147, 148, 151
—runners at, 275
—suburban: Glen Ellyn Hotel and Springs Company, 72; Riverside Hotel, 77; and subdivision development, 73, 77
House moving, 89–92, 100, 110; by Harvey Sheeler, 92; by Tupper brothers, 90
Housing: as consumer issue, compared with food, 349; home ownership, 74; renters and debt collection, 303; shortages, 67; social class and, 82, 94; technology and decline, 82. See also Apartments; Balloon-frame construction; Boardinghouses; Building materials; House moving; "Living in blocks"; Neighborhoods; Public space; Rooming houses; Slums; and suburbs by name
How They Treat Strangers in Chicago, 230
Hulbert, William A., 209
Hull-House: compared with amusement park, 237; employment agency at, 252; and gardens, 140, 140–41; and neighborhood diversity, 109; as semipublic place, 4; slums and, 103. See also Addams, Jane; Neighborhoods; Settlement houses
Hull House Maps and Papers, 105
Humor Club, 173
Hunt, Jarvis, 214
Hyde Park: neighborhood, 45; as suburb, 70; Town of, 67

Ice: cutting of, 131, 132–33; delivery of, 130–32; and the poor, 137; at supermarkets, 144; supply of, 124, 130, 131–35
Illinois and Michigan Canal: cholera and, 320, 321; immigrant construction gangs, 93, 246, 328; and regional growth, 7; survey, 4
Illinois Appellate Court: and Ferris wheel, 215
Illinois Athletic Club, 175
Illinois Central Railroad: commuter trains, 45, 52, 62; and lakefront swimming, 176; office building, 92
Illinois Cycling Club, 192
Illinois Humane Society, 14, 196, 362n.54
Illinois Industrial Training School: and urban fringe, 68
Illinois Society for the Prevention of Cruelty to Animals, 14–15, 362n.54
Illinois, State of:
—automobile licensing by, 58–59
—Bureau of Labor Statistics, 254
—Chicago-Read Mental Health Center, 336, 343

—Constitution: and court fines, 338
—food inspector, 150–51
—free employment office, 253–54, 255–56, 260–61
—General Assembly: and building laws, 98; creates park system, 15–16; debt collection and, 303; drinking age, 232; employment agency reform by, 253–54; food purity law, 118–19; and franchises, 28–29, 33; humane (horse) reform, 14; loan regulation, 309; mandatory physical education, 178; milk pasteurization, 138; outlaws boxing, 209; and public accommodation laws, 264; and railroad speed, 46; and thrift institutions, 69; and tobacco regulation, 196, 197–98; and wage payment regulation, 302, 307
Illinois Supreme Court: on dancing laws, 234; on employment agency regulation, 254; Ferris wheel case, 215; Snell Toll Road case, 44; on teamster tax, 190
Illinois Telephone and Telegraph Company, 34
Illinois Training School for Nurses, 325–26, 326–27
Illinois Woman's Alliance, 196
Illinois Women's Press Club, 175
Immaculate Conception Roman Catholic Church, 104
Immigrants Protective League, 254
Improved Housing Association, 105, 107
Industrial Club of Chicago, 309
Industry: brewing and ice prices, 132–33; brick-making and Goose Island, 95; decentralization and electric motors, 193–94; decline and employment, 273; disease and accident, 244; distilleries and "slops," 136; leather tanning and Goose Island, 103; meat-packing, 132–33; sporting goods manufacture, 173–74; tobacco processing, 194
Infant Welfare Society, 105, 128, 137
Insane: mentally ill at Dunning, 329; treatment of, 333–34
Institutional trap, theme of: defined, 320. See also Bridewell; Cook County Hospital; Dunning
Insull, Samuel: and Mundelein, 74; and transportation, 40
International Harvester Company, 140
Interurban railroads: and amusement parks, 217–18; Chicago, Aurora, and Elgin, 49; Chicago, North Shore and Milwaukee, 49, 238; Chicago, South Shore, and South Bend, 49, 62; and food market plan, 123
Irish in Chicago: Goose Island and, 248–49, 318; potato famine, 93–94. See also Illinois and Michigan Canal
Iroquois Theater Fire, 229–30

Irving Park (suburb), 69
Irvington (suburb), 69
Italians in Chicago: *padrone,* 249; peddling, 276, 281; railway workers, 244–45; restaurants, 149; tobacco refuse, 196; and truck gardening, 116

Jacobs, Jane: on building cycles, 88
Jahn, Frederick, 172, 174
James Allen, 93
Janitors: described, 84
Japanese in Chicago. *See* Restaurants
Jefferson, Town of (suburb), 67
Jefferson Park neighborhood, 46
Jenney, William LeBaron: and Riverside, 70
Jewell, Dr. J. S., 334
Jews in Chicago: and antisemitism, 227–28; charities, 255, 308, 309. *See also* Maxwell Street district; Peddlers
John Drew, 321
John Hancock Building
Johnson, Byron "Ban," 209
John Worthy School, 340
Jones, Amanda T., 119–20
Journal of Risk Management, 352
Joy, Hiram, 132
The Jungle, 119
"Juniper Ade," 278
Juvenile delinquency: Bridewell incarceration, 340; movies as cause, 230; and peddlers, 279; saloons as cause, 230; smoking and, 189, 196; *See also* Youth
Juvenile Protective Association, 197, 231, 233, 235

Kadish's natatorium, 177
Keane, Thomas, 107
Kenilworth (suburb), 53, 71
Kenna, Michael "Hinky Dink," 278
Kennelly, Martin: and Bridewell, 342; and moving and storage business, 87
Kiernan, Dr. J. G., 335
"Kilgubbin" neighborhood, 93–94. *See also* Goose Island
Kinsley, H. M., 148, 262
Kinzie, John, as gardener, 139
Kipley, Police Chief Joseph: and loan sharks, 308
Kitchen Garden Association, 122
Klio Association, 159
Knickerbocker Ice Company, 131, 133–34
Koch, Dr. Robert: germ theory of, 137–38
Kolze, Henry J., 210, 211, 218
Kowalski, Paul, 298
Kroc, Ray, 164–65

Labor:
—service sector economy: African Americans and, 261. *See also* African Ameri-

cans; Employment agencies; Geographical mobility; Waiters; Women
—supply, 244, 270-71; and migration, 260
—unions: and Dunning construction, 336; as patrons of beer gardens, 212; and prison labor, 338; strikes, 212-13, 261; wages, 301; *and by name*
Ladies Christian Union, 251
Lager Beer Riot, 172
Lake, Town of (suburb), 67
Lake Forest (suburb): and H. W. S. Cleveland, 70
Lake Michigan: fishing in, 199; water supply from, 138
Lake Shore and Michigan Southern Railroad, 16
Lakeside Directory of Chicago, 303
Lake View, Town of (suburb), 46-47, 67
Landlord's Protective League, 85
"Laramie" neighborhood, 94
LaSalle Street Tunnel, 23
Launder, James, 310
Lawson, Victor F., 300
League for the Protection of Immigrants. *See* Immigrants Protective League
Legal Aid Society, 309
Levee district, 198-99, 217, 229, 233, 333
Levitan, Solomon, 399n.8
Lewis, Henry, 206
Liberace, 238
Lincoln, Abraham, 14
Lincoln Park, 177
Lipman, Abraham, 403n.42
L'Italia: on restaurants, 149
Little Girl Next Door, 234
"Little Hell" neighborhood: 95, 103, 108, 109, 110; defined, 373n.31
"Living in blocks," 81-82
Loan sharks: 308-9, 314. *See also* Wages
"Loop": definition, 30; and elevated, 32; and house moving, 90-91; street congestion of, 5, 30
Loop Protective Association, 33
Louisiana Purchase Exposition, 238
Lunch hour, 152-53, 155-63
—noon-hour congestion, 30
—ritualistic aspects of, 157
—type of venue: cafeteria, 159; chain outlets, 159, 162-63; company lunch room, 161; "lunch cars," 160; saloon free lunch, 157-58; school, 161, 162, 165; vending machines, 161
—waiters and, 157
Lundin, Fred, 278
Luxembourgers in Chicago: as market farmers, 117
Lyon and Healy Music Store, 25

Macfadden, Bernarr, 201-2
Mackey, Frank, 308

Mail order: and peddlers, 276
Markets: dances in, 225; Haymarket [Randolph Street], 116-17; Market Street [Wacker Drive] Market Hall, 115; Michigan Street [Hubbard Street] Market Hall, 115; night school in hall, 288; South Water Market, 116-17, 143; State Street Market, 115, 143; quality complaints, 117-18. *See also* Dutch in Chicago; Farmers; Food; Maxwell Street district; Peddlers
Marks, Nora: on employment agency cons, 250; on the poor, 319
Martha Washington Home: and urban fringe, 68
Maxwell, Thomas, 207
Maxwell Street district, 103, 285, 287; food vending at market, 126; ice boxes in neighborhood, 135; market closed and moved, 293-94
Mayer, Levy, 234
Maywood (suburb), 69, 71, 72, 73
McConnell, Emmett, 208
McCormick Reaper Company, 94
McDonald, John B., 50
McEwen, Mrs. Fred, 191
McGarigle, William J., 326
McHenry County: and milk, 139
Meat Cooks', Pastry Cooks' and Confectioners' Cosmopolitan Society, 148
Merchants Club, 312
Merriam, Charles, 232
Messengers, 31
Metra rail system, 62
Meywell, Henry, 211
Michigan Avenue, 54, 56; bridge, 151; restaurants, 151
Michigan Central Railroad, 16
Middle class: and neighborhoods, 317; and peddlers, 278. *See also* Real estate: developers and developments; *and suburbs by name*
Midway Plaisance, 181
Midwives, 325
Milk, 135-39; delivery, 61; "Milk Keep," 137; pasteurization, 138-39; purity and wholesomeness, 127, 136
Mills, Fanny, 207
Milwaukee, Wis.: athletic contests at, 171; bicycle excursions to, 180
Milwaukee Avenue neighborhood, 43-44, 52, 299
Milwaukee Avenue State Bank, 297-99
Minorities, theme of: expanded definition, 145-46. *See also* African Americans; Ethnicity; Food; *and groups by name*
Mixed Drinks: on bicycle races, 179
"Model tenements," 105
Moreland (suburb), 74
Morgan, Anna, 174
Morrison, William, 49

Morrison Electric automobile, 50
Morton Park (suburb), 67
Movies: censorship, 234; Central Park Theater, 235; Chicago Theater, 235; and gardeners, 141–42; nickelodeon, 230–31; Nortown Theater, 235. *See also* Theaters
Moving day, 75, 80, 84–87; moving vans, 79, 86–87; superstitions concerning, 86; wagons and, 79
Moving sidewalks, 31–32
Multifunctional centralized institutions. *See* Amusement parks; Centralization; Chicago Board of Education; Cook County Hospital; Department stores; Night schools; Settlement houses; World's Columbian Exposition
Mundelein (suburb), 75

Naperville, dances in, 225
National Anti-Cigarette Association, 197
National Association of Women Stenographers, 252
National Carriage Dealers Protective Association, 61
National Tea Company, 122–23
Neighborhoods: and amusements, 214–15; apartment houses and, 84; and banking, 299; and gardens, 139–42; improvement associations in, 74; local option, 74, 232–33; and the poor, 316; race riots in, 88. *See also* Banking; Ethnicity; Politics; Poor persons; Settlement houses; *and ethnic groups by name*
Nelson, Nell, 250, 258
Newsboys: as peddlers, 275
Newsboys and Bootblacks Home, 281
Newspapers: offices as information centers, 14. *See also* Centralization; Employment agencies; *and by individual title*
New York City: Central Park, 70; Hannah elevated in, 32; milk, 136; restaurant standards, 146
New York Prison Association, 338
New York Times: and Lucy Page Gaston, 200
Night schools, 287–91; teacher qualifications, 288, 289
Niles Center (suburb), 74–75
Noise: and peddlers, 279–80, 281, 293
Noon-Day Rest, 159
Norris, J. W., 245
North Chicago Rolling Mills, 95
Northwestern Christian Advocate: and dancing, 226
North West Plank Road, 43–44
Norwegians: and banking, 298. *See also* Scandinavians
Nuisance complaints, 11–12. *See also* Animals; Noise; Smoke
Nurses, 325–26, 326–27, 344–45

Oak Park (suburb), 45, 71
Oak Park Club, 233
Offices: as semipublic places, 25
Off the Street Club, 185, 189
Ogden, William Butler: as gardener, 139; and squatters, 95
Ogden's Island, 95
Ogilvie, Richard: as governor, 343; as sheriff, 342
Ogontz Club, 159
O'Leary, Mrs. Catherine, 12, 135, 139, 216
O'Leary, James, 216
Olmsted, Frederick Law, 70, 77
Omnibus, 10–11, 19; beer gardens operate, 211; hotels operate, 36
O'Reill, Max: on lunch, 157
Our Lady of Lourdes Roman Catholic Church: moved, 92
Our Most Popular Recreation Controlled by the Liquor Interests, 233
Out of Town, 69

Palmer, Honore, 57
Palmer, Potter, 16, 129. *See also* Hotels: by name
Panoramas, 205–6; *Battle of Gettysburg*, 239; compared with movies, 230; decline of, 208–9; of Fort Sumter, 206; about John C. Frémont, 206; *Mirror of Intemperance and Crime*, 206; about Napoleon, 206; Panorama Building, 208; *Panorama of the Upper and Lower Mississippi*, 206; *Pilgrim's Progress*, 206
Parker, Warren, 10
Park Forest (suburb), 88
Parks, 15–16; amusement parks and, 214–15; athletics in, 175, 177, 183; automobiles in, 57; and beer gardens, 213; bicycles in, 179; consolidation into Chicago Park District, 385n.30; Lincoln Park High Bridge, 347–48; Merrimac Park, 238; and subdivision development, 69
Parmelee, Frank, 10, 16
Pasteurization, 137–38
"The Patch" neighborhood, 310
Patterson, Joseph Medill, 28
Pawnshops, 309–13; charitable, 312; diamond brokers, 306; modern, 314–15
Peddlers, 274–87; compared with union labor, 275; country, 275; and delivery of services, 292, 293; fakirs as, 278; food sales, 117–18, 121, 123, 125, 277; loans to, 308–9; and mail order, 276; Giovanni Mazzo, 277–78; modern, 293; numbers, 275–76; Peddlers and Canvassers Protective Association, 281; Peddlers Protective Association, 281; Peddlers Supply Company, 276; as a problem, 291; selling lunch, 159–60; street musicians, 277–78; and unemployment, 260

Pelham, Laura Dainty, 140
"The Penny Cigarette," 197
Penny Savings Society, 299–300
Peoples Friendly Club, 140
People's Gas Light and Coke Company, 95, 99
Perkins, Dwight, 105
Perry, Herb, 274, 294
Peyraud, Paul, 208
Physical education. *See* Chicago Board of Education
Picnic groves, 211. *See also* Beer gardens
Pickwick Lane, 148
Pilsen: Cigar manufacturing in, 194
Pingree, Hazen (Detroit mayor): and gardens, 140
Plank roads, 43–44, 246
Plan of Chicago: and house moving, 92; and markets, 123; and peddlers, 286
Playgrounds, 10
Pneumatic tubes, 34–35, 40
Poles in Chicago: athletics and, 172; tobacco workers, 197; truck gardens and, 116. *See also* Ethnicity; Neighborhoods
Police. *See* Chicago, City of: Police Department
Policeman Bellinger's cottage, 110
Politics: neighborhood, 318–19. *See also* Chicago, City of: City Council; Chicago, City of: Common Council; Coughlin, "Bathhouse John"; Illinois General Assembly; Kenna, Michael; Powers, John
Pontiac Building, 159
Poor persons: almshouse, 320, 328–29, 331, 333–36; and athletics, 175, 177–78; attitudes toward, 339–42; and food, 120–22, 143–44; and gardens, 140–42; in general, 349; geographical mobility of, 85; and health care, 320–27; homelessness, 314; lifestyle, 243; market anachronism, 287; and milk, 136–39; and neighborhoods, 317–20; and origins of epidemics, 320–21; and technological obsolescence, 353; and time, 314, 350–51. *See also* Bridewell; Cook County Hospital; Credit; Dunning; Food; Housing; Markets; Slums
Porter, Washington, 115–16
Postal Savings program, 300
Postl, Charles, 170–71, 178, 181, 202
Powers, John, 34, 196, 318
Prairie Avenue neighborhood: decline of, 82; and Automobile Row, 151
Prairie Farmer, 139
Prairie State Club, 192
Private space: defined, 4; and class, 349. *See also* Public space; Semipublic space
Prohibition: and beer gardens, 218
Prostitution, 230; and amusement parks, 217; early, 12–13; "The Patch" and, 229; and rooming houses, 82; "The Sands"

and, 229; and smoking, 196, 198–99; white slave recruiting for, 83, 230, 253, 395n.31
Protective Agency for Women and Children, 301, 309
Public behavior, 191; and beer gardens, 213; creating nuisances, 11–12; crowd attractions, 13, 14; etiquette and smoking, 194–95; mob actions, 44, 172; mourning, 14; nudity, 176–77; recklessness with vehicles, 27–28, 50, 56–58; retreat from unpleasantness and danger, 12–13, 38–39; rudeness, 15; slang usage, 263–64, 264; tipping, 264. *See also* Coping; Fads; Public space; Streets
Public space: and bicycles, 180; courthouse square, 328; defined, 11; jail and town square, 337; patriotic events in, 6–7; peddling and, 275–81, 286–88, 292; poor persons and public buildings, 35; public housing, 107–8; street musicians in, 277; in suburbs, 70–71; technology and, 5; theme of, 39; town crier and, 6. *See also* Automobiles; Bridewell; Cook County Hospital; Dunning; Public transportation; Sidewalks; Streets
Public transportation, 44–49; and retail hubs, 303; and weekend travel, 393n.112. *See also* Automobiles; Elevated; Horsecars; Interurban railroads; Metra rail system; Omnibus; Regional Transportation Authority; Streetcars; Subway
Pullman, George, 90, 105
Pullman Company, 257; 1894 strike and bicycle tax, 180, 190; employs waiters, 270
Pure Food Show, 122
Pure Milk Committee, 137

Railroads:
—and amusements: baseball, 209; beer gardens, 209; bicycles, 179; dance steps, 225, 227; and panoramas, 206
—commuter, 44–49, 60, 62–63, 350; and housing choices, 69; railway profit from, 369n.28; and real estate development, 69–75; streetcars contrasted with, 44–45
—conductors, 46
—and country peddlers, 275
—and crime: brings criminals, 337; court witnesses, 337; and vice, 230
—depots, 16, 24, 36–37, 52, 53; Dearborn Station, 37; Grand Central Station, 37; Illinois Central Station, 16, 37; LaSalle Street Station, 37; North Western Station, 37; Union Station, 37
—and food supply, 115–16, 174, 124, 143
—and ice supply, 132–33, 134
—impact on swimming, 176
—and labor: employment, 244–45, 246, 249; and employment agency cons, 247–

48; and mobility of waiters, 267–68, 269; provides labor mobility, 254, 260
—problem of speed, 46–47, 62–63
—promotes restaurant standards, 147
—provides milk supplies, 135–36
—as source of smoke, 51
—and temperance, 160–61
—theater trains, 46
—track elevation and house moving, 92
—*see also individual companies by name*
Raymond, Frank, 56
Real estate:
—advertising, 71, 72–75
—developers and developments, 68–75; S. M. Bloss, 73; Brannigar Company, 74; Britiganwood, 77; Chittenden, 69; J. L. Cochran, 71; Paul Cornell, 45, 69, 70; Dauphin Park, 67, 72; Dr. William B. Egan, 68, 108; Samuel E. Gross, 67, 72–75, 211; E. A. Hill, 73; Samuel Insull, 74; A. Marshall and Company, 69; Maywood Land Company, 69; McElroy and Keeney, 73; McIntosh Company, 74; McLean, Bierbach, 73; E. H. Prince, 71; Richard T. Race, 69; Van Vlisingen and Company, 74; Samuel J. Walker, 70; Charles and Joel Wicker, 69–70
—speculation: Goose Island, 93
—subdivisions: gardening in, 140–42; related to slums, 108
—*see also* Railroads; *suburbs by name*
Recycling: by peddlers, 276
Reebie, W. C., building, 86
Regional Transportation Authority, 62
Reilly, Dr. Frank, 173
Restaurants, 145–65
—ethnic, 149, 151–52; Chinese, 149, 154; French, 149; 148; Greek, 162, 165; Italian, 149; Japanese, 152
—by name: Abson's English Chop House, 148; Gaston Alciatore, 151; Aunt Mary's, 150; Baltimore Dairy Lunch, 159; Berghoff, 148, 151, 154, 164–65; Billy Boyle's Chop House, 148; Boston Oyster House, 148; Casa de Alex, 152; Chapin and Gore, 148; Chicago Oyster House, 267; Chicago Stock Exchange Restaurant, 157; Mrs. Clark Company Lunch Room, 158; DeJonghe's, 148, 154; Delmonico's, 147; Emil Reick lunch chain, 159; Ferris Wheel Park, 214; Forum Cafeteria, 164; The Frogs, 148; Mrs. L. W. Haring, 149; Henrici's, 148, 154, 156, 164, 212; Japanese Lunch Room, 152; Michael Jordan's Restaurant, 41; Joy Yet Lo, 154; Kinsley's, 151, 156, 262; Mrs. Knox, 159; H. H. Kohlsatt, 159, 266; Joseph Chesterfield Mackin, 157–58; McDonald's, 164–65; Milan and Company, 148; Ontra Cafete-

ria, 162; Peacock Cafe, 148; Pittsburgh Joe, 159; Race Brothers, 267; John Raklios, 162–63; Rector's, 148, 151; Relic House, 207; Round Table Inn, 151; Southern Tea Shop, 151; John R. Thompson Company; 159, Toffenetti's, 164; Toothpick Row, 152; Troy Lunch, 159; Weeghman, 159; White Castle, 163; White Tower, 163
—operations of: chefs, 147–48; closing hours, 150; job hierarchy, 265–66; music and, 150; restaurant inspection, 150–51; Sunday closing, 150
—by type: automat, 161; "bohemian" (unconventional), 151; cafeteria, 159, 162; chain restaurants, 164–65; diners, 156; saloons and lunch counters, 150, 157–58
—*see also* Chicago, City of: Department of Health; Food; Lunch; Waiters; Waitresses; Women
Retail Grocers and Butchers Association, 122
Reynolds, Malvina, 88
Risk: accidents, 169, 323, 352–54; avoided through city zoning, 88; avoided through neighborhood separation, 354; crime, 12–13; fire, 84, 103, 169; and food supply, 117–18, 118–24, 142; and housing, 68, 353; ice purity and price, 131, 132–33; in job seeking, 270–71; milk quality, 136–39, 144; moving day, 85–87; to peddlers, 278–79; poverty and types of, 319–20, 324, 325–27, 340–42; reliability of information sources, 353–54; to single women, 82–83; subdivisions and avoidance of, 70–71; suburbs and, 71–72; technological, 352–53; theme of, 169; thrift and, 297–300, 313; traffic, 27–28, 50, 56–58; unemployment and, 243–44, 273; vice and suburbs, 74; workplace inspection, 257. *See also* Employment agencies; Visitors to Chicago
Riverside (suburb), 70, 74
Robertson, Dr. John Dill, 139
de Rochi, Henri, 200
Rodley, W. W. "Clambake," 268
Rodriguez, William E., 123–24
Rooming houses, 81–82. *See also* Boardinghouses
Roosevelt, Theodore, 170–71, 178
Roseland neighborhood: and flowers, 116; and *So Big*, 117
Rosenthal, Benjamin, 107
Rosenwald, Julius, 107, 177
Rosten, Leo, 291
Rubens, Harry, 214
Rumsey, Julian, 151
Rush Medical College, 321, 322, 324
Rush Street Bridge, 22

Sabath, Adolph, 230
Sain, Frank, 342
St. Francis of Assisi Roman Catholic Church, 92
St. John Cantius Roman Catholic Church, 104
St. Louis, Mo.: and Ferris Wheel, 238; market of, 115; restaurant patronage of, 147; unemployed come to Chicago, 246
St Luke's Society: lunch substitute, 158
St. Mary's Roman Catholic Church, 68
St. Stanislaus Kostka Roman Catholic Church, 104
Salmonella poisoning, 144
Saloons: African-American owned, 262; check-cashing in, 309, 302; concert saloons, 236; distinct from restaurants, 150; free lunch in, 157–58, 160–61; as employment agencies and hiring halls, 251, 255, 270; and ice, 133; and morality issue, 230; and special bar permits, 232. *See also* Temperance
Sanitary and Ship Canal, 177, 250, 323
Satter, Mark, 314
Savings and loan societies. *See* Building and loan societies
Scandinavians: aid societies, 252; labor contractors, 249. *See also* Norwegians; Swedes
Schaak, Capt. Michael, 104
Schaumburg (suburb), 43
Schonecker, Joseph, 6–7
Schools. *See* Chicago Board of Education; Night schools
Schufeldt Distillery, 99
The Secret of Suzanne, 199
Semipublic space: and centralization, 354–56; and coping, 38–39; dance halls, 228–30; in early Chicago, 6; factories as form of, 39, 170; gymnasiums and health clubs as, 170–71, 172, 175–77; postbellum, 16–17; rented halls as, 228; smoking regulations and, 195–96, 198; stores as, 25; suburban forms, 70–71; term defined, 4; theme of, 35–38. *See also* Amusements; Baseball: parks; Billiards; Churches; Cycloramas; Dime museums; Gymnasiums; Hotels; Panoramas; Railroads: depots; Settlement houses; Snell family; Swimming pools; Theaters
Senn, Dr. Nicholas, 324
Settlement houses: African Americans at, 177–78; and athletics, 177; Chicago Commons, 103; dancing at, 234; Davis Square Settlement House, 204; Frederick Douglass Center, 177–78; and night school, 289, 293; as semipublic places, 39; services provided, 318. *See also* Hull-House
Sewer system, 7–8

Sheridan Road: automobile speed, 57–58; bicycle path, 191
Sherman, Alson Smith, 131–32
Sidewalk use and signs, 12. *See also* Moving sidewalks; Streets
Silsbee, J. L.: and Edgewater, 78; and moving sidewalks, 32
Sinclair, Upton, 119
Six Flags over Atlanta: carousel moved to, 238
Skandinaven: on community, 47
Skokie (suburb), 74–75
Skybridges: banned, 32
Skyscrapers: and congestion, 30. *See also* Centralization; Loop; Offices; Semipublic space; Streets
Slumming, 233
Slums: and athletics, 177; housing shortages and, 95–96; origin of problem, 93; rear alley, 96, 102; subdivisions and, 96, 108. *See also* Chicago Housing Authority; Housing; Poor persons; Risk
Smith, Perry, 82
Smith, Gen. William Sooy, 71
Smoke: automobile, 51, 56. *See also* Environment
Smoking and Health, 202
"Smoky Hollow" neighborhood, 103
Snell family: Amos J., 42–44, 63; Grace Henrietta, 63; Henrietta, 44; and toll road, 52, 60
Snow, George, 68, 139
So Big, 117
Social class and mobility: and dancing, 227–28; and exercise, 174–75, 175–77; and food, 122–23; geographical separation, 334; and health care, 324–25; and housing, 82, 83–87, 108–9; and information sources, 353–54; and lunch, 153, 155, 156–57; and moving day, 85–87; and peddling, 276; and piano ownership, 303; and privacy, 279–80; and technology, 98–99, 103, 352–53. *See also* Coping; Elite; Middle class; Neighborhoods; Poor persons; Real estate: subdivisions; Slums
Society for the Prevention of Cruelty to Animals: and commuting, 46
Sokols: Bohemians and, 172
South Park neighborhood: depot at, 52
South Side Sayings: on bicycles, 192
Space, urban. *See* Private space; Public space; Semipublic space
Spalding, Albert, 173–74
Special Park Commission, 105
Sports:
—participatory, 171–86, 190–93; archery, 173, 175; baseball, 172; bowling, 173, 176; cricket, 171; fitness and body-building, 170–71, 172, 175–77; golf, 173, 175, 193;

gymnastics, 185; handball, 175; ice skating, 181; racquetball, 175; roller skating, 175–76; running, 171–72; softball, 176; squash, 175; swimming, 176–77; tennis, 173, 182; weight lifting, 173. *See also* Country clubs; Gymnasiums; Health; Swimming pools
—spectator. *See* Automobile racing; Baseball; Boxing; Foot races; Heroes
Sprague, Frank, 26
Stensland, Paul O., 298–99
Stevenson, Dr. Sarah Hackett, 326
Stone, John, 13
Strauss, Nathan, 137
Streetcars: accidents, 49; and amusement parks, 236; automobiles and, 51–53; electrification, 26–27; smoking on, 199; and tunnels, 29–30. *See also* Chicago Surface Lines; Geographical mobility; Tunnels; West Division Street Railway Company; Yerkes, Charles T.
Streets: automobiles and, 51–53, 60; bicycles on, 180, 190; conditions, 7–8, 21, 22; congestion of, 27–28, 30–31, 349–50; dangers of, 12–13; "furniture" of, 31; general use of, 17; grade elevation, 19, 90, 170; informational function of, 14; subsurface utilities and, 32–33; trades, 28, 123; traffic, 11, 27–28, 50, 56–58. *See also* Automobiles; Crime; Horsecars; Horses; Noise; Omnibus; Peddlers; Poor persons; Public space; Semipublic space; Streetcars; Vehicles
Suburbs, 44–49. *See also suburbs by individual name*
Subway: plans, 34
Suder, Henry, 174
Suicide Bridge, 347–48
Sullivan, Louis, 208
Sunday observance: and beer gardens, 211, 213; and markets, 115; and peddling, 280; and restaurants, 150
Swedes in Chicago: cholera and, 328. *See also* Ethnicity; Neighborhoods; Scandinavians
Swift, George B., 214, 215
Swift and Company: ice houses, 133
Swimming pools: in athletic clubs, 172; commercial, 177; in Turner Societies, 172

Taft, William Howard, 300
"Tally-Ho" coaches, 211
Tascott, Willie, 43, 63; and game of "Where's Willie Tascott?" 43
Taxis. *See* Cabs
Taylor, Augustine, 369n.3
Taylor, Charles, 93
Taylor, Graham, 103
Teamsters: and bicycles, 180; companies, 22, 262. *See also* Streets; Vehicles

Technology: backwardness regarding, 109; and ice production, 134–35; social class and, 98–99. *See also* Automobiles; Centralization; Electricity; Elevated; Elevators; Gas lighting; Housing; Risk; Slums; Streetcars; Streets; Telephones; Time; Tunnels; Vehicles
Telephones: and congestion, 31; and health care, 324–25
Temperance: beer gardens and, 213, 214–15; and cooking, 122; and employers, 160–61; Harvey and, 193–94
Tenement Conditions in Chicago, 105
Tennessee: tobacco regulation in, 197
Terry, Luther, 202
Theaters: safety, 229; Schiller Theater bicycle parking, 192. *See also* Movies; Semipublic space
Thompson, James: and 1830 survey, 4
Three Arts Club: housing women, 83
Thrift, 299–300; steamship agents as bankers, 299. *See also* Banks; Building and loan societies; Risk; Time
Time: and appeal of amusements, 206, 208; and city-country relationship, 351; coping and, 350–51; credit purchases and, 302–3; daylight savings, and gardens, 141; and food wholesomeness, 142; freshness of job prospect leads, 271; ice delivery schedules and families, 131, 135; lunch hour, 153; market schedule, 117; night lunch, 160; night schools and, 287–88; pawnshops and, 309–13; peddlers' freedom from time clock, 280; rhythms of the city, 113; seasons and gardening, 139; shift changes, 257; social class and, 314; temporal cycles, 350–51; thrift and, 299–300; wage payment schedules, 301–2. *See also* Coping; Fads; Moving day; Public space; Restaurants: operations of; Semipublic space; Sunday observance; Thrift
Tobacco: cigarette smoking, 195–201; federal regulation, 202–3; smoking by juveniles, 189; "medicated cigarettes," 196; moral condemnation of, 194, 197; refuse recycling, 187, 196. *See also* Industry: tobacco processing; Cubans in Chicago; Gaston, Lucy Page
Towertown neighborhood, 151
Traffic. *See* Centralization; Street
Tramps: and peddlers, 280
Transportation. *See* Automobiles; Elevated; Horsecars; Omnibus; Streetcars; Vehicles
Tribune Tower, 94
Tricks and Traps of Chicago, 13
Trude, Alvin S., 191–92
Tuley, Judge Murray F., 57, 308
Tunnels: freight system, 34–35, 40; river, 8–9, 23, 29–30

Turner Societies, 172–74, 174, 300. *See also* Sports: participatory
Tyler and Hippach Mirror Company, 92

Union Pacific Railroad, 62, 247
Union Stock Yards: closing, 143; and horse market, 9
United Societies for Local Self-Government, 232
United States government: Department of Agriculture, 143; Department of Housing and Urban Development, 344; Department of Labor, 105; and school lunch program, 165; Supreme Court, 47, 264
University of Chicago: and urban sociology, 106
University of Illinois: and urban gardening, 143
University of Illinois at Chicago: and Maxwell Street Market, 293–94; South Water Market, 143
Uptown neighborhood: and apartment lifestyle, 162
Urbanization: and anonymity, 145; and centralization, 114–15; and dining, 163–64; and geographical mobility, 153; and slums, 98; *See also* Coping; Minorities; Private space; Public space; Semipublic space; Time
Ursula (lunch club), 159

Van Cleeve family, 67, 88
Van Etta, Friedman, and Company, 194
Vaux, Calvert, 70, 77
Vehicles: delivery, 61; food trucks, 143; ice delivery, 124, 130, 131–35; private, 27. *See also by individual type*
Victoria, Queen, 171
Visiting Nurses Association, 105, 325
Visitors to Chicago: cause crime, 13; crime victims, 275; and lunch, 153; depot transfer, 16–17; and restaurants, 148; and pawnshops, 311; strikebreakers, 266

Wacker Drive, 123
Wages: and currency exchanges, 309; garnishment, 307; payment, 300–302, 307
Wage Workers Free Collection Bureau, 301
Waiters:
—African-American, 259, 261–70, 272; employment agency, 263; Thomas L. Johnson, 262; strikebreakers, 266
—German, 266, 268
—labor organizations: Bartenders, Cooks, Waiters, and Waitresses Union, 272; Charles Sumner Waiters' Union, 267; Culinary Alliance, 267–68, 272; Federated Hotel Waiters and Hotel Attendants of Chicago, 272; Fitzgerald, 266–67; of

German waiters, 266, 267, 268; Head and Second Waiters National Benefit Association, 269; Hotel and Bartenders International Union, 272; W. Willis Howe, 264; Knights of Labor, 266–67; National Hotel and Restaurant Employee's Alliance, 269; oppose Hotel Keepers Association of Chicago, 263; W. C. Pomeroy, 267; and strikebreakers, 266; White Waiters' Assembly, 266, 267; William Lloyd Garrison Colored Waiters Local Assembly 8286, 266–67
—strikes by, 262–63, 268
—and work: job discipline, 265; employee slang, 263–63, 264; lunch compared with dinner, 157; tipping, 264.
—*see also* African Americans; Hotels; Restaurants, generally and by name; Rodley, W. W. "Clambake"; Waitresses
Waitresses: 259, 263; "grisettes," 13; "pretty waiter girls," 263; as replacements for male strikers, 269; in saloons and hotels, 263; strikes, 259, 398n.114; Waiter Girls Union No. 1, 269
Walgreen, Charles R., 162
Walgreen, Myrtle: serves first drugstore lunch, 162
Waller, Edward, Jr., 212
Wanzer Dairy Company, 136
Ward, A. Montgomery, 160–61
War Garden Production Committee, 141
Warman, E. B., 173–74
Washingtonian Home of Chicago: and Bridewell, 339
Watchman of the Prairies: and dancing, 226
Water: peddling of, 275; purity of, 138; supply improvements, 323
Waugh, Alice, 191
Waukegan (suburb), 50
Weeghman, Charles, 209. *See also* Restaurants, by name; Baseball
Weekly Chicago Democrat, 136; on dances, 225; on hospitals, 321
Welfare: decline of federal, 344–45; indoor and outdoor relief, 328, 336–37, 342–43. *See also* Chicago Housing Authority; Dunning; Poor persons
Welfare Council of Metropolitan Chicago, 343
Welk, Lawrence, 238
Wells, Ida B., 239
Wentworth, "Long John," 12
Werner-Kennelly Moving and Storage Company, 87
Westchester (suburb), 75
West Division Street Railway Company, 44
Western Citizen: and moving day, 75
West Hinsdale (suburb), 70
Wheeling (suburb), 43
Whiskey Row, 155

White Slave Girls of Chicago, 250, 258
Whyte, William H.: on suburbs, 88
Wicker Park, 69–70
Wigmore, John T., 256
Wildwood Club: lunchroom, 159
Wilkie, Franc, 11, 12
Willow Springs (suburb), 340
Wilmette (suburb), 71
Winter: and transit, 26–27
Wisconsin: ice supply from, 133
Woman's Alliance: employment agency, 251–52
Woman's Baking Company, 120
Woman's Canning and Preserving Company, 119–20
Woman's Christian Temperance Union, 197; employment agency, 251–52; fountain, 31; restaurant pay scale of, 269
Woman's Exchange: lunchroom, 159
Women: African-American domestics, 252; athletics, 175, 182; and automobiles, 50–51, 54; as bank customers, 297–98, 304; and bicycles, 191–92; and bowling, 176; and Bridewell, 332, 339; and clubs, 121–22, 175, 252, 317, 335; and household credit purchases, 302–3, 305; dancing and, 204, 218–19; as domestic servants, 247, 252; and Dunning, 335; employment agencies and reforms, 245, 246, 249–50, 250, 251–52, 255; and exercise, 174; in food-processing industry, 119–20; as food purchasers, 114–24, 127, 128, 129; and gardening, 139, 140; hotel employment of, 259; and lunch, 158–59, 162; and lunch clubs and cafeterias, 158–59; as newspaper reporters, 250, 258, 319; and night school, 289, 289–90; as nurses, 325–26; as peddlers, 276, 284; and rail commuting, 45–46, 47–48; as restaurant operators, 149–50; Scandinavian and labor market, 252; and school lunch, 161; and school physical education, 178; "shortage" of, 225; single, and boardinghouses, 82–83; and smoking, 195, 195–96; as stenographers, 252; suffrage, 327; and time, 351; in *The White Slave Girls of Chicago,* 250, 258; as widows, 82, 245, 246, 333; working, 257, 258; World War II and, 272–73. *See also* Moving day; Prostitution; Waitresses
Women's Trade Union League, 252
Wood, Colonel J. H., 206
Woods, Mrs. C. E., 51
Woods Electric automobile, 54

Woodworth, James, 337
"Working-man's trains," 45
World's Columbian Exposition: African-American waiters and, 269; and amusement park evolution, 237; amusements on Midway, 215, 215–16, 220; amusements outside Midway, 208, 239; automobile exhibits, 50; and centralization, 237; drinking water at, 323; elevated lines and, 32; Ferris wheel, 213; food vending, 160; hotels and, 92, 106; labor migration and, 248–49; Lincoln Park High Bridge and, 347; moving sidewalks at, 31–32; processed food exhibited, 118; restaurants at, 148, 149; Viking ship displayed at, 298; Woman's Building at, 289
World War I: and beer gardens, 218; cigarette distribution during, 199; employment agencies, 256, 260; ethnicity and, 202; and food, 118; and gardens, 141; and lunch, 162; and markets, 124; and night school, 290; and peddlers, 287
World War II: and dining out, 164; and gardens, 141–42; and horses, 62; and labor, 272; and night school, 291; and pawnshop, 313
Wright, Frank Lloyd, 78, 105, 212

Yerkes, Charles T., 29; and franchises, 33; and Union Loop, 32; wires and house moving, 92
Young, Ella Flagg: and school physical education for girls, 178
Young Men's Christian Association, 202; and African Americans, 178; and athletics, 177; employment agency of, 246, 247, 255; and night classes, 289
Young Women's Christian Association, 174, 202; employment agency, 251–52
Youth: African-American day nurseries, 252; at amusement parks, 217; and athletics, 177; attend night schools, 288; delinquency and the Bridewell, 340; at Dunning, 335; game of "Where's Willie Tascott?" 43; geographical mobility of, 216–17; orphanages, 170, 321; as peddlers, 282; "slumming" by, 233–34; in slums, 100; and smoking, 196; warned about Dunning, 329. *See also* Amusements; Chicago Board of Education; Chicago Law and Order League; Gaston, Lucy Page; Juvenile delinquency

PERRY R. DUIS teaches at the University of Illinois at Chicago. He is the author of *Chicago: Creating New Traditions* and *The Saloon: Public Drinking in Chicago and Boston, 1880–1920,* as well as numerous articles about Chicago's history. He is coauthor, with Scott LaFrance, of *We've Got a Job to Do: Chicagoans and World War II.*